ISBN 978-1-334-70017-0
PIBN 10600277

Forgotten Books is a registered trademark of FB &c Ltd.
Copyright © 2017 FB &c Ltd.
FB &c Ltd, Dalton House, 60 Windsor Avenue, London, SW19 2RR.
Company number 08720141. Registered in England and Wales.

For support please visit www.forgottenbooks.com

1 MONTH OF
FREE
READING

at

www.ForgottenBooks.com

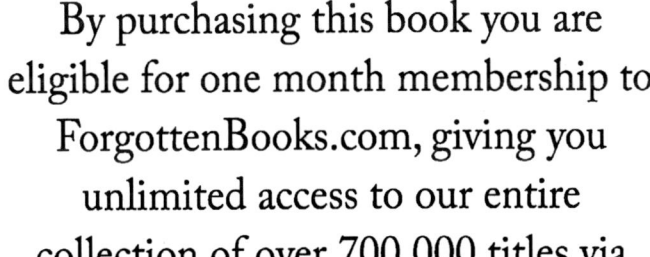

By purchasing this book you are
eligible for one month membership to
ForgottenBooks.com, giving you
unlimited access to our entire
collection of over 700,000 titles via
our web site and mobile apps.

To claim your free month visit:
www.forgottenbooks.com/free600277

English
Français
Deutsche
Italiano
Español
Português

www.forgottenbooks.com

Mythology Photography **Fiction**
Fishing Christianity **Art** Cooking
Essays Buddhism Freemasonry
Medicine **Biology** Music **Ancient**
Egypt Evolution Carpentry Physics
Dance Geology **Mathematics** Fitness
Shakespeare **Folklore** Yoga Marketing
Confidence Immortality Biographies
Poetry **Psychology** Witchcraft
Electronics Chemistry History **Law**
Accounting **Philosophy** Anthropology
Alchemy Drama Quantum Mechanics
Atheism Sexual Health **Ancient History**
Entrepreneurship Languages Sport
Paleontology Needlework Islam
Metaphysics Investment Archaeology
Parenting Statistics Criminology
Motivational

A HISTORY OF ENGLAND

CONSTITUTIONAL MONARCHY

1689—1837

A
HISTORY OF ENGLAN

BY THE REV.

J. FRANCK BRIGHT, D.D.

MASTER OF UNIVERSITY COLLEGE, OXFORD; LATE MASTER OF THE MODERN SCHOOL
IN MARLBOROUGH COLLEGE

PERIOD III.

CONSTITUTIONAL MONARCHY
William and Mary to William IV.
1689—1837

With Maps and Plans

NINTH IMPRESSION

LONGMANS, GREEN, AND CO.
39 PATERNOSTER ROW, LONDON
NEW YORK AND BOMBAY
1902

Printed by T. and A CONSTABLE, Printers to Her Majesty,
at the Edinburgh University Press.

A LIST OF SOME USEFUL AUTHORITIES.

GENERAL HISTORIES.

Macaulay's *History of England*, 1600-1702. Macaulay's *Essays.*
Mahon's *History of England*, 1713-1783. Massey's *History of England*, 1745-1802. Martineau's *History of the Peace*, 1800-1848.
Erskine May's *Constitutional History*, 1760-1860. Ralph's *History of England*, 1689-1727. Pauli's *Geschichte Englands*, from 1814.

BOOKS OF GENERAL REFERENCE.

Cobbett's *Parliamentary History*, to 1803. Hansard's *Debates*, from 1803. *The Monthly Mercury*, from 1690. *The Annual Register*, from 1758. *State Tracts.* Anderson's *History of Commerce.* Maculloch's *Commercial Dictionary.* Eden's *State of the Poor.* Howell's *State Trials.* Macpherson's *State Papers*, 1688-1714. Hardwicke's *State Papers*, to 1727.

FOREIGN HISTORIES.

Documens inédits sur l'Histoire de France (for the Spanish succession).
Sismondi or Martin's *Histoire de France*, to 1789. Von Sybel's *French Revolution.* Lanfrey's *Histoire de Napoleon.* Ranke's *History of Prussia.* Bancroft's *History of the United States.* Mill's *History of India.* Grant Duff's *History of the Mahrattas.* The *Despatches* of Wellesley and Cornwallis. Froude's *The English in Ireland*, to 1800.

WILLIAM III.

Burnet's *History of his Own Time*, 1660-1713. Kennett's *History of England*, vol. iii. Defoe's Works are instructive as to the state of England at this time.

ANNE.

Stanhope's *Reign of Queen Anne.* Coxe's *Life of Marlborough.*
Marlborough's Letters and Despatches, 1702.1712. *Bolingbroke's Correspondence. Life of Sacheverel.*

LIST OF AUTHORITIES

GEORGE I.

Swift's *Drapier's Letters*, etc. *The Stuart Papers*, edited by Glover. Coxe's *Life of Walpole*. Boyer's *Political State of Great Britain*.

GEORGE II.

Hervey's *Memoirs of the Reign of George II.*, 1727-1742. Horace Walpole's *Memoirs of the Reign of George II.*, 1751-1760. Doddington's *Diary*, 1749-1761. Waldegrave's *Memoirs*, 1754-1758. Southey's *Life of Wesley*. Philip's *Life and Times of Whitfield*. Johnstone's *Memoirs of the Rebellion of* 1745.

GEORGE III.

Horace Walpole's *Memoirs of the Reign of George III.*, 1760-1771. *The Letters of Junius*. *The Grenville Papers*. *The Bedford Correspondence*. Buckingham's *Memoirs of the Court and Cabinet of George III*. Russell's *Life of Fox*. Thackeray's *Life of Chatham*. Stanhope's *Life of Pitt*. Wilberforce's *Life*. Malmesbury's *Diary and Correspondence*. *The Cornwallis Correspondence*, 1770-1805. Napier's *Peninsular War*. *Life of Bamford the Radical*. Lord Dudley's *Letters*, 1814-1823. Bell and Stapleton's *Lives of Canning*.

It is not, however, necessary to give a detailed list of authorities, which would be little more than a catalogue of the lives, letters, and memoirs of most of the important men of the time. Of these the number is constantly being augmented, and it is from them and the contemporary tracts, monographs, pamphlets, and fugitive writings that the details of the History must be drawn.

CONTENTS.

WILLIAM AND MARY. 1689-1702.

CONTENTS

CONTENTS

CONTENTS

GEORGE I. 1714-1727.

10

CONTENTS

CONTENTS

GEORGE II. 1727-1760.

CONTENTS

CONTENTS

GEORGE III. 1760-1820.

14

CONTENTS

CONTENTS

CONTENTS

CONTENTS

CONTENTS

CONTENTS

CONTENTS

b 2

CONTENTS

22

CONTENTS

GEORGE IV. 1820-1830.

CONTENTS

24

CONTENTS

WILLIAM IV. 1830-1837.

CONTENTS

26

LIST OF MAPS.

WILLIAM AND MARY.

1689--1702.

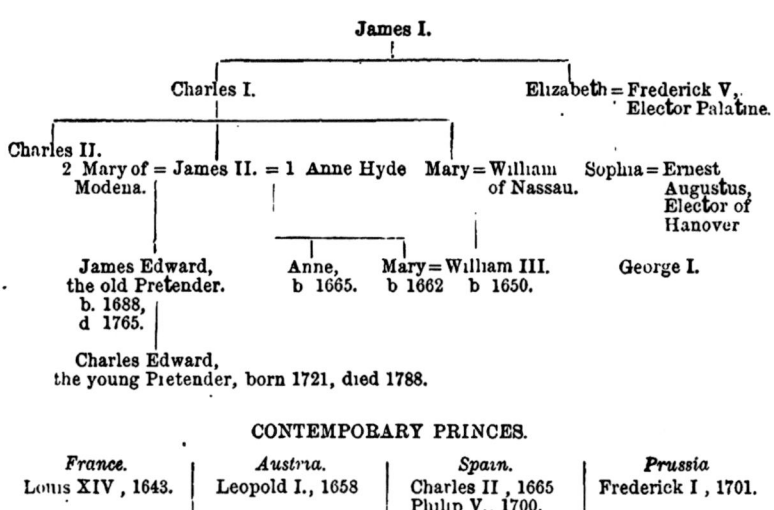

James I.

Charles I.   Elizabeth = Frederick V., Elector Palatine.

Charles II.
2 Mary of = James II. = 1 Anne Hyde   Mary = William   Sophia = Ernest
Modena.   of Nassau.   Augustus, Elector of Hanover

James Edward,   Anne,   Mary = William III.   George I.
the old Pretender.   b 1665.   b 1662   b 1650.
b. 1688,
d 1765.

Charles Edward,
the young Pretender, born 1721, died 1788.

CONTEMPORARY PRINCES.

France.	*Austria.*	*Spain.*	*Prussia*
Louis XIV , 1643.	Leopold I., 1658	Charles II , 1665 Philip V., 1700.	Frederick I , 1701.

Russia.	*Denmark and Norway.*	*Sweden*
Peter the Great, 1689.	Christian V , 1670 Frederick IV , 1699	Charles XI., 1660 Charles XII , 1697

POPES —Alexander VIII., 1689.   Innocent XII., 1691.   Clement XI , 1700

Archbishops.	*Chancellors*
William Sancroft, 1678. John Tillotson, 1691 Thomas Tenison, 1694	(In Commission, 1689.) Sir John Somers, 1693 Sir Nathan Wright, 1700.

CON. MON.   [A]

First Lord of the Treasury.		Chancellor of the Exchequer.	
1689	Mordaunt.	1689.	Delamere
1690	Lowther.	1690	Hampden.
1690	Godolphin	1694	Montague.
1697.	Montague	1699.	Aaron Smith.
1699	Tankerville.	1701.	Henry Boyle.
1700.	Godolphin.		
1702.	Carlisle.		

Secretaries of State.

1689	{ Nottingham { Shrewsbury		1697	{ Shrewsbury { Vernon
1690	{ Nottingham { Sidney		1699	{ Jersey { Vernon
1693	{ Shrewsbury { Trenchard		1700	{ Hedges { Vernon
1695	{ Shrewsbury { Trumbal		1702	{ Manchester { Vernon

BEFORE the Crown was absolutely offered to William, the Convention was eager to reform a number of the most prominent abuses of the last reign. It was shown by the wiser leaders among them that such reforms would entail a mass of legislation which, *The Declaration of Right* to be done well, must occupy several years. It was therefore determined that, for the present, a solemn declaration of principles only should be drawn up. This is known as the Declaration of Right. In it, after enumerating the evils from which the country had suffered, the Lords and Commons declared that the dispensing power does not exist, that without grant or consent of Parliament no money can be exacted by the sovereign, and no army kept up in time of peace. They also affirmed the right of petition, the right of free choice of representatives, the right of Parliament to freedom of debate, the right of the nation to a pure administration of justice, and the necessity, in order to secure these things, *Crown accepted by William and Mary.* of frequent Parliaments. This Declaration having been read to William and Mary, the Crown was solemnly offered them by Halifax, and by them accepted. They were immediately proclaimed amid general plaudits.

Thus was consummated, with scarcely any bloodshed, and by what *Character of the Revolution.* appeared an almost unanimous action on the part of the nation, a complete revolution. . It was not the less a revolution because it was held that the whole Constitution of England passed on in its minutest detail unchanged. By it was overthrown for ever the theory which came into existence under the Tudors, and was brought to perfection under the Stuarts ; henceforward it was impossible that the King should be regarded either as the proprietor of the country, or as a ruler by divine right, the representative of God upon earth. In the place of this theory was substituted that great Whig theory, which, arising among the Puritans, had enjoyed a brief

triumph in the successes of the Great Rebellion, and, violently overthrown at the Restoration, had succeeded in making good its position
during the reigns of the two last Stuarts,—the theory which regarded
the King as reigning by the will of the people and in virtue of an
implied contract with them. As a natural consequence of the position
thus taken by the nation as the supreme power in the State, Parliament, its representative, became in its turn supreme, and although
the change was not yet fully understood, the representatives of the
people were gradually taking to themselves not only the duties of
legislation, but also the executive. The ministry, therefore, however
much they may have been still regarded as the King's ministers,
became by degrees the national ministers, answerable for their
conduct in Parliament, and before long became in fact little else than
the executive Committee of the majority in Parliament.

The unanimity of parties which had secured the triumph of
William was of short duration, nor was his personal   Personal
popularity long-lived.   The apparent coldness of his   unpopularity of
demeanour, his carelessness of the pomps of the Court,   William.
his wretched health, which obliged him to withdraw from London
and establish his Court at Kensington, speedily rendered him personally unpopular ; while, as soon as the general danger which had
caused their union was removed, the fundamental differences which
divided political parties at once made themselves obvious.   Moreover,
the tendency to reaction, visible after all political excitements, began
to show itself.   Two classes were by no means ready to accept kindly
the revolution which had been wrought.   These were the clergy and
the army.   The greater part of the clergy had spent   Discontent of
their lives in inculcating the duty of passive obedience.   the clergy
Although that theory had broken down in practice when the attacks
of the Crown were directed against themselves, they could not bring
themselves to submit without difficulty to a complete reversal of their
political creed, nor could they help seeing that the success of William
implied nothing short of the substitution of the Whig doctrine for that
of monarchy by divine right.· A very large portion of them were
therefore disaffected.   The army, though it had disliked the
introduction of Catholics and of Irish among its
ranks, and was not prejudiced in favour of any theory of   and the army.
monarchy, felt its professional honour injured by the sorry part
it had played in the late events.   So deep was the disaffection
that one regiment quartered at Ipswich broke out into open mutiny,
marched northward in arms, and was only brought to obedience after

a skirmish with some Dutch troops under Ginkel, which had been rapidly sent in pursuit. The signs of general disaffection at the same time were so obvious that it was thought necessary to suspend the Habeas Corpus Act.

Before this happened, William had had to form a ministry and to furnish himself with a Parliament. For this latter purpose, in spite of the opposition of many of the old Tories, who regarded a Parliament not summoned by the King's writ as no Parliament at all, the Convention was changed into a Parliament, and proceeded to act in that capacity. It was not indeed reasonable that a freely elected body, whose choice of a king both sides were willing to allow, should still be regarded upon technical grounds as incapable of settling matters of much less importance. The choice of ministers was a matter of more difficulty.

At the present time the choice of ministers is tolerably simple. The House of Commons having obtained the position of both legislature and executive, the administration is placed in the hands of a Committee of that party which is predominant in the Commons ; the Crown, in fact, having but little choice in the matter. This theory of government, which is a necessary consequence of the Parliamentary triumph at the Revolution, was in the years immediately succeeding that event not understood. The notion of a king whose duties are rather ornamental than real had scarcely entered men's minds The King was still expected to have the direction of the executive, to be, in fact, his own Prime Minister, and to nominate as heads of departments such statesmen as he thought best fitted for the employment, without exact regard to their political views The effect of this was to make the King responsible for the Government; and though the right of impeachment, as exercised in the case of Danby, rested upon the supposition that ministers were responsible to Parliament, the fact was not yet fully recognized. It was this responsibility of the king which had produced the disasters of the Great Rebellion and the late Revolution. The gradual substitution of Parliamentary ministry, which should serve as an intermediate body between the Commons and the Crown, and save the Crown from direct responsibility, is the great constitutional change which was completed on the accession of the Hanoverian house. Such a change becomes absolutely necessary when Parliament has once secured a complete control of the executive ; otherwise it is plain that the acts or proposals of the executive, constantly met by a hostile majority in Parliament,

The Convention changed into a Parliament.

William's difficulties in forming a ministry

Ignorance of the constitutional change

could never be brought to a completion. It also of necessity implies a mutual responsibility among the ministers, who upon essential points must all agree with the Parliamentary majority. These necessary consequences of the triumph of the Whig theory of the sovereignty of the people were little understood even by the best English politicians ; and William, able as he was as a foreign statesman, had never a clear insight into the working of the English Constitution. Nor was his character such as to fit him to occupy the place of an ornamental king.   Thus he both himself intended and was expected by the nation to exercise a supreme influence in the Government, at the same time that the newly won powers of the Parliament were liable constantly to thwart his schemes.   Besides the difficulty which this general ignorance of constitutional principles caused, peculiar difficulties, arising from the manner in which he had obtained the Crown, beset William.   He had been brought to the throne by the Whigs.   By the Whigs he was expected to become a *The Whigs'* party leader.   They looked forward, under his guidance, *desire for* to a triumphant revenge on the party at whose hands *vengeance* they had suffered so much.   On the other hand, William's own wish was to hush the storm of faction, to become King of the whole English nation, not of one party, and to be able to use the resources of England for his great European measures ; he therefore had no intention of becoming a mere party leader.   Again, his view of the duties and responsibilities of a king was a high one, whereas the Whigs, on whom he might be expected to rely, were pledged to give greater prominence to the influence of Parliament.   William's natural tendencies, therefore, when once safeguards for a just Government and personal liberty were secured, inclined him rather to the Tories, whose view of the prerogative was higher.

It was in the midst of these difficulties that William had to select his ministry.   He attempted to conciliate all parties, *William's* with the exception of the extreme Jacobites, and his *ministry.* ministry was a mixed one.   Danby had been mainly instrumental in bringing William to England.   He had indeed in the Convention thrown some obstacles in the way of the Parliamentary change of dynasty, but might fairly look for a high reward.   He was displeased at being appointed President of the Council, a post of high honour, but not of great political activity.   Halifax was appointed Privy Seal.   His intellect, which always saw two sides of a question, was not such as to fit him for decided statesmanship.   The places of real importance, the Secretaryships, were shared between the Tories and the Whigs; Nottingham, the leader of that class who expressed with perfect honesty their willingness to acknowledge any King *de facto*, and Shrewsbury, a young man of great ability and as yet a consistent Whig, were appointed to those places. Neither Treasury nor Admiralty were intrusted to any single individual, but were placed in Commission, both Whigs and Tories sitting at the Boards. At the Treasury, though only third on the Commission, Godolphin, by his superior skill and knowledge, soon became pre-eminent. The purity of the judgment-seat was secured by a careful selection of the ablest lawyers from a list supplied by the Privy Council, while the great places of the Household, where personal rather than political influence was wanted, were chiefly given to William's personal friends from Holland, the most prominent being Overkirk, Master of the Horse, and Bentinck, subsequently Earl of Portland.

By the appointment of his ministers, and by the conversion of the Convention into a Parliament, the apparatus of Government was complete. The Whigs were for a time triumphant. The revenue was

Settlement of the revenue — settled on a peace footing at £1,200,000 a year; the hereditary taxes being given to William for the support of his Crown (a grant which forms the origin of the Civil List), while the Parliamentary taxes intended for the support of Government were granted only for limited periods. The hearth tax, the most obnoxious and unjust of taxes, as it is at once inquisitorial in its action and presses with undue severity upon the poor in comparison with the rich, was abolished. The settlement of the Church, and of the oaths to be

Settlement of the Church. — taken by the holders of places, at once rendered obvious the strength of faction which still existed, and the difficulties which must beset all attempt at impartial government. Three Bills were produced, a Toleration Bill, a Comprehension Bill, for the purpose of so changing the construction of the Church and its Liturgy as to admit numerous Protestant Dissenters, and a Bill for the removal of the Test Act, for the purpose of enabling the King to employ, as he was most desirous of doing, all Protestants in his service. Of these three, one only, the Toleration Act, was carried. In fact the Comprehension Bill, which was introduced by Nottingham, was no doubt intended, after admitting a certain number of Dissenters, to render the exclusion of the rest more absolute. Fear of this rendered the Dissenters themselves hostile to it, and William's personal efforts to produce at once comprehension and relaxation of the Test Act were in vain ; both Bills were thrown out.

There yet remained the question of the oaths of allegiance and su-

premacy.   It was acknowledged on all hands that all lay place-holders
and all newly appointed holders of ecclesiastical prefer-   Oaths of
ments should be obliged to take these oaths, slightly   allegiance and
altered to suit existing circumstances.   The case of the   supremacy
clergy already holding benefices was not so clear.   Many were willing
to accept the new Government peaceably, and it seemed hard that
they should be required to take oaths which gave the lie to all their
former political views.   With regard to the Bishops too, the High
Church Party advanced the doctrine that the Episcopal ordination
was indelible, and that it was impossible for any Act either of
King or Parliament to prevent a man who had once been a Bishop
from being so always.   Against the King's wish the party who were
for the most stringent application of the oaths carried the day.   All
the clergy were required to take them by August 1689 ; if they
had not been taken by February 1690, those clergy and Bishops who
refused them were to be deprived.   Between 300 and 400 refused
the oath, and there thus sprang up that section of the clergy known
as Nonjurors.   The settlement of the country was completed by the
Coronation Oath, which declared that the King would uphold the
Protestant religion as settled by law.   It was a foolish miscompre-
hension of these words, which obviously did not prevent a Parliamentary change in the arrangements of religion, which subsequently
led George III. into his obstinate opposition to Catholic emancipation.
When the oath had been arranged, the coronation took place (April
11), and some new titles were given ; thus Danby became Lord Caermarthen, Churchill Earl of Marlborough, Bentinck Earl of Portland,
and Mordaunt, First Lord of the Treasury, Earl of Monmouth.

When the Government of the country was fairly settled it was
time for William to receive his reward.   Parliament gratified him
by a strong declaration against the policy of Louis abroad, and
assurance of hearty support should he find it necessary   The European
to have recourse to arms.   On the 13th of May war with   war breaks out
France was therefore declared.   William stated that he had no choice
in the matter as France had already begun war upon England.   This
was an allusion to the action of France in Ireland ; for Louis, though
unable to trust James and his English and Irish friends in that
implicit manner which would have rendered his assistance irresistible,
was yet so far convinced that the real key to success against the
coalition was the neutralization of England, that he had allowed James
some assistance in troops.   The other great countries of the coalition
had already declared war with France.   Louis found himself with

one ally only, who did him, if possible, more harm than good,—this was the Porte.   He succeeded in inducing that power to continue its attacks upon Hungary, which was a constant source of weakness to Austria ; but the unnatural alliance between the most Christian King and the great enemies of Christendom gave an opening for the invective of his enemies, which received still further point from his subsequent behaviour.   Unable to sustain the forward position which his armies had assumed in Germany the preceding year, especially when some of his forces were required in Ireland, he ordered a retreat.   What he could not keep he determined to destroy, and

Devastation of the Palatinate — the Palatinate was laid waste with a reckless, unsparing fury, which enabled each country, as it declared war with him, to point out that his conduct was more cruel than even that of his Turkish ally.   It had such an effect on the Continent, that war was declared at intervals of about a month by Austria, the Empire, Spain, Brandenburg and Holland.   William's primary object was attained ; Europe was combined against France.   The resources of England were placed in his hands to support that coalition, but there was yet much to be done before he was free to act.

It has been already related that, on his flight, James stated his intention of finding if possible a new centre of action in Ireland.

State of Ireland — The view was a natural one, for he had throughout his reign been preparing that island as a refuge in case of danger.   He had there acted with more freedom than was possible in England, and gone far to carry out his plans for re-establishing Catholicism. Talbot, Lord Tyrconnel, a perfectly unscrupulous man, was at the head of the Government.   Almost all the other important offices were in Romanist hands.   Rice, chief Baron of the Exchequer, made the law courts subserve the same policy ; he openly asserted his intention of assaulting the Act of Settlement ; all who had or thought they had claims against the actual possessors of land, brought their claims into his court, and no proof was held too weak, no witness too untrustworthy, for the purpose of re-establishing the old Catholics in their possession of the soil.   From private acts he proceeded to public. Charter after charter was forfeited ; municipal corporations re-established, with reckless indifference to all forms of right, on a Roman Catholic basis.   While aldermen in the boroughs thus became Roman Catholic, sheriffs of the same religion were appointed, and in their hands lay the choice of juries, so that the whole legal apparatus was directed against Protestantism.   The army meanwhile had been similarly reorganized ; 6000 Protestant veterans had been disbanded and their places occupied by vehement and disorderly Catholics, who lived, we are told, constantly at free quarters on the Protestant inhabitants.

The arrival of William in England had brought matters to a crisis. The Papists thought their time was at length come. The whole country was full of panic and rumours of a coming massacre. Many of the English fled. The gentry and yeomen gathered themselves together to the towns and strong houses, to attempt if possible to make good for themselves that security which the Government would not give them. The two most important of these centres were Enniskillen and Londonderry. At the former, early in 1689, the Protestant population refused admittance to two companies of Popish infantry which had been ordered to be quartered on them. The gentry collected, drove the soldiers away, appointed Gustavus Hamilton governor, garrisoned the houses round Lough Erne, and held the district for King William. At Londonderry the same process took place. A regiment of 1200 Papists, under the Earl of Antrim, was sent to the city, and the mayor and sheriffs, who by the new charters were Papists, were proceeding to admit them, when thirteen young apprentices of Scotch birth took upon themselves to close the gates, and the Protestant gentry were summoned from the neighbouring country to defend the city. In two days it was strongly garrisoned, and the troops withdrew. It was in vain that Lord Mountjoy, a Protestant, who still remained faithful to James, attempted a compromise. Some few troops under Lundy were indeed admitted, but the country was still held for the Protestants, and Lundy was obliged, in appearance at all events, to accept the new Government.

Panic among the Englishry

Londonderry and Enniskillen garrisoned

Meanwhile William had attempted to enter into negotiations with Tyrconnel. For this purpose he had employed as his agent Richard Hamilton, who had once held a commission in James's army, but who now professed to have changed his allegiance. Hamilton pledged his word that, if he failed in his commission, he would come back in three weeks ; but, forfeiting his promise, he returned to his old allegiance, and became a chief leader on the side of James. But the character of the quarrel was already changing, the real object of Tyrconnel, in common with the greater part of the Irish Catholics, was to uphold neither James nor William, but to destroy for ever the English supremacy. For this purpose he was willing to use the name of James, trusting in fact to the assistance of Louis, to whom he opened his real design. He succeeded in ridding himself of Mountjoy,

William's negotiation with Tyrconnel.

Tyrconnel's object Irish independence

whose loyal influence was likely to thwart his plans, by sending
him on a mission to St. Germains, where James now held his
Court, and where he was at once apprehended. He then summoned
the Irish to arms. .An army of 50,000 Papists was collected, and
many thousands more took arms on their own behalf, and ravaged
the Protestant settlements around them. To complete the Irish
supremacy, Tyrconnel ordered the Protestants to be disarmed. The
His temporary destruction wrought is inconceivable. Property which
success has been estimated at £5,000,000 was destroyed. Whole
herds of cattle were killed and left to rot in the fields ; 50,000 are
said to have been thus killed in six weeks, while about 400,000 sheep
were similarly slain. Unable to withstand this general movement,
the Protestants in the south and west were overpowered, or retreated if possible to the strongholds ot Londonderry and Enniskillen. In those two places the flower of the English settlers stood
at bay, surrounded on all sides by hordes of liberated serfs now in
mutiny against their former masters. An army was ordered to
march northwards under the traitor Richard Hamilton. The Protestants fied before it ; 30,000 of them collected as a last asylum
behind the walls of Londonderry.

The country was in this condition when James, in answer to the
He gets James messages which Tyrconnel had sent him, determined,
over. with the assent of Louis, and with considerable assistance
in officers and arms, himself to visit Ireland. He landed at Cork,
and soon appeared in the capital, while William, unable to act
with energy on account of the difficulties which surrounded him,
was assailed by unthinking men with violent abuse for not taking
stronger measures to prevent those disasters which he was really
watching with the greatest dismay.

On his arrival in Dublin it was gradually brought home to James
that it was no feeling of passionate loyalty which was exciting the
Character of Irish population. Among those who attended his Court
Irish Jacobites. there were two distinct factions. Some Englishmen,
with the loyal feelings which animated English Jacobites, were
anxious to re-establish James and to retain the English influence in
Ireland. Another party, which included Tyrconnel and almost all
the Irish Papists, were fighting to destroy the English supremacy,
they cared not how, and intriguing to secure the assistance of France.
James would naturally have inclined to the former party, but soon
learnt that the power of his partisans was entirely gone.

He made a feeble struggle, and, contrary to the wish of the French and Irish, proceeded himself to the siege of Londonderry. On his march he found that the Protestants, as they retired, had destroyed all the crops and houses behind them. He journeyed through a desert, and when he found that the inhabitants of the city had got rid of their treacherous governor Lundy, had taken matters into their own hands, and appointed Walker, a clergyman, and Major Henry Baker, joint governors, he determined to return instantly to Dublin, there to hold a Parliament. The prosecution of the siege was intrusted to a French general, Maumont, and Richard Hamilton. The defence was so vigorous that the siege was soon turned into a blockade ; and while the gallant city was holding out to the last extremity, the Parliament at Dublin met.

Siege of Londonderry.

As a matter of course, considering the circumstances under which it was collected, it consisted entirely of Catholics. It proceeded to act with a recklessness which might be expected from an enslaved nation suddenly called to power, and from men who for years had been unused to public life. The great Act of Settlement, that compromise which in Charles II.'s reign had settled the share of land to be held by the Protestant emigrants who had followed Cromwell's victorious arms, was repealed. Many thousands of square miles were at a single blow transferred from English to Celtic landlords. The Act itself may have been unjust, but for years it had been the basis of society, and men had acted as though their titles were secure. Its repeal was therefore a violent act of unjust confiscation. Moreover, as far as James was concerned, nothing could be more disastrous, nothing could more surely destroy any influence he might yet keep in England, where it seemed to fore-shadow the justice Protestants might expect from his hands were his reign re-established. Such slight opposition as James offered (for he had the wisdom to see some of the disastrous consequences of the measure) had no effect but to cause profound distrust of himself. Other legislation even more disastrous met with no opposition at his hands. In his want of money he issued false coinage of copper and brass, intrinsically worth perhaps a sixtieth of its nominal value. Thus of course all creditors and mortgagees, who were pretty certain to be Protestants, were ruined. The money was rendered current by threats of punishment against those who refused it. Prices were kept down by law ; and to complete this wild legislation, the great Act of Attainder was passed, containing between 2000 or 3000 names. No inquiry was instituted as to the grounds of accusation against those

Wild legislation of the Irish Parliament

who were attainted, and opportunities were thus afforded for any man who had a personal enemy to introduce his name in the Bill. A limit of time was set within which all those named were bound to surrender themselves to justice or be liable to execution without trial ; while, to prevent the King's mercy from interfering with their vengeance, the Commons passed a law that after November the right of pardon should cease.

Such legislation, sanctioned by James, while it failed to give him

Its effect on English Jacobites. real popularity in Ireland, checked the reaction which was beginning in England. The feeling there grew constantly stronger against the inaction of the Government. The fate of Londonderry and Enniskillen was watched with absorbing interest. A fleet, with some troops under command of Kirke, was at length despatched, but Kirke refused to risk the passage of the river which led from Lough Foyle, and which was now guarded by forts and a boom, and the starving population of Londonderry had the misery of watching the ships as they lay idly in the Lough. But they still held out with astonishing constancy. Their friends in Enniskillen fared somewhat better. They did not confine themselves to defence ; but, issuing from the little island in Lough Erne which surrounded their city, they collected from their enemies a considerable quantity of cattle and ammunition, and lived in comparative comfort and security. At length, in July, the fate of Londonderry seemed sealed. Nearly everything eatable had been devoured,—horse-flesh, rats, salt hides, all that could possibly be converted even into the most objectionable food. It seemed impossible to feed the population in any way for two days longer. At last a peremptory order reached Kirke to relieve the city at all

Londonderry saved. hazards. On the 30th of July, three vessels, two transports and a frigate, sailed up the river, and, after a few minutes of difficulty, broke the boom, and in the evening, at ten o'clock, were anchored at the quay. The city was saved after 105 days of siege and blockade.

The Irish army immediately broke up from its camp and retreated. As it reached Strabane, on its backward course, it received the news

Battle of Newton Butler of another disaster. A great effort had been determined on against Enniskillen, but Colonel Wolseley had been sent to take the command by Kirke, and was successful in defeating at Newton Butler the approaching Irish, of whom nearly 2000 were put to the sword or drowned in a neighbouring lough. The news of this defeat hastened the steps of the retreating army as it returned from Londonderry, and it fled in confusion to Charlemont.

The same week which saw the relief of Londonderry and the battle of Newton Butler was remarkable also for the great defeat of William's army at Killiecrankie. In accordance with the character of the Scotch people, and in some proportion to the cruelty which had been exercised upon them, the Revolution in Scotland took a more violent form than it had assumed in England, for in the North James had been able to carry out more completely those plans which had produced his fall in the southern kingdom. A Church repugnant to the majority of the people had been forced upon them by law; in defiance of the opposition of a subservient Parliament, all the high places had been filled with Papists; nonconformity had been punished with an arbitrary severity and a ferocious cruelty of which England showed no counterpart; the electoral laws also, by requiring from all electors abjuration of the Covenant and an assertion of the King's ecclesiastical supremacy, excluded all but Prelatists from the right of election. Before collecting a national Convention, to consider the state of the nation under the present circumstances, it was necessary to dispense with the Act which excluded Presbyterians from the franchise. The Convention consequently consisted almost exclusively of Whigs, and the change of Government was marked by grave disorders in many parts of the country; nor, though William disliked these excesses, was he able to repress them, and the Episcopal clergy were in many instances most roughly used. There was at first some talk of a union with England, for the national feeling of the Scotch was beginning to yield to the increasing belief that in most points, especially of a financial and commercial character, such a union was very desirable: while many even of the Whigs in England wished for a union of the Churches and the establishment of Episcopacy on some broad and general basis. But the religious feeling of the country was quite averse to such a course, and William was too tolerant a man to wish to apply any coercion to men's consciences. He therefore wrote a letter, in which he did little else than profess his attachment to Protestantism, and his wish if possible to establish the Union. The arrangements he left in their own hands.

Unable himself to be present in Scotland, he intrusted the business to the two Dalrymples, father and son, and to Lord Melville, a prudent man, who, though he had retired abroad during the storm which succeeded the Rye-House Plot, had never committed himself warmly

to either party. James's agents were Graham of Claverhouse, now
Earl of Dundee, and Lindsay, Earl of Balcarras. The Castle of
Edinburgh was in the hands of Gordon, a Jacobite ; and James's agents
hoped that, by their own vigour and by means of the dread inspired
by the castle which commanded the town, they might yet obtain a
predominant influence in the Convention. The first trial of strength
was the election of a President, and before long it became evident
that the Whigs would certainly have the upper hand. They elected
the Duke of Hamilton, and about the middle of March the regular
sittings of the Convention began. At the first meeting, letters from
both King James and King William were produced ;
Letters from
James and
William.
that of James, the production of Melfort, was fitted, like
most of the productions of that statesman, to injure his
master's cause as much as possible. There was no word of repentance, no word of conciliation ; every line breathed an obstinate
determination to continue in the old course, and threats of vengeance
on his enemies. Dundee and Balcarras felt that all hope of maintain-
ing a majority was lost, and having thus failed in their first object,
Dundee tries
to secede
determined to pursue, in accordance with a plan they had
already arranged, a second line of policy, to secede with
their adherents to Stirling, and there establish a rival Convention.
The movement was thwarted by the premature retreat of Dundee.
Edinburgh was full of fierce Western Cameronians, and feeling that
his life was endangered, he hastily withdrew. The news that, with
a party of his old troopers, he had set out for Stirling, holding on his
way a conference with the Governor of Edinburgh Castle, excited the
fears and hatred of the Presbyterians in the Convention
Edinburgh arms
They at once proceeded to rouse the people of Edinburgh
to arms, and to place the town in an attitude of defence, and thus
thwart the idea of secession. They then went on to consider the state
of the nation, and declaring that the late King had forfeited the
throne by misconduct, offered the Crown to William and Mary.
The offer was accompanied, as in the case of England, with a Declaration of Right,—here in Scotland called the Claim of Right,—in
which, without discussing the question, they declared that Episcopacy was abolished. The Crown was then solemnly offered and
accepted.

Yet the difficulties of William were still most severe. The bigoted
Covenanters held aloof from a tolerant King who had not taken
the Covenant ; and a number of extreme Whigs, who were attached
to a monarchy so limited as to be really a republic, put themselves

at the head of a factious opposition, forming among themselves an organization known by the name of the Club. While this powerful opposition was being formed in the Lowlands, war in behalf of the fugitive King actually broke out in the High- _{The Club} lands. Dundee, on his flight from Edinburgh, had remained for some time peaceably in his own house. But letters passing between him and Melfort, James's minister in Ireland, were intercepted. An order was issued to arrest him, with his colleague Balcarras. Balcarras was secured, but Dundee fled towards Inverness, where he found a state of affairs which he was able to turn to _{Dundee escapes} the advantage of James.

The politics of the Highland clans bore little relation to the general politics of the nation. The Highlanders were as yet a half savage race, devoted to their patriarchal form _{Highland politics} of society, and with political attachments which seldom went beyond the head of their tribe. It mattered but little to them whether James or William were upon the Scottish throne. They were equally ready to oppose by violence any Government which interfered with their wild freedom. But among themselves they had bitter tribal jealousies and feuds, and the partial introduction of the feudal system had complicated their relations one with the other. Great chiefs, combining the character of feudal lords and clan patriarchs, had contrived to extend their power, and render other clans besides their own dependent or tributary. The Earl or Marquis of Argyle, Mac Callum More, as the Highlanders called him, head of the great clan of Campbell in Argyleshire, had thus extended his pre-eminence at the expense of his neighbours The power of this chief was great. He could bring 5000 men into the field, and his jurisdiction was so independent as to be hardly second to that of the Crown; consequently all his neighbours looked upon him with jealousy and hatred. That the politics of the head of the Campbell clan were consistently Whig was enough to make all his rivals and enemies Jacobites. But of late years the power of the Campbells had decayed; during the triumph of the Stuart Kings the Marquis of Argyle had been beheaded, and the Earl, his son, had been driven into exile. As the Campbells sunk, the Macdonalds, the chief rivals of their clan, on whose property they had encroached, had risen. But the Macdonalds had a constant feud with the Mackintoshes in the neighbourhood of Inverness, in pursuance of which Macdonald of Keppoch was at this moment engaged in the siege of Inverness, which had made common cause with the Mackintoshes

When therefore Dundee came into that neighbourhood he found the clans already in arms on quarrels of their own. It occurred to
Dundee in the   him that, by taking advantage of the general enmity
Highlands.   against the Campbells, he might form a union of the clans, nominally at all events in favour of King James. His plan met with a partial success. He could not indeed induce the Mackintoshes to join with the Macdonalds, but he secured their neutrality. The eastern clans as a rule followed the same course; but those of the west, more immediate sufferers from the power and encroachments of the Campbells, eagerly leapt at the opportunity of attacking the party of which Argyle was one of the chiefs. Mackay was sent to take the command of the English troops With his regular soldiers he could do nothing against the rapid Highlanders in the mountains, and urged the plan, subsequently followed, of building a line of forts across the country. The campaign produced no event of importance. A cessation of arms occurred in June, spent by Dundee in obtaining succour from James in Ireland, by Mackay in raising troops with some difficulty among the Western Cameronians.

A fresh dispute among the clans renewed the war. The Murrays, of whom Athol was the chief, had not as yet declared for either side. The Marquis of Athol himself withdrew for safety to England, but his eldest son declared for King William, while his steward, who was believed to be in his confidence, declared for James. The two sections of the clan disputed the possession of the castle of Blair Athol,
Battle of   the seat of the chief. It was felt by both parties that
Killiecrankie   the adhesion of this large clan was of great importance,
July 27   and Dundee on one side and Mackay on the other hurried to support their friends at Blair Athol. The castle lies a little beyond the northern end of the pass of Killiecrankie, a ravine through which the river Garry rushes, and which leads from the lowlands of Perthshire to the mountains. The armies were not ill-matched in numbers. Mackay's troops were suffered by the Highlanders to get clear of the difficult pass, and then found themselves in a little valley, with the Highlanders occupying the hills around. As long as it was an affair of musketry, the Lowland troops, many of whom were veterans, held their ground, but when the clans suddenly threw their firelocks from them and rushed with a wild yell on their lines, they broke and fled, with the exception of one regiment, and rushed in helpless flight down the narrow pass. It was the difference in the weapons which caused this strange victory of undisciplined

over disciplined troops. When he had fired his volley, the Highlander threw away his firelock, and was ready in an instant to rush forward with his broadsword. The bayonet at that time in use was so constructed that, when fixed, it filled up the mouth of the barrel. It took some minutes to arrange the clumsy contrivance which turned the musket into a pike. While the regulars were still fumbling with their weapons, the Highlanders were upon them.[1] Mackay brought off such troops as were left with rare coolness, and the death of Dundee neutralized the effects of the defeat. The Highland army passed under the command of General Cannon, who had brought over the Irish auxiliaries, a man of no particular ability. Mackay succeeded in rapidly re-establishing his army. He destroyed the prestige of the Highlanders by defeating a detachment at St. Johnstone's, near Perth; and when a newly raised regiment of Cameronian recruits beat off the mountaineers at Dunkeld, no longer held together by a leader of ability, they broke up and retired to their own glens, and the war was practically over. Mackay concludes the war.

Though William's measures had thus been tolerably successful, although the Revolution was acknowledged in two portions of the Empire, and likely soon to become so in the third, his position in London was most difficult and trying. Success had dissolved the union between the Whigs and Tories, and the triumphant Whigs had time to remember their sufferings in the last reign and to form plans of vengeance. The King desired above all things the cessation of faction and the union of parties, but on every question which arose the Commons displayed a most passionate temper. A certain number of attainders were reversed, and this was well enough ; but when a Bill of Indemnity was brought in, so many exceptions were made to it, that it became in fact rather a Bill of vengeance than a Bill of oblivion. The discussion of these exceptions lasted so long that the Bill had to be dropped for that session. But the intemperate Whig leaders, such men as Howe, Sacheverell, and the younger Hampden, were not contented to be thus balked of their revenge. Fierce attacks were brought against the Lord President Caermarthen, and Halifax, the Privy Seal. The position of Caermarthen was so strong that his enemies were afraid to divide the House against him. Halifax had made more enemies, and was not so firmly supported by the King's influence. The practical mind of William found little to like in the subtle and questioning intellect Factions of the English Parliament Bill of Indemnity dropped Attack on Halifax.

---

[1] Taught by experience, Mackay invented the bayonet fitting round the barrel.

of Halifax ; and as the affairs in Ireland had been virtually entirely
in that nobleman's control, the wretched condition of the Protestants,
the lengthened misery of Londonderry, and the temporary success of
James and Tyrconnel, were all laid to his charge. It was said that
he even purposely neglected Ireland in order to render a new Government indispensable. However, he contrived to escape impeachment
by a narrow majority of sixteen ; and the relief of Londonderry, and
the immediate despatch of Schomberg at the head of a considerable
body of troops to support the Protestant interest, tended to check the
vehemence of the popular anger which was directed against him.

Late in August, the Parliament broke up till October, and all eyes
were turned towards the fate of Schomberg's expedition. His troops
consisted for the most part of raw recruits, scarcely able to discharge
their firelocks. He could not venture to fight with such an army,
but displayed great skill and determination in the manner in
which he overcame difficulties apparently overwhelming.
Several regiments of French Protestant refugees accompanied him ; and while he was lying in the neighbourhood of Dundalk treason was discovered in their camp. The refugees
themselves were trustworthy, but a certain number of other foreigners
had found their way into their regiments, and opened correspondence
with the Irish. Sharp vengeance fell upon the chief conspirators.
But a more terrible enemy than treason attacked the English troops.,
A deadly pestilence arose and carried them off by hundreds : their
misery was unspeakable ; the ties of morality and decorum were
relaxed, the men got drunk sitting on the corpses of their dead comrades, and the horror of the time is well shown by the fact, that
several ships lay in Carrickfergus Bay filled with carcases, and not
a live man on board. The blame of the wretched condition of the
army was traceable to the general maladministration which existed
in the Government. The Chief Commissary was a man named Shales,
who supplied the army with quite uneatable food, drew money largely
for supplies which never reached the troops, and let out the troop
horses, when collected, to English farmers. But it was not only in
the army that this maladministration was visible. Admiral Herbert,
now Lord Torrington, sunk in debauchery, allowed the same offences
to be perpetrated in the navy. It would be unfair to lay this to the
charge of William. The deeprooted mismanagement of the last
twenty years rendered it almost impossible for him to introduce
reforms with any rapidity, nor, with all the weight of foreign affairs
on his hands. could he personally supervise every department. His

*Misery of the
English army
in Ireland.*

own department was well and successfully managed, and the English troops abroad won some honour in a skirmish against the French at Walcourt.

Still it was not to be expected that Parliament, on its reassembling, should be in a better temper than when it separated. It again renewed its violent courses. The necessary supplies were indeed voted; The Bill of Rights, *Parliament meets Oct 19, 1689* by which the Declaration of Right was to be formed into a statute, and which in the last session had been thrown aside because the Lords wished to introduce the name of the Electress Sophia in the succession to the throne, was passed without that amendment; but besides this scarcely any other work was done. On the other hand, the Whig majority proceeded on their course of vengeance. The Earls of Salisbury and Peterborough, Sir Edward Hales *The violence of* and Obadiah Walker were impeached; a Committee *the Whigs* to inquire into the death of Russell and Sidney, known as the Murder Committee, was appointed, and the attack upon Halifax renewed. At length the Whigs, conscious that the King was not well pleased with their vindictive temper, attempted to secure their own permanent supremacy in Parliament. They introduced a Corporation Bill, for restoring all the charters which had been forfeited in the reign of James; and to this, at the suggestion of Sacheverell and Howard, were appended two clauses, the one providing that all who had taken part in the surrender of the charters should be incapable of holding office for seven years, the other adding that all who, in spite of being thus incapacitated, presumed to hold office should be fined £500, and be debarred for life from public employment. These clauses, which would have in fact disfranchized the Tory party in every borough, they attempted to pass through the House by a surprise, when the greater part of the Tory party had returned home for Christmas. But so violent and factious a measure *The Tories* called out all the energies of the Opposition. The *throw out the* country gentlemen came crowding back to town, and, *Corporation Act* after a violent debate, the Whigs were defeated by a small majority. The Tories thought to improve their triumph by reintroducing the Bill of Indemnity without the exceptions, but they quite overrated their strength. Their attempt was defeated by an enormous majority, and a Bill of Pains and Penalties incorporated with the Indemnity Act, which rendered it a mere measure of proscription. But this violent measure was not destined to pass the House. The fierce struggle of parties was so repugnant to the King, any attempt at firm national government appeared to him so hopeless, that, having

William threatens to leave England.

secretly arranged means of retiring to Holland, he sent for his ministers, and told them it was his intention to withdraw from England, leaving the Queen upon the throne. The threat stupefied the Whigs. To whatever excesses their passion may have led them, they felt that their safety was bound up with the prudent chief they had elected. A passionate scene ensued, in which the Tory Nottingham and the Whig Shrewsbury vied with each other in intreating William to forego his plan. At length he

Dissolves Parliament, Jan. 27, 1690, and undertakes Irish war.

yielded, but determined that he would escape from the atmosphere of faction which surrounded him, and himself go to carry on the war in Ireland. Having stated that such was his unalterable intention, he prorogued and dissolved the factious Parliament which he had been unable to bring to reason.

The dissolution brought with it a reaction. The Tories in the New

Tory reaction in new Parliament.

Parliament were as strong as the Whigs had lately been. Even London returned four opponents to the obnoxious clauses of the Corporation Act. As yet the theory of a ministry not having been established, there was no great change, yet the balance among the ministers was somewhat altered. Halifax withdrew from the Government ; the Board of Treasury and the Board of Admiralty were both reconstituted, with a larger proportion of Tories, and Caermarthen attained such an amount of power as to make him virtually Prime Minister. Sir John Lowther was put at the head

Venality of Parliament

of the Treasury, while the purchase of votes, an art at which Caermarthen was an adept, and which for many years to come was constantly employed by the Government, was intrusted to Sir John Trevor, who became Speaker. William had hitherto tried to act without bribery ; he had found his efforts futile, and his influence in Parliament neutralized by the passion of faction. He now, against his own feelings, allowed Caermarthen to have his way. The strange venality of Parliament at this time, and for many years afterwards, may probably be traced to the fact that the secrecy with which debates in Parliament were shrouded prevented the exercise of any wholesome popular opinion upon the vote of the representatives, while the Crown had lost that power of coercing the Opposition which it had enjoyed in the time of the Tudors. It became necessary to purchase what could not be procured by violence, while there was no pressure from without to restrain the cupidity of unprincipled members. With his new Parliament William found himself more free to act.

Its first duty was the settlement of the revenue. This had hitherto been chiefly collected under Acts passed for short terms only. It was now put on a permanent basis. The hereditary revenues, consisting of the rents of royal domains, fees and fines, post office and ecclesiastical dues, together with that portion of the excise which had been paid to Charles II. as the price for the abolition of feudal services, were given to William and Mary. These revenues amounted to about £400,000 or £500,000 a year. The King had hoped to obtain a grant for life of the other excise and custom duties which had been granted to James, and had amounted to £900,000 a year; but the Tory majority felt as distinctly as their opponents that an income which set the Crown free from the necessity of consulting Parliament might prove a source of evils similar to those of the last reign. They therefore gave William for life only £300,000 a year from the excise, the remaining £600,000, which arose from customs, they granted for four years only.

The revenue settled.

On other points the Parliament now acted more in accordance with the King's wishes, although the Whigs produced several embarrassing measures, and attempted to compel all place-holders to take an oath abjuring King James. But William was determined to check the course of vengeance; the known wish of the King enabled the Tories to throw out the obnoxious measure, and the revenge of the Whigs was finally balked by an Act of Grace from the Crown, which took the place of the unfinished Bill of Indemnity.

Act of Grace May 20.

This declared a perfect oblivion for all political offences up to that moment, excepting from the benefits of the Act only such of the regicides as were still alive, and about thirty others; of whom some were either dead or in safety abroad, while the rest, though in England, were suffered to live unharmed. It is a noble addition to the glory of William that, through his firmness and generosity, no blood was shed at the Great Revolution.

Meanwhile the King had been hastening preparations for his war. The number of the troops in Ireland had been raised to 30,000, at length well armed and well provisioned;

Preparation for war.

a fleet, with still more provisions and equipments, was ready to receive the King at Chester. But at that moment it became very difficult for him to leave the country, for the Jacobites had determined to seize the opportunity of his absence for a great effort. Clarendon the Queen's uncle, Dartmouth commander of the fleet which should have opposed William's landing, and Preston

Jacobite plot discovered.

James's last Secretary of State, were the leaders of the scheme. Fortunately their secrets were intrusted to a man named Fuller, who at once determined to turn traitor. He gave over to the Privy Council the despatches from the Queen in France, which had been sewn into his buttons. His fellow-messenger was apprehended ; when convicted and condemned to death, he too confessed, and the chiefs of the conspiracy were in the hands of the Government. Nevertheless it was a terrible time to be absent from home. An insurrection might break out at any moment, and an invasion was threatened from France.

William was determined that, come what would, he would put an end to the disgraceful state of affairs in Ireland. He placed the Government in the hands of the Queen, assisted by a Council of nine,

William goes to Ireland. with Danby for her chief minister, Admiral Russell to advise her on naval, and Marlborough on military affairs, and then crossed to Belfast. Fortunately the two objects of the Jacobites proved incompatible; the threatened invasion so roused the national spirit, that domestic insurrection became impossible. While

Threatened invasion and insurrection William advanced southward, and the Irish army, reinforced by a considerable number of French under Lauzun, fell back behind the Boyne, a great French fleet under Tourville appeared off the Needles. Torrington, the English commander, had been reinforced by a Dutch squadron, yet shrunk from the encounter, and retreated towards the Straits of Dover. The Queen and her Council sent peremptory orders to fight. Jealous of Russell, afraid of risking a great battle with superior numbers, Torrington unwillingly obeyed. With shameful policy, he

Battle of Beachy Head. sent the Dutch squadron forward to bear the brunt of the danger, and left it almost unsupported, till, after exhibiting their usual stubborn bravery, the Dutch were compelled to fall back with their shattered ships, and Tourville swept the Channel unopposed. Almost at the same time as the news of this disgraceful defeat reached London, tidings arrived that the allies, under the Prince of Waldeck, had been beaten by Luxemburg at

Spirited behaviour of England. the battle of Fleurus. But the very misfortunes which seemed falling upon the nation roused its spirit. The Lord Mayor offered the Queen at once £100,000, 10,000 Londoners, well armed for immediate purposes, and six regiments of foot and two regiments of horse, to be raised at once, without cost to the Crown. The same temper was visible throughout England, and suddenly, after three days of depression, hope was again raised in the national mind by the news of the battle of the Boyne.

James had determined to make a stand behind that river, which separates the counties of Louth and Meath, falling into the
sea at Drogheda.   The position was a fairly strong one ;   Battle of the
Boyne
the ground rose immediately from the river, and some of   July 1, 1690.
William's generals scarcely liked to venture upon an attack.   But he
felt that some great blow was necessary to retrieve the disasters of
the last year, and he gave orders for crossing the river at once.   Early
in the morning of the 1st of July the English began to advance.
Young Schomberg was sent some miles up the river, to cross at the
bridge of Slane, and thus turn the left flank of the Irish army.
His success in this movement alarmed Lauzun.   There was a narrow
passage at Duleek, four miles south of the Boyne, where two carriages
could scarcely pass between impassable bogs.   If Schomberg could
secure this pass the Irish would be enclosed in a trap.   It was necessary at any price to avoid this danger ; Lauzun therefore marched to
oppose him, taking with him all the French troops, leaving the Irish
alone to hold the river.   William commanded the left wing, formed
entirely of horse.   He fought his way across the river not far above
Drogheda.   In the centre Schomberg led the main body of the infantry
across the fords of Old Bridge.   The Irish infantry which should
have opposed him, thoroughly demoralized by a year spent under lax
discipline and in habits of plunder, fled at the first onset.   The
cavalry, who had been more carefully drilled under command of
the traitor Richard Hamilton, strove in vain to restore the day.
For half an hour the struggle in the bed of the river was fierce.
The leader of the Protestant refugees was killed, and Schomberg
himself, while rallying these troops, and calling out to them, " Come
on, gentlemen, there are your persecutors," also fell.   But William,
having crossed with the left wing, now came up on the flank of
the Irish, and the passage was secured.   The Irish cavalry were
left entirely unsupported by the infantry.   Fighting bravely, and with
considerable loss, they were slowly driven from the ground.   Their
leader Richard Hamilton was taken prisoner.   James, whose personal
courage it had been usual to praise, turned early from the fight
and fled towards Dublin.   The rout of fugitives hurried through the
pass of Duleek, covered by the French infantry, who had been
resisting young Schomberg's flank attack all the day.   William is said
to have been slack in the pursuit ; Schomberg's death, and his own
exhaustion, after having been thirty-five hours out of the last forty on
horseback, may have been the cause of this.   On neither side was the
loss very great.   Of the English about 500 are said to have been

killed, of the Irish 1500 ; but they were chiefly cavalry, the only trustworthy Irish troops.

James, having reached Dublin, summoned the Lord Mayor and
James's final flight. principal Catholic citizens to the castle. Forgetful of his own speedy flight, he upbraided the Irish for cowardice, and vowed he would never more command an Irish army. He then at once took flight again, hurried to Waterford, and thence by Kinsale to France. Lauzun and Tyrconnel, with the remains of their army, also thought it desirable to evacuate the capital, which William entered in triumph. For a short time he thought of returning to England, for news of the defeat of Beachy Head and of the battle of Fleurus had reached him, and his presence in London seemed necessary. But when he heard of the courageous spirit showed by the nation, and knew that the only use Tourville had made of his victory was to attack and burn Teignmouth, thus still further exasperating the people, he felt that the crisis was over, that he might remain to complete his victory.

He gradually conquered the country as far as Limerick. There
Siege of Limerick. the Irish stood at bay. In the eyes of the French commander nothing could be more useless than the attempt to defend the city. " The walls could be knocked down with roasted apples," said Lauzun. He consequently withdrew his troops, and the Irish were left to themselves, under the command of Sarsfield, the only Irish general who seems to have possessed any military character, and vain though their hopes seemed to Lauzun, the defence of the city was successful. The want of artillery at first checked the proceedings of the besiegers. A daring raid, headed by Sarsfield, destroyed the convoy which was bringing up the siege train. The artillery was buried and exploded, and Sarsfield's party returned unhurt. Then came the heavy rains which occur at this season in Ireland ; the country around the town became a marsh. A final
William returns to England. Sept. 6. vigorous assault proved unsuccessful, and the siege was raised. This check was somewhat balanced by the success of an expedition planned and commanded by Marlborough, which had landed in the south, and in five weeks had conquered both Cork and Kinsale. William returned to England in
Marlborough's success in the south. September, intrusting the government to three Lords Justices, and the management of the war to Ginkel. But no further military operation of importance took place till May in the following year.

The northern and eastern part of the island was in the hands of the English, and brought under some sort of government by the Lords Justices. In that part trade and industry had revived. In the Irish portion of the island, into which the Celtic inhabitants had crowded, there was wild confusion and much distress. Gangs of robbers infested the country, the soldiers were little better themselves than robbers. The currency of James's brass money entirely ruined trade. As usual in Ireland, jealousy of race began to show itself. In the Councils of Regency and of War, to whom the management of James's affairs were intrusted, men not of Irish blood had considerable influence ; they were therefore involved in constant quarrels with the purely Irish party. Some order however began to show itself when Tyrconnel returned from France, accompanied by a French general of ability called St. Ruth. St. Ruth devoted himself with extreme energy to discipline the crowd of disorderly bandits whom he had to command, and prepared as well as he could to oppose the advance of Ginkel, who, seconded by Tollemache and Mackay, moved in the beginning of June from their St. Ruth comes headquarters at Mullingar. The French generals, both from France. now and before, had been of opinion that Athlone was the right spot for the Irish to make a stand. It lay almost in the middle of the island, half on one side, half on the other of the Shannon, separating the provinces of Leinster and Connaught. Ginkel determined that he would take this place, which seemed to him to be the key of the Irish frontier. It was a work of no common difficulty. St. Ruth thought the attempt absolutely hopeless. " His master," he said of Ginkel, " ought to hang him for attempting to take the town, mine ought to hang me if I lose it." The half of the town upon the English side of the river was taken on the 19th, but the real difficulty yet remained. The narrow bridge which joined the two towns was Siege of gallantly defended. There was a ford lower down, but it Athlone. was almost impassable. During the rest of the month the efforts of the besiegers were in vain. At last want of supplies compelled them either to succeed or to retreat. A gallant assault on the ford, which was almost up to the necks of the men, proved successful ; to the astonishment and anger of St. Ruth the town was taken (June 30).

In spite of the advice of Sarsfield and the rest of the Irish generals, who wisely wished to employ their undisciplined troops in a partisan warfare, St. Ruth determined to fight. He fell back about thirty miles from Athlone, to the hill of Aghrim, where his troops occupied rising ground, covered along its whole front by a deep bog ; while along the bottom of the firm ground ran enclosures, which were turned into

breastworks.   Against these difficulties Ginkel marched.   But the
Irish, now well posted and well commanded, showed such firmness,
that it seemed probable they would make good their position, and
evening was already drawing on, when at length Mackay, with the
English and Huguenot cavalry, succeeded in passing
the bog, and placing his troops on the flank of the
Irish army.   At this critical moment St. Ruth was
killed.   With singular folly, his friends concealed his death, not
only from his men, but also from his generals.   Sarsfield had
been ordered to remain immoveable with reserves till St. Ruth
ordered his advance, as the order did not come Sarsfield did not move,
and the victory of the English thus became complete.   The Irish
army broke up, and was pursued with relentless cruelty ; 6000 or
7000 Irish are said to have been put to death as they fled.   The plain
beyond the field of battle was so studded with white corpses, that it
was described as looking like a pasture covered with flocks of sheep.

Battle of Aghrim. July 12, 1691

This battle completed the conquest of Ireland.   The fall of Galway
immediately followed, and Ginkel proceeded to attack for a second
time the city of Limerick.   The chances were now all in favour of the
English, while the Irish were thoroughly disheartened by their late
defeat.   Ginkel's army was well supplied, and all hope of succour was
cut off from the besieged by an English squadron which
occupied the Shannon.   Under these circumstances a
capitulation was granted, the terms of which were fairly
favourable to the Irish.   By the military treaty, all officers and
soldiers who desired it were conveyed to France, under command of
their own generals.   By the civil treaty, the Roman Catholics were
promised the enjoyment of such privileges as they had enjoyed in
the reign of Charles II.   To all who took the oath of allegiance a
perfect amnesty was promised.   It is to the disgrace of England that
this treaty with regard to the Catholics was not kept.   For the time,
however, Ireland was completely subdued, and the
English supremacy established so firmly, that for more
than a century, in spite of the difficulties which more than once beset
the English Government, no outbreak of the Irishry against the
Englishry was even suggested.

Second siege and capitulation of Limerick Oct. 3.

End of the Irish war.

In Scotland, at length, the establishment of the Government was
equally complete.   The members of the factious Club
had gone so far as to make common cause with the
Jacobites.   But in the Parliament which met in 1690,
under the management of Melville as Lord High Commissioner, the

Revolution completed in Scotland

Government succeeded in obtaining a majority. The union among its opponents was at once dissolved. A general acquiescence met the re-establishment of the Presbyterian form of Church government, and no further difficulties of importance were to be apprehended. William could now turn his attention to the affairs of England and of the Continent.

In England, from the middle of 1690, the Jacobite intrigues continued. The lenity shown by William, after the abortive efforts of the Jacobites during the threatened French invasion, encouraged further conspiracies. It seemed certain that William's presence would be required abroad, and that again during his absence an opportunity would be offered for striking a blow against the Government. In December 1690, a meeting was held of the leading Jacobites, and it was determined that Preston should be sent to St. Germains. He was to beg James to return to England, bringing with him a sufficient French force to secure his success, but at the same time, in the name of the Jacobites, he was to intreat him to allow the Protestant religion to remain undisturbed, and to rule in strict accordance with law. Besides this general letter, separate papers were intrusted to Preston, especially one from the nonjuring Bishop Turner, apparently in the name of Sancroft and his brother Bishops. He also took with him notes as to the most vulnerable points of the coast. But the captain of the ship which was engaged to take him over thought it wiser to inform Lord Caermarthen what he was doing, and just as the messengers thought they were safe out of the river, a vessel of remarkable swiftness belonging to Lord Caermarthen's son suddenly appeared alongside, and they were discovered hidden among the gravel which formed the ballast of their vessel.

Jacobite plots in England.

Preston's plot thwarted.

The capture of Preston, and the disclosure of the Jacobite plot, allowed William to go abroad, leaving the complete investigation of the treason to his ministers in England. On the Continent his diplomacy had been singularly successful. He had brought together a great coalition, and had succeeded in winning the Duke of Savoy, whom the King of France had reckoned among his allies, and whose territory closed the passage of the French to the Spanish dominions in Italy. Success would have cemented the coalition, and induced Denmark and Sweden, which were still wavering, to join it. But in rapidity of action a coalition is seldom a match for a single power, and Louis was able to forestall the action of the allies, and capture the important fortress

William's successful policy abroad.

of Mons, in spite of all William's efforts to relieve it. But this first success, though damaging to the coalition, produced no very important military events ; the advantages of the French both in Spain and Italy were counterbalanced by the disasters which befell their allies First crisis of the war over. the Turks in Hungary, and the main armies in Flanders under William and Luxemburg were content merely to watch each other. The first crisis of the war was in fact over. The centre of the coalition was William ; his strength was derived from his position as King of England ; deprived of that position, he would have lost most of his influence, and the only chance of depriving him of it had been the success of the Irish. It was in Ireland, therefore, that the real crisis of the war had arrived. The defeat of James at the Boyne in 1690, and of St. Ruth at Aghrim almost exactly a year after, had thus rendered all hopes of destroying William's position futile. Once again, in the following year, the same critical situation of affairs arose. With the battle of La Hogue the success of James became hopeless, and though the war continued for many years, there is no other point in it which can really be called critical.

The causes which led James still to cherish hope, and which James's hopes upheld by the treason of the ministry induced him to persuade Louis to contemplate that invasion of England to which the battle of La Hogue put an end, are to be found in the conduct of the Jacobite party in England : for while William's attention was constantly turned to the Continent, treason found its way among his own immediate ministers. Uncertain even yet of the stability of the new Government, three of the greatest among them determined to be safe on either issue. Admiral Russell, and Godolphin, head of the Treasury, succeeded in obtaining written pardons from James ; and Marlborough, whose previous treachery might have been supposed unpardonable, made such a show of repentance, that he obtained the same favour, promising in exchange, when he should be in command of the English troops, to bring them over to and of Marlborough. the enemy. But even the treachery of Marlborough partook of the greatness of his character. His views reached far beyond this commonplace act of treason. He was already devising plans by which the fate of England and of Europe should be in his own hands. As his schemes were not yet ready, though the opportunity he had mentioned to James arose in Flanders, he contrived to excuse himself from performing his promise. But before long circumstances led him to believe that he might carry out his treacherous plans in a way more in accordance with his own wishes. The session of Parliament had been a somewhat stormy one. The immense emoluments of place-holders had excited the anger of the Opposition, and although the extreme measures suggested, which went so far as to cut down all official salaries to £500, had destroyed all attempts at wholesome reform, there was much continued discontent against the Court. There had been bitter quarrels also between the Upper and Lower Houses upon new arrangements of the Treason Law which had been suggested, and all parties seemed to be combined in mistrust and dislike of the favours lavished on foreigners. This state of affairs seemed to open the way for Marlborough's intrigues. In fact, years of rivalry and several bloody wars, coupled with constant outrages on one side or the other on distant colonies, had rendered the Dutch at least as hateful to the English as the French; nor was the feeling diminished by seeing many of the greater and more lucrative offices in the hands of members of the hated nation. By working on this feeling, Marlborough hoped to induce Parliament to petition the King to discharge all foreign troops, a line of conduct which at a subsequent period was actually followed. Once rid of these troops (and he thought it impossible that William, situated as he was, could withstand a formal Parliamentary request), Marlborough relied on his own ability to induce the English army, which was very jealous of William's liking for his own Dutch troops, to further his views. The absolute authority which his wife exercised over the Princess Anne enabled him to secure her adhesion to his plans. She wrote friendly and repentant letters to her father. With the army at his command, and with the Protestant heiress inclined to favour his projects, Marlborough would declare for James, and secure his return without the danger of foreign invasion, without the shedding of a drop of blood. Such at least was the story he told the Jacobites. Men who knew his character mistrusted him. It was more likely, they thought, and this seems to have been his real plan, that he would declare not for King James, but for Princess Anne herself. He would thus become indirectly the ruler of England, and as such the head of the European coalition, and the arbiter of Europe.

Luckily for William, even the Jacobites looked with suspicion on the scheme; Bentinck received information of Marlborough's treachery. The King, placed on his guard, stripped him of all his offices; and when Anne, who knew well the reason of his disgrace, persisted in ignoring it and in

Marlborough is deprived of his offices. Jan. 10, 1692.

bringing the Duchess of Marlborough to Court, the spirit of the Queen was roused, and a bitter quarrel broke out between the sisters. The full details of the plot were not at the time known, and a false plot, invented and brought to light by a wretched informer of the name of Fuller, gave Marlborough an opportunity of ostentatiously clearing his character. He was thus regarded as a martyr to the jealousy of William, and to an unreasonable dislike of her sister on the part of the Queen.

The Queen's quarrel with the Princess Anne.

Although for the time the danger of Marlborough's treason seemed to have been escaped, it was undoubtedly the knowledge of its existence, and of the feeling prevalent among William's other ministers, that encouraged James still to retain hopes of success in England.

Before passing to the events to which those hopes gave rise, an incident must be mentioned which, though it had but little effect at the moment, has been always considered as a blot on William's character, and added point to the bitter attacks directed against him towards the close of his reign. Melville had proved unequal to the task of governing Scotland, and the management of the affairs of that country had passed almost entirely into the hands of the Dalrymples, father and son, the elder of whom was President of the Court of Session, having been lately raised to the peerage by the title of Viscount Stair. The son, known as the Master of Stair, was appointed Secretary for Scotland, resident in London. To him now fell the duty of pacifying the Highlands, where the civil war continued to smoulder. Unable to give the Highlanders any effectual support, James had told them that they were at liberty to make peace with the conqueror. It has been already mentioned that local politics had more to do with the conduct of the Highlanders than any question as to the reigning dynasty, and that their hatred directed against the head of the Campbell clan arose largely from the condition of dependence to him in which they found themselves, and which was due in a great degree to unpaid arrears of rent. It was determined now to adopt a plan which had been formerly suggested, and to expend some £15,000 in relieving them from their difficulties. The distribution of this money was unwisely intrusted to Breadalbane, himself a Campbell, and too much interested in the encroachments of that house not to be unpopular. He was profoundly and justly mistrusted by the Highlanders, and the negotiations for the distribution of the money proceeded but slowly, the chief leader of the opposition to the settlement being

Massacre of Glencoe. Feb. 13.

Macdonald of Glencoe, one of that tribe which had suffered most from the growth of the Campbells. Pressure was put upon the Highlanders to bring the negotiation to a conclusion. A proclamation was issued, promising pardon to all who, before the 31st of December 1691, should swear to live peaceably under the existing Government. All who refused to take this oath were to be regarded as public enemies. As the Government appeared to be in earnest, the chiefs yielded, making it a sort of point of honour to yield as slowly as possible. In this foolish contest of honour Mac Ian of Glencoe was unfortunately the victor. Not till the very day named did he appear at Fort William to take the oaths. When he arrived there he found to his dismay that there was no magistrate to receive them, and he was compelled forthwith to set out through the winter snow to Inverary to find a magistrate. The journey was so difficult that it was not till the 6th of January that he reached Inverary. Under the circumstances, the sheriff there consented, though after the prescribed date, to receive the oath, and sent it, with a certificate stating the circumstances to Edinburgh. The slowness of Macdonald had played into the hands of his enemies the Campbells. Breadalbane and Argyle were at one in their determination to use their advantage, and they found a ready assistant in the Master of Stair, whose views, free from all local feeling, were of the sternest description, and who thought the Highlanders should be treated as uncivilized barbarians. He had been disappointed at the submission of the clans, and rejoiced at the opportunity of making one example. By his means the certificate granted by the sheriff appears to have been suppressed, and an order was drawn up and laid before William, in which, along with other instructions to the commander of the army in Scotland, were these words with regard to the clan of Glencoe : " It will be proper, for the vindication of public justice, to extirpate that set of thieves." William signed the order, probably without carefully reading it, almost certainly without understanding what Dalrymple meant by extirpation. His scheme was one of the utmost barbarity. A detachment of soldiers was sent into the glen as though on a friendly mission. They were kindly received and hospitably kept for more than a week. Then, at a fixed date, when other troops were to have stopped all the passes, they suddenly fell upon their kindly hosts and cruelly murdered them. The plan was but partially carried out. The passes had not been stopped, and not more than thirty-eight of the Highlanders were actually killed. But the villages were destroyed, the cattle driven off, and it is unknown how many more perished as they fled in the dead of winter in the wild mountains which surrounded their glen.

It was just after this event, in March, that William went abroad to resume the Continental war. As usual, his absence was the time of danger for England. An invasion from France had long been planned, and was on the point of taking place. Excited by the constant untruthful account of his agents in England, encouraged by the artful and well-planned treachery of Marlborough and William's other ministers, James had never ceased to press upon Louis the wisdom of an assault upon England. His urgent instances had always been met by the opposition of the war minister Louvois. Conscious that his superiority lay in the organization of large disciplined armies in the field, and led by the experience of his life to look to the great operations of regular warfare on the Rhine and in Italy as the real sources of greatness for France, that minister had always set his face against little wars. He was moreover jealous of the influence of Lauzun at the Court of St. Germains, and had repeatedly pointed out what was very true, the falseness of the Jacobite accounts, the weak character of James, the total untrustworthiness of his resources, and the consequent necessity which would be laid upon France of carrying out such an invasion, in fact, entirely unaided. He had dwelt also upon the strong national feeling of the English, repeatedly exhibited when an invasion was threatened, and the uncertainty, even were the attempt successful, of the continued assistance and alliance of a Prince so ignorant and selfish as James. Nevertheless, in this instance James was right, not that all and more than all that Louvois urged was not true, but that the separation of England from the coalition, the command of the sea, and the blow which would be dealt to William's influence, were worth any sacrifice which France might make. Louvois' arguments, however, had hitherto prevailed ; the assistance given to James had been but slight. But Louvois' death (which took place on the 16th of July 1691) opened brighter hopes to the exiled King. Louis was at length persuaded ; and a vast plan was made which, had it been carried out as intended, might well have been successful. An army was secretly collected during the winter on the coast of Normandy. Two fleets were assembled at Brest and at Toulon, numbering together 80 ships of the line, and placed under the command of Tourville and D'Estrées, to convoy this army to England. James, misled by his hopes and by the double-dealing of Russell, believed, and made Louis believe, that the English fleet was thoroughly

The side notes read: **Threatened invasion of England.**

disaffected. Secure in this belief, it was without much anxiety that
the invaders found the spring far advanced, while still the weather
prevented the junction of the fleets.

But meanwhile all secresy had been lost. The Queen in England,
and William in Holland, had put forth all their energy, Battle of
and a combined Dutch and English fleet of 90 ships La Hogue.
was in the Channel under command of Russell. At May 19.
last one French squadron, that of Tourville, consisting of 44 ships,
made its appearance. It was supposed that, weak as it was, it was
sufficient for all necessary purposes; it could probably beat the
Dutch contingent, and the English fleet was of no account, for
neither Russell nor his men were likely to fight. Relying on this
false belief, Louis issued peremptory orders to his admiral to cover the
invasion, and fight the enemy wherever he met them. But James's
folly had already gone far to thwart any hopes based upon the
temper of the English. He had issued a Declaration, the work of
his counsellor Melfort, excepting from all hope of pardon, not only
a long list of gentlemen by name, but whole classes of Englishmen, all
judges, jurymen, and lawyers who had been employed in any of the
prosecutions of Jacobites, all magistrates who did not instantly
(regardless of where they might be) make common cause with him
upon his appearance, all spies and informers who had divulged his
secrets, even the insignificant fishermen of Sheerness who had hin-
dered him on his first attempt to escape from England. So ridiculous,
so ill-judged was the Declaration, that, far from suppressing it, the
English Council reprinted it, and distributed it largely, with a few
pungent criticisms of their own. Even Jacobites had to confess that
at least 500 men were excepted. It is easy to conceive the effect of
such a Declaration, when contrasted with William's noble Act of
Grace of the preceding year. What James's folly had thus half done
the Queen's sagacity completed. Urged on all sides to apprehend
known Jacobites, with the denunciations of a plot, perfectly fictitious
indeed, but none the less very plausible, the creation of a rascal of
the name of Young, just placed in her hands, and fully conscious of
the intrigues of Russell her admiral, she wrote a noble letter, expressing her trust and reliance on the patriotism of her fleet, and sent it
to Russell, with orders to read it to the captains of his fleet. Russell,
at heart a Whig and a devoted lover of his profession, hesitated no
longer. He would fight, he said, though King James himself were in
the hostile fleet. He went from ship to ship, encouraging the crews,
and when Tourville bore down upon him there was no sign of faint-

                                                              [C]

heartedness in the English fleet.   Overpowered by numbers, the French fleet fled, broke into fragments, and was destroyed piecemeal. But twelve of the largest ships, with Tourville himself, took refuge under the Forts of La Hogue, under the eyes of James and Marshal Bellefonds, commander of the army.   There, as they lay in two divisions in shallow water, they were attacked on two successive days by a flotilla of English boats, under Admiral Rooke ; and under the guns of the forts, which were supposed to render them quite secure, they were taken and burnt, while James looked on and saw the destruction of this his last hope.

This great victory over the French, the first which the nation had won for many years, drove the people wild with delight. All the more heavy was their disappointment at the feeble manner in which it was followed up, and at the ill success of the war in the Netherlands in the latter part of the year.   An expedition against St. Malo failed through the jealousy of its commanders.   The broken fleet of Tourville, unable to keep the sea, assumed a new form.   French cruisers and privateers covered the ocean, and hundreds of English merchantmen fell a prey to them.   The commercial world suffered more heavily from the individual enterprises of men such as the privateer captains Jean Bart and Dugouay Trouin than from the great united fleets of France, and almost regretted the victory which had called to life such enemies.

The chief incidents of the war in the Netherlands—the fall of the great fortress of Namur, and the battle of Steinkirk— were very characteristic of the art of war at this period. It was a time of slow, methodical, and scientific movement in the field, but of great advance in the art of attacking and defending fortresses, which in the hands of Vauban and Cohorn was so far perfected, that for more than a century no important change was made in the system they advocated.   Louis did not press his advantage ; after taking Namur his army was diminished by detachments sent to other quarters, and William thought he saw an opportunity of striking a heavy blow against his weakened opponent. A traitor in the English army had habitually informed Marshal Luxemburg of every movement of the allied troops.   His correspondence was discovered, and with a pistol at his breast he was forced to write false information which William dictated.   Having thus, as he hoped, misdirected the vigilance of his enemy, the King determined upon a surprise.   The unexpected difficulties offered by the country prevented its success.

Second crisis of the war over.

Subsequent ill success of the fleet.

Fall of Namur. June 30.

Battle of Steinkirk. Aug. 4.

Luxemburg got his troops into order with extraordinary rapidity, and the English division under Mackay soon found itself hotly engaged. It was successful in its first efforts, but the household troops of Louis were sent against it, and Count Solmes withheld the supports which should have come to its assistance. The division was nearly destroyed, and the anger of the English blazed up fiercely against the Dutch general, who, set over the head of the English commanders, thus basely deserted their troops.

It was thus, with many causes of discontent, that, upon the return of William to England, the Parliament assembled. Mis-management had neutralized the great victory of La Discontented Parliament Hogue; the discovery of Preston's plot had not been Nov. 4. followed by a single act of justice upon the Jacobites; a sharp quarrel had broken out between the Queen and her sister, which, as Marlborough's treachery was unknown, seemed merely capricious and causeless; the war in the Netherlands had been a mere disastrous repetition of the last year's campaign; William's chief misfortune was commonly attributed to the mismanagement, or perhaps the treachery of the Dutch general; the House of Lords had been alienated by the apprehension of two of its members, who had been put to their recognizances, and no further charge brought against them; the harvest in England had failed, so that corn had doubled its natural price; and the police had grown so lax that highwaymen in gangs of twenty and thirty infested the country, and robbed almost within sight of London. Both Lords and Commons consequently entered warmly upon the consideration of the state of the nation. But the continued jealousy which existed between the two Houses brought their inquiries to nothing. As yet neither Ministry nor Opposition was sufficiently organized to secure the advantages either of stable government or of thorough reform. The administration was carried on as before with all the evils of a Ministry divided against itself, in the presence of a factious and disorganized Opposition.

Some important steps were however taken with regard to finance. There was still a tolerably unanimous feeling in favour The Land Tax. of the war, and money had to be procured. In the arrangements for supplying the necessary money, the financial talents of Charles Montague, a young and rising member of the Whig party, first became conspicuous. Early known as a man of letters, and the author in company with Prior of "The Town and Country Mouse," he had been introduced to the King by his patron the Earl of Dorset, and, after strengthening his position by a marriage with the Dowager

Countess of Manchester, had entered political life, and had been appointed one of the Lords of the Treasury in 1691. The financial measures recommended consisted of a reorganization of the Land Tax and of the first establishment of Government loans.* The extraordinary expenses of Government had in early times been met by subsidies. These subsidies were levied both on moveables and on land, but were chiefly supported by an assessment on the land at the nominal rate of four shillings in the pound. Land had increased greatly in value as the demand for it increased, while gold and silver had fallen greatly in value after the discovery of America. In the assessment for subsidies neither of these circumstances was taken into consideration. The four shilling land tax had come in reality to be less than twopence in the pound. During the Commonwealth, and subsequently, a different method of taxation had been followed. The sum to be raised had been first determined, and each landowner had been called upon to pay a proportional share. In 1692 the Land Tax was reintroduced and reorganized. A new valuation was made, and upon this basis a tax was annually laid upon the land varying from a minimum of one shilling in time of peace to four shillings in times of emergency. Four shillings on this new valuation produced about £2,000,000. This sum fell considerably short of what was required. In addition, therefore, a loan, which is the origin of the National Debt, was raised. Money was plentiful in the country, and was so easily obtained, that bubble companies and stock-jobbing had become rife. Montague determined to turn some of this superfluous wealth to the use of the country, and to spread the payment of the debt over several generations. The plan at first adopted in raising these loans was not exactly the same as our present method of perpetual funding. The lenders were life annuitants, and the interest of the loan was secured on new duties on beer and other liquors. As each annuitant died his annuity was divided among the survivors, till their number was reduced to seven, who would at that time be naturally in receipt of an enormous interest on their original loan. After that, on the death of each of those seven, his annuity lapsed to Government. The whole debt would therefore be extinguished at the death of the longest-lived annuitant.

Origin of the National Debt. Jan. 20. 1693.

The money thus collected was soon spent upon another disastrous campaign. Louis, in spite of the exhausted condition of his country, made extraordinary efforts in all directions. As far as the English only were concerned, the two great events of the campaign were the battle of Landen and the destruc-

Disastrous campaign. 1693.

tion of the Smyrna fleet. Louis, using his late conquest, Namur, for his point of departure, had formed two armies, one under Boufflers, the other under Luxemburg, and hoped to repeat the triumph of former years by the capture of either Liège or Brussels. But he found it was impossible to take either of those cities without fighting a pitched battle with William. In spite of the earnest request of his generals, he withdrew to Versailles, and removed the army of Boufflers to the Rhine. Though thus weakened, Luxemburg, by a threatened attack upon Liège, induced William to reduce his forces to save that town, and then falling upon him at Landen, defeated him after a battle, the stubbornest and bloodiest of the war. William's skill somewhat neutralized the effect of his defeat, and Charleroi was the only new acquisition of the French in the Low Countries.

Battle of Landen. July 19

The loss of the Smyrna fleet made perhaps even greater impression upon the English than the defeat of Landen. The fleet, in which was accumulated more than a year's supply for the Eastern markets, and which numbered 400 ships, was to be convoyed in safety from London through the Straits of Gibraltar. After passing the Channel unopposed, the English admirals, supposing that the danger was over, withdrew towards England with their ships of war, and the trading fleet passed onward, guarded only by Rooke with about twenty men of war. Off St. Vincent it fell in with the whole combined navy of France, for the squadrons of Toulon and Brest had joined, and were lying in wait for their rich prey off the coast of Spain. The convoy was completely broken up, many vessels destroyed, while the others fled for safety in all directions. The loss of the English was estimated at many millions. The disaster would certainly have been much worse had not two Dutch ships which formed part of the convoy gallantly sacrificed themselves, and engaged no less than eighteen of the enemy's fleet.

Loss of the Smyrna fleet. June.

In other parts of Europe the armies of France were equally successful. Catalonia had been invaded and Rosas taken. Catinat had defeated the Duke of Savoy in the great battle of Marsiglia (Oct. 3). The Turks had compelled the Germans to raise the siege of Belgrade. Yet, in spite of these successes, France was so worn out, that hints of a desire for peace began to reach the English King.

The possibility of being called upon to settle this great point, and the necessity of taking speedy advantage of his enemy's weakness, brought more clearly home to William the great difficulty which had

beset his reign. For the position which was necessary to enable him
William's to engage authoritatively in the affairs of Europe, for
difficulty with the money required for the pay of his army, and for the
regard to his
Parliament subsidies by which alone the allies were kept true to
their engagements, he was dependent upon Parliament. For at the
Revolution the Parliament had taken upon itself the supreme
authority of the nation. Yet upon that Parliament he was unable
to rely ; for the representative body, though conscious of its power,
had not yet learnt to use it advantageously. It was that worst
of all forms of supreme power, a large disorganized assembly. Well
aware that, both as head of a confederacy and as a general, freedom of
action was necessary for him, William had kept as far as possible
the management of foreign affairs in his own hands, and had sought
to win the favour of all parties by a judicious impartiality. In the
main he had been well supported in his foreign policy ; but faction
was so rife, the increasing divergence of opinion so great, and the
capricious character of the Lower House so evident, that he could
take no important step with confidence. He could not answer for a
year's continuance of the war spirit, nor be certain that any steps he
might take with regard to peace would be acknowledged even by
his own ministers. It became necessary, if possible, to introduce
some order and organization into this uncertain body. It would be
better to risk a formal opposition of a certain number, and be sure of
unanimity in his own administration, than to be at the caprice of a
He forms a popular assembly. William therefore listened to the
united Whig suggestions of Sunderland, and determined to place
ministry. himself entirely in the hands of the Whig party, that
party to which he owed his elevation to the throne, and which was
pledged to the continuation of the war. During the next two years
a change in ministry was gradually carried out, which ended by the
establishment in 1696 of the first united ministry in English history.
It was led by the chiefs of the Whig party, of which the leaders
were Somers, Halifax, Russell and Wharton (known afterwards as
the Junto).

Parliament during these years was occupied in financial arrangements to meet the constant drain of the war, and in perpetual party
struggles which terminated in the complete triumph of the Whigs,
and in the substitution of the leaders of that party for their Tory
rivals in all the chief offices of the administration. The first trial of
strength between the parties arose upon the question of the naval
administration of the former year. The whole nation smarted under

the disasters which had followed on the great victory of La Hogue, which the Whigs had attributed not only to the malad- *Party struggles.* ministration of the two Tory admirals to whom the fleet had been intrusted, but also to treachery. It was impossible, they argued, that Louis could have denuded the Channel of his fleet, and allowed a junction of his admirals so far south as St. Vincent, unless he had had good reason to believe that the rich prey he desired would fall into his hands but weakly guarded. The Tories, who were unable to deny the maladministration, were anxious to exclude the word "treacherous" from the motion. The Whig party was however triumphant, and by a considerable majority the word was retained. But though the general assertion of treason was thus made, the Commons, as was not unusual, shrunk from fixing the treason upon any particular person, and each individual accused was acquitted by a small majority. Enough had been done, however, to give the King a fair opportunity of re-establishing Russell, the great enemy of Nottingham the Secretary, at the head of the Admiralty, and thus taking one step towards his Whig ministry. It was impossible for Nottingham to remain in office with Russell; he was consequently removed from the Secretaryship, and a fresh vacancy thus created, which, after some delay, caused by the conscientious scruples of Shrewsbury, who felt keenly the fault he had once committed in tampering with the Jacobites, was filled by that nobleman, one of the Whig chiefs. At the close of the session, therefore, William found himself with most of his chief officers belonging to the Whig party. Trenchard and Shrewsbury were Secretaries. Russell was the head of the Admiralty. Somers was Lord Keeper, and Montague Chancellor of the Exchequer. The only two Tories of importance left were Caermarthen, Lord President, and Godolphin, at the head of the Treasury. But the character of the latter minister led him to devote himself almost exclusively to his official business, of which he was master. Caermarthen was therefore, in fact, the only important element of discord in the administration.

Montague owed his elevation to the continued success of his financial plans. A fresh loan, known as the Lottery Loan—because though the whole rate of interest was low, in exceptional cases chosen by lottery it was very high—was successfully negotiated, *Establishment* and more important than this, the Bank of England *of the Bank of* was triumphantly established. Banking with private *England.* goldsmiths had come into fashion within the last two reigns, when the convenience of cheques in the place of ready-money payments had become obvious, while the advantage to the banker who had the use of the ready money was also plain. The fault of the system was its insecurity, which had been proved by the not unfrequent bankruptcy of one or other of the banking goldsmiths. A Scotchman of the name of Paterson had some years previously suggested the plan of a national bank, by which the Government should obtain some of the advantages of the banker, and the public, while gaining the convenience of cheques, should have a better security than private goldsmiths offered. This scheme Montague now adopted. He borrowed rather upwards of a million, and formed the lenders into a banking company, allowing them to treat the loan to Government as part of their capital, the interest of which, secured upon taxes, gave them the requisite supply of ready money. They were bound to pursue no other business except banking, yet, even with this restriction, so desirable did the plan seem, that it was at once triumphantly carried through. As a contingent advantage to Government, it is to be observed that the company, which included many of the chiefs of the moneyed interest, were pledged, for their own preservation, to support the present settlement of the throne. Their existence depended upon the regular payment of the interest upon their loan, which it was scarcely possible that the Jacobites, if successful, would pay. The importance of this point became very obvious afterwards, when, in more than one crisis, the credit of Government was saved by advances from the Bank. One other important measure

The Triennial Act passed. Dec. 1694. was carried by this Parliament, and that also was in accordance with the principles of the Whigs. This was the Triennial Act, limiting the duration of Parliament to three years. The King, always jealous of his prerogative, had already once refused his assent to this Bill; but now, having placed himself in Whig hands, he withdrew his opposition, and the Bill was passed.

He was indeed in no position to enter into a struggle with his Parliament. A great blow was falling on him, which unhinged him more than any difficulties or defeats had yet done. This was the

Death of Queen Mary. Dec. 20. death of his wife, who had sickened of the smallpox, and, after a short illness, died on the 20th of December 1694. Her death caused universal sorrow in England and among the Protestant interest on the Continent, while it raised the hopes of James and his friends, who believed, not without a show of reason, that William succeeded in holding his place chiefly by means of the popularity of his Queen. Their hopes proved ill founded, for though at first the King seemed so broken-hearted that he declared he could never again lead an army, when once he had conquered his first grief, he resumed his old energy, and success such as he had never yet met with attended his efforts both at home and abroad.

Meanwhile in England there was no cessation in the strife of parties. The Whigs pursued their triumphant course, and combined to remove the last of their opponents from the Government. Trevor, a Tory, had in the early part of the reign been made Speaker of the House, chiefly for the purpose of carrying out Caermarthen's plans of corruption. Employed in corrupting others, it was not likely that he should be himself above corruption. Suspicions of his venality having arisen, the Whigs proceeded to examine the accounts of the City of London and of the East India Company, which, after much contest, had obtained a renewal of its charter. The Committee found that the City had paid Sir John Trevor in the preceding session 1000 guineas for forwarding a local Bill. The proof was too clear to be questioned. Trevor from the chair had to put the question whether he was guilty or not of high crime and misdemeanour, and to declare before all men that "the Ayes had it." He saved himself from the unutterable ignominy of announcing his own expulsion by feigning illness. A new Speaker, Foley, who did not belong clearly to either party, was elected in his place.

The accounts of the East India Company afforded the Whigs even greater triumph. Sir Thomas Cook, who was the head of the Company, confessed to having disbursed very large sums to secure the charter, but would give no particular accounts. The Commons, determined not to be thwarted, passed a Bill condemning him to refund all the money thus spent, in addition to a heavy fine, unless he made a full confession. In the Upper House the Bill was strongly opposed by Lord Caermarthen, now Duke of Leeds, who, laying his hand upon his heart, solemnly averred that he had no personal interest in the matter, and was moved by public considerations only. It was finally arranged that a joint Committee of the two Houses should inquire into the expenditure of the money that had been secretly spent, and that if Cook confessed he should be held guiltless. The joint Committee met; the King and the Duke of Portland, whose guilt in the matter had been suggested by the Tories, were proved perfectly innocent. But £5000 were traced, if not to the Duke of Leeds himself, at all events to his confidential man of business. Articles of impeachment were made out against him. They could not, however, be brought forward, because the man of

(margin note: Expulsion of Trevor for venality, March 1695.)

business, who would have supplied necessary evidence, had made his escape to Holland. The Duke of Leeds continued to assert his innocence, but confessed that he had allowed money to be paid to his steward, considering this a very different thing from taking it himself. It also appeared that the money had been refunded the very morning of the first sitting of the joint Committee. Though foiled of their impeachment, the Whigs and the Commons had done their work. Leeds was obliged to retire from active life, and was never afterwards employed in the administration. The sole discordant member of the Government was thus got rid of.

and of Caermarthen.
May.

Abroad likewise affairs took a turn more favourable to England and the Whigs. Just before the death of Mary the war had entered into a somewhat new phase. The navies of the two great powers had transferred the scene of operations to the Mediterranean. Thither Tourville had gone from Brest, and thither Russell, with the English fleet, had followed him. He had found means to keep the French fleet in harbour, and to do good service to the general cause by the relief of Barcelona, which was on the point of falling into the hands of the French.

Success abroad.
June 1694.

The absence of the French fleet from Brest, which led to the supposition that the harbour must be unguarded, seemed to afford an opportunity for an attack in that quarter. An expedition was planned; the forces were intrusted to Talmash, while the Duke of Leeds' son Caermarthen commanded the fleet. It gave occasion for a new act of villany on the part of Marlborough; though the plan was kept a profound secret, he contrived to worm it out, and as had happened once or twice before in his career, he used his knowledge only to lay the details of the plan before James, and to secure the destruction of the English expedition. Vauban, the great French engineer, was sent down to re-fortify the place. Every vantage-ground was crowned with batteries, and into the trap thus laid for him Talmash had rushed headlong to meet his death, in company with 700 English soldiers (June 7, 1694). Marlborough's treachery in this instance was rather personal than political. Talmash alone of the English generals could in any way compete with him, and he knew that at his death or failure William, who it must be recollected did not know the full extent of his treachery, would be obliged to restore him to his command. His treacherous plan succeeded. He was again employed, though so thoroughly mistrusted, that William

Treachery of Marlborough.

refused when he went abroad to give the regency to Anne, which he well knew would be but to give it to Marlborough. But the death of Mary, which occurred at the close of the year, while it excited the other Jacobites to action, for a time rendered Marlborough true to William ; for it was followed by a reconciliation between the King and the Princess Anne, and Marlborough was now content to wait till the King's death for the completion of his designs. The more earnest Jacobites followed a different course, and it was in the midst of a conspiracy aimed against his life by Fenwick, Charnock, and Porter, that William set out for Flanders (May 1695).

In that country he had no longer the same formidable enemy with whom to contend. Luxemburg was dead, and his place was ill supplied by Villeroy and Louis' illegitimate son, the Duke of Maine, who was sent to learn the art of war under him. As Flanders was expected to be the great seat of war, the bulk of the French army was placed under Villeroy in that country. Boufflers, with 12,000 men, guarded the Sambre. William, however, had set his heart upon regaining Namur Judicious feints deceived Villeroy as to his intentions, and suddenly his own army, that of the Brandenburgers and that of the Elector of Bavaria, marched straight against the city. Boufflers had just time to throw himself with his troops into the town. A body of troops under the Prince of Vaudemont had been, left to watch Villeroy in Flanders. When that general advanced, the Prince could not hold his isolated position, and only succeeded in making good his retreat through the cowardice of the Duke of Maine. Villeroy advanced almost unopposed. He took the towns of Dixmuyde and Deynse, the garrisons of which, contrary to the terms of capitulation, were sent prisoners to France ; and hoping by threatening the capital to draw William from Namur, he approached and ruthlessly and uselessly bombarded Brussels. But, undisturbed by Villeroy's manœuvres, William energetically pursued the siege. He was assisted by Cohorn, who had originally fortified the town, and had seen it taken by the skill of his great rival Vauban. Vauban had since much increased the fortifications, and Cohorn was eager to regain his honour by capturing it. At length, after some fierce assaults, in which the English under Lord Cutts, who for his bravery under fire got the nickname of " the Salamander," had greatly distinguished themselves, the town surrendered, but the castle still held out. It became evident to Villeroy that the actual presence of his army could alone raise the siege. Drawing troops from all the neighbouring

Campaign in Flanders. 1695.

garrisons, he approached with 80,000 men. But William now felt himself strong enough to give him battle without withdrawing from his operations. For three days the armies remained in presence, and William lay expecting the attack, but Villeroy judged his position too strong to be taken, and withdrew. The fate of the fortress was now sealed, but Boufflers thought that his honour demanded that he should stand an assault; nor was it till the English had succeeded at the cost of 2000 men in making a lodgment in the place that he consented to treat, and for the first time in history a French marshal surrendered a fortress to a victorious enemy. Having gone through the ceremony of surrender. Boufflers was much surprised and enraged at being arrested on his road to France. His angry exclamations against the breach of the terms of capitulation were met by the reply, that William was only following the example of Louis with regard to the garrisons of Dixmuyde and Deynse. He was kept in honourable imprisonment till those garrisons were restored.

Surrender of Namur. Aug. 26.

It was thus no longer as a beaten and unfortunate, though skilful general, that William returned to England. The Triennial Bill having come into operation, the present Parliament would have come to a natural conclusion the following year. It had on the whole acted so much in favour of William and the Whigs, that William, could he have prolonged it, would probably have been willing to do so. But he wisely judged that it would be better to call his new Parliament while still popular from his successes, than to wait the chances of the future year. The event proved that he was right. A brilliant triumphant progress through England was followed by the return of a Parliament with an immense majority favourable to the war and to the Whig interests. Four Whigs were returned for London. Westminster followed the example of the neighbouring city, and so great was the enthusiasm that even the great Tory leader Seymour, whose interest in Devonshire was believed to render his return for Exeter sure, was defeated in that town. The Parliament thus assembled had very important work before it, and, acting in unison with the King, his ministry, and the whole country, carried it through to a noble conclusion.

William's triumphant return. Oct. 10.

New Whig Parliament. Nov. 22.

This important work was the. re-establishment of the currency. The English coin had originally been of hammered metal, it was constantly liable to inequality in weight, and being left with raw edges, easily clipped. In

Re-establishment of the currency.

Charles II.'s reign this defect had been partially cured by the use of machinery, and words had been printed round the edges of the coin ; but as the bad hammered coinage was allowed to be current side by side with the new milled coinage, the better coinage had either been hoarded or had left the country, as invariably happens, when some part of the coinage of the country is of less intrinsic value than the rest. Consequently the evil became worse. Coin was more constantly clipped, and as it wore out was more easily counterfeited. Its defects at length became so obvious that shopkeepers refused to take it except by weight ; thus causing heavy suffering to the lower orders, who generally received their wages by tale, and had to pay by weight, and every little transaction became the occasion of a dispute. So far had the evil gone, that when trials were made in different parts of the country, the coinage had proved on an average to be little more than half its proper weight. A re-issue of coin seemed absolutely necessary. Some were for postponing the difficulty by keeping the present money in circulation till the end of the war. Some suggested that the nominal value of silver should be raised. Fortunately the arrangements fell into the hands of four able and determined men, Somers, Montague, Locke the philosopher, and Newton the mathematician. They decided upon immediate action, and would not listen to any suggestion for the alteration of the standard, which would in fact perpetrate a fraud upon all creditors. Two important questions met them. By whom should the inevitable expense of the re-issue be borne ? How could the inconvenience of the short supply of coin during the recoinage be best alleviated ? Two schemes recommended themselves chiefly to their attention. Locke proposed that, after a certain fixed date, the coin should be valued by weight only. This prevented any deficiency in the circulating medium, as the present money would not be withdrawn from circulation, but it threw the whole expense of bringing the nominal and real value of the coin into harmony, not on the Government, but on the individual possessors of the coin. It was evidently fairer that, where the evil was a national one, the nation should bear the expense. Somers suggested that, with extreme secresy, a proclamation should be prepared, saying that in three days the hammered coin should pass by weight only, but that those who held it might bring it in parcels to the mint, where it should be counted and weighed, and immediately restored, with a written promise of a future payment of the difference between the nominal and real value of the coin. Thus the money would be withdrawn from circulation only for the short time necessary to count it, while the nation would subsequently pay the difference. But for this plan secresy and suddenness were necessary, or the intervening period would have given opportunity and temptation for unlimited mutilation of the coinage. Secresy would have rendered it impossible to consult Parliament, and Montague, in the existing state of party feeling, shrank from the responsibility this implied. It was therefore determined to act in a perfectly honest, simple and straightforward manner; and immediately on the opening of Parliament, a Bill was framed in accordance with certain resolutions previously taken. By these it was declared that the old standard should be kept up, that milled coin should alone be used, that the loss should fall on the nation, not on individuals, and that the 4th of May following should be the last day on which hammered coin should be allowed to be used. The advantage of the good understanding between the Government and the Bank now became evident. To meet the expense of the new coinage £1,200,000 was wanted. The Bank advanced it without difficulty on the security of a window tax, which took the place of the much hated hearth tax, and which lasted on almost to our own time. At last the critical day, the 4th of May, drew near. Fortunately the country was in an enthusiastic mood. Two great Jacobite plots, closely connected, which had been concocted during the previous summer, had been discovered. These were Berwick's plot for a general insurrection of the Jacobites and for an invasion from France; and a plot concocted at St. Germains, intrusted to Barclay, for the assassination of William on his road from Kensington to Richmond. Invasion and assassination are the two forms of conspiracy which the English people cannot bear; and the full discovery of these schemes, with the proved certainty that both Louis and James were fully conscious of all their atrocious details, roused the nation for an instant to an unusual unanimity of enthusiasm, and enabled Parliament to set on foot a great association, signed by hundreds of thousands, who pledged themselves to stand by the King, to support the war, and to pursue with vengeance any attempt upon his life. Good tempered and loyal though the people were the crisis was a fearful one. The operations of the mint were very slow. £4,000,000 of the old coinage lay melted in the treasury vaults. As yet scarcely any new silver had appeared. Money was not to be had either for trade or for private payments. Large employers somehow contrived, with a certain quantity of the old coinage which had not been clipped, to pay the wages. But the greater part of England lived on credit; and it is probable that even thus the crisis would scarcely have been got over, had it not been for an expedient of Montague's, who issued Government securities, bearing interest at threepence a day on £100. These are what are known now as Exchequer bills, and form a floating debt due by Government. They were eagerly used, and with the paper issues of the Bank and the free use of cheques and credit by all, the dangerous time was tided over.

But the most alarming feature was not the difficulty in the commercial world, but the difficulty felt by Government William's want and by the King himself in provisioning the troops and of money. carrying on the war. In the midst of the commercial crisis the Bank of England had met with great difficulties; the goldsmiths, who had always hated their great rival, took the opportunity of attempting to destroy it by villanous means, they bought up all the Bank paper on which they could lay hands, and suddenly bringing it forward, demanded immediate payment. The Bank directors with great courage gained time by refusing to pay the nefarious claim, and referring their enemies to the courts of law. By means of calls on their subscribers they continued to pay by far the greater part of the private and just claims upon them, but they did not appear to be in a position to assist the King when he suddenly wrote home to say that £200,000 were absolutely necessary.

William had hoped that his wants would have been met by the establishment, in accordance with a favourite plan of The Land Bank the Tories, of a Land Bank, as a rival to the Bank of a failure England. This somewhat absurd scheme had been invented by a projector of the name of Chamberlain, who supposed that every proprietor of land possessing that security ought to have the disposal of at least as much money as his land was worth, and therefore suggested a bank which should lend money entirely upon landed security, overlooking the difficulty that land is not always at hand and payable on demand as money is. Harley, the representative of the Tories, now offered to advance the Government £2,500,000 at 7 per cent. The payment of his interest was to be secured by a tax upon salt. If half that sum should be subscribed before August, and half of that half paid up, the subscribers were to be incorporated as the Land Bank. This Bank was expressly intended to suit the wants of the country gentry, and to injure the moneyed interest. The company was therefore bound to lend no money but on mortgage, and to lend on mortgage at least half a million a year. It was not allowed to receive more than $3\frac{1}{2}$ per cent. interest on these mortgages. Now,

as the ordinary rate of interest on mortgages was nearly 7 per cent.
it was plain that no capitalist would lend his money at half of the
ordinary profits. It might have been plain also that the landed
gentry whose chief object was to borrow were not likely to lend.
It was not therefore very obvious where the capital was to come from.
The King, however, hoping to obtain money on easy terms, headed
the list of subscribers with £5000. When the Land Bank was
called upon to advance its promised loan, it was found that the
whole subscriptions consisted of no more than £6200. So eager was
the Government for money, that it offered to give the Bank its charter
in exchange for a loan of £40,000 only, but the subscriptions never
rose beyond £7500, and the scheme proved completely abortive.

The King was compelled therefore to apply to the Bank of England,
The Bank of which by his patronage of the Land Bank he had done
England supplies his best to injure. True to their political creed, a full
the money.
Aug. 15. court of subscribers consented to advance the necessary
£200,000, without one dissentient voice. The Government was
saved, and the connection between the Bank of England and the
Whig party sealed for ever. Meanwhile, Newton's efforts as Master
of the Mint had been ultimately successful. Provincial mints had
been established, and from them and from the mint in London
£120,000 of coin was turned out every day. By August the crisis
was over, and a period of unbroken commercial prosperity began.

But although marks of commercial prosperity were already
visible, the financial difficulty was not entirely over. When
William, who had been abroad during the worst of the difficulty,
opened Parliament upon his return (Oct. 20), he had to confess
that, although the crisis had passed without disturbance in England
or great disaster abroad, there was still need for some exhibition of continued firmness on the part of Parliament. In fact, the
plan of reducing the standard of the coin was so plausible, and had
impressed itself so deeply on the ignorance of the masses, that a
very large party both in and out of Parliament were still anxious to
have recourse to that step, and till all chance of such a measure was
gone no speculators were willing to put the new money in circulation,
and it was constantly hoarded. Consequently a scarcity of money
still prevailed ; and not only in England, but throughout Europe,
there was a very general feeling that England was ruined, that the
source of wealth which had hitherto supplied the European coalition
with the means of war was dried up, and that peace was inevitable.
But in the midst of these difficulties the triumph of the Whigs was

complete. The Parliament stood firm, and carried by a triumphant
majority three resolutions, which destroyed all the
hopes of the enemies of England. First, that the
Commons would assist the King to prosecute the war
with vigour; secondly, that under no circumstances should the
standard of money be changed; thirdly, the Parliament pledged
itself to make good the deficiencies in Parliamentary funds established since the King's accession. The first promise was at once
abundantly fulfilled by munificent grants for the war; the second
caused the immediate production of the hoarded coin; while upon
the third was framed Montague's plan known by the name of the
General Mortgage. Taxes set apart to meet the interest of various
loans had proved insufficient. The deficit was no less than £5,160,000.
It was now ordered that, should the proceeds of the old funds
and new taxes now set aside for the purpose prove insufficient, the
general funds of the country should be charged with the liquidation
of the debts. By such means as these the credit of the country was
finally re-established.

Credit of England restored.

The discovery of the Assassination plot, and the enthusiasm to
which it gave rise, has been already alluded to. It was
one of two Jacobite conspiracies, matured in the middle
of the crisis, when it was a common belief that the Government would
never be able to pass securely through the dangers which surrounded it.
One of these conspiracies was for a general rising of the Jacobites
and a simultaneous invasion of England from France. The completion of this plot was intrusted to James's natural son, the Duke of
Berwick, and in it, had it been carried out, would have been involved
all the best of the Jacobite gentry of England. But side by side
with it was a baser conspiracy, among the more unprincipled and
desperate friends of James, for the assassination of the King. The
management of this conspiracy, which is known by the name of the
Assassination Plot, was intrusted to Sir George Barclay, a Scotch
refugee. It seems certain that the scheme was sanctioned by James
himself, as Barclay was sent over with a few select followers and a
considerable sum of money, authorised to do any acts of hostility
which might conduce to the service of the King. It was also
certainly known to the Duke of Berwick, who was informed of every
step in its progress. He was too honourable himself to take a
declared part in it, but did not feel called upon in any way to interfere in the matter. His own mission proved unsuccessful. The
English Jacobites were willing to rise, but not till a French army

The Assassina-tion plot

appeared in the country. On the other hand, Berwick could only
assure them that, after the failures which had already taken place, no
French army would enter the country till the Jacobites were actually
in arms. On this point the negotiations broke down, and Berwick,
unwilling to be mixed up with the darker schemes of Barclay,
hastened to leave England before the fatal day should arrive. This
day, the 15th of February, had been already fixed. Barclay had
succeeded in collecting about fort men, some supplied from
France, some English Jacobites of desperate character. With these
it was determined to assault the King on his return from hunting in
Richmond Forest. Every Saturday he was in the habit of going
thither, crossing the Thames by boat near Turnham Green. The
spot chosen was a narrow swampy lane leading up from the river.
But, just before the time fixed, William received from Portland
information that there was a design upon his life. He was induced
to postpone his hunting, although he gave little faith to the information, which had been received from most untrustworthy sources.
But in the course of the following week fresh information was brought
by a gentleman of the name of Pendergrass, who was known to be
an honourable man. Every precaution was taken to allay the
suspicions of the conspirators, and on the very day when the attempt
should have been made several of the leaders were arrested. The
troops were set in motion, the Lord Lieutenant of Kent repaired to
his county, and Russell hastened to take command of the fleet to
oppose the intended invasion. French troops had been already
collected at Calais, and Louis, who had been informed of the scheme,
though he had not actually authorized it, had determined to take
advantage of the opportunity its success would offer.

The measures taken proved sufficient. When the King went in
state to Parliament, and explained what had been done, the enthusiasm
of the House was roused. Two Bills were rapidly passed,
the one suspending the Habeas Corpus Act, the other
ordering that the Parliament should not be dissolved
by the death of William, and an association was set on foot by which
the House of Commons bound itself to stand by King William, to
avenge his murder, and to support the order of succession settled by
the Bill of Rights. Throughout the country the feeling excited was
very strong. Means were taken in all the cities of England to search
thoroughly for conspirators, the house of one of them was razed to
the ground by the populace, and one after the other most of them
were captured. Three of them, Charnock, King and Keyes, were

brought to trial. Only a few months before, a Bill which had occupied the public attention through several sessions had received the royal assent. By this the procedure in the case of trials for treason had been changed. Before the passing of that Bill a prisoner charged with treason had not been allowed to see the indictment before he was brought to the bar. He could not put his witnesses upon oath, nor compel their attendance, nor was he allowed the service of counsel, while the Crown enjoyed all the advantages of which he was deprived. The Bill enacted that all the above-named disabilities should be removed. The opposition to this Bill had been grounded chiefly upon the advantage it appeared to give to traitors at a time when the Government was notoriously open to their attacks ; and Parliament had, by way of compromise, postponed till the 25th of March 1696 (at that time the beginning of the new year) the operation of the Act. The prisoners claimed, not without some show of reason, a postponement of the trial till that date. But their request was overruled, the trial was proceeded with at once, and they were all condemned and executed (March 24).

Arrest and execution of the conspirators.

But, by the witness of two of the informers, Porter and Goodman, a more important person had been implicated, if not in the present plot, yet at least in one of a similar nature which had been set on foot immediately after the Queen's death. This was Sir John Fenwick, a man highly connected, who had brought himself prominently forward as a Jacobite intriguer, and had earned the personal dislike of William by a public insult to the Queen. By the law of Edward VI. two witnesses were necessary to prove the guilt of treason, and Fenwick's chief hopes lay in his being able to bribe either Porter or Goodman to leave the country. His first attempt on Porter failed. Porter informed the Government, received the money, and gave up the agent who offered it him. Fenwick then attempted to gain time by making a confession. This was drawn up with great art : while none of the real facts were brought to light, accusations, only too well founded upon fact, were brought against Marlborough, Godolphin, Russell, and Shrewsbury. It was asserted that Marlborough had promised to bring over the army, Russell the navy, while Godolphin only held office by the leave of the exiled King. William, with great wisdom, although he knew how much truth there was in these accusations, absolutely ignored them, and ordered the trial of Fenwick to be proceeded with without delay. But some of the contents of the confession became known, and the

Trial of Sir John Fenwick. Aug.

Whigs decided that, for the honour of the party, it could not be passed over in silence. Godolphin, the last remaining Tory in the Government, they would have been unwilling to acquit; he was induced to resign, and the course was now clear. It was of the highest importance that a real confession should be got from Fenwick, but this he now refused to give, as he had just received information that his agents had contrived to get Goodman, the second witness against him, out of the country. Exasperated by seeing, as they thought, the enemy, who had tried to undermine the character of their chiefs, slipping from their grasp, the Whigs brought the question before the House. The confession was voted false and scandalous, and rather than let their victim escape, in the heat of their anger, they determined to have recourse to the dangerous expedient of a Bill of Attainder (Nov. 13). This attempt, which, as it superseded the law of the land by an exercise of the power of Parliament, had an unconstitutional and revengeful appearance, met with the strongest opposition, but was carried in the Lower House by a small majority. The question became one of party, and finally, after a long struggle, it passed the House of Lords by a majority of only seven. Great interest was made for the prisoner, His execution. but William refused to listen to any request for pardon, Jan. 28, 1697. and Fenwick was executed. William's inflexibility is better explained by his desire to shield the Whig party, whom Fenwick would certainly have accused during his trial, than by the supposed existence of a personal hostility between himself and his prisoner.

This troublesome business having been got rid of, the session Complete closed in complete triumph for the Whigs, among whose triumph of the Whigs. leaders promotions were freely distributed. Somers was April 16. raised to the Peerage and made Lord Chancellor, Russell became Earl of Orford, and Montague became First Lord of the Treasury. This triumph of the party reached its climax in the course of the year, when the war was brought to an end, and the policy of William and the Whigs vindicated by the signature of the Peace of Ryswick.

During the critical year 1696 want of money had paralyzed the action of both armies in the Netherlands, the destruction of the Louis desires French magazines at Givet had rendered it difficult for peace. Louis to maintain his troops, while William, though England was by no means exhausted as France was, was as completely hampered by the want of ready money. Louis had indeed in the course of the year made overtures for peace, but the improvement in his prospects, caused by the conduct of the Duke of Savoy, who had deserted the coalition, joined his army to the French under Marshal Catinat, and successfully insisted that Austria and Spain should declare the neutralization of Italy, had induced him to recede from one of the fundamental conditions of peace—the recognition of William as King of England. The negotiations had been broken off, but succeeding events induced Louis, in 1697, to renew his proposals. The Assassination Plot had failed ; William was more popular and better supported than he had ever been ; the country had passed successfully through its period of crisis, had emerged more powerful than ever and more determined to support the war, and the great French military project for the capture of Brussels had been thwarted by the rapidity of William's movements. Louis therefore now, for the first time in his life, offered reasonable terms, consenting to resign many of the conquests he had made during the war, to give back Lorraine to its Duke, Luxemburg to Spain, Strasburg to the Empire, and to acknowledge the King of England. William, who was never carried away even by his most impetuous   Opposition of feelings, much as he hated France, at once recognized the   the coalition. justice of these offers and the wisdom of accepting them. He found however much difficulty in managing the coalition. The two great powers who had done the least to support the war now did all in their power to frustrate the pacification. Spain, moved by a foolish vanity little suitable to its weak condition, made demands which it was impossible that Louis should grant, while the Emperor, moved by selfish policy, would have been only too glad to continue a war, carried on chiefly at the cost of England, till the death of the Spanish King, which was every day expected. He would then, he imagined, be able to secure by means of the European coalition his succession to that monarchy. At length, after many difficulties, plenipotentiaries from France and the coalition were assembled (March 1697), the one party at the Hague, the other at Delft, and conferences were held at Ryswick, which lies nearly equidistant between these two towns. But the ceremonies of diplomacy, the ridiculous details of precedence, seemed to promise that the negotiations would be dragged out to an interminable length. William was not to be so treated. Having made up his mind that peace was desirable and that the terms offered were fair, he was determined that the peace should be speedily made. While the plenipotentiaries were wasting their time at Ryswick, a series of private meetings took place between Portland and Marshal Boufflers, between the

armies, a few miles from Brussels. A few meetings sufficed to
settle the terms, which were reduced to writing on
the 6th of July. Beyond the general terms of treaty
already offered by France, some personal questions between William
and Louis had to be settled. The French king solemnly pledged
himself to give no countenance to any attempt to subvert the existing
government of England. For form's sake a similar promise was
given by the English king. Mary of Modena was to receive
whatever sum of money the English Law Courts held to be her due;
and though Louis, with his usual magnanimity, refused to stipulate
that James should leave France, it was understood that he should
withdraw either to Avignon or to Italy. Spain and the Emperor
still refused to accept the proffered terms. Louis declared that, unless
they were accepted by the 21st of August, he should no longer hold
himself bound by them. The day passed, and, as was to be expected,
the French King raised fresh demands ; he would no longer surrender
Strasburg. But the opposition of Spain had already been crushed.
The disasters of the year had brought that country to reason ;
Vendome had captured Barcelona, and a French fleet, joined by the
buccaneers of the West Indies, had taken and sacked Carthagena.
William therefore, though much vexed at the obstinacy of the Emperor,
which involved the loss of Strasburg, found himself able to accept
the new terms, in concert with all the great powers of the coalition,
with the exception of the Emperor, and at length, on the 10th of
September, a treaty was concluded between France,
Holland, Spain and England. France surrendered all
the conquests made since the Treaty of Nimeguen, and
placed the chief fortresses of the Low Countries in the hands of Dutch
garrisons; William was recognized as King of England, Anne as his
successor, and all assistance was withdrawn from James. A month
later the Emperor also consented to treat. By this second treaty all
the towns acquired since the Peace of Nimeguen, with the exception
of Strasburg, were restored, together with Fribourg, Brissac, Philipsburg, and all French fortifications on the right bank of the Rhine.
Lorraine was restored to its Duke, Leopold, who granted however
a passage through his dominions for French troops. The Elector
of Cologne was recognized, and the rights of the Duchess of Orleans
upon the Palatinate compromised for money. William and the
European coalition were thus triumphant. Louis had for the first
time to withdraw to his own boundaries, and the succession of England
was secured. At the same time France gained what had now become

Terms of peace.

Treaty of Ryswick. Sept. 10.

absolutely necessary, time to recruit her strength, and leisure to prepare for that great struggle which all men saw to be imminent, when the death of Charles II. of Spain, without a direct heir, should leave the succession of that great monarchy to be disputed among the various claimants.

The joy of England at the conclusion of the war was enthusiastic. The King made a triumphal entry into London, and was everywhere received with enthusiasm. The crowning point of his reign had been reached. Almost without knowing it, he had solved the great constitutional question of the time, and, supported by a ministry in harmony with the Commons, and the national representatives in harmony with the people, had triumphantly brought to conclusion the great objects of his life, established the Protestant succession in England, and proved to Louis the necessity of respecting the rights and feelings of the rest of Europe.

On the very day after the rejoicings to celebrate the Peace of Ryswick, on the 3rd of December 1697, the Parlia- *The Parliament* ment, which had hitherto shown itself so firm in sup- *reduces the* port of the Crown, so unanimous and vigorous in its *standing army.* action, met for its third and last session. William had every right to expect a period of peace and prosperity. But, unfortunately, the very success for which England was rejoicing brought with it the seeds of faction and division. For at once a question had to be settled, on which the Whig party was itself divided, and on which the national feeling was on the whole strongly opposed to the King. The establishment of peace naturally involved the question of the fate of the great army, numbering more than 80,000 men, which England had kept up for the last nine years. The nation, suffering heavily from taxation, was not likely to be willing to continue in peace the efforts made during war. It was, moreover, a deeply ingrained feeling among the country gentry of both parties that a standing army in time of peace was an intolerable evil. The Tories had indeed already adopted the policy which long marked the party. They would have wished England to confine itself, even in war, to the pursuit of success upon the sea, which they regarded as her natural element, and to have withdrawn as far as possible from all the complications of Continental policy. But, even setting aside this view, the experience of both parties led them very naturally to regard an army in time of peace as the inevitable instrument of tyranny. While the Tories remembered with horror the triumphant Ironsides of Cromwell, the Whigs recalled with no less detestation the importation of Irish troops at the close of the last reign, and London overawed by the great camp at Hounslow. On the other hand, William, with his eyes fixed abroad, with a profound mistrust of France, and certain knowledge of the rapid approach of another great Continental quarrel, could not bring himself to approve of the breaking up of an army which he had brought to such perfection. The ministry, under his immediate influence, and guided by the far-sighted sagacity of Somers, believed, like the King, in the approach of fresh danger, and thoroughly disbelieved in the efficacy of half-drilled militia to withstand such well-trained troops as Louis had always at his disposal. The national feeling was, however, too strong to be withstood. A resolution was passed that the number of soldiers should be reduced to the same amount as had been kept on foot after the peace of Nimeguen, a resolution which was liberally construed by the Government to mean 10,000. On other points the ministry and the Parliament remained at one. It was in vain that an attack was directed against William's lavish grants of Crown lands, in vain that an accusation of peculation was directed against Montague, it resulted only in a formal declaration on the part of the Commons of the great services of that statesman.

Montague's success as a financier had indeed reached its culminating point in this session by the temporary settlement of the question with regard to the Indian trade which had so long excited the commercial

The East Indian trade.

public in England. It has been incidentally mentioned that the renewal of the charter to the East India Company in 1693 had produced the fall of Lord Caermarthen. The Company, originally consisting chiefly of Whigs and incorporated by royal charter, had, in the hands of Sir Josiah Child, who exerted an almost dictatorial authority in its management, allied itself closely to the Tories. Its monopoly had also become very unpopular, as the increase of capital and the great receipts of the Indian trade had excited a wish among the mercantile community to enter more largely upon that branch of traffic. As early as 1691 an association of its enemies had been formed, which, although it was not chartered, was commonly spoken of as the new Company, and had succeeded in obtaining a request from the Parliament to the King that he would give the old Company the three years' notice of the withdrawal of its charter which was legally required. An accidental illegality had in fact just then invalidated the charter. It was to procure its restoration that, in 1693, Cook, to whom Child had now relinquished much of his authority, had so lavishly expended the secret service money.

some of which had been traced to Caermarthen. His bribery was successful. The charter was renewed by the King, but the Parliament, at the instigation of the new Company, took a different view of the question, and declared that every man had a right to trade, unless debarred by Act of Parliament. This declaration of the limits of the constitutional power of the Crown in matters of trade William could not venture to oppose. From that time onwards, therefore, the trade had been legally free, but the power of the Company had been so great in the Indian seas, and its conduct so oppressive, that it had been impossible for free traders to carry on their business with any success. Again, in 1698, the question was strongly pressed upon the attention of Parliament, and again the old Company found strong supporters in the Tory party, while the Whigs upheld the demands of those who wished to participate in its advantages. There was a division in the views of the opponents of the Company. Some were eager for perfect freedom of trade, while others joined in the general feeling of the nation, that, although the present monopoly was a bad one, some sort of restriction was still necessary. It was understood that to advance money to Government was the surest way to obtain its support, and the old Company offered £700,000, at four per cent., as the price of the renewal of its charter. But Montague, anxious for money to relieve the embarrassments of the Government, anxious to establish a second great Whig society of capitalists, who Formation of would support him as the Bank had already done, be- India Company lieved that he saw his way to gaining those ends by 1698. opposing the Company, and brought forward a plan by which he hoped to secure the support of both sections of its opponents. He suggested the formation of a company, to be called the General Company, and proposed that a loan of £2,000,000, at eight per cent., should be advanced to Government, and that the subscribers should receive the monopoly of the Indian trade, but be free from the obligation of trading as a joint-stock society unless they should afterwards wish it. He carried the Bill for its formation through Parliament, and, in spite of the forebodings of his enemies, found that the immense sum which had been promised was readily subscribed in two or three days. The Bill was carried on the 3rd of September, but, on the 5th of the same month, the greater part of the subscribers declared their desire to become a joint-stock company, which was therefore chartered by Act of Parliament by the title of the English Company trading to the East Indies. The struggle between the companies was found to be so destructive to English trade, that, in 1702, arrangements for their union were made. A

The two Companies united. 1708.

common court of managers was established, their stocks equalized, and trade carried on under the name of the United Company of Merchants trading to the East Indies. But each company still traded with its own separate stock. Many inconveniences still attended this division of interests, and at last, in 1708, upon the award of Lord Godolphin, a final and complete union was made ; and, as the separate adventurers who had not joined either company were bought out, the monopoly again fell into the hands of the great United Company. But though his plan was thus ultimately a failure, for the moment Montague had all the credit of another great financial triumph, and the Whig party might reasonably expect that, in spite of the one single defeat with regard to the standing army, their position would be as good in the new Parliament as it had been in that which was just closing.

Meanwhile the King's personal attention had been as usual directed

William's attention directed to the Spanish succession.

rather to foreign than to home politics. The great question which at once occupied the minds of diplomatists after the Peace of Ryswick was the succession to the throne of Spain. It seemed very improbable that Charles II., a miserable hypochondriac, should live much longer. At his death there threatened to be a general scramble for his vast possessions. Early in the year, an embassy of unusual grandeur had attended Portland to France. The question had been there opened, and a corresponding French embassy under Tallard had subsequently and with the same object been sent to London. On the dissolution of Parliament the scene of negotiation was transferred to Holland. The question was one of great intricacy and difficulty.[1] It was not easy

[1] Philip III., 1598-1621.

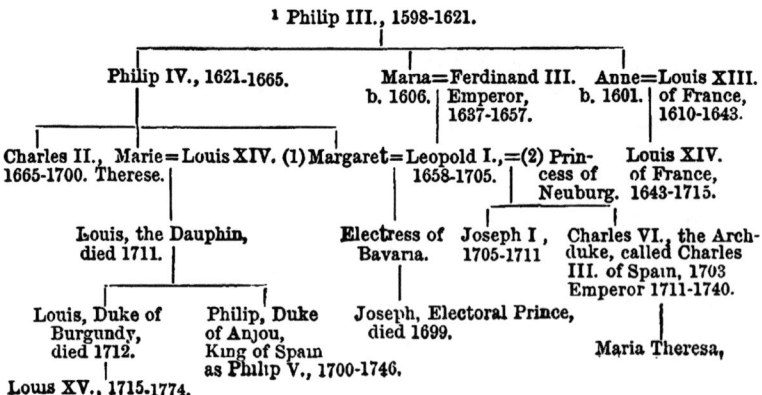

to point out the legitimate successor, even had it been possible to
allow the Spanish monarchy to pass unbroken into the hands of any
of the claimants. The eldest of Charles's sisters had married Louis
XIV., a younger sister had married Leopold of Germany. Leopold
was himself Charles's first cousin, grandson of Philip III. In direct
descent, therefore, the Dauphin stood next to the Spanish king.
Next to him came the offspring of Leopold's first marriage with the
Spanish Princess, namely, the Electress of Bavaria, but she gave over
her right to her son, the Electoral Prince. The third in order was
the Emperor Leopold. But the marriage of the Infanta with Louis
had been accompanied by a formal renunciation of her rights, sanctioned by the Cortes. The marriage of the second Princess with
Leopold had been attended by a similar renunciation, not sanctioned
by the Cortes. The marriage of Leopold's mother with the Emperor
had been attended by no renunciation at all. Thus, if the renuncia-
tions were valid, the claims in accordance with them came in exactly
the opposite order to the claims by order of descent. But the change
in the balance of Europe involved in the accession to the throne of
Spain of a prince of either the imperial house of Germany or the
royal house of France was of far graver importance than the mere
legal rights to the throne. Both Leopold and the Dauphin, conscious
that Europe would not submit to their acquiring Spain for themselves, had handed on their claims to representatives, who might be
considered as comparatively harmless. Leopold had substituted for
himself the Archduke Charles, his son by a second marriage, the
Dauphin his second son Philip. But, in spite of this arrangement,
France, England and Holland had considered it dangerous that the
Spanish dominions should pass entire into the hands of either of the
claimants, and the negotiations of this year were directed to forming a plan for dividing them with some sort of equality among the
three. The product of these negotiations was the First   First Partition
Partition Treaty, definitively signed at the Hague on   Treaty.
the 11th of October. By this the bulk of the Spanish dominions—
Spain, the Indies, and the Netherlands—was to pass to the least
powerful of the three claimants, the Electoral Prince. France was to
receive Guipuscoa in the north of Spain, and the Two Sicilies ; the
Austrian competitor was to be satisfied with the Milanese. The
treaty had been arranged as quietly as possible, but the republican
institutions of Holland were not favourable to secresy. Rumours of
what had been done reached Spain. The desire of the King and
the Castilians was to preserve at all hazards the integrity of the Empire.

Charles was therefore persuaded to make a will, and to declare that candidate whom France and England seemed most to favour, namely, the Electoral Prince, heir to his whole dominions; and thus for a time the matter rested.

Having thus temporarily settled his position abroad, William returned to England with the hope of a peaceful session. The hope was singularly falsified by the event. The great Whig party, so noble and united in adversity, had fallen to pieces, and a Tory reaction begun. The greatness and success of its measures had left room for faction. The unpopularity both of William and Montague affoided opportunity for the attacks of malcontents. On the assembling of Parliament after the new elections (Dec. 6, 1698), it became evident that a large number of unknown men who had been elected, although nominally Whigs, intended to make common cause with the extreme Tories, and that this united faction, under the title of the Country Party, would form an opposition against the Crown. The last session had already marked out the lines this opposition would take. The points at issue would be the maintenance of the army, the distribution of Crown grants, and the conduct of individual members of the ministry. On the first of these points the King did not act wisely. Unable to understand the insular politics in favour with the English, he insisted that the ministry should propose a standing army of 20,000 men. Afraid to introduce a Bill which they knew they could not carry, the ministry suffered the initiative to slip from their grasp, and a private individual was allowed to propose that the number of troops should be further lessened to 7000, and that all those 7000 should be born Englishmen. In spite of the efforts of the ministry the Bill was carried, and William found himself compelled to order the departure of his favourite Dutch guards. Hurt to the quick, he seriously formed the intention of quitting England. He even drew up his farewell speech, and was only moved to remain by the earnest prayers of Somers and by his own returning wisdom.

New Parliament.
Tory reaction.
Dec. 6, 1698.

The Country Party.

Dismissal of the Dutch guards.

Assured of their majority, the Opposition proceeded to attack the late ministry. Their favourite object was Montague, who had laid himself open to their assaults by the pride and luxury which he had exhibited in his good fortune, and still more by the indecent rapacity with which he seized on the valuable place of the Auditorship of the Exchequer, worth at least £4000 a year; this he placed in the hands of his brother, to be held until he should want it. The next victim was Russell, Lord Orford, whose administration only escaped censure by a single vote. And before the session closed, the third point, that of grants of Crown lands, was touched upon in a way which produced much after disaster. The method used on this occasion illustrates a point deserving of notice. The Revolution had placed the supreme power in the hands of Parliament; but Rivalry between the two Houses. Parliament itself consists of two elements, of two Houses drawn from different classes. Besides the general party struggles, besides the frequent contests between King and Parliament, and subsequently between Parliament and people, there was therefore a class rivalry between the two Houses, which had shown itself already on more than one occasion during the reign, and was rendered more prominent now by the fact that the party feeling in the Upper House was on the whole decidedly Whig. The weapon which the Commons intended to use in this strife was their exclusive right of introducing money Bills. Those Bills the Upper House had the power of rejecting entire, but not of amending. The Commons now " tacked " or appended to the Bill for the Land Tax a clause appointing seven Commissioners to inquire into the manner in which the forfeited land in Ireland had been granted out. This obnoxious clause the Lords were compelled to pass, or to reject the Bill entirely, and thus stop the supplies. Though keenly feeling the coercion put upon them, by a plan which would have proved fatal to the Upper House had not the good feeling of the nation and the strength of popular opinion ultimately compelled the Commons to abandon it, the Lords passed the Bill, feeling probably that the present occasion was scarcely important enough for a great constitutional struggle. The Money Bill having been passed, the King, in some anger, prorogued the Parliament (May 4).

As usual, when Parliament was not sitting, William withdrew to Holland, a habit which, now that the war no longer necessitated his presence there, increased his unpopularity in England, and the session of Parliament which he returned to meet in November 1699 was still more stormy than the last.

The discontent in England was backed up by more serious discontent in Scotland. The whole of that nation might The Darien scheme. be now reckoned among the enemies of the Court. For, during the recess, on the 5th of October, certain news had reached England of the failure of the great Darien scheme, and the complete destruction of those wild hopes of wealth and greatness which had been for the last four years buoying up the Scotch nation. Paterson,

the same man whose scheme for the Bank of England had in the
hands of Montague proved so successful, was the originator of this
disastrous project.   He had persuaded himself that the natural
wealth of a country has nothing to do with its prosperity.   The
commercial cities of the ancient world, and Venice and Holland in
modern times, had risen to greatness and wealth without any territorial possessions of importance.   He believed that he could reproduce this phenomenon in the case of Scotland.   The scheme of
Columbus had been to introduce the wealth of the East by a short
and direct route into Europe, and thus to destroy the traffic of the
Venetians.   He had found his plan thwarted by the interposition of
America ; and the discovery of a passage round the Cape of Good
Hope had turned all men's attention in that direction, and had
been the great source of wealth both to the Dutch and Portuguese.
But the plan of Columbus had never been quite forgotten, and
Paterson now thought to renew it by establishing a line of communication across the Isthmus of Darien.   The Scotch were to colonize and
occupy the isthmus, which would become, in the view of the projector,
the great emporium of the whole Eastern trade.   Although he did
not explain the details of his scheme, it was listened to with enthusiasm by his fellow-countrymen ; and in 1695, an extraordinary Act
passed the Scotch Parliament, and received the assent of the Lord
High Commissioner, authorising the formation of a Corporation,
half the capital of which was to be held by Scotchmen, with the
monopoly of the trade with Asia, Africa, and America for thirty-one
years.   With the exception of foreign sugar and tobacco, all its
imports were to be duty free.   Every servant of the Company was
free from imprisonment and arrest.   The Company was authorized
to take possession of unoccupied territories and exercise legal rights,
and the King promised to obtain satisfaction at the public charge
if foreign powers assaulted it.   Subscriptions to the amount of
£200,000 and upwards were speedily forthcoming, and a branch
of the Company established itself in London.   There, however, the
absurdities of the plan were at once discovered, and it met with a
very cold reception.   Any colony, to be useful, must be either in
America or in the Spice Islands ; now interference in America would
not be tolerated by Spain, nor would Holland look on quietly at the
occupation of the Spice Islands ; a maritime war was in fact inevitable ; Scotland, single-handed, could scarcely hope to carry on such a
war, and England would almost infallibly be drawn into it, and this on
behalf of a Company which, by changing Scotland into a free port,

would virtually make it an enormous centre for smuggling to the
extreme detriment of English trade. The attention of the King was
drawn to the subject. He expressed his entire disapprobation of the
scheme, and dismissed the Lord High Commissioner and the Secretary;
but the law was made and could not be rescinded. In 1698, in the
midst of wild enthusiasm, 1200 colonists set out from Leith, with
Paterson among them, and reached Darien in safety, and there
established their colony, but almost immediately came into contact
with the neighbouring Spanish governor, and the inevitable war began.
At first, however, the reports were favourable, and in the following
year a new armament of four ships and 1800 colonists left Scotland
for Caledonia, as the new settlement was called. They had not
been gone long before news arrived at New York that the colony no
longer existed, and that the wretched remnant of its inhabitants had
sought refuge in New England. In fact, the climate had proved
eminently unhealthy, in spite of the assertions of Paterson. Provisions had failed, and, worn out and enfeebled, the colonists, feeling
themselves entirely unable to repell the assaults of Spain, determined
to withdraw. After miserable suffering, a few of them reached New
York, and the second expedition arrived in Caledonia to find only
uninhabited ruins. They determined upon reoccupying these, rebuilt
the fort, and during the few healthy months continued, though with
heavy losses, to carry out their operations. But before long a
Spanish fleet appeared before the town, and an army, marching across
the isthmus from Panama, blockaded it on the land side. Resistance
was impossible. Already 300 of the new-comers had died, the
survivors promised to depart within a fortnight, and on the 11th
of April left the colony for ever. The disaster was regarded by the
Scotch as a national injury on the part of England. The Company
had throughout excited great anger in the Southern kingdom; the
colonial governors had done all they could to discourage the colony
when it arrived, and the Scotch were ready to trace this opposition to
national jealousy,—to attribute it even to William's partiality for his
Dutch subjects, whose trade might have been injured. In truth, the
whole business was a proof, as William pointed out to the House of
Lords, of the difficulty of managing two countries with different
interests under one Crown, and the necessity of a closer union
between the nations.

It was thus, supported by the discontent of Scotland, that the malcontents of Parliament resumed the question of the man- New Parliament.
agement of the royal property. After a fruitless attack Nov. 16, 1699.

upon Somers, who had indeed received a grant, but one against which no reasonable complaint could be made, they proceeded to follow up the work of the last session, and to act upon the recommendation of the seven Commissioners who had been appointed by the tacked clause of the preceding session. The Crown lands had been constantly dealt with according to the King's pleasure, without parliamentary interference. In early times, however, they had been regarded as a trust. Parliament had frequently demanded that the King should live upon his own revenues, and Acts for the resumption of grants had been passed, the last being that immediately following the battle of Bosworth. Since then the gift of the Crown had been considered a perfectly sound title. Whatever dislike, therefore, William's lavish grants to his Dutch favourites had excited, there would have been very great difficulty in calling in question his right to make them. The use to which the forfeited lands which had fallen into William's hands after the Pacification of Limerick had been put was more open to objection. A Bill ordering them to be applied to the public service had been interrupted and left incomplete, and the King had promised that the Commons should have another opportunity of considering the question. As they had since taken no steps in the matter, he seems to have considered himself free to act as he pleased. Of the forfeited lands, which amounted to about 1,700,000 acres, a fourth had been restored to its ancient possessors, according to the Limerick Pacification. Some of the rest had been mercifully given back to Irishmen, some to men like Ginkel and Galway, who had distinguished themselves in the Irish wars, but by far the larger portion had fallen to the King's personal friends, such as Woodstock, the eldest son of Portland, and Keppel, Lord Albemarle. The Commission could not arrive at unanimity, and sent up two reports. But that of the majority, which was very hostile to Government, was alone accepted by the Commons. It ridiculously over-estimated the grants at a sum of £2,600,000, and at the same time declared that very undue leniency had been shown to the Irish. Had these grants not been made, and the confiscations properly exacted, much of the present heavy taxation, they said, might have been spared. The Commons, longing to be free from taxes and hating the Dutch favourites, took up the matter with factious warmth, and the Resumption Bill was passed, vesting all the forfeited lands in the hands of trustees, and offering large rewards to informers who would point out lands which ought to have been confiscated. They even, with palpable injustice, included in

Irish forfeitures.

Resumption Bill passed. April 10, 1700.

their inquiry lands which had never been forfeited. Expecting opposition from the Upper House, they again tacked this Bill to the Land Tax Bill. The Lords now determined upon a struggle. Little as they liked the Dutch favourites, they could not allow themselves to be thus overridden. Their opposition was, however, unsuccessful ; the nation felt with the Commons, and foreign affairs had reached a crisis which rendered peace at home necessary to the King. The quarrel was pressed so far as to threaten a complete breach between the Houses, and a fatal blow to the Constitution. By the influence of the King the Lords were induced to yield, and the triumphant Commons were passing to fresh assaults on the King's friends, when, having passed the Land Tax Bill and thus supplied himself with money, William suddenly prorogued the Houses.

Parliament prorogued. April 11, 1700

The necessity which had driven him to this step was the reopening of the question of the Spanish succession. In January 1699 the Electoral Prince had died. The whole question thus assumed a new shape, and William's undivided attention was required. For the same reason, probably, and to allay the opposition in the House, he thought it necessary to remove Somers from office, and to place the Great Seal in the hands of Sir Nathan Wright. The Second Partition Treaty, which the King was now engaged in arranging, was such as was rendered necessary by the death of the third claimant. The bulk of the Spanish dominions was now to be given to the Archduke. It was to him

Second Partition Treaty.

that now Spain, the Indies, and the Netherlands were assigned, while Milan, which had formerly fallen to his share, was to be transferred to France, to be ultimately exchanged for Lorraine, a German fief, very important to round off the French dominions. But again these arrangements were upset. Portocarrero, the Spanish minister, was in the French interest, and supported by Harcourt, the ablest French diplomatist. By playing upon national feeling, which was strong against any partition, these statesmen excited the anger of the Spaniards against William, who had already incurred their enmity by his fancied support of the Darien scheme; and Charles was at length impressed with the absolute necessity of making another will. The events of the late session had given rise to the belief that William was not really master of England, while the visible greatness of France seemed to afford the best chance of keeping the Spanish monarchy undivided; the will was therefore made in favour of the Dauphin's son Philip, Duke of Anjou, who was declared heir to the whole of the Spanish dominions. The treaty was not well received in

England. While one party clamoured that too much was given to France, another complained of the injustice of forestalling the wishes of the Spanish people, and there was a general feeling of anger at the secresy with which the treaty had been arranged, a treaty which might easily draw England into a foreign war, and which had been concluded entirely without consulting Parliament. This anger reached its highest point when, in November, the King of Spain died, and Louis, in defiance of all his treaties, accepted his grandson's great inheritance. William had determined that the whole responsibility should lie with himself, trusting in his own diplomatic skill ; he had been beaten at his own arts, and his great treaty was absolutely useless.

In fact, there was no time when the King had been so unpopular or his enemies so strong. Nearly every class, except his own immediate followers among the Whigs, were alienated from him ; the mass of the people had suffered from heavy taxation, the nobles were sore at the unwise preference given to foreigners ; the whole nation shared in this feeling, and disliked his constant absences from home ; the scandal of the Irish forfeitures had just been brought to light ; the country gentry remembered with anger the failure of their Land Bank, and saw with envy the increasing importance of the moneyed interest. One thing was plain, that nothing could be done with a Parliament so adverse as the last, with a ministry so powerless as the late holders of power had proved. William therefore dissolved the Parliament, summoning a new one for the following February ; and, freeing himself from the old ministry, called to his councils Rochester, the late Queen's uncle and the head of the High Church Tories, with Godolphin and Sir Charles Hedges. For the present his only hope lay in the possibility of a general European war ; of this as yet there was but little sign. Austria had indeed refused to acknowledge the new King of Spain, and withdrawn its ambassador from Madrid, but in other countries it seemed as if the will of the late Spanish King would be quietly accepted. William himself could do nothing, and for the time was compelled to submit. His new ministry entreated him to acknowledge Philip; his Parliament showed no disposition to support him in any hostile steps against France. Two questions which he placed before them in his opening speech were, the succession of the throne of England, the settlement to which had been rendered necessary by the late death of the Duke of Gloucester, the young son of the Princess Anne (July 29, 1700), and the position which England should assume in the face of the

[Side notes:] William's unpopularity.

New ministry. Dec. 1700.

New Parliament. Feb. 1701.

altered aspect of European politics. It was in vain, upon this latter point, that he attempted to urge them to energy. The King of France had driven the Dutch to acknowledge Philip, by suddenly entering the Low Countries, and capturing 15,000 of their troops who had been intended to garrison the barrier fortresses. William and the Dutch States had in vain demanded the withdrawal of the French troops and the surrender of the strongholds. But even this act of aggression did not arouse the Parliament to energy. They acknowledged the obligations of England under the Treaty of 1677, and promised to send succours to the Dutch, but there seemed no immediate prospect of any grants for the purpose. Nor was the other point much more vigorously prosecuted. A Bill of Succession was indeed produced, but nearly every clause seemed evidently aimed   Succession Act. against the King's former conduct. The new sovereign was not to leave the kingdom without leave of Parliament; no person not a born Englishman was to be capable of holding any position of trust, or of receiving any grant from the Crown. England was not to be engaged in war for the defence of any dominions not belonging to the Crown of England. All matters relating to the Government were to be transacted in the Privy Council, and countersigned by such members of that body as should advise or consent to them. Having thus secured, as they thought, the insular position of England, the House proceeded to settle the succession upon the Electress Sophia of Hanover. Thus, though the Protestant succession was secured, a Bill which William had hoped would be a singular expression of popular sympathy with his own efforts was in fact a vote of censure on many of the acts of his reign.

While public business was thus proceeding languidly, the whole energy of the House was directed against the old Whig leaders and against the House of Lords. Impeach-   Impeachments against the Whigs. ments were hurried on against Lord Portland, Lord Orford, Lord Somers, and Montague, who had now become Lord Halifax. Against each of these the main charge was the share they had taken in the Partition treaties. But, in the case of Portland and Montague, there were additional charges in reference to the grants and dilapidations of the royal revenue, for which they were said to be answerable; while against Somers and Orford was alleged a ridiculous story concerning their participation in the notorious exploits of Captain Kidd. This man had been sent out by private enterprise to destroy piracy in the Indian Sea, and had there himself turned pirate. Both Somers and Orford had subscribed to the original enterprise. Somers, as Chancellor, had sealed Kidd's commission. It was now ridiculously suggested that they had all along known of his piratical intentions. But, while sending up these impeachments, the Commons felt absolutely certain that the Whig majority of the Lords would at once acquit their victims, for it was well understood that the measure was not one of justice but one of faction; they therefore passed an unjustifiable address to the King, praying him to dismiss the four Peers from his Council, even before the impeachments were heard. The House of Lords produced a counter address. The Commons demanded longer time to complete their impeachments, but the Peers were determined to bring a matter on which their judgment was in fact foregone to a speedy issue, and had now both law and, right on their side. They therefore positively refused to extend the time, and the 17th of June was fixed for Lord Somers's trial. Westminster Hall was fitted up with the usual preparations for impeachment. The Lords marched in all pomp to their judgment-seat. The Commons, declaring they had been denied justice, refused to appear. There were no accusers, and Somers was declared acquitted.

But many signs had begun to show themselves in the country which induced William to believe that the popular opinion was turning, and he ventured to put an end to the very dangerous fight between the Houses by a prorogation (June 24). What is known as the Kentish Petition was the great sign of this changed feeling. This petition had been sent up by the Grand Jury of Kent. It hinted that public business had been neglected, and the pursuit of personal vengeance substituted, and humbly deprecated the least mistrust of the King, and implored the House to give effect to its loyal addresses by turning them into Bills of supply. So arbitrary was the House of Commons at this time in the assertion of its privilege, that it was only by consenting to remain outside the House, and be personally answerable for their document, that the five gentlemen who brought up this petition were able to get it presented at all (May 8). It raised a storm of anger, was voted scandalous, infamous and seditious, and the five gentlemen were dismissed to prison. But their cause was taken up by the whole Liberal party, and the desires expressed in the petition were brought before the public in much more forcible language in a memorial written by Defoe, and called from its signature "The Legion Memorial." This expression of opinion could not but have been gratifying to the King.

The Kentish Petition.

The Legion Memorial.

Hope was indeed again opening before him. Not only could he feel certain of some support, however weak, at home, but the persistent retention on the part of Louis, in spite of all their clamours, of the Dutch barrier fortresses and the 15,000 troops he had captured had begun to rouse the war spirit of that people. Left more free to act now that Parliament was prorogued, William at once despatched 10,000 troops into Holland, under command of Marlborough, and before long went thither himself, to lay the foundation of a Grand Alliance between England, Holland, and the Emperor. The Grand This treaty was completed in September. But the terms Alliance. of it proved surely how low William's hopes still were. It only declared that it was desirable that satisfaction should be given to the Emperor on account of the succession of Spain, and pledges given for the security of England and her allies. It allowed two months for peaceful negotiations. After that time the contracting powers pledged themselves to attempt the recovery by force of arms of Milan for Austria, and of the barrier fortresses for Holland.

At this moment James II. of England lay dying. With all Europe submitting with ill-dissembled dislike to the late acqui- Death of sition of Spain by the Bourbons, and ready to take any James II. opportunity for disturbing the newly-appointed King, to acknowledge, in contravention of the Treaty of Ryswick, the young Prince of Wales as King of England, was a step full of danger for the French King. It could not have been hidden from Louis, as it certainly was not hidden from his ministers, that the real strength of his present position was the depressed condition of William, thwarted by his factious Parliament; and Louis must have known that nothing was more likely to change that weakness into strength than a violation of the Peace of Ryswick,—the destruction of the one great advantage which England had gained by nine years' expenditure of blood and treasure. But the influence of Madame de Maintenon, who had been won Louis acknow- over to the interest of the Stuarts, and a certain theat- ledging the Pretender. rical magnanimity which seldom deserted Louis, proved Sept. 16. stronger than prudence. At the deathbed of James he promised to uphold the claims of his son, and three days afterwards the young Prince was formally acknowledged by the whole Court as King of England.

No better news could have reached William. Again, as in the time of his first landing in England, his enemy had done Rouses English more for him than any skill or diplomacy of his own patriotism. could effect. The whole nation burst into a flame. Patriotic and loyal addresses came pouring in upon him. Public bodies in all parts of the country passed resolutions full of affection for him. The conduct of the late majority was denounced as factious wrangling, and the cause of the great insult which had been laid on the country ; and the connection between the Tory party and Louis seemed to be rendered plain when the French ambassador was found seated at supper in a well-known Jacobite tavern surrounded by the most ardent members of the Tory party. The King seized the moment of excitement, and, though conscious of the delays it would entail, at once dissolved Parliament. A struggle such as has seldom been seen excited England from end to end, and everywhere it became evident that the reckless conduct of Louis had secured the restoration of the Whigs. London returned four Whig members, Wharton again won back his supremacy in Buckingham, even the virulent Howe was defeated and lost his seat in Gloucestershire. The flame of indignation still blazed high when William met his new Parlia-

New Parliament and ministry. ment on the last day of the year, and, in words of unusual fire, bade them drop their factious disputes, and know no other distinction than that of those who were for the Protestant religion and the present Establishment, and of those who meant a Popish prince and a French government. The ministry was largely changed. Godolphin left the Treasury to make room for Lord Carlisle ; Manchester was made Secretary instead of Hedges, and other Whig Lords were admitted to the Privy Council. It is true that the unanimity was by no means perfect. The Tories were still strong in the House. There was still some fear of the ultimate return of the Stuarts. But the Government was strong enough to pass a Bill for attainting the pretended Prince of Wales, and a still more important Bill abjuring the house of Stuart, and pledging those who took the oath to uphold in turn each successor named in the Act of Settlement. The acceptance of this oath was made requisite for every employment either in Church or State.

It was thus in the full flush of a new victory, with hopes high,

Death of William. and with a well-grounded belief that his life's work of opposition to the encroachments of the French would not after all be wasted, that William, broken down by disease and suffering, died. He had long been so ill that his life had been despaired of, but he was still able to ride. On the 20th of February, his horse, stepping upon a molehill, fell with him, and his collar-bone was broken. This accident rendered his recovery hopeless. He lived just long enough to express his strong desire for a Union with Scotland, and to appoint the Commission which gave the royal assent to the Abjuration Act. On the 8th of March, surrounded by his faithful friends, he breathed his last.

ANNE.

1702–1714.

Born 1665 = George of Denmark.

CONTEMPORARY PRINCES

France.	*Austria.*	*Spain.*	*Russia.*
Louis XIV., 1643.	Leopold I., 1658. Joseph I , 1705. Charles VI., 1711.	Philip V , 1700.	Peter the Great, 1689.

Prussia.	*Sweden*	*Denmark and Norway.*
Frederick I., 1701.	Charles XII , 1697.	Frederick IV., 1699.

POPE.—Clement XI., 1700.

Lord Chancellors.	*Archbishop.*
Sir Nathan Wright, 1700. William Cowper, 1705. Sir Simon Harcourt, 1710.	Thomas Tenison, 1694.

First Lords of the Treasury.	*Chancellors of the Exchequer.*	*Secretaries of State.*
1702. Godolphin. 1710. Poulett. 1711. Harley. 1714. Shrewsbury.	1702. Henry Boyle. 1708. John Smith. 1710. Robert Harley.	1702 { Nottingham. Hedges. 1704 { Harley. Hedges. 1706 { Harley. Sunderland. 1708 { Boyle. Sunderland. 1710 { Boyle. Dartmouth. 1710 { St John. Dartmouth. 1713 { St. John. Bromley.

IN passing to a new reign we pass to no new epoch. No new principles are at work, no new influences visible. The same constitutional growth which had been gradu- ally developing itself since the Revolution makes its way steadily onwards. The sole difference is the difference in the person of the sovereign. In the yet unfixed state of the Constitution this might have introduced important changes, and did in fact, by the absence of

Power of Marlborough.

ANNE
[1702

the strong personal character of William, tend to easier and more
complete development of parliamentary action. But the importance
of the Queen was much neutralized by the complete mastery exercised over her mind by the Duke and Duchess of Marlborough. The
effect of Marlborough's supremacy was to reproduce almost exactly
the circumstances of the former reign. Though an immoral politician,
a self-seeking and avaricious man, Marlborough was too great not to
appreciate the grandeur of William's European schemes. Thus, as far
as European policy was concerned, he passed almost completely into
that King's place, pledged both by his natural intellect and by his
personal interests to pursue very much the same course as William
had taken. It is scarcely going beyond the truth to call the earlier
part of Anne's reign the reign of the Duke of Marlborough; and
he encountered exactly the same difficulties, and was reduced to
exactly the same straits, as his predecessor had been in his attempts
to carry out a national policy without regard to party.

The dissolution of Parliament had followed as a natural consequence
upon the death of the sovereign who had summoned it,
and in whom it was regarded as depending. The new
position which the Parliament had occupied since the Revolution
had naturally modified that view. By a law passed at the beginning of the eighth year of William's reign, Parliament was
allowed to sit for six months after the King's death. It was
therefore with the same Whig Parliament, which had come into
existence just after Louis had acknowledged the Prince of Wales,
that Anne's reign began. The conduct of the Parliament during
the few months of its existence was entirely free from faction. It
completed and applied the Abjuration Bill, on which it had been
busy at the end of the last reign, established an examination of
public accounts, and granted with great unanimity the same revenue
as William had enjoyed; and further, took a first step towards a
measure which William had recommended, and which the failure of
the Darien scheme had rendered almost inevitable, by passing a Bill
for appointing Commissioners to arrange, if possible, for a complete
union with Scotland.

But it soon became evident that both the tendencies of the Queen
and Marlborough's views on home politics would lead to the restoration
of Tory influence. On the Duke himself and on his wife honours and
offices were freely lavished, and the new ministry was
drawn almost entirely from the Tory party. Thus
Godolphin, Marlborough's son-in-law, was made Lord Treasurer;

Nottingham and Sir Charles Hedges, Secretaries of State; Lord Normanby, shortly afterwards Duke of Buckingham, Privy Seal; Pembroke, Lord President; Jersey was given a place in the Council; while offices were found for Seymour and Levison Gower in the Privy Council, from which Somers, Halifax, and Orford were excluded. Yet even already Marlborough's intention in some degree to disregard party was shown in the retention of some Whigs in office, among others the Duke of Devonshire, who kept his place as Lord Steward. More important, with regard to the future history of the reign, was the division which even thus early began to show itself among the Tories themselves. Rochester, who had come over from his post in Ireland, not only desired a much more complete exclusion of the Whigs from office, but also opposed, in pursuance of the accepted policy of the High Tories, the declaration of war. Thus already, before the dissolution which took place on the 25th of May, two facts, which together form the key to the political history of the reign, were visible,—Marlborough's determination to rely upon a mixed Government, and the disinclination of one section of the Tories to support him in his war policy.

In pursuing the future history of the reign there are three subjects which require special attention, the European war, the Union with Scotland, and the parliamentary and ministerial history; and although the war and the history of the ministry constantly affect one another, it will probably tend to clearness if, for the first few years at all events, these three subjects are treated separately.

The opposition of the Tories to the war had been entirely useless. The completion of the negotiations set on foot by William had been intrusted to Marlborough. Immediately, at the beginning of the reign, he had gone to the Hague, and war was declared in London, at Vienna, and at the Hague on the 4th of May. Meanwhile so many Princes had joined the Confederation, originally consisting of England, Holland, and Austria, that war was declared by the Diet of the Empire. The Elector of Brandenburg had been induced to join by the promise of the royal title; the Elector of Hanover and the Elector Palatine had also given in their adhesion. On the other hand, though the brother Electors of the Bavarian House, the Elector of Bavaria and the Elector of Cologne, had at first agreed to remain neutral, Louis felt pretty sure of the course they would ultimately take, and of the friendship of Victor Amadeus of Savoy, whose daughter had married the new King of Spain, and the position of whose dominions rendered his friendship of great value, giving as it did an access into Italy to the French.

The Queen's love for her husband had induced her to wish that he
should be made Commander-in-chief both of the English
and Dutch forces, though utterly unfit for the post, and
Marlborough seems to have honestly attempted to procure this appointment. But the Dutch would not hear of it, and
ultimately Marlborough took the field in July as Commander-in-
chief, with Overkirk as his Lieutenant commanding the Dutch
troops.

Marlborough appointed Commander.

Two points distinguish this war from the preceding one. Hitherto
in all great confederations against the French the
Spanish Netherlands had been in the hands of the confederates, but as Spain was now in close alliance with France, it
became necessary to conquer this part of the Netherlands. And,
secondly, the death of William had been followed by the complete
depression of the house of Nassau in Holland, and the supremacy of
the republican party, which by no means shared in the late King's
hatred to France, and which, from jealousy of all personal authority,
caused the general to be accompanied by field deputies, with a
right of mixing in all councils of war. This was one of the greatest
of Marlborough's difficulties, as the deputies seldom failed to
hamper him, and to throw obstacles in the way of any adventurous plans. Before Marlborough took the field the campaign
had opened. The French had command of the Spanish Low
Countries, of the Duchy of Luxemburg, and, through the friendship
of its Elector, of the territories of the Elector Clement of Cologne,
who was both Archbishop of Cologne and Bishop of Liège. Both the
Rhine and Meuse were thus in their hands and the fortresses held by
their garrisons. The whole southern frontier of Holland, which left
the sea near Ostend, crossed the mouth of the Scheldt, and cutting off
a portion of Brabant, joined the Meuse somewhat to the north of
Venloo, was thus open to them, while by way of the Rhine they had
an opportunity of attacking the Dutch provinces from the east.
While Holland was thus assailable on two sides, the advancing angle of
the French dominions exposed them in a similar manner. The valley
of the Moselle, which leads directly into the heart of Lorraine,
could be attacked either from the north or by a German army coming
from the south by way of Landau. Anxious to secure their frontier
towards the Rhine, the Dutch had early in the year besieged and
taken the fortress of Kaiserwerth, and bent chiefly upon their own

Position of Holland.

security, would have preferred to retain Marlborough and the army in the neighbourhood of that river. But the Duke saw that the passage of the Meuse where it makes the northern frontier of the Dutch Brabant, and an advance southwards towards the Spanish Nether- lands, would necessitate a concentration of the French troops, and transfer the seat of war to that province. In spite of the opposition of the Dutch, he therefore crossed the river at Grave, and proceeded directly south into Spanish Brabant. As he had expected, his ap- pearance there obliged Boufflers to withdraw from Guelders to oppose him ; and although the opposition of the field deputies prevented a general engagement, Marlborough was enabled to secure the eastern frontier of Holland, to take the fortresses of the Meuse,—Venloo, Ruremond, Stevensweerth, and Liège,—to overrun Guelders, Cleves, the Electorate of Cologne, with the exception of Bonn, the whole of the Bishopric of Liège and the Duchy of Limburg, thus cutting off the French from the Lower Rhine.

Meanwhile an attack had been made upon France from the Upper Rhine. The Margrave Louis of Baden, having crossed the river with the German forces, found himself opposed by Catinat, who did not show his usual ability, and suffered the Margrave to besiege and take Landau and to overrun Alsace. The success of the German army was marred by the defection of Bavaria, which, throwing aside its neutrality, declared in favour of France. Villars was detached from Catinat's army to join the Elector of Bavaria ; and as an access was thus opened to the French into the heart of Germany, Louis of Baden had to withdraw from his conquests, and, turning to meet the new danger, suffered a heavy defeat at Friedlingen.

While such was the course of the war in Germany and Flanders, in Italy, Prince Eugene of Savoy, the general of the allies, had, even in the winter, been carrying on operations against The war Marshal Villeroi. That Marshal had been taken prisoner in Italy at Cremona, and had been succeeded by Vendome. A great but indecisive battle had been fought in August at Luzara, after which the armies were left facing each other, the French still occupying the Milanese. The maritime war had been as inde- The war at sea. cisive as that upon the Continent ; an English expedition under the Duke of Ormond had been sent against Cadiz ; it had failed in its original object, but on the way home had succeeded in destroying a Spanish treasure fleet in the Bay of Vigo. In the West Indies, an event occurred almost unprecedented in English history. The English fleet had been defeated in a great battle, not by the superiority of the enemy, but by the treason of its own commanders. Admiral Benbow, who had engaged a superior force of the enemy, after a fight of several days, was deserted by some of his captains. Wounded and dying, he was forced to withdraw. He lived long enough to have his captains condemned to death by court martial.

The campaign of this year was thus wholly indecisive. The English and Dutch had secured the possession of the Rhine and the Meuse; but the German army was threatened in front from Alsace, while its rear and southern flank were exposed to the victorious army of Villars and the Elector of Bavaria: in Italy the French still held the Milanese against the attacks of Prince Eugene. But before the next campaign opened the position of France had changed considerably for the worse. The diplomacy of Louis had hitherto secured the predominance of French influence in both Spain and Italy by the adhesion of Savoy and Portugal to his cause. Victor Amadeus of Savoy had been won by the marriage of his daughter with the King of Spain; but, situated in the midst of great powers, his conduct was almost of necessity shifting, and his policy directed rather to his own advantage and to the interests of Italy than to the more general interests of Europe; the offer on the part of Austria to give up to him the districts of Montferrat and Novara induced him to desert Louis and to declare in favour of the Grand Alliance. The French army in the Milanese was thus separated from France, and its energy paralyzed. By similar means the fidelity of Portugal was also undermined. A promise of a certain portion of the Spanish possessions both in Spain and in America, and a treaty known as the Methuen Treaty, securing to Portugal great advantage in her trade with England, induced her to join the Grand Alliance. The importance of this adhesion was great, as it afforded an opening for the allied armies to act directly against Spain, the possession of which country was the real object of the war. Nor were these defections the only causes of danger which beset France. Disturbances had broken out in Louis' own dominions. The Protestants of the Cevennes, driven to despair by the cruel conduct of the Intendant, Marshal de Baville, and of the Catholic clergy, had broken into open rebellion, and the irregular efforts of the Camissards, as they were called, had become formidable under the skilful guidance of Cavalier, a baker's lad, who showed extraordinary · aptitude for partisan warfare.

(margin note: Savoy and Portugal join the coalition.)

These misfortunes on the part of France were somewhat balanced by the defection, already mentioned, of the Elector of Bavaria; and Louis determined to take advantage of the road to Vienna thus opened to him, and to throw his chief efforts in that direction. Thither therefore Villars marched through the Black Forest, having previously captured the fortress of Kehl opposite Strasbourg. The movement, however, was only partially successful; while Villars wished to march upon Vienna, already threatened by an insurrection in Hungary, the Elector insisted upon moving into the Tyrol. The peasantry of that mountainous district, deeply attached to Austria, thwarted all his efforts to advance, and when Louis of Baden, leaving the lines of Stolhofen, appeared in Bavaria, the Elector was compelled to withdraw and rejoin Villars. Too weak to defeat the Margrave, the combined generals were obliged to content themselves with checking the German troops coming against them from Franconia under Count Stirum at Hochstädt. Villars, who traced the ruin of the campaign to the rejection of his advice, clamoured to be recalled, and his place was but badly filled by Marsin.

Meanwhile, Marshal Tallard had been repairing last year's disasters in Alsace. Brisach had been taken, the Prince of Hesse, with troops from Stolhofen, had been defeated at Spires while attempting to relieve Landau, and that city had been retaken by the French (Nov. 17). In Flanders Marlborough had formed a great plan to conquer Antwerp and Ostend, but had been thwarted by the slowness of the Dutch, and by the defeat of their army under Opdam at Echeren. The Duke had to content himself with the capture of Bonn upon the Rhine, and with further progress upon the Meuse, where he captured Huy and Limburg.

The following year, 1704, saw a change in the ministry at home. Finding himself thwarted by the extreme High Tories, Marlborough had obtained their dismissal, and the admission of Harley and St. John to the ministry. In the meantime Louis was making vast efforts, and had set on foot no less than eight armies. There was to be war at once in Flanders, in Bavaria, in Alsace, in Savoy, in Lombardy, in Spain, and against the Cevennes. To Villars was intrusted the reduction of the Cevennes, which had been vainly attempted the preceding year by the Marshal Montreval. The Duke of Berwick was to ·subdue Portugal, Vendome to act against Savoy, Villeroi to stand on the defensive in Flanders, and the great effort of the year was again to be in Bavaria, where the events of the preceding year promised fresh success. There a considerable French army under Marsin had collected, and thither now was proceeding a fresh army under Tallard, which would raise the forces in the country much beyond anything the Emperor could bring to meet them. Early in May Marshal Tallard led 15,000 troops through the Black Forest, and formed his junction with the Elector. He then hastened back to Alsace, where 30,000 men had been left to oppose the Margrave of Baden.

The position of the Emperor seemed indeed almost hopeless. Critical position While the French and Bavarians were advancing of Austria. directly towards his capital on the west, the Hungarians, under Prince Ragotski, with constantly increasing forces, were approaching Vienna from the east, so that in June it became necessary to throw up works for the defence of the capital. Marlborough watched the coming crisis with much anxiety, and formed a plan of great boldness for the Emperor's relief. It was no less than to march the whole of the troops under his command, and to transfer the seat of war to Bavaria, interposing between Vienna and the advancing Bavarians. Previous experience had taught him that there was no hope of persuading the Dutch to countenance such a plan. To the States he therefore suggested only a campaign on the Moselle, and co-operation with Louis of Baden in the south ; to Godolphin alone he told his secret. At length a threat that he would move upon the Moselle with the English alone, backed up by the influence of Heinsius, the Grand Pensionary, who was his constant friend, induced the Dutch to give their consent to the part of the plan he had disclosed to them. Other obstacles were The march to met with from the other allies, but they were all at length Blenheim. overcome, and early in May Marlborough set out, ostensibly for the Moselle. To keep up this notion he went first to Coblenz, and the French proceeded to collect their armies to meet him. He then went on to Mayence, and it was believed that he intended to act in Alsace. He was there obliged to disclose his real object. He left the Rhine, marched up the Neckar, and advanced through the Duchy of Wurtemberg. On his road to Mondelsheim, he had a meeting with Eugene, who was commanding the Imperial army on the Rhine. To him he told his plans ; and the intercourse of the two great chiefs ripened into unbroken friendship. They were there also joined by Louis of Baden, a punctilious German general of some ability, but belonging to an older school of tactics. Marlborough and Eugene suggested that the Margrave should retire to his lines at Stolhofen, and hold them against Tallard, while Eugene should bring such of the German army as was moveable to co-operate with the English. The Margrave, however, insisted on the place of honour. Eugene went back to the Rhine, the Margrave joined

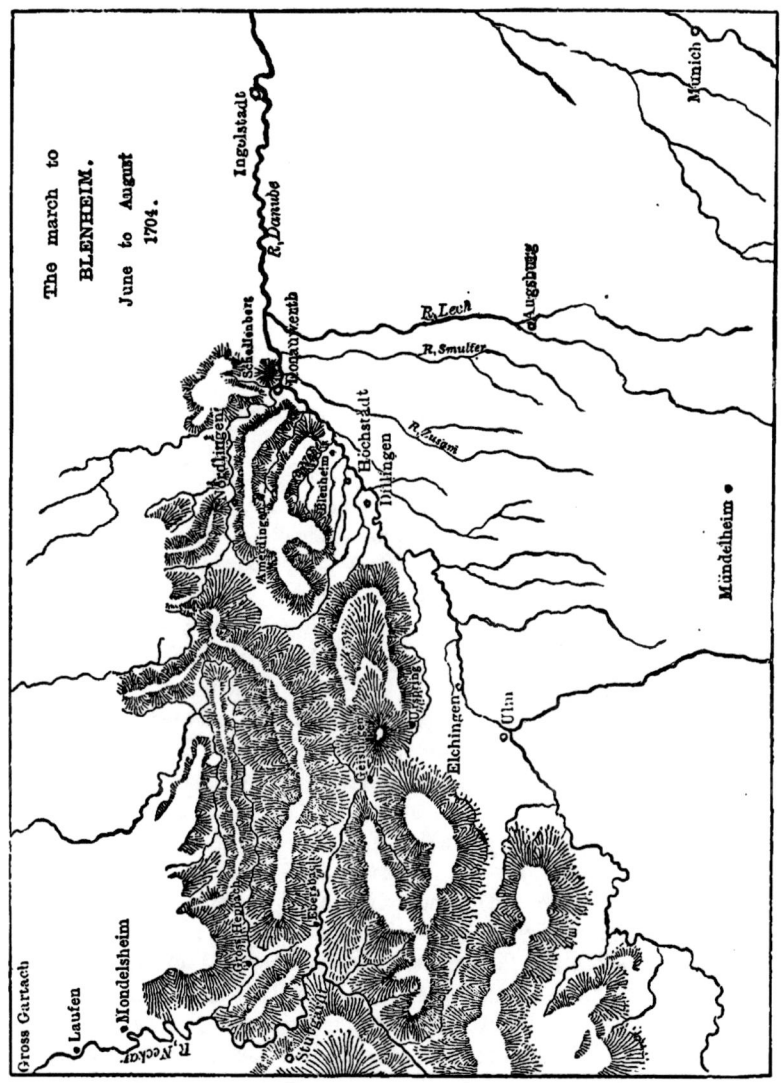

Marlborough; and the difficulty of the chief command was compromised, the generals were to command on alternate days. After making

these arrangements, the armies proceeded on their march through the rough hill country of Wurtemberg. Having crossed the Neckar at Laufen, they followed the course of its tributaries, by Gross Heppach, Ebersbach, and the difficult pass of Geislingen, and finally emerged upon the plains, reaching the Danube at Elchingen, a little to the east of Ulm. The Elector, expecting an attack upon that city, garrisoned it and withdrew, still on the north bank of the river, to Dillingen, further to the east. But Marlborough had no intention of attacking Ulm, he continued his march eastward, determining to pass round and beyond the Elector's army and to secure Donauwerth, which would supply him with a bridge to cross the river, and might be turned into a fortified place for his magazines. With some difficulty he persuaded Louis of Baden to march in this direction. His intention being at length evident, the Elector of Bavaria sent 12,000 men to occupy the strong hill of the Schellenberg, commanding Donauwerth. When the day broke, the English army were at Amerdingen, still fourteen miles from Donauwerth. It was however the day of Marlborough's command. At three in the morning he started on his march, and afraid of allowing the opportunity to slip, though his men were weary from their long journey, Marlborough determined to assault the Schellenberg that same afternoon. The battle was a fierce one, but the allies were entirely successful. The Bavarians fled in disorder. Some thousands crossed the bridge, but the weight of the fugitives broke it down, and a vast number were drowned in the river. The Elector of Bavaria now withdrew to Augsburg, to await the arrival of reinforcements from France. Marlborough and his army crossed the Lech, and proceeded to follow him. Bavaria was at his mercy. He offered the Elector terms of capitulation. They were however refused, and Marlborough was guilty of the one act which is a blot on his military career, he gave the country up to military execution.

The two French generals Villeroi and Tallard, outwitted by Marlborough's march, had meanwhile taken counsel together, and once more Tallard, leaving Villeroi in Alsace, led a reinforcement of 25,000 men to join the Bavarians. He was watched and followed by Prince Eugene, who reached the Danube at Dillingen almost at the moment that Tallard had formed his junction with the Bavarians at Augsburg. As Eugene's reinforcements were necessary, Marlborough fell back to meet him, and soon Eugene, leaving his troops behind him, appeared in person in the camp. Between them they persuaded the Margrave of Baden that the capture of the fortress of Ingolstadt was necessary, and that, as it had hitherto never been taken, it would be much to his honour to reduce it. Thus rid of their pretentious colleague, Eugene and Marlborough arranged their junction, which was finally made, without disturbance from the French, on the 11th of August, a little to the east of Hochstadt, on the north of the Danube. The combined armies of the French and Bavarians had also betaken themselves to the same side of the river, and were now advancing from the west to meet the allied army, should they wish to

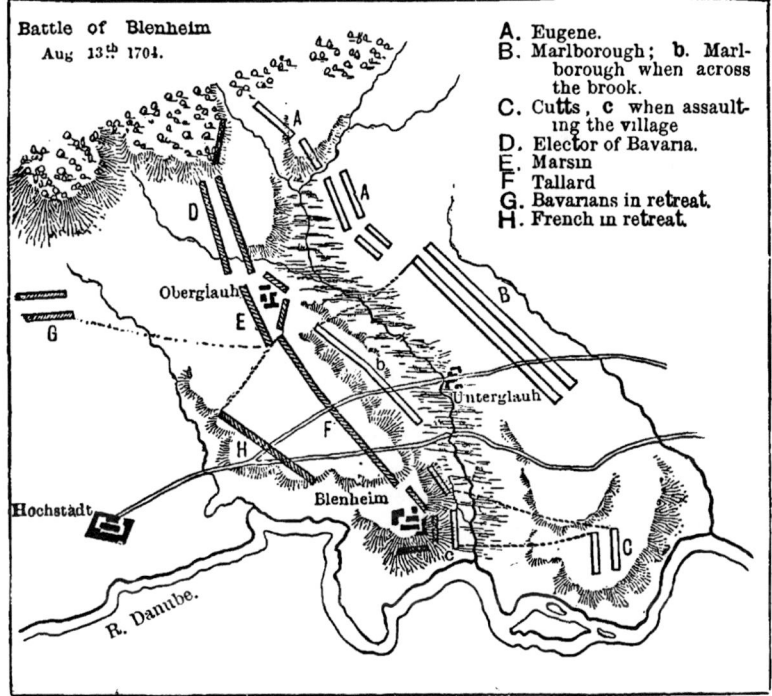

Battle of Blenheim
Aug 13ᵗʰ 1704.

A. Eugene.
B. Marlborough; b. Marl-
       borough when across
       the brook.
C. Cutts , c when assault-
       ing the village
D. Elector of Bavaria.
E. Marsin
F Tallard
G. Bavarians in retreat.
H. French in retreat.

fight. It was believed, however, that such was not Marlborough's intention. Tallard thought he was withdrawing towards Nordlingen, and, as he said after the battle, had intended to fall upon him and fight him on his way thither. *Battle of Blenheim. Aug. 13.*

When it became evident that a battle was to be fought, the French general, advancing from Hochstädt, took up a strong position in the neighbourhood of the village of Blenheim. The hills which lie along the north of the Danube there fall back a little, enclosing a small plain. Across this runs a brook called the Nebel, at the foot of a spur of rising land which runs from the foot of the receding hills to the Danube, where its termination is crowned by the village of Blenheim. The course of the Nebel is full of morasses difficult to pass, but a gradual slope of firm ground leads from it to the top of the rising ground. Along this ridge the French and Bavarians took up their position. The Elector of Bavaria, with Marshal Marsin, occupied the left, where, in the midst of woods, the rising ground joins the hills ; Marshal Tallard with the French occupied Blenheim and the right. Considering Blenheim as the key of the position, Marshal Tallard fortified it with palisades, and placed in it a considerable portion of his infantry, thus depriving himself of their assistance upon the battlefield, and weakening the centre of his army. To the French was opposed Marlborough in person, while Eugene, in command of the right wing, and with a considerably smaller number of troops, led the attack against the Elector. The difficulties he met with prevented Eugene from being early in position, but news were at length brought that he was ready to begin the battle, and Marlborough at once proceeded to the attack. The battle began on the part of the English with an assault upon the intrenched village. It was too strong to be taken, and the assailants were driven back with some loss. But the vigour of the opposition his troops had met with showed Marlborough his enemy's mistake. He determined to direct his chief assault upon the centre of the line. The infantry which were attacking Blenheim were ordered to seek shelter behind some rising ground, and to keep up such a feigned attack upon the place as should give employment to the troops stationed there. Meanwhile, with considerable difficulty, the English army was brought across the marshes, and established in position upon the firm ground beyond. In the French line cavalry and infantry were interlaced ; this arrangement was copied by the assailants. The first effort of the English to ascend the slope was defeated, but after a fierce interchange of fire, a second attempt broke the French cavalry, and destroying the infantry, pierced the centre of the French line. The battle was in fact won, no help could be sent to Tallard by the Elector, a decisive charge of cavalry drove the enemy's horse off the field, and the army fled in two bodies, one towards the river, the other towards Hochstädt. Both were hotly pursued, and of those who fled towards the river thousands perished in the stream. Blenheim still held out, but, cut off from all succour, surrounded by the whole English army, and threatened by the approaching artillery, the gallant garrison was compelled to capitulate, and 11,000 men laid down their arms. The right wing being completely destroyed, the Elector of Bavaria had found it necessary to withdraw his troops from the battle, although they had hitherto held their position against the fierce attacks of Eugene. In the confusion he managed to retire without much loss. The victory, however, was a very complete one ; 60,000 strong in the morning of the 13th, on the 14th the French and Bavarian generals found themselves at the head of no more than 20,000 men. All their tents and baggage, and most of their artillery and colours, had fallen into the hands of the allies. The list of killed and wounded on the side of the allies was about 12,000. Marshal Tallard himself was among the prisoners. Again, even after this defeat, the Elector of Bavaria declined all terms, and his wife, as Regent, had to submit to such conditions as the German Emperor chose to impose. So great was the blow, that the French retreated with extreme rapidity ; they gave up the strong fortress of Ulm, and withdrew beyond the Rhine, whither they were pursued by the allies, who, following separate routes, again assembled at Philipsburg ; nor even there did Villeroi withstand them, but still falling back, allowed them to recapture Landau, during which operation Marlborough completed his work by rapidly marching into the valley of the Moselle and conquering Trèves and Trarbach.

Events of some importance had been taking place in three of the other seats of war. In Spain, Berwick had completely Progress of the war in Spain, the Cevennes, and Italy. worsted the Portuguese, who had been so badly succoured by the English under the Duke of Schomberg that he had been recalled, and Ruvigny, Earl of Galway, a French refugee, put in his place ; while, to balance this, a fleet under Sir George Rooke, having on board the Prince of Darmstadt, and some troops, while returning from an unsuccessful attack on Barcelona, made an easy conquest of Gibraltar, and took possession of it in the name of the English, to whom it has ever since belonged. In the Cevennes, a merciful policy had brought the rebellion to an end, and Cavalier having been offered the commission of colonel in the French army, which he at first accepted and then declined, had been allowed to leave the country. He entered the English army, rose to the rank of general, and was subsequently Governor of Jersey.

Meanwhile affairs in Italy had been assuming a shape which rendered it probable that the great interest of the war would be transferred thither in the following year. Vendome had been rapidly reducing the territory of the Duke of Savoy. One after the other his fortresses had been captured, and no hope seemed left him but in immediate succour, either from the Emperor, who was not likely to give it, or from Marlborough himself.

As was natural after his great successes, Marlborough expected that

Marlborough's plans for 1705. the next year would be one of much importance. Seeing the impossibility of himself assisting Savoy, he had contrived to persuade the King of Prussia to allow 8000 of his troops to proceed to Italy, and to serve under Eugene, who had been despatched thither. His own intention was to follow up his late victory by an invasion of France. He had intended that this invasion should be by the valley of the Moselle, upon which a joint attack was to have been made, by himself up the river, and by Louis of Baden coming from Landau. The plan had been so far foreseen, that the ablest of the French generals, Marshal Villars, was stationed on the Moselle, while Flanders was intrusted to Villeroi, and Marsin continued in Alsace. The weak co-operation of the German Prince rendered the plan abortive, nor did the death of the Emperor Leopold, nor the succession of Joseph the young King of the Romans, increase for any length of time the vigour of the Imperial armies. But while Marlborough was still waiting for the Margrave's assistance, Villeroi had suddenly assumed the offensive, had retaken some of the fortresses of the Meuse, and invested Liège. As usual, on the slightest sign of danger, the Dutch were clamorous for Marlborough's return. His disappointment on the Moselle inclined him to listen to them, and his appearance in Flanders at once re-established affairs. Though disappointed in his main object, he still intended to fight a great battle; but, as usual, jealousy of the allied commanders, and the constant slowness and opposition of the Dutch general, prevented him from bringing on an engagement. He however succeeded in breaking the great line of French fortifications extending from Antwerp to Namur upon the Meuse, and in advancing to the attack of Brussels across the plain of Waterloo, where, but for the opposition he met with among his own colleagues, a great battle might have been fought: he writes, that he felt sure that, had he fought such a battle, it would have been a greater victory than that of Blenheim. However, his difficulties were more than he could overcome. The year passed away without great events, and the French began to think that he had owed his victories to chance. Upon the Rhine, Louis of Baden, though he had been so backward in his support of Marlborough, showed the ability which he really possessed by winning a great battle at the end of the year at Hagenau, unfortunately too late to assist Marlborough in his plans. In Italy, though Eugene won the battle of Cassano, the position of the Duke of Savoy became continually more precarious, and the crisis had not passed.

It was in fact not with either of the great regular armies that the allies this year won any great successes, but with the Peterborough's small and mixed forces in Spain, which had been placed success in Spain under the eccentric but vigorous command of Lord Peterborough. Leaving Galway to prosecute the war in the west, this general, who held with Sir Cloudesley Shovel a joint command of the fleet also, drew the Prince of Darmstadt from Gibraltar, and sailed round the east of Spain. After some successes on the eastern coast, he was eager to march direct upon Madrid. But the Archduke Charles, now calling himself Charles III., who was with him, listened in preference to the suggestions of Darmstadt, who had once been Governor of Catalonia, and trusted much to his influence in that province. The plan of an attack upon Madrid was therefore overridden, and the army proceeded to besiege Barcelona. Serious quarrels occurred between the leaders, for which Peterborough's want of caution was no doubt much to blame, and the siege was on the point of being given up. Already the heavy cannon were withdrawn from the trenches and carried on board ship, when suddenly Peterborough appeared in the tent of the Prince of Darmstadt, with whom he was not on speaking terms, and telling him that he intended to attack the enemy that night, challenged him to follow him. Laying aside his animosity, the Prince at once accompanied him. Peterborough's intention was to capture the citadel of Montjuich, a fort at some little distance from the town itself, and this he trusted to do by a sudden attack when the enemy were off their guard. The attempt was perfectly successful. The English troops followed the defenders pell mell into the walls of the fortress. Scarcely was the stronghold taken than the Spaniards began to advance from the town to retake it. Peterborough rode forward to reconnoitre; a panic seized his troops in his absence, and they were already relinquishing the fort, when he galloped back and rallied them, and fortunately found that their absence had been unperceived. The possession of this citadel was followed before long by the fall of the city, which capitulated on the 9th of October (1705). The greater portion of the troops in Barcelona, and much of the open country, at once declared for King Charles. The kingdom of Valencia followed this example, and in the capital of that province Peterborough subsequently took up his abode. Nor did his successes end there. In the following year, the French, under Marshal Tessé and

King Philip himself, attempted to regain Barcelona. The Count of Toulouse, a natural son of the French King, blockaded it from the sea. Peterborough, moving from Valencia with but 3000 regular troops, did his best to employ Tessé's army, which was 20,000 strong. But the siege went forward uninterruptedly. Already the trenches were within 150 yards of the wall, and an immediate assault was to be expected, when the English fleet under Sir John Leake, second in command, approached. Though his numbers were nearly equal to those of the Count of Toulouse, Leake, a prudent commander, wished to wait for expected reinforcements under Byng. But Peterborough, feeling that delay would be ruinous, determined upon a strange step to compel immediate action. He got on board an open boat and proceeded in quest of the English fleet. After searching for a whole day and night in vain, he at length reached the squadron. Having produced a new commission which had been given him, which gave him full command over Leake whenever he was himself on board, he at once hoisted his flag and gave orders for the attack. But meanwhile, hearing of the arrival of the English, the Count of Toulouse had withdrawn his fleet, the town could be easily approached from the sea, and Tessé thought it better to raise the siege. After this brilliant exploit, Peterborough again wished to march upon Madrid from Valencia, but King Charles, on the advice of his German council, whom Peterborough speaks of by the contemptuous name of "the Vienna crew," determined upon advancing straight through Aragon, and called upon Peterborough to move his troops from Valencia to join him on the march. Meanwhile the army of the west, under Galway and Das Minas, had, after considerable delay, moved upon Madrid also, and had occupied it. They found, however, the feeling there strongly in favour of King Philip. As Aragon and Catalonia had favoured Charles, so, in the spirit of hereditary opposition, the Castilians devoted themselves to the interest of Philip. So strong was the opposition they met with, that the allies had to leave the capital and fall back eastward towards the approaching army of Charles, with whom they formed a junction. But in the combined army there were far too many commanders for vigorous action. Peterborough, the only man of genius among them, found himself constantly thwarted : he put no restraint upon his tongue. Bitter quarrels were the consequence, and he found it necessary to leave the army and betake himself to Italy, which had been his original destination, in order to negotiate with the Genoese for a supply of money.

The same year which saw these sudden and unexpected successes
in Spain was marked by still more complete success against the
French in other parts of Europe.   Marlborough was determined to
wipe out the bad impression which the inactivity of the last campaign had caused.   His own ardent wish was to march with the army
as he had in the Blenheim campaign, and to throw himself into
Italy, where the critical position of affairs still continued.   Finding

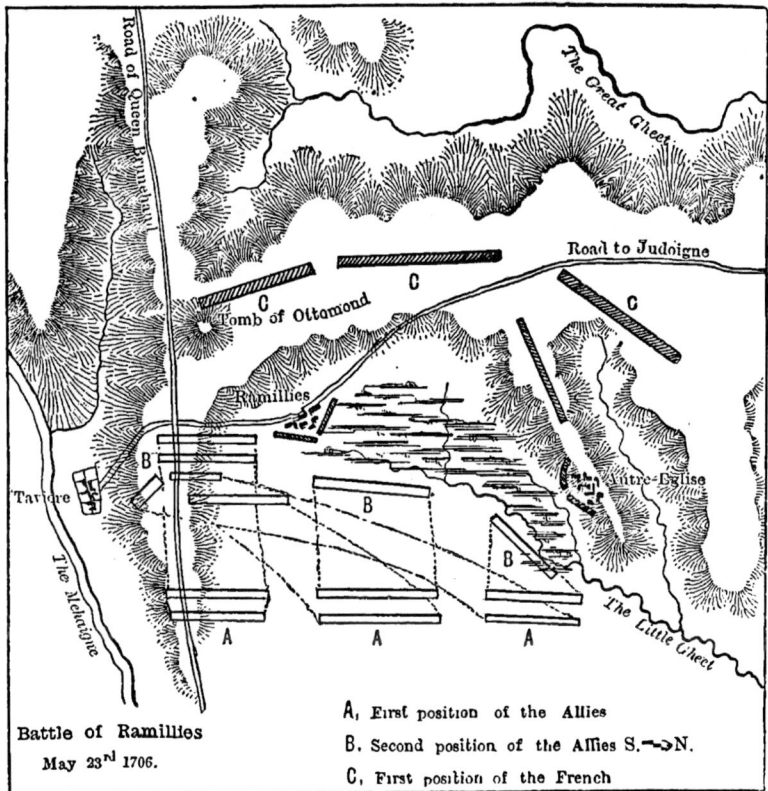

Battle of Ramillies
May 23rd 1706.

A, First position of the Allies
B. Second position of the Allies S.—>N.
C, First position of the French

it impossible to gratify this wish, he determined that he would at least
do something vigorous in Flanders which might serve as a diversion to
his friend Eugene in Italy.   Bringing his army therefore across the
lines which he had broken the year before in the neighbourhood of
the sources of the little river Gheet, he came in sight of Villeroi, with
whose army the Elector of Bavaria, having lost all troops of his own,
was now serving.   The place where the armies met was Ramillies.

Thither Villeroi had drawn his troops, with the intention of covering Namur, which Marlborough's advançe seemed to
threaten. The French general had received instructions
to risk a battle to save that town, and therefore afforded
Marlborough the opportunity he so much desired. The French army
was very strongly posted upon a range of heights forming a semicircle round the sources of the little Gheet river. Their right almost
touched the Mehaigne river, and was covered by the villages of
Tavière and Ramillies. Across it ran an old road known as the road
of Queen Brunehaud, closely adjoining which, in the highest part of
the position, was a barrow known as the Tomb of Ottomond : from
this point the position swept round till it terminated at the village
of Autre-Eglise, being covered from that point by the Gheet and the
marshes in which it rises. The steepness of the heights at Autre-
Eglise, and the river and marsh in its front, rendered the position
almost impregnable, but at the same time made it difficult for the
troops stationed there to act upon the offensive. Marlborough at
once saw that he had the advantage of occupying the inside of a
circle, so that to any given point the movement of his troops was
shorter than that of his enemy's could be. He saw also that the
Tomb of Ottomond was the key of the position. If this was once in
his possession, the whole line of the enemy could be enfiladed. He
ordered therefore a vigorous but false assault on Autre-Eglise. His
feint succeeded ; both the French generals rode to that part of the
field, believing it to be the point of danger. Then Marlborough
ordered the real attack to be made in the neighbourhood of Tavière,
Ramillies, and the road of Brunehaud. He was enabled to draw
troops from his right to strengthen his left in their attack, and after
some warm fighting, especially about the village of Ramillies, the
position was forced, the English troops formed at right angles to
their original position, and pressed onward along the high ground
occupied by the enemy. Villeroi and the Elector found it impossible
to save the day. Fresh difficulty was caused by the breaking down
of the French baggage as it was withdrawing northwards towards
Judoigne. Thus interrupted, the retreat became a rout ; the enemy
were pursued far beyond Judoigne to within two leagues of
Louvain. They did not even rest there ; a hurried consultation
was held by torchlight in the market-place, and the flight immediately continued towards Brussels. The river Dyle, which Marlborough had failed to pass the preceding year, was thus left open.

The consequences of this victory were unexpectedly great. Brussels

(margin note:) Battle of Ramillies. May 23, 1706.

opened its gates to the advancing conquerors; King Charles was proclaimed King in the capital of the Spanish Netherlands; even the
line of the Scheldt was deserted, and Ghent, Bruges, and Oudenarde,
fell into the hands of the allies; the great naval strongholds, Antwerp and Ostend, which had before now sustained memorable sieges,
surrendered, the one on account of some quarrel within its walls,
the other because of its inability to withstand the advancing allies.
The list of conquests is concluded by the strongholds of Menin and
Ath. In fact the effect of the battle was to drive the French entirely
out of the Netherlands; Mons and Namur being the only towns of
importance still remaining in their hands.

The battle even influenced affairs in Italy. The complete disorganization of the French army in Flanders made a change of commanders
imperatively necessary. Vendome, regarded in some ways as the ablest
French general, was summoned from Italy, where he had been acting
successfully against Eugene. He had driven the Imperial army to
retreat behind the Adige; the Milanese had thus been   Saves Eugene
cleared, and Piedmont conquered with the exception of   in Italy.
Turin. Into that last fortress the unfortunate Duke had withdrawn.
For the purpose of taking it, a well-appointed army, under the Duke de
la Feuillade, son-in-law of Chamillart the war minister, but without
other claims to the command, crossed the Alps and invested the town.
It was of the last importance that it should be relieved, and Eugene
determined upon a march, bold even to rashness, for the purpose.
Crossing the Po not far from its mouth, he followed the river upwards upon its south bank. The obstacles he encountered were many;
but Vendome at this critical moment was recalled to Flanders, and
Marsin and the Duke of Orleans, who took the command, allowed
Eugene to cross river after river without opposition, contenting
themselves with following his movements upon the opposite bank of
the river. At length Eugene approached Turin, formed a junction
with the Duke of Savoy, whom the laxity of the siege had allowed
to leave the city with 10,000 men, and passing beyond Turin, turned
his back upon France, and marched against the investing army. The
siege had been carried on without skill, the lines were of immense
length, and severed into various sections by the numerous rivers
which join the Po in the neighbourhood of Turin. Orleans was
eager to lead the troops out of the trenches and risk a pitched battle,
which, as the French had a considerable advantage in numbers,
might easily have resulted in Eugene's defeat. He was overruled
by Marsin, who unexpectedly produced a commission as commander-

in-chief, and the army awaited the assault in their trenches. Even in this position they were badly commanded. Three generals, issuing sometimes contradictory orders, prevented the proper concentration of troops, and when Eugene marched against that section of the works which lay between the Doria and the Stura, not more than a third of the French army is said to have been ready to oppose him. The route of the French was complete, 200 guns, and much stores and money, fell a prey to the victors (Sept. 7). The effect of the victory was greater than the victory itself. It was found impossible to lead the broken troops into the Milanese; they fell back in confusion behind the Alps, thus leaving the force on the Adige to be surrounded by enemies. Piedmont returned to its allegiance, and in fact the whole of Italy was irretrievably lost to France, and compelled to join the Grand Alliance.

The disasters of France had been continuous. Blenheim had secured Germany, and in this year of 1706, Ramillies had been followed by the conquest of the whole of the Netherlands, Turin by the conquest of the whole of Italy, the relief of Barcelona by the occupation of Madrid by the allied forces, although they had subsequently been compelled to fall back towards Valencia. So great were the French disasters that Louis began to think of treating, and suggested as terms on which peace might be made a new Partition Treaty, by which he would consent to acknowledge Queen Anne in England, to give the Dutch the barrier they demanded, to grant great commercial advantages to the maritime powers, and to surrender Spain and the Indies to the Archduke Charles, if only he could preserve for his grandson Philip a kingdom in Italy consisting of Milan, Naples, and Sicily. These terms were very attractive to the Dutch, who thought they had already secured all they required, but were by no means satisfactory to the Emperor, who saw that the barrier given to the Dutch must of necessity be taken from the Spanish dominions in the Netherlands, and therefore from his brother :[1] nor to Marlborough, who, though he confessed he did not believe that the King of France would ever make peace without securing some kingdom for his grandson, was desirous for his own sake to continue the war, and thought the French demand for the Milanese after the great victories which had been won unreasonable. With some difficulty he persuaded Heinsius to reject the terms, and the war proceeded on its course. It might have been better to have

The disasters of the French in 1706

make Louis desire peace

Marlborough rejects his terms.

[1] Afterwards Emperor Charles VI., now called Charles III. of Spain in opposition to Philip V.

accepted Louis' terms. Never again were the affairs of the allies in so prosperous a condition, although the continuation of the war undoubtedly told in their favour by the gradual exhaustion it produced in France.

It seemed indeed in the course of the next year as if the tide of victory had wholly turned. Peterborough had re- The tide of turned to .Spain, and viewing the altered state of victory turns affairs, was now as eager to act on the defensive as he had been before to urge an advance upon Madrid. His advice was again disregarded. The introduction of Sunderland into the ministry at home was unfavourable to him, and he was recalled, leaving the command of Spain in the somewhat incompetent hands of Das Minas and Galway. These generals, determining to act on the offensive, marched out of Valencia towards Madrid, but were met near Almanza by the lately reinforced army of Berwick, and suffered a complete Almanza defeat. The consequence was the loss of Valencia and April 25, 1707. Saragossa, so that Charles was only able to maintain himself in the province of Catalonia. The battle of Almanza was fought on the 25th of April. On the 22nd of the following month, Marshal Stolhofen. Villars completely surprised the Margrave of Bayreuth, May 22. who had succeeded the late Margrave Louis of Baden in command of the Imperial troops on the Rhine. The lines of Stolhofen, which had been so long held against the French, were taken and destroyed. Nor was the advance of the allied army of Italy into the south of France more successful. Eugene and the Duke of Savoy reached Toulon and besieged it. But sickness had much decreased the number of the allies; a considerable detachment had been sent to complete the conquest of Naples, and the appearance of Marshal Toulon. Tessé with a large army, and the threat of an assault upon Aug. 20 their rear, induced them to raise the siege and retire beyond the Alps. Nor was there anything done in. Flanders to redeem the ill-success which had met the allied arms elsewhere. Marlborough in vain attempted to bring the French to a pitched battle. The Dutch had lost confidence after receiving the news of Almanza and Stolhofen, and renewed their old dilatory policy; the rains also somewhat impeded the campaign, which was closed without any important event.

One valuable diplomatic service, however, Marlborough had performed. Charles XII. of Sweden was in the midst Marlborough of his victorious career. Having defeated the Russians diverts Charles at Narva, he had succeeded in driving Augustus. Elector XII of Saxony, from the throne of Poland, and entering Saxony itself, was now in the neighbourhood of Leipsic. Sweden was the old ally of France, and Louis did not let Charles forget it. For a moment there seemed a chance that Charles would follow in the footsteps of Gustavus Adolphus, throw himself and his victorious army into Germany, and ruin the cause of the allies. To deter him from this step Marlborough visited him at his camp, and successfully directed his ambition towards his old enemies the Russians, against whom he shortly marched to meet his ruin at the battle of Pultowa.

The beginning of the ensuing year was marked by a new incident in the war. The hopes of Louis were raised by the reports of the general discontent prevalent in Scotland; a large portion of that nation had seen with dislike the late completion of the Union, and assurances were brought to France of the readiness of the Jacobite party to rise in arms. An invasion was determined on and actually set on foot. The fleet was all ready to sail, when Prince James Edward, afterwards called the Old Pretender, but now known by the name of the Chevalier de St. George, who was to accompany it, was taken ill of the measles. The expedition was postponed for some weeks, and these weeks were enough to destroy its chance of success. Byng with a powerful fleet appeared in the Channel, troops were brought over from the Continent and others collected in England, and though the little squadron succeeded in eluding the fleet and reached the Firth of Forth, there was no sign of a general rising of the Jacobites, and it had to return from its fruitless expedition, glad to escape with safety.

Threatened invasion of Scotland. 1708.

This threatened invasion had of course retained Marlborough in England. It was not till somewhat late that he could join the army. With a slight change of generals the war continued its old course. Villars was employed to reduce Piedmont, Berwick and the Elector of Bavaria were on the Rhine, Spain had been intrusted to the Duke of Orleans, while in Flanders, which was this year selected as the great battlefield, Vendome was to oppose Marlborough, having with him as nominal commander-in-chief the Duke of Burgundy, the heir to the French throne. Marlborough had again formed a great scheme for the campaign. His intention was that the Elector of Hanover, who after the defeat of Stolhofen had taken command of the Imperial troops, should remain on the Rhine, and that Eugene, with whom he again longed to act in co-operation, should form a new army and assist him on the Moselle. The two generals met in April at

Campaign of 1708.

Marlborough's plan.

the Hague, and there agreed that they would make an ostensible plan for the invasion of Lorraine, but that they should in fact join their two armies, and act rapidly and decisively to complete, the conquest of the Netherlands. Eugene met with infinite difficulties in forming his new army, and Marlborough was still single-handed when Vendome began an offensive movement.

The French army had been concentrated at Mons, on the south-west of the Netherlands. It thence advanced northward towards Brussels. Fearing for the capital, Marlborough took up a position to cover it, but suddenly the French marched off eastward, and threatened Louvain. This was, however, but a feint. The real intention of the French was to act upon the western frontier, upon the river Scheldt. The Dutch had made themselves highly un-popular in the Netherlands since they had had possession of that province; the disaffected inhabitants of the great towns on the Scheldt had opened correspondence with Vendome, and were pre-pared to surrender their cities to him. Having therefore drawn Marlborough towards Louvain, he suddenly marched westward to Alost, across the front of the English army, sending forward on his march detachments, to which Ghent and Bruges surrendered without a struggle. As the town of Oudenarde, somewhat higher up the river, would complete the security of these new acqui-sitions, it was determined to besiege it. Marlborough had followed close upon the heels of the French, circling round Brussels so as to defend the capital. He had not ceased to urge Eugene to join him with his troops, which, according to agreement, should have been with him many weeks before. The delay was no fault of the Prince's; he was already hurrying to join Marlborough, when, hearing that it was his intention to fight a battle in defence of Oudenarde, and unable to bring up his troops, he hastened forward alone and joined the English army. Between Marlborough's army and Oudenarde ran the river Dender, which the French determined to hold to cover the siege. Alost, which lies a little to the north of Oudenarde, they already possessed; at about an equal distance to the south, also on the river Dender, was the entrenched camp of Lessines. Could they occupy this they would be in a good position to cover the siege. Marlborough foresaw their intention, and determined to forestall them. Although the river between Lessines and Alost makes a considerable curve, and Marlborough, on the convex side of it, had almost twice the distance to traverse that the French had, he pushed on with such rapidity that he secured Lessines and the pas-

sage of the river before the French columns appeared in sight. It
was now evident to the French generals that Marlborough intended
to fight. They drew in their detachments, and marched rapidly to
cross the Scheldt at Gavre, to the north of Oudenarde. Marlborough
marched direct upon that city, so that the converging lines of march
would speedily meet. It was known that there was much disputing
and ill-feeling between Vendome and the Duke of Burgundy, and
that the latter Prince intended, if possible, to avoid an engagement.
With all speed Marlborough sent forward General Cadogan to secure
the passage of the river, and prepare bridges for his army. After he
had performed this duty, Cadogan rode forward to reconnoitre, and
saw the French troops crossing at Gavre, and, in ignorance of the immediate vicinity of the English, quietly sending out foragers. With
such troops as he had he drove in the outlying posts of the enemy,
who now, apprised of the approach of Marlborough, found a battle
inevitable.

A little to the north of Oudenarde the river Norken joins the
Scheldt, after a course almost parallel to that river.

**Battle of
Oudenarde.
July 11, 1708.**

Between the Norken and the Scheldt an irregular semicircle of hills sweeps with the convex side of one of its
arms at Oudenarde, while the other, surmounted by the village Oycke,
overhangs the Norken; it contains in its hollow two little brooks
which fall into the Scheldt just north of Oudenarde. On the other
side of these brooks, closing the opening of the semicircle, is an
irregular mass of rising ground sloping away northward towards the
junction of the Scheldt and Norken. Vendome gave orders to occupy
this irregular mass and the valleys of the brooks, the arm of the
semicircle between Oudenarde and the course of the brooks being
occupied by Cadogan. But the Duke of Burgundy counter-ordered
his commands, and arranged his troops upon what was doubtless a
stronger position, the range of hills beyond the Norken. But though
stronger for defence, it was much less favourable for an offensive
battle. These contradictory commands cost the French their first
loss. Seven battalions of their troops having pushed forward towards
Oudenarde as far as Eyne, were fallen upon and destroyed by
Cadogan, who thus crossed the brook and ascended the irregular
high land beyond it. Had Vendome's order been carried out the
position of Cadogan would have been very precarious. He was
almost unsupported, although Marlborough was coming to his
assistance with some cavalry, which he led forward for several miles
at a gallop. As it was, however, the English army came up by

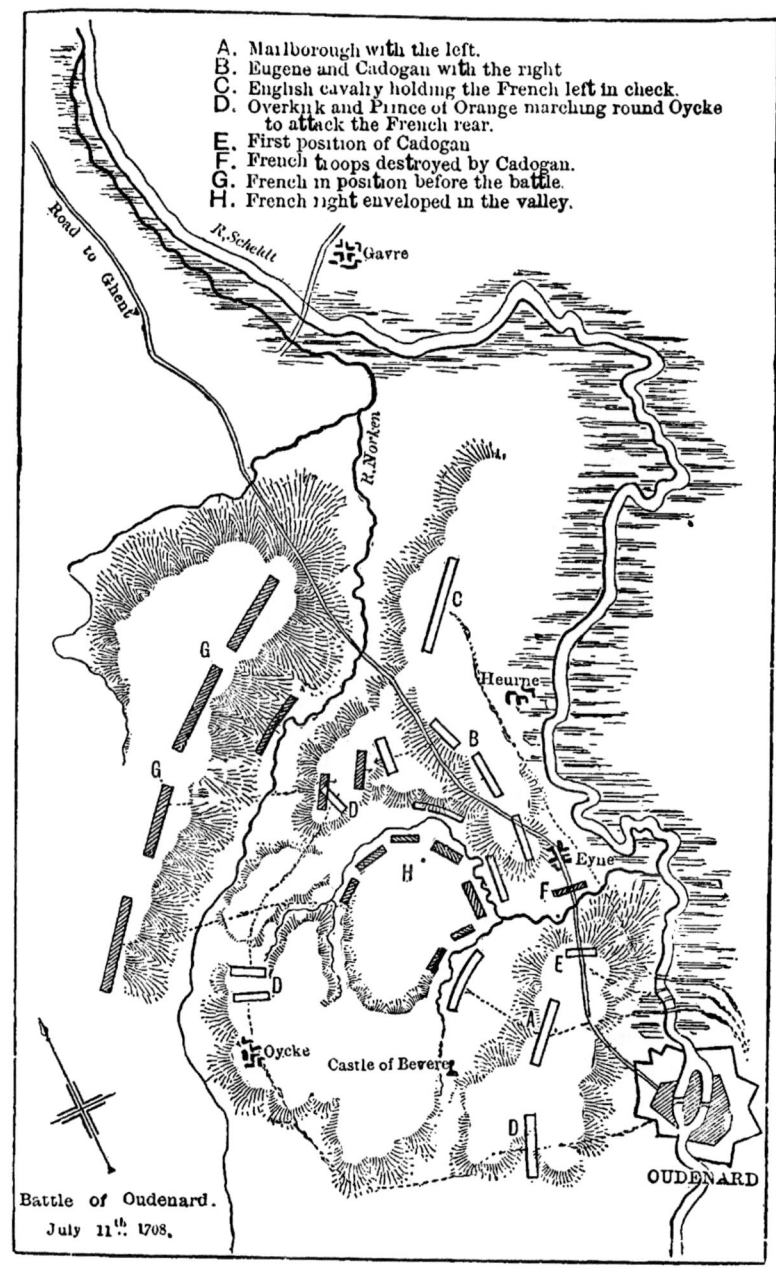

A. Marlborough with the left.
B. Eugene and Cadogan with the right
C. English cavalry holding the French left in check.
D. Overkirk and Prince of Orange marching round Oycke to attack the French rear.
E. First position of Cadogan
F. French troops destroyed by Cadogan.
G. French in position before the battle.
H. French right enveloped in the valley.

Battle of Oudenard.
July 11th. 1708.

degrees, and took position with their left on the semicircle of hills,
and their right supporting Cadogan beyond the brook.   Thwarted
in his first schemes, Vendome now wished to remain beyond the
Norken, knowing that the enemy were wearied with a long march
(it was already four in the afternoon), and that he would have an
opportunity of withdrawing quietly in the night towards France.
The Duke of Burgundy again thwarted him.   He commanded the
right wing, and insisted upon sending his troops forward across the
Norken into the valleys where the brooks ran.   The country was
there broken up with enclosures, and a fierce hand-to-hand battle
was fought with the English right, which Marlborough had intrusted
to Eugene.   The exhibition of all the English cavalry upon the
high lands beyond the brooks held the French left entirely in check;
and while Eugene and the English were disputing the hedges and
enclosures in the valley, Marlborough, passing to the left, observed
that the extremity of the semicircle, which overhung the Norken and
was occupied by the village of Oycke, was unguarded by the French.
He caused Overkirk with the Dutch reserve to march round the hills
to occupy this point, and thus completely envelop the French right.
The effect was the total annihilation of that part of the French army,
and it was owing to an accident alone that any part of it escaped.   The
two extremes of the enveloping English line came so close together,
that in the darkness they fired upon each other.   The mistake was
happily soon discovered, but fearing a repetition of the accident,
the general gave orders rather to let the French escape than to run the
risk of renewing such a disaster.   Some 9000 men thus broke through
at a gap in the semicircle of hills near the Castle of Bevere, and
made their escape to France.   The rest of the beaten army retired
toward Ghent.

Both armies were speedily reinforced.   Eugene's troops arrived
from the Moselle, and joined the English ; Berwick, with part of the
army of the Rhine, which had been observing them, reinforced the
French, but the relative numbers of the troops were not much changed.
Marlborough and Eugene had now to settle upon a further plan of
action.   Before them lay the great city of Lille, one of the earliest
conquests of Louis XIV., newly fortified with all the skill of Vauban.
Siege of Lille. That the allies should cross the frontier and enter
Dec. 9, 1708 France was speedily determined.   But while Marlborough suggested the bold plan of leaving troops to mask Lille, while
the main army marched direct to Paris, Eugene, though by no means
a timid general, urged the more regular course of besieging and

capturing the great fortress which lay in their way before proceeding · further. The arguments in favour of this plan were too plausible to be disregarded. It was decided that while Eugene in person undertook the siege, Marlborough should command the covering army. Even to bring the siege material to the spot was a matter of no small difficulty ; the artillery alone required 16,000 horses, and the progress of the siege was watched by a French army of 100,000. When these preliminary difficulties were triumphantly overcome, there still remained the great fortress itself, occupied by 15,000 men, under the able command of Boufflers. At one time the Dutch deputies were so alarmed at the slowness of the progress made that they urged the renunciation of the project. One of the greatest difficulties experienced by the allied commanders was the provisioning of the army ; the land communication with Brussels was entirely cut off, all provisions had to be brought from Ostend, whither they had been conveyed by sea. The French determined to interrupt this line of communication also, and to destroy one of the convoys which had been intrusted to General Webb, with a most insufficient detachment of troops. It has been suggested that Marlborough was here playing one of his old tricks, that, in his jealousy of Webb, he wished for his destruction, and had intentionally exposed him to this danger. If such was the case he was thoroughly disappointed. When the French troops fell upon the convoy at Wynendale, Webb made a most gallant defence and beat them off. The very slight notice taken by Marlborough in his despatches of this gallant action gives some colour to the rumour. The victory of Wynendale was at all events the turning-point of the siege ; from this time rapid progress was made. On the 22nd of October Boufflers found it necessary to capitulate for the town, while retaining the citadel, and on the 9th of December he marched out of his last stronghold with all the honours of war. The re-conquest of Ghent and Bruges followed upon the fall of Lille.

In other directions the war had been languid. In Spain only had anything been done. There Stanhope had taken the Capture of command in conjunction with Staremberg, the Imperial Port Mahon. general, and had succeeded without much difficulty in capturing Port Mahon in Minorca, a place then regarded as more valuable than Gibraltar, and of the highest importance as affording a safe winter harbour for the English fleet in the Mediterranean.

For some years the exhaustion of France had been great. The finance ministers had been reduced to the most ruinous expedients to maintain the war, and the whole people were suffering terribly.

Exhaustion of France. 1709. To crown their misery, the winter of 1708 was of extraordinary severity and duration. The corn crops were frozen in the ground, the very apple trees perished with cold. Famine threatened to destroy what the war had spared. Louis became very anxious to treat ; and as for some years it had been supposed that the Dutch were inclined to accept a separate pacification, it was to them that Louis addressed himself. The war party was however for the present in the ascendant, and Heinsius, who, as Grand

Louis offers to treat. Pensionary of Holland, exercised a predominant influence in the Council of the Dutch, let it be clearly understood that the Republic would treat only in conjunction with the allies, and that the allied demands would be very high. Louis however despatched an ambassador to see what terms could be made, but he met with a cold reception. The Government in England, especially the Whig members of it, were indignant at the threatened invasion of Scotland in the previous year, and induced the Parliament to vote that the Queen's title and the Protestant succession, the dismissal of the Pretender from

High demands of the allies. France, and the demolition of the fortifications of Dunkirk, should be necessary elements in any treaty : while the Dutch claimed a line of ten fortresses on the Flemish frontier (including some still in the possession of France), and the restoration of Strasburg and Luxemburg. Nor, in exchange for these high demands, was any specific promise of peace given. Such was the position of the French Government, that even these terms were taken into consideration, and Torcy the French minister offered, though he could get no proper passport, to go himself privately and see what could be done to ameliorate them. He found the allies determined to demand at least the resignation of the whole Spanish succession, together with the restoration of Newfoundland to England. This demand put Louis in a difficult position. It was no longer, he declared, in his power to surrender Spain, for his grandson King Philip had a will of his own, and, although he might have been induced to resign Spain for an Italian kingdom, did not choose to become altogether crownless. Louis now reaped the fruits of his former bad faith as a negotiator. The allies, believing that this excuse was fictitious, and alleged merely to gain time, drew up their demands in accordance with the preliminaries, and would promise in exchange for the great concessions demanded from Louis only two months' truce. If in that time Philip could not be induced to resign Spain, the French King was to pledge him-

self to join with the allies to expel him by force of arms. When
Torcy returned with these terrible terms, a Council **Rejected**
was held at Versailles, and amidst tears of indignation at **by Louis.**
the ignominious propositions, it was determined that, in spite of the
necessity of the moment, it was impossible to accept them. Louis
declared, if he had to fight, he would rather fight against his enemies
than against his own children. And now at length, humbled by
reverses, he threw himself on the patriotism of his people; a stirring
proclamation was circulated through the provinces; the King set
the example of patriotism by turning his plate and costly works of
art into money; the whole nation was touched by his humility,
and the war began again with renewed vigour. The allies had
indeed pressed their demands beyond what was either generous or
politic.

Villars, the only great French marshal as yet undefeated, was
intrusted with the duty of checking the victorious advance of Eugene
and Marlborough. His name, and the newly roused **Battle of**
patriotism of the country, raised the spirits of the army, **Malplaquet.**
though they were in want of many of the necessaries of life. Villars,
determined to act upon the defensive, saw Tournay fall without
moving. Thence the conquerors advanced to Mons, the capital of
Hainault. It seemed necessary, if possible, to prevent the siege of
this town. The rapidity of the movements of the allies prevented
Villars from attaining that object, but the investment was scarcely
formed when he crossed the Scheldt at Valenciennes, and appeared
with his army in the immediate neighbourhood. The corner of the
country between the Haine river on the north, and the Trouille on
the east, in which Mons stands, is crossed by a barrier of high ground,
rendered more difficult by large woods and forests. To approach
Mons from the south and west this ridge has to be crossed, and the
only convenient passage is by the *Trouée*, or open gap, between the
woods of Lanière towards the east, and Taisnière towards the west.
Between these woods the high land falls by several ravines into the
plain of Mons. On the crown of the ridge is the heath and village of
Malplaquet. Marlborough and Eugene, supposing that the object of
Villars would be to pass through this gap and attempt to raise the
siege of Mons, brought their army to the foot of the ascending ravines.
But Villars, under whom Boufflers, though his senior in rank, was
serving as a volunteer, feeling certain that at all events a battle
would be fought, determined to adopt a defensive position, and
during the night and day after his arrival at Malplaquet strongly

fortified the flanking woods and the crown of the hill. Marlborough
was anxious to attack before the fortifications were complete, but

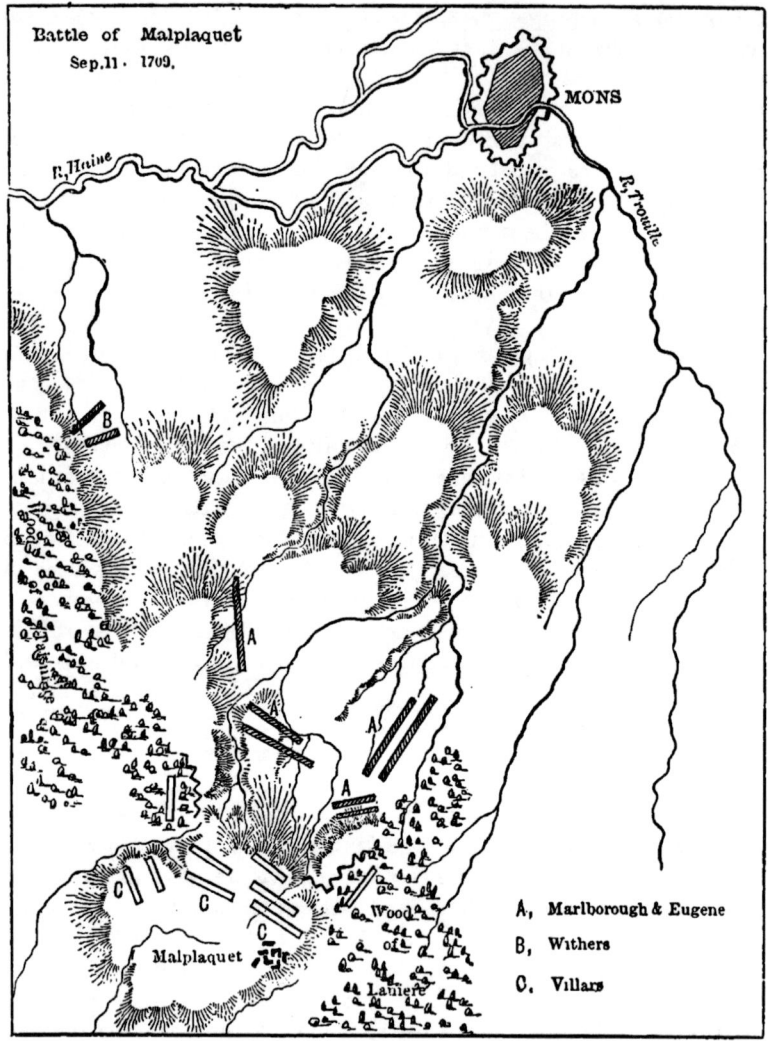

Battle of Malplaquet
Sep.11 · 1709.

MONS

R. Haine

R. Trouille

A, Marlborough & Eugene

B, Withers

C, Villars

Wood

of

Malplaquet

Laniere

Eugene thought it necessary to await the arrival of troops coming
from the siege of Tournay. A day was thus lost, and time allowed
to render the fortifications much stronger. The battle, which began

upon the 11th of September, was the most bloody and hardly contested of the war. In their first assaults the allies were repeatedly driven back, but the pressure upon the wood of Taisnière was so strong, especially when it was outflanked and threatened from the extreme right of the allies under Withers, that Villars had to weaken his centre to hold his ground. Marlborough perceived the weakness and took advantage of it. The entrenchments in the centre of the line were broken through and captured, and thus the position forced. Villars had been severely wounded, and the command had devolved upon Boufflers, who brought off the French army in perfect order, and the fruit of the hard-earned victory was nothing but the field of battle. The English encamped the following night upon the French position, having lost in their disastrous victory 20,000 men. Mons fell, but the campaign had then to be closed.

Thus far it has been possible to follow without interruption the general course of the war, but from this time forward the state of politics in England exercised so decided an influence upon it, upon the negotiations which were to *Summary of political parties from 1702.* bring it to a close, and upon the position and conduct of Marlborough, that it becomes necessary to turn back and trace the history of parties since the Queen's accession. Speaking quite generally, that history consists in the gradual substitution of a Whig for a Tory Government. Rochester and the extreme high Tories were disinclined to a great offensive war, and consequently directly opposed to Marlborough. The Duke, not wishing to break with any great section of English politicians, attempted, as William had done, to govern by means of the moderate men of both parties. But there was a second question which, even after the dismissal of the Tories who disliked the war, prevented the completion of his plan. The Tories were desirous that stringent measures should be taken to support the exclusive authority of the English Church, and in this point were strongly supported by the feelings of the Queen. The Whigs, on whom Marlborough was induced for the purposes of the war more and more to rely, were on the other hand inclined towards more liberal measures. It was upon this point that the second secession of the Tories took place, leaving Marlborough entirely in the hands of the Whigs, and in a certain degree in opposition to the Queen. It was the Whig determination when triumphant to suppress the expression of High Church feeling that produced the complete overthrow of Marlborough's ministry. At the same time, as in the former reign, disputes between the Houses continued.

especially when a Tory majority in the Lower House came into
collision with the constant Whig majority in the House of Lords.

Already, before the Parliament called by the late King had been
dissolved, Rochester and the extreme high Tories had shown their
disinclination to the war, and had besides given proof of a more
exclusive party spirit than suited the views of Marlborough, to whom,
as to William, the affairs of Europe and the conduct of the war were
all in all, and who had no taste for party conflict. As was to be
expected from the character of the ministry, a strong Tory majority
was returned in October to the first Parliament of the Queen's reign.
But Rochester's views were not shared by the whole of his party;

Tory Parlia-
ment.
Oct. 1702.

indeed, the strength of party feeling tended for the time
to give Marlborough the support of the Tories. In
their eagerness to throw blame upon the late King,
they could not refrain from contrasting him with the Duke.
Marlborough had by this time begun his successful career by capturing the towns of the Meuse, and the Commons proceeded to
congratulate the Queen, saying, "The wonderful progress of your
Majesty's armies under the conduct of Marlborough have singularly
retrieved the ancient honour of the English nation." The word
retrieved, intended to imply censure on the late King, was, in spite
of the opposition of the Whigs, carried by a large majority. For the
present then, if merely out of opposition to William, the Tories as

Dismissal of
Rochester.
1703.

a whole seemed pledged to support Marlborough, liberal
grants were made, and shortly after the close of the
session, the Government, resting upon the general feeling
in its favour, felt itself strong enough to get rid of Rochester.
Displeased at receiving no more important office than that of Lord-
Lieutenant of Ireland, he left his government there, and remained
in England. He thus afforded an opportunity to his enemies to order
him to return to his duties. On his refusing to do so, the command
was repeated in a more peremptory manner, and in his anger he sent
in his resignation, which was accepted.

Before this, however, the question of Church government had been
raised in the House, and the storm it excited had caused a somewhat
hasty prorogation. It had been the habit of dissenting members of
corporations so far to do violence to their conscience as to receive the

Occasional
Conformity Bill
thrown out.

Sacrament according to the law of the Church of England
upon their appointment to municipal offices. Having
thus duly qualified themselves, they had continued to
hold office, but had gone back to their old forms of worship. This

habit, known as occasional conformity, was viewed with great jealousy by the Tories. In the first session of the Parliament a bill was brought in to render occasional conformity illegal, and to inflict heavy fines upon those who held office on such terms. The chief supporter of the measure was Henry St. John, afterwards so well known as Lord Bolingbroke. The Bill passed the House of Commons, but its amendment by the House of Lords produced such violent altercations, that the Queen found it necessary to put an end to the session. It was during this session that the Commissioners for the Union with Scotland first held their sittings. The progress of the negotiations which produced the Union in 1706 will be given subsequently.

The Parliament reassembled in November 1703, a month rendered remarkable by the greatest storm ever known in England; it is calculated that no less than 8000 lives were lost in it, while 800 houses and 400 windmills were reduced to ruins. The devastation caused among the forests in the country may be estimated by the fact that Defoe, travelling through Kent, counted 17,000 uprooted timber trees, and then desisted from reckoning them from weariness.

The session was again the scene of a great contest between the Houses. The war was still well supported, and the grants were upon a very liberal scale, rendered necessary ·by the additional troops required for Portugal and Spain, since Portugal had joined the Great Alliance, first under a treaty with Austria, and subsequently under the well-known Methuen Treaty with England. This treaty, regarded as a triumph of diplomacy, was com- _{The Methuen Treaty.} pleted by Mr. Methuen, the English minister at Lisbon, at the close of 1703. It was in exact accordance with the commercial views of the time, and contained but two articles. By the first English woollen manufactures were admitted into Portugal, by the second it was arranged that the duty on Portuguese wines should always be less by one-third than that on the wines of France. It was supposed that this would not only secure the friendship of Portugal, but would also bring much gold and silver, of which the Peninsula was the great emporium, into England, an object regarded as of the first importance under the mercantile system. It was when the Bill against occasional conformity, which had been dropped _{Occasional Conformity Bill again thrown out.} in the preceding session, was reintroduced that the contest began. The ministers who had been eager the preceding year that the Bill should be carried, had, since the resignation of Rochester and the opposition offered by his friends,

grown less eager in their Tory views. In spite of their very lukewarm
support, the Bill again passed the House of Commons by a large
majority. But again it met with great opposition from the Lords,
and was finally thrown out by a majority of eleven. As no amendments had been proposed, there was no room for angry conferences
between the Houses. But an opportunity for quarrel
was found in questions arising from the Aylesbury election. The returning officers for that borough had been
notoriously guilty of tampering with the returns in favour of their
own friends. At the last election the vote of Matthew Ashby had
been rejected. He brought an action against the returning officer,
and a verdict was found in his favour. The case was removed into
the higher court, and three of the four judges of the Queen's Bench
decided that all decisions with regard to votes rested entirely with
the House of Commons. Upon this Ashby brought his case by a
writ of error before the House of Lords, where the decision of the
Queen's Bench was set aside, and the case finally settled in favour
of Ashby. On this the Commons engaged in the quarrel, and
declared that Ashby, by appealing to the law, was guilty of a breach
of privilege. The Lords replied, declaring that the right of voting,
like any other right, might be maintained by an action at the
common law. There for the present the quarrel was left. It seems
tolerably clear that on this point the Lords were in the right, but the
newly won position of the House of Commons inspired its members
with most overweening views of their own importance. In February
of this year (1704) the Queen celebrated her birthday by surrendering
her claim to the first-fruits of ecclesiastical benefices, which were
hereafter to be employed for the benefit of the Church, and which
have since been administered under the well-known name of Queen
Anne's Bounty.

It was with the knowledge and co-operation of Marlborough—
though he had himself taken the opportunity afforded
by the prorogation to go abroad to fight the great battle
of Blenheim—that his friends in the ministry succeeded
in relieving themselves of the rest of the extreme
Tories. For the removal of Rochester in the previous year had by no
means cleared the Government of the party opposed to the active
prosecution of the war. His views were accepted and supported
by Nottingham and Jersey in the Upper House, by Hedges and
Seymour in the House of Commons. Nottingham, true to his
principles, had thrown every obstacle in his power in the way

Marginal notes:

Disputes on the Aylesbury election.

Dismissal of Nottingham, Jersey and Seymour. May 1704.

of a plan which had come before the Council for utilizing for the general purposes of the war the insurrection of the Cevennes. Thwarted in his opposition, after the close of the session, he haughtily demanded of the Queen the immediate dismissal of all the Whigs in the Government, threatening in case of refusal to retire. The Queen, who loved the Tories, would probably have wished to retain him, but she was irritated at the tone of his demand. Her irritation was fostered by Godolphin and the Duchess of Marlborough, and she brought herself to dismiss both Nottingham and his followers, Jersey and Seymour. The ministry had to be reconstructed. But Marlborough and Godolphin were by no means disposed to put themselves into the hands of the Whigs ; they therefore called to office another section of the Tories not adverse to the war. Harley, the Speaker of the House of Commons, was made Secretary of State, Mansell replaced Seymour, the Earl of Kent, a moderate Whig, succeeded Jersey, while the Secretary of War, an unimportant person, made room for St. John.

Replaced by moderate Tories.

These changes did not improve the position of the ministers, as the Tory Party had still a strong majority in the House of Commons. Marlborough's own popularity with the House was shaken, and in the autumn session of 1704, the prevailing feeling showed itself in the form given to the vote of thanks with which the Commons met the victory at Blenheim ; this was so expressed as to place on a level with the great general who had saved the Empire the Tory Admiral Rooke, who had fought an indecisive battle in the Mediterranean, for which many men thought he deserved rather blame than praise, for though almost as strong as the enemy, he had withdrawn from the battle without effecting anything. The Tory temper of the House was again shown by the increased passion with which the Occasional Conformity Bill was introduced and supported. A considerable number of the most vehement Tories were eager to adopt their old method, and to tack it to a Bill for the Land Tax. The Government, and that section of the Tories who followed the newly-appointed ministers, were sufficiently strong to defeat this movement, and the Bill met its usual fate in the House of Lords. As in the preceding session, unable to quarrel with the House of Lords for exercising their undoubted right, the Commons found means of attacking them by renewing the question of the Aylesbury election. Resting upon the decision of the House of Lords, other inhabitants of Aylesbury had sued the returning officers. The House of Commons had committed them to Newgate. The Queen's Bench

Parliament. Oct. 29, 1704.

had refused to interfere; the prisoners demanded a writ of error. The Commons addressed the Queen against the writ, and put the prisoners into the custody of their own serjeant-at-arms. The heat of the dispute rendered a prorogation necessary (March 14).

But the conduct of the Tory majority had tended still further to incline the ministry towards the Whigs. Rooke was superseded as .commander-in-chief of the fleet, Sir Cloudesley Shovel, a Whig, put in his place, and as the three years of the Parliament were now run out, the Government influence was exercised at the elections against all those who had voted for tacking the Occasional Conformity Bill. Even stronger signs were visible of the intention of the Government to form a junction with the Whigs; the ministers began an intrigue with the Junto, promising before long to give the Great Seal to William Cowper (a promise which was shortly after fulfilled), and admitted the Duke of Newcastle to the ministry as Privy Seal in the place of the Tory Duke of Buckingham. Nor was it the Government only which was changing its views. The nation at large, thoroughly interested in the war and disgusted at the conduct of the Tories, returned at the new elections a large majority of Whigs. The growing influence of the Whigs was supplemented by a family tie which connected Marlborough with that party; as Godolphin, whose son had married one of his daughters, formed a link with the Tories, so Sunderland, who had married another, connected him with the Whigs. It seemed as though a bargain advantageous to both sides might be struck between the Duke and the Whig party. The accession of Sunderland to the ministry would on the one side strengthen Marlborough's personal position, and render it more possible for him to carry on his plan of government without parties; while, on the other, it would secure to the Whigs a means of at once influencing the character of the administration. It was determined therefore that Sunderland should enter the ministry, and as there was then no vacant office, he was employed at once as extraordinary ambassador to Vienna, and in the course of the following year (1706) was raised to the office of Secretary of State. His appointment, and the gradual inclination of the Government to the Whigs, was followed, at the beginning of the year 1707, by the creation of several Whig Peers, and by a final breach with the High Tories, when the names of Buckingham, Nottingham, and Rochester were struck from the list of the Privy Council. Marlborough seemed now to have gained his object. The adminis-

Gradual introduction of Whig ministers.

Marlborough's composite ministry. 1707.

tration was a thoroughly composite one. On the one side were a number of Whigs led by Lord Sunderland, on the other a section of more moderate Tories headed by Harley and St. John.

But Marlborough underrated the difficulty of managing a coalition. In his necessary absence abroad this difficult operation was in the hands of Godolphin, always a timid minister, without any real political convictions, and ill qualified for a great party struggle. And such a party struggle was now inevitable. All the ministers were indeed at present willing to uphold the war. On other points their views were diametrically opposed, and both sections were anxious for a more complete admission to power of their own friends. It was the personal influence of the Churchills alone which could support so strange a conjunction. That influence depended upon the favour of the Crown, which by its indirect power of influencing Parliament was practically rather strengthened than weakened by the Revolution. If that favour could be withdrawn the ill-assorted ministry must inevitably fall. This truth was clear to Harley, a man of intriguing character and the leader of the Tory section of the Cabinet. He perceived that it might be possible to Harley, seeing rise upon the fall of the Churchills, and saw how their its weakness. power might be undermined. The Queen was a devoted High Churchwoman; Marlborough and his friends, especially since his growing predilection for the Whigs, were avowedly careless, if they were not Low Church; Harley, on the other hand, had a great reputation for religion and orthodoxy. Again and again patronage had been bestowed on what the Queen considered Latitudinarian principles. Displeased and hurt, she was yet too timid to stand alone, Harley supplied her with the support she wanted. His cousin, Mrs. Abigail Hill, who was a cousin and protégée also of the Duchess of Marlborough, ingratiated herself with the Queen; she was appointed bedchamber woman, and married with the Queen's influence, without the knowledge of the Duchess of Marlborough, to Mr. Masham, a member of Prince George's household. Her quiet, even Intrigues temper formed a happy contrast to the termagant vio- against lence of the Duchess, and Harley succeeded in making Marlborough her his instrument. He roused in the Queen a dread of the subversion of the Church, and she found courage to make several Bishops without consulting her ministers.

The Whig Junto was even more angry than the ministers themselves at this conduct. They suspected Harley's design, and determined to drive him from the ministry. Both parties felt that the crisis had

arrived. One or other of them must become predominant. They both
determined to make their power felt, and by a strange manœuvre
the extremes of both sides joined to attack the ministry. The chief
points of attack were the naval administration,—which, as it implicated her husband, was always a tender point with the Queen,—and
the determination of Marlborough to pursue the course William had
marked out, and to carry on the war chiefly in Flanders.

Failure of the composite ministry. It was in this session of Parliament, which began on
October 23, 1707, that the joint assault upon the Govern-
ment was made. The maladministration of the navy was the chief
topic, but the Tories also introduced a motion in the House of Lords,
recommending a change of the seat of war from Flanders to Spain,
where the battle of Almanza had lately proved disastrous to the
allied armies. Marlborough pointed out in vain that this would
produce an immediate peace with the Dutch, who would feel their
country open to invasion from France; and although the Whigs,
pledged as they were to support the policy of William, could not join
in such a motion, Somers drew up a declaration, embodying both the
disapprobation felt for the management of the fleet, and as much of
the Tory feeling in favour of a change in the seat of war as was possible
for his party to accept. The declaration stated that " it is the opinion
of this Committee that no peace can be honourable or safe to her
Majesty or her allies, if Spain and the West Indies be suffered to
continue in the power of the house of Bourbon." But the manœuvre
of the Whigs in joining in the assault against Government had
been successful; it was not necessary to press the hostile resolution.
Godolphin had been thoroughly frightened, and recognized the
necessity of breaking up the unnatural friendship and of allying himself with one or other of the great parties. With the war still continuing he could not but choose the Whigs. At once entering into
negotiations with the chief of that party, he induced Somers, as
President of the Committee charged with the duty of throwing the
late resolutions into the form of an address, to change the resolutions,
by a slight alteration in the words, from an attack upon Government
into a pledge for the continuation of the war till the French had been
entirely broken. The suggested resolutions mentioned the West Indies,
reflecting on the comparative weakness of our naval efforts, and Spain,
implying a change of the scene of war. The introduction of the

Harley and his colleagues resign. Feb. 11, 1708. words " or any other part of the Spanish monarchy,"
entirely destroyed these hostile allusions. The Whigs
had shown their power, it was no longer possible to refuse

them their reward. It became necessary to break with Harley and the moderate Tories. The discovery that a man of the name of Gregg, a clerk in Harley's office, was in treasonable correspondence with France, threw some suspicions on his master's fidelity, and Marlborough and Godolphin agreed on Harley's dismissal. The Queen was more difficult to move. It required a threat of resignation on the part of the ministers to induce her to give up one who, as she believed, thought entirely with her on Church matters, but she was not yet free from the influence of the Churchills, and she yielded. With him retired St. John, Harcourt, and Mansell, whose places were taken by Boyle, a zealous Whig, as Secretary of State, John Smith as Chancellor of the Exchequer, and Robert Walpole as Secretary of War. Marlborough and Godolphin had apparently triumphed by means of the Whigs, but their victory had lost them the Queen's favour and compelled them to submit to the dictation of the Whig party, who at once set to work to secure office for themselves ; nor were they scrupulous in the means they used, the threat that they would turn their assault on the naval administration directly and by name upon her husband, then on his deathbed, induced the Queen to remove Pembroke and give the Presidency of the Council to Somers. Sunderland, though himself a minister, intrigued with the Scotch Jacobites to throw out the ministerial candidates at the election of Peers held in accordance with the Union. To all this the General and Treasurer had to submit. The administration was completed upon a Whig basis, when Orford was forced upon the Queen as head of the Admiralty.

Marlborough was fully alive to the insecurity of his position. It is often attributed, though perhaps without sufficient reason, to the desire to keep up his personal ascendancy, that he refused the terms offered by Louis; and in the following year the disastrous victory of Malplaquet has also been considered a political battle. A truer view of the case seems to be that, afraid of taking any decided steps, he chose to occupy merely the position of an agent of Government, and obey even against his own convictions the dictation of the Whig party. At the same time, he made two desperate efforts to obtain a position independent of home politics—he applied to the Archduke Charles for the office of Governor of the Low Countries, which would have produced about £60,000 a year, and he also demanded from Queen Anne the position of Captain General for life. In both cases his efforts failed. As far as England was concerned, he probably owed his disappointment chiefly to the conduct of his wife. Finding herself supplanted by Mrs. Masham, she lost all command of her temper, and perpetually outraged the feelings of the Queen by her violent complaints.

The triumph of the Whigs, which had seemed so complete, was of very short duration. Their fall was caused by a fault which had been too prevalent among them since the Revolution—whenever they had the upper hand, they became dictatorial and overbearing. Already they had made themselves distasteful to the Queen by the eagerness with which they had forced themselves into power, and an unnecessary exhibition of that power rendered them distasteful to the people. A certain Dr. Henry Sacheverell, a strong upholder of the doctrine of non-resistance, had preached two sermons, one at the Assizes of Derby, one before the mayor and aldermen at St. Paul's. The mayor, who sympathized with his views, suggested that he should print the sermons, and though the common council, when consulted, declined to authorize this step, the preacher acted on the mayor's suggestion and published both. They became a sort of political manifesto, which was largely circulated through the country. The Whigs were naturally angry at this semi-official production of doctrines subversive of all the principles of the Revolution. They determined to take notice of the sermons, and, foolishly disregarding the advice of Somers, they proceeded by the extraordinary method of impeachment instead of the common process of law. This naturally raised the foolish utterances of a clergyman to the dignity of a party question ; and when they further insisted upon a ceremonious hearing in Westminster Hall, the trial became the fashionable topic of the day. The excitement throughout England was very great. All other public business came to a standstill, and when the Lords, though they found Sacheverell guilty, took a very moderate view of his guilt, and punished him only with three years' suspension, the verdict was regarded as a virtual acquittal, and celebrated as a party triumph. The exhibition of feeling called forth by this trial proved both to the Queen and to her secret advisers how great a hold the Tory party had upon the country. Encouraged by Harley, who loved an underhand intrigue, and by his creature Mrs. Masham, she proceeded to act upon her new-found knowledge, and it became evident how formidable the power of the Crown still was. Without consulting Godolphin, she made the Duke of Shrewsbury Lord Chamberlain. Godolphin, instead of resigning at this marked act of distrust, put up with the affront. Still further emboldened by this weakness, the Queen dismissed Lord

Fall of the Whigs. 1710.

Dr. Sacheverell.

Dismissal of Sunderland and Godolphin. Aug. 8.

Sunderland, whom she had always disliked, and followed up the blow by the dismissal of Godolphin himself. The office of Lord Treasurer was for the time kept in abeyance, but Harley was made Chancellor of the Exchequer, and was virtually Prime Minister. For a little while Harley attempted negotiations with the Whigs, who still retained office, but finding them impracticable, he determined to rest upon the Tories only, induced the Queen to dissolve Parliament, and formed an entirely Tory ministry, the most im- Harley's Tory portant members of which were Harcourt, who became ministry. Lord Chancellor, Rochester, Lord President, and St. Nov. John, who succeeded Boyle as Secretary of State.

It was with this ministry that Louis attempted to renew the in- terrupted negotiations of 1709. The battle of Malpla- Conference at quet and the fall of Mons had forced him to this Gertruydenberg course, and to consent that a congress should be held at 1710. Gertruydenberg. At first Holland refused to treat except upon the preliminaries of the preceding year, and they still demanded the assistance of Louis in ejecting his grandson the King of Spain. Finally, both English and Dutch seemed to have waived this point, but the opposition of Austria and Savoy rendered any general nego- tiation impossible, and the war was resumed.

In Flanders it produced nothing beyond the capture of Douay, but in Spain it was of more importance. There Stanhope succeeded with some difficulty in inducing his colleague Staremberg and The war the Archduke Charles to advance towards Madrid. in Spain. They defeated the Spaniards, from whom French assistance was with- drawn during the negotiations, at Almenara and Saragossa. They pushed on into Castile, and again occupied Madrid. Thus, inasmuch as the war had been fairly successful, it was in favour of the Whigs, although the successes having been chiefly in Spain (the pursuance of the war in which country was a part of the Tory programme), they were less important politically than they would have been had they taken place in Flanders. But whatever advantage the Whigs might have obtained from the war was neutralized when, before the end of the year, events occurred in Spain which entirely altered the com- plexion of affairs in that country. Stanhope's hopes for a successful issue of his enterprise were based on the active co-operation of the army of Portugal. Philip, with his Spanish army, having retired north- wards, there was nothing to prevent the junction of the two armies. But, in spite of the entreaties of the English general, the Portuguese would not move, and as the hope of any successful issue to the negotiations dwindled, Louis again allowed assistance to be sent to Spain, and a considerable army, which the national spirit of the Castilians had formed round Philip, was placed under the able command of Vendome. He at once saw the necessity for preventing the proposed union; and his advance to the Bridge of Almaraz rendered it henceforward impossible. Stanhope was for wintering in Castile, and the army withdrawing from the capital amidst the joyful shouts of the inhabitants, took up a position in accordance with Stanhope's wishes. But the Archduke Charles, who was as uxorious as his rival, could not bear separation from his wife, and hurried home with upwards of 2000 cavalry, the arm in which the allied troops were already overmatched. When it became evident that no hope was to be expected from Portugal, the general saw that to winter in Castile was impossible, and withdrew towards Aragon. But Vendome, smarting under the disgrace he had suffered at Oudenarde, outdid himself. With extreme rapidity, he pressed upon his enemy, who was retreating in two parallel armies, one under Staremberg, the other under Stanhope. With vastly superior forces he came upon the latter general, as he was resting his troops at Brihuega, without the least notion of the close approach of Vendome. Stanhope made a most gallant defence, expecting to be relieved by Staremberg, but hours passed by, and for some unexplained reason, Staremberg did not appear; thus having continued his defence till ammunition failed, Stanhope was compelled to capitulate. The surrender was already completed before Staremberg appeared. His slowness had ruined his cause, but he did what he could to re-establish it; and at Villa Viciosa a great battle was fought, in which both parties claimed the victory. But no fresh victory could have given Vendome more perfect success. Staremberg was obliged to fall back, and reached Barcelona with 7000 men only, the relics of the army which had been so triumphant in the earlier part of the year.

The elections, made while the ferment of the trial of Sacheverell was still unsubdued, produced a strong Tory majority. And it was thus, Harley's policy for peace strong at home and assisted by disaster abroad, that Harley and his Government were able to set on foot their change of policy, and in spite of the failure of the preliminaries at Gertruydenberg, to enter into negotiations for a final peace. It seems probable that from the first Harley's policy was directed to the restoration of the Stuarts, as well as to a return to the main feature of their foreign policy, friendship with France. It is of course possible that his intercourse with the Jacobites was merely

intended to secure his parliamentary position, but certainly his conduct was quite in accordance with the belief that he was in earnest.
The tortuous and underhand manner in which the peace was first set
on foot points in this direction, still more so do the letters of the Abbé
Gaultier, written in the year 1710, which declare that   and restoration
the new ministry had a great consideration for the   of the Stuarts.
Pretender, and that some members of it were working for him only.
The restoration of the Stuarts would be rendered easier by three
things. In the first place it was scarcely possible without the assistance of France. This seems to explain, better than the mere wish
to follow the traditional Tory policy of peace, the immediate steps
taken to put an end to the war, and the very favourable terms
granted to Louis after his disasters. Secondly, it could not be undertaken without the support of the High Church party, which was
very strong. This explains the constant support given by the Government to that party. And thirdly, the success of such a scheme would
have been best secured by the assistance of Marlborough, who was
known to have already frequently intrigued with the Court of St.
Germains. On the other hand the Duke would be the most formidable
opponent. Steps were therefore taken to secure his assistance, and
when that was found impossible, his complete ruin became the object
to be sought.

On his return from his somewhat unfruitful campaign, Marlborough seemed inclined, with his usual selfishness, to   Marlborough
submit to anything for the continuation of his personal   only anxious to
position. We are told by St. John that he expressed   keep his place.
his sorrow for his former wrong step in joining the Whigs. He even
attempted to soften the angry vehemence of his wife, but her fate
was in fact determined by the personal feelings of the Queen. No
entreaties of the Duke, who even threw himself on his knees before
her, could induce the Queen to go back from her wish to deprive the
Duchess of all her offices. She was compelled to surrender her gold
key, and left her apartments at St. James's, having first gratified her
spite by carrying off the brass locks and marble chimney-pieces.
The Duke himself, though he had suffered many indignities, was
permitted to continue the conduct of the war, being assured that
he should be well supported.

Having thus for the time secured themselves from his opposition,
the Government proceeded to open secret negotiations   Secret peace
with the Court of Versailles. The agent employed was   negotiations.
a priest named Gaultier, who had been Tallard's chaplain, and was a

warm friend of the Pretender's cause. This sudden idea of peace
was most unexpected and welcome to the French. "Asking us
whether we wished for peace," says Torcy, "was like asking a sick man
whether he wishes to recover." Gaultier returned with the message
that Louis could not, so soon after the failure of the late treaty,
suggest peace to the Dutch, but he would gladly listen to the mediation of England; a shrewd answer, which at once tended towards
separating England from her allies. The knowledge that a peace
with France was likely, and that all further help from England was
hopeless, induced a French refugee of the name of Guiscard, who
had been prominent in arranging attacks upon France and assistance
to the rebels in the Cevennes, to turn traitor. His correspondence
was discovered, and in despair, upon being examined in the Council,
he determined to revenge himself upon the authors of his misfortune,
and stabbed Harley with a penknife. Harley's popularity was raised
still higher by this attack on him; he was made Earl of Oxford,
and shortly after, on the supposed success of his financial scheme for
incorporating the public creditors into a company to trade in the
South Seas, was made Lord Treasurer. The High Church temper
of the time was further illustrated by the passage of a Bill for erecting fifty new churches in London, and of the Occasional Conformity
Act, now proposed in the House of Lords which had always previously
obstructed it.

The negotiations opened by Gaultier were also continued, Prior
was sent to Paris, and a more specific scheme was set on foot than
had been produced by the verbal negotiations of the spring,
although, unmoved or ignorant of the action of the Government,
Marlborough was attempting to continue his great career. He had
Marlborough's planned a combined movement with Eugene against
plans for the Villars, who had constructed lines near Arras and
campaign of
1711. Cambrai so strong that he boastfully said he had
brought Marlborough to the "non plus ultra." The vigour of
the campaign was checked by the withdrawal of Eugene, who
was required to superintend and guard the Electoral Diet at
Frankfort, which had been summoned to elect the successor
to the Emperor Joseph, who had died on the 17th of April. It
was Marlborough's intention to reduce Bouchain and Le Quesnoy,
to winter in France, and in the spring press forward towards
Paris. His schemes were only partially successful, owing principally to the slowness of the Imperialists. By some skilful
manœuvres he succeeded in passing the formidable lines, and

besieged and took Bouchain, but was unable to carry his great project further.

On his arrival in Paris, Prior found that Louis had authority to treat for Spain as well as for himself, and proceeded Proposed terms to explain the conditions demanded. England no of peace. longer insisted upon the surrender of the ·Spanish crown, but would be satisfied with the pledge that the two crowns should never be united ; Gibraltar, Minorca, and Newfoundland must be secured to England ; Dunkirk demolished, and four towns granted` for trade in South America. Great commercial advantages must be granted both to the English and Dutch, and fortified towns given as barriers for the Dutch in the Low Countries, and for Austria on the Rhine. All this was as yet kept profoundly secret. The negotiation was subsequently transferred to London, and there, in September, eight preliminary articles were drawn up. Louis was to acknowledge Anne and the Protestant succession ; a new treaty of commerce was to be made ; Dunkirk was to be demolished, some fair equivalent being given ; Gibraltar, Minorca, and Newfoundland, with the exception of some fishing rights, were to be secured to the English. In addition to this, the Assiento, or grant ·of the slave trade with America, was withdrawn by Spain from France and given to England. A second set of preliminaries was prepared for Holland, omitting the chief advantages gained by England, but introducing stipulations to secure a barrier and to prevent the junction of the crowns of France and Spain. The Dutch, though much dissatisfied with the desertion of the English, were compelled to give in their adhesion, and Utrecht was appointed as the place where the conference was to be held. Austria was even more outspoken in its anger, and the Imperial minister in London, who was rash enough to express the indignation of his Court in a published appeal to the people, was compelled to leave the country.

Affairs had reached this point when Marlborough returned from his campaign. Entering into communication with his old friends the Whigs, he found that they had formed a coalition Attack on with a section of the Tories under Nottingham, who Marlborough was much displeased at having been excluded from all on his return. the late ministerial arrangements. Marlborough's object was no doubt to join the strongest side. The present position of the Whig party seemed to him so promising that he gave it his adhesion. Nor was he mistaken as things then stood. On the opening Parliament. of Parliament, Nottingham moved, as an amendment to Dec. 7.

the Address, the old Tory resolution that no peace could be safe or honourable to Great Britain or Europe if Spain or the West Indies were allotted to any branch of the Bourbons, and after a hot discussion succeeded in beating the Government by a majority of eight. In the House of Commons, on the other hand, the Government commanded a large majority. Harley and St. John had now to consider what steps to take against this hostile coalition in the Lords. They determined, in the first place, to strike a heavy blow at Marlborough, and the report of a Commission which had been issued to examine into the public accounts afforded them an opportunity of doing so. Basing its assertion on the deposition of Sir Solomon Medina, who had contracted to supply the army in Flanders with bread, the Commission reported that the Duke had received on those contracts large sums of money, amounting on the whole to £63,000, while his secretary, Cardonnel, had also received large douceurs. It also declared that Marlborough had received $2\frac{1}{2}$ per cent. on all subsidies to foreign troops, amounting on the whole to £177,000. Acting on this report, the ministry stripped Marlborough of all his offices. Marlborough was so notoriously avaricious, and his character was so mean, that these charges seemed to the public probable; but, in fact, his reply was tolerably complete. The bread money had habitually been received by every commander-in-chief in Flanders, and had been expended chiefly in obtaining information as to the enemies' plans. The percentage on the subsidies was a free gift from the princes to whom they were paid, and Marlborough had not accepted them without the royal warrant. In the state of feeling at the time these excuses were not much regarded. Having got rid of their most powerful enemy, the ministry made use of the royal prerogative to neutralize the influence of the Lords. Twelve new Peers were created, which gave them a permanent majority.

Having by these strong measures secured their position in Parliament, Harley and St. John proceeded with their negotiations. There

Command of the army given to Ormond. 1712.

was some difficulty with regard to the prosecution of the war while the Congress was sitting. The command had been given to the Duke of Ormond, a man of strong Jacobite principles; he was privately instructed not to undertake any offensive operations against the French, and he consequently informed Villars that he need not be afraid of attacks from the English, although the pressure which Eugene put upon him was so strong that he could not refuse to join in the siege of Quesnoy. His strange lukewarm prosecution of the war, which seemed rather like friendship than hostility, did not pass unnoticed in England. But all complaints were answered by the assertion that the Queen would shortly lay before Parliament the conditions of a peace. In fact, she was only waiting till Philip of Spain should have made up his mind whether to accept an equivalent for the Spanish crown, and retain his rights on France, or remain where he was and renounce those claims. When the answer arrived, preferring the latter alternative, the Queen went down to the House and explained the proposed treaty. Though violently opposed, addresses of confidence were carried. The Queen announces the treaty. June 6.

An armistice was at once declared, and the English troops ordered to separate from Eugene. It was not without a considerable feeling of disgrace that 12,000 English troops withdrew from their old comrades in arms; the English stipendiaries refused to obey the command, and remained with the Prince. A visit of St. John, now Lord Bolingbroke, to Paris, put the finishing stroke to the negotiation, and peace was virtually declared. The campaign, completed by Eugene alone, was unsuccessful. His defeat at Denain, and further successes won over the allies by Villars, inclined the new Emperor to look more favourably upon the peace. The treaties were ultimately signed at Utrecht on the 31st of March 1713. The Emperor's peace, by which the Electors of Cologne and Bavaria were reinstated, was postponed for a year, and was finally completed at Rastadt in the following March. It is certain that the terms gained were infinitely less advantageous than the lengthened and victorious war might have justified, or than those which could have been obtained at the negotiations of Gertruydenberg. The desertion of the Catalans, who had risen in insurrection chiefly at the instigation of the English, was undoubtedly an act of selfishness; and Government would even have sacrificed the advantages of the Methuen Treaty, and granted commercial terms far more in favour of France, had not the moneyed interest proved too strong for it. At the same time, though the Peace of Utrecht was not a glorious one, there is much to be said in its favour; the changed position of Europe, by the accession of Charles to the Imperial crown, had in truth put the questions at issue upon a totally new footing; it would have been quite as disadvantageous to the general European balance that Spain and Austria should have been joined in the hands of the Imperial house as that Spain and France should have been in the hands of the Bourbon Princes. Peace of Utrecht. 1713.

After the close of the great war, the question of succession, rendered more pressing by the failing health of the Queen, came prominently forward. In the midst of the negotiations the Pretender had written a letter to Queen Anne, and Bolingbroke had been throughout in correspondence with him. It is difficult to determine how far Harley was really mixed up in the plot of changing the succession. That he had frequently expressed himself as friendly to the Pretender is certain; but his indolence in business, his constant difficulty in making up his mind, and his love of intrigue, prevented him from taking any strong or definite line in the scheme for the Stuart restoration. With Bolingbroke the case was different. He was unaffected by any Church views, for he did not believe in Christianity; he knew that the part he had already played had rendered him obnoxious to the Elector of Hanover, he had therefore little hope of office after the Queen's death. On the other hand, he was certain of being a trusted minister of the new Stuart king. To help him in the Cabinet he had Bromley, Ormond, and probably Harcourt. But for the success of his plan extreme care was necessary; for the general feeling of the country, though Tory and High Church, was nevertheless Protestant and Hanoverian. An over-hasty declaration of Jacobitism would probably destroy his ministry.

The succession.

Harley's conduct.

Bolingbroke's views.

A new Parliament assembled in February. It was again Tory in its views; and it shows the real object of Bolingbroke's tactics, that the Pretender during the elections wrote to his friends to use their best efforts in favour of the Government. The new appointments also, which were made on the occurrence of vacancies by deaths, show the same Jacobite tendencies. Wyndam became Chancellor of the Exchequer, Athol and Mar two of the chief officials in Scotland. Nor was the Jacobite scheme confined to the appointment of ministers, more immediate practical measures for securing the change of Government were taken. The Cinque Ports were placed in the hands of Ormond, and the entrance of a foreign force into England thus rendered easy; the army was remodelled, and the greater part of those troops which William had organized disbanded; while a plan was set on foot for obliging officers in the army known to be friendly to Marlborough to sell their commissions, which only failed because Harley, either through indolence, or because he really shrunk from supporting the Jacobites, neglected to have the funds

New Tory Parliament. 1714.

Ormond reorganises the army.

ready for the purchase. The Whigs, on their side, also organized themselves for the coming crisis. General Stanhope was regarded as their leader. They seem to have been ready for all emergencies, intending even to employ force, if necessary, to secure the throne for the Hanoverian Elector. In spite of the caution of Bolingbroke, the scope of his plans began to be discovered, and it became necessary still further to blind the nation. Pretending to treat as libels all sugges tions that he was aiming at the restoration of the Stuarts, he intro- duced a resolution that the Protestant succession was in no danger, but his credit was too far shaken to allow of a complete victory. The motion was indeed passed, but the small majority proved how large a section of the Tories was attached to the Hanoverian house, and were willing on that point to make common cause with the Whigs. That party were encouraged to take a further step. Thinking it of the last importance that the Electoral Prince should be in England to take possession of the inheritance of his house on Anne's death, they induced the Hanoverian minister to demand his writ of summons to the House of Lords as an English Peer in virtue of his title of Duke of Cambridge. The Government was thrown into great perplexity; to refuse it seemed to confess their Jacobite tendencies, to grant it was certain to enrage the Queen, who, like other childless sovereigns, was morbidly touchy about the succession, and it would moreover deal a heavy blow at their own plans. The writ was given, but accompanied by a letter from the Queen to the Electress Sophia, couched in such angry language that it is said to have caused the death of that princess, now far advanced in years.

But a schism within its own body was gradually undermining the ministry. Harley, undecided upon all points, and strongly bound by old ties to the Low Church and dissenting interest, could not throw himself heartily into the vigorous policy of Bolingbroke; he was moreover, jealous of the ever-increasing importance of his energetic colleague. The Schism Act, a measure conceived in the most ex- clusive High Church spirit, brought their rivalry to a crisis. It enacted that no person should keep a public or private school, or act as tutor, unless a member of the Church of England, and licensed by his Bishop, thus in fact throwing the whole education of the country into the hands of the Church. Harley, bred a dissenter, and always relying much on the support of the Nonconformist bodies, could not give it his hearty support. With his usual indecision, he played fast and loose with the Bill. But he had lost the ear of the Queen, Bolingbroke and Mrs. Masham had supplanted him, and the favourite so played upon the Queen's High Church propensities, that, after a hot altercation in the Council before the eyes of the Queen, she was induced to dismiss the Lord Treasurer.

In the dismissal of his dilatory rival Bolingbroke saw the removal of the last obstacle to the completion of his schemes, and he was preparing to form a ministry wholly in the Jacobite interest, when the Queen's sudden illness upset all his plans. Had the matter come to the decision of arms, Marlborough, who had just returned from abroad, might, after the treatment he had received at the hand of the Tories, have been trusted to do his best for the Whigs. But, fortunately, the question was destined to meet with a peaceful solution. The Duke of Shrewsbury, in his time the leader of the Whigs of the Revolution, and subsequently guilty of treacherous correspondence with the Stuarts, continued his vacillating policy. The part he had taken in 1708, in persuading the Queen to rid herself of the Whigs, had given him the confidence of the Tory party. But he had never ceased to regret the one false step of his life, and was firmly attached to the Hanoverian succession. His position in the ministry enabled him for the time to become really master of the situation, and to thwart all the schemes of Bolingbroke. With this end in view he arranged a plan with the Dukes of Argyle and Somerset. As the Council was sitting to consider what steps to

The Queen's   take in consequence of the Queen's illness, the two
death   Dukes suddenly made their appearance, claimed their
right as Privy Councillors, were by Shrewsbury's advice admitted, and at once proposed that the Queen, who had for the moment recovered consciousness, should be requested, in view of the coming crisis, to make the Duke of Shrewsbury Lord Treasurer. A deputation, of which the Duke was himself a member, went to her bedside, and persuaded her to give him the White Staff. Vigorous measures were at once taken. Troops were collected, the Elector summoned over, and everything was ready to withstand armed invasion, and to hasten the peaceful acceptance of the legal heir, when the Queen died on the 1st of August.

For several sessions the Parliament had been acting under the

The Union.   new title of the Parliament of Great Britain, the Union
             with Scotland having been completed in 1707. Quite
at the beginning of the reign, in 1702, leave having been given both by the Scotch and English Parliaments, Commissioners had met to make arrangements for the Union. which had always been a favourite

project of William's. Neither party 'were, however, much in earnest, and the members of the Commission were lax in their attendance. There was no difficulty in agreeing upon the main points, but upon trade and finance the claims advanced by the Scotch, who seemed to wish on the one hand for equality of duties, and on the other for exemption from liabilities, were regarded as untenable, and in February 1703 the Commissioners ceased to meet.

On the 6th of May in that year the Scotch Parliament met, under the Presidency of the Duke of Queensberry as Lord Commissioner. Its temper was anything but conciliatory. The ill feeling excited by the Darien Scheme had by no means subsided. The late futile efforts of the joint Commission had still further roused the angry feelings of the people, and there was an idea afloat, by no means without foundation, that the High Church Tories, who were just coming into power, would seize the opportunity for an assault upon the National Church. All these causes influenced the temper of the Parliament, and instead of taking measures tending towards the Union, it seemed bent upon doing all that was possible to render the kingdoms quite separate. The Queen's letter, in which she recommended toleration, was contemptuously neglected, and a strong declaration passed, confirming the Presbyterian Church, " as the only Church of Christ in the Kingdom." Politically, the conduct of the Parliament was even less conciliatory. Resolutions were passed declaring that, after the death of the Queen, no King of England should make peace or war without consent of the Scotch Parliament; though the nation was in the midst of a great war with France, restrictions on the trade in French wine were removed ; Fletcher of Saltoun introduced what were known as the Limitations, by which the authority of the Crown was seriously compromised ; its power of appointing to the great offices of Government was transferred to the Parliament ; and finally, a Bill of Security with regard to the succession was introduced, authorizing Parliament to name a successor from among the Protestant descendants of the royal line, but asserting that whoever that successor might be he was not to be the same as the successor to the Crown of England, unless proper security was given for the freedom of religion and trade. The nomination of the Princess Sophia, hazarded by the Earl of Marchmont, was received with derision and anger. All these Bills, except the last, received the royal assent. But the refusal to pass the Bill of Security was so unpopular, that it was found necessary to adjourn the House without securing any subsidy.

[margin note: Scotch Parliament. 1703.]

In the following year the Parliament again met. It was hoped that a new Commissioner would manage it more successfully,

Scotch Parliament. July 1704.

and the Marquis of Tweeddale was appointed to succeed Queensberry. The policy of conciliation was carried to an extreme, and Godolphin, always a timid minister, allowed Tweeddale to give the royal assent even to the Act of Security.

The hostile feeling exhibited by the Scotch Parliament only went still further to prove what the Darien Scheme had made evident, that the Union was imperatively necessary.

English Parliament. Oct. 1704.

Whigs and Tories therefore combined, when the English Parliament met, in attacking Godolphin for his weakness; and in December, Somers brought forward, and succeeded in passing through both Houses, a law which seemed to threaten war between the countries. After Christmas 1705, all Scotchmen were to be regarded as aliens, the importation into England of the chief Scotch products—cattle, coal, and linen—was prohibited; and as a still stronger threat, it was ordered that the Border towns should be fortified and put into a state of security, and the militia in the northern counties called out. This severe threat was not without its effect. But the anger of the Scotch at the time only grew more vehement. In April of the following year, 1705, Thomas Green, a captain of a ship belonging to the new East India Company, had been seized by the agents of the Darien Company, charged with piracy in the East, and with the murder of a Darien captain. It was afterwards proved that the captain was alive; nevertheless, in spite of orders from the English Council, the Scotch ministers were overawed by the popular feeling, and the unfortunate man, with some others of his crew, was hanged. But England was now determined that the Union should be effected. Tweeddale was removed from his commissionership, and Argyle, assisted by Queensberry, put in his place. This gave Tweeddale an opportunity of forming a third party in the Parliament,

Scotch Parliament. June 1705.

which attempted to hold the balance between those who were for the Union and those who opposed it, and was known by the name of the Squadrone Volante. On the whole, however, this party acted with the Government. The Queen had instructed the Parliament to consider the question of the settlement of the succession, and the appointment of Commissioners to treat. With regard to the first point it proved obstinate, it insisted on first discussing the condition of trade, and could not be induced to name any successor. With some slight alterations, it passed again the Limitations suggested by Fletcher of Saltoun, and added further, that a Scotch ambassador should be present at all treaties involving the two nations. But upon the second point, by the aid of the Squadrone Volante, the Government was successful. The threatened Alien Bill indeed began to have its effect; and it was ordered that the Commissioners should not begin to act till that Bill was repealed. As it seemed to have done its work, this suggestion was attended to, and in November the English Parliament repealed the Act.

Thus then, the chief obstacles being removed, in April 1706, the Commissioners, thirty-one on each side, met. The English Commissioners at once suggested as the prime object of negotiation, that there should be one Kingdom, one Parliament, and one Successor. The Scotch seemed first to desire a Federative Union, but yielded, on condition that their religion should be free, and that their trade should enjoy a general equality of advantage. It was the details, especially of taxation and trade, which gave the greatest trouble. The Scotch insisted on discussing them in detail. It was finally agreed that they should be exempt from terminable taxes, and receive an equivalent for any present loss they might sustain by taking their share in the public debt of England, which was larger than their own. The revenue of England was about £5,700,000, that of Scotland about £160,000. The debts of England amounted to £17,700,000, those of Scotland, taken roughly, to £160,000; that is, England owed three and a half, Scotland only one year's revenue. The equivalent fixed was £398,000, which was employed to pay off the whole Scotch debt, to dissolve the Darien Company and indemnify its shareholders, and for other Scotch purposes. The other questions were easily settled. The title of the United Kingdom was to be Great Britain, the national flags were to be incorporated in one. The Scotch taxes amounted to little more than a fortieth of the English. Had this been observed as a basis of representation, they would have had but thirteen members of Parliament. But this being held too few, they were granted forty-five members, which was about a twelfth of the whole House of Commons. The same proportion was taken for the basis of the arrangement of the Upper House, and thus of the whole Scottish Peerage sixteen were to be elected to sit in the united House of Lords.

When the Treaty had been settled by the Commissioners, it was brought before the Scotch Parliament, where it met with violent opposition. In one way or another it was objectionable to many classes. The Jacobites saw in it the final destruction of all their hopes of a

The Commissioners meet. 1706.

change of dynasty. The extreme Presbyterians did not believe in a
Union which would leave their Church untrammelled. The views
of the Revolution had gone further in Scotland than in England,
and a considerable body of active spirits had adopted republican
views; to them the establishment of a monarchy backed by the
strength of England was distasteful, as rendering any fulfilment of
their hopes impossible. And the Edinburgh tradesmen recognized
to the full the loss they would sustain by the removal of Parliament
to London. The discussion on the various points went on throughout the whole of the year. The final effort of the
Opposition was to be a great protest, to be produced
at the debate upon the share Scotland was to have in
the national legislature. This protest was to be presented by
Hamilton, as premier Peer, and to be followed by a secession of the
minority. But Hamilton's heart failed him at the appointed
moment, the protest was not presented, and on the 16th of January
1707 the measure was finally carried by 110 votes to 69.

Scotch Parliament. Oct. 1706.

Having been successfully passed through the Scotch House, the
Bill had now to be ratified by the English Parliament. So many
changes had been made that it was possible there might be much
difficulty in securing the easy passage of the Bill. But as the Whigs
and the Government were determined that at all hazards it should
become law, they accepted without question all the Scotch amendments. When the articles of the Treaty had thus been carried through
the House, there yet remained the Act of Ratification to complete
it. It was still possible for the opponents of the Bill to reopen
discussion upon each article in detail. The skill of Sir Simon
Harcourt, the Attorney-General, thwarted this disastrous intention,
by so wording the Bill that the articles themselves were not called
in question, but their ratification alone demanded. He induced all
parties, who were on the whole agreed that in some shape or other
the Bill had better pass, to accept it. With little opposition therefore
it was carried through both Houses, and became law, and the
succeeding Parliament took the name of the Parliament of Great
Britain. Party feeling was at the time very high, and accusations
of bribery were lavishly flung abroad, but a closer examination
appears to prove that these charges were unfounded.

GEORGE I.

1714—1727.

Born 1660 = Sophia of Brunswick.

George II.   Sophia = Frederick William.

CONTEMPORARY PRINCES.

France.	Germany.	Spain.	Prussia.
Louis XIV., 1643. Louis XV., 1715.	Charles VI , 1711.	Philip V., 1700.	Frederick William 1713.

Russia.	Denmark.	Sweden.
Peter the Great, 1689. Catherine I., 1724.	Frederick IV., 1699.	Charles XII., 1697. Frederick I., 1720.

POPES.—Clement XI., 1700.   Innocent XIII., 1721.   Benedict XIII , 1724.

Archbishops.	Chancellors
T. Tenison, 1694. W. Wake, 1715.	William Cowper, 1714. Lord Macclesfield, 1718. Lord King, 1725.

First Lords of the Treasury	Chancellors of the Exchequer.	Secretaries of State.
1714. Halifax. 1715. Carlisle. 1715. R. Walpole. 1717. Stanhope. 1718. Sunderland. 1721. R. Walpole.	1714. R Walpole. 1717. Stanhope. 1718. Aislabie 1721. R. Walpole.	1714 { Stanhope / Townshend 1716 { Stanhope. / Methuen 1717 { Sunderland / Addison. 1718 { Stanhope / Craggs. 1721 { Townshend. / Carteret 1724 { Townshend / Newcastle

ENGLAND had been slow to accept the principle of succession by parliamentary instead of hereditary right; **Probability of a restoration of the Stuarts** since 1688 the struggle had been continuous, it had reached a crisis in the closing years of Queen Anne. The triumph of the Whigs, secured to them by the constant successes

of the War of Succession, had rendered them over-confident, and an
act of foolish severity had been followed by their complete overthrow. The natural inclinations of the Queen, and the weakness of
her character, which rendered her constantly liable to be subjugated
by the influence of those around her ; the talents and intriguing
ambition of St. John, and the energy and compactness of the Jacobite
body resting upon the general Conservative feeling of the nation,
had rendered the return of the Stuarts to the throne a very probable
event. A few weeks only were wanting for the completion of the
plot, and James Edward would probably have been received as heir
to the throne, and the work of the Revolution have been undone.
The unexpected illness of the Queen, the rapidity and energy with
which the Hanoverian Lords of the Council had carried out what
was virtually a *coup d'état*, had destroyed these hopes. When the
Lord Treasurer's staff was placed in the hands of the Duke of
Shrewsbury, all hope of carrying out this counter-revolution with
the aid of the executive was at an end. Although he had more
than once faltered in his allegiance to the Whig party, it was now
well understood that he was endowed with something not far short
of a dictatorship, for the express purpose of carrying out the
enactments of the Act of Succession. Everything was done as
arranged by that Act. There was no difficulty with regard to the
regency ; sealed packets containing the names of those who were
to act as the Council of Regency, chosen by the Protestant suc-

Council of
Regency.

cessor, were in his hands. On their being opened, the
names of eighteen Lords, almost exclusively of the Whig
party, were found, who, together with the seven great officers named
in the Statute, were to act, under the title of Lords Justices, as an
interim Government until the arrival of the new King. It is to be
observed that the name of the Duke of Marlborough was not among
them.

Parliament was to continue for six months before dissolution, and

Peaceful
accession
of the King

everything for the present passed off quietly ; the Civil
List was voted as in the preceding reign ; and on the
18th of September the King and his eldest son arrived
in England. He was not a man to excite enthusiasm. An unosten-
tatious man, used to a Court where his will was law, but where the
manners were singularly primitive and plain, he was little suited to
the peculiar position of an English Parliamentary sovereign, from
whom, along with the possession of but little real power, much
dignity and some magnificence were required. Unable therefore to

comprehend the working of that constitution over which he had come to preside, and without ability sufficient to carry on a policy of his own, he naturally threw himself into the arms of that party to which he owed his Crown. The great offices, several of which had been for the last month united in the hands of Shrewsbury, were therefore distributed among the Whigs. Townshend was put at the head of the Government, and with him were Halifax, General Stanhope, Lord Cowper, Nottingham, and Lord Townshend's brother-in-law, Sir Robert Walpole ; while Sunderland was made Lord-Lieutenant of Ireland, and the Duke of Marlborough (though the King had already shown his well-founded mistrust of him) reassumed the offices of Commander-in-chief and Master of the Ordnance. His power, however, was gone. New Whig ministry.

The establishment of the Hanoverian house had thus very much the appearance of a triumph of a faction. There were no attempts at conciliation, such as had been made after the Revolution, no efforts to give a general and national character to the Government. The King came forward as the head of the triumphant Whig party. This attitude naturally at the time excited much ill-feeling, yet on the whole it was wise. George was not the man to carry out a scheme of comprehensive government which had already twice failed in the abler hands of William and of Marlborough. The questions at issue were too vital to admit of compromise, and the Whig party were wise in their view of the crisis. A crushing victory was necessary to teach both their conscientious and factious opponents a lesson,—the one must yield to the force of circumstances, the other must discover that their only road to office lay in concession to principles which they were too weak to shake. Conscientious upholders of the Stuarts must be taught that their choice lay between submission and the resignation of their claim to be regarded as Englishmen; those who used the Stuarts as a road to power must be led to see that they must henceforward limit their opposition to points of minor importance, that the main principles of government were fixed for ever. Triumph of the Whigs.

But the conduct of the King and of the Whigs, though wise, was such as to drive the Jacobites to extremities, and to render an appeal to arms sooner or later almost certain. The irritation of the high Tories at once showed itself. In January, as the six months had elapsed, the House was dissolved, and on the meeting of the new House in March, it was found, as was at that time usually the case, that the party in power commanded a large Riots in the country.

majority. This however had not been secured without serious riots. In Manchester and the midland counties the riots assumed the form of an attack upon the dissenters, and were so serious as to necessitate the passing of a Riot Act. By this Act, which is still in force, it is enacted, that " If any twelve persons are unlawfully assembled to the disturbance of the peace, and any justice of the peace, sheriff, &c., shall think proper to command them by proclamation to disperse, if they contemn his orders, and continue together for one hour afterwards, such contempt shall be felony, without benefit of clergy."

Having secured their majority, it became evident that the Whigs intended to use their regained ascendancy to the uttermost. The Address, both in the House of Lords and in the Commons, was obviously pointed against the framers of the Peace of Utrecht, and before three weeks were over a secret committee was appointed to consider that peace. Bolingbroke had already fled and taken service with the Pretender. Ormond, who till this time had remained in England, putting himself ostentatiously forward as the leader of the Jacobite opposition, followed his example. Oxford alone awaited his trial. The two fugitives were proceeded against by bill of attainder. The impeachment of Oxford was after a while dropped ; in fact, it was difficult to substantiate the charge of treason against him. It was not till long afterwards that any real proof existed of treasonable correspondence with the Pretender; and it was scarcely possible to twist the faults and weaknesses of the Peace, the desertion of the Catalans, even the surrender, unasked, of Tournay, one of our conquests, into crimes under the law of treason ; nor was the doctrine of the responsibility of ministers as yet sufficiently established to allow the majority at once to answer Oxford's solemn declaration, that he had acted distinctly upon the royal authority. It is true that the plea had been overruled in the case of Danby ; but even in the last reign the Whigs had themselves sought shelter, after the battle of Almanza, behind the royal authority, and it was not till more than twenty years of regular party government had intervened that the doctrine was thoroughly understood and adopted.

Meanwhile the aggressive policy of the Whigs was hurrying on an outbreak of the conspiracy which the timely death of the late Queen had checked. It was widespread. Ormond, until his flight, had been busily engaged in organizing it in England, while Bolingbroke had taken it in hand in France :

Impeachment of the late ministers March.

Jacobite conspiracy.

for then, as always, it seems to have been accepted, that any insurrection would be useless without material help from France. In many parts of the country, particularly in the west, the feeling against the Hanoverian succession was strong, and measures had been taken to secure Bristol and Exeter, and other great western towns. In Scotland the difficulty was rather to restrain than to urge forward the Jacobite feeling. Many causes combined to create a widespread discontent in that country. In the north the feeling of loyalty to an hereditary chief was part of the national character, inwoven with the whole system of clanship. *Disaffection in Scotland.* The national pride was flattered by the thought of a Stuart, a Scotchman, sitting upon the throne of England. Moreover, there was one chief of predominant power whose interests had been always Whig, and jealousy of the ascendancy of the clan Campbell, and of its head, the Duke of Argyle, or Mac Callum More, on this, as on several other occasions, tended to throw all rival clans into the arms of any party of which he was the declared enemy. In the Lowlands other influences were at work. The Presbyterians were not likely to forget the unsparing cruelty of the later Stuarts, and now that they had the upper hand, the tolerated Episcopalians met with no great courtesy at their hands; a constant source of quarrel was thus opened, and the Episcopalians and Catholics might be well expected to seek refuge from the intolerance of their victorious rivals, and a restoration even of their former superiority, in the establishment of the exiled dynasty. But more than that, everything English was unpopular. Two great imaginary injuries were rankling in the national mind. The nation had never forgiven King William's treatment of the Darien Scheme, and was still smarting under the supposed yoke which the Union had laid upon them. Whoever was King of England was their natural enemy, so that, except in those places where settled industry had already felt the advantage of the union with England, there was great readiness to join in any enterprise which would be injurious to her. There were therefore ready to join the cause of the Stuarts in the north all the great clans except the Campbells, and in the south the Episcopalians, and those nationalists who regarded as righteous any act of antagonism to England.

But the movement, both in Scotland and in England, was held to depend on the conduct of France, and it was probable that, under Bolingbroke's able management, assistance would come from that country. The King was indeed *Failure of the Jacobite hopes of French assistance* far different from the Louis of other days. Enslaved by the religious influence of Madame de Maintenou, and surrounded by bitter party disputes with regard to the legitimization of his bastards, his energy was gone, while war and taxes and persecution had much depressed the power of France. Still, irritated by the Whig assault upon his friends in England, the champion as he believed himself of legitimacy, and angry at the opposition raised by the English ministry to his new fortifications at Mardyke, he had used his influence with Spain to procure sums of money for the conspirators, had himself supplied arms, and had allowed a small squadron to be equipped at Havre at the expense of France. The flight of Ormond, the first blow to the conspiracy, was followed, on the 1st of September, by the death of Louis. The Government passed into the hands of the Regent Orleans, whose policy was of a purely personal character, his chief aim being the exclusion of the Spanish house from the succession should the young King die. To secure his plans at home external peace was necessary. Personal friendship, both for Stair the English ambassador, and for Stanhope the English secretary, rendered him still more disinclined to break with England. Hope from France was gone. Bolingbroke saw at once the course affairs were taking, and despatched a messenger to tell the leaders of the conspiracy that, as Scotland could not rise without England, and England could not rise without France, and France had no intention of moving, all thoughts of insurrection had better be dropped.

His prudent message came too late. The Pretender, weary of waiting, had taken matters into his own hands, and a leader had already been despatched to raise the northern counties of Scotland. This leader was the Earl of Mar. At Anne's death Mar was Secretary for Scotland, a man of no very great ability, but who, for his skill in trimming his sails to the wind, had earned the nickname of "Bobbing John." He once more tried to play his old game, but found himself mistrusted, and had to give place to the Duke of Montrose. He now hurried to London, sought favour at Court, took a wife from among the leaders of the Whig party, and having thus thrown people off the scent, hurried back to Scotland to organize the insurrection. His chief influence was in Aberdeenshire, north of the Grampian hills; and there, early in September, he contrived a meeting of the chief clans of the neighbourhood. He was joined by Tullibardine, the heir of the Duke of Athol, who brought with him the Murrays, and by the great clan of the Gordons, with Lord Paumure, from the north of Perth-

Mar organizes the insurrection in Scotland

shire, towards which county he at once began to march. The Pretender could not refuse to support Mar's open movement on his behalf. In October he hurried across France, evading an attempt of Orleans to arrest him, and an attempt on the part of the English ambassador to assassinate him. He reached St. Malo in safety. Thence an expedition under Ormond was to have been thrown upon the English coast. Twice Ormond was thwarted by the weather; his third attempt was too late, the English fleet lay before the port. Had he succeeded in landing, no better fortune would have awaited him; the English Government had already heard of the gathering of the Highland clans, the Habeas Corpus Act was suspended, the more active Jacobites arrested; such troops as were then in England, some 8000 in number, were hurried to the west (for the Scotch outbreak was looked upon only as a feint); some 6000 troops, due from Holland as a guarantee for the Protestant succession, were demanded; fresh regiments were rapidly formed; and the command in Scotland was given to Argyle, the natural opponent of the Jacobite clans. The vigorous measures of the Government had in fact already broken the neck of the conspiracy.

Vigorous measures of the English Government.

But there was still real danger in the North, for Mar had an overwhelming superiority of forces, and before the end of October he had the complete command of Scotland as far as the Forth. Argyle, desirous of confining the rebellion as much as possible to the north and east, attempted to hold the line of that river. Mar, to whom immediate success was everything, and who overrated the strength of his party in England, was desirous of crossing the Border as soon as possible, in order to rally the disaffected round him. He had now about 12,000 men with him, but these were poorly armed, and even this poor equipment was due to no care of Mar's, but to a gallant dash by the Master of Sinclair upon an English ship lying in the Forth. With these troops he would probably have been unable to have passed Argyle at Stirling, even if he had not been prevented from moving by the expected arrival of the Pretender. It was therefore determined that a detachment under Brigadier Mackintosh should be thrown across the Firth, and marched direct for England, while the main body should threaten and retain Argyle upon the upper river. The movement was well executed, and 1500 men passed over at a broad part of the estuary near North Berwick. They thence, after an ineffectual march upon Edinburgh, proceeded unopposed directly south to Kelso, as Argyle was kept from following them by Mar's

Mar's success in the Highlands

One detachment marches into England.

movements. They were here joined by some horse under Lord
Kenmure, and by a few English horsemen under Mr. Forster, with
whom was Lord Derwentwater. One cause at least of the insurrection
is clearly pointed out by a proclamation which was here issued, in
which the chief stress was laid upon the foreign domination imposed
upon the nation by the late Union. Some difficulty was found in
persuading the Highlanders to cross the Border, and the march was
directed therefore in a more westerly direction, following along the
back of the Cheviots, and crossing into England near Longtown in
the direction of Carlisle. Even in spite of this concession to their
feelings, several hundreds of the Highlanders deserted, and the rest
had to be tempted forward by a promise of pay. From Carlisle they
marched up the valley of the Eden to Penrith, crossed the hills to
Lancaster, where they were well received by the many Catholic
families in the neighbourhood, and, foolishly leaving this strong place
behind them, pushed on for Preston on the Ribble. Since entering
England, the command-in-chief had devolved on Mr. Forster, and the
insurgents knew that they were being followed by General Carpenter
with between 2,000 and 3,000 men. Forster—a very inefficient
commander—directed his attention only to the pursuing army, and
discipline was much relaxed. On the 11th of November, General
Wills was marching upon Preston northward from Wigan. To reach
Preston he had to cross the Ribble by a bridge, and then pass upward
along a lane which is described by Cromwell, in 1648, as "very deep
and ill," and which it had cost him four hours to clear. Wills met
no opposition till he reached the town, where a gallant defence was
made behind barricades. The neglect of all proper
precautions is somewhat explained by the fact that
Mr. Forster was unable to attend a council of war held
that morning, having been compelled to take to his bed on account
of "some damage" which he had received "at a convivial entertainment." On the 13th, however, Carpenter joined Wills, the town was
completely surrounded, and the insurgents saw the necessity of a surrender. Much dispute has arisen about the terms of that surrender. It seems probable that Wills used ambiguous language,
understood by the insurgents to contain a promise of clemency—by
himself, as insisting upon an unconditional surrender. Colonel
Oxburgh, Mr. Forster's negotiator, declared upon the scaffold that
the words used were : "You cannot better entitle yourselves to that
clemency than by surrendering yourselves prisoners at discretion."
1500 rebels gave themselves up, among them eight noblemen. As

*and is defeated
at Preston.
Nov. 13.*

however a considerable number of English Catholics had joined the Scotch since entering Lancashire, a good many of the rebels must have made good their escape.

On the same 13th of November on which Generals Carpenter and Wills had joined their forces the insurgent operations in the North had also come to a disastrous conclusion. Mar had moved slowly south and west along the great valley of Strathmore, which leads direct from Perth to Stirling. He was approaching Dunblane when he heard that Argyle with 4000 regular troops was already occupying it. On a neighbouring eminence called Sheriffmuir, a spur of the Ochil hills, the armies encountered. The royalist left wing was unable to withstand the rush of the clansmen, and immediately withdrew towards Stirling. The insurgents had held that their own left wing was secured by some marshy ground, but **Mar is defeated at Sheriffmuir.** Argyle perceived that a light night-frost had rendered the morass passable. He fell with his cavalry upon the left flank of the Highlanders, and drove them from the field. The battle was thus equally balanced, the peculiar curve of the ground rendered any general view of the action impossible, and Mar, on his return from the pursuit of the right wing, finding his own left destroyed, determined to retreat, leaving to Argyle the full advantages of the victory.

The battle of Preston had proved the impossibility of relying upon any formidable insurrection in England. As the royalist troops were collected and armies strengthened, the chances of success **The Pretender appears, but flies before Argyle.** became less every day. Mar remained quiet at Perth, and Argyle and the English saw that delay was wholly in their favour. But in January a new colour was given to the affair by the arrival of the Pretender at Peterhead. He at once assumed the style of royalty, issuing proclamations and appointing a day for his coronation. The English ministry could not believe that so bold a step would have been taken without promised support from France. Immediate action became therefore necessary, and through villages burnt by the Pretender's order, and deep snow which Mar believed impassable, Argyle moved northwards, gradually threatening Perth. From the first James had shown but little military spirit, and now, although the clansmen offered to fight for him to the last, on the 30th of January (1716) the army was withdrawn from Perth across the frozen Tay, and marched along the coast to Montrose, whence James and Mar withdrew secretly to France, deserting their followers, who, still retiring northward, were wholly broken up as an army when Argyle reached Aberdeen on the 8th of February. Like every man that ever bore the name of Stuart, with fair abilities, James was selfish and self-seeking to the last degree. Faithless to his friends, a slave to his sensual passions, he was respectable only in a certain gift of personal bravery, in a sort of grandeur of obstinacy, and in the tenacity with which he clung to his religious creed and his hereditary rights.

As is always the case on the defeat of a domestic treason, strong pressure was brought to bear upon the ministers to induce them to act leniently towards the prisoners. The seven noble prisoners—Derwentwater, Kenmure, Nithsdale, Wintoun, Widdrington, Carnwath and Nairn—were impeached by the House of Commons, all but Lord Wintoun pleaded guilty, and sentence was pronounced. Then every means was brought to bear upon the King —private petitions from the wives of the accused noblemen, supported by the influence of all the ladies of the Court; petitions of ladies to Parliament, and lastly, an address from the majority of the Lords, urging him to reprieve if possible. These efforts were so far successful that all were reprieved with the exception of Derwentwater, Kenmure, and Nithsdale. The two first were executed, the escape of the last was contrived by the skill of his wife, who conveyed a woman's dress to her husband, in which he passed safely out of his prison, personating a lady friend who had accompanied the Countess on her visit, and who remained in his place. Three other important prisoners, Mackintosh, Forster, and Lord Wintoun also made good their escape, which seems to indicate either a strong sympathy on the part of the gaolers, or perhaps a wish on the part of the Government to avoid the necessity of more executions. Of the lesser prisoners, many of the common men were executed or transported; officers who had been in the King's service were summarily shot; but a very large proportion of those captured in Scotland being brought for judgment to Carlisle, in contravention, it was asserted, of the terms of the Union, were punished lightly or released, for fear of exciting fresh national quarrels.

It must not be supposed, however, that the excitement on the part of the Jacobites, or the fear on the part of the Hanoverians, was by any means allayed, and as by the existing Statute of 6 William and Mary, Parliament would be dissolved at the close of the year, and a new election held in the spring of 1717, there seemed great probability of a renewal of the contest, or at least of very serious riots during the election time. With this in view, the ministers proposed that the existing Parlia-

Punishment of the rebels (margin note)

The Septennial Act. April 26, 1716. (margin note)

ment should be continued for a term of seven instead of three years. This, which was meant for a temporary measure, has never been repealed, and is still the law under which Parliaments are held. It has been often objected to this action of Parliament, that it was acting arbitrarily in thus increasing its own duration. " It was a direct usurpation," it has been said, " of the rights of the people, analogous to the act of the Long Parliament in declaring itself indestructible." It has been regarded rather as a party measure than as a forward step in liberal government. We must seek its vindication in the peculiar conditions of the time. It was useless to look to the constituencies for the support of the popular liberty. The return of members in the smaller boroughs was in the hands of corrupt or corruptible freemen ; in the counties, of great landowners ; in the larger towns, of small place-holders under Government. A general election in fact only gave fresh occasion for the exercise of the influence of the Crown and of the House of Lords—freedom and independence in the presence of these two permanent powers could be secured only by the greater permanence of the third element of the Legislature, the House of Commons. It was thus that, though no doubt in some degree a party measure for securing a more lengthened tenure of office to the Whigs, the Septennial Act received, upon good constitutional grounds, the support and approbation of the best statesmen of the time. It was upon these grounds that Lord Somers declared that the measure would be the greatest possible support to the liberty of the country, and Speaker Onslow, with a clear view of the tendency of the Act, believed that it would emancipate the House of Commons from its former dependence on the Crown and the House of Lords. It was however probably the more far-sighted only who saw the advantages to which the Septennial Act would lead. It was meant for a temporary Act, and the reasons for its necessity, as set forth in the preamble, are the expenses of frequent elections, the constant renewal of party animosities, and the probability, " at this juncture, when a restless and Popish faction are designing and endeavouring to renew" the rebellion within and invasion without, of an election being likely to prove destructive to the peace and security of the Government. At the same time it is plain that men's eyes were being opened to the threatened loss of independence of the Lower House, for a private Bill was introduced, and subsequently carried through in a modified form by Government, to forbid the holders of pensions withdrawable at will from sitting in the House.

No sooner was the great question which had held the Whig party

together settled by the suppression of the insurrection, than certain
elements of disunion which already existed in the Cabinet
began to make themselves felt, and a train of circumstances began, which ended in the disruption of the
ministry. The tumult of pardon and execution had scarcely subsided,
when the King, to the great dislike of his ministers, giving way to
those natural inclinations which were for many years to be the chief
weakness of our Hanoverian Princes, insisted upon the repeal of the
clause of the Act of Settlement which restrained the King from leaving
England, and hurried to his hereditary dominions. Stanhope accompanied him as representative of the English ministry,
Townshend being left at home. This separation of the
ministry of itself afforded room for intrigue, and the
state of affairs both at home and abroad supplied a more than usually
appropriate occasion for it; for the hereditary family quarrel had
already broken out between George and his eldest son. It was impossible, however, to ignore his claims to the regency during his
father's absence, nor would Townshend permit them to be overlooked. The King was with difficulty persuaded to put the Government in his hands, with the inferior title of Guardian of the Realm
and Lieutenant, and under considerable restrictions. The minister
in England was thus at once put, in some sort, in opposition to the
King, and in a position which gave great opening for the intrigues
of his enemies who surrounded the King; for a clique, consisting
of the King's Hanoverian courtiers, Bernsdorf, Bothmar, George's
private Secretary Robethon, and Madame de Schulenberg, Duchess
of Kendal, the royal mistress, were full of animosity to the minister.
Like the Scotch followers of James I., they regarded England as a
sort of promised land, and took umbrage at the attempts of the
English ministry to check their rapacity. The mistrust thus engendered was rapidly increased by subsequent events, chiefly connected
with the affairs of the Continent.

As the King entered Hanover with Stanhope, the minister was
met by the Abbé Dubois, an agent of the Regent Orleans,
and negotiations began for the establishment of friendly
relations with France, which mark an entire change in the politics
of Europe. To complete the security of the new succession, it was
regarded as necessary that the Pretender should be removed beyond
the Alps, and that all hope of assistance to his cause from France
should cease. Open hostilities to gain this end seemed out of the
question. Austria was much irritated by the Barrier Treaty, by

First signs of the breaking up of the Cabinet

George and Stanhope go to Hanover.

Negotiations with France.

which the Dutch were secured a line of fortresses in the Austrian Netherlands, garrisoned by the Dutch, but paid by Austria. The Emperor, too, was naturally jealous of the increasing power of the Princes of the Empire, three of whom had acquired kingdoms; the Elector of Saxony was King of Poland, the Elector of Brandenburg King of Prussia, the Elector of Hanover King of England. The temper of Austria thus forbade all hope of re-establishing the Grand Alliance. The withdrawal of support from the Pretender had to be sought by peaceful means; and the Regent, intent on his personal aims, was willing to surrender the cause of the Stuarts, and to destroy the works at Mardyke as the price of peace with England. On these terms negotiations for a treaty, in which Holland was to share, were begun.

The German objects of the King rendered its speedy conclusion an object of the first importance. After his defeat at Pultowa, Charles XII. had withdrawn to Bender, where he had vainly attempted to rouse the Turks to assist him against the Russians. In his absence, Russia, Poland, and Denmark, the countries which in turn he had conquered, combined against his deserted country; and the King of Prussia, for his own ends no doubt, but with some appearance of keeping the balance between the parties, succeeded in neutralizing Pomerania, and in obtaining the sequestration into his own hands of the strong town of Stettin. This arrangement by no means pleased Charles, who hastened home from Bender, hoping by an alliance with England to keep his enemies at bay. The accession of the house of Hanover destroyed this hope. The Elector of Hanover had obtained from Denmark Bremen and Verden, part of the spoils of Charles, and was pledged by his own interests to oppose him. He insisted upon an English fleet being sent to the Baltic, though the question was obviously one of German interest only. Not content with opposing Sweden, George eagerly desired that the fleet should be used against Russia, for that country had invaded Mecklenburg, and intended apparently to appropriate it. Again it was evident that the question was chiefly of German interest. Townshend placed the English view of the affair before the King—it did not matter much who possessed Mecklenburg, but to attack Russia, the chief opponent of Sweden, was to leave Charles XII. free for dangerous designs in favour of the Stuarts, in which he was now almost openly engaged. Fortunately diplomacy induced the Czar to withdraw, and the question was thus solved.

But while eager for war with Sweden and Russia, George was

Danger of Hanover from Charles XII.

naturally anxious for the conclusion of the peace with France, and thought himself purposely thwarted by his minister, when the peculiarities of the Dutch constitution threw delays in the way of its completion, and Townshend refused to break faith and conclude the treaty without the accession of the Dutch. The King's dislike for

Dismissal of Townshend
Townshend, excited by his opposition to his German plans, was sedulously fomented both by his Hanoverian courtiers and by the Earl of Sunderland, who, thoroughly discontented with his subordinate position in the ministry as Lord Lieutenant of Ireland, had joined the King at Hanover, and had entered busily into the intrigues going on there. A letter from Townshend, in which, in order to allow the longer absence of the King, he recommended that additional powers should be given to the Prince in England, brought matters to a crisis. Townshend was dismissed from his office, and offered in exchange the viceroyalty of Ireland. For the sake of the party, and upon some sort of apology from the King, Townshend accepted his new office, and the quarrel was temporarily healed.

During this brief reconciliation, the negotiations which had been carried on at the Hague and Hanover were completed, and a Triple

The Triple Alliance. Jan. 1717.
Alliance was signed in January 1717, by which the clauses in the Treaty of Utrecht having reference to the Protestant succession in England, to the French succession, and to the renunciation of the Spanish King to his claims or the French throne, were guaranteed.

But Walpole and the other friends of Townshend took an early

Changes in the ministry. April.
opportunity of showing their discontent at the treatment of their leader, and it became necessary to dismiss them. The direction of the Government thus fell into the hands of Stanhope, as Chancellor of the Exchequer. Sunderland and Addison became Secretaries of State, and James Craggs Secretary at War. The occasion of the final schism was a demand for a supply to oppose the intrigues of the King of Sweden. The lukewarmness of Walpole's support was so marked that his friends and those of Townshend voted against Government, and the supplies were carried by a majority of four only. The fraction of the Whigs who thus left office at once passed into vigorous opposition; yet the crisis was one which should have overpowered party feeling.

The state of Europe was such as to threaten difficulty, even danger,

Danger to England from Charles XII. and Alberoni.
to England. Two statesmen of unusual ability were at work in Europe; to both of them the fall of the new Government in England was an object, and when their

intrigues for a moment brought them together, there was a brief interval of real danger. These were Charles XII. of Sweden, and Alberoni, the Prime Minister of Spain.

Charles had found himself thwarted in his schemes for re-establishing his power by the opposition of the English King. The same opposition had checked the Czar in his ambitious schemes on Mecklenburg. In union with his minister, Görtz, an adventurer who had passed into his service from that of the Prince of Gotthorp, Charles determined on a new combination of the North to suit the altered politics of Europe. He allied himself with his old enemy the Czar, and despatched Görtz to Holland, to see what he could do in France and England. In each of those countries he found it possible to enter into communication with a large dis-contented minority. In France, the Duke of Maine, irritated at the loss of the position which the late King's will would have given him, had put himself at the head of the older and graver statesmen, who clung to the old policy of enmity with England. In England, the Jacobites were still looking out for foreign support. To both countries Görtz sent an agent,—while Spaar was, if possible, to pro-duce a change of government in France, Gyllenborg was instructed in England to promise the Tories the assistance of 12,000 men under the personal command of the King of Sweden. In seeking assistance for his plans, Görtz had come across another intrigue tending in the same direction. He found in Alberoni a man whose views were for the time identical with his own, and Spanish money found its way largely both to the Pretender and to the Swedish agents. Fortun-ately the English Government obtained information of what was going on. Justly holding that his ambassadorial rights were for-feited by his treason, they apprehended Gyllenborg and seized his papers, and persuaded Holland to act in the same manner with regard to Görtz. The papers thus seized afforded full justification for what they had done. But though thwarted in this scheme, both Charles and the Czar continued to act in unison with Spain against the interests of England. It was to meet this plot that the supply was demanded which caused the final schism in the English ministry. The death of Charles in September 1718, at the siege of Friedrichs-halle, whither he had gone in his haste to secure Norway, the pos-session of which was a part of his bargain with Russia, prevented the Northern branch of the intrigue from bearing fruits, and a revolution in Sweden, which changed it into little more than an oligarchical re-public, removed it for more than sixty years from the scene of history

<small>Charles XII</small>

Alberoni's plots were of more importance. He was one of those statesmen who owe their rise to the democratic character of the Roman Church. The son of a market gardener, of a singularly undignified exterior, he had found means to make himself indis-

Alberoni.

pensable to the Duke of Vendome during the war of the Spanish succession, and had subsequently established his position in Spain by bringing about the marriage of Philip with Elizabeth of Parma. His object was entirely patriotic; he desired to replace Spain in the list of great European nations. For this purpose he set to work with remarkable success to revive the industry and wealth of the country. But his views reached further than this; he aimed at the destruction of the Treaty of Utrecht. By that treaty Austria had gained almost all that Spain had lost. It was therefore against Austria that his designs were chiefly directed. Knowing of the irritation which existed between Austria and England with regard to the Barrier Treaty, and believing that France would be unwilling to do anything to the disadvantage of a Bourbon kingdom of its own creation, he supposed that Austria would be without allies. To secure friendship with England, he even granted her great commercial advantages. The defensive alliance between England and Austria, in 1716, was the first blow to his plan. The subsequent conclusion, in 1717, of the Triple Alliance opened his eyes to the probable policy of France. It was then that he threw himself into the intrigues of the Jacobites and the party of the Duke of Maine, and put himself into communication with Charles of Sweden. Alberoni's chief object was to destroy the Austrian power in Italy. Conscious that Spain had gained in strength by the loss of her widespread foreign dependencies, he had no intention of conquering that country. But he wished to restrict the Austrian power there, firstly, by the establishment of younger branches of the Spanish house in Sicily (at the instant belonging by the Treaty of Utrecht to Victor Amadeus of Savoy), and in the duchies of Parma and Tuscany, where the reigning houses were drawing towards extinction, and to which Elizabeth Farnese had claims; and, secondly, by the increase of the territory of Savoy, which he designed to compensate for the loss of Sicily by the cession of a portion of Lombardy. The possession of Sicily was therefore of the first importance to him. But Austria had already been negotiating with the powers of the Triple Alliance for the exchange of that island for Sardinia. Alberoni himself desired to wait till Spain had acquired more power at home, but the apprehension by the Austrians of a newly appointed Spanish inquisitor roused the anger of Philip V., and, against his will, Alberoni was hurried into war. To prevent the exchange of Sicily he at once took possession of Sardinia, and would probably have proceeded to attack Sicily, when the Powers of the Triple Alliance intervened.

Their offer of mediation involved the renunciation on the part of Austria of all claims on the Spanish monarchy, which had never hitherto been dropped,—on the part of Spain of all claims on the Italian provinces. The exchange of *Opposition of the Triple Alliance* Sicily for Sardinia was to be carried out, and Parma and Tuscany to be given to Don Carlos. Enraged at this offer, the work of men, as he said, " who cut and pared countries as they would Dutch cheeses," Alberoni at once set to work all the apparatus his intrigue had prepared. The anger of Savoy was aroused at the loss of Sicily; the Turks, already at war with Austria, were subsidized and urged to further exertions; Ragotski, Prince of Transylvania, was brought forward to demand his hereditary dominions, to hamper Austria on the east; the Spanish envoy in France busily stirred up faction there; Charles XII. and the Czar were urged to immediate action; and an expedition against England, headed by Ormond or the Pretender himself, was set on foot. The whole of Europe seemed involved. The mediating Powers found themselves likely to be drawn into war. Stanhope was removed from his position as First Lord of the Treasury, and made Secretary of State for the Southern Department, which included foreign affairs, and on June 4, 1718, Admiral Byng set sail from England for the Mediterranean.

The crisis was so threatening that the Austrian Emperor, who had refused to accede to the mediation of the Powers, yielded. England procured for him the Treaty of Passowitz, which secured him from the Turks, bought off at the *Formation of the Quadruple Alliance. August 1718.* expense of the Venetians, from whom they had conquered the Morea; and a Quadruple Alliance between England, France, Austria, and Holland was formed on the basis of the old project of mediation, with this difference, that Parma and Tuscany were to be held by Don Carlos only as fiefs of the Empire. Without open declaration of war, France and England had virtually joined the Austrian alliance. Alberoni, however, persisted in his schemes, but fortune had turned against him. The Spanish fleet, not knowing whether it was peace or war, was fallen upon and destroyed by Byng off Cape Passaro; Savoy, yielding to the pressure of the Quadruple Alliance, accepted Sardinia in exchange for Sicily; the death of Charles XII. broke up the Northern Alliance; the conspiracy in France was discovered when approaching maturity, the Spanish ambassador and the Duke and Duchess of Maine apprehended; of the Pretender's expedition, scattered in the Bay of Biscay, two frigates only reached Loch Alsh in Scotland. A few hundreds of the Highlanders gathered to their standard, but the appearance of English troops put them to flight; the chiefs escaped to Spain, the Highlanders were allowed to fly

Fall of
Alberoni.
Dec. 1719.

unmolested to their hills, the Spanish troops were taken prisoners of war. War having now been regularly declared, the French crossed the Pyrenees, and again and again defeated the Spanish troops; and at length Philip was compelled to dismiss his great minister, and on the 19th of January 1720 acceded to the terms of the Quadruple Alliance.

The affairs in the North of Europe were settled in a similar high-handed fashion. There too a nation, struggling to regain its old preponderance, had to be crushed. The death of Charles XII., and the revolution which followed it, put an end to any chance of Sweden's regaining its position in Europe. The new Government fell back upon the old policy of the country; Bremen and Verden were allowed to remain in the hands of George, and an alliance with England and France was entered into. As a necessary consequence the late allies of Sweden again became its enemies. But the friendship of France and England drove them to peace. Orders were even issued to the English Admiral of the Baltic to fall upon the fleet of the Czar without declaration of war, unless with Denmark, his ally, he consented to a cessation of hostilities. Too weak to resist, Denmark accepted a sum of money and retired from the contest; and the Czar,

European peace
1720.

now standing alone, withdrew, though still in arms, to await a better opportunity for action. The foreign policy of Stanhope had thus been successful, and though unjust and domineering, secured for Europe a peace of twelve years.

Meanwhile the minister had carried out with consistency the

Stanhope's
home policy

politics of his party at home. In acting thus he was met with considerable difficulties. On the one hand he had to manage and repress the meddlesome and rapacious German coterie which surrounded the King, on the other he was met by a strong opposition headed by that party of the Whigs which had left office with Townshend.

In all the chief measures of his administration he found an eager

Opposition of
Walpole

and at times a successful antagonist in Walpole. It was chiefly through his instrumentality that the impeachment of Oxford came to an untimely end. The Lords were persuaded

to refuse to listen to any evidence in support of the charge of misdemeanour before they had heard that on the graver charge Trial of Oxford. June 1717.
of treason. They knew that it was impossible for the
Commons to support the more important charge. A quarrel between
the Houses ended in the refusal of the Lower House to proceed to
the impeachment. The Lords gravely assembled on the appointed
day in Westminster Hall, sat there for a quarter of an hour, and
then, as no accusers appeared, declared the impeachment at an end.
Again, Walpole, regardless of party ties, vehemently upheld the
charges of peculation brought against Lord Cadogan by the Jacobites
in the House headed by Shippen. And again, with great inconsistency,
he opposed the repeal of the Schism Act. The Act for Repeal of the Schism Act. Jan 1719.
restraining Occasional Conformity passed in the last
reign, and the Schism Act of 1714, by which it had been
followed, pressed very heavily on the Dissenters; and Stanhope, whose
views appear in some respects to have been more liberal than those
in vogue at the time, went so far in his wish to relieve them as even
to dream of mitigating the severity of the Test and Corporation Acts.
However, wisely yielding to the advice of Sunderland, he confined
himself to an attempt to get the Schism Act repealed, and succeeded,
after much opposition, in both Houses; but his narrow majorities
show that a more extensive measure would have been useless. The
Test Act continued in force, though rendered practically nugatory
after the beginning of George II.'s reign by a Bill of Indemnity
passed almost every year in favour of those who had evaded it.

On the two last named occasions Walpole's opposition had been
useless. On the more important question of the The Peerage Bill rejected Dec 1719
limitation of the power of the Crown to create Peers
by the Peerage Bill, he fortunately proved too strong
for the minister. Like the Septennial Act, the Peerage Bill was
introduced partly on theoretical, partly on party grounds. The
Revolution had been an aristocratic rather than a popular movement.
The power or rather the influence of the Crown had not been destroyed,
but was in abeyance, the Hanoverian monarchs being as it were in
a state of tutelage to the Whig party, whose strength was in the
Upper House. Popular in language, but aristocratic in feeling, this
party regarded political liberty as best secured by its own predominance, rendered permanent by such institutions as a Septennial
Parliament and an exclusive hereditary nobility. It feared alike the
power of the King and the power of the people, and already the
adoption of the Treaty of Utrecht, carried by the popular will and

by a large creation of Peers, had shown the possibility of a union between King and people which might sooner or later destroy its influence. To guard against such a danger was the primary object for which Stanhope introduced his Peerage Bill. But temporary party interests had as much weight with him as general theory. Stanhope and his friends, especially Sunderland, were in dread of the conduct which might be pursued by the Prince of Wales when he came to the throne. He was on bad terms with his father, and regarded Sunderland as the chief cause of the royal jealousy. It was generally believed that his accession would be followed by a creation of peers from among his own favourites. Thus both on public and party grounds the ministry thought it desirable to limit the royal prerogative. As was natural, the Tories, in their dislike to restrictions on the royal prerogative, and the party of Walpole, who opposed it because it was a Government measure, made common cause against the Bill. By its enactments the Crown was to be restrained from the creation of more than six beyond the existing number of 178 English peerages (the power of creating a new peerage whenever an old one became extinct being reserved), no new peerage was to be created with remainders except to the original recipient and his heirs male; while, to place the Peerage of Scotland on the same footing, the sixteen representative Peers of that country were to give way to twenty-five hereditary Peers nominated by the Crown. The Bill met with little opposition in the House of Lords, but was thrown out by a large majority in the Lower House, where Walpole pointed out "that one of the most powerful incentives to virtue would be taken away, since there would be no arriving at honour but through the winding-sheet of a decrepit lord, or the grave of an extinct noble family."

At the present time a defeat on so important a measure must
Strength of have driven the ministry from office. But the theory
the ministry. of party government was as yet so little perfected, that not only did Stanhope retain his place, but his administration was so strong, that the Whig malcontents thought it better to renew their old connection with it, and both Walpole and Townshend re-entered the Government, the one as Paymaster of the Forces, the other as Lord President. It seemed as if nothing short of some great convulsion could shake so powerful a Government, and, though little apprehended, such a convulsion was near at hand.

It was still early in the history of finance. It was only of late years that the moneyed interest had become so important in the country as to admit of the discharge of the public liabilities by means of large and regular loans. But when once the prac- <small>The South Sea Scheme</small> tice had been begun it had been largely adopted, and during the wars of the reign of Queen Anne the debt had risen from sixteen to fifty-two millions. Ignorant of the resources of the country and of the ease with which such a debt might be supported, the financiers of the day were in constant terror of its rapid increase. A member of the House, a certain Mr. Broderick, was expressing the general feeling when he said, " I agree with the ministers, that until the National Debt is discharged, or in a fair way of being so, we cannot properly call ourselves a nation." But besides the general dread of the amount of the debt, there was a very well-grounded dislike to the high terms on which much of it had been contracted. The money having been borrowed in time of war and difficulty, the terms offered to the lender had been proportionately favourable. A settled Government, the success of the Hanoverian succession, and the continued and rapid increase of wealth which had followed it, had rendered money much cheaper, and Government was paying seven or eight per cent. upon its loans, when private individuals could borrow on good security at four per cent. But the manner in which much of the money had been raised forbad any effort at changing the rate of interest. The loans had been largely contracted in the form of annuities, many of them for ninety-nine years; and of these a considerable portion were irredeemable, that is to say, Government was pledged to the payment of the interest as originally arranged, unless some change could be made with the consent of the creditors.

Financiers had therefore two objects in view,—to lessen the whole amount of debt, and to lower the interest payable on what remained. The establishment of the Bank of England had shown the value, in a mercantile point of view, of the Government credit. It became an understood principle that money lent to Government, and thus secured upon the credit of Government, was an excellent form of capital; and when advances were required, or when it became convenient to substitute a single great creditor for a number of little ones, this principle had been brought into use. Two such attempts had been made, the one by Harley in 1711, the other by Walpole in 1717. Harley, when Lord Treasurer, had found a floating debt (a debt, that is, payable on demand of the creditor) of ten millions, and had got rid of the danger of immediate demand by forming a company of the creditors of this floating debt. The ten millions were

<small>CON. MON.</small>   [K]

founded, that is, the interest and not the capital was paid ; the interest was secured upon the customs, and the fund of ten millions became the capital of the company of creditors, who were incorporated as the Company of Merchants of Great Britain trading to the South Seas, and to whom subsequently the mercantile advantages granted to England at Utrecht were given. These came to but little,—the Assiento, or supply of slaves, and the admission of a yearly ship of 500 tons burden to the American colonies. Even this advantage was lost in the difficulties which arose with Alberoni. The first ship did not sail till 1717, and as far as the South Sea trade went Harley's plan was a failure. But the credit gained by the Company in the transaction was good, other lines of trade were opened up, and the Company became great, flourishing and powerful.

Formation of the South Sea Company. 1711.

In 1717 Walpole had been very desirous to diminish the National Debt. He established the first sinking fund, borrowing £600,000 at only four per cent., using this money to pay off liabilities bearing a higher interest, and applying the money thus saved to the extinction of the debt. He also, taking advantage of the value of Government credit, induced both the Bank and the South Sea Company to accept a lower rate of interest for the money they had already advanced, and to advance between them nearly £5,000,000 more, for the purpose of paying off as far as possible those holders of redeemable debts who refused to accept the lowered rate of interest. The great South Sea Scheme of 1720 was in principle nothing but a repetition of this manœuvre. The South Sea Company, believing devoutly in the power of credit, was anxious to extend itself as far as possible. The Government was so eager for the reduction of the debt that the King had made special mention of it in the speech with which he opened Parliament in the close of 1719. Under these circumstances the proposition of Blunt, director of the South Sea Company, found a ready hearing with the ministers. Between them an arrangement was devised, perfectly justifiable and harmless as far as the principle of it went. The bulk of the Government debt consisted in redeemable and irredeemable annuities, on all of which large interest was paid, and on which that interest must continue to be paid unless the holder of the annuity voluntarily reduced it. There is said to have been about sixteen millions of each class of security. Government wished to bring the whole mass into one general fund, bearing a lower rate of interest, and the South Sea Company was so greedy of the Government credit, that it expressed itself anxious to add the whole of this enormous amount to its

The South Sea Scheme. 1720.

capital. It is plain that any transaction of the sort, as far as regarded the irredeemable annuities, must have been entirely voluntary. All that the Government could do was to allow the Company to persuade the holders to exchange their annuities for shares in the Company. With regard to the holders of redeemable annuities, payment in full must be offered, but that payment might be given in shares of the Company. In other words, those who accepted the exchange became proprietors in the Joint-stock South Sea Company to the amount of their claim on the Government. With regard to the Government, the South Sea Company alone became creditor, instead of a multitude of old annuitants, and was contented to receive henceforward, instead of the seven or eight per cent. the annuitants had received, five per cent. till the year 1727, and after that four per cent. till the capital as well as the interest should be returned, for the fund was made a redeemable one. If the transaction were thoroughly successful the capital of the South Sea Company would be increased by about thirty-two millions, advanced to Government at five per cent., and Government would have to pay five per cent. interest instead of seven or eight, besides having the power of redeeming the capital.

So great were the advantages understood to be gained by this accession of capital in Government hands, that other companies wished to share in them. It was voted by a large majority that these advantages should be put up to public competition. The Bank of England and the South Sea Company set to work outbidding each other, the latter finally proposing terms which were virtually a payment to Government of seven millions and a half. This money was to be devoted to the public service, to pay off public debts redeemable before the year 1723, and after that as much as possible of the capital of the South Sea Company itself. It is plain that for the success of this scheme two things were requisite. In the first place, a readiness on the part of the public to accept the Company's shares in exchange for their Government annuities; without that Government would not be freed, nor would the Company get its increased capital. But this exchange would of course bring in no ready money. Secondly, therefore, a large number of new shareholders would be required to subscribe, paying for their shares in ready money, in order to meet the demands of those holders of redeemable annuities who refused all exchange, and to cover the heavy premium of £7,000,000. Now both of these objects were dependent on the popularity of the Company's shares; and it was in this that the mistake of the arrangement lay ; Govern-

Competition of other companies.

ment had in fact made too good a bargain. By an extensive system of bribes large sums of fictitious capital were invented and distributed gratis among influential members of the Government, and still more largely among the hungry Hanoverian courtiers, whose influence it was regarded as all important to secure. All fear of the success of the scheme was almost immediately removed. So great was the belief in the vast Company, backed up by this huge accession of Government credit, so well had the directors done their business, that a very large majority of the annuitants pressed with extreme haste to accept the terms offered, though those terms were very low. The public were then invited to subscribe the new capital. Five separate subscriptions of upwards of a million were in succession opened, and all filled, with equal rapidity.

It was however in its secondary effects, rather than in its immediate consequences, that the scheme exerted the most extraordinary influence. There was a great deal of money in the country, and there was no satisfactory way of using it. Much had been hoarded, for there were not then as now numerous industrial investments in the market in which small sums could be employed. The apparent success of the South Sea Company, and the promises which it held out for rapid fortune-making, excited the spirit of speculation to the highest degree, and companies sprang into existence with unexampled rapidity. Some were real and serious—waterworks, paving companies, and companies for the improvement of all branches of manufacture. Some were mere transparent impostures—as a company for the importation of Spanish donkeys, for the fixing of quicksilver, or for wheels of perpetual motion. It did not matter much what they were, for the rage for stock-jobbing was such that any hardy promoter of a company might hope to float it at all events till he had himself realized a handsome fortune. Change Alley became a scene of the wildest excitement—people in all lines of life hurrying to buy and sell as during the railway mania of our own time. But among all the companies the South Sea Company maintained its pre-eminence, and its shares rose, till in August the £100 share was worth £1000. The Company continued to promise largely, even fifty per cent. profits. The absurdity and danger of such reckless proceedings began to become obvious. The nominal value of all the shares in all the companies then existing was held to be £500,000,000, or twice the value of all the land in England. But many of these companies, being unchartered, were illegal, and had no right to issue shares,

The rage for stock-jobbing.

and the legitimate companies, especially the South Sea, looked with
jealousy at their illegal competitors. Apparently unconscious how
much their own success depended upon the universal delusion, they
proceeded to prosecute some companies which had acted   Bursting of
illegally. The effect was instantaneous. The nation   the bubble.
began to return to its senses ; the bubble burst, and the stocks of
all unchartered companies fell with extreme rapidity. In the
universal ruin they carried with them the South Sea Company.
The panic was as rapid as the eagerness to purchase had been.
Before the end of September South Sea stock was at 175. The
difference between that sum and the £1,000 which they had touched
will give some measure of the loss involved. The ruin among all
classes was unspeakable.

So great was the desolation that it was found necessary for
Parliament to intervene. Not that the great Company itself was in
any way bankrupt, its shares were still at a large premium, they
never fell below 175 ; not that any law of political economy had
been broken ; Government had never pledged itself to support the
credit of the Company, or to force either its shares or its engagements
on the public ; but simply because private speculation   Punishment of
had caused so vast an amount of misery, and because   the directors
the nation was exasperated at it, interference became absolutely
necessary. Examination into all the details of the plan no doubt
proved a considerable amount of venality on the part of the ministry,
of bribery and fraud on the part of the directors. But even thus it
was freely acknowledged that under no old law had any crime been
committed, and it required a retrospective Act of Parliament and
the creation of a temporary crime to bring the directors within the
reach of punishment. As Gibbon said, the steps taken were in
fact an act of popular vengeance and contrary to justice. The private
property of the directors was confiscated and added to the unallotted
stock to form a fund for the relief of the sufferers ; debts due to the
Company for stock purchased at exorbitant prices but not paid for
were remitted on payment of ten per cent. ; the remaining capital
was divided among the new proprietors. As a set off, the Company
was relieved of £7,000,000 due by it to the Government.

These measures are due exclusively to Walpole, the one man
specially fitted from his financial abilities to deal with the   Supremacy
present crisis, and in whose favour it was remembered   of Walpole
that he had been out of office when the plan was set on   1721.
foot. The official inquiries into the circumstances of the South Sea

Scheme left him indeed in a position of undisputed supremacy in the House. Several members of the Government were implicated in the frauds of the Company; Aislabie, the Chancellor of the Exchequer, was found guilty and expelled the House. The younger Craggs died of smallpox before the inquiry was completed, and his father committed suicide. Charles Stanhope was acquitted by a majority of three only, and although Sunderland was declared innocent by a large majority, public opinion was so strong against him that he had to leave the ministry. In the following year he died. During the angry debates which arose on these matters Lord Stanhope had been attacked with virulence by the Duke of Wharton, and the anger which he had felt had been such as to cause a rush of blood to the head, of which he died shortly before his relative Charles Stanhope was acquitted. There remained no possible rival to Walpole, who with his brother-in-law Townshend returned to power as First Lord of the Treasury. Thus, when the new Parliament assembled, he found himself absolute master of the field, at the head of an unbroken Whig party, supported by an overwhelming majority, and for twenty years maintained his position, to the immense advantage of England and to the lasting security of the reigning house.

Not that the Jacobites were as yet extinct, but they were silenced **Revival of Jacobite hopes.** in Parliament, and had to rely upon conspiracy or foreign assistance. Their hopes in fact were at this moment in some respects higher than ever, for the disturbance and discontent caused by the collapse of the South Sea Scheme, together with the birth of an heir to the House of Stuart in the person of Prince Charles Edward, seemed to afford them an opportunity for greater activity. The Stuart papers prove the existence of a well-organized intrigue, under the management of a Committee of five, Lord Orrery, the Earl of Arran Lord Ormond's brother, Lord North, Lord Gower, and Atterbury Bishop of Rochester. The letters display in a very curious manner the false hopes with which the party were constantly buoyed up. Atterbury indeed showed signs of considerable **Bishop Atterbury's plot.** wisdom, the reintroduction of Walpole and Townshend to the ministry seemed to him a great blow to the cause. "The reconciliation," he writes, "is not yet hearty and sincere, but I apprehend it will by degrees become so. The Tories have no good foundation on which to stand. Disaffection and uneasiness will continue everywhere, and probably increase. The bulk of the nation will be ever in the true interest and on the side of justice. The present settlement will perhaps be detested every day more and more, and yet no effectual step will or can be taken to shake it." The great South Sea Scheme also seemed to him a difficulty. "That body of men, who have increased their capital by £40,000,000, begin to look formidable. They cannot but be the governors of the kingdom." He therefore urged instant action before the Whig settlement had time to ripen or the financial plans to be brought to successful conclusion. Even a few years later the Earl of Orrery wrote, "It is not an extravagant computation that four out of five of the whole nation wish well to you." Nevertheless all these Jacobite writers were obliged to confess, even after the failure of the scheme, that the united Whigs were too powerful, and the general prudence of all classes too great, to allow of any successful movement without assistance from abroad. It is plain also that there were numerous sections and much want of discipline in the Jacobite camp. Atterbury's influence was disapproved of by many; Gower had a band of followers of his own; and James was so alive to this source of weakness that he earnestly pressed for the election of a responsible head, naming the Earl of Oxford as the fittest person for the purpose. These divisions, and the want of self-reliance in the face of the powerful Government, constantly prevented the Jacobites from obtaining success; their agents were perpetually soliciting foreign countries for help, and the chain of foreign diplomacy which Stanhope had wrought was so close, that such ill-advised requests could scarcely fail to reach the ears of the English ministry. Thus a determination to take advantage of the confusion caused by the South Sea Scheme, by the death of Stanhope, which was supposed to have broken the link with France, and by the new election for Parliament, was brought to Walpole's knowledge. The Regent had been asked to supply 5000 men, but Dubois was not likely to overthrow the diplomatic edifice he had so carefully built up. He at once informed the English minister at Paris. And at the opening of the new Parliament George was able to give a short summary of the conspiracy, involving an expedition headed by James and Ormond from Spain and Italy, the seizure of the Tower, the Bank and the Exchequer, and the declaration in London of King James; and at the same time he could state that some of the chiefs, especially the Bishop of Rochester, were already under arrest.

The superiority of the Whig party was now shown in the Bills that were passed relative to this conspiracy. The Habeas Corpus Act was suspended for a whole year, the longest time on record;

sums were granted for an increase of the army ; a tax of £100,000, to be collected from all Nonjurors, was enacted ; and as the evidence was scarcely sufficient to go before a Court of Law, Bills of Pains and Penalties were introduced against some of the subordinate agents, and against Atterbury himself, who was forced to leave the kingdom. At Calais he met Bolingbroke, who had just received his pardon and was returning to England. He had been dismissed by the Pretender after the failure of 1715, and had vowed never again to serve so ungrateful a master. None the less did he continue for the rest of his life to hamper by his intrigues the Whig party. The chief cause of his irritation was

Quarrel between Carteret and Walpole. that his overtures were rejected by Walpole, who already began to show that thirst for power and jealousy of men of great talents which was one of his marked characteristics, and which was the ultimate cause of his fall. Carteret, who with Townshend was now Secretary of State, was his first victim—a man of the most brilliant parts and of unrivalled knowledge of foreign affairs. He had succeeded to much of the influence as well as to the views of Stanhope. Abroad he was inclined to plunge England into the complications of Hanoverian policy. It was in fact natural that with his great knowledge of foreign affairs he should be led to consider them more important than other English statesmen, who then as now were inclined towards a policy of isolation. At home, too, his views were less exclusively those of a Whig partisan than those of his fellow ministers. He feared probably less than the occasion demanded the strength of the Jacobites. He looked upon the sole possession of power by the Whigs on the Hanoverian succession as a necessary but only temporary evil. He was desirous of a far larger admission of the Tory element, and would willingly have admitted Bolingbroke and those Tories who would have accompanied him among the ranks of the ministry, or at all events among the ranks of the ministerial supporters. But to Walpole such views were exceedingly distasteful. He well knew Bolingbroke's ability and feared him as a personal rival. He felt also that if Bolingbroke were instrumental in destroying the Tory opposition, the King could not but feel under considerable obligations to him, and that his own exclusive influence would be shaken. Bolingbroke's overtures were therefore most coldly received, and he withdrew again to Paris, where an intrigue was going on, in which he took a prominent part, and which ended in the fall of his friend Carteret. The intrigue itself was of a very despicable character, and was connected with the marriage of a daughter of Madame de Platen, sister of the King's mistress, the Countess of Darlington. To counteract Carteret, who was employing the English ambassador in the Countess's interest, Townshend sent Horace Walpole as his agent to Paris. The existence of two rival ambassadors, one only properly accredited, brought matters to a crisis. The King, in spite of a strong personal friendship for Carteret, was obliged to yield to the influence of Walpole, and his rival had to withdraw to the Lord Lieutenancy of Ireland.

But although the office given to Carteret was regarded as a retirement, in the present instance it promised to be no sinecure. Ireland was in a state of wild excitement, lashed to fury by the exceedingly able but untrue writings of Swift, who in Excitement in Ireland his Drapier's Letters had by exaggeration and falsehood given an aspect of tyrannical misgovernment to a commonplace and legitimate financial act. There was great need of a new small coinage for Ireland, and Walpole had given a patent in 1722 to a certain William Wood, giving him power to coin farthings and halfpence to the value of £108,000. The contract and quality had been declared satisfactory by Sir Isaac Newton, Master of the Mint. The Irish Parliament declared that the patent would occasion a loss to the nation of one hundred and fifty per cent., an extraordinary assertion based upon the fact that a pound of rough copper in Ireland was worth twelve pence, while a pound of coined fine copper was to be worth thirty pence. But the mint in London gave eighteenpence a pound for its copper. The charge of coinage was fourpence, the duties upon copper imported into Ireland were twenty per cent., and the difference of exchange between England and Ireland rendered a slight diminution of the weight reasonable. Of course, however, it is certain that the patentee made something by the bargain, especially as the voracious Duchess of Kendal had been bribed to obtain it. But all facts and all reasoning were useless against the storm raised by Swift's Letters, and it was not till Walpole had exhibited his usual prudence in accepting inevitable defeat, and cancelling the patent, that Ireland was quieted.

It was not in Ireland only that the financial measures of Walpole met with opposition. For years the tax upon malt had been with great difficulty collected in Scotland. This tax had been changed into a charge of threepence upon every Disturbances in Scotland 1725. barrel of ale. Edinburgh was in commotion, and the brewers refused to brew. Lord Isla, the Duke of Argyle's brother,

was acting as Walpole's agent in the matter. He prudently
declined to interfere, certain that love of profit would speedily break
up the combination.   A public meeting, Walpole tells us, was held,
and the question put by the chairman, "Brew or not brew?"   He
began by asking the man on his right hand.   But he and many
who followed him refused to vote, till at last one bolder than the
rest refused to be bound by the majority and voted "Brew."   The
assembly broke up in some confusion, but before morning there were
forty brewhouses hard at work in Edinburgh and ten in Leith.

The remainder of the reign offers but little of interest in domestic
history, but before Walpole could enter unchecked on that course of
peaceful policy which is the chief characteristic of his long tenure of
office, he had yet one difficulty with Spain to overcome, while at
home there was already springing up that opposition of discontented
Whigs combined with the Tory party, which, under the fostering
influence of Bolingbroke behind the scenes, and led in Parliament
by the ability of Pulteney, was ultimately successful in driving the
great minister from office. Since the adhesion of Spain
to the Quadruple Alliance and the fall of Alberoni, a
Congress had been sitting at Cambrai to arrange the
details of the final settlement of Europe. The chief points at issue
were the renunciation of the title of King of Spain, to which the
Austrian Emperor fondly clung, the Grand Mastership of the Order
of the Golden Fleece, which the Emperor also claimed, and the
restoration to their owners of certain Italian provinces of which
the Emperor had taken possession.   To gain these ends, Spain,
absolutely renouncing the policy of Alberoni, attached itself closely
to France and England, purchased the favour of the latter country
by a treaty of commerce, renewing the Assiento and the annual
ship to the Spanish colonies, and of the former by a marriage-treaty.
This marriage-treaty Orleans was induced to accept in pursuance of
his plan for keeping continual hold of the regency; all views of
ultimate succession were gradually fading from him as the young
King improved in health.   It was a threefold arrangement; the
Infanta Mary Anne, then only three years old, was to marry Louis XV.,
the two daughters of the Regent were to marry the Prince of
Asturias, heir to the Spanish crown, and Don Carlos, presumptive
heir to Parma and Tuscany.   Spain had thus done so much that she
awaited with confidence the meeting of the Congress at Cambrai.
But that Congress was very slow in its operations, and the hasty
Queen of Spain and her ambitious husband began to weary of the

*Spanish
difficulties.
1725.*

ill success of their concessions, and to think that perhaps after all matters might be brought to a more speedy termination by direct action, without mediators, at the court of Vienna. The Spanish Government was the more inclined to this step, because it had been persuaded that the Austrian court would lend no unwilling ear to direct negotiations.

This belief had been forced upon the King and Queen by a strange, adventurous, but very able foreigner, who was Intrigues of rapidly rising into somewhat the same position in Spain Ripperda. that Alberoni had held. This was the Baron Ripperda. A Dutchman by origin, a soldier by profession, he was unusually well versed in the details of business and of political economy. He had taken up all Alberoni's views as to the possible expansion of the resources of Spain, and, thinking there was more room for his ability in that country than in Holland, had had himself naturalized there. He followed the King during his temporary resignation of the Spanish throne, and returned with him on his son's death to the possession of full power. There seems little doubt that throughout Ripperda had been in the pay of the Austrian court, and it was chiefly at his instigation that the Congress at Cambrai was deserted and direct negotiations between the courts opened. He had set before the King and Queen very plausible reasons not only for a negotiation but for a change of policy, no less complete than an entire desertion of the mediating Powers and of the principle of the Quadruple Alliance, and a close friendship with the House of Austria. Spain would thus be freed from the constant encroachments of England upon her trade, and the interference of France, which had been very irksome to the Spaniards since the Bourbon accession, would be avoided. The old question of the Barrier Treaty was exciting the animosity of England and Austria; for Austria, in distinct contravention of the commercial articles of that treaty, which forbade to the Austrian Netherlands the trade of India, had established a great Ostend India Company. And there was another object very dear to the Emperor's heart towards which Spain could lend important aid. It could guarantee the Pragmatic Sanction, pledge itself, that is, to preserve the Austrian succession to the daughter of the Emperor, a pledge which in the case of Spain meant a great deal, as Spain had fair claims to a considerable portion of the succession on the extinction of the direct male line of the Austrian house. With these hopes and with these offers Ripperda set out for Vienna, with the intention of entirely destroying the present arrangements of Europe, of breaking the

existing marriage-treaty with the Orleans princesses, of substituting
for them the Austrian archduchesses, and of restoring Europe to
its ancient attitude by the close alliance of Austria and Spain in
opposition to France and England.

The success of Ripperda's scheme, the completion of his great act of
treachery, was rapidly secured by an act of a very similar description
on the part of the Duke of Bourbon. That prince had an almost
insane dread of the possible succession of the Orleans house to the
French throne; to preclude its possibility he desired the immediate
marriage of the young king. But his betrothed Spanish bride was
but a baby; regardless therefore of all treaty obligations, the Duke
sent her back almost without explanation to Spain, and married the
young King to Maria Leczinska, daughter of the ex-King of Poland.
The rage of the Spanish king knew no bounds; he sent peremptory
orders to Ripperda to bring the treaty with Austria to a
conclusion upon any terms. Under these circumstances
the great Treaty of Vienna was made on the 30th of
April 1725. It consisted of three separate treaties, two public and
one private. By the public treaties the Pragmatic Sanction was
guaranteed; the Spanish ports opened to German commerce; the
succession of Parma and Tuscany promised to Don Carlos; and
Austria pledged herself to use her best influence to secure the
restoration of Gibraltar and Minorca. Had this been all it would
have been fair enough, somewhat humiliating to the countries left
negotiating uselessly at Cambrai, but not otherwise than in accordance with the principles of the Quadruple Alliance.

Treaty of Vienna April 30, 1725

On the supposition that there was no secret treaty the English
Opposition desired that no notice might be taken of the
transaction, and reprobated the action of the Government in forming a counter treaty as Hanoverian. But there can
be little doubt that there was a secret treaty. Its tenor was afterwards disclosed by Ripperda. In it the marriages between the two
houses were arranged; Austria and Spain pledged themselves to
assist the restoration of the Stuarts; and to compel, if necessary by
force, the restoration of Gibraltar and Minorca. The existence of
this treaty before long reached the ears of the English ministers
For some little time the Jacobites had been extremely active. An
envoy had come to rouse the loyalty of the clans, and had found
them not disinclined to revolt; and the Duke of Wharton, one of the
Jacobite leaders, had gone abroad and held ostentatiously secret
meetings with Ripperda. Ripperda's own tongue was none of the

The secret treaty.

quietest, and he boasted constantly of his great plans. The threat against the power of England was rendered more dangerous by the attitude of Russia, where the Empress Catherine, who was receiving large subsidies from the Spanish court, was eager to win for her son-in-law the Duke of Holstein the province of Sleswig, which the Danes had taken from him.

To meet this threatening alliance therefore, on the 3rd of September, the counter Treaty of Hanover was signed between England, France and Prussia, for mutual assistance should either of the countries be attacked. The real intention was to compel the Emperor to relinquish the Ostend Company, and to withstand any attempt on the part of the Pretender. Ripperda had returned in triumph to Madrid; but his success was shortlived. He found himself unable to fulfil the promises he had made to the Austrians; the people of Spain hated him; he was driven from office, and had to seek refuge at the British embassy, where his confessions completely justified the precautions the Government had taken in bringing about the Treaty of Hanover. In spite of his fall the treaty he had arranged still continued effective.

It seemed as if Europe was upon the verge of a great war, divided as of old into North and South, Protestant and Catholic. The indignation excited by the Treaty of Vienna in England was very great. As it was well put in the King's speech, it appeared as if the appropriation of the English trade was to be given to one country, and Gibraltar and Port Mahon to another, as a price for assisting the Stuart Pretender to the English throne. Very large subsidies were granted, and the army and navy increased. A British squadron blockaded Porto Bello, another squadron entered the Baltic to overawe the Russians; the Spanish galleons were seized. The foolish publication of a direct appeal from the Emperor of Austria to the English people excited the anger even of the Opposition, and secured the speedy dismissal of Palm, the Austrian ambassador. A Spanish army proceeded to invest Gibraltar.

But the skilful though selfish policy of Prussia, and the pacific tendencies of Walpole and of the new French minister Fleury, produced an arrangement. The Emperor found that his position was becoming dangerous. Prussia, at once the leader of the princely opposition to the Imperial house, and yet thoroughly German in its tendencies, determined to be neutral. It could not assist the

Emperor in supporting a treaty which by its marriage clauses threatened to put a Spanish prince on the' Imperial throne. The King had hopes of gaining from France some portion of the Juliers succession. But the house of Brandenburg had become of great importance in European politics; neither party could well act without it. Its neutrality induced the Emperor to consent to the signature of preliminaries of peace, signed at Paris on the 31st of May 1727. He agreed to suspend the Ostend Company for seven years, and to refer other disputes to the general Congress. The pacific policy which had produced this arrangement was Walpole's. The skill which had formed the Treaty of Hanover, the dread of which had undoubtedly produced the peace, belonged to Townshend. And here began the ill-feeling between the brothers-in-law which ultimately produced the disruption of their friendship.

Preliminaries of peace. May 31, 1727

The period of this exciting foreign crisis was rendered interesting in England by the rising power of the Opposition to Walpole. At the back of that Opposition was constantly Bolingbroke. Enormous bribes had secured for him the favour of the Duchess of Kendal. Great stress had been brought to bear on Walpole to consent to his complete restitution. But Walpole would go no further than to allow a restoration of property, the attainder and consequent exclusion from the House of Peers was kept constantly suspended over his head. His anger against the minister who thus thwarted him knew no bounds. He set himself to work to form an Opposition. William Pulteney, an old friend of Walpole's, but like Carteret cast off as too able, lent himself to Bolingbroke's plans, and became his mouthpiece in the House of Commons. Between them they established the Opposition paper, the *Craftsman*, and under their influence every measure of the Government was vigorously attacked by the Jacobite or Whig members. Underhand intrigue promised to be even more effectual than overt opposition. The Duchess of Kendal, by dint of bribing, had grown to be zealous in the cause of the Opposition. She was constantly at work on the King, urging the full restoration of Bolingbroke, urging even the admission of him and his friends to the ministry, and the dismissal of Walpole. George indeed held bravely to his old minister. He showed him the insidious attacks which the Duchess put into his hands, and allowed him thus to meet and counteract them. But Walpole himself felt that the constant importunity of the favourite would sooner or later have its effect.

Opposition to Walpole headed by Bolingbroke

He was even, it is said, thinking of withdrawing to the Upper House, when the King's death at Osnabrück, on his return home from Hanover, put an end for a moment to the almost successful intrigue. The King's death. June 9, 1727.

England had been singularly fortunate in escaping the dangers which generally accompany a violent change of dynasty. The attention of the new Government is usually so constantly directed towards the maintenance of its position in the face of the eager opposition of its worsted rivals, that it neglects the external interests of the country, and the nation sinks for a time into insignificance. In the first days of the Revolution the nation had fortunately fallen into the hands of a great statesman, whose wide policy, carried out with consummate ability by the Duke of Marlborough, had raised it to a very high position. At Utrecht it had treated as one of the first European nations. The skill of Stanhope had secured the prestige thus won. It was England which was the chief power of the Quadruple Alliance, her fleet in the Mediterranean which gave the first great blow to the plans of Alberoni. Twice the appearance of her fleet in the Baltic had overawed the North, and when the new European combination brought about by the Treaty of Vienna had threatened the existing arrangements of Europe, it was the diplomacy of England which called into existence the counter Treaty of Hanover. Review of the reign Increased importance of England abroad.

At home the survey of the reign is not so satisfactory. There was deep depravity in both domestic and public life. The licentiousness which had marked the whole Stuart period had lost nothing of its wickedness, but a good deal of its elegance, in its union with the corruption of a small German court. With a king without wit, without taste for the arts, without knowledge of literature, without perception of beauty, and swayed by two ugly, ignorant and rapacious mistresses, we hear with no surprise tales of the coarseness of the time. If possible, the depravity of public life was greater than the private immorality. It is enough to mark the character of the reign that the Lord Chancellor, the Earl of Macclesfield, was towards its close convicted of disgracing the seat of justice by receiving bribes, and was removed with ignominy from his office; that three ministers at least, if not more, were compromised in the iniquitous transactions of the South Sea Company, and that the King's mistress amassed an immense fortune from the bribes by which her favour was purchased. But even worse than this shameless venality was the political infidelity which universally Private and public immorality prevailed. It is this which is the real danger of a disputed succession. There is an uncertainty as to which party may ultimately be successful, which engenders a spirit of political gambling, while for any fancied insults, or any real loss of power, immediate revenge can be sought by a mere transfer, and frequently a secret transfer of allegiance. To this may be added the tendency of compulsory oaths, which men persuade themselves that they may accept as a matter of form, and which therefore weaken all sense of conscientious engagements. There was hardly a statesman of note who had not more or less tampered with the Jacobite party. Even Walpole is not quite clear of the charge, while the whole body of High Tories were in constant danger of drifting into Jacobitism.

Nor was this the only cause leading to low political morality.

Influence of the Hanoverian courtiers

The reigning King was a foreigner in all his habits and in all his tastes. He was surrounded by a Hanoverian court, who regarded England as an instrument for the aggrandizement of Hanover, and formed a centre for all intrigues to win the royal favour at the expense of patriotism. It is strange, indeed, that their influence was less directly felt in English politics, and it is perhaps owing to those very Hanoverian predilections of the King, which are so often urged against him, that their influence was not greater. He was so thoroughly German in language and in thought, he was so incapable of comprehending the English Constitution and manners, that his real interests were entirely centred on his Hanoverian dominions, and in all matters in which they were not concerned he left England to work out its own revolution, and was compelled, moreover, to throw himself wholly into the hands of that party on whom the revolution rested, and with whom it was a matter of life and death to secure the completion of that revolution, and to maintain the security of the Parliamentary King. It was fortunate that that party was guided by the wisdom of Walpole. That jealousy of power which was his chief weakness was itself an advantage, since it tended to exclude from power the Tory party, and gave a united character to the Government, which proved the hopelessness of success to all who did not accept it.

GEORGE II.

1727–1760.

Born 1683 = Caroline of Anspach.

| Frederick = Augusta
d. 1751.   of Saxe-
       Gotha

George III. | William,
Duke of
Cumberland.
d. 1765. | Anne = Prince
of Orange. | Mary = Land-
grave of
Hesse-
Cassel. | Louisa = Frederick V.
of Denmark. |

CONTEMPORARY PRINCES.

France.	*Austria.*	*Spain.*	*Prussia.*
Louis XV., 1715.	Charles VI., 1711. Charles VII., 1742. Maria Theresa, 1745.	Philip V., 1700. Ferdinand VI., 1746. Charles III , 1759.	Frederick William, 1713. Frederick the Great, 1740.

Russia.	*Denmark.*	*Sweden.*
Peter II., 1727. Anne, 1730. Ivan VI., 1740. Elizabeth, 1741.	Frederick IV., 1699. Christian VI., 1730 Frederick V , 1746.	Frederick I., 1720. Adolphus, 1751.

POPES.—Benedict XIII., 1724.   Clement XII , 1730.   Benedict XIV., 1740.
Clement XIII , 1758.

Archbishops.	*Chancellors*
Wake, 1715 Potter, 1737. Herring, 1747. Hutton, 1757. Secker, 1758	King, 1725 Talbot, 1733 Hardwick, 1737 Northington, 1757.

First Lords of the Treasury	*Chancellors of the Exchequer.*	*Secretaries of State.*

1727   Walpole.
1742   Wilmington.
1743. Pelham.
1754. Newcastle.
1756. Devonshire.
1757. Newcastle.
	1727. Walpole
	1742 Sandys
	1743. Pelham
	1754 Legge
	1755 Lyttleton
	1756. Legge
		1727-1757. Newcastle
		     1730. Harrington
		     1742. Carteret
		     1744. Harrington
		     1746. Chesterfield
		     1748 Bedford.
		     1751. Holderness
		     1754. Robinson.
		     1755. Fox.
		     1757 { Pitt
		           { Holderness

THE ascendancy of Walpole was in great jeopardy on the death of
George I. Bolingbroke's intrigues against him, backed by
all the influence of the Duchess of Kendal, had indeed
been thwarted by the straightforward manner in
which George I. had put all complaints against him into
the minister's own hands—a striking instance of that love of justice
and fidelity to old friends which were the redeeming traits of his
otherwise uninteresting character. But Walpole had now to do with
a sovereign whom as Prince of Wales he had always opposed, and
who had been known to use strong expressions of disapprobation
with regard to him. George II., a little, dry man, gifted with the
hereditary bravery and obstinacy of his family, but with very
limited abilities, and a mind far more easily touched by little things
than by broad interests, could not be expected to forget Walpole's
opposition, nor to appreciate his calm, tolerant wisdom. When
Walpole brought him the news of his father's death, he was at once
directed to apply to Sir Spencer Compton, a dull, orderly man,
Speaker of the House of Commons and Treasurer to the Prince of
Wales. Walpole was wise enough to profess friendship for the new
favourite, who even employed the ability of his predecessor to draw
up the speech which the King was to deliver to the Council. For
some days it was believed that Walpole's power was gone. His
usual throng of followers deserted him and crowded to Sir Spencer
Compton's levée. But before any definite arrangements had been
made, Sir Spencer unwisely gave Walpole opportunities for personally
explaining himself to the King. He was thus able to remove
the bad impression the King had received as to his foreign policy,
and to outbid his rivals in the arrangements he proposed to make for
the Civil List, a point very close to the King's heart. He completely
succeeded in winning the Queen to his interests ; and when she heard
that Compton had had to appeal to his assistance in arranging the
speech from the throne, she took the opportunity of impressing upon
George the absurdity of employing a minister who was obliged to
lean for support upon his rival. The Queen's influence, which was
very great, turned the scale in his favour. The ministry continued
unchanged. Compton, feeling his brief importance at an end,
withdrew from the contest, and shortly afterwards accepted the
position of President of the Council as Lord Wilmington.

*Walpole
retains his
position.*

The offer which had proved so effective in securing Walpole's
power consisted of a Civil List increased by £130,000,
and a jointure of £100,000 to Queen Caroline. The Civil

*Increase of the
Civil List.*

List, which had been settled after the Revolution at £700,000 a year from all sources, had proved insufficient, saddled as it then was with a variety of expenses, such as the judges' and ambassadors' salaries, beyond the mere expenses of the Court. Anne had been £1,200,000 in debt, George I. £1,000,000 Walpole now offered to induce the House to raise it to £800,000 a year, allowing the King to claim anything beyond that sum which should arise from the hereditary revenues.

Before long Walpole won the entire confidence of the King himself, but it was at first chiefly on the friendship of the Queen that he relied. She was a woman of very considerable ability. Her intellectual fault indeed was an attempt to know too much. *The influence* She collected around her men of learning of all sorts, *of the Queen.* dabbled in divinity, dabbled in metaphysics, patronized poetry, and delighted in listening to theological discussions, in which she kept the part of strict neutrality, believing it is thought but little on either side. But her influence in bringing forward men of ability, especially in the Church, was very great. Her sense was excellent, and by means of it, in spite of the King's royal immorality, she contrived to rule him absolutely. She thoroughly appreciated Walpole, and together they pursued that policy, which was no doubt the right one for the maintenance of the Hanoverian succession. This *Character of* consisted in the pursuit of peace in every direction— *Walpole's* peace abroad, peace at home. If any point was strongly *ministry.* contested it was given up; if any abuse was unobserved it was suffered to rest untouched; and in general their object was to let the nation learn by its material prosperity the advantages of an orderly and settled Government. As a consequence of this policy the period of Walpole's government was uneventful, and was occupied rather with the great Parliamentary struggle between himself and the Opposition under Pulteney than by any great national affairs.

The chief strength of that Opposition consisted of the discontented Whigs, most of whom were driven to oppose Walpole *Character of* by his insatiable love of power. We have already seen *the Opposition* Pulteney and Carteret forced from the ranks of the Government, and all overtures with Bolingbroke rejected. In 1730, Walpole quarrelled with his old friend and brother-in-law Townshend, who was only restrained by his patriotism from joining the Opposition. In 1733, Lord Chesterfield was added to the list. These leaders had behind them a certain quantity of supporters who took the name of Patriots,

and wished to be regarded as the true old Whigs, looking upon
Walpole with his large majority as seceders from them. There
was much plausibility in this view : for the Whig party under
Walpole seemed to have become closely attached to the Crown, and
was supported principally by Crown influence. As the original
principle of the Whigs had been antagonism to the over-great power
of the Crown, it could be plausibly urged that they had now assumed
the position of their former enemies. The Hanoverian line had
ascended the throne with a parliamentary as contrasted with a
hereditary title ; it had therefore naturally found its chief supporters
among the Whigs. With the Hanoverians that party had entered
upon power. But the Revolution, while practically subordinating
the power of the King to that of Parliament, had constitutionally
left it untouched. The Hanoverian kings did not indeed employ it
to its full, but placed it in the hands of the minister, who, by means
of the royal influence, practically ruled England with as unquestioned a sway as any great minister of the Stuarts. The difference
lay in this, that the power of the Crown consisted in the immense
influence it possessed by means of pensions, places, and the command
of the public money, and worked through the House of Commons,
and not in opposition to it. The patriot Whigs were conscious of
the power of the Crown, and were true to their principles in opposing
it. Their error lay in this, that they did not understand that that
power was formidable only so long as there was a venal House of
Commons. Eager as they thought for liberty, they formed a close
connection with the High Tories and Jacobites, the greatest enemies
of liberty ; and in their eagerness for office did their best to oppose
that Government, which for the present, at all events, was the only
safeguard against the restoration of the Stuarts, for the events of 1745
render it plain that danger from the Jacobites was as yet by no means
over. In fact, however, principle had little to do with the matter,
it was personal animosity to the minister, and anger at exclusion
from office, which inspired the Opposition. Even the party names
" Whig " and " Tory " were beginning to lose their meaning. By far
the greater portion of the House was thoroughly attached to the
Hanoverian succession. Some fifty Jacobites sat in it under the
guidance of Shippen, and a certain number of country gentlemen,
with Wyndham at their head, still retained the title of Hanoverian
Tories. But the Parliamentary struggle lay in fact between different
sections of the Whigs, either of which, whatever their pretensions
may have been when out of office, would probably have acted in

much the same way had they succeeded in obtaining it. It was not till the close of this reign and the beginning of the next that the old party names began again to acquire significance. It had become evident that the power and influence of the Crown, but little diminished, as has been said, at the Revolution, had as it were been placed in commission in the hands of the great leaders of the Whig party, who by means of their own Parliamentary influence, added to the King's power which they wielded, had assumed a monopoly of the Government antagonistic at once to the Crown and to the people. Those who regarded this condition of things as a disturbance of the old balance of the Constitution began to rally round the King, and when George III. resumed into his own hands the power of the Crown and broke with the Whig oligarchy, he found his support in this new Tory party.

To oppose the many able men whom enmity to the ministers had driven into the ranks of the Patriots, the Government had little more than the inert strength of an unfailing majority to show. Besides Walpole himself, whose talents were unquestioned, the Government consisted of somewhat second-rate men, such as Newcastle, whose fussy silliness was a constant theme of jest, Stanhope, Lord Harrington, an excellent diplomatist but no politician, and Lord Hervey, a clever but bitter and effeminate courtier. But the Government was supported on almost every question of importance by a vast majority of the House, whose votes the surpassing skill of Walpole as a manager secured—many of them by small places and pensions, or other "considerations," as bribes were then called. That Walpole reduced the purchase of a majority, a practice by no means unknown, to a system must be allowed. It may be urged in his favour, that he used, but did not cause, the venality prevalent among all public men of the time, and employed it so as to secure what was upon the whole the government most advantageous for England at the time.

The folly of the Pretender spared the minister all trouble with regard to the Jacobites, for James had succeeded in alienating his ablest partisans. He had quarrelled with Atterbury as he quarrelled with Bolingbroke, he had excited scandal by his quarrel with his wife, and had suffered an unworthy favourite, Colonel Hay, or Lord Inverness as he called himself, to supplant all his better partisans in his favour. And when the death of Lord Mar was followed by that of the Duke of Wharton and of Atterbury in 1732, the Jacobite cause fell into the hands of very inferior agents, whose intrigues, insignificant as they were, seem to have been thoroughly known by Walpole.

It was thus with one source of danger practically removed that Walpole resumed the threads of foreign policy. The last reign had closed before peace had been concluded with Spain, and while there were still unsettled difficulties with the court of Vienna, although preliminaries had been signed both in Paris and in Spain by what is known as the Convention of the Pardo. It must indeed have been obvious that the Treaty of Vienna, plausible as it seemed, could not have been a lasting treaty. The Bourbons were upon the throne of Spain, and the close junction of the houses of Bourbon and Hapsburg was an impossible contradiction of all history, especially as the desire which was really the moving passion of the Spanish court, the establishment, namely, of a Spanish kingdom in Italy, was fundamentally opposed to the interests of Austria. At the same time the shadow of the approaching dissolution of his kingdom at his death was constantly overhanging the Emperor. No ideas of present greatness, not even the hope of restoring the Empire to the position it had held under Charles V., appeared in his eyes so important as to secure the reversion of his own estates for his daughter, according to the Pragmatic Sanction, by which, in 1713, he had arranged the succession to his hereditary kingdoms. It was impossible for him to hurry into a general war, which must of necessity prevent the acceptance of that arrangement. There·was already a strongly expressed feeling in Germany against the marriages on which the Vienna Treaty rested, and which might have the effect of placing a Spaniard on the Imperial throne. The threatened secession of his chief allies, and the fear of postponing the acceptance of the Pragmatic Sanction, were sufficient reasons to induce the Emperor to withdraw from his bargain. He therefore accepted the mediation of France, where Fleury, though he probably never forgot the old policy of the country which he governed, always apparently exhibited a love of peace ; and it was agreed that disputed points should be referred to·a general Congress to be held at Aix-la-Chapelle, but subsequently moved to Soissons.

At the Congress the Emperor, afraid of exciting the national prejudices of the Germans, entirely deserted his Spanish allies, and instead of hastening a favourable negotiation, perpetually threw obstacles in the way. As far as England was concerned, the great point at issue was Gibraltar, which Spain had already besieged in vain. The ministry, both before and now, seem

European complications.

Congress at Soissons.

to have regarded the surrender of it as neither impossible nor very injurious ; the view of the nation was very different. But as is so often the case, the Congress came to very little. Spain, finding herself deserted by Austria, and observing that the Congress was falling to pieces by constant delays, had recourse to a direct treaty ; and on the 9th of November 1729 the celebrated Treaty of Seville was signed. It was a defensive alliance between England, Spain and France, to which Holland subsequently acceded. Spain revoked all the privileges granted to Austrian subjects by the Treaties of Vienna, re-established English trade in America on its former footing, and restored all captures. The Assiento was confirmed to the South Sea Company, and arrangements made for securing the succession of Parma and Tuscany to the Infant Don Carlos, by substituting Spanish troops for the neutral forces, which since the Preliminaries had been occupying those countries. *Treaty of Seville. Nov. 9, 1729.*

The Emperor now found that he had outwitted himself. He had clung to the Treaty of Vienna just long enough to irritate two of the great countries of Europe, he had put difficulties in the way of its completion, and hesitated about fulfilling it, just long enough to irritate the third. Old friends and old foes had made common cause. His hopes for the Pragmatic Sanction seemed entirely gone. It was not likely that he would sit down quietly while Spanish troops occupied fortresses in what he considered his dominions. He broke off all diplomatic relations with Spain, sent troops into Italy, and on the death of the Duke of Parma seized his duchy. But all men really knew that the bribe was ready, if they would only give it, to put an end to all his opposition. And the impatient Queen of Spain—angry with the shilly-shally policy of her new allies (who would not insist with sufficient rapidity on the completion of the Seville treaty), throwing over France, which she regarded as the chief delinquent in the matter— joined with England and Holland to offer the long wished for guarantee. Thus at length by the second Treaty of Vienna all the much vexed questions were decided. Austria was glad to accept the terms proposed at Seville, agreed to destroy the Ostend Company, to establish Don Carlos in his duchies, and not again to threaten the balance of European power. And in 1732, under the escort of English ships, the Spanish troops took possession of the disputed fortresses. *Disappointment of the Emperor* *Second Treaty of Vienna. March 16, 1731.*

Both these treaties were arranged in accordance with the pacific views of Walpole. When the second was concluded he was absolute

Complete
supremacy of
Walpole.

master of affairs in England ; for almost immediately after the Treaty of Seville the old jealousy which had long smouldered between him and Townshend burst out, and Townshend had found it necessary to withdraw. Townshend was a proud, rough man, ill fitted to play the subordinate part which Walpole was determined to thrust upon his colleagues. Besides general ill-feeling, several specific grounds of difference existed between them. The first Treaty of Vienna had greatly irritated Townshend, who would have wished to avoid all compromise and to proceed to extremities with the Emperor. The link which had bound the brothers-in-law together had been broken by the death of Lady Townshend, Walpole's sister ; and Walpole's conduct with regard to the Pension Bill supplied a fresh ground of quarrel. The Opposition had discovered, without exactly tracing it to its con-

The Pension
Bill.

stitutional source, the power of the royal influence, and early in 1730 Mr. Sandys introduced the first of those Bills for restraining it which became from this time onwards one of the regular weapons of attack against the ministry. He moved for leave to bring in a Bill to disable all persons from sitting in Parliament who had any pension direct or indirect from the Crown, and proposed that every member as he took his seat should swear that he held no such pension. The attack was exceedingly well judged, for it gave expression to a very general feeling, and Walpole, who studiously avoided shocking the feelings of any large section of the nation, was at some loss how to meet it. But he knew that he could rely upon his great Whig supporters in the Upper House, and of that House Townshend was the leader. Walpole therefore suffered the Bill to pass the Lower House without opposition, so that it was upon Townshend and the Lords that the whole odium fell when, as a matter of course, they rejected it. On these and various other grounds such ill blood sprang up between the brothers, that it is told, though upon doubtful authority, that they nearly came to blows at an entertainment in the house of Mrs.

Retirement of
Townshend.
1731.

Selwyn. It was impossible that both the ministers should remain in office; the influence of the Queen turned the scale in favour of Walpole, and Townshend resigned, withdrawing with unusual patriotism from political life, and devoting himself at Reynham, his house in Norfolk, to the improvement of agriculture. It is to him that we chiefly owe the cultivation of turnips. This change, by allowing a proper rotation of crops, and thus avoiding the necessity of leaving fields to lie fallow, added nearly a third to the cultivable area of England, while by supplying large quantities of cattle-food from a comparatively small space of ground, it enormously increased the food-producing resources of the country.

For two years the ascendancy of Walpole was unquestioned. He was enabled to turn his thoughts to domestic improve- Walpole's home ments. English was substituted, certainly most reason- government. ably, for the ancient Law Latin in all legal proceedings, to the grief it is said of some conservative lawyers, and against the opposition of most of the judges. There was a Committee of Inquiry also into the condition of public prisons, which brought many revolting horrors to light. Both in the Fleet and Marshalsea torture by thumbscrew and otherwise was constant, and the condition of poor prisoners who could not bribe the gaolers was inconceivably horrid. Forty or fifty of them, for instance, were locked up for the night in a cell not sixteen feet square. Gaol-fever and famine were constantly destroying them, so that the deaths at one prison were frequently eight or ten a day.

But it was as a financier that Walpole was most favourably known, and somewhat strangely it was a great financial His financial reform in the year 1733 that almost brought him to ruin. measures. Walpole was desirous of lessening even the weak opposi- 1733. tion by which he was confronted in Parliament; and in the hope of attracting to himself the country gentlemen, he appealed, in accordance with his usual principle, to their love of money, and sought some way to lessen the Land Tax. For this purpose he suggested an excise upon salt. This must have been contrary to his own convictions. He could not have been ignorant how important an article salt is in many manufactures, how necessary an article of purchase even among the poorest. He was in fact taxing the poor and the manufacturing classes for the sake of winning the landed interest, which would be called upon to pay a land tax of one instead of two shillings. The new duty was carried, but by no large majority. The chief argument against it was that it was a step towards a general excise, which, because it seemed to infringe on the rights of the subject by giving revenue officers the right of entering houses, was much detested, and regarded as a badge of servitude. Although the tax upon salt was not really intended as a beginning of a general excise, it was nevertheless true that Walpole had a scheme of that nature in his mind : for it was found after a year's experience that the new tax upon salt fell short by two-thirds of the sum required to admit of the reduction of the Land Tax to one shilling. It was to a new measure of excise that Walpole looked to supply the deficiency. The excisable articles at that time were malt, salt, and distilleries, and the produce of the tax in 1733 was about £3,200,000. When Walpole's project of extending the excise got wind it proved most repugnant to the people. Numerous meetings were held, and many members were instructed to vote against any such attempt. But when the project was brought before the House, then in Committee, it appeared that Walpole, disowning all intention of establishing a general excise, confined himself solely to the duties on wine and tobacco ; and even on those commodities designed no increase of the present duties, but merely a change in the manner of collecting them. In future the dues were to be collected after the manner of an excise from the retailers, and not as heretofore in the form of customs at the ports. Fraud and smuggling were so prevalent that in tobacco alone the customs, which ought to have produced £750,000 a year, produced in fact only £160,000. As these frauds took place chiefly at the ports or along the seaboard, Walpole hoped by taxing the retail trade, and not the importation, much to lessen them. In addition to this, he would have established a system of warehousing without tax for re-exportation, thus making London a free port. It was undoubtedly an excellent plan. As he pointed out, it was the shops and warehouses alone which were under supervision, not the houses of the retailers ; liberty was in no way infringed ; it enabled him to remit the Land Tax to the advantage of the country gentlemen ; the scheme was advantageous to the importer, who could re-export free of duty ; the price of the commodity was not raised. But none the less did it meet with the most violent opposition. Wyndham likened it to the unjust imposts of Empson and Dudley, and Pulteney derided it as a vast plan to cure an almost imaginary evil. The people beset the doors of the House during the debate in great crowds, irritating Walpole till he let fall the unhappy words—" It may be said that they came hither as humble suppliants, but I know whom the law calls sturdy beggars ; " an expression which was never forgiven. The resolution was carried, but by an unusually small majority. On this and subsequent motions a Bill was founded, and in the course of many discussions a new cry was raised by Pulteney, that, as most of the seaport boroughs were already in the hands of one or the other branch of the administration, this was a plan for bringing inland towns under the same influences ; and before the Bill came to a second reading, the ministerial majority of sixty had dwindled to sixteen. The excitement became dangerous; even the army was infected, and Walpole, according to his usual principle, yielded to the violence of the storm and withdrew the Bill. But though thus thwarted, he did not forego his revenge on the defaulters of his own party. Chesterfield, the ablest man in the ministry, Lord-Steward of the Household, was somewhat rudely dismissed. Lord Clinton, the Earl of Burlington, the Duke of Montrose, the Earls of Marchmont and Stair, and by a questionable exercise of prerogative the Duke of Bolton and Lord Cobham, were deprived of their commission in the army,—an arbitrary act not lost sight of by the Opposition.

As Walpole, true to his principles, had purchased peace at home by concession, we find him the next year for the same object keeping entirely aloof from a new war which had broken out in Europe. The Peaces of Seville and Vienna had apparently completed the arrangements of the Treaty of Utrecht, and settled all differences between the courts of Spain and Vienna ; but treaties based upon arbitrary territorial arrangements for the purpose of preserving the balance of power are always very liable to be broken. Neither party considers itself quite fairly treated, and is ever on the look-out for some opening to regain its lost power or to acquire some new influence. The Peace of Utrecht had closed the War of Succession, undertaken solely to establish the balance of power in Europe, and had been exactly such a treaty as has been described. The Peaces of Seville and Vienna had been necessary to modify in some degree its arrangements. A quarrel as to the election of a new King of Poland was sufficient to render for the time all three of them useless. It will be remembered that the French King had married the daughter of Stanislaus, ex-King of Poland. All French influence therefore was now employed to secure his re-election, while the Czarina Anne of Russia and the Emperor strongly upheld the claims of Augustus, son of the late King. A Russian and a Saxon army were sufficient to secure the throne for Augustus ; but the Emperor's interference, although indirect, had enabled Fleury to show himself in his true colours, to listen to that great section of his countrymen who were weary of the lengthened peace, and to bring on a war which promised to be far more advantageous to France than any success in Poland could have been. In his attack upon Austria he was joined at once by Spain : for the Queen, the real ruler of the Peninsula, was still discontented with the losses Spain had suffered by the late treaties, and was besides very anxious to secure a crown for her son Don Carlos, who was already Duke of Parma. There was a short campaign upon the Rhine, where Berwick commanded the French, Eugene the Imperial army. Though the French lost their general before Philipsburg, they were everywhere successful, and when the united armies of Spain and Sardinia threw themselves on the kingdom of Naples, they found no great difficulty in conquering the Austrians, and completing the conquest of that country and of Sicily by the victory of Bitonto. Don Carlos assumed the kingdom as Charles III.

In the face of much obloquy Walpole steadily refused to side with either party; the Emperor, unable to secure his assistance, though he declined the pacific mediation proffered by the Maritime Powers, thought it wise to open direct negotiations with France. Preliminaries of peace were set on foot (Oct. 1735), which ripened in three years into the great treaty called the Definitive Peace of Vienna, by which the Spanish house was allowed to retain Naples and Sicily. Sardinia was rewarded with some frontier towns, among others Novara and Tortona, Lorraine was ceded to France, and the young Duke of Lorraine, Francis, the affianced husband of Maria Theresa (heiress to the Austrian Empire), was persuaded to accept Tuscany in exchange. France and Sardinia again ratified the Pragmatic Sanction. This somewhat trivial war thus completed the incorporation of France, established the Bourbons in Naples, and was the cause of the connection between Tuscany and the Austrian house.

Definitive Peace of Vienna. Nov. 8, 1738.

Walpole had been more than usually anxious to keep clear of European wars, because the time for the dissolution of the Parliament under the Septennial Act was rapidly approaching, and there seemed every reason to believe that the struggle at the coming election would be a very fierce one. The Opposition were already supplied with several very effective cries. The Excise scheme, the arbitrary punishment of his opponents, and his determination to keep up a standing army, would all powerfully excite the people against the minister. Before the dissolution they added one more cry against him by making a strong attack upon the Septennial Act. As most of the Opposition Whigs had voted for this Act, they had always shrunk from demanding its repeal. It required all the skill of Bolingbroke, the wire-puller of the Opposition, to induce the two parties to unite in the assault. The debate is interesting, as showing in a great speech of Wyndham the temper of the Opposition and the sort of charges to which Walpole was exposed. "Let us suppose,"

Increasing opposition to Walpole. 1734.

said Wyndham, "a man abandoned to all notions of virtue and honour, of no great family, and of but a mean fortune, raised to be chief Minister of State by the concurrence of many whimsical events, afraid or unwilling to trust any but creatures of his own making, and most of them equally abandoned to all notions of virtue or honour, a man ignorant of the true history of his country, and consulting nothing but that of enriching and aggrandizing himself and his favourites; in foreign affairs trusting none but those whose education makes it impossible for them to have such knowledge or such qualifications as can either be of service to their country or give weight or credit to their negotiations. Let us suppose the true interest of the nation by such means neglected or misunderstood, her honour and credit lost, her trade insulted, her merchants plundered, her sailors murdered; and all these things overlooked only for fear his administration should be endangered. Suppose him next possessed of great wealth, the plunder of the nation, with a Parliament of his own choosing, most of their seats purchased, and their votes bought at the public expense. Let us suppose attempts made to inquire into his conduct, and the reasonable request rejected by a corrupt majority of his creatures. . . . Upon this scandalous victory let us suppose this chief minister pluming himself in defiances, because he finds he has a Parliament, like a packed jury, ready to acquit him at all adventures. Let us suppose him arrived to that degree of insolence as to domineer over all the men of ancient families, all the men of sense, figure, or fortune in the nation, and as he has no virtue of his own, ridiculing it in others, and endeavouring to destroy or corrupt it in all. . . . Then let us suppose a prince, ignorant and unacquainted with the inclinations and interests of his people. . . . Could there any greater curse happen to a nation than such a prince on the throne, advised and solely advised by such a minister, supported by such a Parliament?" Walpole replied in a speech scarcely less vigorous, unveiling the secret influence of Bolingbroke, attributing to him the whole management of the Opposition, and pointing out his vast ambition and unequalled faithlessness.

Wyndham's speech against Walpole.

The election, after a severe struggle, ended by giving Walpole a large majority, although considerably smaller than he had hitherto commanded. The depression of the Opposition was great, especially as Bolingbroke, weary of all exclusion from power, and involved in quarrels with Pulteney, withdrew to France.

The leadership which Bolingbroke thus resigned fell in some

degree into the hands of the Prince of Wales, not indeed that he
Prince of Wales head of the Opposition. 1735. possessed any of the talents of a leader, but that he formed a rallying-point for all sections of the Opposition. From his first arrival in England, in 1728, there had been the usual differences between him and his father. He had thought himself ill-used in the matter of his intended marriage with Wilhelmina of Prussia, whom, though he had never seen, he pretended to adore. The mutual dislike of the fathers of the proposed bride and bridegroom had broken off that match. He had since married a sensible wife, Augusta of Saxe-Gotha. But it was the parsimony of his father which had principally excited his displeasure. He held his income of £50,000 a year entirely at his father's will, whereas his father when Prince of Wales had £100,000 secured to him. But parsimony was the ruling passion of George II., and nothing could persuade him to increase his son's income. Round the Prince had collected all the great leaders of the Opposition; Pulteney, Chesterfield, Carteret, Wyndham and Cobham were intimate with him, and Bolingbroke was his political instructor. Nor was this all. Although the Queen had a love of literature, and in some ways patronized clever men (especially in the matter of Church preferment), Walpole had always refused to show them the least favour; and as a natural consequence, all the better writers allied themselves closely with the clever men of the Opposition, especially with Bolingbroke, who had always been their friend. Swift, Pope, Gay, and Arbuthnot, were constantly writing vigorously against Walpole. " Gulliver's Travels " are full of strokes of satire against the conduct of affairs. Some of Pope's sharpest lines refer to the Queen's implacability towards her son. The " Beggars' Opera " of Gay was regarded as being directed almost entirely against the Government. The " Quarrels between Peacham and Lockit " were by some thought to allude to the quarrel between Townshend and Walpole ;[1] and in the *Craftsman*, the organ of the Opposition, letters of the most virulent description were constantly published against Walpole. To this brilliant Court it was natural that the younger men rising to notoriety should ally themselves. The intellect of the political world seemed there to be centred, and the specious name of Patriot was apt to attract enthusiastic youth. Pitt and Lyttelton began their political career as members of this Opposition.

---

[1] The applications of the passages in the " Beggars' Opera " must have been after-thoughts, as the play was brought out in 1728, before the quarrel at Mrs. Selwyn's, if quarrel there was, took place.

It was not till the year 1737 that a public outbreak between the King and Prince took place. In the preceding year an event had happened, which, though of little historical importance, has been rendered interesting by Sir Walter Scott in his "Heart of Midlothian." During the King's ab ence in Hanover the Queen was left Regent. Two smugglers, Wilson and Robertson, were imprisoned in the Tolbooth, and tried to escape. Wilson went first, but being a big man, could not get through the aperture they had made. Feeling that he had injured Robertson, on the following Sunday in church he succeeded in grasping one of his guards in each hand, and a third with his teeth, thus giving Robertson an opportunity of escape, of which he availed himself. A strong sympathy was excited for Wilson, and after his execution the soldiers were attacked with stones. Porteous, who commanded the guard, fired upon the crowd. For this he was tried and condemned to death, but, in consideration of the provocation, was reprieved by Queen Caroline. The people, enraged at this, organized a riot, and though notice was given to the magistrates, no efficient means were taken for suppressing it. The gates were locked, and the commander of the troops, frightened by Porteous' example, refused to act. The Tolbooth was broken open, and Porteous hanged to a barber's pole, all with the greatest order and regularity. Having done this, and paid for the rope with which they hanged Porteous, the crowd dispersed, nor could any of the rioters be detected. The Queen, regarding the disturbance as a personal insult to her authority, was extremely angry. It was proposed to abolish the Edinburgh city guard and the city charter, level the gates, and declare the provost incapable of holding any office. The opposition of the Scotch members and of the Scotch nobles was however too great to be disregarded, and ultimately the city being fined £2000, and the provost declared incapable of office, no further punishment was inflicted.

During this year the Prince of Wales had married. But this by no means tended, as it was hoped, to the union Quarrel of the King and Prince 1737. of the Royal Family, for the Prince at once renewed his demands for an increase of income. He determined at length to follow Bolingbroke's advice, and demand that the sum he received should not depend on the King's will, but be permanent and fixed by the Parliament. This threat induced the King to make some overtures, with a promise to give the Princess a jointure. They were rejected, however, and the battle fought out. The great flaw in the organization of the Opposition was then made manifest, for the Tories (forty-five in number) refused to vote in

favour of a Hanoverian prince, and the ministers were victorious.
This dispute was followed by a still more scandalous squabble,
the Prince hurried his wife from the King's residence at Hampton
Court to the empty palace of St. James's when she was on the
point of giving birth to her first child, who would be in the direct
line of succession to the throne. This insult was never forgiven,
and the King gave his son a peremptory order to leave the Court.
He withdrew at once to Norfolk House in St. James's Square,

Death of the which became the centre of the Opposition. The Queen
Queen. remained implacable, refusing to see him even on her
deathbed. Her death happened within a few weeks of this unhappy
quarrel, to the great loss of the King, whose want of intellect she
had chiefly supplied, of Walpole, whose staunch friend she had always
been, and indeed of all England, for by seconding Sir Robert's views
she had been mainly instrumental in securing for it that period of
comparative rest which was so much wanted to re-establish its wellbeing after the troublous time of revolution it had passed through.
It was believed that Walpole's power had rested chiefly on her
influence, and there was a general expectation that her death would
be followed by his downfall. The Opposition were much disappointed
when they found his influence with the King as great as ever. It is

Walpole retains said that with her parting words she had recommended
his influence the King to continue to trust in her favourite minister ;
with the King. and her advice was then as always followed by him. For
though he was not a faithful husband, having had Lady Suffolk
for his mistress during the first years of his reign, and now allying
himself with Sophia de Walmoden, created Countess of Yarmouth,
his mistresses never had any great political influence over him—no
influence at all events comparable to that exercised by the Queen.

The Opposition, though disappointed, by no means relaxed its efforts,

The Opposition and found a favourable point of attack in Walpole's
attacks his pacific tendencies. There were still several points of
pacific policy. dispute unsettled with Spain. The limits between
Georgia and Florida were undetermined. By the Treaty of Seville trade
was established on its former footing between the two countries, and the
commercial relations between them were therefore regulated by the
somewhat indefinite treaties of 1667 and 1670. By these the right
of search and the right of seizure of contraband goods were allowed
to the respective nations. This right was exercised with varying
severity by the Spaniards according to their relation with England
at the time. But the trade of English America had very much

increased, and would not be restrained from seeking legally of illegally the trade of South America. There was no doubt abundant smuggling. Even the South Sea Company, which was allowed to send one ship a year, contrived in fact much to increase that number by sending tenders with her, which secretly replenished her cargo as she parted with it. On the other hand, it is equally certain that the Spanish Guarda-Costas had exercised their authority roughly, and many tales of the ill-usage of British subjects were current. These stories were collected and brought up in Parliament by the Opposition, the best known being that of Jenkin's ear. Jenkin was a captain, who asserted that his ear had been torn from him, and that he had been bidden to take it to his king. "Then," said he, "I recommended my soul to God and my cause to my country." The ear, wrapped in cotton, he was in the habit of showing to his listeners. This claptrap story was most effective in rousing the popular indignation. Walpole resisted the clamour, but met with great difficulties. The King, who was at heart a soldier, now freed from the peaceful influence of his wife, was urgent for war; and in the Cabinet itself Newcastle began to bid for increased power by favouring this desire of the King.

In this eagerness for war, which is frequently represented as a folly on the part of the nation, the people were probably really wiser than their rulers. The state of Europe was becoming such that war was necessary for England, if she was to uphold her position, and to obtain that paramount situation in commerce and on the sea which her people then as now regarded as her due. Walpole's peace policy was certainly directed rather to the aggrandizement of his party than to the general interest of the nation, and in pursuit of it he had allowed himself to be duped by the pacific language of Cardinal Fleury. His attention had been distracted from the broader lines of European politics to the details of the constantly shifting diplomacy of the time. It is now known that, as early as 1733, the Family Compact had been entered into between the two branches of the House of Bourbon, for the express purpose of hampering the trade of England, and with a stipulation for mutual assistance both in war-ships and privateers in case of any encroachment on the part of England. Nor was the agreement a dead letter. M. de Maurepas had been busily and successfully employed in reorganizing the French navy.

Walpole attempted at first to pursue his established policy of peace. He opened negotiations with Spain, supported by such signs of coming hostilities as induced that Court to agree to a convention. Many English prisoners and some English prizes were restored, and compensation was promised to the amount of £200,000. Against this, however, was set £60,000 to be paid by England for the destruction of Spanish ships by Admiral Byng in 1718, and in his eagerness for prompt payment Walpole suffered it to be further reduced to £95,000. The disputed points were left for further negotiation. No mention was made of the right of search; the limits of Georgia were not defined. When this convention became known the popular indignation was great. It was regarded as a resignation of our rights. The ridiculously small sum given for compensation was pointed out, and the payment of £60,000 for what the people regarded as a glorious victory was naturally much resented. It was in opposing this convention that Pitt seems first to have shown his great powers of oratory. The ministerial majority was only twenty-eight. Believing that they could now safely proceed to extremities, the Opposition determined upon seceding from the House. With the arguments all on one side, and the votes upon the other, it was impossible, they said, for them to continue to do their duty there. It was a foolish manœuvre, which, though tried more than once, has never been successful. To the public it invariably appears factious, and as no Opposition has been found determined enough to keep it up for any length of time, it has always been made ridiculous by the speedy return of the seceders. In the present instance Walpole sarcastically thanked the Opposition for their withdrawal, and proceeded at once to pass several measures which would otherwise have been sharply opposed; among others, a subsidy to Denmark for a palpably Hanoverian object— the security, namely, of the little castle of Steinhorst in Holstein.

Negotiations with Spain. 1739.

But though he had carried his convention, and although the Opposition had withdrawn, and Cardinal Fleury had offered the mediation of France, it became obvious to Walpole that he must either declare war or resign. His love of power prevented him from taking the latter and more honourable course, and, to the loss of both power and fame, he suffered himself to be dragged against his convictions into war, which was declared on the 19th of October. The joy of England was very great, although Walpole was full of gloomy forebodings, for, as he himself said, "no man can prudently give his advice for declaring war without knowing the whole system of the affairs of Europe as they stand at present. . . . It is not the power of Spain and the

Walpole declares war rather than resign.

power of this nation only that we ought in such a case to know and to compare. We ought also to know what allies our enemies may have, and what assistance we may expect from our friends." He felt certain that the area of the war would soon be extended, for, although he had successfully used his efforts to maintain friendship with France, he knew that there was an intimate connection between France and Spain which must sooner or later bring the former into the field. Moreover, his information as to the plans of the Jacobites was exceedingly accurate, and while the Opposition were constantly deriding the notion of any formidable organization ‘of that party, he never ceased to be on his guard against it. The justice of his views was at once shown, when the declaration of war called to life the slumbering energy of the Jacobites. Intrigues were immediately set on foot; a Committee was appointed in England; overtures were addressed to Spain; and, as Fleury gradually grew colder and more estranged from England, proposals were made to him also, to which he listened, and promised that he would send a body of troops, probably the Irish Brigade, to support any attempt in favour of the Stuarts; thus would be fulfilled the condition without which the English Jacobites had always refused to rise. It was hoped that the Duke of Ormond and the Earl Marischal might make a simultaneous expedition from Spain.

Meanwhile, Walpole, having once yielded, seemed conscious that he no longer possessed the absolute dominion over Parliament he had so long enjoyed. Wyndham, his chief enemy, indeed had died: but in the ranks of the Opposition were still to be found all those men of ability whom twenty years of exclusive and jealous power had made his enemies; and to his old foes was now added the exciting eloquence and uncompromising energy of Pitt. To oppose this formidable body Walpole stood almost alone in the Commons, supported only by such men as Henry Pelham, a conscientious and sensible but not firstrate man, Wilmington, and Sir William Young, whose ready ability scarcely atoned for his damaged character. In the House of Lords he still counted the Duke of Newcastle, Lord Hervey, and Lord Hardwicke among his party. But Hardwicke and Newcastle were both opposed to his peaceful views, and the latter was already intriguing against his chief. The Duke of Argyle had lately become hostile to the ministry, and had been deprived of all his employments. Walpole thus became the single object of all the Opposition invectives. Every measure for the last twenty years which had either failed or

[margin note: Increased vigour of the Opposition. 1740.]

been unpopular was brought against him. The quarrel had become personal between him and the Opposition. His efforts to retain his power were unceasing. He yielded in the Cabinet as to the manner in which the war was to be carried on ; he gave the chief command of the expedition in the West Indies to his political enemy Vernon ; to secure the Jacobite votes at the next election he even went so far as to enter into correspondence with the Pretender, although probably without serious intentions. But this conduct did but encourage his enemies, and in the last session of Parliament (1741) Mr. Sandys brought forward a motion, which was repeated in the Upper House, for his removal from the King's councils. Walpole so far rebutted the charges brought against him, that; after a defence of great eloquence, he succeeded in throwing out the motion by a very large majority.

Walpole's forebodings were speedily fulfilled. Not only, as we have seen, was the Jacobite party at once again called to life, but his expeditions against Spain were by no means great successes. Anson indeed, although all his other ships were lost, made several successful attacks upon treasure-ships, captured Paita, and succeeded in bringing 'The Centurion' safe home after a circumnavigation of the globe. But Vernon, though successful in taking Porto Bello (when his conduct was vociferously contrasted by the Opposition with that of Hozier in 1726),[1] was repulsed with heavy loss in an assault on Carthagena. France had become thoroughly hostile, and when, on the 20th of October 1740, the Emperor Charles VI. died, it became evident that the war would shortly become European. In spite, however, of these proofs of Walpole's foresight, in spite of his success against Mr. Sandys' motion, the charges which had been brought against him had such an effect at the next election that the Opposition found themselves with much increased strength, and it became pretty plain that the Government would have but a very small majority. The session opened with a series of close divisions. The Opposition succeeded in carrying their Chairman of

Ill success of the war.

---

[1] In that year Hozier, probably by the orders of Government, had hesitated to attack that place. Glover, in his ballad of " Admiral Hozier's Ghost," makes him say,

> " I with twenty sail attended,
> Did this Spanish town affright ;
> Nothing then its wealth defended
> But my orders not to fight.
> Oh ! that in this rolling ocean
> I had cast them with disdain,
> And obeyed my heart's warm motion
> To have quelled the pride of Spain.'

Committees against the Government candidate, and when he found himself at last defeated on the Chippenham election petition, Walpole took the resolution of resigning. A few days later he gave up all his places, and was made Lord Orford. Walpole resigns 1742.

Thus closed the career of the statesman who for twenty years had been the sole guide of English politics. It is remarkable how few great measures can be traced to him; but he probably displayed true wisdom in allowing Review of Walpole's ministry. all reforms, however much they may have been required, to remain for a time in abeyance. The one thing which England required was rest. The last hundred years had been one continual scene of political turmoil. During the whole of that period the Revolution had been slowly working itself out, and the English Constitution had been changing. The power had gradually shifted from the King to the House of Commons. The ministry had ceased to be a body of secretaries, to whom was indeed intrusted the chief management of all national affairs, but who, inasmuch as they were still in theory, and in a great degree in practice, merely called upon to execute the King's commands, might be chosen indiscriminately from all parties. Instead of this it had become, what it has practically ever since been, a Committee of the majority in the House of Commons. In a social point of view, during much of the same period, England had been perplexed by a choice of masters, and in some degree by a choice of religions. Walpole seems thoroughly to have understood this position, and to have set himself steadily to work to complete and give stability to the changes which had been going on. He had seen, that far more important than any further improvements to the Constitution was the establishment on a firm footing of what had already been done. His chief object was therefore to make himself absolute master of the House of Commons. For this purpose he used means which we should now consider disgraceful. He is reported to have acted on the principle that every man had his price. He steadily opposed all efforts for the exclusion of pensioners, not from a wish to increase the power of the Crown, but because he wanted to secure the power of the minister, who he saw must henceforward be the real governor of England. He opposed the Peerage Bill because it threatened to increase the power of the Lords as against the Commons. He persistently refused all attempts at coalition (such as had been contemplated by Stanhope and subsequently proposed by Bolingbroke), because he wanted the ministry to be the representatives of the party which had the majority in the House, and of that party only. He kept a tight hand throughout his administration upon the Jacobites, conscious that the security of the reigning house was the only way of calming the uneasiness which all classes felt while they had any choice of rulers offered them. For similar reasons, with regard to religion, he refused to listen to any propositions for the relief of Roman Catholics, which Stanhope had also contemplated ; and still further to calm religious discords by the sense of one strong paramount Church of England, he also refused all concessions to the Dissenters, although they systematically supported him. In saying, however, that the power had passed to the House of Commons, we must be careful not to regard the House of Commons as a popular assembly. The next phase of our history, the complement to that part of the Revolution which we have now passed, is the struggle of the people to get possession of their own House. At the time of which we are speaking the House of Commons was so filled with nominees of great lords, the electoral body was so limited, and the distribution of seats so arbitrary, that the House of Commons could in no way be regarded as a fair representation of the people, and the great Whig majority rested not on the liberal feeling of the nation, but upon an oligarchy of great Whig nobles. In his foreign policy Walpole was influenced by similar principles. Though the Peace of Utrecht was a Tory peace, its maintenance, and that of the balance of power it had established, was his chief object. Anything was better than that England should be engaged in war. War at once opened the door for Jacobite hopes. War at once touched that material prosperity which was to be the surest claim of gratitude to the reigning house. Moreover, as a financier, Walpole hated war. It was in this capacity, if we set aside his general ability and skill in management, that Walpole was greatest. We have seen how prudently he re-established credit after the bursting of the South Sea bubble, and how wise was his plan in his ill-fated Excise Bill. If some of his measures (as the Salt Tax) were dictated by political rather than economical necessities, it is yet certain that he inspired universal confidence, and owed much of his power to the support of the moneyed interest. His personal character, like that of most of his contemporaries, was not good. A large, coarse-looking person did not belie the coarseness of his tastes. He drank freely, joked coarsely, and had more than one natural child. Although in one of his speeches he plumes himself on having never been charged with corruption, his private fortune was certainly much increased by his ministry, and if we except his collection of pictures at Houghton, there is no sign that he had any appreciation of literature or of the arts. His ignorance of literature, and his contempt for it, is indeed notorious.' He spent vast sums of money in purchasing the services of pamphleteers; scarcely one of them was worth anything. He seems to have regarded writing like any other trade, as being capable of being purchased by the piece. Patronage to literary men he systematically refused; we therefore find all the able writers of the time ranged on the side of the Opposition; and it is for the same reason perhaps that the worst points of his character are those which are more commonly known.

The chief fault of Walpole had been his jealousy of talent; on his fall there was no one in the ministry of sufficient influence to take up the reins which had fallen from his hands. Had there been any great difference of principle between him and the ┊ *The new* Opposition, a complete change of ministry would ┊ *ministry under* naturally have resulted. But both the Government ┊ *Wilmington.* and the Opposition had been in the main Whigs. Any man of commanding intellect might have kept the late ministry together. As it was, a sort of coalition was made. Pulteney, it is difficult to say why, avoided the responsibility of the Premiership, and withdrew into insignificance in the Upper House as Lord Bath. The nominal head of the new Government was Wilmington, that same dull man who had for a moment thought to supersede Walpole at the beginning of the reign. Under him many of the old Cabinet were retained; Newcastle, Hardwicke, and Young keeping their offices. The new element was represented by Argyle, who was reinstated as Master of the Ordnance, Carteret, who succeeded Lord Harrington as Secretary, and Sandys, who became Chancellor of the Exchequer. Of Tories there appeared none, and Chesterfield and Pitt were excluded from the arrangement.

So slight a change in the construction of the Government seemed but a poor termination to the fierce opposition to which Walpole had been subjected. In fact, the rivalry had been one of persons and not of principles. The ministry were compelled ┊ *Character of* indeed, by pressure from without excited by their own ┊ *the new* clamours, to institute a Committee to inquire into the ┊ *ministry.* conduct of the great Prime Minister. But though it consisted principally of his personal enemies, too many interests were at stake to render their task easy; and when their report came, it appeared so trumpery, when compared with the charges which had been lavished upon the minister in Parliament, that it was a mere object of ridicule. It seemed as though the system of Walpole was after all to be continued. Many of his followers still remained· in the Cabinet, as the Pelhams (Newcastle and his brother Henry Pelham), and Yorke, Lord Hardwicke, and even the virtual Prime Minister, his enemy Carteret, was obliged by stress of circumstances to adopt that very Hanoverian policy which had so often been laid to the charge of the late minister. Carteret was a man of genius, but of irregular life, and so capricious, and sudden in his actions, that his administration has been called the drunken administration. Disregarding home patronage for the higher and more exciting work of foreign diplomacy, he found his influence gradually and surely passing into the hands of the Pelhams. It was necessary for him at all hazards to secure the King's friendship; he therefore allowed 16,000 Hanoverians to be taken into English pay, and it was strange to hear Lord Bath, and Sandys, the accuser of Walpole, upholding the Hanoverian connection.

A ministry which showed itself thus inconsistent with its assertions when out of office, and in which the elements of disunion were so evident, could not last long. The death of Wilmington (1743), the nominal Prime Minister, was the signal for its dissolution. The candidates for the Premiership were Pulteney on the one hand, supported by the talents of Carteret, and by the favour which this minister's newly-found interest for Hanover had given him with the King; and on the other hand Pelham, as representative of the party of Walpole, and backed by the influence which he still possessed. The question was settled in favour of Pelham, who, though without commanding abilities and constitutionally timid, possessed much of his late leader's love of quiet and power of management. Carteret continued for some time in power under his new chief; but their union could never be cordial, and before the close of 1744, Carteret—who had by continual flattery of the King's weakness so ingratiated himself with his master that the Pelhams thought their legitimate influence damaged by it—was dismissed. But before the confusion which arose on Walpole's fall had settled down one great point in his policy had at all events been reversed— England had thrown itself vigorously into the Continental war.

Pelham succeeds Wilmington. 1743

Such indeed was the position of Europe that it was impossible that England should hold aloof. But Walpole had at least tried, and with some effect, the power of diplomacy. The death of the Emperor Charles VI. of Germany had opened two great questions for which Europe had been long preparing. One of

these was the succession to the Austrian dominions, which Charles
had attempted to secure for his daughter by means of Question of the
the Pragmatic Sanction, and the other was the suc- Austrian
cession to the Empire. The questions were closely succession.
connected. The most dangerous claimant for the succession to the
Austrian dominions was the Elector of Bavaria, who alone of
the powers of Europe had refused the acceptance of the Pragmatic
Sanction ; he was also the most influential candidate for the
Imperial dignity. The Elector rested his claim to the Austrian
succession upon an arrangement by which, as long ago as the middle
of the sixteenth century, Ferdinand I. was said to have substituted the
heir of his daughter Anne, from whom the Elector was descended, in
the place of any other female heir. A second claimant was the King
of Spain, who regarded himself as the heir of all the rights of a
descendant of Charles V., who, when he divided his empire with
his brother, reserved the right of succession to his own immediate
posterity should the direct male line of Ferdinand become extinct.
Both Bavaria and Spain were close allies of France, and the possession of the Empire by the Elector, or of the Austrian dominions
either by the Elector or the Spanish King, would render the influence of France paramount in Europe. It was necessary for England
to oppose such an increase of the power of the Bourbons. For this
purpose it had appeared necessary to Walpole to re-establish something resembling the Grand Alliance, a union at all events which
should include the maritime powers, Hanover, Prussia (rapidly rising
to a first-rate power), and Austria.

But Prussia had just fallen into the hands of the ambitious
Frederick II., supplied by his father's care with a mag- Ambition of
nificent army and with a full treasury. He saw that Prussia.
the opportunity had arrived for making good certain long pending
claims upon a portion of Silesia, and without declaration of war,
occupied the disputed territory, and marching into Bohemia, entirely
defeated the Austrian troops at Molwitz. He was however yet so
far German at heart, that he was willing to guarantee the election of
Maria Theresa's husband to the Empire, and to support the Pragmatic
Sanction, if his claims in Silesia were satisfied. To induce the
Austrian princess to accept these terms became the object of English
diplomacy. It was thwarted by Maria Theresa herself. A strange
infatuation had taken possession of the Austrian ministers during the
close of the late Emperor's reign ; in spite of his action in the Polish
war, they believed in the pacific tendencies of Fleury, and relied

upon the friendship of France. All overtures on the part of Frederick were therefore disregarded, all appeals from England set at naught. The foolish dreams of Austria were dispelled when Frederick, thus repulsed, threw away his last remnant of German feeling and entered into close alliance with France, offering to renounce the claims which he had upon the Duchy of Berg, and to give his vote for the election of the Bavarian Elector to the Empire if his claims on Silesia were guaranteed.

Thus Maria Theresa found herself standing alone in Europe, supported by England only, which indeed supplied her willingly with subsidies, but still directed its chief efforts to persuading her to purchase Frederick's friendship by the cession of Silesia. In accordance with the convention with Prussia, in August 1741, two French armies were poured across the Rhine, one passing through Swabia to assist the Elector in a direct advance on Vienna, the second through Westphalia. So little was England prepared for war, that the King, as Elector of Hanover, was obliged to declare the neutrality of his Continental dominions for a year, a step which excited great anger in England, where the war spirit ran high, and which was a fresh source of complaint against Walpole. At this crisis of her danger Maria Theresa found assistance in that part of her dominions where she had least right to expect it. The hand of the Hapsburgs had been heavy upon Hungary, yet thither she betook herself, and yielding back to them almost the whole of their constitution, excited the warlike magnátes to enthusiasm by confiding to their charge her person and that of her child. As they crowded round to kiss the infant's hand, the hall rang with the shouts, "We will die for our king, Maria Theresa!" A moment's breathing space would allow time to bring the levée en masse of Hungary into the field : the opportunity was afforded by the diplomacy of England, which induced Frederick, who saw with jealousy the advancing power of France and Germany, to check his victorious march and sign a secret treaty at Kleinschnellendorf. The gathering forces of Hungary, the withdrawal of Frederick, and the errors of the Elector and of the French, who were jealous of each other, changed the face of the war. The march to Vienna was postponed for the capture of Prague. The withdrawal of the invaders to Bohemia allowed the Austrians to make a counter blow. As the Elector Charles Albert hastened to Frankfort to secure his election as Emperor, Khevenhuller, with the Austrian troops, was approaching his capital of Munich. Again, at the earnest entreaties of France, Frederick deserted his

[margin note:] Position of Maria Theresa.

engagements and renewed the war, but, unable to hold his advanced position at Olmutz in Moravia, he too fell back upon Bohemia, where the war was now centred.

The changed aspect of affairs was completed by the conduct of England : the pride of the country had been touched by Vernon's failure at Carthagena ; the neutrality of Han- *England supports Austria.* over had caused great discontent ; and when, in February 1742, Walpole had been driven from the ministry, the first act of his successors had been to increase both army and navy, to vote large subsidies to Maria Theresa, to induce the States-General to follow the lead of England, and to send an army of 30,000 English and Hanoverians into the Low Countries.   It was understood that, although as yet but auxiliaries in the main quarrel, it was the rivalry of France and England which was again to be decided in arms. Both the arms and diplomacy of England were successful.   In the Mediterranean the fleet under Commodore Matthews forced King Charles of Naples to neutrality, and allowed Sardinia, driven by the ambition of Spain to side with Austria, to defeat all the projects of the Bourbons in that country ; while the urgent instances of the ambassador at Vienna at length prevailed, and Maria Theresa was induced to give the price which Prussia demanded,—Silesia was conceded by the Treaties of Breslau and Berlin in June 1742. Frederick once more threw over his allies, and the French and Bavarians stood alone in Germany.   They were unable to make head against their enemies, their troops were shut up in Prague, and only after a brilliant but disastrous retreat did a shattered remnant of 14,000 men reach a place of safety in January 1743.

The tide of victory was then already turned when the English made their first appearance in Europe, acting in conjunc- *The English army in Flanders.* tion with some 18,000 subsidized Hanoverians.   The command of the English army, which to the number of 16,000 had been all the last year lying inactive in Flanders, was given to Lord Stair, and the object of the allies was to drive the French entirely out of Germany, and if possible invade Alsace and Lorraine, on which the eyes of the Austrians, who had but lately lost them, were constantly fixed.   To oppose the movement an army under the Duke de Noailles entered Franconia, and the various divisions of the British army and their allies from Hanover were set in motion towards the Maine.   With characteristic slowness, Stair proceeded to collect upon the Maine an army of 40,000 men. Towards the Maine also on the south De Noailles betook himself with about 60,000. Stair lay idly awaiting his 12,000 Hanoverians and Hessians who had not yet appeared, and thus gave De Noailles opportunity of securing the south of the river and holding most of the passages across it. Having waited long enough to be thus

Battle of Dettingen. outgeneralled, Stair suddenly changed his plan, and, without receiving his reinforcements, marched up the

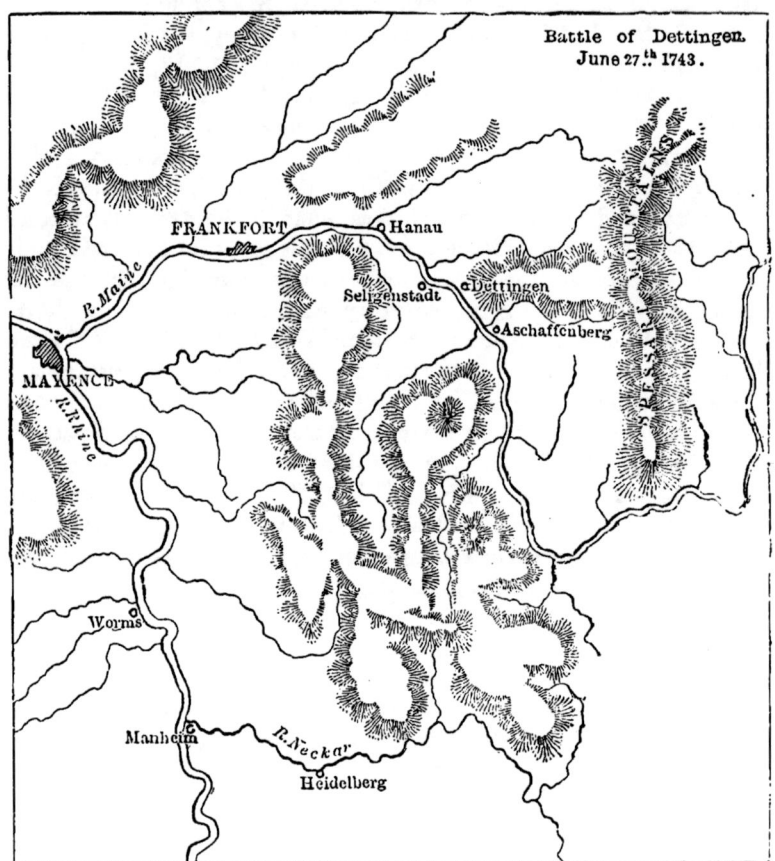

Battle of Dettingen.
June 27.ᵗʰ 1743.

river towards Franconia. He passed Hanau, where he established his chief magazines, and moved towards Aschaffenberg. Between these two towns branches of the Spessart mountains approach the Maine, and about half way between the two is the large village of Dettingen. From Dettingen to Aschaffenberg extends a narrow plain, entered by a somewhat difficult passage between the mountains and river at Dettingen. On reaching this plain the English found themselves outmarched by De Noailles, and thus cut off from Aschaffenberg. It was while thus entangled that they were joined by the King and the Duke of Cumberland. The King found the army cut off from the supplies it had hoped to draw from Franconia, and in danger of being separated from its magazines at Hanau also. Thither it was determined if possible to secure a retreat. As the English believed that the enemy was higher up the river than they were, and that they should be closely pursued, the King took command of the rear as the post of danger, but De Noailles had already forestalled them. He had at once moved down the river so as to put himself between the English and Hanau, taking up his position at Seligenstadt. He sent some 23,000 men, under his nephew the Duc de Grammont, across the river to occupy Dettingen. These troops occupied a very strong position behind a swamp and a ravine made by a watercourse. De Noailles' main army lay on the southern bank, but bridges of communication were made between the two divisions, and cannon placed on the south bank to play upon the flank of the retreating English. Escape seemed almost impossible, especially as the English were in entire ignorance of these movements. On finding his advance checked at Dettingen, George at once left the rear and put himself at the head of the army. There seemed no course but to cut a way through De Grammont's forces. This commander, however, believing himself engaged with the advanced troops of the English army only, and thinking to crush them, rashly left his strong position and crossed the ravine. He found himself in front of the whole English army. The King's horse had run away with him, and he had dismounted and put himself at the head of his troops, and addressing them a few inspiriting words, led them to the attack with much gallantry. De Noailles saw the destruction of his plans and hastened to retrieve the error of his nephew. His efforts however were useless. The mass of infantry, led by his Majesty in person, broke through the enemy, whose loss was so great that De Noailles recalled them beyond the Maine. The retreat towards the bridges became a rout, and they left more than 6000 dead and wounded upon the field. The King wisely determined to get out of his dangerous position as soon as possible, and pushed on that night to Hanau, leaving his wounded to the mercy of the French commander, who treated them exceedingly well. Stair, as hasty in the moment of victory as slow in his preliminary movements, urged **immediate pursuit, but was overruled by the King. On receiving the** expected reinforcements he again urged advance, but jealousies had sprung up between him and the German commanders. He was disgusted at the rejection of his advice, and talking loudly of Hanoverian influence, sent in his resignation, which was accepted.

The objects of a further advance however were obtained without bloodshed. The French army in Bavaria had been beaten backwards **Effect of the** by Charles of Loraine,[1] and had retired behind the Lauter **victory.** into Alsace, whither De Noailles, finding himself unsupported between two enemies, also withdrew. The victorious allies pushed on after them, the King to Worms and Prince Charles to beyond the Rhine opposite Alt Brisach. The new Emperor was thus left without allies, and concluded (July 1743) a convention of neutrality with the Austrians, and withdrew to Philipsburg.

A favourable opportunity for peaceful arrangements seemed **Negotiations** to have arrived. Prussia had gained its object; **for peace.** French intervention had failed; the Austrian suc- **July.** cession was secured; the only open question was what was to be done with the expelled Emperor. George and his favourite minister Carteret, who were at Hanover, undertook the negotiations. George, as Elector of Hanover, and Carteret, from his general interest in foreign politics, took a German and not an English view of the situation. It was George's object, as Elector of Hanover, to appear as a paramount power among the other electors, and to form a strong alliance in the Empire entirely in his own interests. For this purpose he had naturally,—considering the antecedents of his second kingdom England, regarded a close alliance with Austria as of the utmost importance. At the same time, as a Prince of the Empire, he had no strong wish that the Imperial dignity should be constantly in Austrian hands, and was quite willing to allow the validity of the election of the Emperor Charles. In conjunction with Carteret, he therefore agreed that Charles should retain the Imperial title upon condition of renouncing all claims on Austria, of allowing the validity of the vote of Bohemia in all affairs of the Empire, and of dismissing the French from the fortified places they still held within the Empire. He even consented to insist upon the restoration by Austria of Charles's hereditary dominions, Bavaria (now to be erected into a kingdom), and upon the payment of a large sum to the Emperor to support his dignity. Had this treaty been completed, George would have appeared as the mediator of the peace of the Empire, as the champion of the rights of the princes, as the defender of the Austrian dominions, and altogether as the chief

---

[1] Brother of Francis, Maria Theresa's husband.

power in Germany. To a certain point the interests of the people of England had been the same as that of their King. But their real enmity was against France, and under the guidance of a Whig aristocracy, they would have wished to pursue their traditional policy of opposing the Bourbons, chiefly at sea. The arrangements of the proposed treaty by no means suited them. They had long been clamouring against the German tendencies of the King, they had seen with extreme dislike the employment of subsidized Hanoverian troops, and now positively refused to pay a subsidy to the Emperor —a Bavarian prince and the hereditary friend of France.

To the astonishment of the negotiating Powers and the shame of Carteret, the proposed treaty was suddenly broken off. England wanted war with France, and considered it could be best carried on by close alliance with Austria, *Treaty of Worms. Sept. 13, 1743.* which was only too glad to continue the war, with the hope of retaining its hold on Bavaria and rewinning Silesia. A treaty known as the Treaty of Worms therefore took the place of the former pacific arrangements. England, Holland, Austria, Saxony, and Sardinia, agreed to assure the Pragmatic Sanction and the European balance, while Sardinia undertook the armed defence of the Austrian dominions in Italy. It was met by a counter treaty known as the League of Frankfort, the most important members of which were France and Prussia; for the elevation of Hanover implied the degradation of Prussia, and the promise of the King of Sardinia set free Austrian troops *League of Frankfort April 5, 1744* which the Prussian King believed would be used only for the purpose of reconquering Silesia. The European contest was thus assuming a more general and intelligible form; England and France, hitherto auxiliaries, appeared each at the head of a great league, and it was their interests, and indirectly the supremacy of the sea, which were now at issue.

Even yet no declaration of war between England and France had been issued, but it was natural that the French, aware of the real character of the war, should use every means for distressing England. Early in the year it set on *Threatened invasion of England.* foot an attempted invasion of England in favour of the Stuarts. An army of 15,000 was collected at Dunkirk, and placed under the command of the best French general, Marshal Saxe, while fleets were collected at Toulon and Brest for the invasion of England and to support a Jacobite rising. The Brest fleet came out of harbour and approached the English coast. The English fleet was drawn into pursuit; and for the moment the coast of Kent was unguarded. A considerable portion of the French army was on board the transports and had sailed. Once again England owed its safety to the weather. A violent storm blowing direct upon Dunkirk, prevented the movement of the rest of the transports, scattered those already at sea, and the loss was such that the French ministry abandoned their design, and Marshal Saxe was appointed to command the army in Flanders. The naval armaments and this open support of the Pretender gave rise to warm complaints of breach of treaty on the part of our envoy at Paris; as his complaints were listened to with disdain, a formal declaration of war was at length made.

On the Continent the selfish policy of the French, who could think of nothing but the extension of their own boundaries, ruined
Progress of
the war. the success of the war. The Netherlands were invaded and rapidly overrun; Savoy and Piedmont conquered; but these successes on the extremity of the scene of action did not tend to the conclusion of the war. Frederick of Prussia advanced through Bohemia and took Prague, and thus saved France from a threatened invasion of Alsace; but, unsupported by his allies, he fell back from the Austrian dominions, and upon the death of the Emperor (Jan. 20, 1745) was unable to prevent the election of the Prince of Tuscany, husband of Maria Theresa, who ascended the Imperial throne as Francis I. Maximilian, the son of the late Emperor, had shown himself willing to accept the views of Austria; by the Treaty of Fuessen (April 22, 1745) he renounced all claims to the Austrian succession, promising to recall his troops from the French armies, and to give his vote to Francis, husband of Maria Theresa, who on her side recognized the election of his late father, and restored all her Bavarian conquests. Again it appeared that general negotiations might have been possible. But Carteret had been
Changes in
the ministry.
Nov. 1744. driven from office, and the Whigs under Pelham were bent on carrying on their hostility with France. His unpopular Hanoverian tendencies, and the offhand manner in which he had treated the Pelhams, secured Carteret's fall. His place was taken by Walpole's old colleague Harrington. With Carteret withdrew Lord Winchelsea and several others, thus affording Mr. Pelham an opportunity for carrying out that form of administration to which his timidity urged him. In exact contrast to Walpole, he dreaded opposition, and sought to make friends of all parties, and to establish his ministry on what was then called a broad bottom. He persuaded Chesterfield and Pitt to give up their

opposition, and the former to accept the Lord Lieutenancy of Ireland. To the Tory Lord Gower he gave the Privy Seal, and even Sir John Hind Cotton, an undoubted Jacobite, was given a place about the Court. This was not done without great opposition from the King, who disliked Chesterfield and Pitt for their opposition to his Hanoverian schemes, and had a natural mistrust of Tories and Jacobites. The effect of these changes was almost to suppress opposition in the House. The ministry, now including most of the leaders of the Opposition, satisfied with a change of principles, made but little change in practice. The reunited Whig party felt that, as they were engaged in an open war with France, they were, even while subsidising Germans, carrying out their true policy. Pitt openly declared that he no longer opposed subsidies in face of the present state of affairs abroad. He pointed out that the object of the war was somewhat changed, that, the minister who rested wholly on his foreign influence being removed, they were no longer fighting solely in the interests of Austria, but to secure an equitable peace for themselves and their allies. However this may have been, the system of German subsidies went further and further. The Hanoverian troops were for the present dismissed, but their pay was added to the Austrian subsidy. Saxony was bought, the Elector of Cologne was bought, and so was the Elector of Mayence ; and next year (1746) 18,000 Hanoverians were again taken into English pay. Robert Walpole lived just long enough to see the dangers he had kept aloof for twenty years gathering round England. He died in March 1745, leaving England plunged deep in a Continental war, with constantly increasing grants for military service, and consequently increased financial difficulties, and on the eve of the most determined and dangerous effort which the exiled family ever made for the recovery of their crown.

German subsidies granted. 1745.

The war still continued under the mistaken conduct of the French. But neither their successes against England at Fontenoy, nor the invasion of the young Pretender which they supported, nor their victory over the Sardinians at Basignano, were the least decisive. As Frederick, who felt himself deserted, bitterly said, the victories might as well have been won on the banks of the Scamander. What he could do singlehanded the Prussian King did. He defeated the Austrians at Friedberg, and again upon the Sohr. He conquered the Saxons at Kesseldorf and occupied Dresden. But seeing clearly that his allies were bent upon their own ends, he

again listened to the anti-Bourbon diplomacy of England, made a
separate peace with Austria, and the Treaty of Dresden (Dec. 25,
1745) closed the second Silesian war. But, in spite of the withdrawal of Prussia, the general war continued. Early in the spring
a French army under Marshal Saxe invested Tournay. The Netherlands were occupied by an allied army of English and Dutch. There
Campaign in   should have been 28,000 English and 50,000 Dutch,
Flanders   but, although it was their own country that was threatened, the Dutch were so dilatory that the allied army numbered little
more than 50,000. These were under the Duke of Cumberland and
the Dutch general the Prince of Waldeck. The Duke, who was
young, was somewhat controlled by the Austrian Marshal Konigsegg,
and had with him as his military guide General Ligonier. With
these troops the Duke advanced to the relief of Tournay. Marshal
Saxe, whose forces were much superior in numbers, could afford to
leave 15,000 men to continue the siege, while, marching southward
along the river, he occupied a very strong position to cover his
operations. The position was rendered almost unassailable. The
French faced southward; on their right was the river Scheldt, with
the fortified bridge securing their communication and retreat, and
the village Antoing. A narrow and difficult valley ran along
their front from Antoing to Fontenoy, and their left was covered
by the wood of Barré, on the right of which a redoubt had been
constructed. The whole of this position was fortified with field-
works and abattis, with the exception of a gap between Fontenoy and
the wood of Barré, where the difficulties of the approach were held
to be of themselves sufficient. It was resolved to assault this terribly
strong position. To the Dutch was intrusted the attack of the French
right, with the villages Antoing and Fontenoy; to the English the
attack on their left. The attack of the Dutch was without energy,
and failed, and the Prince of Waldeck, withdrawing his troops to a
safe distance, kept them unemployed the remainder of the day. A
Battle of   similar want of energy was exhibited by General In-
Fontenoy.   goldsby, who had been instructed to assault a redoubt
May 11, 1745.   on the left of the French and to clear the wood of Barré.
Finding more opposition than he expected, he withdrew when the
enemy were on the point of abandoning their redoubt, and demanded
further orders. The English and Hanoverians, on the other hand,
energetically assaulted the unfortified gap between Fontenoy and the
wood. Regardless of the flanking fire by which they were decimated,
they pushed across the ravine and up the opposite hill. The space

was narrow, and they advanced, without deploying, in a solid column 10,000 strong with a face of about forty men. The ground was too rough for their cavalry, which therefore advanced in their rear. In this solid formation, with astonishing heroism and determination, they pushed on, crushing all opposition, and unchecked by frequent cavalry charges. They won the crown of the position, cut the enemy's centre, and were moving onwards towards the bridge of Calonne, threatening thus to cut off all retreat from the broken army. The victory seemed decided, and Voltaire allows that, had the Dutch only moved, the French must have been inevitably routed and destroyed. But the Prince of Waldeck never stirred. Fresh troops could therefore be brought from Antoing and Fontenoy to repel the victorious column. In this work it was the Irish Brigade which chiefly distinguished itself, and at last when, by the advice of the Duc de Richelieu, four cannon were placed right in front of the column so as to fire down its whole length, finding itself wholly unsupported, the heroic body began to give ground. It retired as it had come, slowly, disputing every yard, and entirely without confusion. When it reached ground where cavalry could act, that arm, hitherto useless, covered the retreat, and the whole army fell back to Ath. Tournay was treacherously surrendered, and the allies had to content themselves with covering Brussels and Antwerp. This wonderful unsupported advance, though useless for the battle, and purchased with immense loss of life, was for long a just source of pride to the English soldier.

It was the necessity of withdrawing troops for the defence of England which had rendered the campaign in Flanders after the partial defeat of Fontenoy so disastrous. Prince Charles Edward, though bitterly disappointed by the failure of the expedition in the preceding year, did not leave France; and as the French ministry, occupied with their continental affairs, refused him further assistance, he determined to go alone and unsupported to Scotland, and throw himself on the loyalty of his friends there, although in all his previous negotiations with them they had refused to think of a rising unsupported by foreign troops and arms. *Prince Charles Edward lands in Scotland.* Scraping together what little money he could, and purchasing a small supply of firearms, the Prince embarked at Nantes in a privateer. He was escorted, without the knowledge of the Government, by a French man-of-war, in which his stores were placed. On the passage to England they encountered an English vessel, which, though unable to capture the French man-of-war engaged it so vigorously that it had to withdraw to France to refit, and it was in the little privateer, 'La Doutelle,' thus stripped of his supplies and with only seven companions, that the Prince reached the Hebrides. In this plight he met but a cold reception, and it was not without considerable persuasion that Macdonald of Clanranald and other gentlemen of that tribe joined him. Their chief, Sir Alexander Macdonald, and the head of the Macleods, on whose assistance he had relied, kept aloof. Of more importance even than the Macdonalds was the adhesion of Cameron of Lochiel. This chief seems to have been won, against his better judgment, by the persuasive power of Charles, who undoubtedly had in an unusual degree the art of attracting adherents. While still in the extreme west of the mainland Charles was joined by Murray of Broughton, who had been his chief agent, and whom he appointed his Secretary of State. The Prince had reached the mainland on the 25th of July; it was not till the 30th that information was received by the Government that he had left Nantes, and he had been three weeks in Scotland before it was known in London. On the 19th of August the insurrectionary standard was raised in the solitary valley of Glen Finnan, where the aged Marquis of Tullibardine, the rightful heir to the dukedom of Athol, read Prince Charles's Commission of Regency. This ceremony was graced by the presence of a considerable number of English prisoners, who had been captured a few days previously by Lochiel's followers as they were marching to reinforce Fort William.

Scotland is cleft in sunder by a great valley running from the Beauley Firth in the north-east in a south-westerly direction to the salt-water lake Loch Eil. This valley, at present occupied by the Caledonian Canal, forms the basin of a chain of lakes, by far the largest of which is Loch Ness, occupying nearly half of the north-east end of the valley. Between its northern extremity and the sea lies the town of Inverness; at its southern end was Fort Augustus, one of the forts established to keep the Highlands in check, while, where the valley reaches Loch Eil, there was the still more lonely post of Fort William immediately under Ben Nevis. It was in the close neighbourhood of this fort that Charles's followers were first collected, and it was while trying to strengthen it that the royal troops had first come into collision with the insurgents. The tribes to the north of Inverness, as well as Sir Alexander Macdonald and Macleod, were either well-affected or held in neutrality chiefly by the influence of Duncan Forbes of Culloden, Lord President, who had also contrived for the present to attach Lord Lovat, head of the Frasers, to the Government interest, so that it was with the western clans only that Charles began his expedition.

The English military commander in Scotland was Sir John Cope, who had altogether about 3000 men under his command. Cope marches against him All this time the King was absent from England, and orders had to be issued by the Lords Justices. They approved how-ever of Cope's plan for immediately marching into the Highlands and crushing the insurgents if possible among the mountains. With this intention, leaving his dragoons behind him, Cope set out from Stirling along the direct north road towards Inverness. At Dalwhinnie, which is now a posting-station on the great north road, the military road made by Marshal Wade branched off to Fort Augustus, which it was Cope's object to reach and relieve; the main road passed onwards to Inverness. The mountain which forms the south-east side of the great valley in which Fort Augustus lies has to be crossed. It is called in this place Corrie-Arrack, and to cross it the road winds in steep zigzags. The Highlanders had got possession of this difficult pass, and intended to destroy Cope's army while ascending the zigzags. Their disappointment was great when they found that he had turned aside at Dalwhinnie, and was in hasty march for Inverness. By this means he probably hoped to strengthen the loyal clans of the north and to draw the Prince's army in pursuit. He however left the road towards the capital quite unguarded. Charles at once pushed on and crossed the Badenoch mountains to Blair Athol, from whence the great road runs, without any obstacle, through the Pass of Killiecrankie into the plains of Perthshire. He rested a few days at Charles avoids him, and gains Edinburgh Perth, where he was joined by Drummond, Duke of Perth, and by Lord George Murray, the Duke of Athol's brother, a man of considerable military experience and capacity. He then crossed the Forth a little above Stirling, the dragoon regiments which had been left there retiring before him, and advanced rapidly towards Edinburgh. The Castle of Edinburgh was secure, but the town had no adequate fortifications, and the inhabitants doubted long and painfully as to whether they should open their gates or not. The news that Cope, on learning his mistake, had taken ship and had already reached Dunbar, encouraged them to think of resistance, but their determination vanished away after a skirmish called "the canter of Colt-Brig," when two regiments of dragoons ran away, and did not stop till they reached Dunbar. Negotiations were set on foot, but were cut short by the surprise of the town by the Highlanders. On

the 17th of September Charles took possession of Holyrood House, and
it seemed as if the inhabitants of Edinburgh were by no means sorry to
Cope lands receive him. He could not rest long, however, as 'Cope
at Dunbar. was marching along the Firth from Dunbar. He expected to meet his enemy between that town and Edinburgh, but the
Prince marched along the hills to the south of the Firth, and Cope
was surprised to find his enemy again beyond him. He was then near
Prestonpans. He changed his face at once, and lay with his back
to the Firth and his face to the hills, as he believed in an unassailable
position, separated from the Highlanders by a morass. But Charles
was bent on fighting, and a narrow pathway through the morass to
the eastward was pointed out to him. Down this he led his forces
so as to gain a position eastward of the English, who had again to
change their face, looking now directly eastward, with their backs
to Edinburgh. Their infantry were in the centre, their cavalry on
Is defeated either flank. The battle is said to have been decided
at Prestonpans. in six minutes. The rush of the Highlanders renewed
Sept 21 the panic among the dragoons, who all took to their
heels. The infantry stood with their flanks exposed, and as their
fire did not check the Highlanders, they were soon engaged at close
quarters, where the Highland target parried the bayonet thrust, while
the right hand was free to use the claymore. The line was soon
broken, and it is said that not more than 170 escaped death or capture.
The cavalry, taking Cope with them, did not draw bridle till they
reached Berwick.

Some preparations had been made in England to withstand the
advance of the rebels. Marshal Wade was at Newcastle with
Indifference such troops as he could collect, the Dutch were called
of England. upon to supply, in accordance with their treaty, 6000
men, and some regiments were recalled from Flanders. But throughout the population of England there was now, and through the
whole campaign, a strange carelessness as to which side should prove
victorious. The Revolution had been, comparatively speaking, an
aristocratic movement. It had moved the power from the Crown
only to put it in the hands of the nobles. Parliament was so far
from being an adequate representative body, that the disputes carried
on in it excited no very warm interest in the nation at large. At
times indeed it was necessary for the Opposition to excite the people
by some national cry; but that Opposition had uniformly employed
the most violent language against the Hanoverian influence and the
minister of the Hanoverian King. Such partial views therefore as

the people had been allowed of what was going on among their governors had all tended rather to direct the loyalty, which was then so inherent a characteristic of the English, towards the exiled house. Except in the matter of religion, the people at large were able to discover but little difference whether their king was a Stuart or a Guelph; and on this occasion the assurance had been carefully spread that the privileges of the Church of England would not be touched; indeed one of Charles's difficulties arose from the jealousy of his Protestant followers. The class who had gained by the Revolution was that class which Walpole and Walpole's policy had chiefly favoured—the middle class; but as usual the middle class was apathetic and slow to risk anything unless for some personal object. At first therefore it was the Government, unaided by the people, which had to check the insurrection. It will be seen that afterwards the aristocracy offered, though in a very selfish manner, to come forward, and that some towns, especially in Scotland, awoke to their responsibilities, but on the whole it was the Government alone which had to act by means of its soldiers, and England had been stripped of soldiers for its foreign wars. On the other hand, the Jacobites had seen the insurrection of 1715 so thoroughly futile, and had during Walpole's long administration so settled down under the existing Government, that only a few of the more enthusiastic took a real interest in the quarrel.

Had Prince Charles advanced immediately after the battle of Prestonpans he would have found himself almost unopposed; but by the time he had collected some money, gathered in his reinforcements, organized his army, and persuaded the Highlanders to cross the border, Marshal Wade's army had increased to 10,000; the Dutch and English troops had come from abroad; there was a second army under the Duke of Cumberland formed in the centre of England; the guards and trained bands had marched out to Finchley and formed a third body, which the King declared he would himself lead. To turn the position of Wade at Newcastle it was determined, as in 1715, to march along behind the Cheviots and enter England by Carlisle; and the clans (about 6000 strong) crossed the Border on the 8th of November. Carlisle yielded without much difficulty, and on the recommendation of Lord George Murray, who now assumed the military command of the army, it was determined to advance into the heart of England. In two bodies they marched up the Eden over Shap Fell to Lancaster and to Preston; the Prince winning the heart of the Highlanders by wear-

Charles marches into England as far as Derby.

ing their dress and marching at the head of the second division, as strong and unwearied as the best among them, for he was gifted with a fine athletic body, which he had further trained by constant exercise. His carriage he insisted upon offering to the aged Lord Pitsligo. His care for his followers, of which this is an instance, tended much to endear him to them; he was at this part of his life adorned with many of the best graces of a king; his clemency was the constant complaint of his sterner counsellors. It is said indeed to have encouraged more than one attempt at assassination. Towards his enemy, the Elector as he called him, he was also studiously merciful and dignified. In all negotiations with his followers or with the French the safety of the Hanoverian Elector and his family was bargained for; and even when £30,000 was put upon his head, dead or alive, after entirely refusing to make a counter proclamation, he insisted on offering only £30. This was indeed afterwards overruled, and a larger reward offered, but he even then said he felt sure no follower of his was capable of winning it, and the proclamation ended : "Should any fatal accident happen from hence let the blame lie entirely at the door of those who first set the infamous example."

The army passed Preston, that ill-omened town to the Stuart cause, in all haste, entered Manchester, where they met with more recruits than usual, skilfully deceived the Duke of Cumberland into the idea that they were marching towards Wales, got past his army, and had nothing between them and London except the camp at Finchley. They reached Derby, but there Lord George Murray and all the commanders unanimously advised retreat. It was true that they had eluded both Wade and Cumberland, but those commanders with their armies were following them close; the slightest check before reaching London, and their little army of 5000 would be enveloped by 30,000 men; it would surely be better to fall back upon their supports in Scotland, where Lord Strathallan had a force of some 3000 or 4000 men. Charles was unable to hold out against these arguments, backed by all the men of military weight in his army, and very sullenly and unwillingly at length gave his consent to a retreat. It is plain that the Scotch chiefs had been thoroughly disappointed in the neutrality of the English population, were beginning to fear for their own heads, and thought it more prudent as well as more practicable to separate the two kingdoms, and establish

but retreats, to the relief of the Government

Charles at all events at first as King of Scotland. This determination was an immense relief to the Government. Whether a further march would have been successful or not, it is certain that the Government regarded its chances of suc. cess as very great, and London was stricken with panic ; the Bank was reduced to pay in sixpences ; the Duke of Newcastle is said to have seriously thought of declaring for the Pretender ; the King sent some of his valuables to the river ready for embarkation. The camp at Finchley was by no means completed ; Wade and Cumberland were so far behind that they scarcely hoped to come up with the Highlanders ; the occupation of London would have been the signal for a French invasion, and probably for a great Jacobite rising in England. The day on which the news of the advance to Derby was known was called Black Friday.

The retreat was very rapid, and, as was natural, now that the soldiers were in bad humour, by no means orderly. The insurgents were closely pursued by the Duke of Cumberland, who came up with them, but was checked in a skirmish near Penrith, and passing through Carlisle, which was speedily recaptured by the English, reached Glasgow, where they established themselves, and by means of large requisitions succeeded in refreshing and reorganizing themselves after their rapid march. They had marched 580 miles in 56 days. After a week's rest they advanced to besiege the Castle of Stirling, which was defended by General Blakeney. Being joined by the Scotch army under Strathallan, with whom were some French soldiers, and Lord John Drummond, a general in the French service, the Pretender's army reached the number of 9000, the largest he ever commanded. Wade, who had grown slow from age, was superseded by General Hawley by the advice of the Duke of Cumberland. He was an officer of some experience, but little talent, and of a ferocious disposition. He was nicknamed the Lord Chief Justice, and as Horace Walpole tells us, "was brave and able, with no small bias to the brutal." He profoundly despised his enemies, and advancing to relieve Stirling Castle, took up his position at Falkirk without even ordinary military precaution. He was not even present with his army, but was enjoying, with some of his officers, the civilities of Callendar House, where the Countess of Kilmarnock, whose husband was with the Pretender, was entertaining and delaying them. There are two roads between Stirling and Falkirk ; some troops were sent forward by the straight road to deceive the English, while the main body under Charles swept round to the south. They were then separated from the English by a high rugged heath called Falkirk Muir. When the news of their approach was brought to Hawley, he

Charles besieges Stirling. Jan. 3, 1746.

Wins the battle of Falkirk. Jan. 17.

hastened to the field, and led his cavalry rapidly forward to try and
secure the crest of this hill. It was a race between him and the
Highlanders, and they succeeded in winning it. Hawley fell back to
lower ground, and arranged his troops, with their right upon a broken
ravine which descended to the plain. His artillery got hopelessly
jammed in a morass. The battle began with a charge of the royal
cavalry on the left, which was met by a steady fire from the Highlanders, from which the dragoons as usual fled, all but one regiment.
The Highlanders, then rushing forward, entirely broke the centre and
left of the royal army, but their rush was checked by the ravine
on the right; the royal troops there held their own, and being joined
by the one steady regiment of cavalry, were enabled to make an
orderly retreat. One of the flying regiments had fought well at
Fontenoy, and Lord John Drummond, who had been present
at that battle, believed that their retreat was a feint, and by his
advice further attack was suspended. Charles had shown considerable skill in bringing his troops with their back to the wind, so that
the driving storm and cold January wind might beat full in the faces
of the English troops.

The Duke of Cumberland, who had been detained in the south of
England in expectation of a French invasion, was
indignant at this defeat, and declaring that he would
himself willingly lead the broken remains of Hawley's army against the Highlanders, got himself appointed commander. He was a young man of great energy, with the hereditary
bravery of his family, and an active if not a very able general; he
had, moreover, won the confidence of the army at Fontenoy. He
was a man however of violent passions, and at present roused
almost to ferocity by the success of the Highlanders, which touched
his pride both as a military man and a prince of the Hanoverian
house. The Pretender did not follow up his success, but persisted,
from a false sense of honour, in the siege of Stirling, and allowed
the broken English army to be reconstituted. He was however
obliged to desist from this project by a memorial signed by all his
chiefs, and presented by Lord George Murray. Some coldness had
arisen between the Prince and his followers ever since the retreat
from Derby, and the present prudent counsel tended still further to
widen the breach. The army was divided into two bodies, and marched
rapidly towards Inverness, where they were to unite. Cumberland
hastened in pursuit. Inverness was easily mastered, and the neighbouring clan, the Mackintoshes, joined the Prince. But the English,

Cumberland
takes command
of the army

now fully on the alert, prevented the arrival of any supplies from France, and the army was suffering from want of provisions and money. Cumberland's army was meanwhile well supplied from the sea, and marched towards Inverness along the coast from Aberdeen. The passages of the rivers, Spey, Findhorn, and Nairn, were but weakly disputed, and on the 14th of April the royal army entered the town of Nairn. That night Charles slept at Culloden House, the seat of President Forbes, who had fled on his approach. Want of provisions, and the habit of the Highlanders of returning at times to their homes, had reduced his army to about 5000, and of these many were absent from the standards in Inverness and elsewhere searching for food. It was determined, at the suggestion of Charles and Lord George Murray, to attempt a night surprise, but the darkness of the night *He defeats Charles at Culloden, April 16,* and the weariness of the men prevented its success, and the hour proposed for the attack still found them four miles from the English posts. They fell back to Culloden Moor. Murray and some others wanted to retire, but Charles and some of his more reckless followers from France, in overweening trust in the dash of the Highlanders, insisted upon fighting. The men of Athol, the Camerons and the Stuarts, had the right of the line under Lord George Murray, while the Macdonalds, who claimed that position ever since the battle of Bannockburn, sulkily received orders to occupy the left. Taught by former experience, the Duke of Cumberland ranged his army in three lines, with cannon between every two regiments, the second line being drawn up three deep, and arranged as men now are when forming square to receive cavalry. The opening cannonade was wholly in favour of the English, and observing the loss of his followers, Murray advanced with the right. Wearied and harassed as they were, the Highlanders broke through the first line, and captured two cannon, but the firm formation and scathing fire of the second line threw them into hopeless confusion. On the left of the Highland line the Macdonalds, aggrieved at their position, remained immoveable, in spite of the urgent entreaties of their commander, in spite even of the touching words of Macdonald of Keppoch, who cried as he fell, " My God, have the children of my tribe forsaken me !" They afterwards fell back and joined the second line. They were however now outflanked, and their retreat threatened, and though there were some thoughts of trying to retrieve the fortunes of the day with the unbroken left, the more prudent officers regarded the battle as lost, and compelled Charles to fly. He went first of all to Lord Lovat's residence, but, finding but a cold reception from that scheming villain, who was trying to keep well with the Government, while he had sent his son and clan to join the Prince, he fled onwards till he reached the Castle of Glengarry, beyond Fort Augustus. The broken fragments of his army were collected, about 1200 in number, by the skill of Lord George Murray at Ruthven in Badenoch. But Charles gave up the struggle, and sent orders that they should look to their own safety. The insurrection was over: vengeance began. The cruelty with which that vengeance was executed gained Cumberland the nickname of "The Butcher." In the pursuit after Culloden but little quarter was given, and acts of brutal ferocity stained the glory of the day. Some wounded Highlanders who had crawled to a farm building were deliberately burnt to death in it. The prisoners were kept in want of the necessaries of life, and many of the wounded put to death in cold blood. Cumberland fixed his headquarters at Fort Augustus, and harried the neighbouring country with every species of military execution. Acts of cruelty and of wild license were done chiefly at the instigation of General Hawley, but not without Cumberland's knowledge. The Duke was however, and rightly, hailed as the saviour of England.

and cruelly suppresses the rebellion.

For five months Charles was a solitary fugitive in the Highlands and Hebrides. He frequently had to trust his secret to the poorest Highlanders, but the high price set on his head never induced them for a moment to break their faith. His best known escape took place in South Uist, whither he had been tracked very shortly after the battle of Culloden, and where he was surrounded by upwards of 2000 men. Flora Macdonald, a young lady visiting Clanranald's family, succeeded in bringing him safely through this difficulty by procuring from her stepfather, who was an officer in the King's army, a passport for herself and a female servant. In this disguise she took Charles with her into Skye, where, making his secret known to the wife of Sir Alexander Macdonald, who was in the King's interest, she by her means got him put under the charge of Macdonald of Kingsburgh, who brought him to a place of safety. We are told that his height and want of grace in the management of his petticoats, especially in passing the watercourses, very nearly betrayed him. Flora Macdonald afterwards married the son of Macdonald of Kingsburgh. At last, on the 20th September, attended by Lochiel and a considerable number of other fugitives, he set sail

Charles escapes to France.

for France from Loch-na-Nuagh, the very spot where he had landed fourteen months before.

Thus terminated a most romantic piece of military history, astonishing both in the success which the small body of Highlanders were able to gain and the rapidity with which their successes were brought to an end. Had Lord George Murray been a worse general, and had the Scotch chiefs had less at heart the separation of Scotland from England, the success of the enterprise might have been different. At the two critical periods of the war, at Derby and after the battle of Falkirk, Charles was probably right in disliking any retrograde movements. No doubt, on purely military grounds, his opinion was wrong; but a body of half-trained enthusiastic Highlanders are nothing unless victorious. The marked change visible in their retreat both from Derby and from Stirling, on both of which occasions great disorder and want of discipline arose, shows that the moral side of the movement was not sufficiently considered by the generals. On the other hand, Lord George Murray showed great skill in hoodwinking and passing the armies both of Wade and Cumberland, and much good judgment in refusing to introduce regular drill or arms among the Highland regiments. The Lords Balmerino and Kilmarnock were beheaded for their share in the conspiracy, and Lord Lovat, wily though he had been, was convicted on the evidence of the Prince's Secretary of State, Murray of Broughton, who turned King's evidence, and executed. Many stringent measures against the Highlanders were at once passed, such as the Disarming Act, the Act to forbid the wearing of the Highland dress, and more important, an Act for the abolition of heritable jurisdictions, by which the arbitrary power of the chiefs of the clans was destroyed, and regular tribunals under responsible judges established.

At the very time that the Highlanders were still in the country England had passed through a ministerial crisis. The Pelhams had found themselves thwarted and in danger of being supplanted by Granville (Carteret); *Ministerial crisis Feb. 1746* for although they had succeeded in driving him from the ministry, he was still the King's favourite—a position which he had earned by constantly seconding the royal wishes with regard to foreign politics. The chief opponents of these views were Pitt and Chesterfield, and the Pelhams now determined upon bringing matters to a crisis by demanding the admission of Pitt into the ministry. The King, influenced by Lord Granville and Lord Bath, refused to admit him, and the Pelhams, their friend Lord Harrington

(Stanhope), and their whole party resigned. The King at once instructed Lord Granville to form a new Government. He undertook the task, but three days sufficed to show that the King's favour was no match for the Parliamentary influence of the great Whig party, of which Newcastle was the acknowledged leader. Much against his will, the King had to receive back his old ministry upon any terms they chose to propose, and Pitt became first Vice-Treasurer of Ireland, and shortly afterwards Paymaster of the Forces. In this position he was enabled much to increase his popularity, by rejecting the vast profits which it had been the habit hitherto for the Paymaster to make. That officer had been in the habit of receiving a large percentage upon all foreign subsidies, and of using as his own the interest accruing from the large balance of public money he had constantly in hand. These profits Pitt rejected, and at once established a reputation for disinterestedness.

The insurrection in Scotland had had considerable effect upon the continental war. The campaign in Flanders, where the Austrians had been deprived of English succour, had been very unfavourable, and after the battle of Raucoux, the French, under Marshal Saxe, had mastered nearly the whole of the Austrian Netherlands. But, deprived of their Bavarian allies by the Treaty of Fuessen, of the Prussians by the Treaty of Dresden, and all hearty support from Spain by the death of Philip V., they began to think of peace, and negotiations were opened at Breda. Lord Harrington, having fallen under the King's displeasure for his conduct in the ministerial crisis, had resigned, and Chesterfield was called from the Lord Lieutenancy of Ireland to become Secretary of State. He at once began to use his influence, which was very great, both from his social gifts and from his eloquence, in favour of peace, so that there seemed some hopes of a cessation of the war. It was pursued however without check during the whole of the next year. In Holland the appearance of 20,000 French within the frontier roused the national spirit, and the people, disgusted with the dilatory conduct of their republican chiefs, rose in revolution ; they again looked for safety to the house of Nassau, and the young Prince of Orange, a son-in-law of George II., was made hereditary Stadtholder. In conjunction with the Duke of Cumberland he took command of the army in Flanders, but was defeated with much loss to the English at the battle of Laufeldt. The great fortress of Bergen-op-Zoom was taken, and at length Maestricht, on the safety of which Holland depended, was itself besieged. To balance these disasters, the course of the

Effect of the rebellion on the continental war.

war in Italy had been constantly disastrous to France. The Austrians, freed from the pressure of Frederick on the north, were able to act with vigour. They were so successful that Genoa was taken, and Provence itself invaded ; and though in the following year the Austrians were driven from France and Genoa regained, the war in that direction closed with a complete victory over the French at Exiles, and the French troops withdrew to their own country, not to appear in Italy again till the renewed vigour of the Revolution plunged them afresh into a career of conquest. Meanwhile, however, in spite of these disasters upon land, England had been steadily gaining its real object. Holland, whose political importance had almost disappeared, and which had become a faithful follower of England, was still more closely joined to that country by its late revolution. Upon the sea disaster everywhere met the French. Their colonial empire was attacked, Cape Breton Island was captured, and the St. Lawrence and Canada thus laid open to the English. Their navy gradually dwindled away, till it was represented by three or four ships only. They were wearied of the war, and alarmed at the immense addition to their debt. The Dutch were disappointed at the want of success which had attended their revolution ; and the English were satisfied with the destruction of the French marine. All parties were thus at length ready to listen to a reasonable peace.

It was therefore determined to hold a congress at Aix-la-Chapelle. Moreover, the Pelhams had now resumed in some degree the pacific policy of Walpole, and the apparent certainty of the fall of Maestricht brought matters to a crisis. On the 30th of April the preliminaries were signed between France, England and Holland, without waiting for the agreement of Austria and Spain. The terms of those preliminaries befitted the causeless war which they terminated. The chief condition was the complete mutual restoration of all conquests, and the return of each party to its position before the war. There were, however, some slight changes ; Parma was to be given to the Infant Don Philip ; the cessions of Austria to both Prussia and Sardinia were to be secured, and Spain was to restore the Assiento Treaty and the right of a periodical vessel in the South Seas to the English, while the fortifications of Dunkirk towards the sea were to be destroyed ; in exchange for its losses Austria received the complete guarantee of the Pragmatic Sanction and the acknowledgment of the Emperor. The restoration of conquests touched even India, where the conquest of Madras and the resistance of Pondicherry to the English arms had

(margin notes) Treaty of Aix-la-Chapelle Oct. 1748

Results of the war

raised in the minds of the French well-grounded hopes of founding a colonial empire. Taking the war as a whole its results were these : Holland had disappeared from the rank of great nations ; it was evident that it could not defend itself against France. Austria, though it had lost Silesia, had learnt the strength to be derived from the military resources of its eastern provinces. Prussia had proved itself a predominant power in Europe. England had secured its maritime supremacy. France had exhibited its growing weakness, had lost its best opportunity of re-establishing itself upon the sea, and under a show of magnanimous generosity had made plain to the world its total absence of good government, of good administration, or good diplomacy.

The period of the premiership of Henry Pelham is marked by the absence of parliamentary contest. Taught by the stormy close of Walpole's career, he so far deviated from his master's precepts, that, instead of wishing to stand alone in his government, his chief object was to conciliate all parties, and the broad ministry over which he presided included nearly all the men of striking talent in Parliament. There was no opposition worth mentioning, except a little clique who gathered round the Prince of Wales, and at whose head was Doddington. It was not till the death of Mr. Pelham in 1754 that the strife of parties again began.

Pelham's conciliatory government.

Meanwhile the system of subsidies to foreign powers was quietly carried on, even Pitt ceasing to raise his voice against them. The lull of party strife, and the strength of his position, enabled the minister, who was a good financier, to alleviate what was then considered a very threatening danger to the country, and at the same time to demonstrate the firm and constant increase of the national wealth. He determined to introduce a measure (1750) for the reduction of the debt, which was at that time about £78,000,000, paying an interest of £3,000,000 a year. This sum was at that time regarded as very formidable. But Pelham, rightly thinking that the country could well bear the amount of debt, directed his attention not to diminishing the capital but to lowering the rate of interest. This plan had indeed been carried out constantly since the time of William III., and as the operation had been always successful, it marks the increased confidence of the nation in the Government, and the increased wealth of the nation, since money could be procured at gradually cheapening rates. Under William III. eight per cent. had been given : under Queen Anne the interest had been reduced

His financial measures. 1750.

to six : under George I. to five and to four ; Pelham now proposed
to reduce it to three per cent. In spite of some natural opposition
the Bill was carried. Those who were unwilling to receive the
reduced interest, and there were few such, received their capital from
money borrowed at three per cent. The rest accepted the terms,
which were three and a half, for the next eight years, and three per
cent. after 1758. The annual saving was more than half a million,
and Smollett says that Europe saw with wonder England reducing
the national obligations immediately after a war which had almost
ruined Europe. Three millions was indeed a considerable charge
upon a revenue amounting to about £8,523,540. This was derived
from four principal sources ;—more than £3,800,000 from Excise
and Malt Tax, £1,900,000 and over from the customs ; £1,637,608
from the Land Tax, and the rest from the stamp duties and other
small sources. The late war had cost the nation upwards of
£30,000,000, and many financiers, not foreseeing the enormous development of the national resources which the next half century would
produce, took a gloomy view of the financial position of England.
But, as we have seen, the ease with which Pelham completed the
reduction of the interest proved that there was considerable wealth
in the country.

Indeed, although the great industrial period had not yet quite arrived,
both commerce and manufactures were making consider-
able strides, and that wealth was accumulating which
was to find its employment in the next decade. Several
branches of foreign trade had been relieved from restrictions—whale
and herring fisheries, the African trade and the silk trade had all
been relieved, while manufactures had been steadily increasing. As
early as 1715 silk spinning had been introduced at Derby ; and the
woollen manufactures, which, with the silk, were heavily protected,
were of great and increasing importance. The use of cotton, which
was to change the whole face of Lancashire, was regarded most
unwisely as injurious, and but little use was made of it except for
mixing with silk and wool, and in a small degree for exportation.
Protection of silk and wool even went so far that penalties were
laid on the wearing and selling of calico goods. Both in Birmingham
and Sheffield metal works were largely established, and silver plated
upon other metals, which was introduced at Sheffield in 1742, was
soon widely used under the title of Sheffield plate. Improvements,
too, had also been made in the stocking-frame, and, in 1738, John
Kaye had invented his shuttle, which doubled the amount of work

which could be done. But while cotton was as yet scarcely thought
of, and improvements in the old manufactures were only introduced
by degrees, the second great source of English wealth was discovered
and set to work. The quantity of iron in the United Kingdom is
very large, but keen observers complained that, while there was plenty
for our own supply and for exportation, we still imported largely from
America, where it could be worked cheaper. This was because it
had been thought necessary that iron should be smelted with charcoal,
and as carriage was as yet wholly by land and expensive, it was only
when iron occurred in woody districts, such as Surrey and Sussex, that
it could be worked with advantage.. The occurrence of the termination
Hammer in the name of several villages in Surrey marks this old
state of things. The railings round St. Paul's Cathedral were regarded
as the great achievement of the southern ironworks. In 1740 means
were discovered of working iron with pit-coal, which at once opened
an almost unbounded sphere for industry. The discovery is attributed
to Dr. John Roebuck of Birmingham, who, in the year 1759, established the great Carron ironworks in Stirlingshire. It is curious
that a similar plan should have been regarded as one of the bubbles of
the South Sea year. Agriculture was still in a backward condition,
especially with regard to implements. The plough was still a rude
machine, chiefly of wood. Turnips were still crushed with the beetle.
Cultivators, and other means of assisting or saving the trouble of
ploughing, were unknown. But in the east of England, at all events,
the value of frequent manuring was understood ;—turnips and other
root-crops had taken the place of fallow, and a limited rotation of
crops was in vogue. The use of the drill, although invented in 1732,
was little known. All these improvements were however gradually
getting introduced, as the waste lands or great common fields were
by degrees enclosed. Suffolk, where this had been early done, was
at the head of agricultural improvement.

During the period of parliamentary quiet which preceded Pelham's
death, two or three measures of permanent interest were passed.
Reform of the   In 1751 the reform of the Calendar was proposed and
Calendar.   carried triumphantly through Parliament, chiefly by
1751.   the exertions of Chesterfield, Lord Macclesfield, and
Bradley the astronomer. The Julian Calendar, in which the length
of year was slightly miscalculated, had been reformed by Pope
Gregory XIII. in 1582, and this reform had been gradually adopted
in all countries in Europe except England, Russia, and Sweden.
England is said to have rejected it from hatred of the Papacy. The

effect was, that while the year in every other country began upon the 1st of January, in England it began on the 25th of March; while, as compared with other countries, there was a difference of eleven days in computing the days of the month. The change proposed was, that the year 1752 should begin upon the 1st of January, and that eleven days should be suppressed between the 2nd and 14th of September, so that the third of that month should be called the 14th, and that henceforward such changes should be introduced as would make the solar and legal year coincident. The chief practical difficulty was in the matter of payments. It was settled that these should not be put forward. It is thus that the 5th of April, the 5th of July, the 10th of October, and the 5th of January, still remain the days on which the dividends of the public funds are paid. This change met with a good deal of ignorant opposition. The common Opposition election cry was, " Give us back our eleven days."

In 1753 a Marriage Act, usually known as Lord Hardwicke's Act, was brought in, to decrease the number of the formal Lord Hard- acts which constituted a pre-engagement, in which a man wicke's
Marriage Act. might be entangled by carelessness and against his own 1753. will, and, secondly, to check very rapid marriages. At this time the facilities given to marriage enabled heirs and heiresses to marry without consent of their natural guardians—a practice still further supported by a quantity of broken and disreputable parsons who hung about the Fleet Prison, and were known as Fleet Parsons, whose performance of the ceremony was binding, and who could of course always be procured for money. By the new Act marriages must be performed in the parish church, after publication of banns, or by special licenses granted by the Archbishop, and on payment of a heavy sum. Any clergyman solemnizing a marriage in contravention of these restrictions is liable to seven years' transportation. A Bill for the naturalization of Jews, although carried, had to be repealed before the popular uproar. The Bishops, who had supported the measure, drew upon themselves the larger share of the popular indignation. They were indeed at this time unusually liberal in their views. Decay of
In the earlier part of the reign Queen Caroline, in the Church. whose hands the appointments had chiefly been, had carefully selected men of good repute and of liberal tendencies; in opposition to the general feeling of the clergy, she confined her appointments almost exclusively to Whigs. It is possible that this conduct, however praiseworthy in itself, may have tended to increase the general laxity among Churchmen and Dissenters, which had already begun to

be visible before the death of Bishop Burnet. Since that time a variety of causes had combined to increase it. Thus, the separation of the Church from the State in their political views, the Church being chiefly Jacobite while the State was Whig ; a similar division between the Bishops and their clergy, and between the Universities, and the Government, and the Bishops, all tended, by loosening the bonds of authority, to the decay of the Church. The falling away of the Dissenters, and the entire defeat of the Roman Catholics, had also removed all competition ; and while thus unnerved, the Church had been called upon to answer the requirements of an increasing population and of growing towns. It had, moreover, to combat the very general growth of that scepticism which was so rife in France, and which was one of the remarkable symptoms of the coming revolution.

It was this state of public morality which induced the Wesleys to

Rise of the Wesleyans. 1730.

begin their effort at a revival of religion, and to establish and organize the great body of Wesleyan Methodists. They began their career at Oxford, where they collected a small band of followers, deeply impressed with the necessity of heartfelt religion. The most prominent among them was Whitfield, who, after a youth passed in the humble avocations of a waiter in the "Bell Inn" at Gloucester, was now struggling to educate himself for the Church as a servitor at Pembroke College. In his zeal for religion, Wesley went as a missionary to Georgia. He met with no great success there ; but on his return, in 1738, he found that his society had grown, and had reached even London. Whitfield had been ordained, and had become renowned for his eloquence. He it was who, while working at first among the colliers at Kingswood near Bristol, introduced that field preaching which became the main instrument in the spread of Methodism. It was some time before Wesley could bring himself to adopt this custom ; but it afterwards became his constant practice. A separation soon occurred between Whitfield, who was extreme in his views, and Wesley, who had separated himself from the Moravians, with whom he had at first worked, but who in England at least were guilty of many extravagances. The withdrawal of Whitfield made Wesley undisputed chief of the new sect, and to him was left its organization. His agents were for the most part energetic, half-educated laymen, who all looked to Wesley as their absolute chief. His object was not to separate from the Church, he himself said, "Our service is not such as supersedes the Church service : we never designed it should ;" and only a very little while before his death, he said, " I declare once more that I live and die a member of the Church of England, and that none who regard my judgment or advice will ever separate from it." What he tried to do was to bring religion within the reach of those who, either by character or by the line of life they pursued, were unlikely to be reached by the ordinary apparatus of the Church, and to excite among his hearers a more true and enthusiastic religion than the formalism at that time prevalent. His society was to be not the enemy, but the handmaid of the Church. Its organization was strict and admirable. The preachers moved on in constant succession from district to district, so that neither preacher nor hearer should grow weary of monotonous work. A conference, consisting of preachers whom he selected, was held every year. The Methodists were divided into classes, with a leader to each class, and a weekly class-meeting was held. Love-feasts were also established, and any grave sin was visited by exclusion from the society. The effect of this earnest and well-arranged effort at reform was very great ; not only on the Methodists themselves, who were principally among the poorer classes, especially miners and people out of reach of ordinary Church influences, and who at his death in England and America numbered nearly 110,000, but also on the Church, by exciting that warmth and emulation which we have seen was at the time so much wanted. Although its influence was thus great and excellent, it must not be concealed that, as was natural, enthusiasm produced some eccentricities which will explain a good deal of the opposition which Wesley undoubtedly met with among the higher classes and among careless Churchmen.

As in wealth and religion, so in its political tendencies, this period was one of growth and of preparation for the more important half century which was to follow. In that period was to begin the second phase of the political change introduced at the Revolution :—the gradual assertion by the nation of their right to proper representation in Parliament. There were signs that the people at large were already growing weary of the influence of a few great nobles, of the squabbles of aristocratic parties for their own personal aggrandizement, and of the secresy in which the conduct of their nominal representatives was veiled. It is thus that the Opposition could generally rouse an almost irresistible expression of feeling by appealing from the overwhelming majority of Parliament to the passions of the nation. It was thus that Pitt, regarded as a disinterested and patriotic man, without any of the usual sources of influence, became the most popular and powerful statesman in the country; and thus when, in 1752, Mr. Murray charged with interrupting the high bailiff at a Westminster election, refused to kneel to the House, and. was consequently imprisoned during the session, he was led in triumphal procession by the sheriffs of London and Middlesex. Indeed, the privileges claimed for the members of the House might alone have sufficed to excite opposition. We hear that the very rabbits, fish, and footmen of the members were taken under the august protection of the House.

The term of the existing Parliament was just over, and it seemed as if the same quiet course would be pursued in the following one, when all such ideas were overthrown by the unexpected death of Henry Pelham. His death broke the tie which connected so many

Pelham's death gives the Government to Newcastle. 1754.

able men of varying opinions, and it became evident that parliamentary and party struggles would again occur. The King is said to have exclaimed, "Now I shall have no more peace." Upon the Duke of Newcastle fell the task of attempting to continue the existing Government. He himself took his brother's place at the head of the Treasury; he appointed Henry Legge as his Chancellor of the Exchequer. But it was not easy to supply Pelham's place as leader of the House of Commons. The choice seemed to lie between Henry Fox, who was Secretary at War, a friend and protégé of the Duke of Cumberland, Pitt, who was Paymaster, and Murray, who was Attorney-General. Pitt, personally disagreeable to the King, and moreover at this time in ill health, was not to be thought of; Murray's ambition was confined to the law; the Duke therefore applied to Fox. But they quarrelled about the arrangement of patronage, of which Newcastle was very jealous; and ultimately Sir Thomas Robinson, a man of no mark, was made Secretary, and given the management of the House. Pitt and Fox combined to render his position ridiculous and miserable. "The Duke might as well send his jackboot to lead us," said Pitt to Fox. Before the new Parliament had been assembled a month it was found necessary to make terms with Fox, who was given a seat in the Cabinet, although remaining in his subordinate place. This caused a permanent estrangement between the two statesmen. With Fox's assistance Newcastle got through the year.

But Newcastle was not the man to uphold a ministry during a

Approaching danger from India

time of such difficulty as was evidently approaching. Everything pointed to a speedy renewal of war. At the Peace of Aix-la-Chapelle the limits of our American colonies had been left undefined; while in India, where Dupleix and Labourdonnais had inflicted heavy blows on the English during the war, although the nations were at peace, the French and English contrived to continue their rivalry by allying themselves with native princes, and Clive had already rendered his name famous by the defence of Arcot and the restoration of English power in the Carnatic.[1] Thus there were dangers both in the East and in the West. In America the main object of the French was to secure the valley of the Mississippi, to connect by this channel their Canadian colonies with those upon the Gulf of Mexico, and thus to confine the English to the strip of country between the Alleghany mountains and the sea. The English would thus be constantly threatened on all sides, cut off from direct intercourse with the Indians, and from all hope of any extension of their settlements towards the west. The French began their encroachments by erecting forts on the Ohio river, which were to secure the connection between the Mississippi valley and Canada. A colonial war, in which the name of Washington first becomes prominent, arose from these encroachments. And this local warfare continued, till it became necessary for the Government to take the matter up. A force under General Braddock was therefore despatched against Fort Duquesne on the Ohio; but his careless stupidity led him into an ambush, where he himself and a great number of his troops were killed.

and America.

In spite of these hostilities, and although the existence of unsettled questions had caused a very uneasy feeling between them, France and England were as yet nominally at peace. And Newcastle, wholly unfit to conduct a great war, and eager to temporize as long as possible, seems to have tried to confine the war to matters affecting the prosperity of the American colonies. Thus Admiral Boscawen was sent out with orders to watch the French fleet, and attack it if it appeared bound for the Gulf of St. Lawrence. The consequence was an engagement, in which the French lost two ships. The rest of the fleet, to the disappointment of the English people, reached its destination. So again, Hawke's fleet in the Channel received strange and contradictory orders. One party in the Council wished to act openly and declare war. Newcastle suggested that no orders should be given to Hawke, but that he should be sent out to cruise, and that he should be ordered not to attack the French fleet unless he thought it worth while. Finally, instructions were given him to attack line of

Newcastle tries to confine the war to the colonies.

[1] For the consecutive history of India, see p 1113.

battle ships, but nothing smaller, and to spare trading vessels. He had not been gone a week when orders reached him to destroy everything large and small between Cape Ortegal and Cape Clear. The consequence was a large capture of prizes, and a not unfair outcry from France and the rest of Europe against the strange conduct of the English in seizing vessels without a declaration of war.

It was plain that war could not much longer be delayed; and the King's thoughts turned as usual to his continental dominions. Although the importance of the crisis was universally felt, he was content to leave England in the hands of a regency ; and as soon as Parliament was over, just before Boscawen sailed, he hurried to Hanover. Next to France, the object of George's dread was Prussia. More than one cause of quarrel had arisen with that country. Frederick had refused to assist in securing the election of the Archduke Joseph (afterwards Joseph II.) as King of the Romans, a project which Newcastle and George had deeply at heart, believing that it would preserve the European balance and strengthen Austria against the French. Deprived of Frederick's assistance, the plan came to nothing. In 1753, again, a dispute had arisen about some ships captured in the late war, and condemned, as Frederick asserted, unjustly by the English Admiralty courts. To such an extent had the irritation against Prussia increased, that it was confidently believed that Frederick intended to assist the Pretender in another attack upon England, taking advantage of the disturbance to secure Hanover for himself. Against Prussia, therefore, George began contracting great subsidiary treaties with the continental princes. The most important of these were with Hesse and with the Czarina of Russia. A factory, says Horace Walpole, was opened at Herrnhausen, where every prince that could muster and clothe a regiment might traffic with it to advantage.

George's anxiety for Hanover.

He makes sub- sidiary treaties against Prussia. 1755.

It became Newcastle's duty to carry these contracts through Parliament. He knew the opposition they were certain to meet with, and the necessity of finding some strong support in the Lower House ; but his Cabinet was there represented by no man of mark. He had recourse to Pitt, who held the office of Paymaster, but he positively refused to support the subsidies. His colleague Legge went further, and refused to sign the warrants which were to open the Treasury. Newcastle had then recourse to Fox, and succeeded in securing his services by removing Robinson, and making Fox Secretary of State. But the introduction of the

They are opposed by Pitt.

address at the opening of Parliament in the autumn, when the Russian and Hessian subsidies were recommended, was the signal for an open mutiny in the ministerial camp. It was attacked in vehement words by Pitt, who, in a well-known passage, likened the new coalition to the junction he had once seen of the Rhone and the Saône; the one a gentle, feeble, languid stream of no depth, and the other a boisterous, impetuous torrent. Newcastle had no alternative but to discharge both Pitt and Legge from their offices.

Meanwhile the courage of the nation had sunk very low. There was a dread of an immediate French invasion; and the Government so thoroughly lost heart as to request the King to garrison England with Hanoverian troops. This dread was kept alive by a simulated collection of French troops in the north. *The French capture Minorca. May 1756.* But, under cover of this threat, a fleet was being collected at Toulon, with the real design of capturing Minorca. The ministry were at last roused to this danger, and Byng was despatched with ten sail of the line to prevent it. Three days after he set sail the Duke de Richelieu, with 16,000 men, slipped across into the island, and compelled General Blakeney, who was somewhat old and infirm, to withdraw into the castle of St. Philip, which was at once besieged. On the 19th of May—much too late to prevent the landing of Richelieu —Byng arrived within view of St. Philip, which was still in the possession of the English. The French Admiral, La Galissonnière, sailed out to cover the siege, and Byng, who apparently felt himself unequally matched—although West, his second in command, behaved with gallantry and success—called a council of war, and withdrew. Blakeney, who had defended his position with great bravery, had to surrender.

The failure of Byng, and the general weakness and incapacity of the ministry, roused the temper of the people to rage; and Newcastle, trembling for himself, threw all the blame upon the Admiral, hoping by this means to *Newcastle resigns Nov. 1756.* satisfy the popular cry. But Fox, his chief supporter, was in no mood to risk anything by fidelity to so weak a chief. He therefore resigned the Seals; and as Murray insisted upon either resigning or being made Lord Chief Justice (which office was given him), Newcastle, without support in the Commons, found himself obliged to resign also.

It was hoped that Fox and Pitt might come in together, but their quarrel was irreconcilable. After some negotiations, therefore, the Duke of Devonshire was made First Lord of the Treasury, and Pitt

First Secretary of State and real Prime Minister. The measures of the new Government were in strict accordance with the principles of the party which Pitt represented.

The Hessians were dismissed, a Bill was passed for increasing the militia, by which 32,000 men were to be called out; reinforcements were sent to America; the enterprising and warlike character of the Highlanders was enlisted on the side of order by the formation of Highland regiments, a step which did more towards the pacification of the country than any measures of coercion. Pitt also did what he could to dissociate himself from the conduct of Newcastle with regard to Admiral Byng. A court martial held upon that officer had been bound by strict instructions, and had found itself obliged to bring in a verdict of guilty, though without casting any imputation on the personal courage of the Admiral. On his accession to power Pitt was courageous enough, although he rested on the popular favour, to do his best to get Byng pardoned, and urged on the King that the House of Commons seemed to wish the sentence to be mitigated. The King is said to have answered in words that fairly describe Pitt's position, "Sir, you have taught me to look for the sense of my subjects in another place than the House of Commons." The sentence was carried out, and Byng was shot on the quarter-deck of the 'Monarque' at Portsmouth (March 14, 1757). But the new ministry was of short duration. Pitt found himself unable to stand up against the dislike of the King, and the want of that Parliamentary influence which Newcastle's position as head of the Whigs, and his long course of corruption, had gained him. He was summarily dismissed. The King tried to get back Newcastle and his subservient ministry (whom he used to speak of as "Newcastle's footmen"), and, after a period of intrigue, Pitt had to consent to a compromise, giving his own talents and popularity, and accepting in exchange the great Parliamentary support of Newcastle. To this ministry Fox was persuaded to give his adhesion, and to accept the lucrative post of Paymaster-General. Thus was formed that strong Government so gloriously known as Pitt's ministry.

While these ministerial changes had been going on in England, our dispute with France as to the limits of our American colonies had become blended with a quarrel of quite a different origin, which was to plunge Europe into a general war for several years. As early as 1745, before the signature of the Treaty of Dresden, the Courts of Vienna and Dresden had entered into some sort of arrangement for curtailing what they regarded as the undue pre-eminence of Prussia. After that treaty the Empress Queen seems to have been still more anxious for some similar plan, and almost immediately after the termination of the War of Succession, had entered into relations with the Czarina Elizabeth of Russia ; a treaty had been agreed to, to which there were added secret clauses, providing that any movement on the part of Prussia against either Russia, Austria, or Poland, should be held wholly to invalidate the Treaty of Dresden ; and in the result of a success of their arms, it was arranged that Prussia should be divided between the three countries. These arrangements are sometimes spoken of as the Treaties of Warsaw and of St. Petersburg. To this treaty the Elector of Saxony, who was also King of Poland, was a party, though without signing. In 1754, magazines and armies were prepared in Bohemia and Moravia ; the Saxon army was collected at Pirna ; and finally, in 1756, adroit flattery addressed   <small>Europe prepares</small> to Madame de Pampadour, the reigning mistress at the   <small>for war</small> French Court, induced France to join in the alliance. Louis and his ministry, ignoring the really vital question which was then at issue with England, reversed the traditional policy of France, rejected the proffered alliance with Prussia, and threw the country headlong into a European war, in close alliance with its old enemy the Austrian House.

In accordance with the traditions of European policy it was England, not France, who should have appeared as the ally of Austria. But a coldness had been gradually springing up between the Courts. The Barrier Treaty of Utrecht, by which the Austrian Netherlands were debarred from the Indian trade, was a constant   <small>Alliance be-</small> cause of uneasiness. The part which England had   <small>tween England</small> taken in mediating the Treaties of Breslau and Dresden,   <small>and Prussia</small> which ceded Silesia to Prussia, had been mistaken by the Austrian Court ; although in fact both wise and friendly, it had excited deep displeasure. Thus, when an alliance was mentioned, the terms proposed by Austria were so high that the English Government had no choice but to refuse them. Under these circumstances, as Hanover could not be left exposed wholly without friends, England turned to the opposite party and allied itself with Prussia.

Frederick had already entered upon the war. The appearance of hostile preparations had aroused his suspicions. He demanded a plain answer as to the intentions of the Empress Queen, and on receiving an evasive reply, he determined upon striking   <small>Frederick's first</small> the first blow, although he knew that his nation num-   <small>campaign.</small>

bered but 5,000,000, while the number of the allies could not be estimated at less than 90,000,000. He passed rapidly through Saxony, blockaded the Saxon army in Pirna, and, collecting all his forces, defeated the Austrians under Marshal Braun at Lowositz (Oct. 1, 1756). After this victory he rendered the relief of the Saxons impossible, and the whole army surrendered at Pirna. Frederick occupied Dresden, and there found and published copies of the secret treaties, which fully justified his conduct. The French had made a false step in plunging into the continental war. They were already successful in the Mediterranean; already the over-bearing conduct of the English, in laying a nominal blockade on all the ports of France, had excited the general indignation of the Continent. The real policy of that country was to direct all their energies to the colonial and maritime war with England. It is probable that they thought to wring from George concessions in the colonies in exchange for the security of Hanover, which lay exactly between the contending parties. But Pitt at once apprehended the error they had made, and saw a great opportunity for raising the power of England. He knew that when France was busied in the endless difficulties of the European war, England, while subsidizing foreign troops, could employ her real power in completing her colonial empire. He therefore braved the charge of inconsistency, and threw himself heart and soul into the defence of Hanover and the support of Frederick. To under-stand how complete his apparent change of views was, and his courage in openly avowing them, the principles of the party which he had hitherto represented must be remembered. Though a section of the great Whig party, they differed in their views both as to foreign and domestic policy from the main body of the Whigs. To both the power of France was an object of dread. But,—while the official Whigs desired to check it by the preservation of the balance of power in Europe, by close connection with the continental powers, by money subsidies, and by occasional assistance of troops,—Pitt and his friends thought that, as England was an island, its natural policy was to depend upon the navy; that as trade was our proper business, so the navy was our proper strength; that we did but weaken ourselves by entangling ourselves with foreign politics; that our army should be entirely defensive, and that we need have no fear of invasion while we commanded the sea. Thus while one party upheld the necessity of subsidies and a considerable standing army, the other wished for no

Supported by Pitt.

Foreign policy of the various parties in England.

subsidies, a strong militia, and a powerful navy. The differences were not less in their respective views of home policy. The main body of the Whigs were desirous of retaining quite unchanged the Constitution as settled by the Revolution, and held that power must be secured by parliamentary influence and the distribution of patronage. In Pitt's more liberal view, parliamentary influence should have been unnecessary—a Government pleasing to the people, which a good Government would naturally be, would want no other support. Pitt's alliance with Newcastle and his acceptance. of his parliamentary influence was as entirely opposed to this view as his maintenance of subsidies to the European powers was to all appearance opposed to his former views of foreign politics. But circumstances had arisen which to his mind entirely altered the position of England, and he frankly declared that it was for the sake of England that Hanover was threatened, and that he would win America for them in Germany.

The object Pitt set before him in his new ministry was to raise the national spirit. For this purpose he threw himself with all his vehemence into the war, and his energy became visible in every department. He at once assumed the whole conduct of foreign affairs, leaving to Newcastle the jobbery he so much liked ; it is even said that the Admiralty had orders to sign his despatches and instructions without reading them. But he was met with difficulties arising from the bad Government and the bad appointments which he found on entering office. It was thus, with wholly inefficient generals, that he set to work to do what he could in the year 1757. True to his general view of employing England chiefly on the sea, it was to expeditions to the French coast that he at first looked for success. Before he was well seated in the ministry such an expedition had been despatched against Rochefort under Admiral Hawke and General Mordaunt. The fleet acted well enough, but Mordaunt and his soldiers brought the expedition to ruin, though Wolfe volunteered to capture the town if he might be intrusted with 500 men. In America the same want of success met the English. Lord Loudon was there commanding in chief, a man who was incessantly busy and never did anything ; he was graphically described by Franklin as resembling a St. George and the dragon on the sign of an inn, always mounted on a galloping horse, but never advancing a step. Under such leadership the attack on Louisburg failed. Worse than this was the disaster which attended our troops in Germany. The Duke of Cumberland, bold and active,

Disasters of the year 1757

but no general, allowed himself to be outmanœuvred by Marshal D'Estrées, suffered the French to cross the Weser unopposed, was beaten at Hastenbach, and while attempting to cover the fortress of Stade, was surrounded by the French and compelled to sign the Convention of Klosterseven, by which it was agreed that his army should be entirely broken up, the auxiliaries sent to their homes, and the Hanoverian troops go into cantonments. To complete the misery of the situation, Frederick had himself suffered a disastrous defeat at Kolin, in Bohemia, while covering the siege of Prague. The extraordinary campaign which saved Prussia does not belong to our history; it is enough to understand, that with extreme rapidity he threw himself towards the western extremity of his widespread dominions, and filled the gap which Cumberland had left open. The great victory of Rosbach, in the neighbourhood of the Saale, over the French and Imperialists, rendered that flank secure for the present. Suddenly darting back again into Silesia, where his affairs had not been going prosperously in his absence, he completely defeated the Austrians at the battle of Lissa, north of the river Schneidwitz, and thus rendered that flank secure also.

This year, so disastrous in Europe, had been marked by the signal success of our arms in India, whither Clive, who had come home after his brilliant successes in the Carnatic, had again returned as Governor of Fort St. David. He had been summoned to Bengal to revenge the horrors of the Black Hole of Calcutta, and had there laid the foundation of the English power by the brilliant victory of Plassy.[1]

The disasters which had met the English arms in all directions moved the anger of Pitt, and he determined on a thorough change of

generals. In the place of Cumberland, who had shown his inefficiency in the last campaign, Ferdinand of Brunswick, a worthy disciple of Frederick's, was appointed to command the army of Hanover; and as the Convention of Klosterseven was repudiated by the English, he found the defeated army at Stade ready to receive him. Loudon gave place to Amherst and Wolfe. It was in America that the English troops were chiefly employed. The mouth of the St. Lawrence was guarded by Cape Breton Island and Louisburg. At New York the Hudson falls into the sea, and from its mouth there runs northward, nearly into the valley of the St. Lawrence, a valley and chain of lakes, of which the first is Lake Champlain. The fortress which holds the road is Ticonderoga. On the Ohio, as already mentioned,

Change of generals. 1758.

Success in America.

¹ See p. 1119.

was Fort Duquesne, where Fort Pittsburg now is. The French possessions were to be attacked by each of these three points. Amherst and Wolfe, with a fleet under Boscawen, were to capture Louisburg. Abercrombie was to push up the Hudson and take Ticonderoga, while to Forbes was intrusted the capture of Fort Duquesne. Working hand in hand, without jealousy, Amherst and Boscawen succeeded at once in capturing Louisburg, which had last year been supposed unassailable. Fort Duquesne was also taken. Ticonderoga, strong from its situation in the midst of water and marshes, resisted all efforts, but the line of junction between Canada and the Mississippi was effectually cut.

In Europe the same energy was visible. The army of Ferdinand was reinforced by a considerable number of English troops. Prince Ferdinand was opposed by the Count of Clermont, an unusually incapable general, who had in fact never before seen troops in the field. He succeeded in clearing Hanover and driving the French behind the Rhine at Creveld. He there defeated them with a loss of some 6000 men, but found himself unable to retain his advanced posi- tion, and recrossed the river. Pitt had often asserted that, much as he wished to uphold the cause of Frederick, nothing would induce him to send British blood to "the Elbe, to be lost in that ocean of gore." But this successful campaign induced him to change his view, and a considerable body of troops, about 12,000 in number, under the Duke of Marlborough and Lord George Sackville, were sent to join Prince Ferdinand. These same officers had just been employed in executing one of those joint military and naval expeditions which Pitt seems at first to have thought the proper means by which England should assist in a continental war. Like all such isolated expeditions, it was of little value. St. Malo, against which it was directed, was found too strong to be taken, but a large quantity of shipping and naval stores was destroyed. The fleet also approached Cherbourg, but although the troops were actually in their boats ready to land, they were ordered to re-embark, and the fleet came home. Another somewhat simi- lar expedition was sent out later in the year. In July General Bligh and Commodore Howe took and destroyed Cherbourg, but on attempting a similar assault on St. Malo, they found it too strong for them. The army had been landed in the Bay of St. Cast, and, while engaged in re-embarkation, it was attacked by some French

Victory of Creveld. June 23, 1758

Expeditions to Cherbourg and St. Malo.

troops which had been hastily collected, and severely handled.   In
spite of this slight check it was plain that the tide of victory had
Campaign of   changed.   The campaign of King Frederick had been
Frederick.   marked by chequered fortune.   He had found the siege
of Olmutz, in Moravia, beyond his strength, but upon the east of his
dominions had won a great victory over the Russians, under General
Fermor, at Zörndorf (August 25) ; and though he suffered a heavy
defeat by a night surprise at Hofkirchen, he managed his retreat so
ably, that before the end of the year he had rid Saxony of the
Austrians and again secured Silesia.

The success which had marked the course of the British arms in
all parts of the world continued to attend them, and this year (1759) is
Victories of   one of the most glorious in our military annals.   Horace
the year   Walpole remarks, that "it was necessary to ask every
1759.   morning what new victory there was for fear of missing
one."   In January came the news of the capture of Goree in Africa, in
June the news of the capture of Guadaloupe, in August of the victory
of Minden, in September of Lagos, in October of Quebec, and in
November of Quiberon.   The contrast between the England of 1757,
crouching in fear within its own limits and crying for help to
Hanover and Hesse, and the England of 1759 is indeed striking.
There was again a threatened descent of the French upon England,
but there was now no craven fear of such an event.   Pitt had raised
the temper of the people.   The threat was regarded not only with
indifference, but as a means of acquiring further triumph.   England
could well defend itself.   The militia was called out and mobilized ;
the fleet was so large and in such order that it could efficiently watch
all the French ports.   Boats for the expedition were building at
Havre ; Rodney anchored in the harbour and bombarded it for fifty
hours, destroying most of the boats ; Boscawen was watching De la Clue
at Toulon ; Hawke was watching Conflans at Brest.   Thurot, in Dunkirk, was also blockaded.   This arrangement of fleets produced in the
course of the year two great naval victories.

The French desired to connect their scattered squadrons.   For this
purpose De la Clue attempted to come out of Toulon and to join the
fleets in the north of France.   As he passed round Spain, Boscawen,
Naval victories   whose duty it had been to watch him, fell upon his fleet
of Lagos and   off Lagos.   Three of his ships were taken and two
Quiberon   destroyed, while eight vessels, which had been separated
from him, were lost as they came through the straits ; so that, with
the exception of two ships, the whole of his squadron was annihilated.

This was in August. Three months later (Nov.) a still greater success met the English navy. Sir Edward Hawke attacked the Brest fleet under Conflans off the point of Quiberon. He had been driven from his watch by stress of weather, and Conflans had taken the opportunity to come out of harbour, hoping to destroy a detached squadron which was off the coast. But Hawke's return was too quick for him. He made a junction with the detached squadron, and thus, superior in force to the French, drove them back towards the coast. The French withdrew among the rocky islets near the mouth of the Vilaine. It was blowing a gale, and the rocky coast was full of danger. But Hawke replied to the representations of his pilot by giving him peremptory orders, that whatever the risk might be, he was to lay his ship alongside of the French admiral's. " You have done your duty in showing me the danger, now you are to obey my orders and lay me alongside the Soleil Royal." The victory was complete : two French ships struck, four were sunk, and the rest, all damaged, ran for shelter to the Vilaine. This blow, together with the complete destruction of Thurot's squadron, which had come out of Dunkirk and made a landing in Ireland, completed the practical annihilation of the French fleet. The total loss up to this time of the French navy was sixty-four ships, without counting Thurot's squadron. During the same time the English had lost but nine.

But the great victory of the year was the capture of Quebec. To secure Canada was one of Pitt's chief objects. Louisburg and Duquesne had already fallen, and the country itself was thus open to his attack. The French army was under the command of an excellent general, the Marquis de Montcalm, who had his headquarters at Quebec. General Amherst was the English commander-in-chief, but subordinates of more than usual vigour were necessary for him, and Pitt, who had kept his eye on Wolfe since the attack on Rochefort, and had seen his energy at the siege of Louisburg, disregarding all claims of seniority, intrusted to him the attack on Quebec. This was originally to be a combined movement. Amherst was to march up by Lakes Champlain and George, take Ticonderoga and Crown Point, where Abercrombie had failed last year, and thus reach the St. Lawrence. Generals Prideaux and Johnson were to take Fort Niagara, and then, passing down Lake Ontario into the St. Lawrence, to join in the attack on Quebec, securing Montreal on the way. Though both these latter expeditions were successful, the difficulties met with rendered them so slow that the

Capture of Quebec

combination failed. The plan was Pitt's own, and was probably too extensive ; it may be doubted whether he had sufficient knowledge of what it is possible for an army to do. Wolfe, with 8000 men, embarked in the squadron of Admiral Saunders, and reached the Isle of Orleans in the St. Lawrence river on the 13th of June. The expedition experienced no disasters in the way, having fortunately captured a vessel with some excellent charts of the river.

Quebec lies on and below the rocky edge of a plateau on the left or northern bank of the St. Lawrence, just above the junction of the St. Charles river, which thus covers its eastern side. On the other side of the St. Charles the ground again rises and continues in a rugged and difficult mass, till it sinks where the river Montmorency falls into the St. Lawrence in a lofty waterfall. The ridge between the Montmorency and the St. Charles is called Beauport. On this Montcalm's army was in position, precluding the possibility of investing Quebec, to which he had access by a bridge across the St. Charles. On the other or Quebec side of the St. Charles, the heights on the edge of which the town is built extend up the St. Lawrence, and are called the Heights of Abraham. They were believed to be inaccessible to an army. The Isle of Orleans lies in the St. Lawrence from the mouth of the Montmorency till almost opposite Quebec harbour. As long as Montcalm's army occupied the line of Beauport Quebec could not be invested. In that position the army was unassailable. To draw him from it therefore was Wolfe's great object. For this purpose frequent feints were made, but were all unavailing. One assault indeed near the mouth of the Montmorency was attempted, but the English were beaten off. Nor were the defenders of the town idle ; again and again were fire-ships sent down, but the skilful vigilance of Saunders rendered all such efforts unavailing. A battery or two were erected and the town was bombarded, but this did little or no good. It seemed plain that from the Isle of Orleans nothing could be done. The army was moved in succession to two points higher up the river and above Quebec. But Montcalm would not move ; he was content to send an army of observation up the river, and the besiegers lost all hope of the succours they had expected from Amherst and Johnson. On the 9th of September, Wolfe wrote a despatch in which he seemed quite to despair of success. Within a week Quebec was taken. The bold design occurred to him of surprising the Heights of Abraham, and thus compelling Montcalm to fight. He ordered feints to be made both up and down the river while he quietly collected boats. As it was, they were so few in number that his army had to cross in two divisions. Very early in the morning of the 13th of September he began his attempt. With immense toil, up a passage so narrow that at times only one could pass, his soldiers forced their way, and even dragged up one piece of artillery, and when the morning came Montcalm found between three and four thousand men in position opposite to him upon the heights. To cover Quebec it was necessary for him to withdraw his troops from Beauport and to cross the St. Charles. This he at once proceeded to do, and the battle began. Early in the day Wolfe, who was on the right wing, was wounded and carried to the rear, but before he died he had the gratification of knowing that the victory was secured. Both armies lost their first and second in command. Five days afterwards Quebec was surrendered. Wolfe was but thirty-three when he died; he entered the army at fourteen, and had seen much service; a shy, retiring, domestic man, of unprepossessing exterior and weak frame, he owed his promotion entirely to the feeling of confidence which his sound sense and chivalrous energy inspired. It is much to the credit of Pitt that he should have found out his merits, and having found them out have ventured to place so great a responsibility upon so young and unprepossessing a person.

While all the efforts in which the English were engaged single-handed had thus been successfully carried out, they had also, in conjunction with their German allies, won on the 1st of August the great battle of Minden. The French had early in the year taken possession of Frankfort. Their army, strongly reinforced—for the new ministry of the Duc de Choiseul began by being very energetic,—was divided into two; the northern corps under Marshal Contades,· the southern army about Frankfort under De Broglie. An attempt of Ferdinand to regain Frankfort was frustrated by De Broglie, who beat him at the battle of Bergen. The two French armies then joined, and pressed upon the Prince till they drove him behind Minden, a town on the left or French side of the river Weser. It became clear to Ferdinand that a battle must be fought to save-Hanover. He therefore advanced southwards up the Weser, carefully keeping his communications with that river open, while the object of the French seems to have been chiefly to separate him from it. By spreading his army so as to give it the appearance of weakness, though it was in reality capable of rapid concentration, he induced the French to leave an extremely strong position they had taken up upon Minden Heath, with their right covered by

Victory of Minden.

the town, which was in their possession. A body of troops, apparently detached, upon the extreme left of the allies, and close to the Weser, was the bait by which the French were attracted. They hoped by destroying this ill-supported detachment to cut the Prince off from the river. But as De Broglie approached what he believed to be the weak point, he was surprised to find the whole allied army in array before him. Ferdinand by this clever trap brought his enemy to an engagement upon his own ground. The battle consisted in great part of a series of charges of French cavalry on compact bodies of the English and Hanoverian infantry. Weary with their futile exertions, the cavalry, who formed the centre of the French line, gave way. The line was broken, and a charge of cavalry alone was wanted to complete the destruction of the army. Three aide-de-camps were sent in succession to Lord George Sackville, bidding him charge. He pretended not to understand the order, and said he must consult the Prince in person. The same order was given to the Marquis of Granby, who commanded in the second line, and a vigorous charge made, but time had been wasted, and it was too late. The victory was however rendered tolerably complete by a body of 10,000 men, whom Prince Ferdinand had had the courage and foresight to detach from his army, although he was already numerically weaker than his enemy, for the purpose of cutting the enemy's communications. Lord George Sackville was tried by court martial and dismissed from all his military appointments.

The story of the British victories of the year is completed by the success of their arms in India, where the siege of Madras was raised, much of the Carnatic secured, and Wandewash taken by Colonel Coote.

It is necessary to say a few words about the war carried on under Frederick's own eye. The plan of the campaign was much the same as the last. The Russians advanced to gain the Oder, and fought and won the battle of Zullichau over General Wedel, after which they were joined by an Austrian army under Loudon. Against this united force the King advanced, leaving Daun's army already threatening Berlin. He met Saltikow and Loudon at Kunersdorf. The Russian position was forced, seventy cannon taken, and the victory appeared complete, when suddenly Loudon advanced with his troops and altered the fate of the day. In these two last battles the Prussian forces had been weakened by 30,000 men, and the King, feeling certain that he was at the end of his resources, made every arrangement for committing

Frederick's fourth campaign.

suicide. Unaccountably the enemy did not advance, and he had time to collect a few troops. But fortune was still against him; his general, Fink, with 12,000 men, was surrounded, and had to surrender at Maxen; Dresden had fallen into the hands of Daun. After this reinforcements from the army of Prince Ferdinand enabled the King to continue the campaign, till the extreme cold of winter made it necessary to go into winter quarters. The following year Frederick still made head against his gathering enemies. He was unable indeed to save Berlin from the hands of the Russians, but he rescued Silesia by the victory which he gained over Loudon at Liegnitz, and at his approach the Russians fled from his capital. He then turned his arms against Daun, who was still master of Saxony. The fearful battle of Torgau was fought, where the victory was secured to the Prussians, but at the cost of 14,000 men; the Austrians are said to have lost 20,000. This was the last pitched battle of the war.

Battle of Torgau. 1760.

The constant success of his schemes raised Pitt to the highest eminence of power. His ministry was unopposed. Year by year he was enabled, without difficulty, to carry through the House a subsidy of £670,000 to the Prussian King, and to set his estimates at from twelve to twenty millions, a sum before this unheard of. His power over the House was absolute; members were actually afraid of replying to him, and the only difficulty which met him was the temper of his relative Temple, who insisted upon receiving the Garter, and almost shipwrecked the ministry by his selfish claims. It was at this moment of prosperity that the King suddenly died, and, as had long been expected, a change took place in the counsels of the Sovereign.

Pre-eminence of Pitt.

The King dies Oct. 25, 1760

GEORGE III.

1760—1820.

Born 1738 = Sophia-Charlotte of Mecklenburg-Strelitz.

George IV.	Frederick, Duke of York. d. 1827.	William IV. (Duke of Clarence.)	Edward=Victoria Duke of of Saxe- Kent. Coburg. d. 1820. Victoria.	Ernest, King of Hanover. d. 1851.	Augustus, Duke of Sussex. d. 1843.	Adolphus, Duke of Cambridge. d. 1850.

Charlotte = King of Wur- temberg.	Augusta.	Elizabeth=Fred- erick of Hesse- Hom- burg	Mary=Duke of Glou- cester.	Sophia.	Amelia.

CONTEMPORARY PRINCES.

France.	*Germany.*	*Spain.*	*Prussia.*
Louis XV., 1715	Francis I.,	Charles III., 1759.	Frederick II., 1740.
Louis XVI., 1774	Maria Theresa, }1745.	Charles IV., 1788.	Frederick William
Republic, 1793.	Joseph II., 1765.	Ferdinand VII. 1808	II., 1786.
Napoleon, 1804.	Leopold II., 1790.		Frederick William
Louis XVIII., 1814.	Francis II., 1792.		III., 1797.

Russia.	*Denmark.*	*Sweden.*
Elizabeth, 1741.	Frederick V., 1746.	Adolphus, 1751.
Peter III., 1762.	Christian VII., 1765	Gustavus III., 1771.
Catherine II., 1762.	Frederick VI , 1808.	Gustavus IV , 1792.
Paul I., 1796.		Charles XIII , 1809.
Alexander, 1801.		Charles XIV., 1818.

POPES.—Clement XIII., 1758. Clement XIV , 1769. Pius VI , 1775. Pius VII , 1800.

Archbishops.	*Lord Chancellors*
Thomas Secker, 1758.	Lord Northington, 1757.
Frederick Cornwallis, 1768.	Lord Camden, 1766
John Moore, 1783.	Charles Yorke, 1770.
Charles Manners Sutton, 1805.	In Commission, 1770.
	Lord Bathurst, 1771.
	Lord Thurlow, 1778.
	Lord Loughborough, 1783
	Lord Thurlow, 1783
	Lord Loughborough, 1793.
	Lord Eldon, 1801.
	Lord Erskine, 1806.
	Lord Eldon. 1807.

First Lords of the Treasury.

Oct.	1760.	Newcastle.
May	1762.	Bute
April	1763.	Grenville
July	1765	Rockingham.
July	1766	Grafton.
Jan.	1770.	North.
March	1782.	Rockingham.
July	1782.	Shelburne.
April	1783	Portland.
Dec.	1783	Pitt

Chancellors of the Exchequer.

Oct.	1760.	Legge.
March	1761.	Barrington.
May	1762	Dashwood.
April	1763	Grenville.
July	1765	Dowdeswell.
July	1766.	C. Townshend.
Sept.	1767.	Mansfield.
Dec	1767.	North.
March	1782.	Cavendish.
July	1782.	Pitt
April	1783	Cavendish.
Dec.	1783.	Pitt

Secretaries of State.

Oct.	1760	Pitt. / Holderness.
March	1761	Pitt. / Bute
Oct	1761	Egremont. / Bute
May	1762	Egremont. / G. Grenville.
Oct.	1762	Egremont. / Halifax.
Sept	1763	Sandwich. / Halifax
July	1765	Conway. / Grafton.
May	1766	Conway. / Richmond.
Aug.	1766	Conway. / Shelburne.
Dec.	1767	Weymouth. / Shelburne.
Oct.	1768	Weymouth. / Rochford.
Dec.	1770	Sandwich. / Rochford.
	1771	Suffolk. / Rochford.
Oct.	1775	Suffolk. / Weymouth.
Nov.	1779	Hillsborough. / Stormont.
March	1782	Fox. / Shelburne.
July	1782	T. Townshend. / Grantham.
April	1783	Fox / North.
Dec.	1783	Carmarthen. / Sydney.

ON the 25th of October news was brought to the Prince of Wales that his grandfather was dead. It was an event which must have been for some time expected, and George III. and his friends were prepared for it. His training had been somewhat peculiar. The Princess of Wales, his mother, had kept him much secluded, and his education had been chiefly withdrawn from the hands of the distinguished men whom the King had given him as governors, and intrusted to sub-preceptors of the Princess's own choosing. Her constant friend and adviser in this and other family matters had been Lord Bute, who had thereby acquired the greatest influence over the young King. It was understood that henceforth his advice would chiefly regulate the policy of the Crown. His influence and that of the teachers he had selected, some of them it is believed nominated by Bolingbroke, had all tended politically in one direction, so much so that complaints had been made, though uselessly, to the late King of the unconstitutional precepts which his heir was being taught. The views with which the young Prince's mind was filled were those which Bolingbroke

Bute's influence over the young King. 1760.

had developed in "The Patriot King." The beneficent rule of a powerful monarch governing his people by his own will, but for their good, was the ideal he had been taught to set before him. It was pointed out to him that since 1688 the will of the sovereign had been held captive by that great Whig party which had produced the Revolution and secured the Hanoverian succession. And it had been impressed upon him that it was his duty to free the prerogative from this state of servitude, and to annihilate party government by restoring to the Crown its freedom of choice and action. It was with the deliberate intention of carrying out this plan that the King began his reign. Nor was the plan, had it been properly executed, either impossible or unjust. It was felt that the old party divisions were in fact obsolete, that Whig and Tory, in the sense of Hanoverian George's view and Jacobite, were things of the past; and that it was of royalty. highly detrimental to the public service that able and loyal men should be excluded from all share of the Government because, very frequently on only hereditary grounds, they belonged to a party opposed to the great Whig connection. Yet such had been the case. Parliamentary contests had, till Pitt's accession to power, been nothing but greedy struggles for place and power between two sections of the Whig party which had separated in 1716. Had the King made use of his present popularity, and of that advantage which he possessed over his predecessors in his English birth, to exercise his prerogative of choice in selecting eminent men from all parties for his ministry, and had he taken for his chief minister a man who stood well with the nation, the feeling of the country would almost certainly have gone with him. Unfortunately his somewhat narrow intellect and his restricted education made him unable to take a wide view of his position, filled him with a vehement prejudice against the whole Whig party, and made him rest for support on the personal friendship of a second-rate man, who laboured under the unpopularity attending his Scotch birth and his supposed favour with the Princess of Wales.

The behaviour of the young King was at first all that could be desired. In his family relations indeed he was nearly always respectable. He still further added to his popularity by directing a change in the law with regard to the judges, so that their commissions no longer terminated with the death of the King. They henceforward held their commissions for life, unless deprived of them at the joint petition of the two Houses of Parliament. They were thus rendered absolutely independent of Court favour.

The six months which elapsed before the dissolution of Parliament passed without any great changes, although there was no lack of indication of what was coming. The King's name was constantly put forward. Newcastle, who had kept all patronage in his hands, found places filled without his knowledge, and complained that he was met with the uniform answer that it was the King's desire ; and Bute openly rebuked Lord Anson for filling the Admiralty boroughs without consulting the King. With the dissolution of Parliament the changes in the ministry began. Legge gave place at the Exchequer to Lord Barrington; Charles Townshend became Secretary at War, and Dashwood, another follower of Bute's, took the place that Townshend vacated, while four days afterwards (March 25th) Bute was appointed one of the Secretaries of State in the place of Lord Holderness, who had been removed and handsomely compensated. The admission of Bute to the ministry could hardly fail to produce the dismissal of Pitt, for on the great question of the day they were in direct antagonism. Bute, in pursuance of his policy of opposition to all that the Whigs had done, was determined if possible to break off the English connection with the Continent ; and, unable to see the difference between buying troops from a Prince of Hesse and assisting the greatest monarch of the time in a war from which England was reaping nothing but benefit, he intended to refuse the payment of the King of Prussia's subsidy, and was strongly bent upon peace.

Frederick's own campaign of 1760 had closed, as has been already said, with the dreadful battle of Torgau, and the same year Prince Ferdinand had held the French in check, worsting them at Warburg, but had been unable to keep them out of Göttingen and Cassel; and the hereditary Prince of Brunswick, detached to the siege of Wesel, had been defeated at Kloster-Campen. In 1761 the campaign was continued, and the Duke of Broglie was driven back to the Maine and beaten at Langen-Saltza. But Prince Ferdinand was not strong enough to keep what he had regained. The French again advanced, and in June the Prince of Soubise joined the Duke de Broglie, and they together moved forward to the Lippe. They were defeated at Kirch-Denkern, but the effect of the victory was small, and both armies closed the year in much the same position as they began it. These campaigns, resulting in little but loss of life, and the exertions which they entailed, and which had brought France to the verge of bankruptcy, had become intolerable ; and early in the year De Choiseul had induced

[margin note: First signs of change. 1761.]

[margin note: The campaign of 1761 produces a desire for peace.]

both Austria and Russia to consent to negotiations at Augsburg. But as the connection of England with the continental question was accidental, and her quarrel with France quite separate from it, it was thought expedient that a separate arrangement should be made between the two countries. For this purpose M. de Bussy was in June sent to England and Mr. Hans Stanley to Paris.

The terms offered by the French were not unreasonable. The difficulties lay in Pitt's views as to the rights of England, which were

Separate negotiations between France and England. June 1761.

undoubtedly very high. He had, as he said that he was able to do, raised England from her degradation. He had done this by means of a successful war, and had no mind to lose his work or to consent to what would be but a mere cessation of hostilities. He would have, he said, no new Peace of Utrecht. Choiseul's first offer (on the 26th of March) was, that each of the belligerents should keep what they held in Europe on the 1st of May, in West India and Africa on the 1st of July, and in India on the 1st of September. Pitt refused this, insisting that

Pitt opposes peace.

the date fixed in all cases should be that of the signature of the treaty. He was hoping in fact that fresh victories would improve his position; nor was he disappointed. Before the end of July Belleisle, an island which must be considered an integral part of France, Dominique in the West Indies, and Pondicherry in the East, were added to our conquests. The territorial arrangements were for the most part easily settled; but three demands of the French Pitt obstinately refused to grant. These were the restoration of one of her African settlements and Belleisle in exchange for portions of Germany then in her possession—these Pitt demanded without exchange; secondly, compensation for prizes taken before the declaration of war; and lastly, the withdrawal of all English troops from Germany. As the first of these demands was not unreasonable, as the second was obviously just, and the third belonged, and could probably have been transferred, to the general Congress, Pitt would scarcely have refused them had he not seen reason for believing that the propositions of the French were hollow. The fact is, he was already beginning to suspect, and more than suspect, the existence of a treaty inimical to English interests between France and Spain. Ever since the accession of Charles III. to the Spanish throne, in the year 1759, the two Courts had been gradually approaching one

Suspecting the existence of the Family Compact.

another; and the policy which Marlborough's wars had been designed to check was gradually winning its object. In July De Bussy, on presenting the draft of the proposed treaty, appended to it certain claims on the part of Spain, desiring that these might be settled at the same time as the French claims. Pitt was naturally indignant at this, and haughtily replied, that France was "not at any time to presume a right of intermeddling in such disputes between Great Britain and Spain." The Spanish minister, General Wall, owned that he was cognizant of the measure, but expressed peaceful wishes with regard to England. However, though Bristol, the English minister at Madrid, had been so completely deceived that he continued to assert the friendly disposition of the Spanish Court, the correctness of Pitt's surmises became evident, when in August the arrangement known as the Family Compact was signed. By this treaty the Bourbon houses of Spain and France contracted a close and perpetual alliance. Besides France and Spain the Bourbon Princes of Naples and Parma were to be admitted to it. There was a secret clause binding Spain to declare war on England if peace was not made before May 1762. The knowledge of this treaty induced Pitt not only to break off negotiations, but to determine upon war with Spain, for which he immediately made preparations, planning a great expedition against Havannah in the West and Manilla in the East Indies. With his usual haughtiness, he urged these measures upon the Council, but Temple alone supported him. **Pitt resigns.** He indignantly declared that he would not be respon- **Oct. 5, 1761.** sible for measures he did not manage, and on the 5th of October resigned. Thus terminated that splendid administration which had raised England from the depths of degradation to a position of first-rate importance in Europe.

Bute was at once practically supreme in the Council, although he had yet to rid himself of Newcastle. He was afraid of **Bute virtual** Pitt's popularity, and did his best to injure him by **minister.** persuading him to accept a pension, and the title of Lady Chatham for his wife, hoping by that means to make it appear that Pitt was not hostile to his Government, or at all events to wreck his popularity, which rested largely on the public belief in his disinterestedness. Lord Egremont became Secretary in his place. Before the year was over Pitt's wisdom was vindicated. The change of ministry in England and the safe arrival of the treasure-ships, which Pitt would have forestalled, changed the tone of the Spanish Government, and even the pacific Bute found it necessary to declare war in January 1762. Already the impossibility of Bute's peaceful view **War with** was demonstrated, but he none the less prevented the **Spain.** payment of the Prussian subsidy; although this looked **1762.**

very like a breach of faith, it could be urged in extenuation that Frederick's need was much lessened by the death of the Czarina and the accession of Peter III., a devoted friend and admirer of the Prussian King. Bute's policy was indeed so completely opposed to that of his predecessors, that there is reason to believe that he even used his influence to induce Russia to withdraw from its new alliance. This change of policy afforded Newcastle, who was conscious that he was sooner or later to be got rid of, an opportunity of leaving the ministry with dignity. On his resignation Bute at once named himself Prime Minister, and proceeded to carry out, in some points at least, his favourite principles. These were peace at almost any price, and the abandonment of continental connections, the increase and restoration of the power of the Crown, and Government without bribery. But these aspirations degenerated in practice into a war, which was successful owing to his predecessor's arrangements, a vindictive assault upon the Whig party, and the most shameless corruption ever practised in England. The expeditions which Pitt had planned were carried out. Martinique, held to be impregnable, and with it Grenada, St. Lucia, and St. Vincent, were captured by a squadron under Rodney, and this was but a stepping-stone to the capture of the still greater prize — Havanna. The expedition against the Philippine Islands was equally successful.

But Bute, in his eagerness for peace, did not even wait to hear the result of the expeditions, but at once reopened peace negotiations with France. Left to himself, he would have taken no account of the last great conquests. Councillors less anxious for peace succeeded in getting them exchanged for Florida. In November the peace was **Terms of the peace Nov. 3, 1762.** signed. The conditions were much the same as those of the preceding year. Canada passed wholly to the English, the French retaining St. Pierre and Miquelon, with the rights of fishing. England kept Tobago, Dominica, St. Vincent, and Grenada, but restored Martinique and St. Lucia. Minorca and Belleisle were to be exchanged. The French evacuated their conquests in Germany, but on the other hand—and this was a concession Pitt had refused—Goree was restored to France, and the English army was withdrawn from Germany. In India the French were to have no military establishment, but their factories were restored. All the Spanish claims on England were rejected. On the whole, the peace, though it did not destroy the House of Bourbon, as Pitt would have wished, probably gave England as much as she had a right to expect. The conclusion of the treaty was rendered easier by Frederick's continued successes in Germany. Although the Czarina Catherine, who had succeeded Peter, had reverted to the old policy of Russia, and withdrawn her troops from Frederick's assistance, he had been able to retain his superiority throughout the campaign. Prince Close of the Seven Years' War. Ferdinand had gained fresh successes in Westphalia, and had taken Cassel from the French ; while Prince Henry, Frederick's brother, had won a victory at Freiberg, which closed the Seven Years' War.

Bute, while thus obtaining peace, though in a way so irritating to our German friends that England stood henceforward absolutely without allies, had been carrying on his vindictive attack upon the Whigs. The opportunity selected for this purpose was the passage of the peace through Parliament. Grenville, a man of firmness, but without commanding abilities, and deficient in tact, had taken Pitt's place as Leader of the House of Commons. Attack on the Whigs. Feb. 10, 1763. But he was not regarded as strong enough to make head against the opposition which was expected, for the Whigs of all sections, conscious of Bute's designs against them, were beginning to combine. Bute selected a man of greater powers to assist him. He bargained with Fox (whose conscience was not scrupulous when money was to be made) to assume the lead of the House. It was hoped that he might bring some Whigs with him. This he found himself unable to do, and with consummate audacity set to work to purchase a majority. The Paymaster's office became in fact a shop for the purchase of votes, £200 being the least price given. Against such a majority all efforts were of course useless, and the peace received the approbation of Parliament. After this victory vengeance began. The Duke of Devonshire, the head of the great Whig house of Cavendish, for declining to attend a Cabinet Council, was rudely deprived of the office of Chamberlain, and the King with his own hand scratched his name off the list of Privy Councillors. All place-men who had voted against the peace were dismissed. Newcastle and Rockingham were removed from their Lord Lieutenancies, and even the meanest officers of the administration—tax-gatherers and customhouse officers, who owed their places to Whig patronage, were removed. Bute appeared triumphant. Even the cider tax, a ridiculously unfair excise suggested by the ignorance of Dashwood, his Chancellor of the Exchequer, was carried by a large majority in his Bute resigns April 8, 1763 venal House. Suddenly Bute resigned. It is difficult to explain why. Perhaps it was because he was conscious of the unpopularity he had incurred. His Peace of Paris was distasteful to the nation; he had driven from office Pitt, the favourite of the people; he was a Scotchman; the voice of scandal constantly coupled his name with • that of the Princess Dowager of Wales, and the odious name of favourite was indissolubly attached to him. Whether well or ill founded, his unpopularity had reached such a pitch, that he was afraid to leave his house without a bodyguard of prize-fighters. Perhaps experience had taught him his unfitness to conduct the Government. Perhaps, and this was the general belief of the time, he preferred the irresponsible power of the favourite to the dangers and responsibility of

He names
Grenville as his
successor.

the minister. He named Grenville for his successor,— and as he had always used him as his creature, he probably still hoped to find him a pliant tool. In this he was disappointed; and though for a few years he doubtless had much private influence with the King, this part of his career has been much exaggerated, and he himself complained bitterly of the King's ingratitude.

With Grenville the Secretaries of State, Lord Egremont and Lord Halifax, were regarded as holding the direction of public affairs.

The Triumvirate
ministry.
1763.

This ministry has therefore been sometimes called The Triumvirate. Bute found them by no means ready to accept his interference, and soon began to intrigue against them. Grenville more than once complained to the King of his want of confidence. The sudden death of Lord Egremont gave an opportunity for a change in the ministry, and Bute so far changed his former policy as to recommend the King to send for Pitt. A long interview with the King, in which Pitt stated the necessity of bringing back some of the Whig connection to power, left him with the impression that he was to be minister, and he wrote to the Whig chiefs accordingly. But two days after, on a second interview, he found matters changed. The King wished the Earl of Northumberland, Bute's intended son-in-law, to be Prime Minister, and desired several of the present ministry to be retained. This Pitt would not hear of, designating Temple, Devonshire, and others who had just fallen under the King's displeasure, as his colleagues. The negotia-

Bedford joins
the ministry.

tion was broken off. Probably on the day which intervened between the two interviews Bute had changed his mind. In carrying through the peace negotiations he had been assisted by that section of the Whigs which was under the influence of the Duke of Bedford. It is to this section that Fox belonged. The Duke, though of a retiring character, was now induced to accept office by a false rumour, that Pitt had expressly declared that he would not admit him to any Government of which he was the chief. A mixed ministry of the followers of Grenville and Bedford was formed, and is generally known by the name of the Bedford Ministry. The Secretaries of State were Halifax and Lord Sandwich, a man of mean character and licentious morals.

The new ministry met Parliament on the 15th of November, and both Houses were at once occupied with questions with regard to Wilkes. The unpopularity of Bute had found expression in numerous pamphlets. Among the Opposition writers was Wilkes, member for Aylesbury, who, in conjunction with an author of the name of Churchill, had established a paper, *The North Briton*, in which the favourite and his Government had been very roughly handled, and which won popularity by unreasoning general assaults upon the Scotch nation. He had so far exceeded the usual practice of pamphleteers of the time as to write the names of his opponents at full length, instead of employing initials. When the King had prorogued Parliament (April 23rd) on Bute's resignation, he had spoken of the peace as honourable to his crown and beneficial to the people. This produced an attack in the famous No. 45 of *The North Briton*. Grenville had at once proceeded against the author. A general warrant (that is, a warrant in which no individual names are mentioned) was issued against the authors, printers, and publishers of the paper, and under it Wilkes was apprehended, his house and papers being also ransacked. He at once became a political martyr. The chiefs of the Opposition, Temple and Grafton, visited him in his prison, and he proceeded to try the validity of his arrest. Chief Justice Pratt, before whom the case came, held that Wilkes was exempted from arrest by his privilege as a member ; for a member of Parliament is free from arrest on all charges except those of treason, felony, and breach of the peace, and a libel, he said, could not be construed as a breach of the peace. But though the law had failed to punish him, he was pursued by the vengeance of the Government; he was deprived of his commission in the militia, and his supporter, Temple, was removed from the Lord Lieutenancy of Buckinghamshire. The result of the trial was received with public rejoicings in all corners of England. This dispute between Government and a scurrilous writer, of most licentious morals, would be scarcely worth mentioning, although it occupied nearly the whole session, were it not one of the proofs of the want of harmony existing between Parliament and those whom Parliament

The trial of Wilkes. 1763.

was held to represent. It was one of several incidents which showed that the venal House of Commons, consisting of nominees of the Court or great families, was rapidly ceasing to command the obedience of the people, and that the machinery of the Constitution was thereby becoming dislocated.

The question at once came before both Houses. In the House of Lords it assumed a personal form. Lord Sandwich, a former friend of Wilkes, and his associate in his greatest debauchery, but now Secretary of State, did not think it unbecoming to produce an obscene parody on Pope's "Essay on Man," of which Wilkes was the author, and demand his punishment. The book had never been · published; fourteen copies had been privately printed; it had come into Sandwich's possession when Wilkes's house was ransacked, and afterwards by tampering with Wilkes's printer. Sandwich complained of it as a breach of privilege, for it was addressed to him. "Awake, my Sandwich!" it began, instead of "Awake, my St. John!" of Pope's Essay, and ridiculous notes were added, attributed to Warburton, Bishop of Gloucester, who had annotated Pope's work. In the House of Commons Wilkes rose and complained of his imprisonment as a breach of privilege, but he met with little sympathy. By a large majority No. 45 was voted to be a seditious libel, and ordered to be burnt by the common hangman. A dangerous riot was the consequence, nor was the operation completed till a jackboot and petticoat, the popular emblems of the Princess of Wales and Lord Bute, were committed to the flames to share the fate of the obnoxious publication. Further proceedings against Wilkes were postponed by a duel in which he was engaged

Wilkes is expelled by the Lower House. with a Mr. Martin, who had grossly insulted him, and in which he was wounded; but he was eventually expelled from his place in the House. On the two constitutional questions which were involved in this quarrel—the construction to be given to the privilege of members and the legality of general warrants—the popular party was defeated, in spite of the powerful support of Pitt. In opposition to the Courts of Law, Parliament held that privilege could not cover a seditious libel; and Grenville and his majority contrived to shelve a resolution which was introduced declaring the illegality of general warrants. The whole question excited the intensest interest; the House is said to have once sat for seventeen hours. Wilkes, unable to withstand all the assaults upon him, had, in spite of his popularity, been obliged to withdraw to France.

Grenville and his ministry had hardly completed this quarrel, in which they had wantonly embroiled Parliament and people, when they took a fresh step which, though well intentioned, was destined, from the way in which it was carried out, to lose England the best of her colonies.

The thirteen American provinces owed their origin to many different causes, and were very distinct both in their character and laws. There was, in the first place, the group of New England provinces, Connecticut, Massachusetts, New Hampshire (which included what is now called Vermont), and Rhode Island ; these owed their origin to the Pilgrim Fathers, and though the first zeal of their Puritan religion had died away, much of the stern character of their original founders remained among the population : their capital was Boston, almost surrounded by the sea, and already a port of very considerable importance and wealth ; the Hudson formed their boundary towards the west. Then there came a group of provinces originally belonging to the Dutch, and known as the New Netherlands. These had come into the hands of England during the war between Holland and England in the reign of Charles II., and had been granted to the Duke of York. New Amsterdam became New York, and Fort Orange, higher up the stream, Albany. Another part of the same grant was New Jersey, lying between the Hudson and the Delaware. This had been given for payment by the Duke of York to Lord Berkeley and Sir George Carteret ; the western part had been subsequently parted with by Berkeley to the Quakers, and the whole province, which was surrendered to the Crown in the reign of Queen Anne, was therefore known commonly as the Jerseys, and was peopled almost exclusively by Quakers, Presbyterians and Anabaptists. Spreading from their colony in New Jersey, the Quakers, under their great leader William Penn, had occupied the large province of Pennsylvania, with its capital Philadelphia lying inland to the west. One other province belongs to this group, Maryland, which was regarded as a sort of appendage to Pennsylvania, but had a separate assembly of its own ; the governor however was generally the same as the Pennsylvanian governor. Below these two groups were three great colonies, owing their origin to less easily defined sources. Virginia, south of the Potomac, originally founded by Raleigh, had then (by a grant of King James I.) passed into the hands of merchant adventurers. Behaving badly, and quarrelling with their colonists, they were deprived of their rights, and in 1624 the colony became a Crown colony. It had been peopled principally by Church of England men and by men of good English birth. As the oldest colony it was the best peopled, while the birth and character of its proprietors, who resembled English gentlemen, caused them to be regarded as the aristocracy of the colonies. The two Carolinas had been granted to a number of proprietors in the reign of Charles II., but, as in most other cases, the original proprietors had quarrelled with the people, and sold their rights to the Crown. Below these Carolinas was Georgia, founded for philanthropic purposes as a refuge for insolvent debtors and persecuted Germans by General Oglethorpe, the originator of the inquiry into the English prisons in 1728. The only power not English now in North America was that of Spain, which had received a portion of Louisiana from the French in exchange for Florida, which they had been obliged to cede to the English. French influence had disappeared after the Peace of Paris.

There was an infinite variety of religion, law and government Constitution of in these provinces, but in all a certain assimilation the provinces. to the English Constitution ; a house of assembly, an upper house or council, sometimes elected, sometimes nominated by the governor, and the governor himself in the Crown colonies nominated by the King and the proprietors in conjunction. The population appears to have been about two and a half millions.

The old view of the use of colonies was that they should be employed Restrictions entirely for the advantage of the mother country. It on colonial was held that, by the mere fact of their existence, and trade. for the protection they received, they were bound by a debt of gratitude. They were thus the constant subject of mercantile legislation in favour of the mother country, and by the existing navigation laws very close restrictions were laid upon their trade. By those laws the colonies were prohibited from procuring a large number of articles—those, namely, which formed the chief manufactures of England—anywhere except from the mother country. They thus became naturally one of our principal purchasers. Although their imports into England were considerable, the balance of trade was constantly against them—that is, taken as a whole, they constantly owed large sums of money to England. This balance had, of course, from time to time to be made up by payments in actual money, which was chiefly procured by the colonies by means of illicit trade, carried on partly with the West India Islands, but chiefly with the Spanish colonies of America, and was illicit chiefly in that it broke the customhouse regulations of Spain. The colonial illicit or free trade, as it was called, was regarded in point of morality as something quite different from European smuggling. It was carried on openly and systematically by the best colonial merchants, and enabled the colonies to get rid of their timber and those wooden products known under the name of lumber, and also of a considerable quantity of their farm produce which would otherwise have been wasted. A wise minister would not have thought of meddling with such a business, which was in fact the only means by which the colonists were enabled to carry on conveniently their trade with England. But Grenville, with his narrow and legal turn of mind, could see no difference between colonial smug- General suppression of smuggling. gling and smuggling in England. This he was deter- pression of mined to put down, and not content with the ordinary smuggling. means of repression, English men-of-war were employed in all directions as customhouse vessels, and naval officers, people said, were degraded into customhouse officers of the King of Spain. The effect was a crushing blow to the trade of America. And, as if to render the position of the colonists still more distressing, in 1764 a series of enactments were made, laying duties upon various articles for the benefit of England,—at the same time declaring for the first time the right of England to raise a revenue from her colonies ; and while the quantity of money in America had been considerably diminished by the stoppage of the free trade, the present Act was rendered more irksome by ordering all the duties imposed to be paid in hard cash into the English Exchequer. It was coupled, too, with another Act stopping the use of paper money in America. Taken together, this series of arrangements had therefore produced the following effects—a large branch of commerce, the chief source of ready money, was destroyed ; at the same time more ready money was demanded by England ; and the colonists saw themselves prevented even from carrying on their domestic trade in the ordinary channels.

These measures had produced retaliation from the Americans ; it had been determined that as little trade as possible should be carried on with England. Lamb was not to be eaten, and lambs were not killed, in order to increase the stock of sheep for the supply of the wool which was England's great manufacture ; and in all other possible ways men denied themselves European luxuries. It has been said that the preamble of the Act for the new duties stated the necessity for raising a revenue from the English colonies, The Stamp and at the same time Grenville had proposed a Stamp Act.

Act as one of the means of raising such revenue. With singular want of wisdom, though with kindly feeling, he put off bringing in a Bill for the establishment of this tax, which would be an article of excise or inland duty, till the assemblies of the different colonies had stated their views with regard to it. The Americans, though probably without any real legal grounds, drew a line between the levying of customs and the imposing of an inland tax. It is probable that by the strict letter of the law they were liable to both, for even the Long Parliament had only granted temporary exemptions from taxation. But when their attention was drawn to the intentions and claims of the English Parliament, and when a tax, new in fact though perhaps not in principle, was suggested to them, and a year given them to talk it over, it was natural that their opposition should be roused. Five colonies sent petitions against the new measures, but they were wholly disregarded, and the Stamp Act passed without much opposition in Parliament.

The ministry seemed unusually strong—it had triumphed over

The King's Illness

Wilkes; and its financial policy, though ruinous, had been accepted—when suddenly the King became alarmingly ill, suffering from that loss of intellect which afterwards incapacitated him from reigning. In alarm at this illness, on his recovery he desired a Regency Bill to be passed. The natural person to have appointed Regent would have been the Queen. The King had been hastily married in the first year of his reign (1761) to the Princess Sophia of Mecklenburg, a marriage which, as it was contracted chiefly by the influence of the Princess Dowager and Lord Bute, and without the will of the King, for the purpose of withdrawing him from his dangerous love for Lady Sarah Lennox, might have been expected to turn out ill, but which became in fact a happy life-long union. The King however, instead of suggesting, as was natural, that his wife should be Regent, desired to keep the appointment in

The Regency Bill. 1765.

his own hands. The Government objected to this, without limitations, and suggested that the King's choice should lie among the Queen and the members of the Royal Family resident in England. When this Bill was brought forward it was pertinently asked who the Royal Family were ? and it became evident that the ministry did not themselves know how to define it. They ultimately concluded, however, that the Princess Dowager was not a relation of her own son. In making this ridiculous assertion, and insulting the Princess by excluding her name, they were probably instigated by the dread of a Bute ministry in case anything should happen to the King. In pursuance of this policy, Halifax hurried to the King, and persuaded him that the unpopularity of the Princess Dowager was such that the introduction of her name in the Bill would infallibly be followed by its omission on the demand of the Commons, and the Princess thus exposed to public insult. The King, taken off his guard, and naturally wishing to spare his mother so public a mark of disrespect, consented to the omission of her name. The Bill was brought into the House of Lords and passed, limiting the regency to the Queen and the descendants of the late King and Queen resident in England. When the Lord Chancellor—an honest man—explained to the King what he had done, he was much disturbed, but no entreaties of his could move Grenville to change the Bill. Upon its introduction into the Lower House the absence of the name of the Princess was at once remarked, and a large majority voted for its introduction; thus making obvious to the King the shameless trick of which he had been the victim. For this he could not forgive Grenville and Bedford, and at once began arrangements for getting rid of them.

For this purpose he called in the assistance and experience of his uncle the Duke of Cumberland, whose upright and consistent conduct had given him an authority and importance which he had not sought. He was a firm Whig, and had of late years regarded Pitt as the real head of that great party. To him therefore the Duke now applied. In a long interview Pitt explained his views and stated his terms. He demanded that an alliance with the Protestant powers of Europe should be entered into, to balance the Family Compact, that general warrants should henceforward be declared illegal, and that officers dismissed for political reasons should be restored. Everything seemed to promise success, but Pitt wished to see Temple, to whom he was bound by ties of relationship, party, personal friendship, and even pecuniary assistance. After his interview with Temple it was evident that some obstacle had arisen, and the negotiation was broken off. The fact is, that Temple, infinitely Pitt's inferior, had come to terms with George Grenville, and was planning a family Grenville ministry; and Pitt's lofty view of his obligations to his brother-in-law prevented him from breaking with him. The King was thus thrown back, bound hand and foot, into the hands of his old ministry. They would consent to remain in their places if the King would pledge himself to dismiss Bute from his friendship, to get rid of Fox, now Lord Holland, from the Paymastership, turn Mr. Stuart

[margin note: Negotiations for a change of ministry.]

Mackenzie out of his place as Privy Seal for Scotland, make Lord Granby Commander-in-Chief instead of the Duke of Cumberland, and give Ireland to the ministry, which meant the dismissal of the Earl of Northumberland, Bute's son-in-law, from the Lord-Lieutenancy—a mere set of personal and vindictive conditions, contrasting finely with Pitt's political demands. Such as they were the King was obliged to accept them, but he could not bring himself to like or trust his ministry, and after a strong, though not perhaps unduly strong, representation from Bedford against the underhand employment of the King's influence against his own ministers, he determined that he would rid himself of them, even at the cost of accepting the Whig Houses. Pitt was again applied to, talked honestly and simply to the Duke of Cumberland, stating as his terms an European alliance, the abolition of general warrants, the repeal of the cider tax, and a change in American taxation, thus in his two sets of terms clearing himself of all complicity with the follies of the present Government. But Temple refused to take the position of Prime Minister except

Pitt retires into private life.
as the head of a Grenville administration, and Pitt with infinite sorrow gave up the negotiation, sold his house at Hayes, and declared his intention of retiring to Somersetshire, where an admiring stranger had lately left him the house of Burton-Pynsent.

The Duke of Cumberland, finding that Pitt was by some means separated from the great Whig party, applied directly to its acknow-

Ministry of the Whig Houses.
ledged family chiefs, who agreed to form a ministry, putting forward as their head Lord Rockingham, a sporting man of sound sense and large possessions, but no power of language or popular government.[1] Under him were the Duke of Grafton with no parliamentary experience, General Conway, a sensible man, but without any of the gifts of leadership, to whom was intrusted the management of the House of Commons, and the veteran Duke of Newcastle, to whom was given the Privy Seal, with a special perquisite of the patronage of the Church. With the exception of Lord Chancellor Northington, there was in fact scarcely any one of the requisite degree of efficiency in the ministry. Its life could not be a long one. It is fair to say that Burke, who was now first introduced to public life by Lord Rockingham, speaks highly of him for enlargement of mind, clear sense, and unshaken fortitude.

This weak Government found on its hands a question of difficulty

---

[1] He seldom spoke. When Lord Sandwich was one day attacking him, a friend asked him, "How could you worry a poor dumb creature so?"

too great for it. The Stamp Act had been very badly received in America; there had been riots in many of the towns, involving much loss of property; the collectors had been obliged to reᴸounce their offices, and the stamped paper had been destroyed. Virginia had solemnly protested in regular form through the House of Burgesses; and a Congress of delegates of nine or ten of the States had met at New York (October), and passed resolutions, claiming for the provincial assemblies the exclusive right of taxation. At home the merchants had begun to feel the *Question of American taxation.* effects of the self-denying determination of the Americans, in a diminution of their trade, and of the enforcement of the laws against smuggling, in the impossibility of getting money payments for their goods. The sum due is stated variously at two to three millions. During the recess of Parliament the writings and proceedings of the ministry had an air of weakness, and finally, unable to act vigorously themselves, they determined to put the matter into the hands of Parliament.

In January Parliament met, and on the 14th the subject was brought before the House. There was a great debate. Burke then made his maiden speech, and was followed by Pitt, who had not yet expressed his views, and had indeed absented himself from the House for a year. Expectation was raised to the highest pitch, and in a magnificent speech he declared, what till that moment had in England been scarcely thought of, that Parliament had *no right* to tax the colonies, for taxation and *Return of Pitt, and his declaration of views. 1766.* representation went hand in hand. He however, like the Americans, drew a line between taxation and customs. Customs he regarded in the light of trade regulations, and therefore in the hands of the Imperial Legislature. After a speech of weak acquiescence from Conway, Grenville made an able reply; he exposed the fallacy of distinguishing between taxes and duties, alleged many instances of the taxation of unrepresented bodies, and charged the Americans with ingratitude for declining to pay for a war so entirely in their own interest as the last. Pitt, though he had spoken, was, contrary to the rules of the House, called upon by the general voice to speak again. He rose, and declared himself ready to answer Grenville on every point. His reply was such as a statesman must make to a lawyer. "I rejoice," he cried, "that America has resisted; three millions of people so dead to all the feelings of liberty as voluntarily to submit to be slaves would have been fit instruments to have made slaves of the rest." He had not come down with the "statute book doubled down in

dog's ears to defend the cause of liberty," and as to gratitude, he
supposed that all the bounties to America were for English purposes.
There was a trade with America of £3,000,000 a year, and it was
trade which carried England through the last war. " This you owe
to America, and shall a miserable financier come with a boast that
he can fetch a peppercorn into the Exchequer to the loss of millions
to the nation?" He closed by stating his belief that England could
crush America to atoms, but the triumph would be hazardous. If
she fell she would fall like the strong man; she would embrace the
pillars of the State, and pull down the Constitution with her. He
advised the immediate and entire repeal of the Stamp Act, but that
the other rights of Parliament, apart from taxation, should be clearly
declared. There was no doubt much weight in Grenville's instances
of imperfect representation, but they were not wisely urged against
Pitt, who in his first speech had himself pointed out in very tren-
chant words the wretched state of the representative system in England. Indeed, he almost alone seems to have understood the real
meaning of the Wilkes riots, and to have wished to bring Parliament
and the people into harmony. Pitt's bold speech encouraged the
ministers to act, and after a long examination of witnesses, among
The Stamp Act whom Franklin, who had come over as an agent to
repealed. oppose the Act, was the most important, the Repeal of
the Stamp Act was proposed and carried amid the enthusiasm of the
mercantile and liberal world on the 21st of February. For this time
Pitt's political wisdom had saved England from a disastrous breach
with her colonies.

Once embarked on a policy of repeal, the Rockingham ministry
continued to reverse the acts of its predecessors. The trade of
America was again fostered, and Dominique and Jamaica were
made free ports; the obnoxious cider tax was ameliorated, general
warrants were condemned, as was also the practice of depriving
military officers of their commands for political opposition. General Conway was himself the last victim of this practice. Foreign
manufactured silks were also prohibited, and thus the clamours of
the Spitalfields weavers were silenced, which, during Grenville's
administration, had produced a riot directed chiefly against the Duke
of Bedford. But, in spite of these healing measures, the Government
was never strong. The King detested it as being distinctly a party
Weakness of Government, and the abilities of the ministry were not
the Govern- conspicuous. They tried in vain to induce Pitt to join
ment. them. Upon the failure of this negotiation the King

was glad to have recourse again to that great man. For the third time since the close of his administration Pitt had the destinies of the nation in his hand. Twice his Quixotic attachment to his friend Lord Temple had ruined his plans. He had always aimed at a broader basis of government than mere personal or party connection, and during his great administration had succeeded in acting independently. There was something therefore in common between him and the King, though no doubt their view of the destruction of party was different. To Pitt it meant the selection of able men of all political connections, under his own pre-eminent guidance, to form a ministry, which should work for the national good, and be responsible to the nation. To the King it meant the selection of efficient administrators, without any pre-eminent minister, and answerable to himself. There was apparently, however, enough in common between them to induce Pitt to accept the administration, and to break off his connection with Temple, who insisted, as a condition of his support, that the whole of the Rockingham party should be dismissed. Pitt, on the other hand, determined on a fusion with that party. Rockingham himself left the ministry, but his chief sup-

porters remained under Pitt. Grafton was nominally Prime Minister and First Lord of the Treasury, Conway and Shelburne were the Secretaries of State, Charles

Pitt becomes Lord Chatham and Prime Minister. July 1766.

Townshend Chancellor of the Exchequer, Lord Northington became Lord President, and was succeeded as Chancellor by Pitt's friend Pratt, Lord Camden. Pitt himself surprised the world by taking a peerage as Lord Chatham and the small office of Privy Seal. In acting thus he no doubt miscalculated his strength ; he felt himself unable from his growing infirmities to continue to lead the House of Commons, and believed, as he had indeed good right to believe, that his personal character and influence would enable him, in whatever position he might be, to blend the ministry from whatever party he chose them into an harmonious administration. The effect did not answer his expectations. His acceptance of a peerage was regarded as the acceptance of a bribe, especially as his avowed principle in the selection of his colleagues was the same as that rendered so unpopular by Bute and the King—the destruction of party. He thus lost his popularity ; of party influence he had little or none ; he was deficient in knowledge of party tactics, which during his great administration had been in the hands of Newcastle. His natural arrogance had grown on him, and was rendered worse by his irritable state of health. He tried to win the Bedford party, but would not give them enough. He introduced a number of Tories and courtiers into the administration, and thus shocked the great Whig party ; and when, as shortly happened, illness obscured for a time his intellect, the ministry lost all cohesion and fell to pieces.

But though thus failing as a tactician, it was impossible for Pitt to be in office without setting on foot magnificent and beneficial plans.

Chatham's comprehensive plans. He immediately began the new foreign policy which he had so often sketched. Mr. Hans Stanley was despatched to the Courts of Berlin and St. Petersburg to cement an alliance against the house of Bourbon. But at Berlin he met but a cold reception. Frederick, whose character was as mean and selfish as his abilities were great, did not care in the least for the defence of Protestantism or for the safety of England, now that his own safety did not depend upon her friendship. Indeed, since Bute's withdrawal from the war he had hated England heartily, and alleged the want of continuity in English policy as a reason for engaging in no alliances. In truth, his mind was already fixed upon his wicked plan for the dismemberment of Poland. Pitt, now Lord Chatham, was thus foiled at the outset, and his foreign policy failed. Two other great schemes he was unable to bring to completion; one for the better government of Ireland, and the other for what he saw would speedily become a matter of the greatest importance—the regulation of our Indian conquests. He intended to do what we have but lately seen done,—assume for the Crown the sovereignty of India, and confine the Company to their proper and mercantile pursuits.

In the midst of these vast schemes, having given indications that he contemplated a Reform Bill, an India Bill, the pacification and better government of Ireland, alliances which would have forestalled the great alliances of his son, and a plan which might perhaps have retained America, Chatham fell ill at Bath, and the Government ceased to have a natural head.

While Chatham was thus absent from his post his reckless Chancellor of the Exchequer brought in a scheme for again raising revenue from America. The sum was indeed a very small one—£40,000, and raised upon tea, glass, and paper, and therefore falling, it might be urged, under the head of those mercantile arrangements which the colonies admitted the right of Parliament to make ; but in the present state of affairs in America it was a mere act of madness. The repeal of the Stamp Act had been made conditional on

Chatham's illness and mental failure. Jan. 1767.

Townshend's financial measures.

the repayment of property injured in the riots. This the Assemblies had agreed to only with much grumbling, and the Assembly of New York had gone so far in its opposition to a requisition for supplying necessaries to the troops that it had been suspended. While America was in this irritable condition Townshend's measure came to inflame the smouldering mass.

What Chatham had spoken of as the rotten part of the Constitution was, early in the year 1768, brought into full play. Corruption of There was a general election, in which bribery and Parliament. the purchase of seats were shamelessly employed. 1768. £4000 is said to have been the average price of a small borough. Oxford offered to re-elect its members for £7500, to be applied to the liquidation of a corporation debt ; and to show how ridiculously inefficient the representation was, it may be mentioned that in a population of eight millions there were only a hundred and sixty thousand voters. The people were by this time beginning, though perhaps somewhat blindly, to feel that the representative body did not really represent them, and, as usual, they fixed upon one individual, and that not a very worthy one, as a representative of this feeling. Wilkes had already been a popular martyr and the victim of the vengeance both of King and Parliament. He now Wilkes elected presented himself for election in London. He was for Middlesex. there rejected, but immediately afterwards elected by 1768. a large majority in the county of Middlesex. His election produced riots in London, and the Government—contrary probably to their own judgment, and urged by the King—determined to interfere. Wilkes was apprehended as an outlaw, and riots ensued, which were suppressed only by the use of the troops. Twenty people were killed and wounded. The military were not only acquitted when tried upon the charge of murder, but were rewarded by Government. The anger of the people increased, and in the riots which ensued in various parts of England the point immediately at issue was complicated with other social questions, many depressed trades taking the opportunity of exhibiting their discontent. The Government which had to deal with this difficulty was the Duke of Grafton's—Chatham immediately upon his recovery had retired from it, and Lord Shelburne had also left it. Grafton, without views of his own, had become the mere tool in the hands of the King and his party. George was set with dogged obstinacy upon the suppression of insubordination in America and the destruction of Wilkes in England. Under such circumstances the war with the people was carried to extremes. When a vacancy occurred in the representation for Middlesex there was a fresh contest, and Glynn, a partisan of Wilkes, was elected. In the attendant riots a life was lost; the pardon of two men who were convicted, though perhaps on insufficient evidence, for having caused the death, still further irritated the people. Wilkes's petitions were neglected, and on his publishing a severe letter against Lord Weymouth, Secretary of State, the House, instead of leaving the matter to the Law Courts, declared it a breach of privilege, and unable to pronounce a libel against a Peer a breach of the privileges of the Commons, they proceeded, perfectly illegally, to have Wilkes arrested and brought to the bar of the House, and there tried for libel. Wilkes avowed the letter, and Lord Barrington, Secretary of War, and one of the " King's friends," moved his expulsion. A new writ was issued for Middlesex, and Wilkes was re-elected almost unanimously. The House voted that he could not sit, and a fresh writ was issued, and Wilkes was again unanimously elected. Another election was ordered, and this time the Government contrived to get about three hundred votes for Colonel Luttrell against eleven hundred given for Wilkes. The House declared that Luttrell was the member. So iniquitous a decision raised Wilkes into the position of a great popular leader, and was not carried without many vigorous protests from the most influential members of the Liberal party. It tended much to lessen the power of the ministry; both great cities and great counties held meetings to express their want of confidence in the present representation and to ask for a dissolution.

Nor did the ministry strengthen itself by its dealings with America. The new imposts of 1767 had been received with great indignation by the colonists, especially in Massachusetts. There the governor, Francis Barnard, seems to have been totally destitute of all power of conciliation. He was backed up by Lord Hillsborough, Colonial Secretary, scarcely more temperate than himself. The Assembly, in its quarrel with the governor, issued a circular letter to the other colonies, calling for their co-operation against the new taxes. They refused to retract this step at the command of Lord Hillsborough, and were dissolved. The difficulties of the crisis went on increasing. The customhouse commissioners were foolish enough to capture and detain an illicit trader; serious riots were the consequence; the commissioners were mobbed and their houses robbed. The spirit of resistance spread. The Society of Sons and Daughters of Liberty, who refused to use imported goods, multiplied in other colonies. The view of the Government was not conciliation, but coercion. Troops and ships of war were crowded into Boston. In England the feeling was strongly against the Americans. Coercive measures were recommended and applauded; Francis Barnard was raised to the rank of a Baronet; the conduct of the people of Boston gravely censured in Parliament; and at length Bedford's section of the Whigs produced a motion which could hardly fail to excite resistance. The Duke moved, and the Parliament applauded his motion, that as it was probable that American juries would sympathize with their countrymen, the rioters might be withdrawn from their country, in accordance with an obsolete law of treason of the reign of Henry VIII. This measure, which seemed to deprive the colonists of their first rights as Englishmen, met with deserved execration both at home and in America. But to crown all, and to put the ministers quite in the wrong, some general action on their part was wanting. This want was supplied when the conciliatory efforts of Grafton were defeated in his own Cabinet. He suggested the removal of all taxation of America. English pride forbade the Council to accept a measure which they thought derogatory to the rights of an Imperial nation. Therefore, for the mere purpose of asserting the right, they agreed to the removal of all taxes but one, and insisted that the tax on tea should be kept. Thus the original principle of the right to tax was upheld, and the sting still left to rankle in the minds of the Americans.

The unpopularity which their conduct had brought on the ministry was increased by the vigorous and bitter assaults of Letters of Junius. This anonymous writer, probably Sir Philip Junius. Francis, lost no opportunity of attacking, with the greatest animosity, the Duke of Grafton and his supporters, not even sparing the King, and by his bold assaults, excellent style, and by the mystery which hung over him, drew upon himself much public attention, and directed men's minds to all the weaknesses of the administration.

The incompetency of the ministry was indeed becoming obvious. In the first place it was divided within itself. The Weakness of Prime Minister, with the Chancellor and some others, the ministry. were remnants of the Chatham ministry and admirers of Chatham's policy. The rest of the Cabinet were either men who represented Bedford's party, or members of that class whose views are sufficiently explained by their name, "the King's friends." Grafton, fonder of hunting and the turf than of politics, had by his indolence suffered himself to fall under the influence of the last-named party, and unconstitutional action had been the result which had brought discontent in England to the verge of open outbreak. Hillsborough, under the same influence, was hurrying along the road which led to the loss of America. On this point the Prime Minister had found himself in a minority in his own Cabinet. France too, under Choiseul, in alliance with Spain, was beginning to think of revenge for the losses of the Seven Years' War. A crisis was evidently approaching, and the Opposition began to close their ranks. Chatham, yielding again to the necessities of party, made a public profession of friendship with Temple and George Grenville; and though there was no cordial connection, there was external alliance between the brothers and the old Whigs under Rockingham. In the first session of 1770 the storm broke. Notwithstanding the state of public affairs, the chief topic of the King's speech was the murrain among " horned beasts,"—a speech not of a king, but, said Junius, of " a ruined grazier." Chatham at once moved an amendment when the address in answer to this speech was proposed. He deplored the want of all European alliances, the fruit of our desertion of our allies at the Peace of Paris; he blamed the conduct of the ministry with regard to America, which, he thought, needed much gentle. handling, inveighed strongly against the action of the Lower House in the case of Wilkes, and ended by moving that that action should at once be taken into consideration. At the sound of their old leader's voice his followers in the Cabinet could no longer be silent. Camden declared he had been a most unwilling party to the persecution of Wilkes, and though retaining the Seals, attacked and voted against the ministry. In the Lower House, Granby, one of the most popular men in England, followed the same course. James Grenville and Dunning, the Solicitor-General, also resigned. Chatham's motion was lost, but was followed up by Rockingham, who asked for a night to consider the state of the nation. Grafton found it nearly impossible to prop up his falling ministry ; the Great Seal went, as Lord Shelburne said, a-begging. Charles Yorke was indeed induced to take it in spite of his former political connections, but, overwhelmed apparently by the coldness of his former friends, he committed suicide. Grafton thus found himself in no state to meet the Opposition, and in his heart still admiring Chatham, and much disliking business, he suddenly and unexpectedly gave in his resignation the very day fixed for Rockingham's motion.

Camden, Granby and Grafton resign.

The Opposition seemed to have everything in their own hands, but there was no real cordiality between the two sections. The

Rockingham party despised the City friends of Chatham, who, under
the leadership of Lord Mayor Beckford, had become pro- Want of cordial
minent in the Wilkite riots, and since that time by a alliance among
somewhat impertinent use of the right which the City the Opposition.
possessed of directly approaching the King with petitions.   They
dreaded also the paramount influence the Grenville party were nearly
sure to possess in any joint Government.   On the other hand,
Chatham despised the half measures and moderation constantly
advocated by the Rockingham party.   The King, with much quick-
ness and decision, took advantage of this disunion.   To him it was
of paramount importance to retain his friends in office, and to avoid a
new Parliament elected in the present excited state of the nation.

There was only one of the late ministry capable of The King sends
assuming the position of Prime Minister.   This was for Lord North
and avoids a
Lord North, Chancellor of the Exchequer, and to him dissolution.
the King immediately and successfully applied, so that while the
different sections of the Ópposition were still unable to decide on any
united action, they were astonished to find the old ministry reconstituted and their opportunity gone.   The new Prime Minister was a
man whose unwieldy person and want of grace seemed little to fit
him for the command of a popular assembly.   His frame was bulky,
his action very awkward, and his shortsighted, protruding eyes,
swollen cheeks and over-large tongue, enabled Walpole to compare
him to a blind trumpeter.   But under this awkward exterior he had
great capacity for business and administration, and much sound
sense; he was a first-rate debater, and gifted with a wonderful sweet-
ness of temper, which enabled him to listen unmoved, or even to sleep,
during the most violent attacks upon himself, and to turn aside the
bitterest invectives with a happy joke.   With his accession to the
Premiership the unstable character of the Government ceased.   Resting on the King, making himself no more than an instrument of the
King's will, and thus commanding the support of all royal influence,
from whatever source derived, North was able to bid defiance to all
enemies, till the ill effects of such a system of government and of
the King's policy became so evident, that the clamour for a really
responsible minister grew too loud to be disregarded.

Thus is closed the great constitutional struggle of the early part
of the reign—the struggle of the King, supported by the Triumph of the
unrepresented masses, and the more liberal and inde- King's policy.
pendent of those who were represented, against the domination of
the House of Commons.   It was an attempt to break those trammels

which, under the guise of liberty, the upper classes, the great lords
and landed aristocracy, had succeeded after the Revolution in laying
on both Crown and people. In that struggle the King had been
victorious. But he did not recognize the alliance which had enabled
him to succeed. He did not understand that the people had other
objects much beyond his own. He saw that they felt thus far with
him, that they disliked the comparative servitude in which he was
placed, that they felt hurt at the coercion frequently brought to bear
upon him by the dominant faction, that they were willing and
anxious to assist him in breaking those ties of party, which were
little else than the ties of faction and class. Seeing this, he did not
recognize that the people were equally disinclined for the establishment of personal government, that they wanted to strengthen the
Crown and to weaken the Whig party, chiefly as a means of attaining to a more complete system of self-government. He believed that
his own power and his own skill had been chiefly instrumental in
the success which had met his efforts. He had no intention of allowing any of the fruits of that success to fall to any but himself. Kind-
hearted and well-meaning, he wished to govern for the good of his
people, but he distinctly wished to govern for them and not to let
them govern for themselves. It is thus that during the ministry of
North, and of those who preceded him, the royal influence was constantly employed in repression,—repression of all popular movements at home, repression of all attempts at liberty in the colonies ;
and this principle Lord North, backed by a servile House of Commons,
was able to uphold.

The House was indeed notoriously under ministerial influence, and

Grenville's
reform of elec-
tion petitions.
1770.

one of the last acts of Grenville was to attempt a reform
in one particular at least. Disputed elections had
hitherto been referred to a Committee of the whole
House, and had thus become the merest party questions, in which
the right and wrong of the case was never thought of. Grenville's
measure, which was carried against considerable opposition, gave the
cognizance of such questions to a select Committee, with judicial
powers, and themselves bound by oath. Even thus justice was not
secured, and though the number of the Committee was subsequently
again decreased and fresh measures taken to secure fair decisions,
it has lately been found necessary to put the settlement of election
petitions into the hands of some of the regular judges. This important measure closed the career of Grenville ; before the year was out
he died. Thus Lord North found himself relieved from an able

opponent, while the Opposition lost one of its chiefs, and became still more disorganized. About the same time the death of the Marquis of Granby, who by his popularity had formed a link between Chatham's party and the rest of the Opposition, still further weakened that body, and left North with comparatively easy work on his hands.

It was the American question which still pressed for solution. Profound anger had been aroused by Bedford's vindictive proposal, and by the maintenance even in a single instance of the right to tax. Hitherto the quarrel had *Increased irritation in America.* been principally with the New Englanders, but a more general opposition was evidently approaching when the aristocratic province of Virginia came forward to take the lead. When a solemn demand in the House of Burgesses for the repeal of the obnoxious measures of the English Parliament had only produced a dissolution of the House by the Governor, Lord Bottetort, an organized opposition was formed by men who subsequently became the chief actors in the War of Independence. A declaration, signed by Washington, Patrick Henry, Randolph and Jefferson, was issued against importing British goods till the restrictions of 1767 had been withdrawn. In Massachusetts the cry against the troops and the King's ships was continued, and there too the legislative assembly was prorogued. The complaint made against the number of soldiers kept in the province, and the consequent danger of collision, was not groundless. On the 5th of March a riot took place ; and though Captain Preston, who commanded the soldiers, gave no orders to fire, the troops were unable to command their temper, and some blood was shed. This "massacre," as it was called, did much still further to embitter the feelings of the people of Boston. It is pleasant to see that even amidst the wild political excitement Preston and his soldiers got a fair trial, and, being defended by John Adams (afterwards President), were acquitted. This fray happened the very day that Lord North in England announced his determination *Lord North upholds Lord Hillsborough's policy.* of clinging to the policy of Lord Hillsborough, and said he was ready to remove all taxes except that on tea. In vain was it pointed out to him that the value of the tax was little more than £300 a year, and that the Americans had now made up their minds on the principle, and did not care for the mere lessening of burdens. He persisted in his view, saying that the Americans deserved no indulgence, and his motion was supported in the House, by 204 against 142. For a brief space the American question seemed settled. Massachusetts and Virginia still continued loud in their expressions of discontent, but in most parts of the continent the question now seemed rather a small one, and the hostile measures against English trade were generally disregarded.

This period of quiet lasted about three years, during which the ministry of Lord North constantly acquired strength, though there were not wanting signs of the great faults which characterized its policy. In the affair of the Falkland Islands, indeed, in spite of the outcries of the Opposition, there seems to have been no real lack either of prudence or firmness. These desert islands had been occupied by the English as a point of importance in the South Seas. Both French and Spaniards had turned their attention to them also, and a Spanish settlement, called Fort Soledad, had been formed on one of the islands. The English had, however, no idea that their neighbours intended to dispossess them, when, in June 1770, a force of Spaniards from Buenos Ayres arrived off Fort Egmont, and obliged the garrison to retire. This outrage in the midst of peace very nearly plunged the nation into war with Spain and France; for it was Choiseul who was the instigator of the difficulty, and the skill of Harris (afterwards Lord Malmesbury), Chargé d'affaires in Spain, would probably have failed to avert it had not Madame Dubarry, who had lately gained complete influence over Louis XV., seized the opportunity to overthrow the minister. On his fall Madame Dubarry's clique, D'Aiguillon, Terray, and Maupeou, became paramount in France, and, as might be expected under such circumstances, that country ceased for a time to have much influence in European politics.

Affair of the Falkland Islands

The unpopular character of the Government had prevented even its energetic and successful demand for the restoration of Fort Egmont from passing without censure in London. Murmurs against the press warrants had been heard, and opposition to them had been overruled chiefly by Chatham's influence. But the feeling of discontent broke out in full force the following year. Great jealousy had always been felt in Parliament as to reports of the debates held there, and such meagre accounts as had been published, from the memory of hearers or other private sources, had habitually been brought out under some disguise and with an affectation of secrecy. In 1770 this habit had passed into disuse. The Commons, already angry with the House of Lords for having excluded strangers, and indignant that, while the Lords secured secrecy their own debates were

The liberty of reporting Parliamentary debates

publicly reported, resolved to enforce the existing orders against some
of the printers of reports. Among others, one Miller was summoned
to be reprimanded. He however refused to come, saying he was
a livery-man of the City. A messenger sent to fetch him was himself apprehended and taken before the Lord Mayor, Brass Crosby, and
Aldermen Oliver and Wilkes. These magistrates supported the
arrest and held the messenger to bail. The House was very indignant. As the Mayor and Oliver were members, they justified in
their places in Parliament what they had done, and were committed
to the Tower. This was a sign for a renewal of the riots attending
the Wilkite difficulties. Mobs filled the streets, and Lord North was
ill used. The City took up the part of its members, who lived in
prison at the public expense ; and although the law courts held
that the City was in the wrong, appearances became so threatening
that the House let the matter quietly drop ; and on the prorogation
in May the prisoners were allowed to leave their confinement in
triumphal procession, and the question was not again raised. This
secured for ever the liberty of reporting.

In spite of this victory the popular party in the City was losing
ground, and Wilkes was not the name of power it once   Lord North's
had been ; while within the walls of Parliament the   ministry
                                                       gathers
ministry was constantly acquiring strength and the   strength.
Opposition becoming more and more broken up. Grafton had again
consented to return to office; Lord Sandwich, a follower of the
Duke of Bedford, accepted the Admiralty. Lord Suffolk, the
leader of what was left of Grenville's party, became Secretary of
State. The Opposition was thus reduced to the party of Rockingham and such few followers as consistently clung to Lord Chatham,
but these two sections could never work well together, and the three
Whig propositions of the year were all lost by want of union. The
want of harmony between the Parliament and the country, and the
consequent need of some reform, had been shown by the late quarrels
in the City. Chatham brought in a Bill with that object, embodying
his old plan of increased county representation. This, as it seemed
the only manner of securing an addition of independent members, and
as there was not yet in existence an important manufacturing and
industrial element unrepresented, was probably the best measure that
could have been taken. But it did not find favour with the Rockingham party, and was put aside. The same fate attended an effort on
the part of the Rockingham party to define the law of libel, and to
give the jury in such cases the right of settling not only the fact of

publication, but the character of the libel. Chatham thought that
measure should have been left for him, and a ridiculous struggle
between the two Whig sections in the House was the result. On the
third question, the dissolution of the present Parliament, which had
been the favourite object of all the City opposition and addresses,
Chatham found himself almost alone. While thus all effective
opposition disappeared, Lord North found his chief parliamentary
support in his law officers. Thurlow, his Attorney-General, and
Wedderburn, his Solicitor, afterwards Lord Loughborough, brought
—the one the weight of great legal knowledge, very strong sense, a
wonderful power of invective, and a determination of character
almost brutal ; the other a time-serving readiness and facile elegant
eloquence which was always at the service of his chief.

Excellent as the King's domestic life was, he did not escape the
family discomforts which so constantly attended the
house of Hanover. Two of his brothers gave him much
displeasure by their marriages. The Duke of Cumber-
land,[1] a man of libertine life, after scandalizing the world by appearing
as defendant in a case of criminal conversation, married Mrs. Horton,
a sister of that Colonel Luttrell who had been forced upon the electors
of Middlesex ; while the Duke of Gloucester now declared his marriage with Lady Waldegrave, an illegitimate daughter of Sir Edward
Walpole. To guard against such marriages in future, the Royal
Marriage Bill was passed, which forbids any member of the Royal
Family, unless children of princesses married abroad, to marry before
the age of twenty-five without the King's consent. After that age
they must give a twelvemonth's notice of their intended marriage,
which may be completed unless it be petitioned against by both
Houses of Parliament. A more real disgrace than these
marriages was the fate 'of George's sister, Caroline
Matilda, Queen of Denmark. Her husband was a dis-
gusting and licentious sot, whose villanous conduct so changed her
naturally good disposition, that it was not found difficult for her
enemies to gain credence for a story which connected her name
in a disreputable manner with a certain Struensee, at that time
favourite and Prime Minister in Denmark. This man, a physician
by profession, had acquired absolute control over the King's mind,
and had speedily risen to power. His enemies were of course
numerous, and the opportunity offered them by the Queen's conduct only too favourable. Struensee and the Queen were suddenly

Royal Mar-
riage Law.
1772.

Fate of the
Queen of
Denmark.

---

[1] The old Duke of Cumberland had died in 1765.

apprehended by night, and the Queen, after some remonstrance from King George, allowed to retire to Zell, where she died after a few years, protesting her innocence. Struensee, however, was executed, and confessed the crime with which he and the Queen were charged.

From such comparatively trivial matters as royal marriages and misconduct it is necessary to turn to what forms one of Division of Poland the darkest passages in the political history of Europe. England, · under the guidance of a ministry bound to support the selfish policy of a King whose real aim was solely the aggrandizement of the Crown, had held selfishly aloof from foreign affairs. France had just disgraced the last capable and vigorous minister she possessed, and lay supine under the hands of the King's scandalous mistress. So these two great countries, to their eternal disgrace, looked calmly on while the Eastern powers, without reason or plea of reason, dismembered an old kingdom and reduced a noble people to slavery. The institutions of Poland were very different from those of the rest of Europe, and such as lent themselves easily to the plans of encroaching neighbours. Since the failure of the house of Jagellon (1572) the monarchy had been elective. So great a Constitution of Poland. prize had naturally attracted the notice of foreign powers, who sought to secure the advancement of their own interests by obtaining the election of some favourite candidate of their own. Faction within the country was the inevitable consequence, and the arrangements of the constitution made faction permanent. There was no middle class. The nation had not gone through the same processes as other Western people. Nobility was easily obtained, and each member of the nobility ranked as the peer of all Its peculiar institutions the rest. Below the ranks of the nobility came the serfs. Political power, and also most of the executive, was vested in this wide aristocratical democracy. Usually delegates of the nobles constituted a governing house. Sometimes the whole body could, and did, claim the right of legislating. In the delegates' house one veto could check the progress of any law. If to this is added that the nation was divided by fierce differences in religion, it will be seen that no fairer field for foreign intrigue can be conceived. Nor, in spite of their individual bravery, were the Poles in a position to withstand force; the nobility still clung to their old habit of fighting on horseback, so that, at a time when modern warfare had fairly begun, there was no infantry but such as consisted of serfs. The strength of the army still consisted in an irregular body of light horse. Well might the Czarina Catherine say that anything might be had from Poland for the trouble of picking it up. She had made the experiment. On the death of Augustus of Saxony, in 1764, Russia had compelled the Poles to elect a late favourite of the Empress, Stanislas Poniatowsky, and from the time of his election had in fact treated Poland as her own property. It had been the hereditary policy of France to withstand Russian influence in Poland, and during Choiseul's ministry this policy was continued. The Turks were induced to make a war with Russia, which, though disastrous to them, no doubt somewhat lengthened the dying agonies of Poland. The confederates, who opposed in arms the reigning king and the Russian party, chiefly on the ground that they had insisted on the rights of the dissidents or dissenters in opposition to the orthodox Catholics, received constant though secret help from France. The conduct of Austria also was as yet ambiguous, and, judging by its natural interests, should have been opposed to that of Russia. On such hopes the confederates rested. Occasional success lured them on more rapidly to inevitable ruin. But France was too far away to give real help. Choiseul fell before the intrigues of the Dubarry party, and neither nation nor ministry was in a temper or position to pursue with energy a distant and unselfish policy. On the other hand, Austria speedily began to see more advantage in joining the prosperous and rising powers of Eastern Europe than in trying to prop up against them a falling cause. It became evident that Russia would soon be absolute master of the kingdom. Frederick of Prussia could not see such an accession to the power of his dangerous neighbour without taking some corresponding measures, and as a Prussian army entered and pillaged ruthlessly all the northern provinces, it became plain that there existed some understanding between Frederick and th Empress. The movement of Austrian troops, at first supposed to be friendly to the confederates, soon proved

Treaty of Partition.
that Maria Theresa, however grandly she might write and speak, had joined in the conspiracy of robbers; and before the year 1772 was over the treaty made early in the year was declared; and the necessary concessions were wrung with much violence from the King and legislature, absolutely unable to assert any will of their own. The final ratification took place in May 1773. The kingdom was to be partitioned. Each of the three great neighbours was to receive a portion somewhat in proportion to its size. Russia got 87,500 square miles; Austria 62,500; Prussia only 9,465 square miles, but these containing the best and most industrious part

of the nation. What remained was formed into an hereditary monarchy in the house of Stanislas. It is fair to say, as an excuse
for the supineness with which England looked on at this vast
national crime, that the best and wisest of her statesmen had systematically directed their attention to the depression of the house
of Bourbon. In the system of balance of power, as then understood, nothing was regarded as so likely to prove a check on the
power of that house as the increase of the influence of Russia.
Any movement in favour of Poland must have been in union with
France and in opposition to Russia, and would have tended at first
to reverse that action, which was generally regarded as most consistent
with the safety of English interests. In the face of recent facts
(1871), it may be clearly evident that the dangers of Europe come
from the East and not from the West; but it is not fair to blame
statesmen or nations because they did not foresee the French Revolution and its consequences, nor to throw indiscriminate censure on the
whole system of the balance of power because it has sometimes
produced disasters. As long as the social constitution Balance of
of Europe remains the same as it has been since the power
breaking up of the feudal system, as long as the feeling of nationality survives, in some form or other the balance of power is a
necessary safeguard to national independence. The fictitious divisions
into which Europe has by dynastic influences been forced, and the
maintenance of which has been the chief cause of the disrepute into
which the system of balance has fallen, have disappeared, or are
disappearing, before more natural and truly national divisions ; but
until these in their turn give way to some wholly new industrial
organization the undue preponderance of one nation must be an object
of dread to all the rest, and their efforts must be directed, as events
afford opportunity, to diminishing that preponderance.

It is fair also to say that the ministry had enough upon their
hands already. Although there had been a comparative American
cessation of the troubles in America, there had been affairs
many signs that they were by no means over. The more 1772
advanced leaders, indeed, in Massachusetts were too determined in
their views and too skilful as managers of agitation to let the friends
of the English connection, though doubtless considerably the larger
part of the population, carry the day through their inactivity. The
discontent of the colonies had been sedulously kept alive by the skill
and vigour of the leaders of the Opposition party. In the midst of
constant quarrels with their governor, Hutchinson, an American by

birth, the Massachusetts leaders appointed a committee of twenty-one for the purpose of organizing opposition to the Government. This step was followed by Virginia, where, in 1773, a corresponding committee of still wider scope was appointed; and at length two events occurred which entirely destroyed all hope of a peaceful accommodation. These incidents were the publication of some letters of Hutchinson, and an arrangement with the India Company which had in reality no connection with the quarrel. In June 1773, certain letters were laid before the House of Representatives of Massachusetts purporting to be written by Hutchinson, their governor, and his brother-in-law, Oliver, Lieutenant-Governor. These letters, written in 1767 and the two following years to Whately, the private secretary of Grenville, were of a private and friendly character. They took a view favourable to the Government, and stated the opinion of the writer, that a firm exhibition of authority would best tend to check the colonial discontent. The letters had been forwarded from England by Dr. Franklin, who was acting as agent for Massachusetts. As they were private letters, and Mr. Whately was dead, it is impossible that Franklin should not have known that they had come into his hands by unfair means. He had not the least right to use them. Indeed, on sending them to America he made a stipulation that they should not be published. Of course such a stipulation in the heat of a political quarrel was intended to be broken; and they were not only produced and read, and acknowledged by Hutchinson, but published. Their effect was very great; it seemed to the Americans as if the English Government had been urged to all its acts of severity by a party of traitors among themselves. The House of Representatives at once addressed the King, warmly demanding the removal of Hutchinson from his place as governor, since he had, they said, betrayed his trust, and given private, partial, and false information to Government. The petition was sent to Lord Dartmouth, who had succeeded Lord

Dunning's petition rejected 1774. Hillsborough as Colonial Secretary, by him it was laid before the King, who referred it to the Privy Council. The Council, consisting chiefly of "the King's friends," met in January 1774. Franklin, as Colonial agent, was present. The petitioners were represented by Dunning, the great Opposition advocate. The administration had unwisely given the affair the air of a Government question by naming Wedderburn, the Solicitor-General, as Hutchinson's counsel. Dunning contented himself with saying that the petitioners had no impeachment to make, no facts to prove; they only appealed to the King's judgment. With most unwise want of reticence, Wedderburn, feeling himself in the presence of a very favourable audience, gave vent to a furious diatribe against America, and more especially against Franklin—a man, he said, to be shunned by all honest men, from whom men would henceforth hide their papers; in short, a thief. The Council heard, laughed, and applauded. Franklin stood unmoved, no muscle showing how much he felt the insult, but it did not miss its mark. For him from that day no accommodation was possible, and the brown suit in which he stood was put by, to be worn again only when the treaty declaring America independent was signed. The petition, in which a people had expressed their earnest and passionate feelings, was declared frivolous and vexatious, and Franklin was removed at once from his office of Deputy Postmaster for the colonies.

Wedderburn had, no doubt, in his violent invective only expressed the feeling of most of the English nation; only a few weeks after the meeting of the Privy Council news had reached England which was not likely to render the bitterness between the two people less. In 1772 the India Company had come to Parliament demanding a loan. Much censure had been thrown on their officers and their manner of action, and alterations had been insisted on, which placed the Company very much at the mercy of Government. As a sort of compensation a Bill was brought in in their favour, by which they were enabled to export their teas from their London warehouses to the American colonies free from the English duties, and liable only to the much smaller duty to be levied in the colony. This measure would allow the India Company to get rid of a large surplus stock of tea then lying on hand, and would enable the colonists to buy their tea considerably cheaper. To the colonists however it bore another aspect. The whole plan seemed to them a scheme to surprise or bribe them into compliance with the very measure of taxation they were so strenuously opposing. This belief was supported by the fact, that all the consignees who were to receive the tea were warm partisans of England, and was fostered by the whole body of tea merchants and free traders, who saw themselves likely to be driven from the market by this direct tea trade. The opposition party took means to organize a resistance. The consignees were duly warned. The tea ships entered Boston harbour, but the captains were so fully convinced of the futility of their speculation, that they would willingly have again withdrawn. Some little customhouse formalities detained them; and meanwhile they were boarded by a body of men dressed as Mohawks, who tossed the

[margin note: The India Company's difficulties 1772]

obnoxious tea into the sea. Similar steps, though less violent, were
taken elsewhere, and none of the tea sent over under this disastrous
law found its way into the market.

Such violence, and such contempt of authority, exasperated the
minds of the English people. Lord North seems still to have
inclined to conciliatory measures, but the remnant of the Bedford
party, always particularly bitter against America, was too powerful
for him, especially as the King's opinion, before which North always
yielded with fatal weakness, was thrown into the scale on the side
of severity. Two measures were devised to punish the refractory
colony. By the first, known as the Boston Port Bill,
the customhouse, and consequently all the trade, was
moved from Boston, and the port was declared closed;
in fact the thriving town was rendered desolate. The warehouses
stood empty, the docks and quays were deserted. Salem was chosen
to take the place of Boston; but so strong was the feeling against
the Bill, that the very merchants of Salem, though the benefit
would have been all theirs, petitioned against it. The anger excited
by the Bill was not confined to Boston; a feeling of indignation
pervaded all the colonies. Their sympathy was soon increased by
fear for their own liberties; for a second Bill was
introduced, abrogating the old charter of Massachusetts.
Its popular constitution was to be destroyed, and the
colony was to become in the strictest sense a Crown colony; the
council was to be named by the Crown instead of by the people;
and the judges, magistrates and sheriffs were to be nominated and
removed by the governor without consulting the council. All the
other colonies naturally felt their charters insecure.

The Boston
Port Bill.
1774

Massachusetts
government
Bill

In fact, all seemed to show that the critical time had come. Attempts were indeed made subsequently at reconciliation,
but they were hollow, and the proposers of them knew
that they were hollow. Henceforward an appeal to arms became
almost certain, and the idea of claiming independence, as yet only
existing in the minds of a few of the leaders, began to become prevalent. Virginia at once threw in her lot with Massachusetts. A
fast was ordered on account of the Boston Port Act, and the governor
dissolved the assembly. The leaders met at the Raleigh Tavern, and
agreed upon a form of association against trade with England. Washington, hitherto hopeful of reconciliation, declared his readiness to
raise 1000 men at his own cost for the support of the people of Massachusetts. In spite of all Government opposition, most of the colonies

Crisis of the
quarrel

accepted the lead of Virginia, kept the fast, and agreed to the association, while, as a chief step in the direction of general revolt, a Congress was summoned at Philadelphia, and attended by representatives of the assemblies of twelve colonies, Georgia alone being absent. The English, too, understood that the two great Bills were little short of a declaration of war. Hutchinson was recalled, and General Gage was made Governor of Massachusetts, while Boston was filled with troops. Of course a quarrel between the new governor and the assembly was inevitable. The assembly was dissolved, and refusing to disperse, collected and sat at Concord, constituting thus in fact a rebel government, whose orders were implicitly obeyed. Gage had been obliged to fortify Boston Neck ; as a counter measure the Concord assembly established a permanent committee of public safety, organized 12,000 militia, and enrolled *minute men*, or picked men from the militia bound to serve at a minute's notice. While things were thus drifting into war in Massachusetts, the General Congress issued a Declaration of Rights, setting forth the rights of the colonists as Englishmen, and declaring that the late Acts were infractions of these rights, and must be repealed before America would submit, and passed a resolution forbidding importation from England, the use of imported goods, and after the interval of a year exportation to England also. These, and other acts and papers of the Congress, Acts of the General Congress acquired much weight by being to all appearance issued unanimously, an important advantage which was only gained after a trial of strength, in which the views of the advanced leaders were carried by a majority of one. When defeated on a scheme of reconciliation proposed by Mr. Galloway, and considered as a test question, the minority wisely accepted their position, and desisted from all protest, so that all the acts of Congress might have their full weight.

A general election in England in September of this year made it plain that the temper of the people was no less bitter General election. and determined in the mother country than in the Anti-American feeling of the colonies. A large ministerial majority was returned nation ready to support any acts of coercion. The Opposition began by demanding papers in an amendment on the address, but the real struggle did not begin till January, when Chatham Chatham's again expressed his opinion, moving the immediate motions for reconciliation. repeal of the obnoxious statutes of the preceding year 1775. and the withdrawal of troops from Boston. The majority against him was overwhelming ; none the less did he at once set to work, with Franklin's help, to prepare a scheme of reconciliation, though Franklin had probably neither much hope nor much wish that it should succeed. It was at first fairly received by Lord Dartmouth, the Colonial Secretary, but again Lord Sandwich and the Bedford party overawed their more temperate colleague, and it was rejected with scorn. The wisdom of some step in the same direction

North's measure for the same purpose.

seems however to have been plain to Lord North, who in a short time produced a scheme of his own. This did not go further than to say, that so long as the colonies taxed themselves with the approbation of King and Parliament no other taxes ought to be laid on them. It was much too late for any such trumpery measure.

It was indeed too late for any schemes of reconciliation, and the appeal to arms began. General Gage, who in spite of his representations had been left without reinforcements during the winter, could not see the

Skirmish at Lexington. April 1775

preparations made for arming and supplying the militia, carried on by the provincial Congress, without taking some measures to prevent them. In April he determined to destroy the stores at Concord. Some militiamen, who were being drilled at Lexington, only dispersed after firing upon the troops ; and when the soldiers, after destroying such of the stores as had been left at Concord, began their homeward march, they found themselves assaulted from behind every hedge and cover, and were compelled to seek refuge in a very distressed condition with a body of troops who had been sent to support them. The English loss was 270, while the rebels lost less than 100 men. This slight success raised the spirits of the colonists; militiamen crowded in from all quarters, and General Gage was blockaded in Boston. The rebels even ventured to attempt an expedition against the neighbouring province of Canada. A Bill passed

Canada Bill

the preceding year in England had given a constitution to Canada. This colony, nearly wholly French, neither understood nor valued English institutions, and was firmly Roman Catholic in its religion. The constitution was wisely conceived in a more arbitrary spirit than would have suited Englishmen, and with great liberality established the Roman Catholic worship. The Americans, unable to see the wisdom of this, and Puritan in their own religious beliefs, fancied that Canada must be smarting under its wrongs, and that they should find hearty sympathy there. In this belief, and to open the road thither, two New Englanders raised troops on their own responsibility—Arnold, a horse dealer, and Ethan Allen —and advanced against the forts which held the valley of Lakes

George and Champlain, which, with the valley of the Hudson, forms the natural road from New York to Mon- Fall of treal. They speedily seized Ticonderoga and Crown Ticonderoga May. Point.

· The first question which met the second General Congress was whether they should take upon themselves the responsi- The second Con bility of these actions or accept the conciliatory resolution gress assumes sovereign of Lord North. There was no hesitation on the part of authority the Congress. Lord North's proposition was thrown aside at once; orders were issued against supplying any British force or officer; a national name was assumed—*The United Colonies;* coercive measures were decreed against any province which should refuse to recognize the authority of Congress; and on the flimsy excuse of a contemplated invasion from Canada, the actions of Allen and Arnold were acknowledged, and an attack on Canada organized. These were acts of rebellion and war, and the Congress, conscious that the die was cast, proceeded to appoint a commander-in-chief. Their choice fell upon Colonel Washington, a Virginian gentleman, and a member of the Congress, who had seen some service in the late frontier wars, and was much respected by his province. He was a powerful, somewhat silent man, of very strong sense, and great powers of self-control, possessing that commanding influence which is given by strong passion and enthusiasm habitually Washington subdued, but just visible under a constant and calm chosen com- exterior. His unquestioned honesty, his hatred of dis- mander-in-chief order, and his great simplicity of character, fitted him well to give dignity to a cause which ran the risk, if it fell into inferior hands, of degenerating into a selfish and riotous uproar.

Washington at once hurried to the seat of war, but before he arrived another battle had been fought. A narrow Battle of channel separates Boston from another town of the name Bunker's Hill. of Charlestown, behind which rise two masses of high June 17, 1776 ground, known as Breed's and Bunker's Hill, from which Boston is commanded. Breed's Hill is the nearer of the two to Boston. It was natural to suppose that General Gage, whose forces had been raised to 10,000 men by reinforcements under Generals Clinton, Howe and Burgoyne, would assume the offensive, and at all events try to secure these hills. The Americans attempted to forestall him, and some rude defences were thrown up on the ridge of Breed's Hill. About 2000 English were sent to dislodge them. The Americans fought well, more than once the English drew back before their fire, but rallied by Clinton, they eventually took the position, driving the enemy, more than twice their number, in disorder along Charlestown Neck, where they were open to the fire of our ships. More than 800 of the English fell in the desperate struggle.

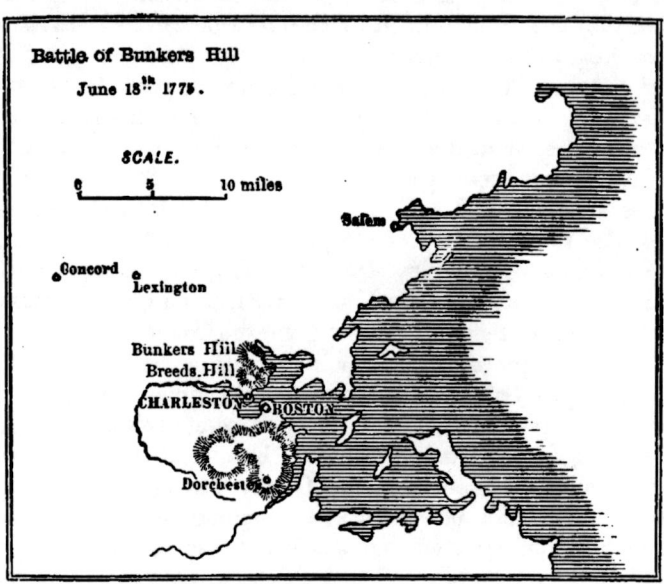

Battle of Bunkers Hill
June 18th 1775.

SCALE.
0   5   10 miles

Concord
Lexington

Salem

Bunkers Hill
Breeds Hill
CHARLESTON
BOSTON
Dorchester

Although the insurgent troops were justly proud of the gallant

Condition of the American army.

stand they had made against disciplined forces, the army when Washington joined it was not such as a general would wish to command. Even in the late battle well authenticated cases of cowardice had occurred among the officers. The militia regiments of the various states regarded each other with jealous eyes; there was no sort of uniformity of dress, no trace of soldierly bearing; the soldiers showed little subordination to officers scarcely better than themselves; and, worse than all, there was a fearful deficiency of powder. It taxed the ability and temper of their new general to the 'full to bring the motley crowd into order. He exacted the sternest discipline, drew a sharp line between the officers and men, procured hunting shirts to supply the lack of uniform, and by unremitting toil gradually produced a tolerable army. Why General Gage looked quietly on while this process was being carried out it is difficult to say. Even setting aside the lack of ammunition, of which however he was fully informed, he had troops enough to have destroyed the enemy which were blockading him without difficulty, and might thus perhaps have ended the war at a blow.

The slowness which characterizes the English generals at the beginning of the war is probably to be traced to the prevalent idea that reconciliation was still possible, and that the terrible extremity of civil war might be avoided. Even at this very time the Congress was sending to the King a last appeal ; but this document, known as the Olive Branch Petition, was not received in England. There was a technical objection to it which secured its rejection ; it purported to come from the Congress—an illegal and unrecognized body. The Americans could scarcely indeed have expected that it would have produced any effect. It held out no hope of concession, but expressed only vague wishes for reconciliation. It probably served the turn of those who sent it by allowing them to throw the blame of the future war entirely on the English. It might have been wise on the part of the ministry, even thus late, to have accepted overtures of peace, but it would have been a stretch of wisdom which no man had a right to expect; for the Congress had undoubtedly by its action assumed a position of complete independence and hostility which a Government could scarcely be expected to overlook. *The Olive Branch Petition.*

Even before the Olive Branch was sent the Congress had determined to take advantage of the successes of the preceding year, and had organized, under Generals Montgomery and Arnold, an attack upon Canada, which General Carleton was ill prepared to repel with less than 1000 British troops. While Montgomery crossed Lake Champlain and pushed on to Montreal, Arnold, with incredible labour, had made his way up the valley of the Kennebec, and so down the Chaudière, to Quebec. Unable to prevent the junction of the armies, Carleton hastened to throw himself into the capital, and upon the Heights of Abraham succeeded in checking their advance, with the loss of Montgomery their leader. Arnold could do no more than keep up a nominal blockade, so ably was the defence conducted, and the general who superseded him, meeting with no sympathy from the Canadians, was forced to withdraw in disorder beyond Lake Champlain. *Attack on Canada*

Meanwhile the dilatory conduct of Gage, who had now been succeeded by General Howe, had lost Boston to the English. Washington had at length found himself strong enough to take and

fortify the Dorchester Heights, which commanded the English lines on
Boston Neck. A general engagement, which could scarcely have

**Howe retires
to Halifax.
March 1776.**

ended otherwise than favourably to the English, would
have still rendered the town tenable, and Howe was
inclined to bring on a battle. But a continued course
of bad weather frustrated his plans, and thinking that for military
reasons New York, where the royal party was strong, would make a
better base of operations, he determined to withdraw; he accordingly
removed all his troops to Halifax, there to await promised reinforcements. So long were the fresh troops in coming that Howe
had to leave Halifax without them. There was considerable
difficulty in supplying him. The military arrangements of England
have been constantly found inefficient at the opening of a war; it
was only by purchasing troops at an exorbitant price from the Duke
of Brunswick and the Landgrave of Hesse that the immediate want
could be supplied. It was therefore only on a limited scale that
Howe was enabled to carry out that plan for the arrangement of the
troops which was afterwards continued during the war; and which
consisted of making New York the centre of operations, to be supported by two subsidiary forces, the one acting in the Southern
States, the other from Canada. In pursuance of this plan, he
despatched a force against Charleston, in Carolina, under General
Clinton, while he himself moved to Sandy Hook, thus threatening
New York, whither Washington had hastened from Boston. He
was there joined in July by his brother, Admiral Lord Howe,
and found himself, with his reinforcements and with the troops
which had been sent to Charleston and had returned upon the
failure of the expedition, at the head of nearly 30,000 men.

Lord Howe brought with him full powers for himself and his

**Fresh offers of
conciliation
rejected**

brother the general, empowering them, in accordance
with a late Act of Parliament, to receive the submission
of any colony, and after such submission to grant pardon
and redress. An Imperial nation, defied by its colonies and not yet
beaten, could hardly offer more, and to those not thoroughly conver-
sant with what was going on in America, it must have seemed that
there was every chance of such terms being accepted. Never as yet
had the chances of the insurgents seemed so small. It is true that
the revolt had become universal; but the spirit of the commercial
population of the Northern States was severely tried, and seemed to
be yielding under the depression of trade caused by the war. The
English army was for the time actually more numerous than that of

Washington, whose troops, nominally but 27,000 strong, were diminished by illness or absence. Those who remained were in a miserable condition, and consisted chiefly of men enlisted for short periods, who could scarcely be properly drilled before they returned to their homes. But the state of feeling was no longer what it had been. It was no longer a question of pardon or redress. The more earnest and violent men had, as is usual in civil commotions, been coming more and more to the front. The idea of a total separation from England had been rapidly gaining ground; republican and democratic principles had made their appearance; the writings of Thomas Paine had been published, and so largely were his views received, that a declaration, issued by the aristocratic State of Virginia, served afterwards as the model for the Declaration of the Rights of Man issued by the revolutionists of France; and already, before the arrival of Howe with his offer of pardon, the extreme party had determined to check all lukewarmness and put an end to all chance of reconciliation by taking an irretrievable step. In June, Lee of Virginia proposed in Congress that the colonies should declare themselves independent. The numbers on division proved to be exactly equal, but Dickinson, the writer of the "Pennsylvanian Farmer's Letters," and the leader of the moderate party, consented to withdraw, and the motion for independence was thus carried by a majority of one. The document itself is not a very powerful one, but shows how abstract political views had become mingled with the original questions in dispute. It is based on the Declaration of Virginia, recapitulates all the real or fancied grievances of the colonies, and, with curious political dishonesty, attributes them all to the personal tyranny of the King. The Declaration of Independence, issued on July 4th, reached Washington's army just before Lord Howe's arrival; it of course rendered his pacific mission fruitless. The colonies had assumed the position of an independent nation, and claimed to be treated with all the respect due to such a position. Howe's letters to Washington were even returned unopened, because they were not addressed to him by his full military style and title.

Declaration of Independence July 4, 1776

To the English nothing now remained but to take advantage of the superiority of their troops. An attack upon the lines of Brooklyn, at the end of Long Island, separated from New York only by a narrow channel, was ordered. The Americans, in about equal numbers, came out of their intrenchments, and for the first time during the war a battle was fought in the open

Battle of Brooklyn. Aug. 27

CON MON.   [s]

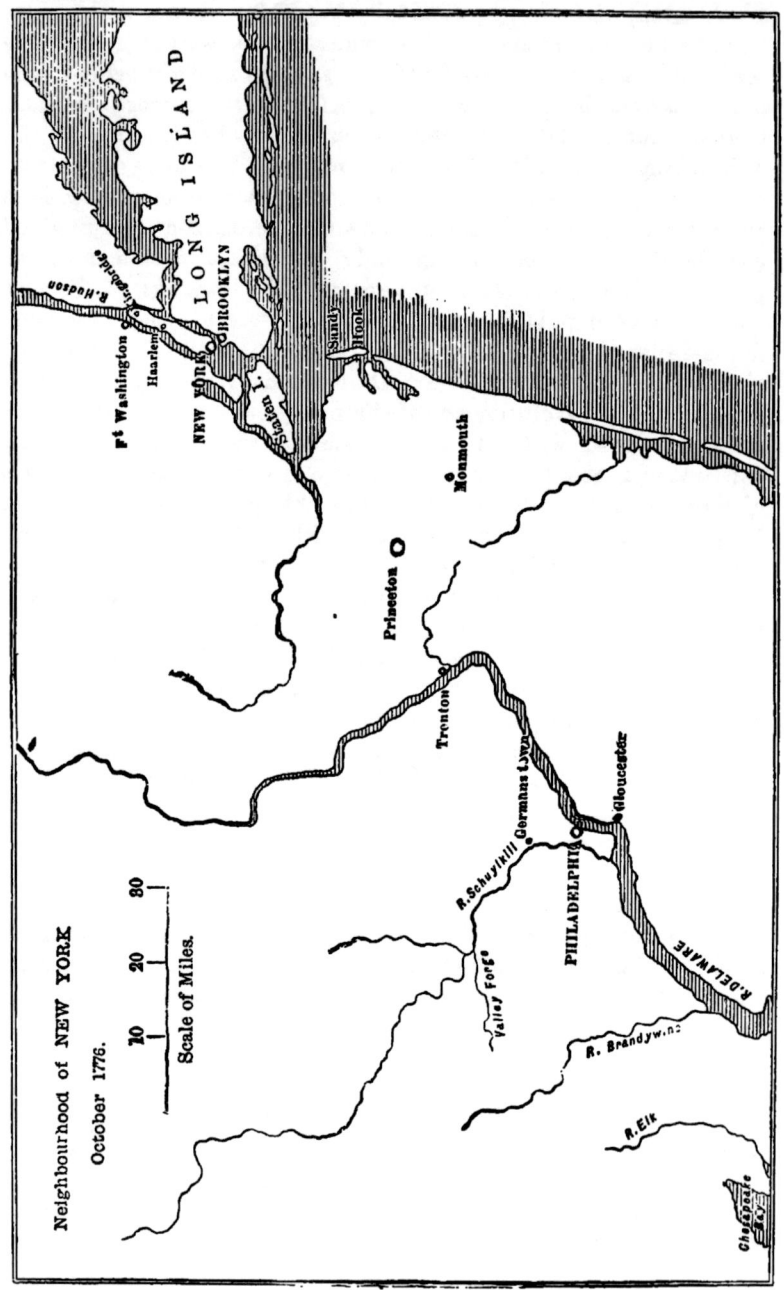

Neighbourhood of NEW YORK

October 1776.

Scale of Miles.

10   20   30

field.   The victory of the English troops was immediate and complete.
It was due only to Howe's want of vigour in pressing his success
that Washington was able to withdraw his army to New York,
whence, finding it impossible to hold his ground, he retired ultimately
to the mainland, taking up a position at Kingsbridge, and leaving the
city in the hands of the English.   It was plain that the temporary
militia of the colonists was useless against regular troops, and in
spite of its republican dread of a standing army, the Congress at
length listened to Washington's repeated representations, and authorized the enrolment of some regular troops.   But for more than
a year he was compelled to do his best with his old militia, and
nothing but the continued and incomprehensible slowness of the
English generals saved him from disaster.   Step by step he was
driven backwards, till he was compelled to cross the Delaware and
leave the whole of the Jerseys in the hands of the English.   The road
to Philadelphia seemed open, and the Congress, in fear, withdrew to
Baltimore.   But the English, when they found that all the boats on
the Delaware had been removed, quietly withdrew into winter
quarters upon a very extended line, and waited in hopes of being
able to cross the river on the ice.   The time thus wasted lost
them all the advantages they had won, and gave Washington an
opportunity to recover.   Eager to strike some blow which should
raise the spirits of the colonists and enable him to fill the ranks of
the army, he determined to take advantage of the weak and extended
line of the English.   On Christmas evening, trusting to the effects of
the day's debauch, he crossed the river, and surprised and captured
the garrison of Trenton.   Cornwallis, who had the command of the
advanced troops of the English, came to the rescue, but Washington
by another night march swept round the English army, Washington
and captured or destroyed two regiments at Princeton. recovers New
                                                        Jersey.
He was unable to secure, as he had intended, the supplies Jan. 3, 1777.
at Gloucester, but before long he succeeded in clearing New Jersey
of the English, and confining them, as before, to New York and Rhode
Island.

Howe remained idle till June, thus allowing much time to the
Americans, to whom time was everything.   But in June preparations
for a great joint movement were matured.   Not only Threefold plan
was the main army in New York again to resume of the English
the offensive, but advantage was to be taken of the possession of
Canada, and an attack organized from that country.   This branch of
the combined movement was placed under the command of General

Burgoyne. The cleft made by the valley of the Hudson is continued northward by the Lakes George and Champlain, and a natural
road thus formed from Canada to New York. Down this the
Canadian army was to march, assisted by the co-operation of Clinton,
who was to lead troops from New York to meet it. Thus the disaffected provinces of New England would be severed from the rest
of America.

Howe's army, which was now comparatively powerful, was expected
to make its way through the Jerseys, and to complete the project of
last autumn by capturing Philadelphia ; but, finding
Washington ready to oppose his advance, he suddenly
withdrew his troops and embarked them in the fleet.
He appeared for a moment off the mouth of the Delaware, but again,
finding more obstacles than he had expected, took to the sea, and
sailing all round the promontory between the Delaware and the Bay
of Chesapeake, ultimately arrived at the top of that piece of water at
the Head of Elk, nearly as far from Philadelphia as when he started.
The time spent in making this long circuit enabled Washington to
be fully prepared to cover Philadelphia. He took up his position
in Brandywine Creek. He was there quite outmanœuvred. While
one division of the English held the ground in front, another marched
round and fell upon the rear and left flank, and completely routed
his army. He still tried to hold the line of the Schuylkill, but it
was passed by the English with little difficulty, and Philadelphia
occupied. The capital was thus in the hands of the English, but the
expeditionary character of the attack prevented it from being so
effectual as a steady advance would have been, while it rendered the
conquest nugatory by separating it entirely from New York, the
real basis of operations. In some degree to correct this error, it
became necessary to secure direct access by sea by the capture of
the forts which held the mouth of the Delaware. For this purpose
the English army was divided, one portion remained at Germanstown to hold Philadelphia, and the rest were moved to
the siege of the forts. Washington took advantage of
the weakness of his immediate opponents and attacked
the troops at Germanstown. At first he was successful, but a panic,
such as not unfrequently seizes young and half-disciplined troops,
changed his half-won victory to defeat. The forts of the Delaware
were at length captured, and the operations of the English seemed
to have been thoroughly successful.

It was indeed a moment of intense depression in the American

[Margin notes:]
Howe's expedition against Philadelphia. Sept. 1777

Battle of Germanstown. Oct. 4.

army; nothing but the extraordinary patience and steadfastness
of Washington could have saved it.   Half-disciplined   Washington
troops, many of them inclined to desert, or to leave   reorganizes the
their standards as soon as their short time of enlistment   army.
was over, thousands without shoes, a commissariat ridiculously
incompetent and notoriously fraudulent, a civil power inclined to
meddle and complain of the military arrangements, such were some
of the difficulties with which he had to contend.   He managed in
spite of all to keep his army together, and to induce his troops to go
into winter quarters at Valley Forge, a wild but strong position
among the hills on the Schuylkill river a little above Philadelphia.
News from the North came to cheer him in his distressed condition.

Though successful in itself, the real object of Howe's expedition
had not been obtained, it had not enabled the army of New York to
go to the assistance of Burgoyne, and that general had   Burgoyne's
been compelled to surrender with all his army on the   disasters
17th of October.   In June he had advanced along the west side of
Lake Champlain, and had taken the fortress of Ticonderoga, Fort
Anne, and Fort Edward on the Hudson.   Hearing that the Americans had supplies but slightly guarded at Bennington, on the road to
the Connecticut river, he sent a small detachment to secure them.
This was the beginning of his misfortunes; the difficulties proved
greater than was expected, the expedition failed and had to retire in
haste, with the loss of all its artillery.   However, trusting to the
co-operation of the army from New York, and of a force which was
to make its way from the great lakes by Fort Stanwix down the upper
Hudson and join him before Albany, Burgoyne continued to advance.
He collected thirty days' supplies and crossed the Hudson, thus
cutting himself off from Canada, and relying for safety upon his
power of opening communication with New York.   The militia of
the neighbouring district at once rose behind him, thus completely
severing his communications.   His Indian auxiliaries had left him;
he could not rely much on his Canadian troops, and now found
himself in face of General Schuyler with 16,000 men.   The help on
which he had calculated did not come, Lieutenant Colonel St. Leger
failed before Fort Stanwix, and Clinton was unable to leave New York.
Burgoyne attempted an assault on the American position before
Behmus's Heights, north of Stillwater, but failed.   To advance seemed
impossible, he therefore ordered a retreat, though this was scarcely
less difficult.   He had told Clinton that he could hold out till the
12th of October, and when that day came he was still close to

Saratoga, and now neither retreat nor advance was possible. His boats upon the lake, which afforded him his sole means of procuring supplies or of transport, had been destroyed; he had no choice but to make some sort of surrender. On the 17th of October a convention was signed by which he surrendered his whole force to General Gates, who had assumed the chief command of the American troops. His army was allowed to march out of camp with the honours of war to the bank of the river, there to lay down their arms, and to be forwarded to England, under promise not to serve again during the war. Though the reception of the prisoners by both generals and men was most generous, and though Burgoyne lived as a guest in General Schuyler's house, the terms of the convention were not honestly fulfilled; Burgoyne, indeed, was allowed to return to England, but the main part of the army was detained in America for several years. The blame of this breach of treaty is held to attach to Congress only, and not to Washington.

The autumn session of 1776 had been opened with a speech full

Effect of American affairs on the Parliament. Oct 1776. of the successes of the English arms. The battle of Brooklyn, the fall of New York, the expulsion of the invaders from Canada, were all topics of congratulation. The feeling of the nation went with the Government, and the opposition in Parliament dwindled to a very small minority; but in spite of their weakness they continued to urge conciliatory measures, and at the beginning of the session, both in the Upper and Lower House, amendments in that sense were moved to the address. So plain was it, however, that such efforts were wholly useless, that Lord Rockingham's party ostentatiously retired from all public questions, attending the House only during private business. Fox indeed, who had left the ministry in 1774, and had become the foremost champion of the American cause, remained in his place, but the rest of the party did not reappear, till, finding their step worse than useless, they took the opportunity of a debate upon the Civil List to return to public life.

This debate arose on a demand for an increase to the Civil List of £100,000 a year, and £600,000 to pay off the debts already owing.

Increase of the Civil List. Under the existing circumstances the necessity for the measure was obvious, for the King's ordinary tradesmen were unpaid, and his servants' wages in arrears. The Civil List already amounted to £800,000 a year, and the known personal frugality of the King and Queen rendered the disappearance of so large a sum the more scandalous. In fact, nearly £600,000 had been spent since 1769 in secret service. It was easy to explain the insufficiency of the Civil List and the permanence of the ministerial majority in Parliament; not only had the Pension List been largely increased, but there were a swarm of sinecure officers about the Court, from grand falconers in the House of Peers to turnspits of the kitchen who sat in the House of Commons. The Civil List was increased, but the grant was accompanied by a strong expression, on the part of Sir Fletcher Norton, of the feeling of the House, that under the existing pressure of taxation such extravagant use of public money was much to be blamed,—words which were subsequently formally accepted by the House as their own.

The session closed with another effort on the part of the Opposition. On this occasion it was Lord Chatham who led the attack. He returned, after two years of illness, and still swathed in flannel, to move an address, urging the King to arrest the misfortunes in America. The measures he advised were unconditional redress of grievances, and repeal of all penal statutes; in other words, he would have granted all the demands of the Americans with the exception of their independence. But, while urging moderate counsels with regard to America, he blazed out at the idea of an alliance of the colonists with the French, and demanded instant war. His motion was of course lost. His fears of an alliance with France were not however unfounded; already, before the Declaration of Independence, Silas Deane had been sent over to Europe to try and make some arrangement. If the confession of the culprit is to be believed, Deane's handiwork was to be seen in the nefarious plans of a man called John the Painter, who in the December of the preceding year (1776) had attempted to fire the dockyards of Portsmouth. Again, immediately after the Declaration of Independence, Adams and Franklin had been sent over as accredited agents to make a commercial and defensive alliance with France. But though they had been well received both by the ministry and by the salons of Paris, where for the time Franklin was the fashion, their representations were mistrusted, and no real help was given. The French had no wish to engage in a failing cause, and continued to keep up an appearance of friendship with England, even, at the instigation of our ambassador, issuing, though probably intentionally too late, a *lettre de cachet* to stop the Marquis of Lafayette from sailing to join the colonists. He had no difficulty in avoiding it, and was present with Washington during the Philadelphian campaign. But the Court of France was in fact only watching

Chatham's motion. May 30, 1777.

American intrigues with France

the turn of events. The news of the defeat of Burgoyne had scarcely

reached Europe before the independence of America was acknowledged and a commercial treaty made. In case of France becoming involved in the war with England, this treaty was to be extended into one by which France engaged to supply military assistance on the sole condition that America should never acknowledge the supremacy of Great Britain.

Already, by the time of the meeting of Parliament for the autumn

session, rumours of Burgoyne's difficulties had reached England, though no news of his final disaster had arrived. The danger of war with France, to which Chatham had alluded in the spring, seemed to increase, and men's thoughts began to turn towards the great statesman who had before saved England in similar difficulties. Nor did Chatham refuse to respond to the general expectation; not for many years had he shown such activity as in this session. In moving an amendment on the address, he demanded the withdrawal of all troops from America, stigmatized with due severity the employment of savage Indians in the war, and strove to rouse the national spirit against France. But the energy and eloquence he exhibited throughout the session were unavailing. He consistently upheld the view that conquest of America was quite impossible, that it was worse than useless to carry on the war, and that all the demands of the colonists should be granted with the exception of independence. This, he said in the strongest words, it was impossible for England to grant. He relied, no doubt, on the natural hostility between the colonists and France, and it is possible that, had he been placed in office, his policy might have been successful. He was loved and trusted by the Americans ; concessions from his hands might have been received. He was feared by France; his plan of removing the troops from America would have left the resources of England free for a foreign war ; his threats and his name might have deterred the French from war. But certainly no other man could carry out such a policy, and so it was generally felt; North himself acknowledged the impossibility, and was anxious to resign ; Lord George Germaine (Sackville), who, disgraced at Minden as a military man, had become as member of the Government the chief supporter of repressive measures in America, was also preparing to give up his post. The ministry seemed on the point of giving way, and indeed the necessity for such a step was increasing rapidly. Early in December came the terrible news of Saratoga,

and three weeks later the preliminaries of the treaty between France
and the colonies were agreed upon, though the French ministry
had not scrupled to cover their intentions by false statements on the
matter.

The Opposition began to feel triumphant. Though still quite
outvoted in the House, they knew that the majority turned with the
ministry, whatever it might be; but they did not sufficiently reckon
on the King's obstinacy. He had been right in his boast at the
beginning of his reign; he was thoroughly English; he reflected and
sympathized with the most vulgar feelings and prejudices of the
people. The disasters in America had called out considerable
enthusiasm in England; money had been largely subscribed for
keeping up more troops, and the temper of the nation was evidently
for pressing the war with energy, regardless of con-   The King
sequences. In vain did Lord North express his desire   insists on Lord
to resign, and declare the necessity of conciliatory   office
measures. The King, strong in the popular feeling, reproached him
for intending to desert him, as he called it. On further pressure he
gave him leave to apply to Chatham and the Whigs, but only on the
absurd condition, that they should join the present ministry, serve
under Lord North, and carry out the same policy as the existing
Government. He would not hear of the ministry being put frankly
into Chatham's hands. As usual, Lord North yielded, and consented
to stay in office. He even consented to bring in bills absolutely
reversing all his own policy, and which could have come with good
grace only from the Opposition. His Conciliation Bill, now in the
hands of the ministry, was carried without difficulty, and all
American demands, short of independence, were granted;   Lord North's
all officers appointed by Congress acknowledged, and   Conciliation
commissioners, with the most ample powers to discuss   Bill
and arrange all points of quarrel, appointed. North still wished that,
as this was in fact the Opposition policy, the Opposition should have
the duty of putting it into effect; but the King and the course of
events were too strong for him. The Conciliation Bill had hardly
passed when an open rupture with France took place.   Rupture with
The treaty concluded on the 6th of February was notified   France.
in insulting terms to the English Court. Such a treaty was followed
by the inevitable withdrawal of ambassadors, and war with France
was in fact upon us.

To the Opposition it seemed as if the play had been played out.
They were inclined for immediate submission. If England could not

conquer America alone, what hope was there of conquering America joined with France with the whole house of Bourbon in its wake? They urged the immediate recognition of the independence of the colonies. Such, as has been before explained, were not the views of Chatham; his spirit rose with the idea of war with his old enemy, and he relied on his own ability, not indeed to conquer, but to conciliate America while he crushed France. His plan was never put to the test. On the 7th of April the Duke of Richmond moved in the House of Lords that all troops should at once be withdrawn from America, and a peace concluded, which of course implied the independence of the contracting parties. Chatham, very weak and ill, and against the advice of his friends, went down on purpose to oppose the motion. Scarcely able to walk, his feeble steps were supported by his son William and his son-in-law Lord Mahon. After hearing the Duke of Richmond's motion, he rose with difficulty, and resting on his crutch, and with his eyes looking unnaturally vivid in his shrunk face and under his great wig, he proceeded to make a vigorous reply. His voice was very low, and at times his memory failed, but here and there his eloquence rose to its old pitch, and he again thrilled his hearers as he recounted the dangers which England had outlived, and demanded whether the country which but seventeen years ago was the terror of the world " was to stoop so low as to tell its ancient inveterate enemy, Take all we have, only give us peace." . The Duke replied in a weak speech; and Chatham rose again, eager to answer him, but before he could speak he was seen to gasp, to lay his hand

Death of Lord Chatham. May 11, 1778

upon his heart, and to sink back, apparently dying. The death of this greatest of English statesmen put an end to all hope of a new policy. Unless the Americans received the conciliatory measures of Lord North well—which was most unlikely—the war must be fought out. Every honour was paid to the memory of Chatham. He was voted a public funeral in Westminster Abbey, and a monument, which is placed over the door at the west end of the Abbey, and represents him with his arm raised in the act of speaking. His debts were paid and a large pension settled on his family. Four Lords protested against these honours and the ministerial people kept chiefly aloof from his funeral. But the feeling of regret and admiration was universal. The Duke of Richmond's motion was of course negatived, and it remained to be seen what the Commissioners could do.

Before that question could be answered a subject was brought before the notice of Parliament and nation which was destined to

play an important part and to take the place of the American contest as a party test. This was the question of Catholic relief. The
laws still existing against the members of the Roman Catholic religion
were most severe in character. They had been enacted   Laws against
chiefly in the reign of William III., when England was   Roman Catholics
still in mortal terror of the restoration of the malign   repealed.
influence of the Stuarts and their religion, and they bore the marks of
their origin; many of them were indeed, as Dunning said in seconding
the motion for their repeal, a disgrace to humanity. Sir George Savile,
member for Yorkshire and a great Whig leader, moved the repeal of
some of them; he had no intention, he said, of touching the whole penal
code against Catholics, and was willing to substitute a test; but he
moved the repeal of some of the most obnoxious laws. These were
the law which punished the celebration of Catholic worship as
felony in a foreigner, as high treason in a native, and the laws by
which the estates of Popish heirs educated abroad passed to the next
Protestant heir, by which a Protestant heir could take possession
of his father's or other relative's estate during the lifetime of the
real proprietor, and by which Papists could acquire property only
by descent. The first law was so monstrous, and the others so evidently tended to foster the worst forms of family division and public
informing, that their repeal met with little opposition. Dundas,
Lord Advocate, promised a similar Bill for Scotland. This was the
beginning of opposition. The Scotch were indignant at any sign of
toleration, and organized a resistance which speedily spread into England. The Protestants found a mouthpiece in Lord George Gordon,
a young man of slender intellect, and nearly mad on religious topics;
although his principles were so unsettled that he died a Jew, he now
threw himself with frenzied vehemence into the Protestant movement. The King, with his usual power of sympathizing with the
narrower views of his people, took up the same side, and during the
remainder of the reign Catholic emancipation served as a test by
which to try whether his ministers would be subservient or not.

Meanwhile the Commissioners under the Conciliatory Bills had
reached America (May 1778). It was at once plain that   America rejects
they were too late. The French alliance had been made   conciliatory
known, and the Americans were as yet full of enthu-   offers.
siasm for their allies. For a time the influence of Washington had
been shaken. His toilsome but inglorious work of reconstituting the
army of Valley Forge had been unfavourably contrasted with the
brilliant success of Saratoga; Gates, a man in every way his inferior,

had been set up as his rival, and placed at the head of a war committee, which overruled Washington's advice and wishes. But the ridiculous failure of a plan which, in the interests of the French, the committee had suggested for attacking Canada had brought the Congress to reason, and their trust in Washington had been restored. The division of interests which had threatened the rising republic was thus healed, and the Commissioners found a unanimous feeling against entertaining their suggestions. Nor had the success of the English been such as to assist their views. After a winter idly spent in Philadelphia, Sir William Howe had been succeeded by Clinton, who had found it necessary to withdraw his army to New York, which with Rhode Island were the sole possessions left to England. The answer which the Commissioners received was therefore very decided. No such questions as were raised could be considered till the fleets and armies of England were withdrawn or the independence of the colonies acknowledged. The Commissioners could only retire, leaving behind them a manifesto threatening the utmost severities of war.

But, in spite of the confidence which the French alliance aroused in the minds of the Americans, the immediate effect of the treaty was not advantageous to them. A joint attack upon Rhode Island brought to light the dislike and jealousy between the new allies which Chatham had foreseen. The timely arrival of the English fleet compelled the French admiral, d'Estaing, to leave the coast. The Americans thought themselves deserted and gave up the siege. Their general, Sullivan, published an indignant general order, and addressed to

Effect of the alliance between America and France.

d'Estaing a sharp remonstrance. In deep dudgeon, he ceased for the rest of the year to assist the Americans, and acted wholly for French interests, trying to excite a national sympathy in Canada, and finally sailing away to the West Indies. For the time the French were almost as unpopular with the colonists as the English. In other respects the year's campaign was rather in favour of England. Georgia was occupied by an expedition sent from New York, and the Island of St. Lucia was captured from the French. But the object of the alliance was really obtained, for the war was no longer confined to America.

Resting on the support of the King, and backed in its American policy by the general feeling of the nation, North's ministry, in spite

Weakness of North's ministry.

of the poor success which had attended our arms in America, had hitherto had an appearance of strength. It was now, after a struggle of a few years, to succumb to a succession of difficulties which brought to light its inherent inefficiency. The extension of the sphere of the war brought the first danger. A powerful fleet had been sent into the Channel under Keppel, which at the mere rumour of the approach of a superior fleet of the French retired. When strongly reinforced, it brought the enemy to action off Ushant, but after some hours' fighting the two fleets withdrew, without the slightest advantage on either side; not one ship of either nation had struck. To shield himself from the natural indignation felt at so ridiculous a result, Keppel tried to throw the blame on Palliser, his second in command. As Keppel was in opposition, and Palliser a Lord of the Admiralty, the recriminations of the admirals were taken up by their respective parties, and a vehement parliamentary war arose. At length Keppel succeeded in obtaining a court martial, but the people as well as the Parliament had joined in the quarrel; there were violent demonstrations in his favour, and the case being in fact prejudged, the trial ended in his triumphant acquittal. A far less complete and unqualified sentence of approval awaited Palliser when he in turn was tried. Already it was evident that the hold of North's ministry was shaken; it had now to face a direct attack in Parliament. Burgoyne and Howe, both members of the House of Commons, were eager to throw all the blame of the recent miscarriages upon the shoulders of the Government; and an attack on the Admiralty was so successful, that Lord Sandwich was only rescued by a narrow majority from censure by the declaration of Lord North that he would resign were the censure carried. In his difficulties Lord North made some overtures to the Whigs, but all negotiations were rendered abortive by the restrictions placed on them by the King, who would indeed allow new ministers to be introduced, but would hear of no new measures. With the fatal facility which marred his character, North yielded to the King's stronger will, and remained in office against his own convictions, a mere official to carry out the policy of his master. His difficulties were further increased when Spain followed in the wake of France and also declared war; and the united fleets of the two countries assembled, apparently with the intention of invading England. In spite of a considerable exhibition of national spirit, it was all Sir Charles Hardy, who had command of the Channel fleet, could do to cover the coast of England and postpone a general engagement. Fortunately, though the allies were vastly superior in numbers, their ships were ill supplied and scarcely seaworthy, and they found it necessary to withdraw to their respective countries, leaving the Channel free.

But it was not only from abroad that dangers were gathering round England. The Irish, whom the people and Government of England have always regarded as a colony, and treated in the same spirit of jealous selfishness that had alienated the Americans, began to think of following the example of these colonists Their trade had always been avowedly governed and confined to suit, not Irish, but English interests. In addition to the usual restrictions, they had been suffering from an embargo on their provision trade with America, and their other industries were sinking in the general depression. When they saw Lord North proposing conciliatory measures, and promising relaxation of trade restrictions to America, they not unnaturally began to raise their claims to similar indulgences. Their requests were so reasonable that some small relief was given, but Lord North was afraid to carry out to the full a policy of free trade in face of the vigorous opposition of the great trading cities of England, where, with true commercial selfishness, any chance of a new competitor was regarded with vehement dislike. Burke was brave enough to speak heartily in favour of the Irish, in spite of instructions from his Bristol constituents; his bravery cost him his seat at the next election. With their fair claims thus trifled with, the Irish again learnt a lesson from America. What could not be got by asking might be yielded to an armed nation. On the pretext of an intended attack by the French on Belfast, soldiers were demanded. But Ireland had been denuded of troops for the American war; no troops could be sent. The inhabitants had now their excuse for arming themselves. Quite without disturbance, and with loyal protestations, volunteer corps sprang up all over the country; by the end of the year, in spite of the influence of Government, they numbered 50,000 men. In the presence of this army, with the Dublin companies in arms before the doors, the Irish Parliament of 1779 met. The national cause had found an energetic and eloquent leader in Henry Grattan. He moved an amendment to the address, demanding free trade as the national right of Ireland. The amendment passed unopposed, and was carried by the volunteers in triumph to the castle. Encouraged by this success, backed by the armed force around them, and by the populace of the city, the Parliament proceeded to the strong measure of granting supplies for six months only. Such events at once attracted attention in England, and votes of censure were moved by the Opposition on the Irish policy of the Government. But Lord North had also learnt wisdom from American affairs, and early

Difficulties in Ireland

in 1780 he passed Bills acknowledging the commercial equality of Ireland and a free export of their chief commodities.

But even Ireland was by no means the last of Lord North's troubles. The feeling against government by influence had been steadily on the increase. With characteristic selfishness, the mass of the people had sympathized with the war, which seemed to some rebellion against the natural supremacy of Englishmen, and which others saw clearly was a revolt against that commercial system which they regarded as the chief safeguard of their own interests. But want of success, increased taxation, and a diminution of trade, began to change the current of opinion, and men observed with jealousy the impossibility of carrying any measure against the influence of the Court. The King had completely triumphed, and by means of his friends, his pensioners, contractors, and sinecurists, could at all times command a large majority in Parliament. The Whigs, finding that influence which they had so long wielded thus transferred to other hands, began to see the enormity of such a system, and the great leaders of the party, whose territorial power was very great, put themselves at the head of a reform movement which soon became important. In the autumn of 1779 motions for economical reform were brought into the House of Lords. They were rejected; but in December the general feeling, and the determination of the Whigs to create an organization outside the House, were shown by a great meeting in York, attended by a large majority of the freeholders of the county. This influential meeting was followed by others of the same sort in many counties, and the organizers of the party went so far as to establish committees of correspondence on the model of the committees in America. Twenty-three counties and many large towns, in spite of the constant opposition of the Government, sent up petitions like the one agreed to in Yorkshire, demanding a reduction in exorbitant emoluments and the abolition of sinecures. Sir George Savile presented the Yorkshire petition on the 8th of February, and three days afterwards Burke introduced a great measure for economical reform of which he had already given notice. Lord North found it so impossible to oppose him, that the Bill passed almost unanimously into Committee. It there, however, encountered a most vigorous resistance, and was finally destroyed piecemeal. But the movement, once started, continued its course. Mr. Crewe introduced a Bill to deprive revenue officers of their votes, and Sir Philip Clerke another for the exclusion of contractors from the

(marginal note: Difficulties from the reform spirit in England.*)*

House. Outside the House the pressure became heavier and heavier, till at length, on the 6th of April, after a great meeting of the people of Westminster, where Fox had harangued, and which was thought sufficiently dangerous to demand the presence of troops, Dunning rose in the House, and after blaming the ministry for their under-hand obstruction to Burke's Bill, produced the startling resolution, that "it is the opinion of this Committee that the influence of the Crown has increased, is increasing, and ought to be diminished." This resolution, with a very slight alteration, he was enabled to carry against Government by a majority of eighteen. It was followed by two other resolutions in the same direction, one declaring the right of the House to reform the Civil List, the other that the abuses complained of should be immediately redressed. Both were carried. But when the House again met, and he proceeded to more detailed motions, Dunning found that the corrupt body he addressed, though willing enough to affirm abstract resolutions, had no real liking for reform. His majorities rapidly diminished, and finally no action was taken upon the resolutions which he had carried.

Scarcely had the ministry managed to escape from Dunning's resolutions when a new danger came upon them. This time they did not stand alone. All parties in the House had to join to repel a common enemy. It has been mentioned that a measure of Sir George Savile's for the alleviation of the penal laws against Roman Catholics had been carried, and that the motion of introducing a similar measure for Scotland had caused much displeasure in that country. The feeling spread, and Protestant associations formed themselves throughout England, and fixed upon the crackbrained Lord George Gordon for their chief and representative. The agitation had been kept up during the last year, and now Lord George wanted a great demonstration and petition to be got up. He declined to present the petition unless accompanied by 20,000 followers, who were to meet in St. George's Fields, adorned with blue cockades. Instead of 20,000, some 60,000 men were present, and proceeded to march across London Bridge to the Parliament House. There, in Palace Yard, they held their position unmolested, while they attacked and ill used any obnoxious Peers, or broke into the lobby of the Lower House, and, with their excitement kept alive by addresses which Lord George delivered from the staircase above, demanded that their petition should be at once attended to. Lord George was brought to some reason by a threat of personal violence if he continued his foolish behaviour, and the military at

The Lord George Gordon riots June 1780.

length arriving, the immediate precincts of the Parliament House were cleared. But though foiled in their wish to intimidate the House, the mob were by no means satisfied, and the unaccountable and timorous delay on the part of the executive, whether ministry or magistrates, allowed the riot to reach such a height that it could be with difficulty controlled. That night the chapels of the Sardinian and Bavarian embassies were burnt, and after a day of comparative quiet, the mob, finding itself unopposed, proceeded to renewed acts of violence. For four days London was in its hands. The prisons were broken open, Catholic chapels burnt and sacked, the shops of Catholic tradesmen pillaged, and the houses of those who were known to be favourable to the Catholic claims either destroyed, as those of Lord Mansfield and Sir George Savile, or kept in a state of siege. Johnson tells us how he saw the mob, quietly and undisturbed, destroying the sessions house in the Old Bailey. Horace Walpole found Lord Hertford's house barricaded and the lord himself and his sons loading their muskets in expectation of an assault. On the 7th the tumult rose to its height. This was the fifth day of the riots. The town was so intimidated that blue flags and strips of blue were shown on most houses, and few came out without the blue cockade. The rioters had long since passed from under the control of their religious leaders, and were guided by leaders of their own. On this day more than one attack was made on the Bank, headed by a fellow mounted on a brewer's horse, with a harness of the chains of Newgate jingling about him. More chapels were sacked, more prisons opened. No less than thirty-six fires were blazing at once. The most fearful scene was in Holborn, where Mr. Langdale's distillery was broken open and set on fire. There, amid the flames fed by constant supplies of spirit, the wretched rioters flew upon the liquor, drinking the gin from pails, or lying grovelling and lapping it from the kennel; many died of actual drunkenness, many more perished helplessly in the flames. It was time that something should be done, yet the ministry and magistrates alike shrank from doing anything. There was a notion abroad that the military might not act till an hour after the Riot Act had been read by a magistrate, and courageous magistrates could not be found; nor was it forgotten that on previous occasions soldiers had been harshly treated by juries for over zeal. The emergency was one which well suited the dogged and courageous character of the King. On the 7th he summoned a Privy Council, and put to it the question whether the soldiers might be employed without the machinery of the Riot Act. None of the members of the Council would take the responsibility of recommending such a course, and the Council had almost separated without doing anything, when George called upon Wedderburn, who was present as legal assessor, to state the view of the common law. He unhesitatingly said that a soldier did not cease to be a citizen, and might, and should, interfere to prevent acts of felony. This was all the King required. There were 10,000 troops in London, and he now felt he might act energetically. Orders were sent to Lord Amherst, the commander-in-chief, to that effect, and that evening and during the night such vigorous measures were taken that the mob was at once crushed and the crisis over. The numbers killed and wounded by the military were not less than 500, and probably very many more, as many were carried off privately. Undoubtedly the King's decision on this occasion saved London. Of the prisoners some twenty-nine were executed. The Lord Mayor was tried and convicted of criminal negligence. Lord George Gordon was arrested and foolishly tried for high treason. Wedderburn had meanwhile become Lord Chief Justice, and before him he was tried. The Judge's address was more like the pleading of an advocate than the charge of a judge, and people felt it so; the turn of feeling also had a little changed, and Lord George was acquitted. He died, a Jew, in 1793 of gaol distemper caught in Newgate, where he had been confined for libelling the Queen of France. When the House of Commons again assembled the gigantic Protestant petition was considered. It was met by five resolutions, the joint work of the political enemies Burke and North, which declared the continual approval of the Commons of the late Act of Toleration.

Trial of Lord George Gordon.

In the midst of these difficulties at home there had been some rays of comfort from the success of both fleet and army abroad. Early in the year Rodney had been placed in command of a fleet which was to act in the West Indies. On his way out he had instructions to relieve Gibraltar, which had been closely invested since the beginning of the war with Spain. While carrying out these orders he met the Spanish fleet off Cape St. Vincent and gained over it a complete victory. Four line of battle-ships were taken, four destroyed, only four made their escape. Gibraltar was then relieved, and Minorca also, so that Rodney could write home that the English were masters of the Mediterranean. He thence proceeded on his way to the West Indies, where De Guichen, with the French and Spanish fleets, could not be brought to an engagement, and where for the time nothing was done. Though Rodney's successes and

Gleams of success.

Rodney's victory.

those of Admiral Digby in the Bay of Biscay were somewhat neutralized by the capture of our West and East India merchant fleets, ably
planned and carried out by the Spaniards off the Azores, they raised
the spirits of the Government, coupled as they were with cheering
news from the army.   Just as the Gordon riots were suppressed, information arrived that Charleston, the capital of South Carolina, had
fallen into our hands.   On several occasions during the   Capture of
war the eyes of the commanders had been turned south-   Charleston.
ward.   The feeling of loyalty was less shaken there than in the more
northern provinces, and it seemed desirable that the efforts of England
should not be confined to one little spot along the whole of the
enormous seaboard of America.   Savannah in Georgia had already
been taken, and in pursuance of a general plan for acting on a more
extended basis, Clinton moved with the bulk of his army from New
York and besieged Charleston.   The siege was carried on with vigour
and skill, and General Lincoln found himself obliged to surrender.
Clinton set actively to work to reduce the Carolinas.   Virginia,
one of the centres of disaffection, would thus be between two fires,
and something more tangible might be effected than had yet been
done by the army at New York.   In fact, the interest of   The interest of
the war was now transferred to the South, for though   the war passes
Washington and the main American army still lay about   to the South.
New York, its effect there was only to neutralize the English army
opposed to it, while the active operations which led to the end of the
war were carried on at Carolina and Virginia.

Before describing the final struggle, it will be well to see the
difficulties under which the English laboured.   The war had become
a world-wide one.   Not only had the two maritime powers France
and Spain engaged in it, but it was plain that our old rivals the
Dutch were soon going to do so also.   Before the end   England alone
of the year an unusually strong instance of our deter-   against all
mination to insist on the right of searching neutral ships,   Europe.
when a convoy was searched and captured under the guns of the convoying ships of war, had raised the anger of the Dutch to   War with the
a high pitch.   The capture of a vessel containing Mr.   Dutch.
Laurens, late President of the American Congress, and proofs that he was
engaged in making an alliance with the States of Holland, rendered it
impossible to avoid a declaration of war, and Holland was added to our
armed opponents.   Nor was this all.   The same odious rigour of search
nearly brought all the nations of the North upon us.   The Empress
of Russia had suffered from it at the hands of the Spaniards.   She

therefore, acting probably at thé instigation of the King of Prussia,
constituted herself the champion of neutral rights, and
succeeded in uniting the nations of the North in an
armed neutrality in support of the doctrine that neutral
ships made neutral cargoes, and that nothing was contraband of war
except what had been definitely made so by treaty. In other words,
she claimed for neutrals the right of carrying the property of belligerents unmolested, a right which virtually told against the English
only, whose main hope lay in keeping dominion of the sea and
stopping the trade and supplies of its enemies. The Armed Neutrality
also upheld the now generally received principle that a blockade to
be respected must be efficient, that is, that there must be sufficient
force before a blockaded port to prevent the entrance of trading
vessels. The whole maritime power of Europe was thus arrayed
against England, and yet it was only by keeping the upper hand
at sea that she could hope to carry out successfully her attempts
on land. It was impossible to pour large armies into America and
to subdue a continent without some easily accessible base of operations. This base the sea afforded. It will be seen in the sequel
that the loss of naval supremacy was the immediate cause of the
disaster of Yorktown.

Armed neutrality of the North.

But as yet the arms of England continued to be successful. Clinton,
leaving Cornwallis to command in the South, had hastened back
from Carolina to New York, that he might be ready to oppose the
French fleet, whose arrival had been threatened. In June the expected armament arrived, consisting of seven line of battle-ships
and 6000 men under the Count de Rochambeau. The rapidity with
which Rhode Island was at once occupied and placed in a state of
defence thwarted the efforts of the English to regain it, but the
British fleet was so much stronger than that of the enemy that a
blockade was maintained around the seaboard of the province, which
paralyzed all action on the part of the French for the rest of the year.
This forced inactivity of Rochambeau gave rise to one of the best
known episodes of the war. Washington left his headquarters to
meet the French general and concert measures for action
if possible. His absence was used for the purpose of
carrying out a piece of treachery which had long been hatching.
General Arnold was in command at West Point on the Hudson, a
position of great importance, as it prevented the occupation of the
valley which affords direct communication between New York and
Canada. Married to a royalist wife, with a feeling that his un-

Arnold's treachery.

doubted genius was not sufficiently valued, and smarting under a public reprimand for some dishonest practices into which he had been led by his poverty and love of ostentation, Arnold had for some time been in secret correspondence with Clinton, making arrangements for changing sides, and handing over to the English the important post of which he had charge. The correspondence had been carried on through Major André, a young and very promising officer, now Adjutant-General of Clinton's army. Washington's departure seemed to offer an opportunity for carrying out the plan. To complete the negotiation a personal interview was required, and Major André, with instructions from Clinton not to enter the lines of the enemy and to wear uniform, repaired to the neighbourhood of West Point. When day dawned the interview was not over, and André was induced to continue it in a house within the American lines. On leaving he was also imprudent enough to dress as a civilian. He had already passed the lines on his homeward journey, when he was accidentally met and stopped by some militiamen; he avowed himself an English officer, but presented a pass from Arnold; the pass was disregarded, he was searched, and papers found in his boot. Under these circumstances there were about him all the outward marks of a spy, and as such he was treated. Much to the anger of the English, Washington, refusing to hear any representations in his favour, brought him to trial before a court of American officers, by whom he was condemned. *Trial and death of Major André.* He even rejected the last prayer of the enthusiastic soldier, that he might be saved from a felon's death, and had him hanged, with all the usual attendant circumstances of disgrace—a piece of stern but perhaps necessary justice, and, in spite of the outcry raised at the time, apparently in strict accordance with the laws of war. Timely information of André's capture enabled Arnold to escape from his house, where Washington was momentarily expected, and to obtain shelter on board the English man-of-war which had conveyed André to the ill-fated meeting. Washington was surprised on reaching Arnold's house to find no host, but it was not till he had paid a visit to West Point, and found the commander absent there also, that he discovered the real state of the case.

While things were thus at a standstill round New York, the war had been actively prosecuted in Carolina. Alarmed by the fall of Charleston, the Americans had sent General *Campaign in Carolina.* Gates to take the command there; they regarded him as their ablest general, and he figured in some degree as a rival to Washington.

He found the English in possession of a line of country extending from Pedee river to Fort 96. The main body of the English, under the command of Lord Rawdon, lay in the neighbourhood of Camden, towards the centre of this line. Against this position Gates advanced; his march was a very difficult one; he had to make his way through a rough uncultivated country, where provisions were not to be obtained; for several days his troops had to subsist on the peaches which are there almost indigenous. He was able, in spite of these difficulties, to bring into the field a force numerically double that of the English, who were no more than 2000 strong. His troops, however, were unable to withstand the attack of a well-disciplined force. On the left and centre they at once threw down their arms and took to flight. The troops from Maryland and Delaware upon the right showed, it is true, more firmness, but the victory of the English was complete, and Lord Cornwallis, who had hurried up to assume the command, improved it to the utmost. Colonel Tarleton, an officer of indefatigable energy, pushed rapidly forward, and succeeded in surprising Colonel Sumter, a partisan officer, on the Catawba, and the whole army moved steadily forward to Charlotte, with the intention of invading North Carolina. A slight check sustained by a body of loyal militia, however, alarmed Cornwallis, and, together with the smallness of the number of troops at his command, induced him to postpone his forward movement till the following year. In the interval he and Lord Rawdon, his second in command, were guilty of acts of most impolitic severity. Such prisoners as could be proved to be deserters from the royal army, or to have once accepted the royal Government and to have subsequently joined Gates, were hanged. Some of the disaffected residents of Charleston were deported to Saint Augustin, while the property of others was sequestrated. Rawdon in fact went even further, and ventured to set a price on the head of every rebel. Such acts went far to alienate the people, and by weakening the security of the communications increased the difficulties of the following year, and tended to neutralize the effects of a very promising campaign.

The same success which had attended the English arms in Carolina followed the efforts of the fleet in the early part of the next year; Rodney captured from the Dutch, who had joined the coalition against England, the enormously wealthy island of St.

St. Eustatia captured. 1781.

Eustatia. Much of the property collected there belonged however to English owners, and a vast clamour arose when the admiral declared it all prize of war. He asserted, and It subsequently became plain, that the island was used as an entrepôt for the collection of goods which were afterwards to be supplied to the enemy. Other charges brought against him, accusing him of hasty and over rigorous action, afterwards proved to be equally ill founded, for fortunately both military and naval commanders were members of Parliament, and had full opportunity of vindicating themselves before the House, and of stripping the charges against them of the exaggerations which surrounded them. Thus General Vaughan was charged with forcible removal of all Jews from the island, but was able to produce a written document from the Jews themselves thanking him for his considerate treatment of them.

These successes soon proved to be delusive. The coalition against England was becoming too powerful to be withstood. *Delusive character of these early successes.* Already a great drawn battle with the Dutch had been fought off the Doggerbank, and Sir Hyde Parker had been compelled to withdraw his shattered fleet into English quarters; and it soon became evident that we had for the present lost our supremacy of the sea, or at least were unable to keep a commanding superiority in all parts of the world at once, for to such dimensions had the war grown. Thus the French made an attack upon Jersey, which was only saved, when it had already fallen into their hands, by the intrepidity of Major Pierson, a young soldier of twenty-five, who himself lost his life by almost the last shot fired; another and more successful expedition under the Duke of Crillon assaulted Minorca; while a great armament setting out from France parted midway across the Atlantic, thus becoming two fleets, one of which, under Bailli de Suffren, was able to give us full employment in the Indian waters, while the other, under De Grasse, raised the naval power in the West Indies above our own. Rodney found himself unable to save the Island of Tobago, and, broken by the climate, was compelled to return to England. Nor was his successor Sir Samuel Hood more fortunate; a detached squadron was found sufficient to counterbalance the English fleet in the West Indies while De Grasse sailed with the bulk of his fleet to the American coast, where his arrival at once turned the balance against us, and deprived us of that command of the sea which was absolutely necessary for our success. The fatal effects of this loss were soon to be apparent.

The first warlike event of the year was an expedition under General Arnold (who had obtained a command from his new masters) directed against Virginia, in the hope that such a diversion

might assist Cornwallis in what was intended to be the main effort
of the year. It produced however no great effects beyond the
destruction of a considerable amount of property, and when Cornwallis set himself in motion, he found himself faced by a more
formidable opponent than General Gates. At the instigation of
Washington, Nathaniel Greene, a self-made general, who had risen
from a blacksmith's forge, had been given command in the South.
He proved himself a man of great vigour and tenacity, and though
invariably beaten when opposed to any large body of English troops,
he contrived to recover so quickly, that the barren name of victory
was usually all that was left to the English. The campaign opened
by the defeat of Colonel Tarleton, who had rashly attacked the
Americans under Morgan at Cow-pens ; nor could Cornwallis succeed
in getting between the victorious general and Greene's army ; their
united forces were compelled however to fall back before Cornwallis'
advance till they had evacuated the whole of North Carolina.
Political necessities checked the English advance, and Cornwallis
attempted, without much success, to consolidate the royal influence in

Battle of Guildford Courthouse. March 15. the province; but, by the middle of March, Greene found
himself again in a position to re-enter Carolina and
to give battle to Cornwallis in the neighbourhood of
Guildford. He occupied a position at Guildford Courthouse; as
usual the English were victorious, as usual they reaped nothing from
their victory, for Cornwallis, finding his troops much diminished in
numbers and not meeting with the assistance he expected from the
inhabitants, was compelled to fall back upon Wilmington. Greene
did not long pursue him, for by thus withdrawing to the coast he
had laid open the road into South Carolina, where Rawdon had been
left with a small detachment. Greene saw his opportunity, and
pushing boldly southward, again approached the English post at
Camden. Afraid to attack Rawdon without reinforcements, he
occupied a strong position upon Hobkirk's Hill, about two miles from
Camden. There Rawdon thought it prudent to attack him, and
he was driven from his position. The ludicrous insufficiency of the

Hobkirk's Hill. April 25, 1781. English troops (there were but 900 engaged in the
battle) again prevented them from using their victory,
and Greene was enabled, without risking another engagement, to
compel Rawdon to withdraw his troops to the immediate defence of
Charleston.

Meanwhile two courses had been open to Cornwallis at Wilmington ; he might either hurry in pursuit of Greene and assist the

hard pressed army of Rawdon, or push northward and effect a junction with the Virginian expedition, which has already been mentioned, under Arnold and Phillips. To pursue the first course was to give up all his previous successes, to relinquish all hope of striking a decisive blow ; for independent action his own army, numbering only 1500, was too small : he decided therefore to march northward, and in May formed a junction with the expedition, by which the number of his troops was raised to 7000. He left Wilmington on the day on which the battle of Hobkirk's Hill was fought. Till the heat of summer compelled a cessation of active fighting, Cornwallis was always superior to his enemy ; but as the autumn advanced, the Americans, who had been constantly reinforced, were again a match for him. The three English armies were then acting— Position of the the main body, 10,000 strong, under Clinton at New English armies. York—Cornwallis' army, about 7000 strong, on the coast of Virginia— Rawdon's handful of men, now under the command of Colonel Stewart, a little in advance of Charleston. Before the close of the year the whole of South Carolina and Georgia were lost, with the exception of Charleston and Savannah; for Greene, coming down from his summer position on the Santee Hills, had succeeded, after a very severe struggle at the Eutaw Springs, in obliging Battle of Eutaw. Colonel Stewart to retire to Charleston Neck, leaving Sept. 8. the whole open country to be overrun by the Americans.

The position of Cornwallis was also becoming critical. Cut off from support on the south, his only hope was to fight his way northwards to join Clinton, or to receive large reinforcements from this general by sea ; but it was not likely that Washington would allow his army to be neutralized by the English troops in New York. . It was almost certain that he would turn his attention southward, join General Wayne in Virginia, and render a northward movement Cornwallis in of the English impossible. The only real hope was from Virginia. the sea, but the sea was no longer a secure basis of operations. The English fleet, now under the command of Admiral Graves, who had succeeded Arbuthnot, tried its strength against De Grasse in September. The action was indecisive, but it became evident that, when all the fleets were joined, the French could muster thirty-six sail of the line in the Bay of Chesapeake, while the English force was no more than twenty-five. But as yet the English did not acknowledge the naval superiority of their enemies, and Cornwallis, acting as he believed, though apparently erroneously, on instructions from Clinton, took possession of Yorktown, a village on the high southern bank of York

river, and there awaited assistance. The defensive position thus
taken up by the English army and the want of energy shown is
explained by the news which had reached Clinton, that the French
were thinking of withdrawing if the war should last beyond the
current year. He believed that, could he contrive to weather the
difficulties which surrounded him, the opposition of the Americans,
unable to stand alone, would on the loss of their allies disappear
without further effort on his part. His hope was not unfounded; it
was in truth a critical moment for the Americans. At a meeting
between the American generals and De Grasse, the Admiral had
declared that he had orders not to remain longer than November;
the nation was on the verge of bankruptcy; the New England States,
with the selfishness which had marked them throughout, were ready
to give in. It was thus absolutely necessary for Washington to act quickly and to win some striking success.
What Clinton therefore ought to have foreseen happened;
Washington turned his attention towards Virginia, and undeterred
by an assault on the New England States which Clinton attempted
as a diversion, the mass of the American army began steadily to gather
round Cornwallis. The position which he occupied was not a happy
one, it was in fact untenable without command of the sea, which,
as has been mentioned, had already been lost. He occupied the
southern bank of the York river, there about a mile wide, and on
the northern side the little village of Gloucester. The fortifications
were of no great value, and the advanced posts were at once withdrawn upon the receipt of a despatch from Clinton, stating that there
was every hope that the fleet, with 5000 men, would attempt to relieve
the army, and would leave New York for that purpose in about ten
days' time. This was a fatal error, as it gave the enemy positions
commanding the works. The besiegers numbered 18,000, their large
and powerful artillery being in part supplied by the French ships. The
first parallel was completed on the 9th of October; the fire from it
was overwhelming: on the 11th the second parallel was opened, nor
could the bravery of the besieged prevent the capture of two advanced
redoubts on the 14th, which were at once included in it. It now
became evident to the besieged that the expected reinforcements had
failed them, and after a brilliant sally, during which many of the
enemy's guns were spiked, Cornwallis, finding all his guns silenced
and his ammunition drawing to a close, felt that he had to choose
between surrender and an effort to withdraw his troops from their
untenable position. He determined to attempt the latter plan; his

American armies close round Yorktown.

scheme was a desperate one; his troops were to be transported in open boats to Gloucester, they were there to break through the enemy's lines, which were not strong in that direction, to seize the horses of the besiegers and of the neighbouring country people, and make their way to New York. The boats with their loads had already crossed once when a storm arose which rendered the further prosecution of the plan impossible, and when morning dawned Cornwallis had no alternative but to make terms. He agreed to surrender all his troops as prisoners of war, and on the 19th of October, 4000 British soldiers who remained fit for work marched out with the honours of war between the long lines of the French and American army and laid down their arms. It is worth mentioning, as a strange little piece of professional arrogance, that when marching between the lines of French Cornwallis on the one side and Americans on the other, the English compelled to officers saluted punctiliously all the French officers as surrender. Oct. 18, 1781. belonging to a regular army, but refused any acknowledgment to the Americans. This was virtually the close of the war. The infant Hercules had strangled its second serpent, as was afterwards portrayed on Franklin's medal.

The close of the war under such circumstances of failure could not but bring with it the fall of the ministry. The news New session of arrived at a striking time, but two days before the Parliament. Nov. 27. opening of the session. With such a weapon in their hand, and with the stored-up rancour of ten years of opposition, the leaders of the Whigs pressed motion after motion against the Government. Fox and Burke vied with each other in their Tottering bitter assaults, and the young Pitt, who had come into condition of the Parliament as member for Appleby, on the nomination Government. of Sir James Lowther, rapidly assumed a high position on the same side. The Budget was in itself a proof that Lord North was yielding; the estimates were so small, that he had to explain that he intended to give up all notion of a war on a "continental plan by sending armies to march through the provinces from South to North;" he would henceforth content himself with holding some important harbours on the American coast. Outside Parliament, in the metropolitan counties, vigorous opposition meetings were held, and the public anger was raised to its climax by a succession of misfortunes which befell our arms. Admiral Kempenfeldt found himself completely outnumbered in the West Indies, and the whole of the Windward Islands, except Barbadoes and Antigua, were lost. Minorca, which was regarded as of even more importance than Gibraltar, and the key to the Mediterranean, surrendered after a gallant defence. The Bailli de Suffren thwarted an expedition against the Cape of Good Hope. At the same time at home the Irish difficulties, which will be treated of more at length afterwards, were becoming most threatening. Under these circumstances, a motion by General Conway, that the war on the continent of America should be discontinued was lost by one vote only, and a repetition of the same motion a week later was carried by a majority of 234 against 215. Lord George Germaine, who was pledged to the continuance of the war, withdrew from the Government, and finally a direct vote of no confidence on the 15th of March was only lost by a scanty majority of nine. North saw that further struggle was hopeless, and on the 20th compelled the King to allow him to declare the administration at an end. He went out of office with his usual tact and good humour. A great attack had been arranged for that evening, which was to be led by Lord Surrey; he and North rose at the same moment, and the cries from the rival parties could not be quelled till Fox rose and proposed a formal motion that Lord Surrey be first heard. With admirable presence of mind, North rose and said that he would speak to that motion, and prove its inutility by declaring his government at an end. There is a well-known anecdote of his persistent good humour; expecting a long debate, the Opposition members had sent away their carriages, and as they stood awaiting them shivering in the drizzling rain, Lord North passed through them to get into his. "Gentlemen," he said, "you see the advantage of being in the secret," and drove off.

North's resignation was the complete defeat for the time of the King's plans; but George III. was a man of the most obstinate and determined character, and he by no means intended as yet to give up the fight. The Opposition which had formed the alliance to drive North from office consisted of two sections. First, the old or Revolution Whigs, as they liked to call themselves, who, true to their aristocratic principle, had chosen for their leader the wealthiest but by no means the ablest man among them, Lord Rockingham, an agriculturist, a sporting man, of respectable talents and much honesty, though without any of the gifts of oratory which are necessary for the management of a public body; and secondly, those Whigs who had owned the leadership of Chatham, and who now followed the Earl of Shelburne; a party less tied by aristocratic connections, and representing, as far as could then be represented, the real liberal interests of the country.

Defeat of the ministry on Conway's motion.

Lord North's resignation.

Shelburne refuses the Premiership.

To avoid the necessity of putting himself into the hands of his particular enemies, the Whig families, it was to this section that the King at once applied. But, as Chatham had always found, it was of itself far too weak a party in Parliament to form a satisfactory ministry. Moreover, the eagerness with which Burke and Dunning had of late years demanded financial reform, and the share they had taken in driving North from office, made it impossible for their claims to be ignored. Shelburne therefore refused the King's request. The King's discomfiture seemed quite complete when Rockingham accepted office. The ministry consisted of equal num- New Whig bers of the two sections of the Liberals. Rockingham, Government Keppel, Lord John Cavendish, the Duke of Richmond, and Mr. Fox, of the one party ; Lord Shelburne, Camden, General Conway, Lord Ashburton (Dunning), and the Duke of Grafton of the other. Strangely enough, the balance between them was held by the Tory Lord Thurlow, the King's personal friend, who remained in the position of Lord Chancellor. Pitt haughtily refused to accept any subordinate office.

Three great questions at once presented themselves to the new administration,—to pacify the clamours of Ireland, to The three complete the economical reforms to which they were questions which pledged, and by means of which they hoped to regain met it. some of the power of which the successful policy of the King had robbed them, and to bring to conclusion as honourably as possible the American War.

In Ireland the agitation had been constantly on the increase since the conciliatory measures of Lord North in 1780. The agitation Free trade had been granted, but this step towards in Ireland. independence had opened the way to still further demands ; if they had followed the Americans thus far, why not follow them a step further and demand legislative independence also ? The legislative superiority of England rested mainly upon two Statutes, Poynings' Law, or the Statute of Drogheda of the reign of Henry VII., by which all Bills brought forward in the Irish Parliament, except such as regarded money, were subject to revision or suppression by the English Privy Council, and the Statute 6 George I., which asserted the right of the English Parliament to legislate for Ireland. No sooner had Grattan succeeded in his first agitation, than he proceeded, in spite even of the wishes of his friends Lord Charlemont and Burke, to set to work the same machinery for the purpose of obtaining the reversal of these statutes. As early as April 1780 he had produced, though unsuccessfully, a motion in the Irish Parliament declaratory of Irish independence. Since that time his position had become stronger, disputes in Parliament had excited the national feeling, the volunteers had completed their organization, and appointed Lord Charlemont their commander-in-chief. A great meeting of deputies from the volunteers had been held at Dungannon, which had· accepted to the full Grattan's propositions. With this great armed power behind him, and reinforced by the influence of the Roman Catholics, whose interests he had lately espoused, Grattan was enabled on the 16th of April to bring forward a final and successful address declaring the perfect legislative independence of Ireland. It was carried unanimously through both Houses. In face of this pressure, though not blind to the almost inevitable evils of a dual Government, Fox and Shelburne yielded the point, and the two obnoxious Statutes were unconditionally repealed.

The ministry had entered upon office supported by a vast agitation
Economical throughout the country, by county meetings, societies and
reforms. corresponding associations, and these allies outside the walls of Parliament were eager for very sweeping measures of reform in all directions, especially financial reform, limitation of the influence of the Crown, the purity of the House, and reform of the representation. All these measures had a political as well as an economical side. They all formed portions of the avowed politics of the Whigs for breaking the power of the Crown. Both revenue officers and contractors assisted to uphold Government influence ; the votes of the revenue officers were said to command no less than seventy boroughs, and contracts, given not because advantageous to the public, but for political purposes, were but so many indirect bribes. But the voice of the statesman is apt to be singularly tempered by his accession to office, and the Government Bills which Burke introduced in June proved but a weak reflection of his former measure. Certain obvious abuses were removed, secret service money was diminished, and a smaller share of it allowed to the Treasury ; the Pension List was cut down to £90,000, and £300 fixed as the outside limit for a single pension ; the Lords of Trade and some other unnecessary officials were abolished ; but the expenses of the Principality of Wales and the Duchies of Lancaster and Cornwall, together with many useless offices of the Household and public offices, were untouched, and the whole saving effected was only about £72,000 a year. Burke in thus limiting his propositions was doubtless acting under pressure from his colleagues. His own sincerity was proved by the limitation

which he set to the inordinate emolument which as Paymaster he derived from his own office.   But the honesty of the ministry as a whole was somewhat compromised when they forestalled the action of their own Bill, and hurriedly granted large pensions, varying from £2600 to £3200, to Lord Grantham, to the Chancellor, and to Colonel Barré. Still further proof that a limitation of the royal power and not real reform was the object in view, was given by the reception accorded to a measure for parliamentary reform introduced by William Pitt. Chatham had always seen and asserted that some measure of parliamentary reform was necessary if influence was to give way to any true national representation.   But though constantly inveighing against Government influence when in the hands of their opponents, the Whig oligarchs, to whom parliamentary influence was as necessary as it was to the King himself, had no idea of lessening their own power, and Pitt's measure for increasing the representation of the counties, then the chief homes of independence, though ably supported, was defeated by a majority of twenty, swelled by the open opposition of some of the ministry and the lukewarmness of others.   Fox and the Duke of Richmond however supported him.   Divisions in the Cabinet upon so important a question, scandals such as the Barré pension and the unsatisfactory carrying out of promises of economical reform, tended to lessen the popularity of the ministry.   But it was the management of the great question of all, the completion, namely, of an honourable peace, which displayed chiefly the weakness of the administration.

As far as America itself was concerned the fall of Yorktown had virtually put an end to hostilities, and the declared policy of England reached no further than the retention of certain posts and harbours.   It may be a question whether this was wise, for it is certain that the condition of the Americans was very deplorable.   Bankrupt and impoverished, the Congress was in no condition to support the army in a state of efficiency, and from its factions and intrigues had so lost public confidence, that Washington was earnestly intreated to make himself dictator, and take the management of the country into his own hands.   But it was impossible for the Whigs, after the language they had used in Parliament, where they had not scrupled to rejoice at American successes, and to speak of the American armies as *our* armies, to think of anything but peace at once and on any terms.   But though the war with America thus died out, that with the allied powers of Europe was by no means ended.   Spain and France had joined the Americans with the cry of independence, absurd enough from such monarchies, but with the real object of destroying the power of England, and reversing the humiliating terms forced upon them by the Treaty of 1763. The Dutch had joined the coalition for commercial objects of its own; they were desirous of destroying the English Navigation Act and of restoring the freedom of the sea. The moment seemed to have arrived when all these wishes could be gratified, and negotiations for a general peace were therefore of a twofold character and by no means easy to complete, as America was pledged not to conclude a treaty without her allies. A further complication arose from the peculiar arrangements of the English ministry, by which American affairs fell to the lot of Shelburne as Home Secretary, while Fox, his rival in the ministry, in his capacity of Foreign Minister had the duty of negotiating with the European powers. As Dr. Franklin, the most important American diplomatist, was at this time in Paris, that city became the centre of negotiations, and thither both ministers sent agents. Mr. Oswald, on the part of Lord Shelburne, began to open the business with Franklin, while Mr. Thomas Grenville was accredited as plenipotentiary from Fox to arrange matters with M. Vergennes, the French minister. With singular ingratitude, the Americans, though bound not to *conclude* a treaty without their allies, thought it right to complete all the arrangements except the actual conclusion secretly and separately with the English, although they had not thought it beneath them to let their allies undertake all the more arduous parts of the war. Although there was some difference of opinion as to the exact manner of granting the independence of America, all parties in England were agreed that it should be granted, and as this was the sole point at issue between the countries, there was little to be done but the arrangement of boundaries and some minor details.

Very different was the case with the French; when the basis of the

Exorbitant demands of France

Treaty of 1763 was proposed it was absolutely refused. It was plainly asserted that the very object of the war had been to annihilate that treaty, and hints were thrown out that England would be expected to surrender even a large part of her East Indian dominions. "Your arms are too long," said M. de Vergennes, "why not be satisfied with Bengal?" Before the year was over events happened which caused the French to lower their tone. The fall of Yorktown and the subsequent failure of the arms of England had made them believe that her power was gone, and they confidently looked forward to the success of two great enterprises then on foot to complete her discomfiture. De Grasse, with a large fleet, was to join the Spanish fleet in the West Indies, take troops on board, and seize Jamaica. The fall of Minorca had set De Crillon free to complete the fall of Gibraltar, with a vast armament which he had been engaged in organizing. To Rodney was intrusted the duty of protecting Jamaica ; he determined to prevent the junction of the enemy's fleets. A line of frigates within signal distance extended from St. Lucia to the French position at Martinique, and the enemy had not been two hours at sea before he was in pursuit. After some ineffectual efforts he succeeded in getting to the windward of the enemy, and on the 12th of April brought the French fleet to action. The number of the fleets was exactly equal. The superiority in number of men and weight of metal was in favour of the French. The battle is famous for the introduction into naval tactics of the manœuvre called breaking the line. Before this time it was usual to meet the enemy in line, to close up ship to ship, and win the battle chiefly by hard fighting. The new manœuvre consisted in advancing in column against the enemy's line, passing through it, thus breaking it in half, and enveloping one of the halves with the whole fleet. On the present occasion its use resulted in a complete victory. The English took or destroyed eight ships ; the loss of the French was very great, being much increased by the crowded state of their vessels, which had on board the soldiers intended for the Jamaica expedition.

In spite of this great success, the ministry continued its efforts at peace, but so long as there was any hope of securing ⟨Siege of⟩ better terms by the capture of Gibraltar the French ⟨Gibraltar.⟩ would not come to the point. Nor did the change of ⟨Sept. 13.⟩ ministry caused by the death of Rockingham change the aspect of affairs. Gibraltar had now been three years besieged. British fleets had twice forced the blockade and relieved the garrison. General Elliot's defence was vigorous, and inspired his troops with confidence. In the last November a great sally had destroyed the greater part of the enemy's works, but now a final effort of the united house of Bourbon was to be made. De Crillon, fresh from his success at Minorca, took the command, and neglecting the attack from the land side, set his hopes on a terrific bombardment to be conducted from the sea. He constructed ten huge floating batteries, with walls of wood and iron seven feet thick, shot proof and bomb proof ; a fleet of more than forty first-rates was in the harbour, and a fire from 400 pieces of artillery, in answer to which the English could produce but 100, was to annihilate the fortress. Elliot was not disheartened ; trusting to the natural strength of the place in other directions, he con-

centrated the whole of his fire upon the terrible batteries. For a
long while they seemed absolutely impenetrable, but at length the
constant stream of red hot shot took effect, and at mid-day their fire
slackened. Before midnight the largest of them burst into flames,
and eight out of the ten were on fire during the night. The siege
was over, and the fleet, which still waited in the hope of meeting
Lord Howe on his arrival with a relieving squadron, was driven
from the harbour by the weather before he came, so that he was able
to enter and relieve the garrison unmolested.

This great success, following so close upon the West Indian victory,

Changed tone of French demands. made it plain to the allies that England was by no
means so prostrate as they had imagined, and there was
no longer much difficulty in settling the preliminaries
of a peace. France accepted readily the offers which had been
rejected in the earlier part of the year. The partial cession, under the
Treaty of Paris, 1763, of the small islands St. Pierre and Miquelon off
the mouth of the St. Lawrence was completed, and the fishing round
Newfoundland regulated. Tobago in the West Indies, and the establishments of Senegal and Goree in Africa, were ceded to France. In the
East Indies the French were permitted to retain their commercial
establishments, but without military occupation. The treaty for the
destruction of Dunkirk was formally given up. With these slight
Terms of peace. Jan 20, 1783. concessions France had to be satisfied. Spain kept
Minorca; and the Floridas were given up to her—
better terms than she had a right to expect. England received
in exchange the Bahamas, which she had already reconquered,
and the right of cutting logwood in Honduras. Holland, with
whom the English Government had in vain attempted a separate
treaty, gained nothing by her rejection of those overtures, but was
obliged to agree to a mutual restoration of conquests, with the exception of the seaport town of Negapatam, which remained to the
English. A provisional treaty had already been made with America,
by which the independence of the States was formally declared,
boundaries settled, and commercial relations re-established. The
only difficulty was the claim for compensation for loss of property
raised by the American loyalists. This however was waived.

The duty of concluding these treaties had not fallen to the same
Death of Rock-ingham. Divi-sion of the Whigs. ministry as had begun them. The composition of the
Rockingham ministry had not been such as to secure its
stability; it consisted, as has been said, of two distinct
and equally balanced parties. A rivalry between the leaders of

these parties was inevitable, especially when one of them was a man so self-asserting and so conscious of his claims as Fox. United for a moment under the nominal leadership of Rockingham, a man of great influence though of slender ability, their union was at once dissolved at the death of that nobleman. Fox refused to serve under Shelburne, to whom the King at once offered the Premiership, and though several of the old ministers retained their places, the greater part followed their leader, and a split, which proved to be final, arose between the two sections of the Whigs. The new min- The Shelburne istry included, as Chancellor of the Exchequer, William ministry. Pitt, as yet but twenty-three years of age. Already his July 1782. oratorical power and his aspiring genius had made him one of the first men of the House, and he was regarded as a worthy successor of Chatham. Till this period he and Fox had been on friendly terms, and usually on the same side on political questions, but he had his father's hatred of faction, or the introduction of personal motives into politics, and bitterly reproached Fox for his conduct in leaving the Government. Henceforward they were avowed opponents. Fox's own explanation of his conduct was as follows. He said that he had written by the King's orders to Mr. Grenville, then at Paris, to authorize him to offer to the American agents "to recognize the independence of the United States in the first instance, and not to reserve it as a condition of peace." At the same time an official letter, for the same purpose, was sent by the Earl of Shelburne to Sir Guy Carleton in America. Mr. Fox, suspecting that this measure though consented to in the Cabinet, had not the entire approbation of some of his colleagues, had, in order to prevent any misconception, purposely chosen the most forcible expressions that the English language could supply; and he confessed that his joy was so great on finding that the Earl of Shelburne, in the letter to Sir Guy Carleton, had repeated his very words, that he carried it immediately to the Marquis of Rockingham, and told him that their distrust and suspicions of that noble lord's intentions had been groundless, and were now done away. "Judge then," said he, "of my grief and astonishment when, during the illness of my noble friend, another language was heard in the Cabinet, and the noble Earl and his friends began to consider the above letter as containing offers only of a conditional nature, to be recalled if not accepted as the price of peace. Finding myself thus ensnared and betrayed, and all confidence destroyed, I quitted a situation in which I found I could not remain either with honour or safety."

The Whig love of office had not been satiated by a four months' tenure of it, nor had Lord North's party taken kindly to their loss of power, and in their greedy desire for personal aggrandizement, Fox and North, who a few months before were speaking of each other as the most corrupt of the human species, found it consistent with their dignity to combine to eject Lord Shelburne's Government. They chose as their test question the terms of the peace. Lord North, probably, conscientiously believed that they might have been more favourable. Fox had himself offered much larger concessions to Holland, and had not disapproved either of the American or French terms, nor did he now offer the smallest suggestion as to what better terms might have been procured. In parliamentary influence, however, the coalition was quite irresistible, and at the opening of the session in the spring Lord Shelburne found himself in a minority

The coalition ministry under Portland. upon resolutions which had been moved condemnatory of the peace. He at once resigned. After a few

April 1783. ineffectual struggles the King had to accept the coalition ministry. Nothing could have been more distasteful to him; he found himself suddenly robbed of the whole advantage of twenty years of political scheming; he had triumphed on the fall of the Chatham administration, and for years had been served, as he would wish to be served, by a very able, popular, upright, but obsequious minister, only now to be thrown back, apparently bound hand and foot, into the hands of the hated Whig oligarchy. His policy had produced a disastrous war, an enormous augmentation of the National Debt, and an all but universal cry for a better system of economical government and national representation; while the Whigs, taking advantage of the opportunity which the ill success of royal Government gave them, had succeeded in regaining, as it appeared, an unassailable superiority. In parliamentary influence they were overwhelming; they numbered among their party Fox and North, the two ablest debaters in the House, and Burke, the greatest orator. They had also the long official experience of Lord North's party. Against them were the few remaining members of the old Chatham party, with no influence on which to rely, and upheld almost solely by the brilliant promise of young Pitt. The nominal head of the new Government was the Duke of Portland, for, as usual with coalitions, a man of no great ability was elected as the nominal chief. Fox and North were equal Secretaries of State, Lord John Cavendish was Chancellor of the Exchequer. The Cabinet was completed by Lords Keppel, Carlisle, and Stormont. The great strength of the new ministry was speedily shown ; a second Bill for parliamentary reform was rejected by the large majority of 144.

This ministry, which seemed so irresistible, was doomed to be of short duration, and the factious movement, which seemed to have thwarted for ever the policy of the King, proved in the sequel the means of establishing his policy for the rest of the reign. The cause of this sudden change of fortune was the necessity for some legislation with regard to the affairs of India, but before relating the final struggle it will be necessary to give a brief sketch of the course of events in that country.

For this purpose the history can be broken conveniently into two periods. There are two classes of difficulties which the Sketch of the English have had to overcome. First, the rivalry with history of other European nations, and secondly, the opposition India. to their gradual encroachment offered by the native chiefs and native tribes. The first of these periods may be held to close at the Peace of 1763, and includes the formation and establishment by the English of the three Presidencies of Bombay, Madras, and Bengal, and the practical destruction of all other European influence.

The India Company sprang into existence in the first year of the seventeenth century. In December 1600, the Indian Foundation of Adventurers were formed into a chartered company, the India Company. their monopoly being at first granted for fifteen years, 1600. and subsequently in 1609 rendered perpetual, but revocable at three years' notice from the Government. It was the intention of the Company to dispute the trade of the East with two nations who had already made good their position there. The discovery of the Cape of Good Hope in 1497 by the Portuguese under Vasco da Gama, had been followed by nearly a century during which Portugal showed extreme energy both in arms, in literature, and in mercantile pursuits. The western coast of India, from Goa northwards to Ormuz in the Persian Gulf, was more or less completely conquered by the Portuguese from the native rajahs. In 1580, Portugal was conquered by the Spaniards ; its greatness was at an end. The Dutch had already established important factories both in India itself and in the Spice Islands, and had with success contested with the Portuguese their monopoly of the Indian trade. It was in emulation of the Dutch, and taking advantage of the depression of Portugal, and in pursuance also of their systematic opposition to Spain, that the English Company was formed.

At first this trade was small but very lucrative. The attention of the Company was chiefly directed to the exclusion of interlopers, or free traders, who interfered with their monopoly. Their chief factories were Surat, near Bombay, which brought them into immediate conflict with the Portuguese, against whom they assisted the native princes, and Bantam, in Java, which placed them in conflict with the Dutch, at whose hands, in 1623, they suffered the famous outrage known as the Massacre of Amboyna, where ten Englishmen were put to death upon their confession of conspiracy against the Dutch extorted by torture. Both these positions were obviously inconvenient, and tended to permanent hostilities. Some more secure situation was desirable, and in 1640 the Rajah of the Carnatic allowed the Company to purchase ground close to the deserted Portuguese settlement of St. Thomé; and the Fort of St. George and the town of Madras rapidly rose to importance. This town took the place of Bantam. The marriage-treaty of Charles II. with Catherine of Braganza gave the town and island of Bombay to the English, and it took the place of Surat. In Bengal all three rival powers had factories upon the Hooghly, a branch of the Ganges. Not long after the transference of their business from Surat to Bombay the English became involved in some petty hostilities in Bengal, and were compelled to resign their factory, and found a home lower down the river at a village called Chutternuttee. They were in fact in great danger of being driven from the country, but they managed to mollify the anger of Aurungzebe, who was at that time on the throne of the Moguls, and in 1698 obtained a lease of the village, there built Fort William, and founded the town of Calcutta. The Revolution in England threatened for a time to destroy the India Company. A great rival company, called the New India Company, was formed, and was supported by the majority of the Commons. But finally, in 1708, the quarrels were adjusted, and the Companies coalesced to prevent the destruction of both, which threatened to follow their eager competition. Their whole capital was made to consist of £3,200,000, lent to Government at five per cent.; and they had the right of borrowing one million and a half more. Repeated prolongations of their privileges were made; in 1712 to 1736, in 1730 to 1769, in 1743 to 1783. Their three settlements formed separate presidencies or seats of government, unconnected one with the other, each governed by a president and council. Events in Europe had practically destroyed the rivalry of Portugal, which had lost its energy, and moreover, in its dislike of Spain, had become the close

Foundation of Madras, Bombay, and Calcutta.

Decline of Portuguese and Dutch competition.

ally of the English. The stress even of the Dutch competition was very greatly slackened. That country also, in its dread of France, was generally friendly to England, and from the position of its settlements its commercial importance was rather in the islands than in the mainland of India.

Aurungzebe had died in 1707, after a very long and glorious reign. He was the most successful of that line of Indian Emperors generally spoken of as Great Moguls, and the inheritor of a vast empire founded by Baber, a descendant of Timor the Tartar, who died in 1530, but whose work was carried on by his successors, notably by the great Emperor Akbar, whose reign ended in 1605. Aurungzebe carried the arms of this victorious empire, now stationed at Delhi, over nearly all the mainland and peninsula of India. His chief opponent was Sivajee, the founder of the Mahratta dynasty. This chief, who was never conquered, died young in 1680. On his death for a time the glories of the Mahratta dynasty declined. The head of this people, the Rajah of Satara, like other Eastern monarchs, became merely a nominal ruler, his Peishwa or Prime Minister, whose abode was Poona, became the real head of the race, but like by far the greater part of the Hindoo rulers of India, the Peishwa acknowledged the supremacy of the Mogul Empire. Wherever the Mahommedan arms had been really victorious, the provinces were in the charge of Subahdars, or Viceroys of the Emperor; the great bulk of the Peninsula, known as the Deccan, being in the hands of the greatest of their Viceroys, called the Nizam. The death of Aurungzebe was the signal for the dissolution of this great power.

Decline of the Mogul Empire. 1707.

In the midst of the prevalent dissolution a new and most dangerous rival of the English Company arose. This was the French Company which had been established under Louis XIV., and which, like the English and Dutch, had an establishment upon the Hooghly called Chandernagore ; a settlement eighty miles south of Madras called Pondicherry ; and to represent our settlement on the Malabar coast, the two islands of the Mauritius or Isle of France, and the Isle of Bourbon, won respectively from the Dutch and Portuguese. In 1744, when the Companies first came into active competition, two men of great genius were at the head of the French Presidencies; Labourdonnais at the Mauritius, and Dupleix at Pondicherry. The dissolution of the Mogul Empire has been not inaptly compared to the break-up of the Western Empire of Charles the Great. All the provincial governors who were at all in a position

Competition with the French Company.

to do so, while keeping up for a time their nominal dependence upon
the central court of Delhi, rendered themselves practically independent. It was of this state of dissolution that Dupleix, with singular
ability, took advantage. As he gazed upon the shattered fragments
of the decaying empire, on the rising independence of Hindoo rajah,
mogul and nabob, and observed the constantly increasing power of
the Mahrattas from the Western Ghauts, Dupleix formed the opinion
that India was not for the natives, but for European conquerors, and
as Dutch enterprise had sought another direction, and Portugal was
Grandeur of a failing power, the only countries that could compete
Dupleix's for the high position were France and England. Having
schemes. settled upon his opponents, he settled also upon his
means of offence. The French Company and its officers must become
at once the nominal feudatories of the Mogul Empire, and without
present conquest must so mingle in all the affairs of the native
princes, and so assist them by means of native levies drilled in the
European fashion, as virtually to master them all. In other words, he
invented that system by the application of which the English power
has subsequently been formed. The war of the Austrian Succession,
which broke out in 1744, supplied him with his opportunity. A network of alliances was formed around the English settlement, and kept
together by the skill of Dupleix and of his wife, a woman of Portuguese
extraction and of extraordinary talents. But Dupleix's activity was
crossed by the equal energy of Labourdonnais, who, with a fleet
hastily gathered, captured Madras. The English inhabitants surrendered upon terms, the town was to be repurchased for £440,000.
This was in strict accordance with the views of the French Government,
but not in accordance with the views of Dupleix, who wished to
drive the English from the Peninsula. A hot dispute arose between
the two governors. Dupleix induced Labourdonnais to withdraw
upon a false promise of surrendering Madras; and Labourdonnais
returning to France, was there, with the ingratitude the French
always showed to their colonial governors, subjected to several years
of imprisonment and a trial, which was the immediate cause of his
death. Retaining Madras, and with the aid of the Nabob of Arcot,
Dupleix was proceeding, in 1747, to complete his conquest by the
capture of Fort St. David. The approach of the English fleet saved
the fortress, and even enabled the English to make a counter attack
upon Pondicherry. It failed, and the fame of Dupleix and the French
Success of was at its height among the natives when the Peace of
Dupleix. 1748 compelled the restitution of conquests. But the

plans of Dupleix were such that no war between the nations was necessary to enable him to carry them on. It was native quarrels he desired, and such quarrels arose at the death of the old Nizam El Mulk of the Deccan. His throne was disputed by his son Nazir Jung and his grandson Mirzapha Jung. At the same time Chunda Sahib appeared as a claimant for the viceroyalty of the Carnatic. Both the pretenders found their cause adopted by Dupleix, who understood well how secure his position would be did he succeed in establishing by his own power a Nizam of the Deccan and a Nabob of the Carnatic. Aided by the Marquis de Bussy, as great as a soldier as Dupleix was as a diplomatist, in 1749 the pretenders and the French won a victory at Amboor, in which the reigning nabob was killed. His son, Mahomet Ali, took the title of Nabob of Arcot, but was obliged to retire to Trichinopoly, while the whole country was in the hands of his rival. Thus successful in arms in the Carnatic, Dupleix was equally so by intrigue in the Deccan. In 1750, as the French approached Nazir Jung's army, a conspiracy which Dupleix had hatched broke out, and Nazir was murdered. Mirzapha acknowledged his debt of gratitude to the French, and it was at Pondicherry that he entered upon his rank, rewarding his European allies with the government of the whole country from Cape Comorin to the Kistna. Dupleix appeared to have gained his object. The Company of which he was the governor was accepted as a ruling power in India; the great princes of the neighbourhood both owed him their crowns. The only place still holding out against his authority was Trichinopoly, and thither he directed all his efforts.

It was then that England at last found a champion in Robert Clive. Unable to summon troops sufficient to relieve **Defeated** Trichinopoly, he determined to attack Arcot as a diver- **by Clive.** sion. The plan succeeded. Arcot fell almost without a struggle. 10,000 men were detached from the armies of Dupleix and Chunda Sahib at Pondicherry, but their attempt to recapture Arcot was a signal failure; and when Clive secured the assistance of a band of Mahratta horse under Morari Row, the siege was raised, and was followed by a victory over Rajah Sahib, son of Chunda Sahib. Taking the Pagoda of Conjeveram on the way, Clive, in 1752, turned towards Fort St. David, but was recalled to fight Rajah Sahib, whom he again conquered in the battle of Coverpauk. He was then at leisure, in conjunction with Major Lawrence, who had come to assume the command, to raise the siege of Trichinopoly; and when the besiegers were themselves besieged in the islands of Seringham

in the river Cauvery, and when Chunda Sahib was there killed, the
failure of Dupleix's measures was complete. The war indeed continued some time longer. Bussy upheld the French nominee, Salabat
Jung, in the Deccan ; Dupleix still kept up hostilities in the Carnatic.
But as his fortunes failed, his employers deserted him. In 1754 he
was recalled. A treaty was made between the Companies, and
Dupleix died in poverty and misery a few years afterwards in Paris.

In 1753 ill health had compelled Clive to go to England. In 1755
he returned to India as Governor of Fort St. David, of which he took
possession on the 20th June 1756, having on his way assisted in the
destruction of Gheriah, the sea-girt stronghold of the pirate Angria,
who had long been the terror of the Bombay merchants. On the
very day of Clive's arrival at Madras, Surajah Dowlah, the Nabob of
Bengal, a young man of about nineteen years of age, cruel, effeminate,
and debauched, had captured Fort William and Calcutta. Shelter
afforded to a defaulting revenue officer of his, and the increase of the
fortifications of Fort William, roused a quarrel between him and the
English. He advanced upon Calcutta and captured it, and the
world was horrified by the tragedy of the Black Hole.

The Black Hole
of Calcutta.
June 1756.

The prisoners, 146 in number, were thrust into a narrow
chamber some twenty feet square, whence, after a night
of unspeakable horrors, but twenty-three wretched survivors were
dragged the following morning before Surajah Dowlah and sent as
prisoners to his capital at Moorshedabad. The horrors of the Black
Hole of Calcutta were beyond expression terrible ; the heat of the
night was intense, and as the agonies of thirst and suffocation came
upon them, the prisoners struggled to the windows for a mouthful of
fresh air, careless that they trod to death their fallen comrades ; they
insulted the guards in hopes that they would fire upon them ; many
died in raving madness. Mr. Holwell, the chief of those who
survived, was so broken that he was unable to walk from the prison.
When the news of this fearful event reached Madras, it was at once
determined to take vengeance upon the Nabob. After some difficulties
Clive was appointed to the command, and though four months were
wasted, partly by contrary winds, partly by the jealousy of the various
English commanders, by the middle of January 1757 Calcutta was
regained. This success and a night attack upon his army excited in
the mind of the Nabob such a dread of the English that he consented to enter into an alliance with them. The temporary cessation of hostilities with the natives and the arrival of reinforcements
gave Clive an opportunity to destroy the French settlement of

Chandernagore, although the Nabob, to whom the presence of the French as a counterpoise to the English was of great importance, had taken it under his protection. This act of open contempt for his authority excited Surajah Dowlah's anger anew, and afraid to oppose the English openly he entered into secret negotiations with the French, and intreated M. Bussy to march from the Deccan to his assistance. His intrigues became _{Clive's treaty} known, and were met by counter intrigues : it was _{with Meer} determined to depose him, and to place Meer Jaffier, his _{Jaffier.} general, on the throne ; and in order to deceive one of his agents named Omichund, who threatened to betray the conspiracy unless bribed by an enormous sum of money, Clive was guilty of forging the name of Admiral Watson. The treaty to which the false signature was appended promised the bribe, but was a sham treaty. On the real treaty which Admiral Watson had signed Omichund received nothing. The plot being ripe, Clive openly advanced towards Moorshedabad, the Nabob's capital, and on the 23rd June 1757 won with his troops, numbering in all some 3000 men, the _{Battle of} great victory of Plassey over 30,000 of the Nabob's troops. _{Plassey.} That battle secured the power of England in Bengal. _{June 23, 1757.} Surajah Dowlah fled ; Meer Jaffier was placed upon the throne. A sum of nearly £3,000,000 was paid to the Company, to which was given the entire property of Calcutta itself as far as 600 yards beyond the Mahratta ditch, and the zemindary or feudal tenure on payment of rent of all the country between Calcutta and the sea. The English thus had firm footing in Bengal, and before 1760, when Clive was again compelled to seek England, he had made two other steps in advance. In support of Meer Jaffier, he had advanced against and conquered Shah Allum, the Great Mogul, and for ever freed himself from competition of the Dutch by capturing the whole of a large squadron which they had sent to the assistance of their factory at Chinsurah in opposing the advance of the English.

The following year saw the final fall of the French power in India. While Clive was securing Bengal, the breaking _{Final overthrow} out of the Seven Years' War had renewed the hostilities _{of the French} _{power in India.} in the Carnatic. On this occasion Lally was the _{1761.} champion of the French. But able and vigorous as a soldier, his ill-usage of the natives, his eager temper and satirical tongue, surrounded him with disaffection both among the Indians and his own troops. At first his advent was marked with success. In the course of 1758 he captured and destroyed Fort St. David and retook

Arcot. But, early in the following year, the disaffection of his troops and the arrival of Admiral Pocock prevented him from bringing to a successful issue an assault on Madras, and from this time onwards the English retained constant superiority. Colonel Coote, a soldier of Clive's training, took the command; and on the morning of the 22nd January 1760, won over the French the great battle of Wandewash. The European troops alone were engaged. It differed from other Indian battles in this respect, and was a national victory won upon Indian soil. Coote's sepoys, on congratulating him on his victory, thanked him for having shown them a battle such as they had never yet seen. The battle of Wandewash did for Madras what Plassey did for Bengal. The troops of the English and their allies gradually closed in round Pondicherry, and in spite of a firm and splendid resistance, that sole remaining stronghold of the French power surrendered in January 1761; and Lally, like his predecessors, returned to France only to meet with persecution from his employers, and finally death upon the scaffold. The Portuguese, Dutch, and French had thus all disappeared from the political world of India, though they still kept up trading stations at Pondicherry, Chandernagore, and Chinsurah. England had secured a sovereign position in its three Presidencies.

The further growth of the Empire was at the expense of native tribes, and carried on in the midst of strange domestic mismanagement. The English Government at Calcutta, left without the guiding hand of Clive, soon drifted into fresh quarrels with the natives. Mr. Vansittart was left as governor, and already, in 1760, he had thought it desirable to remove Meer Jaffier, the Company's creature, from the throne of Moorshedabad, and replace him by Meer Cossim, his son-in-law. The step was an unwise one. The new viceroy was of less malleable materials than his predecessor, and speedily came to look with great anger at the constant breaches of the revenue laws perpetrated by the English traders. He quarrelled especially with a gentleman who occupied the advanced factory of Patna high up the Ganges. To be out of the influence of Calcutta, he withdrew his capital from Moorshedabad to Monghir, and all seemed tending towards war. It was in vain that Mr. Vansittart went himself to Monghir, arranged for the payment of inland duties, and received as a sign of peace a present of £70,000. An embassy sent from Calcutta to complete the pacification was fallen on and murdered at Moorshedabad, and under the circumstances war became inevitable. The advance of the

English was rapid and triumphant; Moorshedabad fell, and after a nine days' siege Monghir itself was taken. The Nabob found it necessary to fly, but before he fled, with the assistance of a renegade Frenchman called Sombre, he committed a crime similar to that of the Black Hole of Calcutta. On the 5th October 1763 the whole of the English residents of the Patna factory (150 in number), enclosed within their prison walls, were shot down or cut to pieces, and their mangled remains thrown into two wells. One alone escaped. The Rajah and his instrument Sombre fled into the district of a neighbouring nabob, Sujah Dowlah of Oude, at whose court was tarrying, in a condition between exile and prisoner, the Mogul Shah Allum, who had been driven from his throne at Delhi by the advance of the Mahrattas. Sujah Dowlah had been appointed vizier, and virtually wielded all the power that was left to the descendants of the Moguls. With these allies Sujah Dowlah advanced to meet the English, and suffered, on the 23rd of October, at Buxar, higher up the river than Patna, a terrible defeat at the hands of Major Munro. The fruit of the victory was the person of Shah Allum himself, and backed now by his authority, the English pressing on in their victorious course, the following year entered Allahabad, the chief city of Oude.

Massacre of Patna. 1763.

Battle of Buxar. Oct. 1764.

Victory in war and increased dominion had only increased the maladministration of the India Company, which reached such a pitch, that in 1765 it became necessary again to despatch Clive to the scene of action. This was not done without the most vigorous opposition. Two great parties had long divided the India House in London. Mr. Sullivan had for some time exercised a paramount authority there. Clive had appeared as his rival. Both parties lavished their wealth in creating votes, and a factious struggle arose in the heart of the Company. At length the general voice seemed to declare that Clive alone could restore order in the mismanaged Presidency. Clive saw his opportunity. He publicly refused to go out as long as Sullivan occupied the place of chairman of the Court of Directors. The proprietors were so frightened by this threat, that when the day of election of directors arrived, Sullivan found himself unable to carry more than half of his list of directors, and Clive's friends were triumphant. He was sent out with full powers, and authorized to override the opinion of the Council, although usually the governor was entitled to only one vote. The struggle for bribes

Maladminis-tration of the Company.

Clive returns to India May 1765

and ill-gotten gain was carried on to the moment of his arrival. Only a few days before he landed the viceroyalty of Bengal had been sold, contrary to all justice, to the illegitimate son of Meer Jaffier for £140,000. But the scene was speedily changed. In two days Clive and the Committee who accompanied him had mastered the state of affairs and declared their dictatorial authority. At the dread of his name alone Sujah Dowlah sought peace. He compelled Meer Cossim and his agent Sombre, who had organized the massacre of Patna, to leave his dominions, and a treaty was made in accordance with Clive's view, that for the present it was better to strengthen than increase our dominions. By this treaty Sujah Dowlah retained his provinces, surrendering only the districts of Corah and Allahabad, which were given as an imperial dominion to Shah Allum. In return the provinces of Bengal, Orissa, and Bahar, were granted for all administrative purposes to the Company, who thus became nominal as well as real princes of India. The Nabob of Bengal was pensioned with a yearly income. This was the beginning of a system which played a great part in our Indian history. By this means the Company were secured a revenue of two millions. But even yet Clive thought it imprudent to place the administration in European hands, and selected as native Prime Minister a Mahommedan, Mahomed Reza Khan. This choice was made deliberately, in spite of the claims of Nuncomar, the chief of the Bengal Brahmins. The rivalry between these two chiefs bore notable fruit afterwards. Having settled our difficulties with the natives, Clive turned to domestic reforms; he deprived the military of a large allowance, called "double batta," which they had received from Meer Jaffier, and quelled, with incomparable vigour and sagacity, a mutiny which arose in consequence; he forbade civilians to receive presents from the native princes, and restrained officials from engaging in private trading, while he himself set an admirable example of disinterestedness. Unfortunately he was unable to superintend the execution of his plans, but was compelled by ill health to return to England (Jan. 1767).

While the events that have been mentioned were going on in Bengal, the southern Presidency had had its own difficulties to contend with. Immediately above the plains of the Carnatic lies the hill country of Mysore, and there a new power had been established by the ablest opponent we ever met in India, Hyder Ali. A Mahommedan of low birth, a freebooter, a rebel, and commander-in-chief of the Mysore army, he succeeded at last in establishing himself on the throne of the Hindoo Rajah.

Affairs in Madras; rise of Hyder Ali.

Sometimes in confederation with the Nizam of the Deccan, some-times with the Mahrattas of the Western Ghauts, Hyder kept up a continual war with the English. His army of 100,000 men was organized in the European fashion. Though unable to write, his retentive memory enabled him to be a most dangerous diplomatist, and though beaten in the field, his activity kept the English army in constant movement and exhausted the Company's resources. To such an extent was this the case, that Clive's reforms were counter-balanced, and in 1769 Indian stock fell sixty per cent.

Such threatening appearances in the commercial career of the Com-pany, the constant scandal of their factious struggle in London, and the anomaly becoming every day more striking of a body of merchants exercising, and exercising very badly, sovereign rights over large conquered districts, excited the attention of Parliament. Chatham, as has been mentioned, intended to have enforced the rights of the Crown; and the Company only escaped some interference of the kind by offering to establish supervisors of its own and to pay the English Government £400,000 a year. But in 1773 matters had become much worse; a fearful famine had devastated Bengal, corpses choked and infected the Ganges, the fish and fowl became uneatable, more than half the population are said to have been swept away. It was felt that no properly conducted Government could have permitted such an evil; and when in 1772 the united effects of the Madras wars and the Bengal famine reduced the funds of the Company to so low an ebb that they had to demand of Parliament a loan of a million sterling, legislation became inevitable. At the beginning of the year a Committee of inquiry had reported, and again in the autumn another secret committee had been named; upon their report Lord North formed what is known as the Regulating Act. By this he granted the Company their loan, relieved them of their annual tribute to the State, and allowed them to export their bonded tea, with what disastrous effects in America has been already seen. In exchange he confined their interest to six per cent. till the loan was paid, and afterwards to eight per cent.; and, proceeding to the organization of their government, he established a supreme court upon the English model, made the Governor of Bengal Governor-General of India, and appointed by name in Parliament a new Council. Warren Hastings, already Governor of Bengal, was made the first Governor-General; Barwell, a member of the existing Council, was continued in his office. General Clavering, Colonel Monson, and Philip Francis, were named

Famine in Bengal, 1770.

Regulating Act, 1773.

as the new members. During the discussions relative to this Act much blame had been thrown on Clive, and though a formal vote of censure was mollified by the words, that "Robert Lord Clive did at the same time render great and meritorious services to his country,"

Death of Clive the trouble he underwent preyed upon a morbid mind and a body weakened by disease so much that he committed suicide (Nov. 1774).

The interest which has hitherto centred upon Clive is now transferred to the career of Warren Hastings. An Indian statesman by profession, and thoroughly acquainted with the wants both of native and European populations, he had entered upon the duties of the Government of Bengal in 1772. The post was not a light one: in India a people in the last stages of distress, a Government full of abuses, a small dominant population who believed their sole duty was to acquire wealth rapidly; in England a factious and fluctuating body of governors whose chief object was high dividends. Such were the conditions under which Hastings had to act.

Hastings Governor-General. A change in the management of the land tax produced a larger revenue with less oppression; the country, freed from marauders, was in a better condition to pay taxes; but this was little. Rumours were afloat that Reza Khan, the finance minister, was peculating largely. On the accusation of Nuncomar, his old rival, he was apprehended by Hastings, who either believed the charges or acted in obedience to the Company's orders. On examination he was acquitted, but not replaced in his office, nor was Nuncomar appointed to succeed him; the administration was kept in English hands. The Viceroy, an infant, was deprived of half his allowance, and a quarrel having arisen between our old ally Shah Allum, who had made friends with the Mahrattas, and the English, Allahabad and Corah were resumed and sold to the Vizier of Oude for fifty lacs of rupees. More than that, for a further sum of forty lacs English troops were basely let to that prince to destroy his enemies, the neighbouring Afghan conquerers of Rohilcund. All these measures seem to have been dictated primarily by a desire for an increased revenue. It was at this crisis that the Regulating Act took effect, and the new councillors arrived in the Hooghly. The man of the most importance and activity among them was Philip Francis, who is now generally accepted as being the author of " Junius' Letters." The other two always voted with him, and all three came out with strong prejudices and a determination to oppose Hastings. The new Governor-General therefore found himself at once in a permanent minority, for, as before, he had but one vote in the Council. Barwell, the Indian member of the new Council, always voted with him. There arose therefore a fierce struggle for power, and the new councillors made haste to seek on all sides grounds for attacking Hastings. It was understood that they were willing to receive any charges against him. Nuncomar, who had been heavily disappointed at not receiving the vacant place of Reza Khan, charged him with having been bribed to pardon that great official; and Francis and his partisans determined to confront Nuncomar with Hastings at the council board. The Governor-General rightly refused to preside at what was virtually his own trial; but upon his dissolving the Council the three new members declared it not dissolved, and continued the inquiry. Fortune placed in the hands of Hastings the means of freeing himself from this awkward dilemma. A private charge of forgery was brought against Nuncomar, and he was tried before the new supreme court. It is impossible to say how far this charge was fostered by Hastings, he himself asserted upon oath that he had nothing whatever to do with it; at all events it was carried to its conclusion, and Sir Elijah Impey and his colleagues found the charge proved, and condemned Nuncomar to death. Impey, an old school-fellow of Hastings, whose career showed him not to be above suspicion, is by many held to have acted corruptly; but his colleagues entirely agreed with him, nor does it seem that he did anything worse than import into India the habits and feelings of Europe when he suffered the sentence of death to be carried out. No doubt this was a shock to the moral feelings of the Hindoos, to whom forgery was not the grave offence that it is to us. However this may be, the death of Nuncomar secured the supremacy of Hastings. There was no one brave enough to bring charges either true or false against one whose vengeance seemed to have struck down the head of their religion. His supremacy was soon still further secured; by the death of Monson he found himself, by means of his own casting vote, master of the Council. One more violent struggle took place, after which he was able to act according to his own judgment, although constantly thwarted by Francis. In the height of his difficulties he had lodged a conditional resignation with his agent in London, and his agent, alarmed by the news from India, had presented it. Suddenly, in the midst of his triumph in Calcutta, a ship arrived with a new member of the Council and the news that the Governor-General had resigned. Hastings positively refused to ratify the act of his agent, which he declared was unauthorized by him. The bitter contest which arose from this subject was brought before the Supreme Court of Justice for arbitration. Sir Elijah Impey again settled the question in Hastings' favour.

Hastings could now turn his thoughts to what was his constant object, the aggrandizement of our power in India, and his view
His opposition to the Mahrattas. seems to have been to enter into close alliances with the great Mahommedan Princes, the Nabob-Vizier of Oude and the Nizam of the Deccan, to render them dependent on the English by means of large subsidies, and by their assistance oppose an effectual barrier to the great and increasing power of the Mahrattas, whom he regarded as the most dangerous rivals to the English. Affairs in the dependent Presidency of Madras gave him an opportunity for carrying out this policy. Mismanagement and peculation had been as rife there as in Bengal. The Rajah of Tanjore, a Mahratta prince, had been dispossessed in favour of the Nabob of Arcot, an old ally of the English. This measure was disallowed by the directors at home. Lord Pigot was sent out as governor to re-establish the Rajah. The same struggle between the Governor and his Council as had been seen in Calcutta took place in Madras, but proceeded to even greater extremities. The Council arrested Lord Pigot, who died a prisoner in their hands. Thus the policy of restitution was crushed, and the claims of the Mahratta Rajah of Tanjore were neglected. In Bombay, too, constant disputes had arisen with the Mahratta chiefs of Poonah, so that the whole of that great confederacy was ready for war. To appreciate the importance of such a war, it must be remembered that the Mahrattas had spread over much of India. The descendants of Sivajee, like the descendants of most Indian conquerors, had sunk into *rois fainéants* at Satara, delegating their real power to their viceroy, called the Peishwa of Poonah, whose office was hereditary. Dependent offshoots of this power had established themselves in the hills of the Malwa under the great princes Sindia and Holkar; in Berar under a prince called the Bonslah, in Gujerat under the Guicowar, and in the extreme south in Tanjore; while bands of Mahratta horsemen had, as we have seen, seized upon Delhi, and expelled for a time Shah Allum, the Great Mogul, who had however made terms with them, and was now again seated upon his ancestral throne. With this vast power, already on bad terms with both the southern Presidencies, it was discovered that the French were intriguing. With his usual vigour Hastings was determined to forestall war, which he saw was inevitable. For this purpose,

in spite of the opposition of his Council, an army was at once despatched southward to act through Bundelcund. The command was given to Colonel Goddard. But Hastings, who seldom acted a straightforward part, intrigued at the same time with the Bonslah and with Rajonaut Rao, a deposed Peishwa, now a refugee in Bombay. Upon the news that France and England had declared war, still further energy was infused into military affairs ; and Chandernagore, near Calcutta, and Pondicherry, just south of Madras, two French settlements, were captured. The Mahratta war was not without its reverses. The Bombay army was surrounded near Poonah, and escaped only on ignominious terms ; but Goddard upheld the honour of the English arms, and defeated Sindia and Holkar, while Captain Popham took the almost impregnable castle of Gwalior. The war was regarded as of sufficient importance to require the presence of the veteran General Sir Eyre Coote, who was despatched from England to take the command.

But all prospect of carrying out the ambitious schemes of Hastings for subjugating the Mahrattas was suddenly clouded. Hastings' policy News arrived in 1780 that Hyder Ali, who had long thwarted by Hyder Ali's been watching his opportunity, had pounced upon advance. Madras. He saw the English engaged in a vast Indian war, he knew that their arms were not successful in America, he expected the speedy arrival of a large French force, his time had come at last, and he flung himself in irresistible numbers upon the Carnatic. The English were virtually taken by surprise ; one army under Colonel Baylie was destroyed, a second under Sir Hector Munro saved itself by rapid flight. In a moment Hastings comprehended the new situation of affairs ; the news reached Calcutta on the 23rd of September, on the 25th he was ready with a complete new plan of operations. He offered peace and alliance to the Mahrattas ; he embarked all available troops for Madras ; in virtue of the supremacy of Bengal, he ventured to suspend Whitewell, the incompetent Governor of Madras ; he gave the command to Sir Eyre Coote, and sent also vast sums of money thither. It was to sustain this great effort, without if possible diminishing the gains of the Company, that Hastings committed the rest of those acts of oppression which were afterwards alleged against him. To supply the greed of his employers he had sold British troops to destroy the Rohillas ; in his great struggle for power he Conclusion of had strained the law in the case of Nuncomar ; to support the Mysore his Mahratta and Mysore wars he stooped to actions of war.

injustice and cruelty. The return of Sir Eyre Coote re-established affairs at Madras, he won a great victory at Porta Novo and a
second at Pollilore. The general peace in 1783 put a conclusion to
the war, which had been continued by Tippoo upon the death of
his father Hyder Ali. Hastings had succeeded in concluding a
treaty with the Mahrattas, and had his hands free for carrying on
with energy operations against Mysore, the Dutch, and the French
fleet under De Suffren. All the Dutch settlements had been captured; five great indecisive battles had been fought between De
Suffren and Sir Edward Hughes; but no striking advantages had
been won over Tippoo, who had even met with some successes on
the Malabar coast. With the European nations terms had been arranged in France; with Tippoo a peace was made on the conditions
of the mutual restorations of conquest.

To return to the conduct of Hastings. On the first alarm of war with
Robbery of   Hyder Ali, he had demanded troops from Cheyte Singh,
Cheyte Singh. the Rajah of Benares, as from a feudatory of the Empire.
This demand was annually renewed, together with the customary
tribute of £50,000. Upon this being delayed it was raised to £500,000.
This was still unpaid when Hastings determined to make a personal
visit to Benares. He entered the city with an absurdly inadequate
guard, and put Cheyte Singh under arrest; an insurrection was the
consequence, and Hastings was for a time confined to his house by
the populace and in imminent danger of his life. Perfectly calm and
unmoved in the midst of his dangers, he yielded not one step; he
succeeded in letting the neighbouring troops hear of his danger;
Major Popham came to his rescue, and routed the people of Benares;
Cheyte Singh was driven from his country, a new rajah, with a
much enlarged tribute, was put in his place; his fortress at Bidzegur
and all his property was seized. Hastings at once proceeded to
similar acts in Oude. He entered into a nefarious compact with
the Nabob to rob his mother and grandmother of their money.
These two ladies lived at Fyzabad, the ancient capital of Sujah
Robbery of the Dowlah; his son, the reigning Nabob Asaph Ul Dowlah,
Begums of Oude had withdrawn to the new city of Lucknow. The
Begums possessed large landed property and Sujah Dowlah's
treasure; it was agreed between Hastings and Asaph Ul Dowlah
that this should be taken from them, the landed property going to
the Nabob, the money being received as payment for heavy arrears
due from the Nabob to the English. A lengthened siege and
partial famine did not effect the purpose of the plunderers; it was

found necessary to seize, to imprison, to starve, and torture two aged eunuchs, the princesses' chief friends and ministers, before treasure to the amount of about a million could be wrung from them; the excuse alleged for such unmitigated wickedness was that the Begums had intrigued for an insurrection in Oude. Again Sir Elijah Impey was on the spot to give his voice in favour of Hastings when the rumours on which these charges were based were submitted to him.

Whatever excuses might be found for such actions, in the difficulties of Hastings' position and the peculiarity of Indian Displeasure in habits, it was certain that the condition and rights of England. a Company which had become a sovereign ruler, and was at once under the necessity of demanding a loan to avoid bankruptcy, and guilty of what could not but sound to English ears as acts of the cruellest oppression, must form a chief topic of parlia- Parliamentary mentary discussion. Accordingly, in 1781, two com- inquiry, mittees had been formed to inquire into the affairs of 1781. India. Their reports were strongly condemnatory of the Company's government, and the Secretary of State for the time being accordingly demanded Hastings' recall. To this the directors, as by law they had a right to do, refused to listen, but the matter could not be dropped, and immediately after the formation of the Dundas's Bill, coalition ministry Mr. Dundas produced a Bill for the 1783. regulation of India. His view was that the Governor-General's power should be increased, and the office given to some great independent nobleman such as Lord Cornwallis. Not only was this Bill regarded as a party measure, and by no means of sufficient breadth for its object, but also it was felt that the subject was one which should be handled by Government itself. In pursuance of this view, in the autumn session of the same year Fox's India Bill. Fox brought forward his great India Bill. The faults Nov. to be remedied were sufficiently obvious; a trading company had by a strange turn of fortune become a governor of large provinces, and had again and again engaged in extensive wars. It was plain that the functions of the merchant and the governor were not only distinct but antagonistic. The claims of the proprietors for large dividends, and the duty of the directors to work for the financial benefit of their employers, was certain to blind them to acts of injustice which had a tendency to fill their coffers. The main principle of any great India Bill must have been the resumption by the Crown of its inherent Imperial rights, which it had suffered accidentally to fall into disuse. Accordingly, Fox proposed that all the authority which the Company had exercised should be transferred to a body of seven commissioners, nominated in Parliament and capable of holding office for four years, after which the vacancies occurring in that body were to be filled up by the Crown. To them, as trustees, was to be transferred also the whole property of the Company. But the management of this property and the commerce of the Company was placed in the hands of a subordinate council of directors, proprietors each of them of £2000 stock, acting under and subject to the orders of the superior council. The vacancies in the subordinate council were to be filled by the Court of proprietors. There were additional stipulations for the purpose of checking monopolies, the acceptance of presents, the hiring out of British forces, and changes in the tenure of land, regulations in fact attempting to remove the principal known abuses of the Indian Government. The Bill was a thorough and great Bill, and the magnitude of the subject, and the freedom which the Government enjoyed from any party pledges in the matter, should have raised it out of the sphere of party politics, but it was at once furiously assaulted. There were Objections to it. raised against it two objections, corresponding to the two councils which it proposed to erect. First, it was urged that it was incompatible with the dignity of the Crown that patronage so enormous as that of India should be vested even for a time in any hands but those of the King himself.[1] As Lord Thurlow said, when the Bill was before the House of Lords, "the King will in fact take the diadem with his own hands and place it on the head of Mr. Fox." What rendered this defect more glaring was, that the new committee was named in the Act, and that all seven members of it were strenuous supporters of the present administration, so that a fresh and overwhelming source of influence was secured to Mr. Fox's friends. It was urged, secondly, that even granting the necessity and wisdom of such a transference of political power, the establishment of the second council for the management of the commerce of the Company was a violent and unnecessary infraction of chartered rights. Bad financial management, as apart from their political conduct, could not be alleged against the Company, nor did it seem probable that commerce would be better managed under the direction of a parliamentary Committee, even though working through a subordinate council of merchants, than if left exclusively

---

[1] The patronage was worth more than £300,000 a year; besides the governor and the councils, there was one place of £25,000 a year, one of £15,000, five of £10,000, five of £9000, one of £7500, three of £2000, and so on.

in mercantile hands ; besides, no later than 1780, the charter of the Company had been renewed, and to deprive it of the superintendence of its own trade was a manifest breach of that charter. Such were the objections raised by the Opposition, and they were largely echoed in the country, where the coalition, as is generally the case in England, was highly unpopular. The feeling out of doors is shown by a well-known caricature which represents the triumphal procession of Carlo Fox Khan, crowned and riding on a state elephant. However, the Bill was triumphantly passed through the House of Commons, where the coalition majority was overwhelming.

But the King, who hated his ministers, and whose pride was touched in its tenderest point by this Bill, was determined that it should never become law ; rather than suffer such indignity he would refuse his assent to the Bill, exerting a prerogative which had lain dormant since the reign of William III., or take refuge, as he was fond of threatening, in Hanover. He was saved from either alternative by a plan suggested to him by Lords Thurlow and Temple, which, although open to the charge of being uncon- *The King procures its* stitutional, prevented the Bill from passing the Upper *rejection.* House. These two noblemen, using the hereditary right of British Peers to advise their sovereign, drew up and laid before George a strong memorandum against the Bill, which they called "a plan to take more than half the royal power, and by that means disable his Majesty for the rest of his reign ;" and Temple suggested that the Bill might be stopped in the House of Lords if the King would authorize him to express his wishes. The King upon this supplied him with a paper to show to any Lord he pleased. The purport of it was, that "his Majesty allowed Earl Temple to say that whoever voted for the India Bill was not only not his friend, but would be considered by him as an enemy, and if those words were not strong enough, Earl Temple might use what. ever words he might deem stronger and more to the purpose." The effect of this intimation, acting upon the minds of waverers and of those who prided themselves in the name of King's friends, was to secure a majority against the Bill. On the 17th of December it was lost by nineteen votes, Lord Stormont, a member of the ministry, voting against it. The King thus assumed the strange position of the opponent of his own responsible ministers. In fact, *His conduct un-* he felt the power of the hated Whigs closing around *constitutional.* him, and thought any measure justifiable which would free him from their grasp and enable him to assume that position which had been the constant aim of his policy. Moreover, he no doubt relied somewhat on the unpopularity excited by the coalition, and on the apparently unprincipled and factious conduct of the united leaders. That his conduct is incompatible with constitutional monarchy there can be no doubt. If he disliked his ministers' measures he had one straightforward course open to him;—he should have dismissed them; if their majority was overwhelming, he should have dissolved Parliament; if he could not command a majority in the new Parliament, he was bound to submit. An underhand opposition to ministers, who are alone responsible to the nation, is entirely destructive of that confidence which is necessary to the very existence of a constitutional monarchy. Of course the uproar raised in the House of Commons was great. Motion after motion condemnatory of the action of the King in the House of Lords was carried by great majorities. The ministry determined that the responsibility of removing them should be left to the King, who, perceiving the necessary consequence of his late step, on the 18th of December, sent the under secretaries to tell the ministers they were dismissed, refusing even to see them personally.

Ministers dismissed

The great Whig party and the great following of Lord North being thus removed from office, it became a question where a ministry was to be sought. The only party remaining was the little section of Chatham's followers, headed by the young Pitt, and reinforced by a portion of the Tories, with whom they may now be considered as incorporated, although for several years Pitt's policy was decidedly Liberal. To this youth of twenty-four the King appealed for assistance, and, relying on his own genius, he had the audacity to accept the struggle, though conscious that he must be defeated on every division. There followed a scene unparalleled in parliamentary history. The Cabinet had to be drawn almost exclusively from the Upper House; Lord Thurlow became Chancellor, Earl Gower President of the Council, Duke of Rutland Privy Seal, Lord Carmarthen and Lord Sydney Secretaries of State, and Lord Howe First Lord of the Admiralty, and this, with Mr. Pitt himself, was the whole Cabinet. In the House of Commons he could rely only on Dundas and his cousin William Grenville. When the writ was moved for a new election for Appleby on Pitt's taking office, it was received with shouts of laughter; no pity or favour was extended to the new minister; Dundas could hardly get a hearing on ministerial business, motions of great· importance were pressed on even though Pitt had not yet taken his seat, and so certain

Pitt accepts the Premiership. 1783.

did Fox feel of restoration to office, that he wrote to a friend in Dublin that he would not dismiss one member of his household till after the 12th of January. On that day Pitt was to make his appearance as Prime Minister. An address *Factious violence of the Opposition 1784.* had been delivered to the King praying against either an adjournment or dissolution, for this was the step which Fox's party chiefly feared. On a favourable reply to this address, short Christmas holidays had been allowed, and the House had to meet again on the 12th. In those few days Pitt had got ready an India Bill, but before he was allowed to produce it Fox had succeeded in carrying no less than five motions against the Government, one of them pointing to "unconstitutional abuse of his Majesty's sacred name." In spite of this Pitt produced his Bill, which was similar in character to the Bill he afterwards carried; on its first reading there was no division, on the second reading, although it was thrown out, the hostile majority, which had been already diminishing, was no more than eight.

Things began to look a little more encouraging for the minister. He determined with great wisdom to give the Opposition rope, and urged them to constant violence by an obstinate *Firmness and sagacity of Pitt* refusal to say whether he meant to dissolve or not. The language of the Opposition had been so violent that the reaction was becoming strongly marked in the country. "It was a contest," said Dr. Johnson, "whether the nation should be ruled by the sceptre of George III. or by the tongue of Fox." All attempts at mediation failed, although many independent members attempted to effect it. Fox's hope was, that if Pitt continued to avoid dissolution the 25th of March would arrive without a new Parliament. On that day the Mutiny Bill expired, and he hoped by refusing to renew it to compel his rival to resign. But the tide had now fairly begun to turn; Pitt's bravery was exciting the sympathy of the people, while the unmeasured virulence of Fox and his party was constantly damaging them. Pitt, too, had won great admiration by refusing for himself, although his private means amounted to scarcely £300 a year, a rich sinecure called the Clerkship of the Pells. This, with a somewhat ironical pride, he had given to Colonel Barré in exchange for the pension which the Rockingham ministry had so scandalously given him. The threats that supplies should be stopped seemed to many moderate people factious and improper, and numerous addresses poured in from the Corporation of London and other towns. On the 8th of March Fox played what may be called his last card; he brought in a paper under the threatening title of "Representation to the King;" after many hours of debate it was passed by a majority of one only. It was plain that the victory of Pitt was secure and that the Opposition had ruined themselves.

Pitt's victory.

Accordingly, when on the next day the Mutiny Bill came on there was no opposition, and having by firmness and moderation fairly weathered the storm, Pitt on the 25th recommended the King to dissolve the Parliament. The elections made it evident that the feeling of the nation was entirely with Pitt; no less than 160 of Fox's friends lost their seats—"Fox's martyrs" they were jocosely called. Several great contests took place, the most notorious of which was that for Yorkshire, where Wilberforce was brought in triumphantly in opposition to the great territorial houses, and that for Westminster, where Fox himself stood against Lord Hood and his old colleague Wray, who had become a ministerialist. The poll was kept open forty days, amid scenes of indescribable excitement. For twenty-three days Fox was at the bottom of the poll, but at length the strenuous canvassing of his friends, added to the charms of Georgiana, Duchess of Devonshire, and other lady politicians, succeeded in placing him second on the list. As more votes however were registered than there were voters, obviously some fraud had been committed, and a scrutiny was granted. Meanwhile, as the Whigs held illegally, no return was made, Westminster was unrepresented, and room had to be made for Fox in the close borough of Kirkwall. It was not till the following session that Pitt, who, with some want of liberality, upheld the conduct of the High Bailiff in refusing the return, was defeated in the House on the subject. The representatives took their seats, and Fox got £2000 damages from the Bailiff.

Dissolution of Parliament and defeat of Whigs 1784.

The great party struggle of the last year, which had terminated in the utter discomfiture of the Whigs and the establishment of the new Tory party under Pitt, had not left much time for the real requirements of the State. India, Ireland, the finances, parliamentary reform, were all matters which pressed for immediate attention. Firm in his parliamentary majority and in the support of the King, Pitt proceeded to handle them. The finances were naturally in a bad condition at the close of an unsuccessful war. The funds were standing only at 56 or 57, the unfunded debt was upwards of £12,000,000, and there was a considerable deficiency in the Civil List. One of the principal sources of the revenue was destroyed by systematic smuggling of tea. Men of otherwise respectable character and consider-

Pressing measures.

Pitt's Budget.

able capital were embarked in this trade. Large vessels brought their tea, and lay off at some distance, distributing their cargoes to small vessels, which landed them here and there on the coast. Regular receiving-houses were established and lines of carriers which brought the tea to the towns. It was estimated that the smuggled tea was at least as much as that which paid duty. Pitt lowered the duty both for this article and for spirits, the other great smuggled commodity, so as to withdraw the temptation from the smugglers. The deficit was made up by a house and window tax; this is known as the Commutation Tax. An Act called the Hovering Act was also passed, which extended the limits of the authority of the revenue officers to four leagues from the coast. Half the unfunded debt Pitt funded, and made up the deficit, which he considered a little below a million, by taxes on various commodities. These arrangements though they show no great novelty, were much applauded at the time.

Having thus cleared the way for general legislation, Pitt proceeded to bring in his India Bill. It was very like the one which had been defeated the preceding year, and was probably chiefly the work of Dundas. The fate of Pitt's India Bill. 1784. Fox's Bills had shown the strength of the India House, while the necessity for some Government control was acknowledged by all parties. The present measure was therefore one of compromise. A new ministerial department was established which should exercise the whole political control of the Company; this was to be called the Board of Control. By it was laid the foundation of that system of double government which continued in force till 1858. All business was to be carried on in the name of the Company, which retained the whole patronage except the appointment of the commander-in-chief, and other higher functionaries, whose appointment was subject to the veto of the Crown; but the Board of Control absolutely dictated the political conduct of the Government. Thus the chartered rights of the Company were left untouched; the balance of influence was not upset by a sudden change of patronage; the Board of Control, being ministerial, passed in or out of office with the ministry, but India was secured against mercantile views of policy by its political management being withdrawn from the hands of a merchant company. It was certainly a less complete Bill than its predecessor, it could not be a permanent arrangement, but tided over the present difficulty, and was carried without serious opposition.

Much more difficult was the settlement of Ireland. The rational

and patriotic demands of the volunteers, which had led to the legislation of 1780 and 1782, had been satisfied by those measures, but had been followed, as is always the case in
Ireland, by agitation of a more revolutionary character. The leadership of the movement had passed from Grattan to Flood, rather a
demagogue than a statesman, and the volunteers, a national and
patriotic body, gradually dwindled to nothing, and in their place
arose a clamorous and revolutionary democracy. The cry put forward was for parliamentary reform, the urgent necessity for which
was indeed obvious. In a Parliament of 300, 116 seats were held by
nominees of no more than 25 proprietors. The Government commanded 186 votes, pledged to them in exchange for the possession or
hope of offices or pensions, 12 members were regarded as honest supporters of the Government, the regular Opposition was about 82, 30
Whig nominees, and 52 members of the popular party. To this Parliament Flood introduced a sweeping measure of reform. A scene
of wild uproar was the consequence, the Bill was thrown
out by a large majority; no better success attended its reintroduction in a more moderate form. The mob rose in
wild disorder, and acts of ferocious cruelty were perpetrated. The
leader of this movement outside Parliament was Napper Tandy, an
ironmonger, who did not scruple to intrigue with the Court of France.
Some of the lower priests were also engaged on the popular side, but
as Flood refused the franchise to the Catholics in his proposition, the
main body held aloof from the movement. This state of disorder
Pitt intended to improve by reforming the Parliament in a more
practical and moderate manner and by commercial arrangements.
All attempts at parliamentary reform had however to be abandoned;
but the minister felt that before any vigorous measures could be
adopted it was necessary to grant justice to the people. He determined therefore to complete the work of 1780, and to establish real
commercial equality between England and Ireland. At the same
time he strongly held that equality of privilege implied
equality of burdens. In accordance with this view
eleven resolutions were brought into the Irish Parliament and
accepted without much opposition. By these the restrictions of trade,
which had already been removed as far as regarded Europe and the
West Indies, would be removed in like manner with regard to the
rest of the world; and with regard to imports, England and Ireland
would become one nation, so that goods landed in Ireland could be
re-imported into England without further duty. In exchange for this,

all the hereditary income of the Crown, which was derived chiefly from customs, beyond the sum of £656,000 was to be applied to the support of the Imperial navy. Thus the money paid would bear a direct proportion to the advantages gained by Ireland by the extension of her trade. Pitt, sure of the economical soundness of the principles on which this Bill was based, only courted full discussion. He underrated the selfishness of the commercial interest. On the resolutions being introduced to the English Parliament, the strongest opposition was raised by merchants and manufacturers, afraid of a fresh competitor; and Fox and Burke, the first of whom was confessedly ignorant of the laws of political economy, turned the opposition to their party purposes. The Bill had to be altered considerably, restrictions with regard to the Asiatic trade had to be continued, thus seriously diminishing the advantage granted to Ireland, while Pitt laid himself open to the charge of encroaching upon the newly-earned independence of that country by trying to establish the commercial superiority of England, since all this commercial legislation was to emanate from the English Parliament. The Whigs took immediate advantage of this error, and, unable to stop the Bill in the English Parliament, used all their eloquence to inflame the patriotic feeling of the Irish. The Bill in its changed form was therefore rejected in Dublin (August), and Pitt began to feel the necessity for that great measure which he completed eighteen years afterwards. If either true parliamentary reform was to be brought about or commercial equality to be established, not only legislative equality, but legislative *union*, it was plain, would be necessary.

[sidenote: Selfish commercial opposition.]

[sidenote: Pitt recognises the necessity for a union.]

This was not the only defeat which the ministry suffered. It was no more successful in its efforts at parliamentary reform in England. In fact, the interest felt in the question had begun to flag; it had been raised to its utmost by the separation between the representatives of the people and the people they represented, which had been so obvious during the administration of Grenville, and by the long and disastrous triumph of royal influence under Lord North. But Pitt's success rested entirely upon the will of the constituencies after the late dissolution, and the people were on the whole satisfied with their representation. But with Pitt, as with his father, the reform of Parliament had always been a favourite object; he now produced a Bill by which he hoped to win all parties to his side, but its very timidity weakened its popularity. He proposed to disfranchise thirty-six rotten boroughs,

[sidenote: Failure of Pitt's Reform Bill.]

and to give the seventy-two seats thus gained to the counties and to London and Westminster. Thus far he was true to his old plan, but afraid of the opposition of borough proprietors, he consented to recognize as a part of the Constitution their rights of proprietorship, and designed to set apart a fund of £1,000,000 to satisfy the claims of the possessors of the boroughs which he wished to destroy. Such as it was the Bill was rejected by a majority of seventy, and Pitt regarded the question henceforward as settled against him. It is to be observed that all these measures, whether successful or not, were such as we should now speak of as Liberal measures.

The success of the Government in its financial schemes, on the other hand, was marked, although the arrangement which at this time excited most admiration has since been recognized as based upon an absurd fallacy. Alarmed at the great increase of the National Debt, and inspired with an honest wish to reduce it, Pitt produced his plan for a sinking fund. His taxes had been so successful, and the financial recovery of the nation at peace and under a firm Government had been such, that he found himself possessed of a surplus closely bordering on a million, and suggested that this million should annually be set aside and vested in commissioners to accumulate at compound interest. It was to be beyond the control of Government, and this fund with its accumulations was to be applied, as circumstances permitted, to the reduction of the debt. The principle is obviously sound as far as it goes, that is to say, what a nation saves it can clearly apply to the purpose of reducing its liabilities, but there the matter ends; there is and can be no peculiar and mysterious power in a sinking fund. But this was not seen by Pitt, or by those who approved of his plan, and when times of difficulty arose, the million went on year by year being religiously set aside, although not only one million, but many millions were yearly borrowed for the purpose of covering the current expenses of the year. Interest, and often much higher interest, was thus paid out on the one side in order that a less interest might be gained on the other. It was not till the year 1828 that this fallacy was finally exposed by Lord Grenville, who, strangely enough, had been the chairman of the committee who first recommended its adoption. It had however been virtually abandoned in 1807. Although he fell into this error, Pitt's financial views were generally broad; thus about this time he entered into a commercial treaty with France, by which, with some very few

His financial success.

Commercial treaty with France. Sept. 1786.

exceptions, prohibitory duties between the countries were repealed, a moderate tariff was established, and the famous Methuen Treaty with Portugal, which had almost excluded French wines, and changed the habits of the English nation, giving them a taste for the hot wines of the Peninsula, was abrogated. He also greatly simplified the custom duties, supplying their place in some instances with excise or customs levied inland, a most beneficial measure, but formerly so unpopular that it had almost proved fatal to the ministry of Walpole, the only great financial minister England had had during the century.

These measures, important as they were, excited little attention in comparison with the threatened impeachment of Warren Hastings. Though, as we have seen, censured, and almost recalled in 1781, the Governor-General had latterly retained his post unmolested, and came home in June 1785 on the natural expiration of his office. At home he was well received, but he had two vindictive enemies in the House of Commons, one, Edmund Burke, whose imagination had always been strongly drawn towards the majestic history of Hindostan, and whose hatred of oppression had been strongly fired by the accounts which had lately been received from India; the other, Philip Francis, the rancorous and defeated rival of the late Governor-General; and Hastings had scarcely arrived in England before Burke gave notice that he should call attention to his conduct. The feeling in England that Hastings had on the whole done a great work was so strong, that, although the ministry had shown him many marks of favour, it is possible that even Burke might have left him untouched had not his injudicious and wearisome agent, Major Scott, challenged inquiry. Burke accepted the challenge, and in April produced specific charges against him, based principally on his war with the Rohillas and on his conduct to Cheyte Singh and the Begums of Oude. Hastings, who was always unable to understand the feeling of the House of Commons, insisted on being personally heard at the bar, and wearied the House by reading a written document of enormous length, which occupied a day and a half in reading. On the first charge, however, with regard to the Rohilla war, a considerable majority was in his favour; it will be remembered that this belonged to the first period of his administration, and it was upon this that he had been already censured; but as Dundas, the original mover of the vote of censure, urged, with much show of right, the fault was an old one, and had been condoned by the subsequent appointment of Hastings as Governor-General

Charges against Warren Hastings.

Hastings and his friends believed that his cause had gained the support of Government and was now secure. Great was their dismay when, upon the second charge with regard to Cheyte Singh, which Pitt supports was brought forward by Fox, Pitt rose and declared, that them. although he regarded Cheyte Singh as the vassal of the Bengal Empire, and liable to be called on for assistance, he could not but regard the infliction of a fine of £500,000 for the non-payment of £50,000 as ridiculously and shamefully exorbitant. On these grounds, he said, he should support the charge, all his friends voted with him, and Fox's resolution passed by a majority of forty. This entirely changed the aspect of affairs, but the lateness of the season (June 1786) rendered it necessary that the completion of the charges should be postponed till the next year. In the February of that year Sheridan, in a speech occupying five hours and forty minutes, produced the charge with regard to the Begums of Oude. So striking was this piece of oratory that it was deemed necessary to adjourn the House lest the excitement produced by it should prevent cool judgment of the matter. Again, and with the same result as before, Pitt both spoke and voted in favour of the charge. Consequent impeachment On these and other charges Burke, in May, founded a 1787 resolution of impeachment, and proceeding to the Upper House, impeached the late Governor-General, who was taken into custody and admitted to bail. The trial did not actually begin till February 1788.

Another question which now arose, and which was in the next year to be of the greatest importance, was the conduct Conduct of the Prince of and character of the Prince of Wales. True to the tradi-Wales. tions and customs of his family, he had allied himself to the enemies of his father, and not only in his political but in his domestic life had much outraged the King's feelings. From the respectable and somewhat repellant family life of the Court, the princes, one and all, took refuge in a disorderly and licentious life. The stern propriety of the father, and the somewhat unlovely rigidity of the mother, undid the work which their thoroughly domestic character should have done. The Prince of Wales had everything in his favour upon his entrance into life. Good-looking, of pleasant manners, of considerable ability, and views at all events nominally liberal, there was nothing to prevent his great popularity. Unfortunately the profligacy of his life, which the world might have pardoned, was the mark of a thoroughly depraved character, which led him into breaches of honour. This fault became very obvious in the year

1787. For some time he had been clamouring for the payment of his debts, and on the King's refusal to discharge them, he had in a huff reduced his establishment and pretended to live like a private gentleman.   Meanwhile he had been entangled in an awkward love affair. Mrs. Fitzherbert, a Roman Catholic lady, had attracted his attention, and refused to listen to his advances unless he would marry her. This he did.   Now, by the Act of Settlement, marriage with a Roman Catholic invalidated all claims to the throne, but by a second statute, the Royal Marriage Act, any marriage contracted without the royal consent was null.   By pleading the second, the Prince could therefore avoid the action of the first, but by so doing was virtually taking away the character of his wife, and obviously evading the law.   With this slur upon his character, he came to the Parliament for the payment of his debts.   The charge against him was raised by Rolle, the member for Devonshire, and Fox, completely duped by his royal friend, was induced to give the fact a flat denial.   The Prince completed his treachery by afterwards disavowing his instructions to Fox.   Such conduct naturally produced a temporary coolness between them.   After so strong a denial, however, it was impossible to refuse the Prince's demand, and his debts were paid, to the amount of £160,000.

The work of the last year was completed by the commencement, in February, of the trial of Warren Hastings.   The trial took place in Westminster Hall, the Peers sitting as judges, presided over by the Lord Chancellor, and the accusations being supported by the managers appointed by the House of Commons, assisted by the most eloquent men in England, among their number, Fox, Burke, Sheridan, and Wyndham.   The very talents of the accusers, together with the exaggerated and unlawyerlike style of Burke, tended to the safety of the accused.   The trial became a mere exhibition of rhetoric ; people crowded to hear the speeches, but withdrew as the legal points were argued, or the evidence produced, while Burke's language was so intemperate that the Lord Chancellor and even the House of Commons censured him. At the same time, in 1789, the gradual change of popular feeling was shown in the trial of Stockdale for libel against the promoters of Hastings' trial.   He was prosecuted at the demand of the Commons, at the Government expense, but was acquitted.   Three years afterwards Burke himself renounced sixteen of his charges, and all interest in the end of the trial gradually disappeared.

The year was marked not only by the completion of old questions.

Trial of Warren Hastings. Feb. 1788.

but by the appearance of a new one. Pitt called attention to the slave

Mot on for
regulating the
slave trade
May 9. 1788

trade. The horrors of this trade had for many years been before the public, and the opposition to slavery had so far been organized, that it had been determined to assault—what it was believed might be overthrown without much difficulty—the actual trade in slaves, and leave the abolition of slavery itself for a future occasion. The horrors of the trade could scarcely be exaggerated. Ships built for the purpose were employed, in which the allowance of room for a slave was five feet and a half in length by one foot four inches in breadth. The extreme height between decks was five feet eight inches, but this was occupied by shelves, upon which the slaves were packed. Sixteen hours a day they remained below, chained to the deck, fed upon a pint of water and two feeds of horse beans. Such conditions of life, for weeks together, in the tropics, not being conducive to health, they were brought up and forced to jump upon the deck, under the influence of the whip, for the sake of exercise. If any difficulty arose, they were tossed overboard without scruple, and English law courts held underwriters answerable for such loss, as arising from the natural perils of the sea. No charge of murder, or even manslaughter, was ever dreamt of. These facts were substantiated by a Committee, presided over by Whitbread, to which a motion of Sir W. Dolben for regulating the trade had been referred, though the witnesses had previously enlarged on the excellence of the ships and the merry dancing of the slaves. But before any real action could be taken, an event occurred which for a moment threatened the stability of the ministry.

In November, after some months of illness, the King was declared

The King's
Illness.
Nov. 1788

incapable of carrying on the business of the country. His illness assumed the form of insanity, and even if he should survive, as was thought doubtful, it seemed plain that a regency would be inevitable. The King's physicians, following the ignorant practice with regard to lunatics which obtained at that time, prescribed the strictest and most galling constraints, separated the King from his wife, refused him the use of knife and fork and razor, and intrusted him to coarse and cruel servants. Having by this means intensified the symptoms, they proceeded to pronounce them incurable. Fortunately for the King, Lady Harcourt was bold enough to recommend Dr. Willis, who, originally a clergyman, had for nearly thirty years been managing a private asylum for lunatics, where he had met with much success. On being summoned, he at once declared he could cure the King, and the Queen and Pitt placed him in his hands with implicit confidence. Thus when, after some prorogation, Parliament assembled in December, a committee which had examined the medical evidence expressed a hope of the King's recovery. Armed with this report, Pitt moved for an examination of precedents before arranging the regency, while Fox, forgetful of the Prince's late duplicity, and clutching eagerly at the power which seemed just within his grasp, asserted that precedents were useless, as "the heir-apparent had an inherent right to assume the reins of government." As Pitt immediately pointed out, this was to rob the Parliament of all power in the matter, although it had twice been regarded as competent to change the succession to the throne. The vehemence of the Whig party in fact overreached itself, and enabled Pitt, who firmly believed that he was on the point of being driven from office, with a somewhat ostentatious show of carelessness as to the favour of the future King or Regent, to produce a Bill nominating indeed the heir-apparent as the Regent, but under strict limitations. The principle he laid down was that, as the King would in all probability recover, he should, on resuming his functions, find things as little altered as possible. He therefore refused to the Prince of Wales the right of making Peers, or granting places, in reversion or for any term except during his Majesty's pleasure, while the care of the King's person and household was left in the Queen's power. Nothing, probably, but the feeling that the Prince was thoroughly immoral could have allowed Pitt to produce so stringent a Bill. It was not indeed passed, for the necessity of passing it was prevented by the recovery of the King. This had been the work of Dr. Willis, who, by mingled kindness and firmness, the removal of all the ridiculous restraints the King's doctors had laid upon him, had succeeded in restoring his self-respect and bringing him back almost to his usual state of sanity, although for some weeks longer he persistently believed, while showing the tenderest affection for the Queen, that he was deeply in love with one of the ladies of the Court.

Pitt's faithful adherence to George during his illness, and the firmness with which he had insisted on keeping things unchanged, though at the risk of total loss of favour for himself, bound the King to him more closely than ever, and for many years to come his position was quite unassailable. Up to this time Pitt's policy had been enlarged and liberal in all directions. He had contrived to realize his father's plan, and resting on the authority of the Crown, but independent as a minister, had destroyed the monopoly of power so long held by the great Whig factions.

This he had done without subserviency and without deserting the
.Liberal principles in which he had been trained, but he could not
but feel that he rested primarily on the royal support, and insensibly
his policy had become the royal policy, and he was pledged to support the influence of the Crown. This gradual and almost unobserved
change was called into active exhibition by the events which were
happening in Europe.

GEORGE III.—*CONTINUED.*

1789—1820.

First Lords of the Treasury.		Chancellors of the Exchequer	
Dec	1783	Pitt	Dec. 1783. Pitt.
March	1801	Addington.	March 1801. Addington.
May	1804	Pitt	May 1804. Pitt.
Jan	1806	Grenville.	Jan. 1806 Petty.
April	1807	Portland	April 1807. Perceval
Oct.	1809	Perceval.	June 1812. Vansittart.
June	1812.	Liverpool.	

Secretaries of State.

June	1789	{ Carmarthen. { W. Grenville.	Jan.	1806	{ Spencer. { Fox.
June	1791	{ Dundas. { W. Grenville.	Sept.	1806	{ Spencer. { Howick.
July	1794	{ Portland. { W. Grenville.	April	1807	{ Canning { Hawkesbury
March	1801	{ Pelham { Hawkesbury	Oct.	1809	{ Wellesley { Ryder.
May	1804	{ Harrowby { Hawkesbury.	Feb.	1812	{ Castlereagh. { Ryder.
	June	1812	{ Castlereagh. { Sidmouth.		

THE year which followed the King's recovery saw the opening of the Great Revolution in France. This event produced ultimately an entire alteration in the character of Pitt's **Effect of the** policy, and a split between Burke and Fox which **French Revolu-** virtually annihilated for the time the Whig party, and **England.** rendered Pitt absolutely pre-eminent; but it was not till more than a year had passed that its full effect was felt in England, although from its first outbreak it had a tendency to exaggerate party differences, and brought into more striking contrast the principles of those who, like Pitt, desired the maintenance of a strong royal power, of those who, like Burke, looked no further than the establishment of an aristocratic constitution, and of those who saw with pleasure every advance towards the realization of those dreams of class equality which for more than a century had been stirring in Europe. When at length the influence of the Revolution became irresistible, England was in a position abroad to take a leading part in the European opposition to its principles, and at home social changes had occurred which rendered such a course of policy inevitable.

Although Pitt was probably aware that he was not a great war minister, or fitted, as his father had been, to inspire the nation with enthusiasm in the midst of danger, he by no means forgot to uphold the dignity of his country ; and his management of foreign affairs certainly raised England from the depres. sion into which she had sunk after the loss of her colonies, and the disadvantageous peace contracted with France and Spain at the close of the war.

Political development of England.

One of the first instances in which this reviving spirit was shown was the affair of Nootka Sound. Spain, raising the arrogant claim that to her belonged the whole west coast of America, seized an English ship in Nootka Sound, in Vancouver's Island, and destroyed our settlement there. Upon this, Pitt, drawing closer his alliance with Prussia and Holland, and going so far as to increase largely the number of men in the navy, managed to exact from Spain a withdrawal of this claim and a restoration of English property, granting in exchange an assurance that illicit trade with the Spanish colonies should be checked.

Affair of Nootka Sound.

But far more important than this single exhibition of determination against a country so decayed as Spain was the successful policy which Pitt pursued with regard to the general policy of Eastern Europe. The first opening which occurred was in Holland. In that country there existed, as usual, a constant strife between two great parties, the party of the Republicans and the party of the Prince of Orange. Of old the republican party had meant the party of the aristocratic and wealthy merchants of the country. The party of the Prince of Orange had almost without exception been favoured by the bulk of the people. But ideas had been rapidly growing ; republicanism had assumed a somewhat different meaning. The war between ruler and aristocracy had been changing to a rivalry between the ruler, supported by the lovers of order and fixed authority, and those whose views were of a more democratic stamp. But the democrats of Holland still regarded themselves as the legitimate descendants of the republican party, and inherited the foreign policy of their predecessors. Like them, they sought the support and assistance of France, while the Stadtholder and his friends regarded England as their chief support. The agitation in Holland had been so vigorous that the Prince of Orange had been forced to withdraw to Nimeguen, leaving the Government in the hands of his rivals (1785). Here was a manifest danger to England. If the democrats remained in possession of the country Holland would become little else than a dependency of France, instead of what it had so often been, the

Forms an alliance with Holland.

firm ally of England. At the present moment France was more particularly ready to give it support. Vergennes, the French minister, was anxious to retain some sort of prestige for the Government, which was rapidly sinking in power and credit under the reckless and wasteful management of Calonne. No better opportunity could have been afforded him than the chance of undertaking a successful piece of diplomacy, or of war, in behalf of a democratic party, whose opinions had much in harmony with the rapidly increasing revolutionary feeling of France. Moreover, the commercial world of France was full of hostility to the late treaty with England; and as Vergennes had contracted that treaty, he hoped to wipe out some of his unpopularity by raising difficulties as to the completion of that part of it which touched upon the French trade with India. There the Dutch and French interests both led them to oppose England as far as possible, and a war would almost certainly have commenced had not Vergennes died. At the same time Calonne gave place to Lomenie de Brienne, and it was uncertain what course he would pursue. The question was brought to a crisis by a curious act of ill-judged violence on the part of the democrats, who seized upon the person of the Princess of Orange while she was visiting the Hague (June 1787), probably in the hope of attempting some reconciliation. As the Princess of Orange was the sister of the King of Prussia, he was able to use the attack upon so near a relative as a fair pretext for interfering on behalf of royalty. He marched 20,000 men to the frontiers under the Duke of Brunswick, thus affording Pitt the opportunity he desired of reconnecting England with European allies. He made common cause with Prussia, promising the assistance of the English fleet, and sent to demand from France an explanation of the 15,000 men they had assembled at Givet. The French refused an explanation, promised assistance to the States-General, and proceeded to send their troops into the country. The united arms of Prussia and England were successful, the Stadtholder was restored to power (Oct. 1787) with even less restriction than usual. The friendship thus begun ripened into alliance ; and Holland, now entirely in the English interest, joining with England and Prussia, a sort of triple alliance was entered into for securing the peace of Europe, and to support the principle of the balance of power, in which Pitt was a firm believer.

The rising influence of Russia was the great object of Pitt's dread. The progress of that country was very threatening; its vast bulk and unknown resources, and the success which *His efforts to oppose Russia*

had hitherto attended its progress since the time of Peter the Great,
had rendered it a very formidable element in the European system.
Chatham had indeed regarded its growth as advantageous to Europe,
the counterpoise at once to the power of the French and of the
Prussians. His son took a different view, justified by the evident
attempts of the Empress to increase her power at the expense of
Turkey, and thus to secure the Black Sea, if not the Mediterranean,
and by the ever-increasing influence which she exercised over both
Prussia and Austria. Even the great Frederick had found himself
obliged to court his formidable neighbour; again and again his
brother, Prince Henry, had visited St. Petersburg; while Joseph II. of
Austria was entirely led away by the Czarina's greatness. Already the
greater part of Poland had been absorbed by that Empire; there
now remained two powers at either extremity of the great mass of
Russia which might easily have suffered a similar treatment. These
were Turkey and Sweden. In the year 1787 the aggression for which
Europe was waiting took place. The Emperor Joseph had a meeting
with the Czarina, and travelled with her in her carriage as she went
to visit the Crimea. He was there thoroughly dazzled by the greatness of the scheme which she unfolded to him. Turkey and Greece
were to be conquered, and the old Empire of the East to be re-
established. In exchange, it was hinted that something like a
Western Empire should be constituted, and Italy, as of old, be placed
under the Austrian sway. But the success of the Czarina and the
Emperor was hampered by the sudden and vigorous assaults upon
Russia from the side of Sweden under its King Gustavus III. This
attack in its turn threatened to be neutralized by the intervention
of the Danes, who were connected in friendship with the Czarina.
Such, then, was the position of affairs which Pitt had to consider,
in reference always to what he believed of vital importance, the
European balance,—on the one side, Austria, Russia, and Denmark;
on the other, Turkey and Sweden.

There were three countries against which Pitt could put in practice
Alliance with   what appears to have been his fixed plan of European
Prussia, Holland action; desirous of peace, and thinking few questions
and Sweden.   of sufficient importance to authorise him in plunging
Europe into war, he hoped, by a show of superior power on the part
of himself and his allies, to uphold the dignity of England and the
existing balance of power. He began with the weakest. He drew
closer his friendship with Prussia, and his threats in union with
that power detached Denmark (Oct. 1788) from its allies. thus

ridding Sweden of the enemy in its rear, and allowing it to carry on its aggressive movements, which seemed so successful as a diversion in favour of Turkey. An alliance with Holland, Sweden, and Prussia secured the maintenance of peace on the part of Denmark. He then turned to Austria; for the danger from the joint attack on Turkey had become really imminent when the strong fortress of Oczakow fell (Dec. 1788) into the hands of the Czarina's favourite Potemkin. The opportunity was favourable. Joseph II. had died, in 1790, just as all his plans, whether of aggressive ambition on the side of Turkey or of domestic reform in Flanders, had seemed to terminate in failure; while in Flanders a spirit of insurrection, too powerful for him to suppress, had been excited by certain reforms which he there introduced. Indeed, domestic dangers had threatened him on all sides. His successor, Leopold, was desirous of securing the friendship of French and German powers to aid him in his election to the Imperial Crown; and under threat of an immediate invasion from Prussia, which Pitt had instigated, and impressed with the rising danger to all monarchies from the events which were occurring in France, he consented to conclude Procures the Convention of Reichenbach. in August 1790 the Convention of Reichenbach and to withdraw from the Turkish war. Twice, then, Pitt's policy of intervention, combined with threats, but without actual warfare, had been thoroughly successful. The position of England began to stand higher abroad, and the country had again been brought into close connection with its old German allies.

His third intervention was less successful. The Czarina, left to herself both by friends and enemies, persisted in her course, and the fall of Ismail in December was marked by astonishing barbarities. Pitt thought to act upon Fails in his intervention with Russia the Russian Empress as, in conjunction with Prussia, he had acted upon Austria. He demanded that a peace should be made upon the *status quo* before the war, and threatened to support his demand by arms. An increase of the fleet was indeed ordered, but Pitt was mistaken both in the temper of the English and in that of the Russian Empress. The isolated threat of one country standing without allies did not seem to her very terrible; to the people of England the danger of a Russian aggression was of little importance. Pitt found it necessary to change his policy and withdraw his threat, and was content to allow Russia to conclude a peace by which she obtained the territory between the Bug and the Dniester and the fortress of Oczakow (Jan. 1792).

But it was not only in its political position that England had
developed with extraordinary rapidity after the American War. The whole condition of those industrial
arts which give work to the lower orders was
changed, and an enormous impulse given to the employment of
industry. In spite of the constant complaints of those who
were bent upon asserting the decline of the nation, the population
had been gradually increasing ever since the Revolution of 1688;
the rate of increase in the thirty years preceding 1780 was about
40,000 a year. This increase of population had already begun to
call fresh land into cultivation; between 1760 and 1770 no less than
a thousand enclosure Bills were passed. The improved processes of
husbandry did even more than the mere extent of cultivable area to
increase the productive power of agriculture. But this agricultural
production could never have increased at the rate it did had it not
been that the proportion between consumers and producers of food
was rapidly being altered; for it was this period which changed
England from an agricultural to a manufacturing country, and placed
the weight of population, which had hitherto been greater in the
South, entirely in the North. By successive steps all the great improvements in spinning and weaving were introduced; the discovery
that iron could be worked as well with pit coal as with charcoal gave an
immense impetus to the second great branch of industry; and the improvement in the steam engine, which enabled machinery to be worked
irrespective of local peculiarities, spread the manufactures, which had
hitherto nestled among the hills for the sake of obtaining water-power,
into all parts of the coal-producing districts. This burst of industry of
necessity produced great economic changes. The employment of labour
in manufactories tended to increase the population rapidly. The increase of numbers, the growth of wealth among the manufacturers, called
into activity more skill in agriculture, and demanded the occupation
of more land. Land to which recourse is had under this pressure is
naturally the worse land; it therefore requires more labour to produce its crop, and the most laboriously produced crop sets the value
of the whole; the prices of the necessaries of life began rapidly to
rise. Though the use of machinery made many things cheaper, and
improved methods of husbandry prevented prices from rising as they
would otherwise have done, as a general rule, while the price of
luxuries decreased, the price of necessaries rose. Wages did not rise
with a proportionate rapidity, and it was still a question whether, if
the French war had not intervened, the relation between food and

Industrial development of England.

consumption, between prices and wages, would have been satisfactorily arranged. It was however evident that all these improvements, while they created great wealth for the middle and mercantile classes, by no means rendered the position of the mechanic and artisan easier, while, at the same time, higher and more intelligent employment, and the more sedentary life led by the mechanic, were well suited to foster habits of thought, and to make the half-educated man a shallow reasoner, ready to accept crude ideas as to the measures best fitted to produce improvement in the social position of himself and his class ; and such ideas, emanating from France, had been for some time widely spread among the people.

Thus, while England had gradually resumed her commanding position abroad, and was ready with allies to join in any external movement, and while the growing wealth of the mercantile world was rendering it daily more certain Active condition of England abroad and at home. that any such movement would be in a conservative direction, the people—increased in numbers and intelligence, but not bettered in their general condition—were becoming ready to lend a willing ear to any measures which promised to improve the political position of their class. And it was just at this time that the French Revolution broke out.

On the 5th of May 1789 the States-General of France was assembled for the first time since the year 1614. The causes of this momentous event, which produced nothing less than a complete change in the history of the world, were of Causes of the French Revolution ancient growth ; the explosion had been slowly preparing ever since Louis XIV. had completed the mistaken policy of centralization, and had been able to say that the King and the State were one. The power and importance of the Crown had been secured at the cost of the destruction or degradation of all the conservative elements of society. The nobility, deprived of their local power, had been summoned to the capital to swell the splendour of the Court ; without duties they still continued to enjoy privileges, while the administrative power was practically centred in the hands of the royal intendants; they were exempt from direct taxation, and known to their tenantry and dependants only by the feudal dues which they exacted, and by certain remnants of feudal services they could still claim. The judicial body, the "nobility of the robe," held their position, not by merit or by legal knowledge, but by purchase. The upper clergy were drawn to the Court like the nobles, and lived in splendour, while the village curé had hardly the means of livelihood. The people, oppressed by unjust taxation, excluded from all hope of bettering their condition, saw themselves deserted by their natural guardians and leaders, who seemed to enjoy wealth wrung from their toil, and honours earned by no merit of their own, but solely on the ground of birth. The misery of their position was aggravated by the constant recurrence of famines, and they saw with rage the corn trade so manipulated by men in the highest position as to all appearance to increase the scarcity. But an oppressed people will suffer long in silence unless the temper of the class above them be such as to favour the expression of their discontent. Such a temper had been called into existence among the thinking middle classes by the growth of sceptical and rationalistic philosophy.   Drawn originally from English sources, from the writings of the philosophers of the English Revolution, this form of thought had found its exponent in Voltaire, from the keen shafts of whose wit no abuse and no institution was secure.   Montesquieu had pushed the same spirit of inquiry into political and constitutional questions, and Rousseau, more sentimental and spiritual in his views, had supplied a firmer but no less revolutionary basis to society than was afforded by the purely negative teaching of Voltaire. The literary power of these men make them the best known exponents of the spirit of the time, but the spirit itself was prevalent everywhere. Thus, while the institutions of the country were radically bad, they were exposed to the fiercest and most destructive criticism, and ideas of the possibility and rightfulness of a happier state of things were suggested to the public mind. The conduct of the Court and Government was not of a character to blunt the criticisms directed against them ; the finances were in a state of hopeless disorder. The accession of Louis XVI. had for a moment raised hopes of a change of system ; Turgot, an honest and able man of the widest views, was summoned to the ministry. But as his plan included of necessity retrenchment on the part of the Court and the taxation of the privileged classes, Court, nobles, and magistracy made common cause against him, and he found their opposition too strong for him. The same fate attended every effort at reform. Minister after minister was called to office, content either to follow the old course, which was inevitably leading to bankruptcy, or obliged to yield before the selfish opposition of the privileged classes. In turn, Clugny, Necker, and Calonne withdrew discomfited. At length, in 1787, the Cardinal Lomenie de Brienne accepted the difficult post. Like his predecessors, he soon found that there was no resource but the extension of taxation This brought him into collision with the Parlement, the chief court of justice, whose members were drawn from among the privileged class.. They contrived for a while to give their opposition the appearance of a popular movement against the power of the Crown : they even went so far as to declare that the right of extending taxation resided in the States-General alone. It was in vain that the King superseded the Parlement, and produced a new and by no means injudicious constitution ; the mention of the States-General had seemed to open a new view to the people ; nothing short of them would now be accepted. The new constitution fell hopelessly to the ground ; the King found it necessary to recall Necker, the only minister who had enjoyed any popular confidence, and his triumphant return was speedily followed by the meeting of the States.

The assembling of the States-General, which was by many regarded with hope as the close of the difficulties of France, proved but the beginning of troubles. The unprivileged classes had at length obtained the means of expressing their wants, and would be satisfied with nothing short of complete revolution. Unfortunately, the King, a well-meaning man, with a real love for his people, was of a slow intellect, and easily guided by those around him. He fell into the hands of the princes and courtiers, and was induced to make common cause with the privileged classes, which were at first the real object of attack. When the Commons, or Tiers Etat, declared themselves the real representation of the nation, and changed the States-General into a National Assembly, he attempted to check them by a royal sitting, only to find his authority disregarded. The Commons assembled in the Tennis Court at Versailles (June 20), swore to perfect the constitution, and became the dominant power in the nation. An attempt to check their further advance by force of arms, the collection of troops around Paris, the removal of the popular minister Necker and the appointment of the Marshal de Broglie to the command of the army, drove Paris to insurrection. The thorough untrustworthiness of the army was proved ; the Bastille fell (July 14) ; the National Guard sprang into existence ; and a revolutionary Commune at the Hôtel de Ville governed the capital. The power of the sword passed into the hands of the people. Though the Assembly continued the work of the constitution, though, on the 4th of August, the aristo. cracy, in a moment of wild enthusiasm, surrendered all its old feudal rights, the mistrust of the Parisians, aggravated by the famine and the difficulty of subsistence, continued to increase. The Court im-

Assembly of the States-General May 5, 1789

prudently gave colour to its mistrust, Lafayette, at the head of the National Guard, desired to get the management of the Revolution more entirely in his own hands.   On the 6th of October a crowd of National Guards and starving women marched to Versailles and brought the King in triumph to Paris.   He was followed by the

The King brought to Paris. Oct. 6.

National Assembly, which henceforward worked under the eyes of the Parisian Commune and people.   The prestige of royalty disappeared, the King was in fact a prisoner in his own capital; the power had passed even from the National Assembly, and was centred in the people of Paris.

Such scenes, marked by acts of sanguinary vengeance on the part

Excitement produced in England.

of the people, and showing the absolute powerlessness of the old system of Louis XIV., could not fail to excite the strongest interest in Europe.   Nowhere was this more the case than in England.   To some it appeared that our great enemy was perishing before our eyes of its own natural decay; while from another point of view, to lovers of liberty, there was a whole world of hope in the vigorous life exhibited by a people, downtrodden as the French lower orders were believed to be; to another party the hurried and irregular vehemence which had marked the changes in France seemed proof only of an anarchy shocking to all respect for form or antiquity, and sad evidence against the possibility of an orderly growth of reform.   "The French have shown themselves," said Burke, "the ablest architects of ruin that have hitherto existed in the world.   They have done their business for us as rivals in a way which twenty Ramillies or Blenheims could never have done." "How much is it the greatest event that ever happened in the world and how much the best," said Fox after the taking of the Bastille. While a third view, and this at first was Pitt's, rested complacently on the possible approximation of the Government of France to a constitutional monarchy similar to that of England.

The three years which elapsed between 1789 and the end of 1792

First reactionary movement.

drew more distinctly the line which separated the two first of these opinions, and proved that the third was untenable.   It was clear from the first which of them would ultimately gain the upper hand among the governing classes in England.   Already, as early as March 1790, a proposition for the relief of Protestant Dissenters, and for the abolition of Test and

Rejection of the Abolition of Tests and of the Reform Bill

Corporation Acts, which had been lost by only a small majority the preceding year, was thrown out by overwhelming numbers.   A Bill for the reform of the representation, introduced by Flood, though Pitt had several times himself brought the subject forward, met with a similar fate; and shortly before the meeting of the new Parliament on November 25th, Burke issued what may be regarded as the manifesto of his party in his work entitled "Reflections on the French Revolution." It was **Burke's** called forth by signs of the sympathy which the French **"Reflections** **on the French** Revolution was meeting in England. Its more enthusi- **Revolution."** astic admirers had determined to reap what advantages they could from the present state of excitement, and two societies—the Constitutional Society, founded a few years before, and the Revolution Society, an old established body connected with the Dissenting interest, and intended to support the principle of the Revolution of 1688—had entered upon a course of renewed activity. On its anniversary, in November 1789, the Revolution Society had not only listened to an inflammatory and revolutionary discourse by Dr. Price, a Unitarian minister, but had also sent an address of sympathy, signed by Lord Stanhope, their President, to the National Assembly, by whom it had been rapturously received. It was upon this text chiefly that Burke wrote. His book had a wonderful success, 30,000 copies were speedily sold, and writers have been found bold enough to imply that the safety of Europe was owing to this work. In truth, Burke saw more clearly than those around him the inevitable course of the Revolution; he foresaw its excesses and its miserable end in a military despotism; he saw, too, that it must of necessity become prose- lytizing. Terrified by these dangers, and unable to conceive the excellence of any government unlike our own, which was at that time a highly aristocratic limited monarchy, he did not see the truths which the French Revolution embodied, and which, had they been wisely directed and not rudely assailed, would have allowed Europe to pass into the new and inevitable phase of progress for which it is still struggling, without the constant outbreaks of passion on one side or the other which have marked the last seventy years. This work drew forth many replies, the most important of which were Macintosh's "Vindiciæ Gallicæ" and Thomas Paine's "Rights of Man,"—the first a temperate and excellent work of the man who was afterwards to be one of the greatest philosophical statesmen in England, the other the rough but sensible production of a revolutionist by profession.

The sentiments which Burke had declared in his essay he soon took an opportunity of declaring in Parliament. The **The Canada** question before the House was a new constitution for **Bill.** Canada. This was called for by the extremely antago- **1791.**

nistic character of the inhabitants of the two parts of the colony.
The inhabitants of Lower Canada were French, and used to French
habits, those of Upper Canada entirely English. The province was
in future to be divided, and the constitution of the Upper Province
assimilated as nearly as possible to the English model. Hereditary
peerages even were to be established. The Bill, granting as it did a
sort of self-government to the colony, was a wise one, but Fox opposed
it, and took the opportunity of speaking in high praise of the new
constitution of France. Some days afterwards, upon the same
measure, Burke arose and proceeded to reply, inveighing strongly

Breach between Fox and Burke. May 6, 1791. against the Revolution. His own side vociferously called
him to order; he persisted in his speech, deploring that
he should be obliged to break with his friends, but ready,
as he said, to risk all, and with his last words to exclaim, "Fly from
the French constitution." Fox whispered there was no loss of friends,
but Burke rejoined, " I have done my duty at the price of my friend;
our friendship is at an end." Fox rose afterwards, and with tears
in his eyes repeated that he regarded Burke as his master and
teacher in politics, but he could not withdraw what he had said in
praise of the French constitution; and thus the friendship of years
was severed, and Burke was ranked with the ministerialists.

But it was not only in Parliament that the strong division of
The Birmingham riots. July 1791. opinion caused by the Revolution was beginning to be
evident. The conservative temper of the upper and
middle classes was shown clearly in the riots at Birmingham. The friends of the Revolution had determined to have
a public dinner to celebrate the anniversary of the taking of the
Bastille. The dinner was chiefly planned by Dr. Priestley, a Unitarian minister, a man of much scientific repute. Hearing that his
movement was unpopular, he attempted to postpone the dinner, from
which he was himself absent; some eighty persons however met, and
in the evening a fierce riot broke out against them; from Thursday
till Sunday the riots continued, Dr. Priestley's house and library
were destroyed, and much wanton mischief done. It was constantly
reported, though never proved, that the magistrates of the district,
far from trying to check the rioters, had been seen urging them on.

Up till this point Pitt had certainly shown no sign of yielding to
Pitt's policy as yet unchanged. the conservative feeling of the country. He had declared
distinctly that he intended to pursue a policy of neu-
trality, to hold carefully aloof from any interference in the domestic
affairs of France, and had even entirely neutralized the effect of the

Convention of Pilnitz (Aug. 1791) by refusing to accede to the project of concerted action on the part of European powers which had there been broached. He even felt so certain of the continuance of peace, that his Budget, in the spring of the year 1792, was framed entirely upon a peace footing. He suggested the diminution of the number of sailors by 2000 ; he allowed the subsidiary treaty with Hesse to come to an end, and drew up a plan for the reduction of the interest of the Funds from 4 to 3½ or 3 per cent. He even continued his measures of improvement; he again supported, in a speech of unusual excellence, the immediate abolition of the slave trade, although without success ; while, in conjunction with his great opponent, he carried through a Bill for a change in the libel law known as Fox's Libel Bill, which placed in the hands of juries the right of determining not only the fact of the publication of a libel, but the more important question whether the matter published was in its character libellous or not. The opposition offered to this Bill by Lord Chancellor Thurlow cost him his position ; the Great Seal was put into commission. But the crisis had in fact arrived. The events which had taken place in France, and which continued to take place during the year 1792, and the corresponding excitement aroused in England, were gradually driving the minister to the persuasion that his peaceful policy of non-intervention was no longer tenable.

After its removal to Paris in October 1789, the Assembly, now under the influence of the Jacobin Club, and watched by the Parisians, proceeded rapidly in its work of destruction and reconstitution. All local arrangements and provincial powers disappeared when France was divided into Departments; the Crown lost its hold upon the judicial system, which was now grounded upon a popular basis; the Church became a department of the State, and the necessities of the State were supplied by selling its vast property, or, as purchasers were not forthcoming, by issuing bills payable in Church lands, called assignats. It became plain that the power of the Crown, and with it the power of the executive, was entirely disappearing. Nothing could save it but one of two courses—the King might become a traitor to his country, throw himself into the arms of his brother potentates, and begin a war of kings against peoples, or, withdrawing from his capital, rally round him all the conservative elements which yet remained in France. This was the plan of the one great man of the Revolution, Mirabeau; but Mirabeau died in April 1791; and in June of the same year the King adopted the other

Progress of the French Revolution.

The King's flight to Varennes. June 1791

and worse course, fled from Paris, and was arrested at Varennes.
He was brought back a prisoner, and remained with suspended authority till the Assembly in September, hurriedly completing its work
of constitution-making, resigned its office.   The King then resumed
his authority at the head of the new monarchical constitution, but with
power strangely clipped, and with an Assembly the leading members
of which, the Girondins (so called because their leaders were
representatives from the Gironde, a district near Bordeaux), eager and
ambitious men, preferred theoretically a republic, and believed that
their power would be best secured by plunging France into a war.
It is not in fact true to assert, as is commonly done, that it was the
attacks of the combined monarchs of Europe which drove France to
war.   Much sympathy was no doubt felt for the disasters of the
The Girondin   royal family, and the representations of the emigrant
ministry de-   nobles and princes had met with some success in Russia
clares war.
April 1792.   and Sweden.   But both those countries were far off.
The more immediate antagonists of France—Austria and Prussia—
were prevented by their domestic jealousies, their fear of Russia,
and their relations with Poland, from thinking seriously of an open
assault upon France.   It was for their own ends that the Girondins
stirred up the war spirit in France, and it could best be fostered by
exciting the popular feelings by suggestions of interference on the
part of foreign kings with the new-born liberty of the country, and
by hinting that the King himself was a party to this conspiracy.
Thus, taking advantage of the strong sympathy which foreign
courts expressed for the cause of royalty, the Girondins demanded, in an
overbearing tone, immediate and satisfactory replies to their diplomatic
questions, and failing these, declared war upon Austria in the month
of April 1792.   Their declaration of war was speedily followed by the
reality of that union between Austria and Prussia which they had
falsely urged as an excuse for it.   But the Girondins had overreached
themselves: by exciting the popular feeling against the King they
had played directly into the hands of the Jacobins: and when the
King, in June 1792, discarded his Girondin ministry and attempted
to rule with something like independence, it was only with the aid
of the Jacobins that they ultimately returned to power.   For it was
by this extreme party, still further excited by the injudicious and
The King   threatening manifesto which the Duke of Brunswick
suspended.   had issued on the 25th of July, and by the ill success of
Aug. 10.
        the opening of the war, that the great insurrection of
the 10th of August was carried out.   The King was suspended from

his functions, the Tuileries were taken, and though the Gironde was nominally restored, the power of the State was really in the hands of the Jacobins and the revolutionary Commune. The Legislative Assembly lingered but a few weeks longer, to give place in September to a National Democratic Convention. The brief space Massacres of between the 10th of August and the 21st of Septem- September ber was filled by the terrible consequences of the unbridled triumph of the people. The royalist prisoners were murdered in the prisons, the revolutionary Commune established in Paris, and when the Convention met, in the midst of fear at home and fear Declaration of of the advancing· Prussians abroad, its first step was the Republic. of necessity the declaration of the Republic and the Sept 21, 1792 dethronement of the King.

Almost on the same day that the Convention opened, the advance of the Prussians had been suddenly and unexpectedly Revolutionary checked. Dumouriez had occupied the Passes of the character of Argonnes, Kellermann had fought the "cannonade" of the war. Valmy, and the Prussians, bargaining for a safe retreat, began to hurry homeward with ignoble speed. From this time onward the character of the war changed, and became really dangerous to Europe. A party more energetic than the Girondins was now in power. Dumouriez had always recommended the conquest of Belgium for political reasons ; but war assumed a different aspect now that it was in the hands of the Jacobins ; it went hand in hand with the propagation of revolutionary ideas. The victory of Jemmappes opened the road to Belgium ; in the South, Nice and Savoy completed the desired frontier of the Alps ; and the temper in which these conquests had been achieved was rendered obvious when, a few days after the battle of Jemmappes, the celebrated decree of the 19th of November was issued, promising fraternity to all nations desirous Edict of of liberty, and when, two days afterwards, Savoy was Fraternity. formed into a new department as the Department of Nov. 19, 1792. Mont Blanc. If further proof was needed of the character of the war, it was afforded by the peremptory orders which were issued to disregard all treaty obligations and to open the navigation of the Scheldt, which treaty after treaty, guaranteed by France and other countries, had closed, and the opening of which could not but bring France directly into opposition both to Holland and to England. The chief points to be remembered as affecting England are the declaration of war with Austria, sought by the French, and upon old fashioned principles ; the fall of the Girondins, practically completed on the 10th of August; the union of Austria and Prussia produced by the war, but not contracted formally till after the death of Leopold; the advance of the allies; the consequent establishment of the Jacobins; the massacres of September; the summoning of the Convention; the check to the allies at Valmy; the renewal of the war of aggression upon different principles and with different success, those principles being illustrated by the ordering of the opening of the Scheldt and the appropriation of Savoy; while in Paris the completion of the second stage of the Revolution was marked by the suspension and trial of the King.

It was thus, with an enlarged knowledge of the principles and Change of inevitable course of the French Revolution, that Pitt had opinion in England as to to choose his conduct, and that in the course of this year the Revolution. (1792) the English people finally divided itself into parties, and in Parliament the old party names of Whig and Tory, which had in fact since the Hanoverian succession lost their significance, assumed a new meaning. The first movements of the Revolution were generally hailed with enthusiasm in England. In the grand march of the first days of the States-General and National Assembly there was nothing at first obvious to shock English feeling. On the surface it appeared only as if France had discovered, and was determined to realize, the same truths which England had already discovered; the people and the Crown appeared to be preparing to act hand in hand against the monopoly of the privileged classes, against the Divine right of kings, and for the establishment of that official royalty which already existed among us. To the leaders of the Whigs, who still erroneously believed that that party was the really Liberal party, there was everything to excite enthusiasm in the movement of the people, while Pitt himself could scarcely fail to recognize that the very same process was being carried out to which he owed his own elevation. But, by extraordinary mismanagement on the part of the French Court, and by the sluggish, uncertain character of the King, it came to pass that the cause of royalty became unfortunately and indissolubly connected with the cause of the privileged classes. The direction of the Revolution was shifted, and the assault was directed not only against them, but against the Crown ; and not only against the Crown, in the sense that hereditary kingship was attacked, but also against all vigorous executive of which the King, even in his official capacity, might be regarded as the representative. Now Pitt's administration may be regarded as a popular triumph due to the union of King and people. It was

quite untrue in England that the interests of the Crown and aristocracy were one; the power of the Crown, in so far as it was antagonistic to the power of the great families, was favourable to liberty.
Nevertheless, the ideas of the French Revolution did in fact receive
considerable sympathy in England, as was rendered more and more
visible daily. The amount of that sympathy assumed an exaggerated
appearance under the influence of the fear and horror created by the
excesses in Paris, and the relation of classes which had not existed in
England, but which those who sympathized with the Revolution chose
to believe existed, did in fact arise. The choice seemed again to be
offered between people and King. And all the privileged classes,
and all the propertied classes, recognizing that a strong executive
meant order, and that a strong executive was represented by the
King, speedily made their choice, and gathered round the King.

There was thus formed a new Tory party, having for its watchword, " The Old Constitution," refusing to listen to any
sound of reform or change, regarding every measure in
a popular direction as a preliminary to popular excesses,
the dominion of the uneducated, and the reign of socialistic ideas.
At the head of this party Pitt, of late so liberal, placed himself, supported by Burke, the late Whig leader. Conscious of the strength
he had himself derived from the Crown, conscious of the advances
in liberty he had been able to obtain by means of his alliance with
it, and thoroughly shocked with the disorder and violence of France,
Pitt determined that of the two elements of the Constitution, which
seemed to be coming into opposition one with the other, it was the
Crown which at all hazards required the firmest support. To this
new Tory party, before long, the greater part of the Whigs gave in
their adhesion. But as a new Tory party was formed, so was a new
Whig party. Certain large-minded men, such as Grey, saw no reason
why a panic should check such obvious improvements as had already
been set on foot. Certain vehement party men, such as Fox and
Sheridan, of large and warm hearts, rejoiced when their feelings led
them in the same direction as their political opposition, and formed
together a small but united band, to whom the French Revolution
was admirable, to whom war with France was wicked, and every
attempt at the repression of disorder a wanton act of tyranny.

It has been already pointed out that both the social and constitutional condition of England afforded a good ground on
which sympathy for the Revolution might take root.
Not only were the numbers of the labouring classes

*Formation of a
new Tory
party.*

*Sympathy with
the Revolution
among the
lower classes.*

largely increased, not only was the condition of the labouring class changing for the worse, the relations between capital and labour were in a much less satisfactory state than they now are, every form of combination among workmen was regarded as a crime, the line between class and class was very strongly drawn. Country people were complaining, in England as in France, of the absenteeism of landlords, the employment of harsh middlemen, and the general resort of all gentry to London. The Test Act and the penal laws were regarded by those who were affected by them as relics of persecution, all efforts to relax them were generally met with scornful rejection, and, before all, the representation was in a condition which, but for its evil effects, might be regarded as simply ridiculous. The sympathy which might thus have been naturally felt was not left without

Revolutionary societies   instruction or direction. Those who most strongly felt its influence speedily formed themselves into societies, by whose means, in conjunction it seems pretty certain with assistance from the French themselves, writings and pamphlets, pointing out every flaw in the condition of England, and often using language which was certainly seditious, were spread broadcast among the people, and even among the soldiers. Of these societies by far the most respectable was one known by the name of the "Friends of the People." Its object was to excite and keep alive an agitation for the removal of the inequalities of the representation. It included many men of the greatest respectability, numbering twenty-eight members of Parliament in its lists, and such names as Lord John Russell, Grey, Sheridan, Erskine, and Lord Lauderdale. Far more dangerous were two active societies which had now established branches in many of the chief towns of England. These were the London Corresponding Society, numbering between 6000 and 7000 members, organized as a secret society, and governed by a small secret committee of five, and a Society for Constitutional Information, consisting of the more advanced and thoroughgoing educated men of the time, and holding opinions of so dangerous a character that the Society of the Friends of the People thought it necessary to disclaim all connection with it. It was to check the action of these societies that the two first retrograde actions of Pitt were directed.

The outcome of the work of the Society of the Friends of the

Rejection of Grey's motion for reform. April 1792.   People was that Grey gave notice of a motion for a general reform of the representation. To this Pitt refused his support. Two things were necessary, he said, to induce a man to support a measure—the possibility of carrying it, and the possibility, when carried, of putting it into execution to the advantage of the people; both these conditions were now absent, not only did he believe that in the present state of feeling the Bill would infallibly be rejected by the House, but also it could not now be carried out without the greatest danger. The motion was therefore dropped, and all chance of carrying reform disappeared. Yet the necessity for it was made very clear by a petition from the same society presented by Grey in the following year, which exhibited in all its nakedness the inefficiency of the representation, and proved that a decided majority of the House was returned in fact by no more than 154 individuals.

But while the respectable reformers were carrying out their efforts by parliamentary means, the two less scrupulous societies went on issuing papers and pamphlets to such an extent, that at length it seemed good to Government to issue a royal proclamation warning the people against seditious writings, and then to proceed to take legal measures against them. *Proclamation against seditious writings. May 21.* This proclamation was issued on the 21st of May, and the address moved in Parliament to thank the King for issuing it may be regarded as the exact point at which the new division of parties sprang into existence, for it was supported by many of the chief leaders of the Whigs, and though an effort made by Pitt to strengthen his party by a coalition with the Whigs failed for personal reasons, the Duke of Portland, Wyndham, Thomas Grenville, and others, came back to their allegiance to the wisdom of Burke, and joined henceforward in the united Conservative party. It is remarkable also for a second point which connects it with the international aspect of the French Revolution. *Diplomacy of M. Chauvelin.* M. Chauvelin had lately been sent over to England, with his far abler secretary Talleyrand, as minister accredited by the French King. But Louis' authority was little more than a shadow, and M. Chauvelin already thought fit to enter upon that peculiar course of foreign diplomacy which was characteristic of the revolutionists; he drew up a strong protest against the Proclamation, and demanded that it should be laid before Parliament. Of course Grenville, the Foreign Minister, had no alternative but to send back the letter, with a sharp rebuke, explaining to him what he seemed to have forgotten, the true position of a foreign minister. This was the beginning of that diplomatic squabble which ended in M. Chauvelin being dismissed from England.

But before the breaking off of diplomatic intercourse, the open sympathy expressed for the changes which had taken place in France had begun to rouse the fear of the governing classes in

England. The proclamation against seditious writings had but
little effect compared with the exciting news of the
10th of August, the massacres of September, and the
retreat of the allies. The societies thought fit to send
deputations with addresses of sympathy to the National
Convention. The Revolution Society sent a present of a thousand
pairs of shoes for the army, and the Corresponding Society, with four
or five others of a similar character, sent a joint address, congratulating the French upon their republican form of government, especially
admiring the outrageous conduct of the mob on the 10th of August,
and even approving the sad events of September. Nor was their
energy confined to words. Riots broke out in several towns both in
England and Scotland. The most important were those in Sheffield
and Dundee. At Sheffield the disturbances took the form of a regular
revolutionary riot. It was on a day appointed for rejoicing for the success of the French arms; a tree of
Liberty was planted, and the procession passed through
the streets, headed by an enormous picture of Dundas and Burke
plunging their daggers into the heart of Liberty. "They are as
resolute and determined a set of villains as ever I saw," writes an
officer who was quartered in the place, "and will gain their object if
it is to be gained ; they have debating societies and correspondence
with other towns ; they have purchased firearms, and are trying to
corrupt the soldiers." At Dundee almost the same events took
place ; again a tree of Liberty was planted, and the cries of "Liberty,"
"Equality," "No excise," "No King," were soon universally heard,
though the ostensible cause of the riot had been the high price of
corn.

This state of affairs—the seditious conduct of the societies, and
the obvious tendency to riot—induced Pitt, in the beginning of December, to call out the militia. This he could
only do legally by alleging insurrection as the excuse,
and it was a somewhat strained construction of the word to apply it
to these outbreaks. But Pitt had now made up his mind not only
for repression in England but for war abroad, and the summoning of the militia was intended in fact as a first step in that direction. It was under these circumstances that an autumnal Parliament
was summoned. The discussions naturally turned upon the conduct
of the Government in calling out the militia, but Fox was unable to
collect more than fifty votes to disapprove of the vigilance of the
Government in internal matters.

Congratulatory addresses sent to France by the societies. Sept.

Riots in Sheffield and Dundee. Nov.

The militia called out. Dec.

Much more really important were the indications of the near approach of war, given by the stress laid by the Govern- <small>Signs of</small> ment upon the decree of November, the opening of <small>approaching war with</small> the Scheldt, and the irregular and unsatisfactory char- <small>France.</small> acter of our diplomatic relations with France. From the beginning of 1793, although there was no declaration of war between England and France, it was perfectly clear that war was inevitable. An Alien Bill was introduced, rendered necessary it was <small>The Alien Bill.</small> urged by the great assembly of foreigners in England, <small>Jan. 4, 1793.</small> chiefly royalist emigrants, but also in part emissaries from the Jacobin government. Foreigners were by this Bill ordered to state the object of their visit to England, to enter their names on a register, and to obtain passports for moving to and fro. The Bill was at once asserted by the French to be an infringement of Pitt's commercial treaty of 1786, which had promised freedom of access to French citizens. It was followed by measures even more stringent. The exportation of all materials of war, the introduction and circulation of assignats, and the exportation of corn whether English or foreign, to French ports, were prohibited. While affairs were in this attitude, the catastrophe for which Europe had breathlessly waited took place. Louis XVI. was guillotined <small>Death of</small> on the 21st of January 1793. A thrill of horror ran <small>Louis XVI.</small> through all classes of society, nearly the whole of <small>Jan. 21, 1793</small> London, and not the Court only, appeared in deep mourning, and orders were almost immediately sent to M. Chauvelin to leave England within eight days. The unofficial connections between him and Lord Grenville had been kept up ever since the King's suspension, but M. Chauvelin prided himself upon being in close connection with the Opposition rather than with the Government, and persisted in separating in his papers the interests of the Government and of the people. He had offered explanations and produced a long letter for the same purpose from Le Brun, the French Foreign Minister, with regard to the decree of the 19th of November, but the explanation was of a character to increase the irritation of the English. He had met every measure of the Government with an angry protest: he justified the opening of the Scheldt; he complained that he was obliged to enrol himself with the other aliens; he declared that the prohibitory Bills were distinct breaches of the treaty of 1786; and he was doubtless glad when the consummation he had aimed at was reached and he was ordered to leave the country.

Some slight pretence was still kept up on the part of the French

Efforts on the part of Pitt for the continuation of peace of a desire to keep the peace. M. Maret, well known afterwards as the Duc de Bassano, was sent over to take M. Chauvelin's place. The object of his mission is really unknown; he simply notified his arrival to Grenville, held no communications with him, and very shortly returned to France to find war already declared. At the same time another indirect offer of negotiation arose, strangely enough in Belgium, where Dumouriez desired an opportunity for a diplomatic meeting with Lord Auckland, our ambassador. It speaks well for Pitt's real desire to treat if treating were possible, that he at once accepted this proposition, holding that a general in command of an army might treat, without any implied recognition of the legitimacy or the stability of the Government which employed him. But though the required leave was immediately sent to Lord Auckland, it arrived too late, war had been already declared. It is a further proof of Pitt's pacific tendencies, that when he agreed to Dumouriez' proposal an embargo had already been laid upon English shipping in the French ports, an act of war which he was willing to overlook as long as any hope of negotiation remained.

But it may be fairly asserted, in spite of all that Fox and his

Determination of the French for war. friends urged, that there was no real opportunity after the massacres of September of treating with dignity with France. While M. Chauvelin was attempting on the 27th of December to explain away the November decree, on the 31st of the same month the Minister of the Marine wrote thus to the seaports of France: " The Government of England is arming, and the King of Spain, encouraged by this, is preparing to attack us. These two tyrannical powers, after persecuting the patriots in their own territories, think no doubt that they will be able to influence the judgment about to be pronounced on the tyrant Louis. They hope to frighten us. But no; a people that has made itself free, a people that has driven out of the bosom of France the terrible army of the Prussians and Austrians, this people will not suffer laws to be dictated to them by a tyrant. The King and his Parliament mean to make war upon us. Will the republicans of England permit this ? Already these freemen show their discontent, and the repugnance they have to bear arms against their brothers the French ; well, we will fly to their succour, we will make a descent upon their island, we will lodge there 50,000 caps of liberty, we will plant the sacred tree, and we will stretch out our arms to our republican brethren; the tyranny of their government will be immediately overthrown." In fact, as has more. than once happened in our history, the disturbance of a few reckless men, which our free constitution permits to show itself without repression, was construed to mean what it might mean in less free countries. Misinformed by their emissary Chauvelin who saw but one party, willing to believe what they liked to believe, and ignorant of the character of the English nation, the French had persuaded themselves that there was a real division between the Government and the people of England, and were eager for the war.

That war they declared on the 1st of February. English interests were so injuriously affected by what promised to be the per- Reasons for manent occupation of Belgium, that sooner or later England the war. must have declared war. The *casus belli* was a difficulty. England was pledged to neutrality, and was bound to France by a close commercial treaty. The only two grounds on which, technically, war could be declared, were the opening of the Scheldt and the destruction of the balance of power by the appropriation of Savoy. England being under distinct pledge not to interfere with the internal condition of France, neither the massacres of September, the establishment of the Republic, nor the death of the King, could with any justice be alleged as a ground of war. The appropriation of Savoy was an evident fact, but it was very plausibly urged that England, being in a state of professed neutrality, had entirely disregarded the invasion of France by the great Eastern powers, and had allowed to pass, without observation, the second partition of Poland. The opening of the Scheldt was no doubt contrary to treaties with Holland which England had guaranteed, but it was very reasonably urged that England was not called upon to plunge into a war unless Holland requested her to do so, and Holland remained studiously quiet. The guarantee of the treaty had been to save Holland from war; it might well seem a distortion of duty to force Holland into war for the preservation of the treaty. There can be no doubt that the Opposition was right in asserting that the war was declared against opinion; the point in which they were wrong was this, that they did not recognize the fact that opinion grown to a religion, a religion become propagandist in its nature, and that propagandist religion in arms was the greatest social danger which could threaten the world. Pitt and Burke saw this; the whole body of Tories and conservative Whigs dimly felt it. But the trammels of ages of diplomacy were too strong to allow of the fact being openly recognised. It was then with joy that the ministry found themselves released from their difficulties by the French declaration of war.

When England engaged in the war a campaign had already been

French successes in the campaign of 1792-3, on the Continent.

fought to the entire disadvantage of the allies. The close of the year 1792 had seen the retirement of the allies from French soil, the battle of Jemmappes, and the occupation of Belgium and Savoy. The accession of England, Spain and Holland to the coalition so far invigorated it that its members believed that a campaign of a few months would complete their work; for dangers surrounded the French Convention on all sides. Dumouriez, a member of the Girondin party, displeased with the conduct of the Jacobin Convention, was meditating defection; the excesses of the governing party in Paris had aroused all the slumbering loyalty of France; La Vendée was in arms for constitutional monarchy and the Catholic religion; and both at Lyons and Toulon the reaction was for the moment triumphant. Dumouriez' treason had an immediate effect. Directly upon the declaration of war he invaded Holland, but seeking rather popularity with his army and the prestige of victory than the success of the plans of Government, he turned aside from Holland, and risked a battle at Neerwinden on the Gheet, in which he suffered a complete defeat from the Prince of Saxe-Coburg; and thus as a defeated general, and without his army, he gave himself up to the Austrians. His defeat and defection allowed the allies to advance along the whole frontier. But their movements were dilatory; instead of marching upon Paris they selfishly preferred to take Mayence, Condé, and Valenciennes; they even committed the mistake of binding the captured troops to refrain from war only against themselves; they were therefore available to suppress the insurrection in La Vendée, and the troops hitherto employed there could be sent to the eastern frontier. The same want of energy continually marked the progress of the allies. The Prussians and Austrians were in fact too jealous of each other, and too much bent upon their interests nearer home to act with vigour. Time was again wasted in sieges. While the Austrians sat down before Le Quesnoy, the Duke of York with the English troops besieged Dunkirk. Their communications were kept open by the Dutch at Menin and Hoondschoote. But the French army, under the vigorous management of the Jacobins, and guided by the military genius of Carnot, was no longer to be trifled with; Houchard fell upon the weak position of the Dutch, and York

was driven to a disastrous retreat with the loss of all his artillery
The success was indeed only momentary; a panic seized the French
troops, and they fell back to Lille, thus affording the allies an opportunity of advancing to the attack of the fortress of Maubeuge, which
closed the road to Paris; but Jourdan, who had succeeded Houchard,
now put in practice Carnot's principles. Hastily gathering 50,000
men, he fell upon half that number of Austrians, and completely
defeated them at Wattigny. Success had also attended the French
against the Prussians on the Upper Rhine. There, too, the terrible
rigour of the new Government had restored the aspect of affairs.
St. Just and Lebas had appeared as conventional commissioners in
Alsace, bringing terror with them. The beaten armies were supplied
and organized. Two young generals of the revolutionary school,
Hoche and Pichegru, were placed in command, and the tide of victory
was turned; the Prussians had to fall back, compromising the
advanced position of the Austrians, and before the close of the year
the French army, which had begun the campaign with a series of
disasters, found itself victorious along the whole frontier line.

The Convention had also been successful in its wars in the
interior of France. After six weeks of bombardment, and against
on the 9th of October, Lyons yielded, without conditions, the royalists
to be given up to the fearful cruelty of Collot d'Herbois; in France.
and the victorious troops hurried southwards to besiege Toulon,
which had placed itself in the hands of the English, and had
admitted the allied fleet to its roadstead. The genius of Bonaparte
is said to have secured its capture. He saw that one fort called the
Equilette commanded the roadstead, and that its possession would
oblige the English, who were the soul of the defence, to withdraw.
The capture of the fort answered his expectation; Lord Hood,
without making terms for the inhabitants, collected such of the
royalists as could crowd on board his ships, and sailed away, having
first set fire to all the stores, and burnt or carried off forty ships of
war (Dec. 18, 1793). The insurrection of La Vendée had also
been suppressed. Intrusted at first to ignorant men, with no
claim to command except the strength of their revolutionary
principles, the Convention troops had been everywhere defeated.
But when Kleber was put in practical command the course of
victory changed. Terribly defeated, and with all their chiefs of
importance mortally wounded, the insurgents determined to try the
fortune of war upon the other side of the Loire. They marched
northwards towards Laval, defeated their pursuers, and had they

made common cause with the Bretons might still have been successful. But trusting to help from England, which never came, they undertook a fruitless assault upon Granville in Normandy. Thinking themselves betrayed, and longing for their homes, the ill-organized mass of peasants insisted on being led southwards : even then there was some life in them. They defeated the republican General Rossignol and threw him back upon Rennes ; but failing in an attack upon Angers, they marched pointlessly towards Le Mans. They were there received with terrible slaughter by Westermann, Kleber and Marçeau ; 18,000 men, women and children were killed, and the rest fled, pursued by the pitiless Westermann. The fugitives reached the Loire, fought one final battle at Savenay near its mouth, where they were all, with the exception of some eight or ten thousand men, either put to death or captured.

Thus revolutionary France had proved itself no contemptible enemy to the united troops of Europe, and established its rule unquestioned in France. It was plain that all hope of an easy subjugation of France was over, and it was with the greatest difficulty that Pitt was able to keep the coalition together; the eyes of Prussia were eagerly bent upon Poland, an easier prey than France. Of increase of territory in Europe England had no hope ; the war had been forced on her, and was honestly a war of opinion. But any cessation of her efforts would have placed her in a worse position than when the war began. Pitt had from the first intended that the country should be indemnified by the acquisition of the French Colonies, and neither he nor the upper classes of England were blind to the advantages at sea which the war afforded them ; it was worth making great efforts to gain the undisputed mastery of the sea both in commerce and in arms. Nor did the large sums of money, raised chiefly by way of loan, appear so ruinous as they really were. The effect of large loans is to increase the wealth of the capitalist at the expense of the working man; nor, as the chief weight of the accumulating taxation falls on posterity, does it become immediately evident. Thus supplied with almost unlimited means, Pitt succeeded in keeping up the coalition, taking into English pay, it is almost true to say, the whole of the Prussian army, and doing nearly as much for the Austrians.

Pitt's difficulty in keeping up the coalition.

Pitt's energy was equalled by that of France, and the Convention had the additional advantage of being free from constitutional rules. Vast conscriptions filled their armies, forced requisitions supplied them with arms and equip-

Continued success of the French in 1794

ments. It was with the Northern army, 160,000 strong, under Pichegru, that the English had most to do. A concentrated march on Paris had been proposed but rejected, and when the campaign opened each army was divided into three divisions, and the duty of marching with 100,000 men on Paris was intrusted to Coburg. Defeated in the centre, the French had met with unexpected success on the left, Clairfait, the Austrian general, having been twice beaten at Moucron and at Courtray. Upon this, Pichegru almost destroyed his centre to strengthen his wings, and the threefold manœuvres became twofold. The key of the campaign was the possession of the Sambre; the Austrians lay in an advancing angle with their left upon that river from Mons to Charleroi. If the French could cross the Sambre they would be virtually in the rear of the Austrians. To this point, therefore, the Commissioners of the Convention, St. Just and Lebas, repaired, and attempted to inspire the troops with something of their own enthusiasm. Again and again the French were driven back. But Carnot's plan of massing troops was at length employed; the greater part of the army, which under Jourdan had been facing the Prussians on the Moselle, was turned northward, and Jourdan took command of 100,000, well known as the army of the Sambre and Meuse, just as the Commissioners had been driven back for the fifth time behind the river. After a sixth failure, the Commissioners insisting upon a seventh effort, the river was successfully crossed, and on the heights of Fleurus a battle was fought in which, though it was not completed, the Austrians were practically defeated. Step by step the English and the Austrians retired, the one towards Holland, the other towards the Rhine. By July the English were behind Breda, the Austrians beyond the Meuse. Want of supplies checked the French advance for a few weeks, but by October the English were driven into the corner between the Yssel and the Rhine, and the army of the Sambre and Meuse had captured Cologne and Coblenz. The occupation of Belgium by the French compelled the Prussians further south also to fall behind the Rhine, the left bank of which was thus in possession of the French army from Basle to the sea. Even south of that point successes had been won. The Sardinian position of Saorgio had been turned, and the passes of the Alps were opened to the French, who were thus in a position to invade Italy on the one hand and Holland on the other. The lateness of the season, and the wretched state of the equipment and commissariat, might have induced the French to be satisfied with these conquests, and few armies would have thought of facing an unusually severe winter shoeless and in rags, for to such a plight had the bad management of the Revolutionary Government brought them. But to this army of enthusiasts the winter was but a useful ally for the conquest of Holland, where a strong feeling in their favour already existed among that large section of the people, who had seen with anger their attempted Revolution of 1787 suppressed by the arms of Prussia, and to whom the Government of the Stadtholder was very distasteful. The failure of the preceding campaign had obliged Pitt to insist upon the recall of the Duke of York, much to the King's displeasure, and Pichegru now found himself opposed to General Walmoden, the Hanoverian commander. But of opposition there was really none. The lines of the three great rivers, the Meuse, the Waal and the Lech, were abandoned without a fight, and crossed by the French, either upon the ice or by means of pontoons ; and finally Walmoden left Holland to its fate, and retreated across the Yssel and the Ems to embark his army safely in Bremen. The

The French capture Amsterdam and the Dutch fleet. 1795. Stadtholder had already fled from the Hague and taken refuge in England. Amsterdam was occupied by the French without difficulty, the ragged regiments waiting patiently in the bitter snow in the streets of the rich city till their quarters were arranged for them without the least attempt at disorder. A striking finish was put to the campaign by the capture of the Dutch fleet in the Texel. The ships were ice-bound, and fell into the hands of a regiment of cavalry, who galloped across the ice to secure them. Holland was at once erected into a republic upon the French model.

But in spite of these continual reverses of the allies, in spite of

Indirect advantages gained by England the perpetual failure of the British arms in the Low Countries, Pitt had not been mistaken in the indirect advantages which the war would give him. The conflagration at Toulon had inflicted an almost irreparable loss upon the French fleet. In Corsica the veteran patriot Paoli had aroused the feeling of his countrymen against France. Nelson and Hood, with 1000 British soldiers serving as marines in their ships, had taken Bastia, which was regarded as almost impregnable, and the people of Corsica had begged King George to accept their crown. While thus in the Mediterranean English supremacy had been established, a still greater success had attended her fleet off the coast of France. By immense exertions a powerful and well-equipped fleet of twenty-six ships had been assembled by Bon St. André and placed under the command of Villaret Joyeuse. It left the harbour of Brest for the purpose of convoying a large fleet laden with flour from America. The English Channel fleet, under Lord Howe, sailed to meet it. In number of ships and weight of metal the English fleet was somewhat inferior, but the Revolution had stripped the French marine of its best officers, who had habitually been supplied by Brittany, now royalist in its tendencies. Bon St. André, originally a Calvinistic clergyman, had all the fearful energy belonging to the Conventional Commissioners, but little of the skill of a seaman, yet he frequently overruled the commands of Villaret Joyeuse. Thus, when the fleets met upon the 1st of June, the French were unable to prevent Admiral Howe from repeating Rodney's well-known manœuvre of breaking the line. The defeat of the French fleet was complete ; one ship went down, and six line of battle-ships remained as English prizes.

Defeat of the French fleet. June 1, 1794

Upon the Continent, however, success had been wholly on the side of the French; the campaign of 1794 and the winter of 1795 had added Belgium, Holland, the left bank of the Rhine, part of Piedmont, Catalonia, and Navarre, to their dominions. The coalition began at once to fall to pieces. As it was plain that there was no further hope of a military promenade to Paris or of territory to be gained at an easy price, the King of Prussia, who had been only kept up to the mark by enormous subsidies from England, made his peace with the French. It was the pressure of England alone which had driven Spain and Holland into the war. Although Pitt had procured a change of ministry in Spain in accordance with his own views, and the substitution of Godoy for Miranda, the Spanish Government now awoke to its true interests. All the advantages of a maritime war of necessity fell to the lot of the English, and Spain saw herself aiding in the destruc tion of the only efficient rival to the English upon the sea, and thus in fact rendering certain her own insignificance on that element. The Spanish Government was therefore willing to treat. Holland, completely conquered, and with half its population preferring the French rule to that of the Prince of Orange, who had been forced upon the country, obtained peace by giving up its chief fortresses, paying a large indemnity, and making an offensive alliance with France against England, by which thirty ships of war were placed at the disposal of the French. Many of the smaller states both of Germany and Italy declared themselves neutral. England was thus practically left without allies, with the single exception of Austria, which was only induced to continue its engagements by a subsidy of four millions and a half. This series of treaties was completed in the course of the year

Prussia, Spain and Holland leave the coalition.

1795, chiefly by Barthélemy at Basle ; the treaty with Tuscany, Feb. 9 ;
with Holland [at the Hague], May 15 ; with Prussia, April 5 ; and
with Spain, July 14.

The campaign of the following year, 1795, was confined to the
Rhine, where Pichegru commanded the army of the Rhine and
Moselle, Jourdan that of the Sambre and Meuse.　Pichegru was
meditating treachery, and lay idle opposite the Black Forest till the
advance of Jourdan from the North to co-operate with him for the
purpose of retaking Mayence forced him into action.　He took
Mannheim, and might have taken Heidelberg, but he wilfully resigned
this advantage, and fell back in disorder upon the lines of Weissem-
bourg, where he signed an armistice with the Austrians preparatory
to joining them.　His retreat had compelled that of Jourdan also.

The English meanwhile had engaged in a lukewarm way in an
expedition which, had it been carried out with vigour,
might have changed the face of affairs.　After the great
destruction of the Vendéan army at Savenay, the war continued
to smoulder both in La Vendée itself and in Brittany.　But north
of the Loire it assumed a somewhat different character ; the open,
simple and heroic devotion of the Vendéan peasantry, who had followed their priests, gentry, and leaders of their own rank to battle,
was wanting, and the hostilities of Brittany assumed rather the form
of brigandage than warfare.　The country was infested with small
bands, who kept up connection with one another by means of private
signals, but who seldom appeared in large numbers, and worked chiefly
by night-surprises and by rapid and secret cutting off of detached
posts.　The chief man of the Chouans, as the Breton insurgents were
called, was Cormatin.　But certain men of higher rank were also
among them; the chief of these was Count Joseph de Puisaye, a man
of considerable energy and ability, who had been a member of the
National Assembly.　De Puisaye saw that irregular warfare could
produce but little effect, and desired to obtain assistance from England, where the Government was supposed to be ready to assist any
endeavour against the French Republic ; an impression kept alive by
the rumours, probably much exaggerated, spread by agents who
were constantly passing and repassing through the Channel Islands
between France and England.

In the autumn of 1794 De Puisaye betook himself to England
and laid his plans before Pitt.　It was suggested that 10,000 British
troops should be joined with the corps of emigrants, and
should land in Brittany and seize Rennes, and thence
push forward at once over Normandy, Maine and Poitou.
It was thought advisable that a prince of the blood should either

Insurrection of La Vendée.

Expedition from England planned.

accompany the expedition or shortly appear upon the scene, and the Count of Artois was selected for the purpose. Lord Moira, favourably known in the American War as Lord Rawdon, was to take command of the English troops. But though speed and secresy were of the first necessity, the expedition hung fire, and news of it reached the ears of the French Government. The reason for this delay was partly jealousy and disunion among the emigrants themselves, partly Pitt's mistrust of the readiness of the French to join him, and his knowledge of the danger of relying on the assertions of sanguine exiles, and partly the discovery of the feeling existing among the royalists themselves in La Vendée and Brittany against the introduction of any large foreign army; for the belief seems to have been prevalent that Pitt's objects were selfish, and that an English army would be rather a danger than an assistance. It is at all events certain that the royalists in Paris, in their dislike that the reaction should be brought about by any means but their own, did their best to injure the expedition. The consequences of the delay were serious. In spite of considerable sums of money sent from England, and a good deal more much cheaper money, consisting of forged assignats, which were exported largely, in the spring of 1795 the skill of Hoche and Canclaux, the generals opposed to the insurgents, and the very favourable terms offered by the Convention, induced the chiefs both of the Vendéans and of the Chouans to accept an amnesty. The terms offered were certainly unusually tempting. A large indemnity of several millions of francs was to be given to the people to repay them for their losses; the houses that had been burnt were to be rebuilt; ten millions were to be given to the chiefs to take up the bonds that had been issued in their names during the insurrection; Charette was to be allowed to keep up 2000 men in the pay of the Government, freedom of religion was to be granted, and there were to be no requisitions in La Vendée for five years. The agreement was made as solemn as possible. The first to accept it was Charette, with whom the treaty was signed with great pomp in the city of Nantes in February. Subsequently, in April, Stofflet gave in his adhesion to the same arrangement, and finally the Chouans did the same. It seemed a proof of their sincerity that they gave up into the hands of the Commissioner of the Convention nearly a million of forged assignats, which they had received from the English fleet round the coast; but on the part of the insurgents it appears that this treaty was illusory, forced upon them by the delay of the English. At length, however, the ministry seem to have been fired with all De Puisaye's enthusiasm, and an army composed at his desire solely of emigrants,

but supplied with English stores and money, set sail from England in June of 1795. On some points his plan was overruled for the worse. For the sake of a good roadstead for the English fleet, it was arranged that the landing should be upon the peninsula of Quiberon, close to Carnac, instead of in the north of Brittany; and again, apparently in mistrust of De Puisaye's partisan system of warfare, it was thought necessary to give him as second in command a royalist emigrant of the name of D'Hervilly, a red tape soldier, who had displayed considerable courage on the 10th of August, but who was a very bad man for the present irregular warfare. It even seemed doubtful whether his authority did not supersede De Puisaye's, and after Quiberon was reached, it was thought necessary to send an appeal to England to settle this weighty question. Meanwhile, after two days of delay, the troops were landed at Carnac. They were received with an enthusiasm so riotous and irregular, that the commander's love of discipline received a severe shock, and he ceased to trust his wild allies. However, in three days they were joined by some 10,000 men, and De Puisaye was eager to rush forward and raise the whole of the neighbouring country, but the answer from England had not yet been received, and the troops waited on in inactivity. At length something was done. A small fort called Fort Penthièvre covers the little isthmus which joins the peninsula of Quiberon to the shore. D'Hervilly proceeded to bring up all his artillery, but before his operations were completed, De Puisaye and a few hundred Chouans had gained possession of the place without difficulty. With his regular troops in the peninsula and holding the fort, and with his Chouans spread along the mainland, De Puisaye was compelled to remain inactive. All the jealousies which existed among the royalists burst out, and even worse than that, time was allowed for General Hoche to increase his 5000 troops, which might easily have been routed, to double that number. He suddenly attacked the invaders, and drove the whole mass, Chouans, emigrants, and all, to the narrow confined peninsula. Their efforts to break loose were unavailing; fresh emigrant troops under Sombreuil came from England. De Puisaye's authority was confirmed, but it was too late. Some republican troops taken in Fort Penthièvre had been admitted to the emigrant ranks. They entered into treacherous correspondence with Hoche's army, and by their assistance the fort was recaptured. The exit from their peninsula was thus entirely closed to them, the enemy's cannon was placed along the corresponding shore, and swept the isthmus and the roadstead, while the republican troops, advancing from the fort, drove the invaders backward into the corner of the tongue of land. They were literally driven into the sea. The scene was a fearful one. Many in despair threw themselves upon their own swords, many tried to reach the boats of the fleet, and were a ready mark for the republican musketry. Some thought themselves fortunate in reaching fishing-boats which were hovering about the coast, but in zeal for their own preservation the boatmen lopped off their hands and suffered them to sink. Some 900, with De Puisaye at their head, reached the English squadron and were saved. About 700, under De Sombreuil, made, as they thought, terms with General Humbert, but the conditions were only verbal, and included, as the French asserted probably with truth, a reference to the Convention. The reactionaries in power were glad of the chance of freeing themselves of the charge of favouring the royalists. Orders were given that the law against emigrants taken in arms should be carried out to the letter. The prisoners were brought out in batches and shot upon the seashore till 700 of them had been killed. After this the fate of the insurgents was sealed. In the following year (1796) the Count of Artois again appeared upon the coast, and Charette and Stofflet were again in arms, but the Count of Artois was content to remain in idleness at L'Ile Dieu, and Hoche succeeded in the difficult work of at once conquering and conciliating all that remained of the insurrection. Charette and Stofflet were both captured and shot.

There can be but little doubt that when war was first declared the feeling of the English people was very strongly in favour of it. Accustomed for years to trust to Pitt, they continued their perfect confidence in him though his *Confidence of the English in Pitt.* policy had changed, and, as we have seen, the opposition in the House of Commons was virtually destroyed. The confidence of the nation was chiefly exhibited in the readiness with which it met all the demands for increased taxation and for immense loans ; in fact, Pitt was strongly supported by the commercial classes. With them the war was in itself popular, they were clearsighted enough to see how vast was the opening likely to be afforded them by the increase of English power upon the sea.

In the year 1793 Pitt gained a fresh right to their gratitude by the assistance he afforded them during a brief monetary crisis which threatened to be very destructive. *Increased by his assistance in a financial crisis.* The year had been one of great financial difficulty. The

sudden expansion of manufacturing industry which had followed
upon the great inventions at the beginning of the reign, and the
increase of commerce which followed the close of the American War,
had rendered necessary a large amount of capital. The want had been
met by a largely increased paper currency. Reckless banking had
become prevalent, and provincial banks issued notes far beyond their
capital. A very slight panic would be enough to cause the collapse
of such a system. It was found that to meet the necessities of the
exchange between England and the rest of the world bullion would
have to leave England. Bullion was already scarce, and the Bank
of England therefore thought it necessary to restrict its issues. This
was enough to cause the failure of a few great houses; a panic
ensued; there was a run upon the provincial banks; out of 350
more than 100 failed. Yet there was in reality quite enough property
both in securities and in goods to enable merchants to meet all
demands. It was only for the moment that there was a deficiency of
money, that is, of the means of exchange. Pitt, with admirable clearness, recognized the real solvency of the country, and authorized the
issue of bills on the Exchequer to the value of five millions. These
were advanced to merchants, who could prove their solvency, against
securities or goods. As these bills rested on the credit of the nation,
they were readily received, the engagements of the merchants were
satisfied by their means, and credit was restored. As it proved, not
more than four millions was borrowed, and the whole sum was speedily
repaid without loss to the nation.

The effect of the complete trust placed in Pitt was to allow him to
give full rein to his new policy. Now that policy was
one entirely of repression, and the effect of it in the long
run, indeed before the year was out, was to divide
England much more sharply into the propertied and non-propertied
classes, and to bring into existence a state of feeling highly undesirable, and which tended much to produce those very evils it was
intended to prevent. While every movement in a liberal direction
was certain to be checked, laws of the most stringent description
were willingly passed, and at first the execution of existing laws,
especially with regard to seditious writing, received great public
support. In this class may be mentioned the Traitorous
Correspondence Act. There has always been great
dislike to tampering with or extending the law of
treason, yet there were but fifty-three members of the House of
Commons who could be found to lift their voices against this Bill,

Effect of Pitt's new policy of repression.

The Traitorous Correspondence Bill. March 15, 1793.

which declared guilty of high treason, firstly, all those who supplied any arms or military or naval stores to the enemy; secondly, all those who purchased lands in France, for the use of assignats rendered the sale of land the chief support of French finance, and the purchase of land was therefore regarded as indirectly strengthening the hands of the enemy ; thirdly, it prohibited all intercourse with France without special license under the Great Seal; and fourthly, the insurance of French vessels by English merchants. The two first of these offences were to fall directly under the old law of Edward III., and to deprive those who were guilty of them of the advantages secured to them by the ameliorations of the law which had since been made, such as the right to employ counsel, and to be furnished with the list of the jury, the necessity of two witnesses to secure conviction, and the lapse of a certain period between the indictment and the trial.

But it was chiefly in the prosecution for seditious meetings and seditious writings that the character of the Government showed itself. The best known of these in the year 1793 was that of Muir. This young man, a member of the *Trials for seditious writings.* Society of the Friends of the People, was indicted for spreading the works of Thomas Paine. He defended himself with great ability upon the ground that he had only aimed at the reform of Parliament. His speech was greeted with loud applause, but the Lord Justice-Clerk summed up most strongly against him, and asserted the strange doctrine that the Government was made up of the landed interest. "As for the rabble," said he, "who have nothing but personal property, what hold has the nation on them?" He sentenced Muir to fourteen years' transportation. The severity of the judges and the frequent trials that the Government ordered had not the effect of checking the popular feeling. Delegates from various parts of Scotland, in concert with the Friends of the People and other societies, assembled at Edinburgh. The leading spirits were Maurice Margarot and Joseph Gerald, agents from London. These delegates assumed the name of a convention, spoke of the first year of the British Republic, and otherwise mimicked their French brethren. In December the law came upon them, and three of them, with Margarot and Gerald, were transported for fourteen years.

Up till this time the people as a whole had been heartily with Pitt; but the course of the year had tended to change their feelings, the war had been by no means the light undertaking expected, and it began to be seen that its *Pitt resists the growing desire for peace,* continuation meant fearful expenses, heavy taxes, and a system of government but little in accordance with the general character of English administration. Some even of Pitt's old friends began to whisper of peace, but his will was not one to yield to opposition. In Parliament he was still supreme, and in this first beginning of difficulties he exhibited the greatness of his energy and his resources. He branded with fierce words, which reminded his hearers of his great father, all who dared to think of peace ; he openly avowed that the idea was impossible till some total change took place in the French Government, thus putting his actions on their true basis. Backed by his commercial friends, he found means to continue the subsidies to Prussia and Austria, he purchased the adhesion of several of the smaller German states, induced the Spaniards to continue a war which was wholly against their own interests, and obliged the lesser Italian states to join the coalition; he even allowed Russia to perpetrate the second partition of Poland, though under protest. With such efforts as these he contrived to carry on his war ; it was not unreasonably that he became the ogre of the French, the one object of their insatiable hatred.

At home he would not abate one jot of his policy. Again the prosecutions went forward. So little had the late action of Government been successful that discontent and the intrigues of the societies were becoming even more envenomed. The English had taken a leaf out of the Scotch book; two of the great societies—the Constitutional Society and the Corresponding Society—determined that they too would have a convention. It seems to have been a far more real and dangerous thing than the Scotch convention. The workmen were stirred up, meetings were held in all the great towns attended by delegates from London, revolutionary songs were composed and circulated, and a considerable number of weapons constructed and secreted. It was the intention of the Convention to overawe Parliament somewhat in the same way as the Jacobin Club overawed the French Assembly. The Government determined to act as strongly as possible against it, and instead of accusing the leaders of seditious practices merely, they thought it advisable to treat their conduct as a great and capital crime, and to bring them to trial for high treason. The leaders arrested were Hardy, Secretary of the Corresponding Society, Adams, Secretary of the Constitutional Society, Horne Tooke, the well-known opponent of Junius, the Rev. Jeremiah Joyce, author of the "Scientific Dialogues," and tutor to Lord Stanhope's sons, Thelwall, a political lecturer of some importance, and three others. A

and continues the prosecutions for seditious writings.

secret committee of the House, having examined their books and papers, reported that there were ample proofs of a traitorous conspiracy for overawing Parliament. Upon this report the Government advanced a step further, and in spite of the eager opposition of the minority, carried through the House the suspension of the Habeas Corpus. Trials for high treason followed both in England and Scotland. In Scotland the prosecution was successful, but the English trials did not go off so smoothly. Hardy was tried first on the 28th of October. Sir John Scott (afterwards Lord Eldon) conducted the prosecution; but although the evidence, if true, tended to show that language of a most seditious character had been used, and weapons and plans of insurrection made, yet the skill and eloquence of Erskine, who laid his chief stress on the grave constitutional danger of any enlargement of the Treason Act, procured an acquittal. The Government was not satisfied, Horne Tooke was also tried. He defended himself with his usual effrontery and humour, and again an acquittal was obtained. Still the Crown persisted, and Thelwall the lecturer was tried; again the accused was acquitted. The excitement about the trials was intense, the speeches of the rival barristers were listened to with extreme interest, and the acquittals were hailed with the wildest enthusiasm. It was plain that a considerable change had taken place in the feelings of the people; the strings of repression had been drawn too tight; the line between class and class was becoming more sharply marked.

The same fact is rendered obvious by the completion in this year of the consolidation of the new Tory party. Ever since the middle of 1792 the Duke of Portland and his friends had voted with Government, but they now openly joined it, and were admitted to some of the best places. The Duke of Portland became Secretary for the Home Department, Earl Fitzwilliam Lord President, and Mr. Wyndham Secretary at War. The one point which connected the new recruits with the ministry was the determination all felt to carry on the war. Pitt was therefore hampered in two directions. When Parliament was opened on the 13th of December 1794, there appeared to be a growing feeling in favour of peace, and Pitt found himself opposed to many of his old friends, the country gentlemen; but his union with the Duke of Portland and his party rendered a change of policy at present impossible. He was in the hands of the war party; afraid of losing their support, and buoyed up by an idle belief in the financial exhaustion of France, he determined still to carry on the war vigorously. As he was quite paramount in Parliament[1] in spite of an increased minority, he had no difficulty in getting leave to raise a loan of eighteen millions, and to guarantee another large loan to purchase the co-operation of Austria. He nevertheless slightly changed his tone, and confessed that he should be satisfied with a peace that gave him security, and allowed later in the session that there was a possibility of treating with the present Government of France.

Amongst other minor difficulties which he had to meet was the

The Prince of Wales' marriage. April 8, 1795. constant embarrassment of the Prince of Wales. Seven years before he had purchased the payment of his debts by a lie concerning his wife; he was now again £700,000 in debt; the only terms on which he could hope to get relieved were that he should marry legally, and the King had chosen for him a Princess of Brunswick whom he had never seen. Lord Malmesbury arranged the negotiation, but unwisely suppressed, what he saw clearly himself, the absolute unfitness of the lady for the position she was to occupy. He found her frivolous, slovenly, and quite deficient in tact. It was impossible but that she should be distasteful to any English gentleman. Very shortly after the birth of her child a formal separation took place, and a scandalous dispute arose, which afterwards turned into a great party conflict. For the present however, the Prince received the price of his unfortunate bargain. The royal message demanding the assistance of Parliament was couched in humble language, and asked only for some arrangement by which the debts should be ultimately paid; but even thus it excited a perfect storm in the House. None even of the Prince's old friends rose to defend him, and Pitt himself, though no friend of the Prince, intreated that the matter might not be examined by a Parliamentary Committee, for fear of the damaging effect of such an inquiry on the principle of an hereditary monarchy. It was finally arranged that the Prince's income should be raised from £72,000 to

---

[1] To show how paramount he was in Parliament, and how powerless the Opposition, it is only necessary to read the list of the Acts which passed Parliament that year. Motion in the House of Peers by Lord Stanhope for non-interference in the internal affairs of France—unanimously rejected. Motion of a like tendency in the House of Commons—negatived. Motion in the House of Peers for facilitating the opening of negotiation with France—negatived. Motion for a vigorous prosecution of the war—carried. Sundry motions for preparing the way for peace with France—negatived. Motion in the House of Commons for inquiring into the state of the nation—negatived. Another to the same intent in the House of Peers—negatived. Motion in the House of Commons tending to a general pacification by Mr. Wilberforce—negatived. Motion of a similar tendency in the House of Lords—negatived.

£125,000 a year, that the revenues of the Duchy of Cornwall should be set apart, which in twenty-seven years would extinguish the debt, and that £25,000 a year more should be devoted to pay the interest. To these enactments was added an extraordinary one, rendering the Prince's servants liable for any contract they should enter into on his behalf, and limiting legal remedy against the Prince to the term of three months.

Such demands upon the public purse seemed very badly timed, when the working classes were suffering very heavily from depression of trade, from famine produced by two bad harvests, and from a constantly increasing burden of taxation. Discontent was in fact increasing widely, great political meetings were held in London and elsewhere to expose the abuses of monarchy and aristocracy. Riots and seditious writings were constantly on the increase, and the Government thought the state of affairs so critical that they determined upon an autumn session. Three days before Parliament met a monster meeting was held under the auspices of the Corresponding Society in Copenhagen Fields. The excitement thus produced found vent in an assault upon the King as he went to open Parliament, one of the windows of his state coach was broken by a stone or bullet; on his return his coach was again surrounded by an angry mob, with shouts of "Bread, bread! peace, peace!" and he only escaped with difficulty by driving rapidly in his private carriage from St. James's to Buckingham Palace. The King, who throughout showed great courage, showed himself in the evening at Covent Garden theatre, where he was on the whole well received. This act of violence produced two coercive Bills, one to suppress seditious meetings, the other to extend the law of treason. Every public meeting was to be advertised by a paper signed by resident householders, and all meetings were liable to be dispersed according to the Riot Act if any two justices thought them dangerous; while by the second law, writing, preaching, and speaking, were created overt acts, thus rendering the offender guilty of treason, and writing or speaking against the established Government was made a highly punishable crime. These Bills were commonly known as the Sedition and Treason Bills. They were not passed without strong opposition, and the use of language on the part of Fox so vehement as to excite still further the anger of the Tories. This party was now enjoying its selfish triumph to the utmost. It became necessary again to augment the taxes, and Pitt hit upon the expedient of levying duties

Sufferings of the lower classes. 1795.

Assault on the King.

upon legacies and successions. The country gentlemen had sufficient influence to confine the Bill to the succession of money and personal property only, and to exclude real property from the action of the Bill. This glaring injustice was not remedied till 1853.

The burden of taxation had much to do with the overtures for peace which were set on foot in 1796. Nearly all classes in the kingdom had become weary of the war. Pitt, as has been seen, had been forced into it against his natural tendencies, and though, when once embarked in the war of opinion, he had used language of the most overbearing character, he was eager, now that he found his hope of a speedy bankruptcy of France frustrated, to bring about an honourable peace. Such an opportunity was offered by the changed character of the French Government. The Directory had held its position for upwards of a year, and seemed to give promise of such stability as would render negotiation possible. This change in the Government of France had been the outcome of a series of revolutions which had followed each other in rapid succession.

Changes in France give hopes of peace.

The Girondins had, contrary to their conscientious opinions, voted for the death of the King. It was in fact an act of suicide. After this it was useless to oppose any demand of the Jacobins; the attempt only produced a violent struggle in the Convention, which ended in the complete overthrow of the Girondins by the insurrection of the 1st of June. In the place of the party thus annihilated the Jacobins found themselves supreme. Upon them henceforward lay the duty of saving the Revolution within and rescuing France from foreign assaults from without. The machinery of Government to which they trusted to obtain these ends was a Committee of Public Safety, in whose hands the full powers of the executive were lodged. As far as the external defence of France was concerned, the restless energy of the new rulers was completely successful. La Vendée, Toulon, and Lyons, the centres of opposition within France, were all reduced. Carnot struck out a new plan of warfare, and found means to employ with success the masses with which an almost unlimited conscription supplied the army, and from this time onwards the French were everywhere successful. But while exhibiting this energy abroad, in France the government of the Committee was in the last degree cruel and tyrannical. Nor could the Jacobins agree among themselves. On the one side was a party atheistical in their religion, communistic in their political views, foul and blasphemous in their

Retrospect of French affairs. 1793.

The Committee of Public Safety.

language. This party, which predominated in the Commune, took
its name from Hébert, the editor of an infamous paper called *Père
Duchesne.* It shocked the feelings of the world by its excesses,
abolishing religion, closing the churches, and holding a blasphemous
service in Notre Dame in honour of Reason. On the other side was
a party, headed by Danton, intent chiefly on success abroad, and
inclined to believe that the work of destruction had gone far enough.
Between the two was the party of the Purists, headed by Robespierre
and St. Just, who looked with equal hatred on the scandalous and
anarchical conduct of the Hébertists and the indulgent and somewhat
loose lives of the followers of Danton. Robespierre was able to
attack and destroy both these parties in turn. The Hébertists were
the first to fall, but very shortly after the same fate befell the
Dantonists.

Atheists and indulgents being thus both removed, Robespierre and
his party were virtually masters of France. Under them The Reign
the Terror knew no relaxation. "The maxim of our of Terror.
policy," said Robespierre, "ought to be to guide the people by reason
and the enemies of the people by terror." Whole batches of victims
completely unknown to each other were sent off together to the
guillotine under pretext of being accomplices in conspiracy. Between
the 20th of June and the 27th of July 1400 people were executed.
But Robespierre and his friends looked forward to some conclusion
of this state of things, desiring to establish a purely moral, stoical,
and deistical Republic. As a first step, the worship of the Supreme
Being was decreed, and a great festivity held, where Robespierre,
decked with flowers, officiated as priest. Thus, too, he began to shelter
the priests and nobles. The idea of the cessation of the Revolution
thoroughly frightened some of the worst among the Committee, and
Robespierre's assumption of authority disgusted them. They contrived to form a coalition with all the discontented parties, Hébertists,
Dantonists, Girondists, Royalists, were all ready to combine against
the one man whose stoical purity seemed to insult them, and whose
cold implacable cruelty gave them no hope if they should offend him.
Robespierre was thus hated by the people, and at enmity both with
the people and the Committee, but was still influential at the club
of the Jacobins, the Convention, and the revolutionary Tribunal.
Knowing that an assault would be directed against him, his wisdom
would have been to strike first. To this course St. Just urged him,
but he seems to have relied upon his influence in the Convention,
and was astonished when he found his friends wholly outnumbered

and a hearing refused him. On the 27th of July he was arrested
Fall of   with Couthon, St. Just, and his brother. He escaped
Robespierre.   and fled to the Commune. For a moment it appeared
as if an insurrection would have reinstated him. But the richer
sections of Paris rallied to the destruction of their tyrant, and on the
following day Robespierre, with twenty members of the Commune,
was dragged to the scaffold.

The party which had overthrown Robespierre were as cruel and
far more depraved than he was. They would gladly have continued
the Revolution in its most odious form. But the Terror once
destroyed, it was impossible to check a reactionary movement. The
revolutionary Committee and Tribunal were modified, the Commune
destroyed, the club of the Jacobins dissolved, and the Girondins
who had escaped execution recalled. Such measures did not please
the mob of Paris, still further excited by the constant continuance of
famine. On the 12th Germinal (April 1), and again on the 1st Prairial
(May 20), they rose in insurrection, invaded the hall of the Convention, clamouring for bread and the constitution of 1793. For
Establishment   six hours a wild tumult raged within the walls. But
of the   soldiers had been collected, and with the aid of the
Directory.
Oct. 1795.   troops of the more reactionary Paris sections order was
restored. This was the deathblow of the democratic party. A
new constitution was drawn up, the executive power was vested
in five directors, and two councils, the one of 500, the other of
250, established. The hopes of the royalists had been raised by the
late reactionary movement. Finding themselves thwarted by the
new constitution, the richer sections and the partisans of reaction
marched on the Tuileries. General Menou proved unequal to his
place, and the task of defending the Assembly was given to Barras,
who chose as his active lieutenant Bonaparte. With a vigour
unchecked by fear of shedding the blood of citizens, this young
officer brought up thirty cannon from the camp of Sablons, and
received the advancing insurrectionists with such showers of grape,
that, though not without a short resistance, they were completely
defeated. This was the first step towards military despotism. The
new constitution came into effect on the 27th of October 1795.

Thus, before it was understood how completely the army had got
Pitt's first   the upper hand in France, how completely from hence-
negotiations for   forward its interests would be military, the appearance
peace.   of something more like a permanent and orderly government in the shape of the Directory seemed for the instant to give

hopes of peace. Towards that point Pitt's feelings had been gradually tending. Even as early as December 1795 he had spoken of the possibility of an honourable peace should a more settled government ever be arrived at in France, and since then much had happened to induce him to lower his tone. In spite of all his efforts, he had seen his great coalition disappear at the Congress at Basle. He had seen the complete ruin of his Quiberon expedition. More than that, all his best tendencies had been shocked by the consequences of his own government at home. But the opening of his eyes to the fallacy of his belief in the speedy bankruptcy of France and its rapid conquest, with which in all his difficulties he had hitherto buoyed himself up, came too late. His application for peace through the Swiss minister (March 1796), which the King announced at the close of the session, met with a very cold reception. For the Government of France, having just been re-established on a new and more dangerous basis, would listen to no terms which implied the restoration of the Low Countries to Austria ; and as it was impossible for Pitt, after his conduct to that country, to suggest any other terms, the negotiations speedily came to nothing.

Indeed, the French Republic had this year reached a pitch of glory unequalled in the palmiest times of the monarchy. Carnot, who was again in power as one of the Directory, had conceived a plan for a campaign of this year upon a gigantic scale. Three armies were to push out from France and strike all of them by the three different roads, of the Maine, the Danube, and the Po, at Vienna. Three young generals were intrusted with the task. Jourdan was given the army of the Sambre and Meuse, Moreau the army of the Rhine and Moselle, Bonaparte succeeded Schérer in the command of the army of Italy. The preceding year the battle of Loano had secured to the French the Riviera as far as Savona, but the troops were destitute of every necessary. Napoleon aroused their enthusiasm by promises, and in a fortnight had separated the Austrians and Piedmontese, defeated the former at Montenotte and Dégo, and thrown them back into Lombardy, the latter at Millesimo, and again at Mondovi, as he pursued them towards Turin, and finally wrung from them a treaty which left him at liberty to pursue the Austrians. Another fortnight was hardly over before he had turned the Austrian position on the Ticino by the passage of the Po at Placenza, driven them from the Adda by the victories of Fombio and Lodi, and having

Napoleon's Italian campaign. 1796.

chased them behind the Mincio, secured the whole of Lombardy to the French. Bonaparte completed the first act of the campaign by securing the line of the Adige and forming the siege of Mantua. He employed some weeks in conquering Italy as far south as Naples, but from this work he was recalled by the approach of an Austrian army to raise the siege of Mantua. Wurmser, marching by the Adige, had entered the city in triumph, while Quasdanowich was approaching by the Chiesa. Bonaparte, giving up every other object for the moment, placed himself between the armies, defeated Quasdanowich, at Lonato on the one hand, and Wurmser at Castiglioni on the other, and thus driving them into the Tyrol, resumed the siege of Mantua. Wurmser made one more effort to raise the siege; again he advanced with two armies, hoping to enclose the French. Davidowich descended the Adige, Wurmser the valley of the Brenta. The battle of Roveredo destroyed the former, while Bonaparte, turning rapidly into the valley of the Brenta in pursuit of Wurmser, came up with and defeated him at Bassano. Thus cut off from Germany, the Austrian general had no resource but to take refuge in Mantua (Sept. 12). The Austrians could not leave their army thus shut up in Mantua, and a fresh effort was made to save it. It was again a double attack, but after three days' fight, Alvinzi, coming from the east, was beaten at Arcola, and the attempt failed. Six weeks later he made one more desperate effort, but was defeated again on the plateau of Rivoli. Alvinzi's attack had been rendered the more dangerous, because upon the Maine and Rhine Jourdan and Moreau had been unsuccessful. There the Archduke Charles had in a certain degree followed the same plans as Bonaparte, and directing his whole force against Jourdan, had compelled the retreat of Moreau also. It was to this victorious general that the Austrians looked to continue their defence. But Bonaparte, in the beginning of the following year, repeatedly drove him backwards, defeated him on the Tagliamento, drove him into the mountains, and defeated him at Neumarck, and finally, having secured the pass of the Semmering, and being within eighty miles of Vienna, he obliged the Archduke to demand a suspension of arms, and opened negotiations known as the Preliminaries of Leoben (April 13), which were completed under the title of Campo Formio on the 17th of October 1797.

On the Rhine and the Maine the two other divisions of the general
Pitt's second
negotiations for
peace. .
plan had not met with the same success as had attended the arms of Bonaparte. Great and astonishing as his progress had been, it did not therefore seem as yet to have closed all

hope of peace, for which in fact it had only rendered Pitt more anxious; and as the establishment of the Directory seemed to promise that permanence to the Government which Pitt had declared to be the indispensable condition of any hopeful negotiations, it was determined in the autumn of this year (1796) to make a fresh effort, this time direct, to negotiate with the Directory. For this purpose Lord Malmesbury was despatched to Paris. The English believed that they had something they could offer in exchange for any restorations France might make. The Cape of Good Hope had been captured in the preceding year, and in the spring of the present year Moore and Abercrombie had done good service in the West Indies. Many of the islands there had been taken, Guadaloupe almost alone remained in French hands. These conquests they offered to restore. But if the French had been unwilling to treat in the preceding year, their successes in Italy had not rendered them more moderate; they were at this very time arranging, at the instigation of the malcontents in Ireland, represented by Wolfe Tone, a plan for the conquest of Ireland under the command of General Hoche, and probably a still greater plan for the invasion of England itself. In fact, there was still the same irremediable objection—the English still felt bound in honour not to resign the Netherlands to France. "On this point," writes Grenville in his instructions to Malmesbury, "your Lordship must not give the smallest hope that his Majesty will be induced to relax." There was also another point in the French diplomacy which rendered the negotiations difficult. They could not understand the position of a plenipotentiary who had not absolutely full powers to act without reference to his own Court, and taking umbrage at the repeated couriers who went to and fro from Paris, declared their belief that the effort at peace was not honest on the part of England, and that Malmesbury had not full powers at all; and finally, De la Croix, a somewhat stiff man of the red tape school, who had from the first behaved with considerable rudeness, wrote suddenly to Malmesbury bidding him leave Paris within eighteen hours. Thus closed the second effort on the part of Pitt to make peace, chiefly important because it clears him from the charge of inveterate determination to continue the war, because it throws the blame of that continuance completely on the French, and because it shows the effect which the lengthened efforts of England, especially the pressure on the finances, were having upon the naturally peaceful and economical mind of the minister.

The preparations for invasion from abroad could not be kept

secret, and fresh and constant efforts had been made to meet them.

Preparations to resist the threatened French invasion. Fresh levies were made both for the navy and for the army; supplementary bodies of militia were raised; plans suggested for the establishment of large bodies of irregular cavalry, and the enrolment as irregular infantry of all those who paid a gun license. More than this, in spite of the pressure on the finances, under which the funds had fallen as low as £53, a new loan of £18,000,000 was raised upon terms which, though we should now think very high, were not then considered remunerative. The loan, which bore a nominal interest of 5 per cent., was issued at £112, 10s.; that is, every £112, 10s. advanced was to represent £100, thus practically reducing the interest to less than 4½ per cent. Pitt found it necessary to make a distinct appeal to the loyalty of the people to raise the loan on these terms; but the temper of the wealthy classes and the amount of riches still existing in England were shown by the extraordinary rapidity with which the subscription list was filled. £1,000,000 was subscribed by the Bank in their corporate capacity, £400,000 by the directors individually; before the close of the first day £5,000,000 was subscribed by different merchants. At ten o'clock on the Monday the doors were opened, and by twenty minutes past eleven the subscription was declared to be full; hundreds were reluctantly obliged to go away. By the post innumerable orders came from the country, scarcely one of which could be accepted, and long after the subscription was closed persons continued coming, and were obliged to depart disappointed.[1] The Duke of Bridgewater sent a draft on sight of £100,000, a similar sum was even given by the Duke of Bedford, one of the staunchest opponents of the war. The Ministry subscribed £10,000 a piece.

Such an outburst of loyalty might have opened the eyes of the French as to the difference between the revolutionary **French expeditions to Bantry Bay and Bristol.** temper of England and of their own country, but their ignorance of the temper both of England and Ireland was extreme; General Clark (subsequently Napoleon's War Minister) was at this very time asking Wolfe Tone whether he thought it probable that in case of a landing in Ireland the Irish Lord Chancellor would join the rebels. On the 15th of December the great expedition for Ireland set sail from Brest. Like so many invasions of England, it was thwarted by the uncertainties of the sea. After a stormy passage a few ships assembled in Bantry Bay; but

---

1 It is a curious fact that the subscription was filled in fifteen hours and twenty minutes; two on Thursday, six on Friday, six on Saturday, and one hour and twenty minutes on Monday.

the general had been driven in another direction; there were no signs of the eager Jacobin uprising which the French had expected, the commanders were afraid to proceed without orders from Hoche, and the expedition straggled back again to Brest, with the loss of four line of battle-ships and eight frigates. A similar untimely fate met a more desperate assault intended for the shores of England. Some 1500 men, two-thirds of whom were liberated galley-slaves, and from their character known as the " Légion noire," were sent under Colonel Tate with the intention of burning Bristol. They landed on the shores of Pembrokeshire, and it needed but the appearance of a few militia and yeomanry under Lord Cawdor (and it is frequently said of a few old Welsh women in their red cloaks and hats) to induce the crew of miscreants to take to flight. The expedition was probably only intended as a sort of forlorn hope to discover in what state of preparation England was, for the negotiations having entirely ceased, the French were thinking of a great attack on England itself.

The idea of invasion was a well-timed one; at no time in the war, either before or after, was England in so critical a condition or its existence so precarious. It had become plain by this time that the strength of England, at all events under the present management, lay in two directions—in its enormous resources and capacity for paying money, and in its fleet. Though such troops as had been employed had exhibited their usual bravery, though when well led, as in India, their efforts had met with great success, it was evident that the present ministry, hampered by their political relations and by the incessant interference of the King himself in the army, was unable to make any real show in the European war. But already in the last four years nearly eighty millions had been added to the National Debt, every variety of taxation almost had been tried both to cover the interest of the accumulating debt and to supply the yearly million to the sinking fund, and men began to think that the sources of money must shortly begin to fail. And yet the subsidized armies abroad had met with nothing but disaster. The North of Germany, including even the King's electorate of Hanover, had been driven to enter into a neutrality. Prussia had in the last year signed two conventions of the most amicable and friendly description with France; and the well-known selfishness of the Austrian Court did not allow it to be questioned that, if it saw its way to permanent advantage, it also would close its disastrous campaign by deserting the coalition. Worse even than that remained behind; it seemed

[margin note: Critical condition of England.]

as if the country was really upon the verge of a national bankruptcy, for the amount of specie was found insufficient to carry on the business of the country. At the same time that the financial strength of England seemed to have been fruitlessly exhausted, her permanent power upon the sea seemed on the point of disappearing also ; for not only had the French been lately turning their attention to their own navy, but the successes of their arms had given them the command both of the fleets of Holland and Spain. Holland, formed into the Batavian Republic, had early purchased peace by promising thirty ships : in the July of the last year Spain had entered into a similar convention, and the whole of her naval resources, as many as forty line of battle-ships, were at the disposal of the French. It was with these combined armaments that the intended descent upon England was to take place. And just as the internal ruin had gone hand in hand with the failure of external financial influence, so it appeared that the new-born naval power of our enemies would go hand in hand with the total dissolution of our maritime force : for disaffection was widely spread among our sailors, and the year was marked by the mutinies of St. Helen's and the Nore.

In point of time it was the financial difficulty which first arose. The difficulty was not what is called a commercial but a monetary crisis. There was no want of credit, there was no want of solid wealth, but there was every chance of there being such a dearth of the circulating medium that the ordinary transactions of business would not be able to be carried on, that it would be impossible to meet engagements as they fell due, and that consequently many houses would be forced to stop payment, and a general bankruptcy be the result, more especially as it seemed probable that at the head of the banks that stopped payment would be the Bank of England itself. The causes of this state of things are not very difficult to understand. The same forces which had been at work to produce the necessary issue of Exchequer bills in 1793 had continued ; the balance of trade had been constantly against the country. The position of Spain, Italy, France and Holland in the ranks of our enemies had of necessity curtailed the number of our purchasers. The necessity of war supplies and several poor harvests had rendered necessary the purchase of much food and of much raw material, consequently to restore the balance large payments in gold and silver had to be made. The great subsidies granted to foreign powers had necessarily been chiefly paid

Monetary crisis.

in specie. Large compensation had been given for the freights and cargoes of neutral ships which had been seized; and the Government for their special purposes had had to borrow upwards of ten millions in specie from the Bank. Threats of invasion had induced people throughout the country to realize their property as far as possible; this had produced a run upon the country banks, which had in turn demanded their deposits from the Bank of England. All these accumulated causes had so lowered the reserve, that on Saturday the 20th of February there was only £1,272,000 in the Bank cellars, and it was known that the demands of the next forty-eight hours would entirely empty them. In this crisis the Bank applied to the Government; a Council was immediately held, although Suspension of it was Sunday, and a proclamation was issued forbid- cash payments. ding payments in cash. A meeting of merchants next day sanctioned this step, promising to accept bank notes as legal tender. On ex- amination the Bank was found solvent, but a Bill was passed pro- hibiting it to pay in cash more than twenty shillings, or to advance to Government more than £600,000. Though only intended as a temporary expedient, this Act continued in operation for twenty-two years, and during the whole of that time the depreciation of the paper money was comparatively slight.

The danger caused by the mutiny was still greater : it was the intention of the French Directory that the fleet of the Texel, composed entirely of the Dutch, the fleet at Brest which had been collected for the invasion of Ireland, and the great Spanish fleet, should combine. Thus, an armament of more than seventy ships of the line would sweep the English fleet from the Channel, and any operations against the island would be rendered safe. But the check The invasion sustained by the Spanish fleet off Cape St. Vincent checked by the victory of St ruined the well-conceived plan. A few days before Vincent, Feb Tate landed in England, the great Spanish fleet set sail 14, 1797. from Carthagena, intending to join the French fleet off Brest and the Dutch fleet off the Texel, and thus secure the mastery of the Channel. Sir John Jervis was Admiral in the Mediterranean, and with him was Commodore Nelson, and though the Spanish fleet had twelve more ships than he had, and 1200 more guns, he determined to fight. He contrived to separate nine Spanish ships from the main body, and took four of the remainder, and though the separated ships joined the line in the evening, and Jervis was still outnumbered, the Spanish fleet retired into Cadiz.

But though the combined invasion was thus thwarted, the whole danger for England, or rather for Ireland, was by no means at an end. Hoche had been removed from the army of the Ocean to the army of the Sambre and Meuse. His mind was constantly bent upon the invasion of Ireland, and, acting under his influence, the Dutch Government, wishing to do something to show that they were not entirely effaced from the list of nations, with great efforts strengthened and equipped their fleet at the Texel till it numbered fourteen sail of the line, and embarked in it their whole army, 15,000 men, for an attack upon Ireland. The Directory, taking umbrage at this independent action, insisted upon Hoche, with 5000 men, accompanying them, and on their refusal began again to get ready their Brest squadron for a similar expedition. To watch the Dutch became the duty of Admiral Duncan, the care of Brest was intrusted to Admiral Bridport with the fleet at Portsmouth. Fortunately for England, the sailing of the fleets was delayed ; had they sailed in the summer, as intended, they would have found England without fleets.

Early in the year a conspiracy was discovered among the crews of the fleet at Spithead, with a view to demanding redress of certain

Mutiny at Spithead. grievances. These grievances were shared in by all the seamen in the navy and were very real. The pay and pensions had never been altered since the time of Charles II., though every necessary of life had risen from thirty to forty per cent.; this neglect was rendered particularly objectionable as the pay and pensions of the army had been increased to suit the times. Many officers were appointed by interest alone, and a system of barefaced peculation was carried on by those who had the duty of provisioning the fleet, for the ships were furnished in a great degree by contract through the purser ; moreover, all the nautical arrangements were at this time remarkable for extreme roughness, almost brutality, for unjust severity of discipline, for arbitrary power vested in the hands of the captain, and frequent misuse of that power. When Lord Bridport, Lord Howe's second in command, signalled to put to sea, every ship in the fleet refused to obey ; and the next day delegates from every ship met in the ' Queen Charlotte,' and the mutiny was organized. The men behaved with perfect decorum, and drew up a petition, asking that their wages should be raised to suit the rise of prices in every direction, and that some improvement should be made in their system of pensions. To the Admiralty they sent a petition, exposing the peculations of the pursers and the unwarrantable hardships to which the sailor was exposed. The

Admiralty acknowledged at once the justice of the claim for advanced wages, but were silent upon the other abuses. This did not satisfy the men: three admirals were sent to treat with them; and when an outburst of anger on the part of one of them broke off the conference, the red flag of mutiny was hoisted and the guns loaded. However, when their demands were granted in full, and a free pardon was sent them from London, they at once returned to their duty. During the whole of the outbreak perfect order had reigned. But the folly of the Admiralty, who, wishing to save their credit, sent down a perverse order that the marines should be kept constantly ready to suppress mutiny, led the sailors to believe that they were being deceived, and a second outbreak was the result. An attempt to suppress it by force on board the 'London' ended in a real mutiny among all the ships then lying at St. Helen's, outside Spithead. Lord Howe, the most popular of the admirals, known among the sailors as "Black Dick," was intrusted with the difficult task of recalling the fleet to its allegiance. With great skill he contrived that while their requests were granted, they should seem to be receiving rather than demanding a favour. He persuaded them to write a letter of contrition to himself, and apparently as the fruit of his good offices, announced to them that an Act of Parliament had been passed securing to them the redress of grievances they had demanded, and that considerable changes were to be made among the officers.

This wholly unpolitical mutiny was followed by a more formidable movement among the ships at the Nore. It began on board the 'Sandwich,' the flagship of Admiral Buckner. As in the former case, delegates from the Mutiny at the Nore. May 18. seamen met on board the 'Sandwich,' but the chief management of the mutiny fell absolutely into the hands of a seaman called Parker, a man of good education, and at one time an officer in the navy, but whose abilities as a leader were spoiled by his arrogant assumption of dictatorial power. Under his influence the demands of the mutineers assumed a political character; they required a revision of the Articles of War, an increase of prize-money, and the dismissal of officers not agreeable to the ships' companies. All efforts to bring the men to reason were unavailing. Lord Spencer himself, the First Lord of the Admiralty, had an interview with Parker, but was met with nothing but insult. After this the mutineers fired upon some frigates who would not join them, and blockaded the Thames. It became necessary to take vigorous measures. Bills were passed without opposition strengthening the hands of Government, and making it felony to hold intercourse with the mutinous ships. Ships were got ready, the navigation of the Thames was rendered difficult by the removal of marks, and batteries were erected along the river. Cut off from the shore, and finding no sympathy among the fleets at Portsmouth and Plymouth, nor among even the most advanced radicals on shore, although they were joined by the fleets of Admiral Duncan, the mutineers began to give way. Ship after ship slipped her cable and escaped from the mutinous fleet, and on the 15th of June the 'Sandwich' herself was brought within range of the batteries. Parker was at once apprehended, sentenced to death, and hanged. But though the firmness of the Government had secured them complete victory, they were too conscious of the real abuses in the navy to be severe. Only four or five executions followed.

The great peculiarity of the mutiny was the ease with which it
Real loyalty of was ultimately suppressed and the proofs of underlying
the sailors. loyalty which are visible throughout it. In the Channel
fleet all the offers of the Admiralty, and even of Parliament, were regarded as delusive till the King's own sign manual was exhibited, upon which all signs of mistrust at once vanished. When one of the ships threatened to leave the fleet and join the French, the guns of the rest of the mutinous fleet were at once turned upon it, and it was carefully blockaded by guard-boats; and again, so far from sympathizing with the mutineers of the Nore, the sailors of the Channel fleet, after their return to allegiance, wrote to the delegates declaring that their conduct was a scandal to the British navy. Even at the Nore, where the mutiny had taken a more political form, every ship but one struck the red flag and hoisted the royal ensign on the King's birthday, and within a few weeks of the suppression of the disaffection, the battle of Camperdown, one of the severest engagements of the time, was chiefly won for England by the crews of the lately insurgent fleet.

It was well for England that the Government of France was at
Disorganization this time so disorganized that no vigorous effort could
of the French be made to take advantage of her deplorable condition.
Government. The place of the assignats had been taken by another
form of paper money called "mandats," but these too had been rejected by the people, who could no longer be brought to believe in paper money of any description. Forced to have recourse to the use of specie, the Directory had also found itself compelled to have recourse

to the old means of raising money ; compulsory loans were established, the receipts of future years anticipated, the national goods sold for whatever they would fetch, and money raised at the most ridiculous interest. These financial arrangements gave rise to much nefarious speculation and stock-jobbing ; the business of the army to still more ; and the newly enriched speculators, emancipated from the pressure of the terror and devoid of all the nobler sentiments of republicanism, were a mere set of selfish voluptuaries. In such a dissolution of morality and public spirit it was plain that the royalists had their chance, and in the year 1797 sufficient members of their party were elected to change the majority of the two councils. The representative body immediately entered into a struggle with the executive Directory; and in that Directory were Barras, a revolutionary at heart though the leader of all the dissoluteness of the time, Barthélemy, the negotiator of Basle, who appears to have been royalist in his tendencies, and Carnot, an upright republican, but yet under the influence of the dread of the old terror. It was plain that if the Revolution was to be saved it must be done by violent means, and Rewbell and Laréveillière, the remaining directors, with the assistance of Barras, determined to save it at the cost of a *coup d'état* carried out by the army. On the night of the 18th Fructidor (Sept. 4, 1797), Carnot and Barthélemy, with fifty of the obnoxious majority, were arrested, and all chance of a royalist reaction was for the time over. Bonaparte was now convinced that the ultimate fate of France must be with the army, in other words, that it must lie with himself, but with great wisdom he determined to wait the turn of events.

While the parties were thus struggling in France, and there seemed a chance of an entire change of feeling, the English ministry, very seriously anxious for peace, again opened   Negotiations negotiations. The Preliminaries of Léoben had in fact   at Lisle. removed what should have been the sole difficulty ; it was impossible that England should continue to hold out on the subject of the Low Countries when Austria had herself entered into a private treaty to abandon them. A passport was therefore demanded, and, somewhat unfortunately, Lord Malmesbury was again fixed upon as the negotiator. He went to Lisle, presented his plan of a treaty, and had every reason to believe that all was going well. England consented to restore all her conquests with the exception of the Isle of Trinidad, the Cape of Good Hope, and Ceylon. But this was at the very moment when the quarrel was at its height in Paris ; intent upon its own affairs, the Directory suffered the negotiations to drag on, and when at length the republican party won their victory on the 18th Fructidor, the negotiations were suddenly broken off on the old ground that Malmesbury had not got full authority. The real reason is obvious,—the party in power, who relied on the army, knew that the power of the army was immensely increased by a state of war.

The termination of the negotiations was at once followed by a vigorous continuation of the war. Lord Malmesbury had been but

Battle of Camperdown. Oct. 11, 1797. a few weeks in England when the Dutch fleet found itself ready at length to sail from the Texel. But the delay—caused by the weather, the absence of Hoche, and the factions of Paris—had almost deprived it of its terrors. Even when the greater part of his fleet had been in mutiny in the Thames, Duncan had maintained the appearance of a blockade; keeping his two faithful ships within sight of the land, he had kept up so regular a succession of signals, as though sending his orders to a fleet outside, that the Dutch never found out that there were only two ships watching them. When at length they sailed Duncan's fleet outnumbered theirs by one ship. He had withdrawn for an instant to Yarmouth roads to refit, but apprised in time, he was enabled to fall upon the Dutch fleet before it had left the coast of Holland. He contrived, although the enemy was in close order, to come between them and the shore, and after a close combat, which recalled the old days of the rivalry between England and Holland, by four o'clock on the 11th of October he had succeeded in capturing the flagship of Admiral Winter, together with seven other ships of the line, two 56-gun ships, and two frigates. The bold manœuvre of passing between the enemy and the shore was a source of some danger, as the fleets drifted close inland during the action, but Duncan skilfully saved both his own fleet and his prizes. The action was watched by crowds from the Dutch shore. This battle put an end to the danger of immediate invasion, though it seems to have inspired the French with a determination to carry on that invasion on a larger scale in the following year, when great preparations were made under the personal superintendence of Bonaparte.

The breach of negotiations at Lisle was followed on the 17th

Peace of Campo Formio. Oct. 17. of October by the completion of the Peace of Campo Formio, which had been begun by the Preliminaries of Léoben. This peace secured to France the possession of Belgium, the left bank of the Rhine, and the Ionian

Isles, and acknowledged the establishment of the Cisalpine Re-
public, consisting of the provinces conquered in Italy from the
Austrians, the Pope, and Venice; while Austria received in exchange
Venice itself and its eastern provinces, Friuli, Istria, and Dalmatia.
France thus lay not only triumphant in Europe, but with the
Rhine for its frontier, and for outposts four republics pledged to
uphold its revolutionary ideas. But in acquiring this position the
rights of peoples had been trampled upon. A few months later saw
Switzerland appended to France, while the occupation of Rome seemed
to give colour to the assertion that the Revolution was atheistical.
The whole turn of events was such as to justify, even to necessitate,
subsequent European interference.

The peculiar manner in which Ireland has been conquered, peopled,
and managed, renders questions regarding this country Complications
most intricate and difficult. There is seldom a single attending Irish
interest to be traced which is not crossed by numerous difficulties.
side winds, which render the development of political questions
crooked and complicated. The Roman Catholic interest, the Protestant interest, the old Irish interest, the Anglo-Irish interest, the
interest of the English ascendancy, the claims of the Presbyterians
as contrasted with the National Church, are constantly crossing and
recrossing. At no time was this complication so great or this difficulty so insoluble as in the years which followed the breaking out
of the French Revolution.

There is one thing, however, which tends to throw a certain light
upon the conduct of the Government of England during Necessity for
these years of difficulty. Pitt and his more intimate the Union.
friends had already firmly decided in their own minds that one cure
only was possible for Irish evils—a close and complete legislative
union with England. The action of the Whig Government in 1782
had been ostensibly in exactly the opposite direction; the triumph
of Grattan and the volunteers had been won when legislative disunion was granted, and what we should now speak of as Home Rule
established. The party which triumphed on that occasion was not
the Irish party, or the Catholic party, but the Protestant aristocracy.
The anti-national character and exclusive nature of the party in
power was shown by the rejection of all Pitt's efforts at parliamentary
reform. The independent Irish Parliament was indeed full of able
speakers; men who carried the art of rhetoric and of clothing little
thought in magnificent language to the highest pitch. But it is not

unfair to take as a sample of the practical excellence of the management of what we may speak of as the Home Rulers, the condition of
the Foundling Hospital in Dublin. It was a noble institution; about
£16,000 a year was spent on it; 120 noblemen and wealthy gentry
were on its committee; yet after just ten years of Irish management,
a committee of inquiry reported that out of upwards of 2000 infants
yearly consigned to its care, the average that survived was 130.
They were sent up in scores, in open baskets, from distant parts of
Ireland, and arrived crushed and half lifeless, to be tossed aside,
without care or inquiry, into the kennel. Twenty-one committee-men
formed a quorum, yet never once, except when places were to be
given away, had that quorum met, and for years the treasurer, to
whom the management had been confided, had been absolutely bed-
ridden. All that can be alleged in excuse for the bad management,
of which this is r. sample, is that the Constitution of 1782 had not
been thoroughly tried. Deprived by law of its power in the Irish
Parliament, yet conscious of the impossibility of allowing the country
to act as if completely independent, the Government had had recourse
to indirect influence for establishing its power. While the franchise
and the representation, all official places and all professions, except
the medical profession, were exclusively confined to the Protestants,
who were also the possessors of nineteen-twentieths of the soil, Government had found it possible by bribery, direct or indirect, to command
a constant majority in Parliament of those who were eager to uphold
the English connection and the Protestant ascendancy. But the
very fact of its thus acting had placed a considerable portion of the
Protestant population in opposition to Government.

Among the Protestants themselves there were formed two great
Irish opposition
to Government.
parties, who may be called roughly Whigs and Tories;
on the one side those placemen and pensioners who supported the English Government, and on the other those aristocratic
families and connections (probably by no means purer or higher-
minded than their opponents) who wished, as the Whig aristocracy
had wished in England, to be masters of the Government, and to
rule Ireland almost as a separate nation. Of these great connections
the typical men were, of the Tories, the family of the Beresfords, led
by the ability of Fitzgibbon the Chancellor, and of the Whigs, the
family of the Ponsonbys, led by the genius of Grattan. Around the
Opposition party there naturally collected those men who were really
reformers at heart, and the Opposition was thus enabled to use cries
and watchwords which were not only specious and plausible, but

which really touched the great evils of the country. The first of these evils was the preposterous amount of Government influence; and the obvious way in which that influence might be reached was by a reform of Parliament, for nothing could be more abominable than the arrangement by which members were elected. It was worse even than in England; by far the larger number of seats were either private or Government property, and nominees were appointed under distinct conditions, and their votes secured by distinct and well-understood bargains; every man's price and every man's expectation were actually entered like a list of merchandise in the Government books. A second point was the fact, that not only all political power, but till the year 1793 almost all social position was denied to the Roman Catholics. On the first of these points the opponents of Government were agreed; they were perfectly willing, for the sake of injuring Government, to press constantly for a large reform bill. On the second point there was a far greater difference of opinion. Grattan, though himself a Protestant and a friend to the Protestant ascendancy, was great enough to urge constantly the relief of his Catholic fellow-countrymen; but the great majority of his friends, however much they might from time to time for political purposes uphold the Catholic claims, were in fact thoroughly opposed to anything which would injure their own Protestant ascendancy. There was thus a sort of show of union between the Protestant nationalists and the Catholics, but at heart disunion and dislike.

Meanwhile, whatever effect upon the Protestant population Home Rule may have had, it had not in the slightest degree alleviated the position of the Irish peasants. Their landlords were still Englishmen, Protestants, conquerors, and harsh landlords. The Church of England still demanded its tithes. The aristocracy and gentry had neglected their duties till, as has been well said, they forgot they had duties to perform; they were hopelessly corrupt, both morally and politically. The independence which the peasantry were taught by the inflated language used in Parliament to believe they had already acquired seemed to them a bitter deception; and their belief in the villany of the rulers who had tricked them, and in the complete slavery and hardship of their own position as Roman Catholics, was envenomed by the expressions which the Opposition allowed itself to use in its assaults on Government. They were thus ripe for rebellion. Indeed, for many years they had been filling Ireland with outrages. All sorts of combinations had been made against rent-collectors and tithe-proctors. In

Munster arose the Society of the White Boys and the followers of Captain Right. Combinations were also directed against the farmers of taxes, who most shamelessly abused their position. Absenteeism was the curse of Ireland. While the middleman of the absentee landlord racked the wretched cotter for his rent, the middleman of the absentee parson racked him for his tithes. They were in the habit of taking their payments in interest-bearing bonds, and when the wretched peasant was unable to meet those bonds, he became practically the slave of the tithe farmer, who compelled him to do his farm work for him as the price of his forbearance to put the law in execution.

The executive machinery of the Government in Ireland was not strong
Weakness of the executive. enough to keep order. The outrages of the Catholics had frequently to be met by the voluntary efforts of their enemies, which soon degenerated into counter-outrages. Thus there arose in Munster a constant cruel war between the two religions. In the north of Ireland it was worse, for the hatred between the religions was there more pronounced. In dread of outrages similar to those of the south, the Protestants began, in the roughest and most illegal manner, to deprive the Catholics of arms, which indeed they had no right to carry ; and the Catholics were driven to form themselves into lawless societies under the name of Defenders, in opposition to which there arose, about the year 1790, the organization of the Orange Lodges; and there, too, a cruel civil war began to be waged.

While Ireland was in this miserable condition, while the liberty
Effect of the French Revolution in Ireland. which the wretched peasantry had been promised had entirely disappeared, while the upper classes of all parties seemed in the last degree degraded, and the ascendancy of the useless and tyrannical Church fixed for ever, the great news of the French Revolution came. Even in more sober England men's hearts were stirred within them at the promise of the emancipation of the human race ; among the suffering passionate Irish, with their impulsive and sanguine dispositions, the effect was far greater. But the class who were at first chiefly influenced by it were not the Roman Catholics—although, no doubt, for them too it seemed to promise at least a share in the franchise,—but the Northern Presbyterians and Dissenters, republican from their origin, and, from the very nature of their religious creed, equally oppressed with the Catholics by a proud and dominant Church, and more keenly alive to that abominable system of government which touched the Protestant more nearly than the Catholic, because he

alone had any share in it. Ulster, and especially the town of Belfast, were the great centres of the republican and Jacobin feelings, together with Dublin, where, as was natural, the more lively, ambitious, and freethinking elements of society were chiefly to be found.

There were thus to be somehow handled and managed by Government a strong, vicious, reckless, constitutional opposi- Difficulties of
tion, in connection with a few men honestly desiring the Government.
the legislative independence of Ireland, and, as a necessary step,
thorough parliamentary reform ;—secondly, a great body of Catholics,
of which the higher and more respectable part desired the gradual
alleviation of their position, and joined with the Opposition,
not from dislike to the English connection, but because the supporters of Government influence seemed inclined to refuse every
demand ; and of which the lower part, in wild misery and excitement, was waging a lawless war both in the north and south ;—and
thirdly, a very considerable body of men, dissenters of the North,
and freethinkers of Dublin, who, touched by the influence of the
French Revolution, desired an entire overthrow of the Government,
and were willing to throw themselves into the arms of France for
the destruction of the English connection.

It is plain that of these sections two were chiefly dangerous—the
Roman Catholic peasant, who hated the Protestant, and Formation of
the republican Protestant, who hated the Government the Society
of United
and hated the Catholic also. While these were separate Irishmen.
it might be possible to play off one against the other. In this the
few reckless men who desired a complete change of Government saw
the cause of their weakness. The most prominent of these was
Wolfe Tone, a young barrister, the son of a Dublin coachmaker,
who for personal reasons as he openly confessed—because certain
suggestions of his had not been well received in England—was the
determined enemy of everything English. Nominally a Protestant,
really a freethinker, to him, and to several others like him,
religious disputes appeared merely ridiculous ; and the brilliant idea
seized him of uniting those two sections of people which were really
dangerous to England—the Northern Republican and the National
Roman Catholic—and of thus forming the great Society of the
United Irishmen. It was plain that great difficulties must arise
in realizing such a scheme. Much as the Protestants of Ulster
hated England, they undoubtedly hated Catholics more ; much as
the Catholics hated England, undoubtedly they hated Protestants
more. Still, it might be the policy of both parties to bury for a

time their great hatred, and to make common cause on that
point which they had in common. Wolfe Tone and his republican
friends, entirely careless of religion, formed an excellent connecting
link. It was with this view that he betook himself to Belfast, to
take advantage of a great celebration to be held there in honour
of the anniversary of the destruction of the Bastille, and there
established his Society, as he seems already to have done in
part in Dublin. Its ostensible views as put forward in the programme were, that the weight of English influence was so great
as to require the cordial union of the people of Ireland to maintain liberty, that the only constitutional way of opposing that influence was reform of Parliament, and that no reform was practicable
which did not include Irishmen of every religious persuasion. Tone
hoped, by thus setting prominently forward the advantages which
each party was desirous of gaining, to win the adhesion of both.

But the Catholics themselves were not a wholly united body.
Disunion among the Catholics. Unable to find any more legitimate means of making
themselves heard, they had, since 1782, intrusted their
interests to a central committee at Dublin, consisting of
some of the most important nobility and gentry of their party, as
well as of others of a more violent stamp. The temper of the
English Government was such, that fairly friendly relations subsisted
between it and the Bishops and more educated part of the Catholics.
Pitt was himself a friend to the Catholic claims in England. · Many
of the restrictions had been already removed from the Catholics
in England and in Scotland, and neither Pitt nor the chief members of his Cabinet thought it impossible that the emancipation of
the Irish should proceed by the same steps as in England. This
feeling was rendered much stronger by the French Revolution. It
seemed impossible that the dogmatic and highly organized Roman
Church should become the champion of disorder and atheism, and
Pitt hoped by attaching them to himself to find in them a support
against the spread of the revolutionary principles which were his
great dread. The Catholics thus became an object of contention to
the extreme parties; on the one side the Nationalists and United
Irishmen sought to win them by holding out hopes of regaining their
supremacy by reform of Parliament, and of a consequent alienation
from English policy which might well involve a complete change in
the Act of Settlement, and the restoration of much property to its
old Roman Catholic owners; and on the other side the English
Government attempted to outbid its rivals, and to attach the Catho-

lics more closely to the English interests, by granting them immediately a large measure of relief. As was natural, this auction terminated in a split among the Catholics themselves. In 1791 a portion of the Committee sent up very reasónable demands in a petition, signed by upwards of sixty names. These petitioners represented the moderate and better part of the Catholics, who would have been willing to accept the legitimate offers of the English Government; but the majority, inspired by the revolutionary feelings of the time, and eagerly desirous for the complete restoration of their position, refused to acknowledge the petition as their own, and drove the sixty signatories from the Committee. They then proceeded to play directly into the hands of Wolfe Tone, entering into close connection with the revolutionary society at Belfast, which they no doubt intended to use as a cat's-paw only, until they should attain that complete Catholic ascendancy, which could scarcely fail to result from a thorough Reform Bill if connected with the removal of religious disabilities.

It may excite surprise that the Government did not, in the presence of the very obvious danger which had arisen, and when the country was full of disturbance, act vigorously in support of the Protestant ascendancy, or at least confine itself to giving such measures of relief as would have satisfied the seceders of the Catholic committee. The Lord Lieutenant, and those who had charge of the government in Ireland, perpetually urged upon the English Cabinet the necessity of supporting the English, declaring that the real contest would ultimately be between the Irish nationalists and the English settlers. But Pitt could not give up his idea that relief to the Catholics was necessary. He suffered Richard Burke, a foolish young man, to act apparently in his name, and to hold out hopes to the more advanced Catholic party. The Cabinet, indeed, subsequently denied having given him any authority, but as undoubtedly Pitt had given him a letter of introduction to the Secretary, it was very hard to prove this disclaimer. Consequently, in the session of 1792, both the Belfast republicans and the Catholic committee sent up petitions to Parliament of a very strong description. They were both rejected, and in their place a measure was introduced by Sir Hercules Langrishe, apparently with the consent of Government, admitting Catholics to the profession of the law, removing restrictions on their education, and repealing the Inter-marriage Act. It was only with considerable difficulty, and by Government influence, that this Bill was passed

Mismanagement of the Government.

[2 C]

through the House, for the Protestant feeling in Parliament was very strong. Langrishe's measure was no doubt a righteous one; but it is a question whether at the moment concession to the Catholics was wise, especially when it was purchased by unpopularity among the Protestants. It seems probable, however, that both now and in his subsequent action, Pitt was influenced by a detestation of the iniquitous means by which Ireland was governed. He did not care much about shocking his majority of pensioners, or weakening English ascendancy, being fully determined that before long that ascendancy should give place to a wider and less provincial scheme of Government, produced by a complete union.

The effect of the measure at first was, however, certainly not salutary. Signs of concession on the part of the Govern-

Increased demands of the Catholics.

ment, and the foolish conduct of Richard Burke, excited the Catholics of the United Irish party to raise still higher claims, and to attempt to insist upon them by overawing the Government. Determined that there should be no mistake as to the real wishes of their party, the committee contrived to summon a general convention of Catholics in Dublin, each parish sending up its representatives. This Parliament met in what was called the Back Lane, under the presidency of Edward Burne, a well-known Catholic merchant of extreme views. The members drew up a petition, demanding the franchise for the Catholics, and sent it direct to England, attempting thus to overrule their own Irish Government. At the same time, Tone and Napper Tandy, the leader of the Dublin malcontents, attempted to arm their threatening counter-parliament with military power, by raising, in imitation of the old volunteers, a body whom they called the National Guards. The vigour of Fitzgibbon nipped this plan in the bud. He issued a proclamation against the assembling of men in arms, and as though to prove how much a little vigour would effect, and how easily the movement might at that time have been suppressed, the muster which should have taken place the following day was attended by three men only, of whom Napper Tandy was one. But the petition of the Convention had been well received in England; the Government there persisted in overriding the wishes of the Lord Lieutenant, and with every appearance of having yielded to pressure, in 1793, Major Hobart, the Chief Secretary, in accordance with instructions from

Catholic Relief Bill passed. 1793.

London, introduced, and by Government influence forced down the throat of an unwilling House of Commons, a second Catholic Relief Bill, admitting Catholics to the grand juries, magistracy, and, finally, to the franchise, at the same time repealing the Act which prohibited the bearing of arms. The Government had now gone as far as it intended to go. It had apparently made its concessions with a bad grace, and to the wrong people. As Lawrence Parsons, a singularly sensible member of the Irish Parliament, pointed out, the Bill gave the franchise, but still refused to the Catholics the right of sitting in Parliament. As the franchise was very low, it virtually threw the power into the hands of the lower Catholics, while excluding the Catholic gentry from their legitimate influence. It was, however, in vain that he urged the admission of the Catholics to Parliament, and the raising of the franchise. The United Irishmen were able to say, that as long as they could vote for Protestants alone the franchise was of little use ; and further, that even had they been able to elect Catholics, the Government influence was too strong to make the change of any avail.

It was then nominally with the cry of reform of Parliament that they continued their agitation. And as the late con-cessions had been apparently granted under a system of threats, the same system of intimidation was pursued. Riots and outrages again broke out in all parts of Ireland. The Defenders again became active. House after house of the Protestants was robbed. Murders of all sorts were committed. In this year alone there were 180 houses attacked in Munster ; while the success of the Convention had been such that the experiment was to be repeated at Athlone. Fitzgibbon indeed postponed the immediate danger by securing the passage of the Convention Bill, which forbade the assembling of such illegal meetings ; and in other respects the hands of the executive were for the time so much strengthened, that although much outrage continued, and discontent was smouldering throughout the country, and the emissaries of the United Irishmen scarcely veiled their revolutionary intentions, their hopes sunk low, and Tone was himself thinking of joining the Government side. He even had an interview with the Chief Secretary, and there was some thought of giving him employment abroad. But just about this time, in 1794, the United Irishmen, losing hope of carrying out their revolution singlehanded, began to think of summoning the assistance of France. It was in this year that one Jackson went as an emissary to France with undoubtedly traitorous designs. One of his comrades, as so often happens in Irish treasons, turned informer ; Jackson was apprehended, and took poison, and died in the dock as the sentence was being pronounced on him.

(margin note: Renewed agitation for reform of Parliament)

Suddenly the hopes of the Irish party received an unexpected
Failure of Fitz-
william's efforts
at reform, Jan.
1795. impulse. In the year 1794 the Duke of Portland and
the Whigs joined the Cabinet. Their point of union
was the war only, in other respects they clung to their
old traditions. Portland, their chief, had been Prime Minister when
the Act for legislative equality had been passed; and when, under
pressure from this section of his party, Pitt consented to send Lord
Fitzwilliam, the heir of Lord Rockingham, to Ireland as Viceroy,
there seemed a great probability that a complete change of policy
was intended. Such indeed was the view of Grattan, who had had
a personal interview with Pitt, and such no doubt was Fitzwilliam's
own view. Such in part was Pitt's view also, but he was half-
hearted in the matter. He was displeased at having to yield anything to the new members of his Cabinet, and though desiring that
the Catholic claims should be granted, he was so pledged to repression that he scarcely thought the present a desirable time for that
measure; while his fidelity to personal friends, and his strong view
of personal claims, made him determined that none of the existing
officers or placemen should be removed. Besides this, the only
statesman of great ability among the Irish, and the only one who
possessed Pitt's ear, was Fitzgibbon the Chancellor, a bigoted upholder of Protestant ascendancy. It was then with very different
views that Fitzwilliam and Pitt regarded the new appointment. How
great this difference was seems to be absolutely proved by a reference to Grenville's letters. In fact, the way in which Pitt yielded
can only be explained by his intending ultimately to produce the
Union. Fitzwilliam's arrival was hailed with enthusiasm by the Irish,
and acting upon his own view of his commission, which he believed
that Pitt shared, he proceeded rapidly to introduce reforms. Fitzgibbon, it was clearly understood, he was not to touch; but the
Attorney and the Solicitor-General, Wolfe and Toler, he removed,
and replaced them by the far better known lawyers, Ponsonby and
Curran. A great outcry was raised at this, but it was slight when
compared with the opposition evoked when the Viceroy proceeded
to lay his hands on Mr. Beresford, Commissioner of the Revenue.
He was the head of one of those great families who obtained their
influence by managing the country for the Government interest,
without any claim on the score of talent. So great was his influence
that a quarter of the places in Ireland were said to be his gift, though
he himself occupied only the unimportant situation of Commissioner
of the Revenue. Every underling and jobber in the country felt his

position endangered, but it wanted more influence than theirs to remove Fitzwilliam. His discomfiture was completed by his own rash rapidity of action. A Bill was planned with the co-operation of Grattan for the immediate granting of the Catholic claims. Fitzgibbon at once took advantage of this, and well acquainted with the obstinacy and over-scrupulousness of the King's character, found means to have it suggested to him that to admit Roman Catholics to Parliament was a breach of his Coronation Oath. The suggestion fell on willing ears; from that time onward it became a fixed idea in the royal mind, from which no effort could remove it.

Fitzwilliam was recalled. Lord Camden, son of Chatham's friend Pratt, succeeded him as Viceroy, with the avowed inten- Fitzwilliam succeeded by Lord tion of restoring the system of Government and the Camden, March policy of Lord Westmoreland. His arrival was marked 1795. by riots in Dublin, in which Fitzgibbon's life was with difficulty saved. Grattan persisted in bringing in the Bill he had begun under Lord Fitzwilliam, but when, after a debate which lasted all through the night, it was finally rejected by a large majority, the rejection was held to be final.

A change came over the spirit of Ireland. Even the more patriotic members began to think that a complete separation An open rebel- from England was their only hope. The Catholic lion begins. committee, feeling that it was no longer of any use, dissolved itself. The Catholics made common cause with the United Irish, and the bolder spirits, scarcely hiding their revolutionary intentions, sought assistance directly from France, whither Tone and Lord Edward Fitzgerald betook themselves; and an insurrection was planned, to be carried out in conjunction with a French army under Hoche. One effect of this was the separation of the Protestants of the North from the disaffected body. Among the townsmen of Belfast revolutionary principles still kept their hold; but the eagerness of the Catholic Defenders and their constant outrages to procure arms threw the great mass of the northern Protestants, whether Churchmen or Presbyterians, on to the Government side. The Orange Lodges were formed and organized. The opposite parties were divided, as seems inevitable in Ireland, by religion; and the first open fight between the two parties took place (Sept. 21) at the village of Diamond in Armagh, a skirmish spoken of as the battle of the Diamond. At all events interests now began to clear themselves. The fight was between Catholic revolutionary Irish and the Protestant upholders of English ascendancy.

This piece of Irish history has been, and will ever be, the subject of the fiercest controversy. It is only by remem-
bering that on one side the accumulated wrath of a
half-savage and badly governed country was making itself terribly
visible for an object which cannot be condemned, yet by means
which were utterly odious; and that on the other side the instinct
of self-defence, the stern necessity of upholding their rule at all
hazards, fear of the ever-threatening horrors of a triumphant and
savage foe, and revenge for the personal miseries already inflicted
upon them, were driving men to cruel though perhaps necessary
actions, that this period can be read in at all a judicial and un-
partisan spirit.

With regard to the savage cruelty of the Irish, it can only be said,
as affording some excuse for their conduct, that they had suffered
much, that they had much to complain of. With regard to the
real danger and lengthened organization of the conspiracy there
is abundant proof, and was then abundant proof in the hands of
the Irish Government, for as usual all the secret committees were
full of traitors. With regard to the conduct of the Government
—which, whatever may be said of it, did not drive the people to
rebellion, for they had long settled upon that—it may be fairly
asked what other means than severity could possibly have been
used. Lord Camden deserves the greatest credit for his moderation, and for the care with which, through two years and upwards,
he avoided bringing on an open outbreak. The only real question
appears to be whether severity used much earlier might not have
altogether frustrated the rebellion. The reason why this severity
was not used is to be found in the conduct of the Whigs in England,
and in the views of Pitt and the Liberal part of his Government,
who sat apart from the scene and could not be brought completely
to comprehend the danger.

To the Irish Government the state of the country was well
known. It was known that Wolfe Tone had gone
abroad, nominally to America, but with the intention
of visiting France, with the full approbation of the
United Committee at Belfast. It was known that in 1795 the plans
of an insurrection had been almost perfected, and that to meet that
insurrection there were in Ireland scarcely any English troops, about
10,000 invalids and fencibles, and a militia half of whom were among
the conspirators. It was also known that assassinations and the
swearing-in of conspirators were of constant occurrence. It is not

surprising that in the year 1796 it was found necessary to pass an
Indemnity Act to cover acts for the preservation of peace which
broke the letter of the law done by the army and magistrates, or
that a Bill should have been passed against assassination, or that
an Insurrection Act, which allowed suspected districts to be declared
beyond the law, and to be placed in military occupation and deprived
of arms, should have been carried. The danger became still more
threatening when it was known that Lord Edward Fitzgerald, the
brother of Lord Leitrim, and Arthur O'Connor, the friend of all
the Whigs in England, had gone abroad, had seen General Hoche
in Switzerland, and arranged with him for a French invasion. At
this time a trustworthy informant told the Government that there
were 200,000 men ready officered, that there were pikes and muskets
for 150,000, and that the militia were almost to a man members
of the United Irish Society. It was then that it became absolutely
necessary for security to raise a trustworthy force. This force,
principally consisting of Protestants, who volunteered immediately
to the number of 37,000, was the yeomanry. It did not, however,
consist entirely of Protestants ; and Camden, in spite of the pressure laid upon him by Parliament and by all who surrounded
him, refused to recognize the Orange Lodges, which would at once
have given him the power he wanted. As it was, the establishment
of the yeomanry certainly saved Ireland, and yet it is here probably
that the great error of the Government showed itself. English
soldiers, if possible, alone should have been used. The traditional
hatred between the religions was too fierce to allow the subjugation of the Catholics to be left in the hands of the Protestant
yeomen.

The invasion which Hoche had planned, in accordance with the
wishes of Lord Edward Fitzgerald and Wolfe Tone, was a very formidable one ; nor, had it succeeded in landing, could it probably
have been otherwise than successful. Fortunately the energy of the
Government had just then struck a most damaging blow at the
insurrectionary movement. Among the other illegal
actions of the army of the North, which had been
under the command of Luttrell, Lord Carhampton, had
been the sudden apprehension of the whole revolutionary committee in Belfast. Neilson, Ore, Russell, and the two Sims, had
been lodged in Dublin Castle. It was to allow of such arrests as
these that almost at the same time the Habeas Corpus was suspended ; for the Government was in the awkward position of

Arrest of the
revolutionary
committee.

knowing the treasonable practices which were going on, and of knowing the authors of them, but of yet being unable to produce proofs, as the information had been received under the seal of secrecy. The importance of this apprehension was much increased by the very complete organization of the United Society. A series of little societies, none of which exceeded eighteen, were linked together, and formed a complete hierarchy through baronial committees, district committees, provincial directories, up to a grand executive directory of five, elected secretly, and known to none but the provincial secretaries, who examined the votes. The military organization was almost as complete. The sudden destruction of the executive committee, whom nobody knew, in fact cut the head of the organization entirely away; till what had happened had been discovered, and a fresh committee elected, there was no power to issue any orders. It is probably to this that is to be traced, not only the apathy, but the apparent goodwill of the people of the South at the time of the French invasion.

The period during which the French expedition, thirty-eight ships of all sorts, was lying in Bantry Bay was one of extreme danger. The strange inactivity of the English navy would have allowed the French to complete their plans at perfect leisure. Fortunately Hoche himself had been separated from the expedition on its passage, and Grouchy, the second in command, shrank from the responsibility of leading without his superior's commands. A hurricane swept the bay, preventing landing, and the ships returned uselessly to Brest. But the apathy of the people was of very short duration. The evident possibility of assistance from France raised their temper. The disturbances in the North were speedily renewed; murder followed murder; Orange retributions followed in their turn, and at last, in March 1797, General Lake was ordered to disarm the conspirators of Ulster. He issued a proclamation ordering all persons to bring in their arms and surrender them, threatening to use force if they were refused. Well informed by his spies, Lake captured 50,000 muskets, 72 cannon, and 70,000 pikes, often, it must be confessed, with cruel severity on the part of the yeomanry, who were his agents. Frequently, but it is believed only when certain information had already been obtained of the existence of arms, flogging and picketing (that is, putting their feet upon sharp stakes) wrung from the wretched peasants the knowledge of their place of concealment. Such conduct, though cruel,

[margin note: Failure of the French expedition to Bantry Bay.]

[margin note: General Lake's success in Ulster.]

had it been exercised throughout Ireland would probably have prevented the worst of the insurrection.

But the Government was hampered in Ireland by a very small, but very eloquent and noisy, opposition in Parliament, and in England by the whole of the Whig opposition in and out of Parliament, constantly crying out against any severity, or any use of other than the civil power; and by the Cabinet itself, which continued half-hearted, disliked severity, looking forward ultimately to a complete change of system, and desired, even by great, concessions, to put off an outbreak till that change could be effected. But it was in fact impossible. The very existence of these champions for their cause, the secession from Parliament of Grattan and his friends, who declared that their voices were now useless, the supposition that the English Cabinet would not tolerate any extreme measures, the certainty that France was still thinking of assisting them, the opportunity for that assistance afforded by the mutiny at the Nore, in which traces of Irish influence are not wanting, drove the leaders to more and more extreme steps. Still more was their confidence raised by the ill-judged conduct of Sir Ralph Abercromby, who was appointed to succeed Carhampton as commander-in-chief. He was the friend of Lord Moira. An ardent Whig, and full of English Liberal views, and used to regular English soldiery, he was disgusted both at the stringent measures and disorderly conduct of the yeomanry he was called upon to command, and shocked its feelings by declaring that their state of disorganization was such as to make them a terror to none but themselves. He even declined to carry on in the South that work which Lake had done in the North, and to disarm Munster. Again General Lake was called to undertake the unpleasant duty. It was no doubt carried out there, in the midst of an almost purely Roman Catholic population, with even more severity, more religious intolerance, and more cruelty, than in the North. It must be observed, however, that at the worst these cruelties could have lasted but a month, for after Lake had held his command about that time the insurrection broke out. When it did break out the Government was partially prepared for it, for treachery at last put the whole secret of the conspiracy into their hands. A certain Mr. Reynolds, a man of small property, had joined the United Irishmen, but frightened at the extent of their schemes, gave information that the Leinster delegates would meet in March at the house of Oliver Bond, one of their chief

Increased difficulties of the Government.

associates¦ The whole committee was there seized, together with letters and papers of the utmost importance.   Many arrests of leaders followed, but Lord Edward Fitzgerald; the chief military leader of the conspiracy, contrived to escape.

The 23rd of May had been appointed for a general rising.   Two days before that date Fitzgerald was arrested, after a desperate resistance.   With a dagger ,he killed one of his assailants, Captain Ryan, and severely wounded Captain Swan ; nor was he secured till Major Sirr, the town mayor, shot him through the shoulder.   He lingered a few days and then died.   Two other leaders, of the name of Sheares, were also arrested, and papers of a most bloodthirsty nature found about them.   In spite of the loss of their leaders, the insurrection broke out on the appointed day.   It was to have opened with the capture of Dublin. This attempt completely failed ; but on all the roads round the city the mail coaches were destroyed, so as to isolate the capital ; and at Naas, Kilcullen, Rathfarnham, and Prosperous, and in other places in the county of Kildare, the military were attacked.   At Prosperous the barracks were burnt, and nearly all the soldiers killed.   In most other directions a brief moment of success, marked by actions of wild savagery, was all that was accomplished.   From Kildare the insurrection turned upon Carlow.   But there timely arrangements were made, and 600 of the rebels perished, while not a single soldier was hurt.   The success of the soldiery was marked by even worse cruelty than that of the rebels ; twenty-eight suspected yeomen were shot in cold blood in the neighbourhood of Dunlaven ; and after the defeat at Carlow, Gordon says : " Executions commenced, as elsewhere in this calamitous period, and about 200 in a short time were hanged or shot according to martial law ; among the rest Sir Edward Crosby, a loyal gentleman, who unfortunately professed Liberal opinions."   But it was where least expected that the rebellion was most formidable.   In Kildare the rebels never gained much head ; but in Wexford, which was regarded as free from disaffection, a regular war arose.   The rebels here mastered the town of Wexford, where they found a gentleman of property, Mr. Bagenal Harvey, to whom they gave the command.   But their real leader was a priest named Murphy.   They succeeded in overrunning the country, but were at last checked by General Johnson before the town of New Ross.   He pursued them to Enniscorthy, and on the 21st of June General Lake succeeded in utterly routing the rebels, and taking their camp on Vinegar Hill.   This was practically a

Actual outbreak of the insurrection.
May 23, 1798

deathblow to the rebellion, though many of its horrors continued in isolated districts.

Two or three days before this battle was fought a new Lord-Lieutenant had arrived in Dublin. This was Lord Cornwallis, who had once before been asked to assume the post, but, frightened at its difficulties, had with- drawn. The recall of Camden may have been necessary if any policy of reconciliation was to be tried, for he was no doubt deeply implicated in the measures of repression which had been taken, and it would have been hard to have aroused confidence in him in the minds of the Irish. Certainly, however, a shadow of blame was allowed to rest upon his conduct which was perfectly unjust. He had been as longsuffering as it was possible to be. He had even at his sorest pressure rejected the employment of the Orangemen, from the dread, which he frequently expresses in his letters, of estab- lishing a religious war, and setting one part of the people against the other. Self-confidence was the chief characteristic of Lord Corn- wallis. The ministers constantly complain in their correspondence of the little information he deigned to give them ; and his view and management of the crisis were based entirely upon his own concep- tion of what had been going on, without consultation with those who had taken part in it. He brought with him a view in some respects erroneous, but which seems on the whole to have led him to right conclusions. He denied that the insurrection was either reli- gious or national ; he considered it Jacobin. The view was, no doubt, entirely erroneous ; yet it induced him to act in the same way that the most careful and enlightened philanthropist would have acted. For the Jacobin leaders, the Dublin and Belfast Pro- testants, he was pitiless ; for the misguided people he had a profound pity. He therefore used all his efforts to conciliate, and speedily after his arrival, with the advice of Lord Clare, an amnesty was published for all who would lay down their arms. It was certainly not the way to put an end most rapidly to the insurrection. It was mistaken for fear, and again and again he found his hopes of conciliating the Catholics disappointed, the reason being that his hopes were based upon a wrong ground. But, nevertheless, this course was exactly the most desirable for England to pursue. It was the conduct of a strong third person intervening to stop an internecine contest. While the country was still disturbed, and parties of brigands were scouring all the out-of-the-way corners (for that was the form the rebellion ultimately took), the chief

[margin note: Arrival of Lord Cornwallis to succeed Camden.]

[margin note: His efforts at conciliation.]

leaders were hanged in Dublin; till, struck with terror, the prisoners, seventy in number, offered to say all they knew if their lives were spared. Anxious to gather from their own lips 'proofs that would refute the constant, plausible, and factious assertions of Whigs in England and Nationalists in Ireland, although the Government knew probably all that could be told, Cornwallis accepted the offer. Arthur O'Connor, who had once before been tried in England, and acquitted because nearly every man of the Whig party had been called as a witness to swear to his character, drew up the confession. But he drew it up in a way to suit his own fancy. All the treasons of which the prisoners had been guilty they not only confessed, but, now that they were safe for their lives, boasted of in the true braggart Irish spirit. Cornwallis refused to receive such a confession ; but not liking to break his word, he allowed the prisoners to give personal evidence before a Committee of Lords, and their evidence was published. Contrary to the wishes of the Home Government, their lives were spared. How thoroughly bad they must have been is shown by the fact that the American minister entreated that the United States might be mentioned as one of the countries to which they should not be allowed to withdraw; the opinions they declared were so immoral and so dangerous, that the Republic must decline to receive them. They were therefore sent to Fort-George, in Scotland, where they remained till the Peace of Amiens.

Before the insurrection was quite completed there was one other short episode which seems to show how little real vitality there is in any national effort in Ireland. A small force under General Humbert, acting probably without orders, landed at Kilala, in Mayo, on the 22nd of August. With only 800 men, and a considerable number of irregular rebels, he advanced against Lake, who had an army of 3000 at Castlebar. These troops, consisting chiefly of disaffected militia, he utterly defeated; they fled with a speed which gained for the battle the name of the Castlebar Races. But on advancing further inland, he found the uselessness of his adventure, and laid down his arms to Lord Cornwallis. The squadron which was bringing him reinforcements was defeated and destroyed by Admiral Warren. Of ten ships but one frigate and one brig escaped. On board of these was Napper Tandy ; while among the prisoners was Wolfe Tone, the man of most ability among the chiefs. He was tried and condemned to be hanged, but committed suicide.

Failure of General Humbert's expedition.

Cornwallis' experience, although it did not diminish his self-confidence, seemed to force on him one fact, the necessity of the Union. He detested the Castle party by whom he was surrounded, he believed in the thorough bloodthirstiness of the Orangemen, he had learnt that conciliation, unless very complete, could have no effect upon the Catholics. He thus arrived at the fact of which Pitt had always been conscious, that under the existing system justice to the Catholics was absolutely impossible; it was imposible to make the Protestant Parliament agree to admit Catholic representatives; and even supposing this to be possible, Catholic representation meant confiscation of Protestant property, and the predominance of the Catholic religion, and rather than submit to that the Protestants would fight. To attempt to make such alterations was wilfully to plunge Ireland into a civil war of extermination. The only way to overcome this difficulty was to establish some paramount authority which should overrule the local and provincial interests of the island, and by a superior power keep the factions from flying at each other's throats. Cornwallis therefore threw himself heart and soul into the Union, supported by Fitzgibbon, now Lord Clare. But it was not carried out without extreme difficulties. Pitt's intention was notified to the Irish Parliament. Here it at once excited a violent agitation, and a thing unheard of in that venal House of Commons, an amendment on the Address, was carried against the Government by a majority of four. Nearly all the great names in Ireland, from Mr Foster the Speaker, to Ponsonby, Grattan, and Curran, were strongly opposed to the Bill. As there was no constitutional way of destroying the Parliament except with its own consent, and as left to itself it seemed plain that Parliament would oppose the Union, means had to be devised to change this state of things. The English supremacy had been systematically upheld by indirect bribery; and when application was made to the same class of people as had hitherto managed that influence, their answers showed that it would not be impossible to carry the same system further. The management of the greater people was left in the hands of Lord Cornwallis, who had a profound contempt for nearly all the Irish except the better part of the Roman Catholics. The whole mass of smaller men was handed over to the management of Lord Castlereagh, a young Irishman of much ready ability, at that time Secretary. To him too was intrusted the duty of arranging a scheme which might be passed through Parliament. By this scheme a million and a half of money

Proved necessity for the Union.

Opposition in the Irish party.

was to be spent in compensation to borough-holders, lawyers who had hoped to improve their prospects by entering the House, and the tradesmen of Dublin. Pitt had in one of his old reform Bills accepted the theory that boroughs were property ; this part of the scheme was therefore passed, the indirect claims were not allowed. The bulk of the Catholic party, to whom hopes were held out, were not disinclined to the Union. In the English Parliament resolutions in favour of the Union were carried without much difficulty. The full force of Pitt's arguments was there felt. It was understood in fact to be a case of· necessity. An independent dual Government could not be worked, nor justice be secured for Ireland, while party and religious differences ran so high, except by the intervention of the calmer and broader spirit of an Imperial Parliament. In the Irish Parliament the opposition was much stronger. But that none may feel much regret at the threatened destruction of that body, it may be mentioned that even now, in its last struggle, it extended the Act of Indemnity so as to throw a shield over the most outrageous cruelty and wickedness on the part of the Protestant suppressors of the rebellion. Fitzgerald, who boasted of having flogged many perfectly innocent people, and of having driven one at least to suicide, was not only acquitted when charges of this description were brought against him, but succeeded in turning the tables and recovering damages from his victims.[1] The interval between the Parliament of 1799 and the Session opening in 1800, which the Government had determined should be the last, was employed in continuing the trade in votes and boroughs. The Marquis of Down-shire, who had seven seats of his own, was the only great borough proprietor who held out. And when the new Parliament met the Government was pretty secure of its victory. Nevertheless, there was a tremendous contest on the first night, when an amendment was moved to the Address, pledging the House to uphold the National Parliament. For fifteen hours the struggle had lasted, when, at seven in the morning, Grattan, who had not sat in the House for some years, was suddenly introduced, just dragged from his bed and very ill, clothed in the old patriotic dress of the volunteers of 1782, and walked up to the table to take the oaths. He had been

---

[1] This worthy gentleman, who used to compel the peasantry to prostrate themselves before him, who flogged a man within an inch of his life for writing a note in French, which he could not understand, and kept another for some days in prison without the slightest shadow of a charge, was rewarded with a considerable pension and a baronetcy.

hurriedly elected immediately after midnight for the town of Wick-
low for the express purpose of producing this *coup de théâtre*. His
speech against the Union was a very fine one, but it did not save
the amendment, which was defeated by a majority of forty-two. The
Opposition was now bidding high for votes. £4000 was declared by
Lord Cornwallis to have been offered for one vote. It is uncertain
to what extent indirect bribery had been carried; it was probably
much exaggerated; but at all events, when on the 18th
of February the resolutions for the Union were brought
in, they were passed by a majority of forty-six. These
resolutions were transmitted to England, and the royal assent was
given to the Bill founded on them on the 2nd of August. By this
the Parliaments of the two countries were amalgamated, Ireland supplying four spiritual and twenty-eight temporal peers, and one hundred
commoners. The Irish Protestant Church was welded with the English
as the United Church of Great Britain and Ireland. Perfect equality
in matters of trade was established. Ireland was to contribute in the
proportion of two to fifteen to the Imperial revenue, and the debts of
the two countries were to be kept distinct. Having gained its object,
the Government had to pay the Bill. £1,260,000 was contributed at
the rate of £7000 a seat. In addition to this, twenty-two peerages
were created, five Irish peers were called to the House of Lords, twenty
advanced a step in the Peerage.

The Union completed. Aug. 2, 1800.

By the treaty of Campo Formio the French were relieved from
their war with Austria, and it was probably the belief
that singlehanded they were more than a match for
England, the object of their particular hatred, which
induced the Directory to break off the negotiations at Lisle. The
victorious army of Italy was transformed into the army of England.
The prospect of wealth to be gained there was held out to the troops,
instead of the promised donation which the finances were in no
position to bear. The command of the army was intrusted to Bonaparte, who assumed an appearance of great interest in the expedition,
and visited the sea-coasts under pretence of arranging for the
embarkation of the troops; but he was not likely to risk his fortunes in England while the sea was commanded by his enemies.
He persuaded the Directory that a more severe blow could be dealt
upon England by a descent upon Egypt, the highroad to India,
whence succour could be sent to Tippoo Sahib, the Sultan of Mysore,
who, after he had been crushed by Lord Cornwallis, was again,
relying for success upon French arms, thinking of renewing war.

Desire of France to invade England.

To Bonaparte private ambition was no doubt a main reason for this resolution. The state of Europe was very threatening. 'A second coalition was getting itself formed. In none of the new republics, neither Holland, nor Switzerland, nor Rome, in all of which constitutions had been forced on the people against their will, was there a cordial love for France. But Bonaparte, who, as he said, did not consider "the pear ripe," was willing that the bad management and failures of the Directory should ripen it before he raised his hands to pluck it. His imagination too, which always played a powerful part in his resolutions, was fired with the notion of an Eastern empire, whence, as he said, he should return and take Europe *en revers*.

On the 19th of May 1798, the army of France, 36,000 strong, sailed

Bonaparte's campaign in Egypt.

from Toulon harbour, escorted by 30 vessels of war, 72 smaller vessels, and carried in 400 transports. The expedition was a strange one; not only was Egypt to be conquered, it was to be scientifically explored, and a number of learned and scientific men were mixed with the generals that surrounded their commander. Before reaching Egypt a strong point was secured to give the French the command of the Mediterranean. The Order of St. John of Malta, by treason and for money, gave up the island to Bonaparte. Thence he sailed on the 2nd of July, and ten days afterwards reached Alexandria.

Thence he marched towards Cairo, which he conquered, after win-

Battle of the Pyramids.

ning on the road the battle of the Pyramids over the Mamelukes, a warrior caste sprung originally from Circassian slaves, who had made themselves masters of Egypt. It was the old story of undisciplined valour breaking itself against the firm squares of a disciplined Western army. Murad Bey, the Mameluk commander, withdrew to Upper Egypt, and the French entered Cairo. Bonaparte at once set to work to organize the country, and in his eagerness to conciliate the people, hinted that he too believed in Mahomet. The absolute atheism, however, of the French troops, and this cynical readiness to change his creed, only exasperated the Turks against him.

Nelson had been watching the port of Toulon, but the French fleet gave him the slip. From the 19th of May till the 1st of August he was in vain pursuit, not knowing where the expedition had gone.

Battle of the Nile. Aug. 2, 1798.

On that day he came in sight of the French fleet, consisting of thirteen ships of the line, one of which was the 'Orient,' with 120 guns, and four frigates. Nelson's own fleet consisted also of thirteen ships, but none of them were larger than seventy-fours, and he had but one frigate and a brig. The enemy were very advantageously placed at anchor along the shore of the Bay of Aboukir. In front of them lay an island with a fort, their flanks were covered by gunboats. They believed their position unassailable. But Nelson quickly determined, from the appearance of the anchored fleet, that there must be sufficient water for his ships between the French and the shore. He boldly ordered some of his vessels to sail inside. The left of the French line was thus enveloped and placed between two fires. Nelson began the fight at once, although it was six in the evening. It raged the whole night. In less than two hours, however, five of the French ships had struck, and at nine o'clock the 'Orient' caught fire and blew up. When the battle closed about six the following morning, nine of the French ships had been taken and two had been burnt. Want of frigates, and the damages sustained by his own fleet, prevented Nelson from pursuing the two remaining French ships, which sailed away almost unhurt. The same causes prevented him from destroying completely the French transports. This victory shut up the best French army with its great commander useless in Egypt, and excited the enthusiasm and hopes of all the conquered countries in Europe.

But meanwhile Pitt had been able to set on foot a second great coalition. Austria, humiliated by the Treaty of Campo Formio, far from discharging her army, had raised its numbers, and demanded some sort of indemnity for the successes of France in Italy and Switzerland. *Pitt forms a second coalition.* Napoleon by his advance upon Egypt had himself forced the Ottoman Empire into war with France. The princes of Germany, though not desiring war, and even now treating with the Directory at Rastadt, could not forget the loss of the empire beyond the Rhine. Russia was also induced to join the coalition ; for changes had taken place both in the internal and external condition of the country ; since 1796, Paul I., a prince of scarcely sound mind, had succeeded Catherine in that country, and Poland having been destroyed, a road was open for him to introduce himself, as had been the constant desire of the Russian monarchs, into the politics of Europe. Prussia, where Frederick William had died, still held aloof in neutrality. The cement of this coalition was as usual English money. Naples, in the winter of 1798, had raised an army under the Austrian General Mack, and attempted to rid Italy of the invader ; but, hated by its own subjects, the weak and tyrannical government was able to effect nothing. The King had to fly in the English fleet, Naples was changed into the Parthenopæan Republic, and the whole of Italy was thus brought under French dominion. The frontier line, then, against which the coalition was preparing to act, extended from the Zuyder Zee to the Mediterranean. Its centre was the mountain mass of Switzerland. Both parties regarded this as the key of the position. But the French spread their troops weakly along the whole length, so that Massena in Switzerland seemed to form the centre of one large army; and to him was intrusted the duty of separating, by capturing the salient angle formed by Switzerland and the Tyrol, the armies of the coalition. The plan was not a wise one. The opening successes of Massena and his lieutenants, which brought the French into the valley of the Inn, did not prevent the Archduke Charles from defeating Jourdan and the army of the Rhine at Stockach, nor Kray, the Austrian general, from beating Schérer at Magnano, on the Adige, and driving him behind the Adda. Massena, with his flanks thus exposed, found himself compelled to retreat also.

These successes on the part of the allies, and the murder of the French envoys to the Congress of Rastadt, excited the French to fresh energy. Schérer was replaced by Moreau. Macdonald, who was holding Naples, hastened to his assistance, and all the armies in the centre were placed in Massena's hands. But Suwarrow, a semi-barbarian, who had never yet been conquered, had arrived to take the command in Italy. He pressed on with great rapidity and success. Moreau was beaten at Cassano (April 27), and fell back behind the Po. He again retired in the direction of Genoa in order to form a junction with Macdonald coming from Naples. Suwarrow was thus able to leave him behind him and threaten the French frontier; the advance of Macdonald however across the Apennines obliged him to turn. He fell upon that general, and after a three days' battle upon the Trebia, beat him, and turned rapidly upon Moreau, who had advanced to Novi, and had there formed a junction with the broken army of Naples. But both Macdonald and Moreau, as unsuccessful generals, were removed, and Joubert was given the command. On the 18th of August, Suwarrow attacked the French at Novi, Joubert was killed, and his troops completely routed. Italy was thus lost to the French; for in Naples Cardinal Ruffo had raised the Calabrians, and with the assistance of the English fleet both Naples and Rome were regained to the coalition. It was on this occasion that Nelson committed that act which is the great blot upon his name. He

Italy regained by the coalition.

had become infatuated with Lady Hamilton, wife of the English minister, through whose influence his fleet had been provisioned before the battle of the Nile, and who was devoted heart and soul to the execrable Government of the Bourbons, exercised practically by the Queen, a sister of Marie Antoinette. To please the Court, Nelson, who arrived at Naples just as the French and Republicans had completed a capitulation with Cardinal Ruffo, broke off the completed negotiation, and insisted upon the Republicans capitulating without terms. They were thus handed over to the cruel vengeance of the Court. 30,000 patriots were thrown into prison, and for six months all those who had taken the least part in establishing the Republic were continually exposed to the danger of execution.

The disasters of the French were to have been completed by a combined attack of English and Russians upon the other extremity of their line. On the 22nd of August, a few days after the battle of Novi, an army under Aber- *The coalition captures the Dutch fleet.* cromby, who was shortly superseded by the Duke of York, arrived at the Helder. The defence of the country was intrusted to Brune, but the allies succeeded in landing, and captured the whole Dutch fleet in the Texel. At this moment the hopes of the allies were very high, and the French, worsted abroad and full of discontent at home, seemed on the verge of destruction.

The news that Bonaparte had been defeated at Acre added still further to their depression. To complete his dreams of Eastern conquest, and to forestall the attacks of an army gathering on that side, Bonaparte had marched into Syria. *Napoleon defeated at Acre. May 21, 1799.* He won the battle of El Arish, took Joppa, where he massacred his prisoners, and advanced as far as Acre at the foot of Mount Carmel. The fortress, which was held by Djezzar, lately a robber, now a Pacha, was not in itself strong, but the French operations were rendered slow by the fortunate capture of their battering train by Sir Sidney Smith, the English commodore. After fifty days a breach was made, but the brilliant example of Sir Sidney Smith and his sailors, who entered the town, encouraged the Turkish garrison to a desperate resistance, which rendered all efforts at assault vain ; Bonaparte had to retreat disappointed. "Had it not been for Djezzar," he said, "I might have been Emperor of the East." The story of his poisoning his sick at Joppa is untrue, though he suggested and defended the step. With a broken army he regained Egypt, but he was still in a condition to beat the Turks near Alexandria, at what the French call the battle of Aboukir ; but while thus victorious, he heard news of affairs in Europe which led him to think that the pear was at length ripened. He slipped secretly from his army, accompanied by his four friends, Berthier, Lannes, Murat, and Marmont, and set sail for France, leaving the army under the command of Kleber.

Before Napoleon arrived the danger of France from without had disappeared. Jealousy had arisen between the Austrians and the Russians, which was not likely to be soothed by the rough behaviour of Suwarrow or the palpable self-seeking of the Court of Vienna. It became necessary to rearrange the com-mands. The war in Switzerland was to be intrusted to Suwarrow, who was to march thither and effect a junction with his Lieutenant Korsakoff, who was already in the country. But before the junction could be effected Massena annihilated the army of Korsakoff at the battle of Zurich (Sept. 26), and when Suwarrow had forced his way over the St. Gotthard Pass, he found himself in the midst of hostile armies instead of meeting his friends. He turned suddenly to the right, and making an extraordinary march among the glaciers and peaks of the Alps, he succeeded in reaching Coire in safety. Believing himself betrayed by the Austrians, he refused to serve again, and retired to Russia, where he died in disgrace. Nor had the Duke of York been more successful in Holland. The character of the country rendered it very difficult to advance, while the want of discipline of the Russians on the right wing entailed a defeat before Bergen. The town was indeed afterwards taken, but loss in battle and by ill health, and the want of all signs of co-operation on the part of the inhabitants, induced the English to sign what must be considered a disgraceful convention at Alkmaar, by which they agreed to withdraw from Holland, and give over 10,000 French prisoners without exchange ; the English how-ever kept possession of the Dutch fleet.

In India the English arms had been more successful. The intrigues of Tippoo with the French having been clearly dis-covered, and efforts at friendly arrangement having proved vain, General Harris, with a considerable army, was ordered in February 1799 to march upon Seringapa-tam. The Governor-General at this time was Lord Mornington, brother of the Duke of Wellington, who himself, as Colonel Arthur Welles-ley, was one of the leaders of the expedition. After two successful skirmishes, General Harris appeared before the capital, which was a strong city well prepared for a siege. In about a month the place was taken by assault and Tippoo himself killed. This success placed

Margin notes:
Jealousies and disasters of the coalition.

Success in India against Tippoo Sahib and the French.

the whole kingdom of Mysore, with a large amount of treasure, in the hands of the conquerors.

On his return to Paris (Oct. 16), therefore, Bonaparte found himself in a position to carry out his plans for personal aggrandizement; and though the great danger from foreign enemies had disappeared, the interior of France offered him every opportunity for laying hands on the Government. It was not forgotten that during his absence the safety of the Republic had been risked, and its hard-won victories rendered useless; and as the incapacity of their present rulers had been even more obvious at home than abroad, all eyes turned to him as the natural saviour of the State. Moreover, now that the first fervour of revolutionary energy had worn itself out, the bulk of the nation desired order, even though earned at the expense of liberty. Of the two Councils that of the Ancients was decidedly inclined in favour of a more settled Government, and it was through it that Napoleon determined to work. The Council of Five Hundred was more difficult to deal with. For a moment Napoleon shrunk before their patriotic and republican cries, but, urged by the Abbé Sièyes, who pressed him to action, crying, "They have put you outside the law, do you put them outside their hall," he recovered courage, and his Grenadiers, entering the hall with beating drums, quietly extruded the representatives. Thus was accomplished the great *coup d'état* of the 18th Brumaire (Nov. 9). The Directory was destroyed; a new constitution, spoken of as the Constitution of the year 8, was established, by which the executive power was vested nominally in three consuls, but really in the First Consul, Bonaparte, who thus became practically Dictator. His measures were anti-revolutionary, his object being to restore confidence and to heal faction. With his thoughts thus turned to the reorganization of France, he desired to be free for the present from foreign wars, and one of his earliest steps was to make overtures with the continental powers. To England he made proposals of peace in a letter addressed immediately to the King (Dec. 25). This was of course a grave breach of the etiquette of courts, and the letter was answered by Grenville in anything but a conciliatory spirit, while the whole blame of the war was thrown upon the French, with whom the English minister declined to enter into negotiations so long as the Government was in the hands of those "whom the Revolution had so recently placed in the exercise of power." Some more correspondence ensued, but the English ministers positively refused to treat. It is certain that Napoleon's offer was merely to

Napoleon returns, and is made First Consul. Nov. 11, 1799.

gain time; on the other hand, the dictatorial tone of Grenville's reply could not but be very irritating to the French.

The weary war therefore continued, and before the year was over the position of affairs abroad had so changed that England was no longer able to maintain the haughty tone which had been adopted. War in the hands of Bonaparte was a very different thing from war in the hands of the Directory. In April the French were again across the Rhine, and the Austrians driven behind the Inn ; while in Italy, though Genoa, the last town in the possession of the French, surrendered, its danger was turned to immediate advantage by Bonaparte. Under pretence of collecting an army for its relief, he massed his troops in the neighbourhood of Dijon, and while all eyes were directed towards the siege, he suddenly pushed across the Great St. Bernard and appeared at Ivrea on the rear of the besieging army. Melas, who commanded the Austrians, at length perceived his danger. He ordered Otto, his lieutenant, to raise the siege, with the intention of concentrating his troops ; his orders were disregarded, and Genoa was taken, but the delay was fatal. It gave time for Bonaparte to re-establish the Cisalpine Republic, and, turning backwards, to place himself between Melas and Mantua, whither that general was now anxious to withdraw. A decisive battle was brought on before Alessandria, from which stronghold the Austrians advanced, on the 14th of June, against the French on the plains of Marengo. The Austrians, more numerous than the French, had apparently won the battle, and by three o'clock the whole French army had retreated. Melas withdrew to rest, leaving what he believed to be a pursuit in the hands of General Zach ; but the French army, reinforced by the reserves, and headed by Desaix, made a great final effort. The Austrians, who had advanced too rashly in the eagerness of their pursuit, were unable to withstand his charge ; they broke, and their victory was changed into a disastrous defeat. On the following day, with the victorious army in his front, and the liberated garrison of Genoa in his rear, the Austrian general, seeing no hope, entered into a convention, called the Convention of Alessandria, by which the greater part of North Italy was surrendered to the French.

An attempt was made to change this Convention into a more general peace, and a Congress was held for this purpose at Lunéville, but the English Cabinet was much divided in its own views, the Austrian Government acted with extreme duplicity, and Napoleon demanded a separate treaty with the two belligerent powers,

[side note:] Napoleon regains the North of Italy.

[side note:] Napoleon's victories.

which Austria, knowing its weakness when separate from England, was afraid to grant. The Congress came to nothing, and in November the army under Moreau renewed the campaign. Battle of
Hohenlinden.
Dec. 2, 1800. The Austrians were determined to hold the line of the Inn, but their troops, very badly commanded by Archduke John, were attacked in the forest of Hohenlinden, and sustained a crushing defeat. Their loss is put at 25,000 men and 100 guns. There could no longer be any question in the matter, and the Emperor had no choice, if he would save his capital, Treaty of
Lunéville.
Feb. 9, 1801. but to sue for a separate peace. By the Treaty of Lunéville (Feb. 9, 1801) the frontier of the Rhine was again ceded to France.

It needed but a breach with Russia to leave England single-handed in opposition to France. The Emperor Paul, but little removed from madness, had seen with disgust the defeat of his troops in Switzerland, and believed that in the joint expedition to Holland his army had been wilfully sacrificed. He was also smitten with extreme admiration for the genius of Bonaparte, who Russia deserts
the coalition. took care to flatter this feeling and to intrigue against English influence. The old question of the right of search gave Paul a pretext to break with his allies. The doctrine of the English, accepted generally as the law of nations, was that a belligerent had the right of searching neutral ships for contraband of war or for property of the enemy. The Northern powers claimed that the neutral flag should cover the cargo, with the exception of contraband of war. This had been their view for many years, and, as has been mentioned, gave rise to the Armed Neutrality of 1780.[1] This view they had not been able to enforce, but it was quite an open question whether ships under convoy of a man-of-war could be searched. On this point the English and the Danes twice came into collision ; but during the summer of 1800 an amicable arrangement had been arrived at. Paul however refused to let the matter drop ; he took it up as an injury to the whole Northern powers, laid an embargo upon all English property in Russia, made prisoners 300 merchant seamen, and renewed the Armed Neutrality, which was joined willingly by Sweden, and under pressure by Denmark also. The English Government at once retaliated by an embargo on the property of the allied nations ; and England was thus left completely singlehanded, for her allies in the south of Europe were much too weak to afford her any assistance, while her maritime superiority seemed seriously compromised by the action of the Baltic powers.

[1] The views of the Armed Neutrality have been since accepted by Europe,

Nor was it only abroad that danger seemed impending. The condition of the country was rendered miserable both by heavy taxes and by the pressure of two years of scarcity. Corn had risen to the unprecedented price of 120 shillings the quarter, a price which could not possibly have been maintained under any reasonable system of political economy. But at this time it was held in the last degree dangerous to admit corn from abroad, partly because it was thought that a nation should trust to its own resources for the prime necessaries of life, partly because it was believed that a diminution of gold and silver, which must inevitably follow from large importations, was a disastrous thing for the nation. Nor was this all, the arrangements of the poor law were such that it became necessary to maintain high prices in the agricultural districts. The received opinion was that the increase of population, irrespective of the powers of employing it, was a distinct advantage. Premiums were given for early marriages, and assistance granted from the rates in proportion to the numbers in a family. The natural tendency was a fearful increase of population, depending for the most part on the rates, which were therefore inordinately high. It thus became possible for the farmers to pursue the plan they have always regarded as most conducive to their interests, and to drive down the wages to the lowest point; the people were reduced to a condition little above serfdom; and to enable the agricultural districts to support the pressure of the rates high prices had to be maintained. The condition of the country districts was thus kept tolerably even, and the burden of the high prices fell almost exclusively upon the industrious population of the towns. It was natural that a House of Commons returned chiefly by the landowners should favour protective duties, which thus rendered them at once absolute masters of their peasantry and threw the burden of their increased expenditure upon the towns. But such a state of things produced much suffering, and suffering produced riots, which the folly and ignorance of the judges increased. From the Lord Chief Justice downwards, they seemed to have combined to throw the blame upon the corn factors, whom they charged with the obsolete crimes of forestalling and engrossing. Punishment was indeed inflicted for the crime of buying corn and selling it at a higher price in the same market. The people naturally took their cue from these blind leaders, and corn riots were very prevalent. It is of course plain that whatever tends to the husbanding of resources and to the equalization of prices is

Internal condition of England.

really advantageous, and that the corn factors, in carrying out the law of supply and demand, were a most useful set of men.

To meet these difficulties Pitt thought it expedient to have an autumn session. He was himself inclined to think that some extraordinary measures were desirable to alleviate the distress, and in the existing state of the law he was perhaps right. But Grenville, a more rigid follower of the principles of political economy, was much opposed to any tampering with the natural laws of supply and demand.[1] When Parliament met the action of the judges was gravely censured, and several remedial measures were introduced, such as bounties on importation of grain, and the prohibition of the use of corn in distilling and starch making, and (though this proved a useless and pernicious measure) of the use of any but brown bread. Large subscriptions were also made to alleviate the distress.

Autumn session. Oct. 1800.

The Parliament which assembled early the following year (1801) was the first united Parliament of Great Britain and Ireland, and but a few days of its existence had elapsed before a great and most unexpected change took place in the position of affairs. There had long been a want of harmony among the members of the Cabinet with regard to the war ; but there had now arisen an even more formidable question. The union had been effected by much bribery in money, titles, and places ; these promises had all been fulfilled. But there was one section of the Irish whose opposition would have been fatal to the measure, but to which such promises could not be made. The tacit support, or at all events neutrality, of the Irish Roman Catholics had been secured by a vague but very well-understood promise that their claims should be considered under the new arrangement. It is certain that both Castlereagh and Cornwallis understood that this was so, and Pitt felt it an imperative duty to make an effort to fulfil this promise. The matter had been talked over in the Cabinet as early as the autumn of 1799, and was formally discussed in the presence of Lord Castlereagh at the end of September 1800. The Chancellor, Lord Loughborough, was at that time in attendance upon the King at Weymouth. He was a man of a base and time-serving nature. At this Cabinet he displayed his hostility to any measure for the relief of the Catholics, and used his opportunity to instil into

Pitt proposes a Catholic Relief Bill. 1801.

[1] The error of Grenville's position lay in this, that the law of supply and demand can only work *universally*. It does not follow that it will act beneficially in a single country under protective laws.

the King's mind that to consent to any such measure would be a breach of his coronation oath. In this he was backed up by Lord Auckland, who had always been a friend of Pitt's, but who was inclined to underhand intrigue, and did not think it beneath him to prejudice the King's mind against Pitt's policy. Matters were brought to a crisis when, at a levée in the beginning of 1801, the King mentioned openly to Dundas that he was aware that such a measure was in contemplation, adding his usual formula, that he "should hold any one who supported it as his personal enemy." It became plain to Pitt that he could hesitate no longer, and although the King sent Addington the Speaker, a personal friend of Pitt's, to persuade him not to bring the matter forward, he sent a letter to George declaring his intention and his determination to resign if he was not allowed to fulfil

Pitt resigns. Addington Prime Minister. 1801. his promises to the Irish. The King wrote back urging him to remain in office and to drop the measure, but Pitt was determined, and the King was forced to accept his resignation. In his place he desired Addington, a man of very second-rate ability, to form a ministry, a duty which, on the advice of Pitt, he accepted. The resignation of the great minister, as it was only personal, did not imply the resignation of the whole ministry, but all the great members of it, Grenville, Dundas, Windham, and Spencer, retired with him. It is pleasant to think that Lord Loughborough's duplicity received no reward, he was excluded from the new arrangements, Lord Eldon, at the King's own request, became Lord Chancellor, and Loughborough had to content himself with the earldom of Rosslyn.

Illness of the King. The shock of parting with a minister he had so long trusted brought on a renewal of the King's insanity, and measures were taken for a regency under the same restrictions that Pitt had before insisted upon. George was at this time so popular that even the Opposition treated him in his illness with every consideration. His popularity, the natural consequence of his well-ordered domestic life, had been considerably increased by an attempt in the preceding year on his life. When entering Drury Lane Theatre a man had risen in the pit and discharged a pistol at him, two bullets passing a very little above his head. The miscreant who made the attempt was a lunatic of the name of Hadfield. The King, always remarkable for his personal courage, had displayed great calmness under the circumstances, and the loyalty of the nation had been much excited. Fortunately, under Dr. Willis's treatment, his illness was speedily mastered, and in the beginning of

March he was declared convalescent. But his illness, which he himself traced to Pitt's conduct, had such an effect upon that statesman,
that he wrote promising never to reintroduce the Catholic question.
His friends did not see why, under these circumstances, he should not
remain in office, but Addington naturally objected to giving up the
place he had just gained, and the Government continued in his hands,
supported by a Cabinet of complete mediocrity, upheld   Character of
for the present by Pitt's influence. It was indeed just   the Addington
such a minister and Cabinet as suited the King's well-   ministry.
known views—safe, conservative, submissive, and without commanding ability. Nor did the great country party object to a change
which freed them from the imperious domination of one so vastly
their superior as Pitt, and placed over them a man whose talents
were not superior to their own, and whom they might hope to guide
rather than follow. Though Pitt acted honestly in the first instance,
it is only too probable that he regarded Addington as a temporary
substitute for himself, and designed to return to power after the
present difficulty was over, and when he had made a public demonstration for the purpose of saving his honour. However this may be,
his somewhat lukewarm support was before long changed into open
enmity. At first, however, he spoke with even exaggerated admiration of the new Cabinet, which in the House was completely successful, while great successes both by sea and land somewhat relieved
the nation from its embarrassing position.

The French army, deserted by their great commander, was left
shut up in Egypt under the command of Kleber, a   The French
man of organizing genius, who bid fair to establish the   army in Egypt.
French influence in that country. He was, however, assassinated by
a fanatical Mussulman (June 1800), and the command fell into the
hands of Menou, a general of but second-rate capacity. Before this
change of command, a treaty, known as the Treaty of El Arish, had
been completed (Jan. 24), by which the French army was to be allowed
a safe return to France. This convention was concluded on board the
flagship, and with the full approval of Sir Sidney Smith ; but, meanwhile, intercepted despatches had made known to the Cabinet the
almost hopeless condition of the French army, and orders were sent to
the Mediterranean that no treaties should be sanctioned by the admiral
which did not insist on the surrender of the French. The Treaty of El
Arish had been concluded without this knowledge and before these
orders had reached Sir Sidney Smith. Moreover, affairs in Egypt
had much changed, for Kleber, indignantly rejecting all idea of sur-

render, had at once proceeded to attack the Turks, had won over them a great victory at Heliopolis (March 20, 1800) and reoccupied Cairo. It became necessary therefore to renew the war, and Sir Ralph Abercromby, who, with Pulteney, had been employed in fruitless expeditions against Ferrol and Cadiz, collecting the troops employed in both expeditions, in number about 20,000, proceeded to Egypt. Troops also under Sir David Baird were ordered to attack the country from India. A landing was forced at Aboukir Bay, under the immediate command of General afterwards Sir John Moore, and on the 21st of March a battle in the neighbourhood of Alexandria was fought, where the French were thoroughly defeated. The English had to deplore the loss of Sir Ralph Abercromby, but General Hutchinson, who succeeded him, continued to act with vigour. The Grand Vizier, with a large but disorderly Turkish army, attacked Cairo, while the English kept Menou besieged in Alexandria. In June Cairo fell, and General Baird having arrived from India, the combined English army compelled Menou to capitulate in Alexandria on the 27th of August. The terms of surrender were honourable. The French army was allowed to return to France, but all ships, together with all the objects of art which the French had collected, became the property of the conquerors. This success, which showed the unbroken vigour of England, tended to accelerate the peace which was gradually becoming necessary for all parties, and for which negotiations were already set on foot in London with the full approbation of Pitt.

Battle of Alexandria. March 21, 1801.

Meanwhile, but a few days after the victory of Alexandria, the cloud which had risen in the Baltic was also dispersed. The renewal of the Armed Neutrality, and the general conduct of Russia, made it evident that that country was engaged in the French interests. A fleet under Sir Hyde Parker, with Nelson as second in command, was despatched to the Baltic. Negotiation was tried with the Danes, but wholly unsuccessfully, and Parker, a dilatory commander, was induced by Nelson's energy to consent to an attack upon Copenhagen. The passage of the Sound was forced without loss, but an examination of the enemy's position showed that they had used the delay which had been given them to great advantage. Shore batteries had been erected and put into fighting trim ; floating batteries established, and the harbour covered with a line of vessels of all sorts four miles in length. Within this lay the Danish fleet. Nelson offered to attack with ten sail of the line ; he was allowed twelve. The attack was made from the south, Sir Hyde Parker on the outside threatening the batteries

Battle of Copenhagen. April 2.

and the vessels at the mouth of the harbour. At ten o'clock on the 2nd of April, Nelson began his attack. Several vessels grounded and were rendered useless, and so hot was the engagement that Sir Hyde Parker thought it better to hoist the signal for discontinuing action. Nelson declined to obey it, and the other captains took their orders from him. Many of the Danish ships had struck, but being constantly reinforced from the shore, continued the fight, it is said, even after they had surrendered. This was probably an accident; but Nelson took advantage of it to write a friendly letter to the Crown Prince. "The Vice-Admiral Lord Nelson," he said, "has been commanded to spare Denmark when she no longer resists. The line of defence which covered her shores has struck to the British flag ; but if the firing is continued on the part of Denmark, he must set on fire all the prizes he has taken without having the power of saving the men who have so nobly defended them. The brave Danes are the brothers, and should never be the enemies, of the English." He then agreed to a truce while the wounded were moved from the prizes. Having taken advantage of the lull to withdraw his fleet from the difficult channel in which they were entangled, he went on shore to negotiate a treaty. To enable him to attack the Russians, he insisted on a long armistice, which a threat of immediate bombardment induced the Danes to grant. The English fleet then sailed against the Swedes, who withdrew, and were left unmolested, while the fleet proceeded against the Russians. On his way, however, Nelson received the news that the capricious despotism of Paul had excited his courtiers to a conspiracy, which, though apparently aimed only at the deposition of the Emperor, had in fact ended in his assassination. The accession of the young Emperor Alexander I. completely changed the policy of Russia. The embargo was removed from the British shipping and the merchant seamen liberated. As the Armed Neutrality still existed, Nelson would have proceeded to strong measures ; but Sir Hyde Parker was satisfied, and though he was recalled, the complete change in Russian policy rendered further action unnecessary. In June a treaty *Peace between* of peace was signed in St. Petersburg, by which the *England and* Armed Neutrality, with its claims, was given up, but *Russia.* the right of search accurately defined. It was also agreed that blockades must henceforward be really efficient in order to be valid. Blockades by proclamation were thus abolished, and could be only sustained when the blockading force was sufficient to enforce them.

Bonaparte was still threatening an invasion of England, and gun-

Preliminaries
of peace.
Oct. 1, 1801.

boats and rafts had been collected at Boulogne. These the Government ordered Nelson to attack, but the attempt was on the whole unsuccessful. However, the supremacy of England on the sea was so great that there could not be much fear of the landing of a foreign army, and the French, defeated in Egypt and thwarted in their Northern policy, were ready to come to terms. In October the preliminaries of a treaty were signed. By this England gave up all its conquests except Trinidad and Ceylon. The Cape of Good Hope was restored to the Dutch, but open to the trade of the contracting parties. "Malta was to be restored to the Knights of St. John,[1] under the guarantee of one of the great powers; Porto Ferrajo was to be evacuated. On the other side, the Republic of the Ionian Islands was to be acknowledged, and the French were to withdraw from Naples and the Roman States; the integrity of Portugal was to be secured; Egypt was to be restored to the Porte, and the Newfoundland fisheries to be placed on the same footing as before the war."[2]

Although the preliminary treaty had been signed, it cost some time and much anxious negotiation before its final ratification in the March of the following year. These negotiations were held at Amiens, on the part of England by Lord Cornwallis, on that of France by Joseph Bonaparte, assisted by Talleyrand. At the opening of Parliament, on the 29th of October 1801, the minister had been able to mention in the King's speech with satisfaction both the

Opinions in England concerning the peace.

preliminary treaty with France and the arrangements with the Northern powers which put an end to the threatened Armed Neutrality. By the bulk of the people the return of peace had been hailed with extreme delight. General Lauriston, who had brought the authority for signing the preliminaries, had been received with a public ovation, the populace had dragged his carriage through the streets, and London and other towns had been illuminated. In completing these preliminaries Addington and his friends had acted with the entire approbation of Pitt, who, at heart cordially disliking war, had brought himself to believe that Bonaparte, having now obtained the supreme power in France, would probably be satisfied; at the same time, as he himself pointed out, Jacobinism had been already checked in England, and the lesson taught to the world that the fruit of Jacobin principles was

---

[1] Malta had been ceded by Charles V. to the Knights of St. John in 1530, after they had been deprived of Rhodes by the advancing Turks. Bonaparte had taken possession of the island in 1798, while on his road to Egypt.　　　　[2] Massey, vol. iv. 636.

terrorism and anarchy, and its end a military despotism. Seeing the isolated position which England now occupied, and believing the causes for further war removed, Pitt accepted the terms of the peace, although the concessions on the part of England, especially the surrender of the Cape of Good Hope, were no doubt great. With the support then of Pitt and of the general feeling of the country, the ministry found in Parliament large majorities in favour of their peace. But Pitt's views were by no means shared by a considerable number of his late colleagues. Grenville, Windham, and Spencer clung tenaciously to their old view that Bonaparte's career was but beginning, that his policy would continue to be one of aggression, that his present offers of peace were delusive, and that for the honour of England and the safety of Europe the war should be continued.

Before the preliminaries were ratified abundant proofs were given that they were right and that Pitt was wrong. Taking advantage of the exhausted condition of the Continent, of the eager desire of Addington to secure peace, and of the position of England, which was not only without allies, but unable while negotiations were still pending to make objections upon the score of treaty rights, Bonaparte hastened to complete his ambitious projects—by the appropriation of those smaller States which had already fallen into a state of dependence upon France (the Republics of Holland, Switzerland, and the North of Italy, now called the Cisalpine Republic), and by the re-establishment of the French colonial power by means of a great expedition to reconquer St. Domingo. His method of proceeding with regard to the Republics was craftily arranged so as to give to the assumption of French supremacy the appearance of voluntary action on the part of the people themselves. For Holland a constitution was drawn up in France of a strongly republican character, which, when rejected by the National Assemblies of Holland, was put to the vote of the whole body of the people, and being accepted by a very small minority, while the rest abstained from voting, was declared established by the national will (Oct. 17, 1801). In Switzerland, not yet ripe for annexation, instructions were given to the French minister to thwart all efforts at the formation of a stable constitution, and to keep things so unsettled that an appeal to France was certain sooner or later to be made, while French troops garrisoned the Republic ostensibly for the purpose of keeping order. Less delicacy was used with regard to Italy. The chief rulers of the Cisalpine Republic were summoned to Lyons, a constitution of Bonaparte's creation given them, and they were ordered to elect as their President Bonaparte himself (Jan. 1802). The expedition to St. Domingo was made still further to advance Napoleon's projects; for thither was sent, to be destroyed by the climate, almost the whole of the army of the Rhine, the only part of the military establishment of France not wholly devoted to him.

Meanwhile the projects for the ultimate annexation of Piedmont and Genoa were carried on, and distinct orders sent to the negotiators at Amiens to withdraw entirely from discussion the affairs of Holland, Switzerland, and the Italian Republics, in other words, to treat with England as if the affairs of Europe were entirely beyond her cognizance. The withdrawal of these points of discussion left little to be settled except minute points with regard to fisheries and prisoners, for Bonaparte also entirely refused to entertain the idea of a commercial treaty with England. The only point of interest left was Malta. According to the preliminaries this island was to be evacuated and to be restored to the Knights under the guarantee of Russia. But a new sovereign was now upon the Russian throne less likely to be under the immediate influence of France. Bonaparte therefore wished to change the terms, to destroy the fortifications of the island, thus rendering it useless in a military point of view, and to place it under the guardianship of the King of Naples; in other words, to render it at once worthless to the English and an easy prey to the French whenever they should desire to reoccupy it. In their eagerness for peace the English ministry consented to be blind to Bonaparte's aggressions, though firm upon the point of Malta, and though they refused to acknowledge the existence of the newly-organized republics. No doubt, what the English meant was that, for the sake of peace, they would bear what Bonaparte had already done, but that any further step would produce war. Bonaparte, on the other hand, argued that the refusal to acknowledge these republics was in fact a resignation on the part of England of the right of interference with them; henceforward that country could not complain although they were incorporated with France. There were thus a number of outstanding questions left unsettled at the peace, which was finally completed on the 27th of March 1802.

Negotiations at Amiens

Peace concluded. March 27, 1802.

But it had begun to be plain to all thinking men that it could be but a short truce; and indeed Napoleon was already writing that "a renewal of war was necessary for his existence, as the memory of old victories was likely speedily to pass away." In fact, he totally mistook the temper of England. Addington's ministry, no doubt, was pledged to peace, and was anxious at all hazards to make it durable. The people of England were indeed weary of the war and eagerly desirous for peace ; but they had lost none of their independence and pride, and anything which should prove either that their honour was attacked, their commercial activity trammelled, or their independence of action limited, would easily produce a reaction, and bring them back to their warlike temper. Bonaparte, while intending to renew the war sooner or later, meant to keep the occasion in his own hands, but, trusting to the weakness of Addington, he pursued a line of conduct exactly fitted to prove to England the absolute necessity for an immediate renewal of hostilities, and which touched the sensitive nation in its most tender points. He never ceased from his course of aggression, thus treating the remonstrances of England as if they were completely worthless and beside the point.

Napoleon mistakes the temper of England.

Continues his aggressions.

In August he annexed the island of Elba, in September the whole of Piedmont, in October Parma and Placentia ; and at length, taking advantage of the carefully fostered disorders in Switzerland, he suddenly occupied that most important military point with an army of 30,000 men under Marshal Ney, and took to himself the title of Mediator of the Swiss Republic. It has been mentioned that he refused a commercial treaty with England at the Peace of Amiens ; this under the plea of a desire for the protection of native commerce he undoubtedly had a right to do ; but he now obliged all the countries dependent on him to adopt a similar course, to exclude English productions, and thus closed half Europe to English trade.

Not content with this conduct abroad, he took upon himself to interfere with the internal affairs of England. His course of policy was such as to be wholly incompatible with a free press ; his underhand machinations were certain to be exposed where such a press existed. On the Continent he had succeeded in enforcing silence ; in England alone an unfettered press was able to direct its assaults both on his policy and his character. No doubt some of the attacks were sharp enough ; especially had an emigrant, one Jean Peltier, established a French paper in London called *L'Ambigu*, which was full of strong invective against the First Consul. Again, the emigrants had not ceased from

Demands the repression of the English press.

forming conspiracies against the French Government, conspiracies
and the expul- which Bonaparte delighted to exaggerate, to mingle
sion of the with doubtful charges of assassination, and to connect
emigrants from
England. (wholly without grounds) with the English ministry.
Those emigrants were enjoying the hospitality of England : Otto,
the French agent in London, was therefore instructed to bring the
matter to the notice of Lord Hawkesbury, and to demand the suppression of the obnoxious papers, and the dismissal of the emigrants
from England. Hawkesbury's answers were at first of a peaceful
and conciliatory character. He replied that he would consult the
law officers on the matter of the press, and would go so far in the
matter of the emigrants as to withdraw them from the isle of
Guernsey. This answer was followed by still more peremptory
demands, requiring effective measures of repression with regard to the
press, the withdrawal of the emigrants from Jersey, the removal
from England of the Bourbon princes, and the expulsion of all
emigrants wearing the orders or distinctions of the old régime.
What rendered these demands more grotesque was the fact that
the *Moniteur*, the official paper of France, was constantly full of
assertions of the complicity of the Government with the attempts of
assassins in France, and of libels on the English Constitution ; there
was even an English paper, the *Argus*, published in Paris, a counterpart of the *Ambigu* of Peltier. To demands thus formulated no
English Government could afford to give a temporizing answer, and
Hawkesbury replied that the freedom of the English press was limited
by English law alone, and that the exercise of hospitality could not be
curtailed. At the same time, as Peltier appeared to have exceeded all
legal license in his writing, an action was commenced against him, and
in spite of a brilliant defence by Macintosh he was found guilty.[1]

Such conduct on the part of Bonaparte was rapidly changing the
feeling of England and rendering war inevitable. It became evident
that, no longer to uphold an aristocratic government, but for our
very existence as an independent country, we must plunge into war.
Consequent As this feeling gained ground, so did the desire that
change of
feeling in
England. when that war should come it should find England in
the hands of its ablest statesmen, and not in those of
an incapable man like Addington. Even from the first, as soon as it
was understood that Pitt, in deference to the King's weak state of
health, had consented to forego the support of the Roman Catholics,
his immediate friends had desired his return to office, and had
regarded as false his position as the supporter out of office of

[1] Owing to change of relations with France the punishment was not carried out.

Addington's weak ministry. Already, in November 1802, Canning, the most eager of his supporters, in conjunction with Lord Malmesbury, had set on foot an address to Addington begging him to resign. This plan had been peremptorily closed by Pitt himself. Indeed, the obstacles in the way of his resumption of office were very awkward. In some sort the creator of the present ministry, and known to have had a share in most of their earlier measures, Pitt could not come forward in opposition till some flagrant instance of incapacity or some great national crisis should justify such a step. The only other hope was that modesty (which was not one of his characteristics) might induce Addington to acknowledge his incompetence, and himself advise the restoration of Pitt to the ministry. Fully aware of these obstacles, and feeling his position an anomalous one, Pitt withdrew for a time from Parliament.

Negotiations for Pitt's return. Nov. 1802.

During his absence the difficulties with France continued to increase, and the signs of Bonaparte's intention of making war sooner or later became more obvious. At length, in January 1803, was published a report of Colonel Sebastiani, who had been sent by Napoleon, nominally for commercial purposes, to examine the resources of Egypt and the East; in fact, so far from being commercial in its character, the report was devoted almost entirely to show with what ease Egypt could be again conquered by the French. It was impossible that such an official document could be issued by a power which was really friendly. At the same time Bonaparte had sent both to England and to Ireland agents who, under the same commercial pretext, were really minutely examining the resources of England and instigating Irish rebellion. Nor was the question of Malta as yet at rest. The project of obtaining a guarantee from the European powers had failed, and in face of the constant aggressions of Bonaparte, it was impossible for England to evacuate the island with the certainty that it would be immediately occupied by the French. But Bonaparte was still anxious to keep the occasion of war in his own hands, and still hoped to impose upon the feeble ministry of England. He summoned Lord Whitworth, the English ambassador, to an interview, in which he declared that he did not desire war, but that he would rather see England in possession of the Faubourg St. Antoine than of Malta, that he was ready to attempt a descent upon England if necessary, but how much better would it be for

Napoleon examines the resources of Egypt, England, and Ireland. 1803.

His interview with Lord Whitworth. Feb. 18, 1803.

England to join with him and share his spoils and his greatness. Two things only were necessary for this,—the suppression of the press, and the removal of Georges, a Chouan leader and emigrant, from English protection. As for the counter-charges of the appropriation of Piedmont and of Switzerland, they were but trifles not worth mentioning. Almost immediately after this the *Moniteur* declared, in its annual account of the condition of the nation, that as long as party government existed in England an army of 500,000 must be kept on foot for defence and vengeance.

. This was too much even for Addington, and on the 8th of March a message was brought down from the King to the Commons, declar-

The militia embodied. March 11, 1803

ing it necessary that measures of precaution should be adopted, alleging for this the great military preparations which were going on both in Holland and in France, which were in fact intended for St. Domingo, but which in the feverish state of international feeling were a just cause of uneasiness. In accordance with this message the militia were on the 11th ordered to be embodied. In spite of all that Bonaparte had done he pretended to be indignant at this step; and at a public reception at the Tuileries accosted Lord Whitworth with passionate words,

Failure of renewed negotiations for Pitt's return.

accusing England of driving him into war. Then at length Addington began to yield to public feeling, and through Lord Melville opened negotiations for the return of Pitt to office. But a frank resignation and an open acknowledgment that Pitt was the better man of the two was beyond him. He stipulated that Grenville and Windham, who had throughout opposed him, should be excluded from the new arrangements. He wished Lord Chatham to assume the position of nominal Prime Minister, while he and Pitt should be equal Secretaries. Pitt was not a man to accept a position of even nominal subordination; he did not even hear Lord Melville's proposition to the end. "Upon my word," said he, "I had not the curiosity to ask what I was to be." And thus England plunged afresh into war, while all her best statesmen were still excluded from office. For the crisis came rapidly nearer. The feeling of the nation was aroused, and Addington could no longer withstand it. An ultimatum with regard to Malta was drawn up, demanding its retention for ten years, its surrender after that period to the inhabitants, and the cession to England in its stead of the island of Lampedusa. Bonaparte was somewhat taken aback by this exhibition of vigour, but as his answer to the ultimatum was not satisfactory, Lord Whitworth demanded his passports, and withdrew from Paris on the 12th of May. The French ambassador left London on the 16th, and on the 18th a declaration of war was published.   War declared. May 18, 1803.

This war was of a distinctly different character from that which preceded it. The one had been undertaken in the interest of aristocracy and of property, in a panic of fear of the growth of the liberty of the people ; now the whole nation was   Character of the war. driven to defend itself, and, while defending itself, Europe also, from the aggressions of a gigantic and all-absorbing ambition. The outbreak of this war marks a change in the career of Napoleon. He had hitherto acted, nominally at all events, as an agent for the propagation of national liberty. He had pretended throughout to be spreading the principles of the French Revolution ; he had met with much sympathy from downtrodden nations ; he had found it easy to overwhelm effete and unpopular dynasties. He was now entering upon a war against the people themselves, and, though success at first attended his arms, when it became evident that it was not assistance against tyrants but subjugation to a foreign power that he brought, the efforts to oppose him became national, and before the uprising of nations he ultimately succumbed. Bonaparte's first step after war was declared corresponded exactly with this change. Crowds of Englishmen had thronged to see   Napoleon arrests all the English in France. with their own eyes the condition of revolutionized France. All the English in France between the age of eighteen and sixty, numbering it is believed about 12,000, were suddenly by a single decree taken prisoners, and kept confined till the close of the war, thus spreading sorrow and discomfort broadcast through England. The pretext was the capture of two ships before war was declared; they were not however captured till after the ambassadors had withdrawn, nor, as has subsequently been made evident, till Bonaparte had himself ordered an embargo to be laid on the English shipping.   .

Bonaparte's interference in the affairs of Ireland had also its share in rendering the war truly national. It had been hoped that the great work of the Union, following the suppression of   He excites discontent in Ireland. the Rebellion of 1798, would have introduced peace and prosperity into the island. Nor at first did the hopes appear ill founded. Both Lord Hardwicke, the Lord-Lieutenant, and Lord Redesdale the Chancellor, appear to have believed in the rapid improvement both of the physical and political condition of the country. The Catholics, although disappointed of their

hopes, seem to have understood the state of affairs which obliged
Pitt to refrain from the further prosecution of their claims, and to
have postponed all idea of present agitation.

But the miserable cultivation and the prevalence of waste lands
in Ireland allowed of the existence of an extremely ignorant and
prejudiced peasantry, and among them it was not difficult to excite
again their old animosity to England. Bonaparte took advantage of
this opening, and while the Peace of Amiens lasted many French
agents seem to have been poured into Ireland, both for the purpose
of inquiring minutely into the resources of the English Government there and of establishing a connection with the discontented
peasantry. Many intercepted letters proved to Government the
existence of these agents; their presence in Ireland was excused,
like Sebastiani's mission to Egypt, by the assertion that they were
merely commercial agents, following a system which had obtained in
France ever since the time of Colbert. Their success was limited by
the distaste of the Catholics for the French Revolution. In spite of
Bonaparte's intercourse with Rome and the establishment of the
Concordat with Pius VII., by which he established Roman Catholic
Christianity as the religion of France, the Catholics could not forget
the destructive doctrines which had attended all the former steps of
the Revolution. It was therefore among the republicans only (not
an influential body) and the ignorant mob that the agitation took any
hold. A leader was found in Robert Emmett, the son of a Dublin
physician, who with his brother had been more or
less implicated in the affairs of 1798. He visited Paris
early in the Peace, had personal interviews with the First
Consul, and returned home ready to instigate the rebellion. The
other leaders were Russell, a religious enthusiast, and Quigley, a professional agitator. About Christmas 1802 the conspirators began
their operations. Arms and powder were collected at depôts in
Dublin, and members of the conspiracy were enrolled. Some of
these informed the police of what was going on. The explosion of
the powder in one of the depôts, and the discovery of pikes there,
still further warned the Government, and Emmett considered it
necessary to hasten the outbreak. Saturday the 23rd of July was
the day fixed for the rising. It proved to be little more than a city
riot. As no soldiery had been brought into Dublin, it was for some
time in the hands of the mob, who plundered and got drunk. The
only important incident of the riot was the murder of Lord
Kilwarden, the Chief Justice, who, returning from his country-seat

*Emmett's
Rebellion.
1803.*

with his daughter and nephew, was met in the streets by a part of the mob and brutally murdered. The arrival at the castle of his daughter, who had contrived to make her escape from the murderers, at length set the military in motion, and the mob was dispersed without much difficulty. The depôt was discovered, with the supply of arms, green uniforms, and the proclamation of the provisional government which was to have been established. Emmett sought safety by pretending to be a French officer; but the French were not liked; his flight was not favoured by the people; he was captured and hanged. The importance of the outbreak lies chiefly in the disclosure of the deepseated hostility of the Irish, and the necessity laid upon the English of establishing a series of coercive laws, which remained in force for many years, and went far to neutralize the healing effect which it was hoped the Union would have exercised.

The declaration of war called Pitt from his retirement, for the war, in the form it had now assumed, seemed to demand the co-operation of all patriotic men. Pitt therefore again appeared in the House; he thought it his duty to see, now that war had come, that no laxity was displayed in its support, and returned to his place, intending, as he himself said, not to join in any opposition to the ministry so long as their measures seemed energetic, but to forget all that was past (and many things had been done of which he could not fully approve) and devote himself to insuring vigour and activity for the future. Few positions could now be more embarrassing than that of Addington. His peaceful plans had come to nothing; and conscious, as he could not but have been, of his own inferiority, and of the general desire under present circumstances for Pitt's return to office, he had now to withstand the powerful attacks of an unusually able Opposition, and the damaging criticism of a so-called *Difficulty of Addington's position.* friend whom all the world regarded as his rival. And it must be owned that Pitt's views were far more in accordance with the views of the Opposition than with those of the minister. Grenville, Windham, and Spencer, the consistent supporters of the preceding war, had entered into a close alliance with Fox, its consistent opponent. Their common view, which was shared by Pitt, was that the condition of the country was so critical that nothing but the ablest possible ministry could be tolerated—that the present ministry, consisting as it for the most part did of the least able members of Pitt's old Government, was wholly incompetent to meet the present dangers, and that the one thing necessary was a great combined arrangement by which the administration of affairs should be intrusted to men of all parties of the widest experience and the greatest talents. They were naturally anxious that Pitt, whose views they knew to be almost identical with their own, should openly join them, but, as has been seen, although he shared their views, he felt himself still bound to give some sort of support to a ministry which he had himself created, and which nominally upheld the same principles which he had always advocated. In this trying position Addington's Government showed

His vigorous measures inefficiently carried out. very creditable activity. Their budgets, with which Pitt had at first been discontented, were now conceived in accordance with his own principles. A considerable portion of the increased burden was borne by taxation, especially by the reimposition of a property tax, and loans were contracted only as far as needful. Militia to the number of about 70,000 were embodied; an army of reserve 50,000 strong, raised by ballot to serve for four years, voted; and by a Bill, known as the Military Service Bill, the enrolment as volunteers of all men between the ages of seventeen and fifty-five provided for. The number of these volunteers speedily rose to beyond 300,000. As the standing army was kept at about 120,000, there must have been of one sort or other upwards of 500,000 armed men for the purposes of defence. The temper of the nation was thoroughly roused. Pitt himself, as Warden of the Cinque Ports, raised and commanded 3000 volunteers, and caused considerable offers of gunboats to be sent in to the Government from the maritime towns.

But great though these preparations were, they were carried out with a dilatoriness and want of energy in which Pitt and the Opposition found much cause of complaint. Windham was an enthusiast for the regular army and disliked the volunteers. Pitt pointed out, that although volunteers were exempted from serving in the militia, they could only claim their exemption when properly enrolled and armed, and the issue of arms was so slow as to throw a great damp upon volunteering, which this exemption was intended to encourage. There was also a great blot in the administration which afforded plentiful room for attack. Lord St. Vincent, great

Increasing opposition. as an admiral, had proved himself incompetent as the head of the Admiralty. In the desire of the ministry for economy many of the gunboats and other ships had been rapidly broken up, and the stores in the dockyards sold, much of them to the French themselves. Attacks directed on these points began to tell. Other circumstances combined to drive Pitt to declare himself. He was perfectly conscious of his own greatness, and of the universal feeling that his present position was unworthy of him, and he believed that he was the right man to be intrusted with the Government in the present crisis. It was with much alarm that he heard that the King's health was again failing. There seemed every prospect that a regency would be necessary. If that regency were established, it was understood that Lord Moira, the Prince of Wales' chief adviser, would be called upon to form a Government. Pitt declared that under those circumstances he should be compelled to decline office ; fearful of being thus permanently removed from the ministry, he thought the time for action had arrived ; if he was to be minister at all he must take steps to become so ; he therefore declared his total want of confidence in the present ministry, and stated his intention, should the state of the King's health permit, of writing Pitt offers to him, stating his views, and putting himself at his to undertake Majesty's service ; he desired, if possible, a broad the Government. Government, but that if the King objected to that he should state his willingness to attempt to form one even upon a narrow basis. He further declared his belief that after the recess the combined Opposition would be sufficiently strong to compel the ministers to resign. Addington also was so conscious of this, that when, on the reopening of Parliament on the 5th of April, the Opposition assault began, he authorized Lord Eldon to enter into communication with Pitt. Through the Chancellor the letter before alluded to was laid before the King. Meanwhile the ministerial majorities were diminishing. The Irish Militia Bill was carried by a majority of twenty-one only, at that time regarded as very small. On the 23rd Fox moved to refer all Army Bills to a committee of the whole House. His motion was rejected by only fifty-two ; while, two days afterwards, on his attack on the Army of Reserve Addington Bill, the ministerial majority again sunk to thirty-seven resigns in a House of 443 members. Upon this Addington April 26, 1804. resigned.

On the 30th Mr. Pitt was informed of the King's desire that he should draw up a plan for a new administration ; he accordingly stated, first in writing, and subsequently (May 7) in a long interview, what he considered best for the country. On Pitt desires three grounds he strongly urged a large and compre- a broad hensive ministry. The war was a national one, and ministry. promised to be both long and expensive ; to induce the nation to make the required sacrifice unanimity was most desirable. To wage war singlehanded was beyond the power of England; but while party divisions were rife in Parliament the confidence of foreign nations could not be gained. And lastly, if the King wished to keep the question of the Catholic emancipation from discussion, it was desirable that there should be no formidable Opposition certain to make use of the Catholic claims as a means of offence against Government. On these grounds the new minister urged the admission of both Grenville and Fox to the ministry; but he here found the King obstinate, Grenville he would admit, Fox never. The course that statesman had followed with regard to the American War, his strong language in favour of the Revolution, his strenuous opposition to the last French war, had rendered him politically hateful to the King. His friendship for the Prince of Wales, and the share which the King believed he had taken in the direction of the Prince's conduct, had excited his strong personal dislike. To these prejudices Pitt, in an evil hour for himself, yielded. He had indeed, as he had already stated, intended to do so. He consented to exclude Fox from his arrangements. But he still hoped to win the support of his old colleague Grenville, and since Fox, with great magnanimity, told his partisans that he had no wish that the King's personal prejudice against himself should influence their conduct, he was not without hopes of strengthening his Government by the addition of some of the Whigs. These hopes were disappointed. The two sections of the Opposition held separate but simultaneous meetings. In one Grenville declared he would not take office without Fox. and his followers accepted his decision; in the other the friends of Fox determined to decline office if their chief was excluded. No resource was therefore left to Pitt but to form his government as best he could upon a narrow Tory basis. The political sections from which he was enabled to draw were his own immediate followers, and such of the late minister's as did not feel themselves pledged to follow Addington in his retirement. The result was not wholly satisfactory. Lord Eldon, the Duke of Portland, Lord Westmoreland, Lord Castlereagh, and Lord Hawkesbury, continued to hold office, Lord Hawkesbury surrendering the important post of Foreign Secretary to Lord Harrowby, and receiving in exchange the Home Office. Dundas, who had been created a Peer as Lord Melville, became First Lord of the Admiralty, while Lord Camden, Lord Mulgrave, and the Duke of Montrose, also became members of the Cabinet, which consisted of twelve, all of

Pitt yields to the King's opposition.

He forms a Tory ministry.

whom, with the exception of Pitt and Castlereagh, were in the Upper House. Several other men of importance were admitted to subordinate offices ; Canning became Treasurer of the Navy, Huskisson one of the Secretaries of the Treasury, and Mr Perceval, the future Prime Minister, remained in the position of Attorney-General.[1]

The change of ministry implied a complete change of policy. As Addington's ministry had been from the first intended Difficulties of as a peace ministry, so the accession of Pitt to office Pitt's position. implied a vigorous prosecution of the war. But it was with very maimed influence that it entered upon its work ; all hope of acting in foreign affairs with the full weight of a great combined national party behind him had disappeared from Pitt's view. The same opposition which had opposed Addington was ready to oppose him ; while Addington himself, unable to act in any great or magnanimous manner, had also joined its ranks, and was in open opposition to his old friend. It was with a majority scarcely larger than that of the ministry he had succeeded, supported by the same mediocre men, and aided in the Commons by one minister alone, that Pitt found himself obliged to encounter the bitter enmity of Bonaparte.

The necessity for energy Pitt probably felt more strongly than any of his contemporaries. Strange incredulity was expressed both by Fox and Grenville as to the reality of the invasion with Real danger which Bonaparte was threatening England. Yet it is from France. certain that the intention of invasion was perfectly real. Bonaparte had determined to carry out the threat he had let drop to Lord Whitworth. In the first place it suited his policy to keep his army together and thoroughly employed. The temper of the Parisians was lukewarm ; he felt that some pressure was necessary to induce them to give him the support his ambition required, and such coercion could in no way be more certainly procured than by exciting the personal devotion and enthusiasm of his soldiers by unfolding before them constant visions of glory. At the same time his exasperation against the English led him to underrate the difficulties which lay in his way, and to believe in the real practicability of his scheme. The minute and careful preparations in which he engaged are incompatible with the idea that the invasion was a

---

[1] Lord Stanhope gives in his Life of Pitt the following list of the broad administration as planned by Mr. Pitt :—Treasury, Mr. Pitt; Secretaries of State, Lord Melville, Mr. Fox, Lord Fitzwilliam. The other offices were to have been given to Lord Spencer, Lord Grenville, the Duke of Portland, Lord Eldon, Lord Chatham, Mr. Windham, Lord Castlereagh, Lord Hampden, Lord Harrowby, Mr. Grey, and Mr. Canning.

mere feint. In all the ports of the Channel boats were being built; even inland towns with any water communication with the sea were busily employed in the same labour. A great basin was constructed at Boulogne, of a peculiar shape, intended to allow of an extremely rapid embarkation of the army, which was encamped upon the neighbouring heights, and fortifications were raised to render the flotilla secure from the sea. Yet in all probability, had the plan been tried, it would have proved a failure. The boats used to transport the troops were to be of several classes and sizes, and the mere action of the tides, which are of great strength and complexity in the Channel, would have been exerted quite differently on these different sized vessels, and would almost of necessity have separated the flotilla; yet the whole success of the movement depended on the simultaneous landing of the army at one point. Moreover, for the passage of heavily-laden and flat-bottomed boats an absolute calm of two days would have been necessary, and a calm of two days is a phenomenon of rare occurrence in the Channel; while, thirdly, success presupposed the complete absence or idleness of the British fleet.

However, whether practicable or impracticable, Napoleon intended to make the effort, and Pitt, in common with the English nation, believed in his intention. The excitement was universal. The country was entirely occupied in drilling and warlike preparations; martello towers were built along the southern coast, beacons rose on every hilltop, a great canal or ditch was dug along the coast of Kent, and Pitt excited the ridicule of Grenville by the energy with which he superintended the numerous reviews which he set on foot through his brother Lord Chatham. Such defences have been derided as ridiculously inefficient, and certainly neither the Kentish ditch nor a few round towers mounting one gun each, nor a half-disciplined militia, could have checked the French army had a landing been effected. The real value of such preparations was the life and energy and courage which they roused in the people. The more real work of the minister was the restoration of the national forces to their full efficiency, and the effort to induce the other countries of Europe to combine in withstanding the dangerous ambition of the French usurper.

Preparations for defence.

With regard to the army the great ministerial measure was the Additional Force Bill. There existed at this time two systems of enlistment, the one for a limited term, the other for the general service; the recruiting officers in these two

The Additional Force Bill

branches had entered into a sort of competition, the effect of which was that very large and quite unnecessary bounties were offered to induce men to enlist on one or other of the two systems. A second difficulty was one which constantly attends a volunteer army, the difficulty of procuring a constant and regular supply of recruits. The intention of the Additional Force Bill was to obviate these two difficulties. Pitt thought that this might be done by raising an additional force of 50,000 men, whence a supply of trained soldiers could be constantly passed into the regular army. There already existed an army of reserve, collected under the Reserve Bill passed by the late ministry, but its full complement of 50,000 had not been reached; there was a deficiency of 9000 men. At the same time the militia had risen much beyond its usual numbers. It was at present 74,000 strong, instead of 40,000 for England and 8000 for Scotland, which was regarded as its normal strength. The present Bill reduced the militia to its old dimensions. The remainder, with the 9000 as yet unraised men of the army of reserve, was to form the additional force from which 12,000 annually were to pass into the army. Parishes were to be assessed at a certain number of men, and if they failed to supply them a moderate fine was to be laid upon them, to go to the general recruiting fund. It was an attempt, in fact, to introduce in some degree the principle of compulsory service, already slightly recognized in the militia. The newly-organized body had this also in common with the militia, that it was connected with the regular army by forming second battalions not bound to serve abroad, but to be used to supply the place of the regular army when it was required for foreign service. It was supposed that there would be no difficulty, when military habits were once formed, in finding the annual 12,000 to feed the regular troops. The whole strength of the Opposition was brought to bear against the Bill, which certainly, in its compulsory clauses, introduced a new principle into the English military system, and it was only with the comparatively weak majority of forty that it was carried through the House. As far as the naval forces Increase of were concerned energy and activity were all that was the navy. required, and these were supplied by Lord Melville. In the first year of his administration he could boast that he had added to the fleet no less than 166 vessels, either completed or in a state of forwardness, while during the same period 600 ships had been docked and repaired.

With regard to foreign affairs Pitt's position did not at first seem hopeful. He wished to follow out the policy of the last war, and to form a third coalition. But Bonaparte was engaged in almost the same process in opposition to England, and the chances at first seemed all in favour of the success of the French in this vast competition. By the Treaty of Lunéville those German princes who had been dispossessed by the advance of the French to the Rhine, and by the withdrawal of Tuscany from the House of Austria, were to be indemnified at the expense of the ecclesiastical principalities of the Empire. This arrangement might have been carried out without much difficulty by the Germans themselves, but the avarice of the great powers Prussia and Austria, and the difficulty which the smaller princes found in obtaining their restitutions, rendered mediation necessary, and an article of the Treaty had thrown the arbitration into the hands of Bonaparte. He had used this opportunity to flatter Russia by suggesting that the Emperor should be joined with himself in the duty of arbitration, to please Prussia by unduly favouring its claims, and to foment all the rivalries of the Germanic body. He had further, on the rupture of the Peace of Amiens, suggested that some of the points at issue should be decided by the arbitration of Russia, hoping thereby to silence for ever any complaints Alexander might have to urge against him, so that neither that power nor Prussia was disposed to be unfriendly to him, while Austria was exhausted under the late heavy blow which had been dealt her, and much occupied by the rivalry of the other German powers. But in spite of this appearance of friendship of both Russia and Prussia for France there were secret causes of hostility between them. Alexander had seen through the somewhat barefaced attempt to purchase his favour by the offer of the position of arbitrator, and while consenting to act as mediator, had continued to urge the injustice of the conduct of the French with regard both to Piedmont and to Germany. To such an extent had the angry correspondence been carried, that a scene had taken place (July 29, 1803) between Bonaparte and the Russian ambassador very similar to that with Lord Whitworth. With Prussia also the ambition of the first Consul had prevented him from completing his work of conciliation. He had displeased that Court by a persistent refusal to withdraw his troops from Hanover. On the whole, the feeling of Lord Harrowby, when he entered upon the plan of forming a coalition, was that his best hope lay in the direction of Russia; but that all Europe would remain quiet till the great invasion of England should either have destroyed that power or

Napoleon attempts to form a coalition.

by its repulse offer a favourable opportunity for assaulting France.

Napoleon's own conduct went far to remove all expected difficulties. No one could have played more completely into the hands of his enemies. A conspiracy was set on foot against his Government by the royalists ; it was principally in the hands of Georges, the breton leader, and of General Pichegru. At the right moment the Count of Artois was to appear upon the scene, and the Bourbons to be re-established. The police and Bonaparte obtained early information of it. Bonaparte made use of his knowledge to foster the conspiracy, and to implicate General Moreau, whom he had always regarded as his rival since the battle of Hohenlinden, and who appears to have been guilty only of having consented to be reconciled to his old friend Pichegru, from whom political differences had separated him. Although there is not the slightest proof of the truth of the fact, it was asserted that the plan included the assassination of the First Consul ; and, determined to make the most of his knowledge of the conspiracy, Bonaparte sent agents, who entrapped two of our ministers abroad, Messrs. Drake and Spencer Smith, into consenting to the conspiracy. Of the real plot they knew nothing, but were led to believe in the existence of some royalist scheme and to lend it their aid. Bonaparte then charged them publicly with having joined in a plan of assassination, demanded, and ultimately (April 1804) succeeded in procuring, their expulsion from Bavaria and Wurtemburg, and sent to all the Courts of Europe a coarse and virulent attack upon the English Government. The reply of Lord Hawkesbury (April 30)—for this took place during the Addington ministry—to the effect that England had the right, and would use the right, of taking advantage of the political situation of countries with which she was at war, justified the conduct of England in the eyes of all foreign powers, and excited a strong feeling against the conduct of the Consul. The conspiracy was followed by a still more startling act of violence. Unable to secure the person of the Count of Artois, who received timely warning of the plot, and burning to strike some blow against the Bourbons, Bonaparte, regardless of the neutrality of the country, sent a body of troops into Baden, there captured an innocent and unoffending Bourbon prince, the Duc d'Enghien, son of the Prince of Condé, brought him into France, had him summarily tried by a military tribunal, and immediately shot. The effect of this great crime upon the crowned heads

[margin note: Napoleon's conduct with regard to Georges' conspiracy]

[margin note: Murder of the Duc d'Enghien. March 21, 1804.]

of Europe was instantaneous, and was not decreased when Bonaparte
threw off all mask of moderation, and gave an outward
form to the despotism he had long practised by declaring himself Emperor. But there were still many difficulties to be overcome before the Courts of Europe could be brought
to see the absolute necessity of forming a coalition. It required a
whole year of negotiation, and of further proofs of Napoleon's
character, before Pitt's object was attained.

Napoleon
Emperor.
May 18, 1804.

The loss of his able Foreign Minister added fresh difficulties to his
negotiations. In December 1804 Lord Harrowby was
disabled by an accidental fall, and had to resign the
Foreign Office. His place was supplied by Lord Mulgrave ; but Pitt was made conscious of the weakness of his ministry
by the severe blow that the loss of one member of it was to him.
Addington, since his retirement from office, had been in open opposition to the minister ; but as their views were generally similar,
and the division between them had been entirely owing to the sore-
ness arising from the manner in which Addington had lost the
premiership, there seemed no reason for a further separation. Addington therefore rejoined the ministry,
taking the title of Lord Sidmouth and the office of
President of the Council, which the Duke of Portland was compelled
by ill health to resign. Pitt's majority was thus increased, although
the strength gained by the adhesion of Addington himself to his
ministry was not much.

Lord Harrowby's
retirement.
Dec. 1804.

Addington
rejoins the
ministry.

While the negotiations for a coalition were continuing, England
carried on the war singlehanded, and before long such
power as Spain possessed was added to that of France.
To support his vast expenditure Napoleon demanded subsidies from
foreign countries under his influence, and a treaty had been made
with Spain, now ruled entirely by Godoy, Prince of the Peace, by
which a considerable sum was annually paid to the French exchequer.
Although this was virtually an act of hostility to England, the
English ministry, aware of the weakness of Spain, had passed it over
in silence ; but at the same time our minister, in February 1804,
declared that the preparation of any naval armaments in Spanish
ports would be regarded as a cause of war. In September the
English admiral on the coast of Spain notified the existence of such
an armament in Ferrol ; a strong note was written to the Spanish
minister, and ultimately the English ambassador retired from
Madrid in November, and in December war was declared. But

Spain joins
France.

already in October, before the declaration of war, the English had seized four treasure-ships, well knowing that the money would sooner or later find its way into the hands of Napoleon. The justice of the action was questioned; but, considering the declaration of the preceding February, and the known fact that Spain paid subsidies to France, the seizure seems to have been thoroughly justified.

While our enemy was thus strengthened by the open adhesion of a country which could at least assist him with ships *Failure of* and convenient harbours, our efforts to weaken his pre- *attempts to* parations for invasion, which were continually being *Napoleon's fleet.* pushed on, were unavailing; descents were made upon the coast and a few outlying boats captured; but the great attempt which was made in October to destroy the flotilla produced no result. The expedition is known as the Catamaran expedition. It was proposed by means of vessels filled with combustibles to burn the flotilla in Boulogne harbour, but when the fire-ships were sent in, they either failed to reach the vessels, or a passage was made for them, and they drifted harmlessly through.

It was only outside the limits of Europe that the English showed a decided superiority, and that great successes kept up the hope of both ministry and people during this fearful period, when the arrival of Bonaparte in England was daily expected, and when as yet all Europe seemed to hold aloof from our alliance. Surinam had been conquered from the Dutch, and in the year 1805 a great *Success of the* war was brought to a triumphant conclusion in India. *war in India* After the capture in 1799 of Seringapatam, the capital *Mahrattas.* of Tippoo Sahib, the ruler of Mysore, the territories of Mysore had been divided by what is known as the Tripartite Treaty between the English, the Nizam of the Deccan, and a descendant of the ancient Rajahs of Mysore, whom Hyder Ali had dispossessed. By these new acquisitions the English had come in contact with the great Mahratta power.

The great empire conquered by this warlike race, which had been founded by Sivajee in the seventeenth century, extended *Extent of the* from Delhi in the north to the Tumbudra, a southern *Mahratta* tributary of the Kistna on the south, and from the Bay *empire.* of Bengal on the east to Gujerat in the west. The authority of the Rajah of Satara, nominal head of the race, had passed into the hands of his minister the Peishwa, who resided at Poonah, in the Western Ghauts. His authority had in turn become nominal, and the empire was broken up among five great chiefs, of whom the Peishwa may be ranked as one. The others were the Bonslah or Rajah of Berar, occupying the north and east of the Deccan, and including Cuttack and the mouths of the Mahanadi in his territories; Sindia, who occupied the north-west of the Deccan and Kandesh, and whose property extended northwards through a portion of Malwa as far as Delhi, of which he held possession, and westward into Gujerat, where he had considerable property; Holkar, who lay almost entirely in the Malwa, north of the Vindyha range of mountains, to the east of Sindia, between him and Berar; and, lastly, the Guicowar, who possessed in Gujerat all except those territories that were in the hands of Sindia. He alone of the Mahratta chiefs preserved neutrality during this great war. To the south of the Mahratta states lay that part of the Deccan which was governed by the Nizam, now tributary to the English; and south of his dominions, touching on its north-west the southern extreme of the Mahratta country, was Mysore. All three Presidencies were therefore in contact with one or other of the Mahratta states.

At the beginning of the century the Mahrattas were at war among themselves, and Holkar, in his rivalry with Sindia, had thought it advisable to expel the Peishwa from Poonah, and to set up a creature of his own there. The deposed Peishwa sought an asylum among the English in Bombay. The presence of the predatory chief Holkar in the south induced the English to occupy their northern frontier in Mysore with an army of observation. While things were in this position the Peishwa offered to enter into a perpetual treaty with the English if they would reinstate him in Poonah. Lord Wellesley was at this time Governor-General of India. He had set on foot a policy which had been much opposed by the authorities in the India House, and the support of which by Pitt had been constantly assaulted by the Opposition. This policy is known as the subsidiary system. It was found impossible, in the presence of the native powers, naturally anxious to rid themselves of the English conquerors, and certain to find ready assistance from the French, to remain in a state of inaction. On the other hand, Wellesley did not think it desirable or just to conquer and annex all the neighbouring territories, which would in fact only have enlarged the sphere of danger. He preferred to establish English influence, to oblige the native rulers to enter into permanent treaties with him, to place the political management of their provinces in the hands of a British resident, to pay for the support of an army largely officered

Lord Wellesley's subsidiary system.

by Europeans, while the native princes, at the same time, retained the domestic government in their own hands. It is now generally allowed that this was a wise system, but at the time the outcry against it was so great, that even after the success of the Mahratta war Wellesley had in fact to yield to it, and returned to England in 1805. While this policy, however, was uppermost, such an offer as that of the Peishwa was certain to be accepted, and at the end of 1802, by the Treaty of Bassein, the English accepted the friendship of the Peishwa, and undertook to restore him.

The threatening attitude of the English compelled the Mahratta chiefs for a time to lay aside their private enmities, and Holkar, Sindia, and the Rajah of Berar made common cause against the invaders. What rendered this coalition more formidable was, that Sindia had established in the Douab, or district lying between the Jumna and the Ganges, a French state in the hands of a certain M. Perron, in which there was a considerable number of troops drilled in the European fashion, and officered by Frenchmen, while in the south, the neighbourhood of Pondicherry, which had been restored to France by the Peace of Amiens, gave an opening to that power to interfere should war again break out in Europe. The first act of the war was rapidly and successfully carried out. General Wellesley marched, in the spring of 1803, from the frontier of Mysore, was joined by Colonel Stevenson with the Nizam's army from Hyderabad, recaptured Poonah on the 20th of April, and by the middle of May had reinstated the Peishwa. The General at that time believed that all disputes with the Mahratta powers would be settled by negotiation. It before long became evident that on the part of the Mahrattas these negotiations were a feint, and that the three chiefs, with their French allies on the north, were still determined to fight, and had designs upon the territories of the subsidiary Prince, the Nizam, who was at the point of death. To withstand this great confederacy a large and well-combined plan of operations was made. To secure unity of action, General Wellesley was invested with supreme authority in the Deccan, General Lake was given similar powers in the valley of the Ganges, while secondary attacks were directed against Sindia's territories in Gujerat under the command of Colonel Murray, and against the Bonslah's province of Cuttack under Colonel Harcourt. The confederation was thus assaulted simultaneously at four points. In the meantime the rupture of the Peace of Amiens had become known. Pondicherry was carefully watched, and French troops recently landed there taken prisoners.

Outbreak of the Mahratta war. 1803

In August General Wellesley left Poonah, Colonel Stevenson acting in correspondence with him further to the east. He marched direct to Ahmednuggur, which he captured, crossed the Godavery river, and arrived at Aurungabad. Meanwhile Sindia had fallen back northward, and in September the two English commanders joined their forces a little to the east of Aurungabad, and advanced to meet him. Sindia's forces, reinforced by sixteen battalions officered by Frenchmen, lay not far from Assye on the river Kaitna; between them and the English extended a range of hills; to prevent their escape the English commanders separated—Stevenson marching by the eastern, Wellesley by the western end of the range. When Wellesley heard that the enemy were moving off, he determined upon an attack without waiting for Stevenson's arrival. To get at the enemy it was necessary to cross the river which was on his right; although assured by his guide that it was impassable, he conjectured the existence of a passage from the appearance of two villages immediately opposite each other on the two banks of the river. He found his conjecture was correct, and his troops, when they had crossed the river, exactly occupied the space between that and another stream on which Assye stands. His two flanks were thus covered. He there with 4500 men entirely defeated Sindia's army, numbering more than 30,000. At the close of the day he found himself in possession of nearly 100 cannon and the whole of the camp equipage. The General mentioned it afterwards as the bloodiest battle for the numbers that he ever saw; the killed and wounded among the English amounting to more than 1500, a third of their entire force. The Mahratta army separated into two divisions, one division under the Rajah of Berar retiring westward as though to attack Poonah. Leaving Stevenson, therefore, to follow the northern division under Sindia, Wellesley hastened in pursuit of the Rajah. Sindia, being close pressed by Stevenson, begged for a truce; but as it was found that his troops were still serving in the army of the Rajah of Berar, and that the truce was merely deceptive, the pursuit was recommenced, and the enemy brought to a final engagement on the plain of Argaum, where they were again entirely defeated. The war in the Deccan was closed by the capture, by the combined armies, of Gawulgur, near the sources of the Taptee river. Two days afterwards, on the 17th of December, the Rajah of Berar submitted, and before the end of the month Sindia also consented to treat. By these treaties

Battle of Assye. Sept. 23, 1803.

Battle of Argaum, Nov. 29.

Subsidiary treaties with Sindia and Berar.

the province of Cuttack was annexed to the English possessions, Sindia was driven entirely from the Deccan, and lost some strong places in the Douab. Both princes entered into subsidiary arrangements, and promised to admit no foreigners but English to their confidence.

These treaties were the consequence of the combined campaigns of Wellesley and Lake; for during the brilliant campaign of Assye in the Deccan, Lake had been carrying on war with equal success in the valley of the Ganges. The French province in the Douab had given but little trouble. Perron had retired from one of his fortresses, Coel, without fighting; his second stronghold, Alleghur, had been captured; his troops had indeed remained to fight, but he had himself surrendered to the English. The capture of Alleghur had been followed by a great victory over the Mahrattas within sight of Delhi. Lake had entered that capital, restored the aged Shah Allum to the Mogul throne, and attached to the English by so doing the whole Mahommedan population of India. He had won further victories at Muttra and Agra on the Jumna, and finally, on the 1st of November, at the same time that Wellesley was carrying out the pursuit which preceded the battle of Argaum, won the great battle of Laswari. The secondary attacks had been no less successful. While Murray had captured Baroach and subjugated the rest of Sindia's possessions in Gujerat, Harcourt had secured Cuttack at the mouths of the Mahanadi and the great temple of Juggernaut. The subsidiary treaties signed at the close of the year were the consequences of this series of victories. In reward for their services Lake was raised to the Peerage and Wellesley made a Knight of the Bath. Holkar alone remained unsubdued. The following year, 1804, he was again in arms, and though thoroughly defeated by General Lake, succeeded in obtaining the support of the Rajah of Berhampoor, and prolonged the war till the close of the year 1805.

The success in India was no doubt of great importance both in sustaining the courage of the people and in cheering the last days of Pitt; but he was not destined to close his life in happiness and triumph. He lived, indeed, long enough to see the great coalition for which he had been working completed, and to receive the adhesion to it of Russia, Austria, Sweden, and Naples; he lived long enough to see the English again triumphant upon the ocean, to hear the news of the greatest victory which had ever attended their arms, and to rejoice at the dispersion of the threatening cloud which for more than a year had hung over the country. But he also lived just long enough to see, as far as his foreign policy was concerned, the whole of his careful structure dashed to pieces, and the complete triumph of his arch enemy at the battle of Austerlitz.

If the close of his life as a foreign minister was sad, a still thicker Attack on Lord Melville. mist of misfortune hung over the last years of his home government. The man on whom he most relied in the ministry was his old friend Lord Melville, who had fairly justified his confidence by the energy and success with which he had reconstituted the navy. It was through him that the Opposition found means to inflict a deadly blow upon the minister. Lord St. Vincent, though his general administration had been weak, had been laudably anxious to improve the condition of the Admiralty, especially Naval inquiries Feb. 1805. in regard to its expenses. He had therefore established a commission of naval inquiry, which from time to time sent in its reports. The last of these, the tenth, had been sent in in February 1805. Even before its publication it was understood to reflect upon Lord Melville's conduct as Treasurer of the Navy, an office which he had held along with several others in Pitt's first administration. On one point he had certainly shown remissness. He had allowed Mr. Trotter, Paymaster of the Navy, to pay public money to his own account at his banker's, and to use it as his own. No loss had accrued to the State in consequence; but no doubt it was a highly censurable misapplication of public funds. But beyond this, it was asserted that Lord Melville had himself acted in a similar way, and undoubtedly there were certain sums unaccounted for. Lord Melville's own account of this matter was, that since his retirement from office he had destroyed all old vouchers; but that even if he possessed them, as he at that time held various offices, and did not keep the accounts entirely separate, he would not have been able to give a satisfactory account without disclosing confidential transactions of Government. This no doubt meant that the money had been employed for some secret service; but his enemies did not scruple to say that he had appropriated it to his own uses. Upon the report Mr. Whitbread founded a parliamentary attack upon Melville, and gave notice that he would bring in a vote of censure upon the 8th of April. Government had now to determine what they would do. Pitt and his own immediate friends, entirely disbelieving the charge against Melville, resolved to withstand it openly. But there was a division in his own Cabinet. Lord

Sidmouth and Melville were great enemies, and, declaring that he regarded it as impossible for Melville to clear himself, Sidmouth warned Pitt that if he persisted in defending him he should be obliged to resign. As this would have been complete ruin, Pitt yielded to a middle course, and determined to request that the inquiry might be referred to a select committee. On the 8th the great debate came on. It was plain that the question would rest with the votes of the independent members, and when Wilberforce, whose character carried great weight, declared that he must support the vote of censure, those members who were pledged to neither party were induced to follow his lead. The anxious moment for division arrived, and the numbers were declared to be equal—216 having voted on either side. The Speaker was then called upon to give his casting vote. The scene is thus described by Lord Fitzharris :—" I sat wedged close to Pitt himself the night when we were 216 ; and the Speaker Abbot, after looking as white as a sheet, and pausing for ten minutes, gave the casting vote against us. Pitt immediately put on the little cocked hat that he was in the habit of wearing when dressed for the evening, and jammed it deeply over his forehead, and I distinctly saw the tears trickling down his cheeks. We had heard one or two, such as Colonel Wardle, say they would see ' how Billy looked after it.' A few young ardent followers of Pitt, with myself, locked their arms together and formed a circle, in which he moved, I believe unconsciously, out of the House, and neither the Colonel nor his friends could approach him." The Opposition were not content with the vote of censure ; although Melville at once resigned his office, Whitbread proceeded to move an address to the King that he should be removed from the King's Councils and presence for ever. The feeling of the House did not justify so extreme a measure, and the motion was withdrawn. But before long the minister thought it necessary so far to yield to public opinion as to have Lord Melville's name withdrawn from the Privy Council.

Vote of censure against Melville. April 8, 1806.

The disagreement between Pitt and Sidmouth upon Lord Melville's conduct terminated in the withdrawal of the Lord President and his followers from the ministry. On the appointment of Sir Charles Middleton, a very old man, to the Admiralty, in which he had been the constant assistant of Melville, Sidmouth took the opportunity of expressing his displeasure and resigned. The charge against Lord Melville was pressed to impeachment. He delivered a defence before the House

Sidmouth resigns. July 7.

of Commons, but it was not regarded as satisfactory. The House of Lords were therefore called upon to decide the question, and when it subsequently came to the vote (June 12, 1806) a very large majority, on all the charges, declared the prisoner not guilty. But Pitt did not live to hear either this declaration of the innocence of his friend or to suffer from the desertion of his colleague Sidmouth.

Parliament prorogued. July 12, 1805.   The impeachment was not carried up to the Bar of the House of Lords till the 26th of June; on the 12th of July Parliament was prorogued, and Pitt did not live to see the opening of another session.

Progress of the war. 1804.   While misfortune was thus following the minister in Parliament, his great plans of European policy had been continued and had at last met with success. In fact, in this matter Napoleon had been his best ally, and had been gradually forcing the great powers of Europe into hostility. The ill feeling which had arisen between the Emperor Alexander and Bonaparte in the preceding year had been increased by subsequent events, and the Czar had been gradually taking up a position of more defined hostility. On the 24th of May 1804, he contracted a defensive alliance with Prussia, though not intending immediate war if it could be avoided. The murder of the Duc d'Enghien and the violation of neutral territory had forced him further in the same direction. So strongly had he resented this act, that it was through his representations to the Diet of Ratisbon (July) that Austria and Prussia, who would otherwise have passed it over in silence, were induced to take any notice of it, and at length, finding his indirect action through the German powers of no avail, he had remonstrated directly with France and withdrawn his ambassador from Paris (Aug. 18). Prussia, though pursuing throughout a weak and vacillating policy which had induced Haugwitz to retire from office, also expressed its disapprobation of Napoleon's conduct by a change of ministry. But instead of seeking to allay its fears, Napoleon still further excited its jealousy by intriguing with the smaller States of Germany, and making a violent inroad into the territory of Hamburg (Oct. 25), to carry off thence the English minister. Austria too, though restrained by her weakness from overt action, in November contracted a treaty with Russia similar to that of Prussia. Very little was wanted to bring all three powers into open hostility with France.

. The character of Alexander gave indeed to Napoleon an opportunity which he ought to have seized. He was full of high-flown notions for the regeneration of Europe, for the more equitable division of states, and some generally established system of public law. With some such scheme his minister Nowosiltzoff came to England in 1805. Pitt speedily modified his views, and proved to him that before so grand a scheme could be realized the practical work to be done was to insist upon the establishment of the terms of the treaties of Lunéville and Amiens. Accordingly, on the 11th of April, the Treaty of St. Petersburg was signed. The two countries pledged themselves to support a general European league, for the purpose of demanding the evacuation of Hanover, Italy, and Elba, the real independence of Holland and Switzerland, and the complete establishment of the kingdom of Naples: they especially pledged themselves not to interfere with the internal government of France, and to close all questions by a general European congress. As England refused to evacuate Malta, the Czar declined to ratify the treaty, and determined to make one more effort singlehanded to avoid war. For this purpose he despatched an ambassador with much more favourable terms than those implied in the late treaty. But Napoleon declined to see him for two months, and in those two months he had had himself declared King of Italy (May 26), had accepted the offer of the Doge of Genoa to comprise the Ligurian Republic in his Italian kingdom (June 3), had created Lucca into a principality for the husband of his sister Eliza (July 21), and had received an ambassador from the Court of Naples with the most stinging threats and insults. The Russian ambassador was therefore recalled, and, though without declaration of war, the coalition was in fact in existence, and arrangements for a general attack upon France began. The coalition was thus the fruit rather of Napoleon's conduct than of Pitt's diplomacy; the occupation of Hanover, the violation of the neutral territory of Baden, the murder of the Duc d'Enghien, the establishment of the kingdom of Italy, the annexation of Genoa and Lucca, and virtually of Holland and of Switzerland, supplied ample reasons to excite the alarm of Europe and to drive the powers into coalition.

But while the coalition was forming, and Napoleon seemed wantonly to be insulting Europe and ignoring the danger of exciting fresh enemies, he was in fact urging on with all rapidity his schemes .for the invasion of England, which he probably hoped might be so successful as to paralyse all action on the part of the European powers. The constantly repeated representations of his naval officers had forced him, much against his

Treaty of St. Petersburg. April 11, 1805.

The coalition practically formed. Sept. 1805.

Napoleon prepares to invade England.

will, to believe that his descent upon England would be impracticable
unless secured by the presence of his fleet. In spite of the general
voice of those who knew the condition of the French navy, he
determined to act with his fleet on the same principles as he
would have acted with his army; a gigantic combination of various
squadrons was to be effected, and a fleet great enough to destroy all
hope of opposition to sweep the Channel. For this purpose the
eighteen ships of the line at Brest under Admiral Gantheaume, the
squadron at Rochefort under Villeneuve, and the Toulon fleet under
Latouche-Tréville, were to unite. The last mentioned admiral was
intrusted with the chief command. Sailing up the coast of France,
he was to liberate from their blockade the squadrons of Rochefort and
Brest, and with their combined fleets appear before Boulogne. But
Latouche-Tréville died, and Napoleon intrusted his plans to Villeneuve.
Those plans, all of them arranged without regard to the bad condition
of the French ships, or to the uncertainty of the weather, were
frequently changed; at one time Villeneuve from Toulon, and Missiessy, his successor, at Rochefort, were to proceed to the West Indies,
drawing the English fleet thither; then Gantheaume was to appear
from Brest, throw troops into Ireland, and thus cover the flotilla.
At another time, all the fleets were to assemble at the West Indies,
and, joining with the Spanish fleet at Ferrol, appear in the Straits of
Calais.

To complete this last measure Villeneuve set sail from Toulon
on the 30th of March 1805, joined Gravina at Cadiz, and reached
Martinique on the 13th of May with twenty ships of the line, and seven
frigates. His voyage was so slow that Missiessy had returned from
the West Indies to France, and the junction failed. In
hot pursuit of Villeneuve, Nelson, who had at length
found out his destination, had hurried. At Martinique
Gantheaume, with the Brest fleet, should have joined Villeneuve;
unfortunately for him Admiral Cornwallis blockaded his fleet.
Villeneuve therefore had to return to Europe alone, sailing for
Ferrol to pick up a squadron of fifteen ships. He was then, at
the head of thirty-five ships, ordered to appear before Brest,
liberate Gantheaume, and appear in the Channel. Back again in
pursuit of him Nelson sailed, but supposed that he would return
to the Mediterranean and not to Ferrol; he therefore again missed
him; but as he had found means to inform the English Government that Villeneuve was returning to Europe, Calder, with a fleet
of fifteen ships, was sent to intercept him. The fleets encountered

Nelson's
pursuit of
Villeneuve.
May 1805.

off Cape Finisterre. The French had twenty-seven vessels, Calder but eighteen, and after an indecisive battle, in which two Spanish ships were taken, he was afraid to renew the engagement, and Villeneuve was thus enabled to reach Ferrol in safety. However, all the operations towards concentration had led to absolutely nothing, and the English fleets, which the movements towards the West Indies were to have decoyed from the Channel, were either still off the coast of France or in immediate pursuit of the fleet of Villeneuve. Nelson returned to Gibraltar, and as soon as he found out where Villeneuve was, he joined his fleet to that of Cornwallis before Brest, and himself returned to England.

The day before Calder had also left nine ships with Cornwallis, who had thus a fleet of thirty-five vessels. He divided them into two equal parts, sending one to Ferrol, and keeping the other to guard Gantheaume in Brest. Meanwhile Villeneuve had not been able to get ready for sea till the 11th of August. Had he then sailed he would probably have encountered with his own nineteen ships Cornwallis' fleet of thirty-five vessels off Brest. Had he indeed postponed his sailing for a few days he would have found Cornwallis' fleet separated, but even then it was improbable that he would have escaped one or other of its divisions. But in fact he did not know of its division, and therefore, acting in the belief of the union of the great fleet off Brest, he was afraid to venture northwards, and with the full approbation of his Spanish colleague Gravina, determined to avail himself of a last alternative which Napoleon had suggested, and sailed to Cadiz. This was a fatal blow to the gigantic schemes of Napoleon. Up till the 22nd of August he still believed that Villeneuve would make his appearance, and in fact wrote to him that day at Brest, closing his letter with the words, "England is ours." As the time for his great stroke drew near he grew nervously anxious, constantly watching the Channel for the approach of the fleet, and at last, when his Minister of Marine, Decrès, told him that the fleet had gone to Cadiz, he broke forth in bitter wrath against both his minister and Villeneuve, whom he accused of the most shameful weakness.

Failure of Napoleon's schemes. Aug.

But Napoleon was not a man who let his success be staked upon one plan alone. Though studiously hiding from his people the existence of the coalition, and not scrupling to have recourse to forged letters and fabricated news for the purpose, he was fully aware of its existence. He knew too of the movements of the armies of Austria and Russia, and had already taken some steps to meet them.

Without much difficulty, therefore, he at once resigned his great

He changes
his plan and
marches against
Austria. plans upon England, and directed his army towards the eastern frontier, determined to wipe out by a great campaign, in which the chances were all in his favour, the disgrace and ridicule of his long-threatened but abortive attack upon England. The largest and best part of the Austrian army was in Italy under the Archduke Charles. On the Inn there were barely 80,000 men, commanded by General Mack. The Russians had yet far to go before they could form a junction with the Austrian troops, and Napoleon, when he first changed his plan on the 25th of August, intended to march by the most direct route to meet the Austrians, and if possible prevent them from crossing the Inn. For this purpose he could bring, counting the army of occupation of Hanover, nearly 200,000 men into the field. The passage of the Rhine was open to him; it was no longer necessary as of old to fight his way through the Black Forest. By pursuing a direct course he would be able to pick up the troops who were in Hanover on his way, and bring his whole army to bear at once upon the Inn. The Austrians, however, little calculating on the rapidity of his movements, believing that the army was engaged on the northern coast, and desirous of securing the assistance of the Bavarian army of 25,000 men, rashly crossed the Inn on the 7th of September, and advanced to Ulm. Their movements were accurately known to Napoleon, who had sent Murat in disguise into Bavaria to watch them; and when he heard that they had taken up their position so far in advance of their base of operations, he formed his great plan for surrounding and capturing the whole army at Ulm.

While Napoleon was thus hurrying off to destroy the Austrian troops, Nelson, having heard of the destination of Villeneuve, and feeling that the fleet he had so long pursued was his fair prey, offered his services to Government. They were gladly accepted, and on the 13th of September he left his home for the last time to take command of the fleet off Cadiz. Thus, each on its own element, the two great nations of Europe, commanded by the two great lead rs of the day, were engaged almost simultaneously in undertakings of the last importance, and almost simultaneously the results of those undertakings became known. On the 19th of

Capitulation
of the Austri
army at Ulm.
Oct. 19. October, Mack, finding himself surrounded and cut off from Vienna, with all hope of relief gone, capitulated at Ulm, and his whole army of 30,000 men laid down

their arms before the enemy. On the 21st of the same month the English and French fleets encountered just within sight of Cape Trafalgar, outside the Straits of Gibraltar.

The fleet of the English numbered twenty-seven vessels, Villeneuve had the command of thirty-three, without reckoning five frigates and two smaller ships. In other respects, in ability of seamanship, and in knowledge of the management of guns, the English were undoubtedly superior. Some days before the battle Nelson had conceived and made known his plan of action. The assault was to be made in two lines; at the head of one Nelson was himself to break the line in the centre, while Collingwood led the second to the attack of the rear squadron. The French were formed in one line, and were sailing in a south-easterly direction. Nelson's plan was therefore calculated not only to destroy the enemy, but also to cut off his retreat from Cadiz and the north. This part of his plan Villeneuve saw through and avoided. He changed the direction of his line, so that the rear squadron became the leading squadron, and the road to Cadiz was kept open. In this order, in full sail, with the wind in their favour, the English attacked and broke the French line. All the advantages of this well-known manœuvre were gained, and by half-past five in the evening, of the thirty-three vessels of the enemy eighteen were in the hands of the English, eleven with difficulty retreated towards Cadiz, and four others, which had formed the leading squadron of the French, were standing out to sea, only to be captured a few days afterwards by another fleet. But the victory was dearly won. Nelson, who had appeared as usual with his orders on his coat, had formed a mark for the riflemen with whom the rigging of the French ships was filled. He fell early in the action, but lived long enough to hear of his complete victory. He died thanking God he had done his duty, and even to the last, mindful of the safety of his fleet, giving orders that it should at once anchor to await a gale whose approach he had foreseen. The storm came as he had expected; a considerable part of our prizes was lost, and three of the French fugitives were wrecked before they reached the port of Cadiz. Of the whole fleet eight vessels alone escaped, which remained blockaded in Cadiz till they fell a prey to the Spanish insurgents.

But though the sea thus passed entirely under the command of the English, though all chance of invasion had disappeared, a crushing blow upon the Continent shattered for the time all hope of permanent opposition to the

Battle of Trafalgar. Oct. 21.

Battle of Austerlitz. Dec. 2, 1805.

advance of Napoleon. The catastrophe at Ulm was followed by a rapid advance upon Vienna. The wisdom Napoleon had shown in concentrating his troops for one great and decisive blow at once bore fruit. The army of Italy was obliged to retreat before the advance of Massena, in time to defend if possible Austria itself. It was too late even for that, and it was compelled to withdraw into Hungary, for the Emperor, desirous of saving the Viennese from the horrors of a siege, had withdrawn with his troops into Moravia, in the hopes of there meeting the main body of the Russians whom Alexander was bringing to his succour. Thither Napoleon pursued him, and there, with his back to the citadel of Brunn, not far from Olmutz, he brought on the great battle of Austerlitz, and before the close of the day the forces of the coalition were completely beaten, losing upon the field 27,000 killed and wounded, 20,000 prisoners, and 133 pieces of cannon.

While these stirring events had been happening, the health of the English minister had been sensibly declining. Cheered for a moment by the news of Trafalgar, clouded though they were by the death of Nelson, the rapidly-occurring disasters of Ulm and Austerlitz, and the dissolution, by the Treaty of Presburg, of the coalition he had so laboriously established, went far to render fatal the disease which was already threatening him. He returned from Bath, still hoping against hope that he might be present at the opening of Parliament, withdrew for quiet to his villa at Putney, and there died on the 23rd of January 1806.

Death of Pitt. Jan. 23, 1806.

The death of Pitt was followed by the break-up of his Cabinet, which was not so constituted as to be able to stand without him. The King did indeed attempt to continue it under the leadership of Lord Hawkesbury; but upon his refusal to accept the responsibilities of the Premiership, the King was obliged to have recourse to the Opposition, and to summon Lord Grenville to his Councils. The admission of Grenville to the ministry implied the admission of Fox; the close political alliance they had formed, the determination they had already expressed, when rejecting Pitt's offers, never to join in any separate arrangements, rendered it quite impossible for either to accept office without the other. In spite, therefore, of the King's anger and dislike, he was compelled to admit his old enemy Fox to the ministry. The basis on which Grenville and Fox had been united in opposition was the strong belief which both felt that in the present crisis a ministry of a broad and national character was required. On this principle they formed

New ministry.

their new administration, which was known by the name of "the Ministry of all the talents." Lord Grenville became First Lord of the Treasury; Earl Spencer and Mr. Windham, members of Pitt's first administration, Secretaries for the Home and War departments; Fox became Foreign Secretary, and his friends Earl Fitzwilliam and Grey (now Lord Howick), the one Lord President of the Council, and the other First Lord of the Admiralty. Lord Moira, Master-General of the Ordnance, represented the friends of the Prince of Wales; while Lord Sidmouth became Lord Privy Seal, and as he insisted on bringing one friend with him into the Cabinet, introduced with questionable wisdom Lord Ellenborough, the Lord Chief Justice. It has since this time been generally held that such a position is incompatible with high judicial duties. Lord Henry Petty, afterwards Lord Lansdowne, was Chancellor of the Exchequer. Before the ministry went out all due honour had been paid to the late minister; a public funeral and monument had been voted, together with the sum of £40,000 for the payment of his debts.

The character of Fox as a statesman was now upon its trial. After thirty years of exclusion from office, in perpetual oppo- Character sition to the King and the general feeling of the upper of Fox. classes, Fox had at length an opportunity of proving the justice of the reliance which men of liberal opinions had always placed in him. Large-hearted, with great warmth of personal affection, and general love of the human race, he had uniformly opposed war, had constantly declared that either the mismanagement or ill-will of the ministers had been the main obstacle to peace : he had believed devoutly in the excellence of the Revolution, traced its excesses to the wanton opposition of the crowned heads of Europe, and still persisted in believing that straightforward and friendly negotiations would bring about a right understanding with Napoleon. The brief period which elapsed between his acceptance of office in January and his death on the 13th of September, sufficed to prove to him the futility of his hopes; and the ministry found itself obliged to take up identically the same position as that of their predecessors. Like his great rival, he closed his life in the midst of the unutterable sadness caused by the complete frustration of those plans on which, according to his view, the welfare of his country rested, with this additional bitterness in his cup that upon him was forced the conviction, not only that circumstances were too strong for him, but that the optimism which had been the very breath of his political life rested upon no solid ground, and that the work to which he had devoted himself, and the maintenance of which,

had perpetually debarred him from a share in the government of the
country, had been wholly misdirected.   That destruction of illusions
which comes to most men in their youth fell upon him when he was
already breaking with age and disease, and when he must have been
conscious that no time was left him to correct the errors into which
he had been led.   It is difficult to conceive a sadder close to a noble
political career than that which fell upon the minister as he discovered too late that the practical logic of facts contradicted all those
high aspirations which had throughout guided his conduct.   So
complete, however, was the proof afforded him by his short ministry
of the futility of his hopes, that his friend Lord Howick, after just
a year of office, was compelled to declare of the late negotiations that
" there never was any opportunity of procuring any such terms as
would have been adequate to the just pretensions and consistent with
the honour and interests of this country; ' one thing is clear, the progress of Bonaparte has never yet been stopped by submission, and
our only hope therefore is in resistance, as far as we can resist his
ambitious projects.' "

The negotiations of which Lord Howick thus confessed the disastrous conclusion were opened by Fox almost immediately after his accession to office.   A few days after his
appointment an unknown person called upon him, and
disclosed a plan for the assassination of the Emperor.   With natural
indignation, Fox caused the man to be apprehended, and while warning Bonaparte that the law of England prevented his lengthened
detention, he promised that it should be long enough to enable the
Emperor to provide against the nefarious plan.   It is not improbable
that the whole conspiracy was devised by Napoleon himself for the
purpose of opening a negotiation with Fox, in whom he believed he
had a sincere well-wisher, and on whose simple-hearted optimism he
believed he could play.   He caused a copy of a speech to reach Fox
in which he expressed his willingness to make peace with England
on the stipulations of the Treaty of Amiens.   This led to a direct
negotiation between Fox and Talleyrand, in which the English minister, in accordance with his views, attempted, as he said, to act upon
the assumption that the countries would treat as two great powers, de-
spising any idea of chicane.   But this was not at all Napoleon's view
of negotiation.   His diplomacy constantly assumed the same form—
separate treaties with different members of the coalition, and the hurried
continuance of aggression during the time that negotiations were pend
ing, so as to compel the treating power either to accept the aggressions

or to break off the treaty. This had been his plan before the Treaty of Amiens, and this he had just repeated after the battle of Austerlitz.

Prussia was already so far pledged to join the coalition that it was on the point of receiving the first payment of a subsidy from England. But Bonaparte succeeded in inducing the vacillating court to break with both its allies. Two separate treaties were made, one at Schönbrunn, by which Prussia withdrew from the coalition, and entered into an offensive and defensive alliance with France, receiving Hanover in exchange for Anspach, which was to be restored to Bavaria, and the Principality of Neuchatel, which was to be annexed to France, and the other at Presburg, in which Austria, having lost all hope of any assistance Prussia might have rendered, was induced to accept the most disastrous terms. The kingdom of Italy was to receive Venice and the Adriatic provinces ; the three German powers which were consistently friends of France—Bavaria, Wurtemberg and Baden—obtained portions of the German dominions of Austria ; the royal title was secured to Bavaria and Wurtemberg ; the rights of the Empire over the immediate nobility were renounced ; the reorganization of Italy was admitted ; and Austria even agreed not to interfere in the affairs of Naples. On these terms the constitution of the Germanic Confederation was guaranteed. It is needless to point out what a seed of hatred was sown by these treaties, in which one of the German powers was humiliated by its ignominious bargain, the other driven almost to despair by the ruthless manner in which it was pillaged.

Treaty of Schönbrunn, Dec. 10, and Presburg, Dec 26, 1805.

It was shortly after this that Pitt died and Fox entered office. There were left of the coalition England and Russia, with whom Napoleon had now to deal. Fox felt, as any honourable man must have felt, that it was his duty to stand by his allies, and to engage only in negotiations in common with them. Napoleon, on the other hand, pursued his old policy, and determined to treat separately ; but while treating he continued the work on which he was then engaged—the erection of a number of small independent kingdoms and principalities in vassalage to France. In February and March he overran Naples and established his brother Joseph as king. In March he ordained a similar fate for Holland, and before June had established his brother Louis there. Numerous other principalities were called into existence for his relations and marshals, and the work was completed by the organization in July of the Confederation of the Rhine, consisting of Baden, Bavaria, Wurtemberg, Hesse-Darmstadt, and several other

Napoleon erects dependent kingdoms. 1806.

smaller states, who acknowledged the protectorate of France, and promised to keep on foot an army of 63,000 men at Napoleon's disposal.

While thus proceeding with his aggressions he was treating with Progress of the both Russia and England. To the letters of Fox had negotiations. succeeded personal negotiations between Talleyrand and Lord Yarmouth, who had been detained a prisoner after the Peace of Amiens. The terms which were first offered to Lord Yarmouth show the contempt with which Bonaparte regarded Prussia, the change in the terms as the treaty continued shows how little intention there was of really coming to an honest arrangement, should it prove possible to separate the interests of Russia and England. At first Talleyrand told Yarmouth that no difficulty would be found in taking Hanover, which had already been given to Prussia, and restoring it to England, or in giving Sicily back to the King of Naples. Sicily indeed Napoleon had not yet conquered; but as the separate treaty with Russia advanced and became more possible, Yarmouth found the terms changing. He was told that Sicily was to be conquered and added to the kingdom of Joseph; and finally, when the treaty with Russia was provisionally signed, although Yarmouth had been assured that the constitution of Germany should be unchanged if peace were made, the Confederation of the Rhine was called into existence. Fox's eyes had been almost opened by this time. The refusal of Sicily, the separate peace with Russia, the interference with the constitution of Germany, led him to see that his friendly negotiations were not likely to lead to much result. He therefore sent Lord Lauderdale, with fuller authority than Lord Yarmouth, to re-establish the old basis of negotiation.. His complaints were listened to, but there were no signs of withdrawal on the part of France. As for the compensation of the King of Naples, it was desirable enough, but it must not be at the expense of France. He might perhaps have Albania, which belonged to Turkey, or Bagusa, which belonged to Austria, or the Balearic Isles, which Negotiations belonged to Spain. While affairs were in this unbroken off. promising situation news arrived that the Czar had Death of Fox. entirely rejected the provisional treaty his minister had signed, and almost immediately afterwards Fox died. The diplomatic intercourse continued about a month longer, and was then broken off.

Fox's friends thus learnt the error of their previous views, and the necessity of carrying on the war with vigour; but Fox's ministry was not entirely without fruit. As he had himself stated, the second great object of his life was the abolition of the slave trade. For upwards of thirty years the horrors of slavery had occupied the minds of a large section of benevolent men in England. In 1783 the Quakers had petitioned against the slave trade. From that time till 1788, Clarkson, a young Cambridge man, had devoted his life to collecting evidence on the horrors of the trade. He had succeeded in interesting in his cause Pitt, Fox, and, before all, Wilberforce; and in that year Pitt had brought the matter before Parliament, and a resolution had been carried to take the slave trade into consideration. Circumstances and the interests of public business had prevented Pitt from entering fully into the plans of the abolitionists, although Wilberforce was constantly urging him to do so. Still, again and again, in 1792 and 1796, Bills had been carried in favour of abolition in the House of Commons, though subsequently defeated in the House of Lords. In 1804, on Pitt's resumption of office, Wilberforce renewed the question, which had been allowed to slumber by the Addington Cabinet, and a Bill for abolition, or rather suspension of the trade for a term of years, was again carried. In the House of Lords it was again postponed, but Pitt tried what could be done by a royal proclamation, which was issued to prevent the trade at all events in the conquered colonies, the possession of which had greatly increased the trade, so that nearly 60,000 slaves were yearly imported in British vessels. In February 1805 a larger measure had been rejected in the House, but on the accession to office of Fox, who was known to be more enthusiastic on the matter than Pitt had been, the hopes of the abolitionists rose high. Nor were their hopes disappointed, though the party against the measure was strong. The West India merchants were all against it, and a number of Tories, with the King at their head, regarded slavery as a natural and scriptural institution by no means to be lightly touched. On the 10th of June 1806, Fox pledged the House of Commons, almost without opposition, to take measures as speedily as possible for abolishing the trade. Even in the House of Lords the minister found that there would be no serious opposition, and determined to produce a Bill to prohibit the slave trade entirely. This Act prohibited slave trading from and after the 1st of January 1808, but as the punishments were only pecuniary, it required a new Bill, introduced by Mr. Brougham in 1811, making slave trading felony, to secure its final extinction. These Bills did not abolish slavery, but only the slave

Abolition of the slave trade.

trade. Fox did not live to bring in the Bill, but it was produced by his colleague Lord Howick, afterwards Lord Grey, on the 2nd of January 1807, and in spite of the opposition of the royal dukes, of Lord Eldon and of Lord Sidmouth (Feb. 3), the Bill was passed by a

The Abolition Bill passed. March 25, 1807. · majority of sixty-six. When it was brought to the House of Commons (Feb. 23) it met with quite an enthusiastic reception, and was passed by an overwhelming majority of 283 to 16. The Bill was rapidly hurried through its other stages, in order that the ministry which had been successful in passing it might have the honour of completing it; for before the royal assent was given it was well known that the Grenville ministry had ceased to exist.

The cause of this rapid termination to a ministry which had

Fall of the Grenville ministry. begun under such good auspices was the attempt again to bring forward the Catholic claims, against which the King was set with immoveable obstinacy. Grenville's conduct was dictated by high policy, and in itself wise, although, if we regard the minister as a mere party politician, in the last degree indiscreet. As he himself told the King, he and the majority of the Cabinet thought that in the present critical state of England it was most necessary to secure content and unanimity at home, and to be in a condition to use to the full the military capacity of every class of his Majesty's subjects. For this reason he was desirous of removing so much of the disabilities both of the Catholics and of the Dissenters as affected their military position. There seems, however, to have been some complication in the matter. The Irish Catholics, headed by Lord Fingal and Mr. O'Connor, were preparing a great petition, demanding not only change in the army regulations, but the admission of Catholics to the offices of sheriff and to corporations; and although Grenville was careful to forestall the presentation of their petition and to avoid all appearance of compromise, it is probable that his measure was in fact in some degree a concession to prevent further agitation; besides which he could not help feeling that the just expectations of the Catholics had not been satisfied at the Union. By a law passed in Ireland in 1793 the Roman Catholics had been permitted to hold rank in the Irish army up to the rank of colonel; but certain restrictions had been

Revival of the question of the Catholic claims. laid on their holding staff appointments. By the Union the two armies of Ireland and of England had been made one, and the anomaly had therefore arisen, that officers capable of holding their rank while in Ireland were incapable of so doing when they came to England. The ministry determined to remedy this glaring anomaly, and at the same time to remove the disabilities which tended to exclude the English Dissenters from the army. For that purpose a clause was added to the Mutiny Bill of the year. Some of the High Tories in Parliament, such as Lord Eldon and Mr. Perceval, thought it unnecessary, and the King's friends, as Lord Sidmouth and Ellenborough were called, offered some opposition, but on the whole the proposal was regarded as reasonable. The intention was notified to the Viceroy in Ireland, and the King himself was finally induced to consent, at the same time declaring that he would not allow any further step in the matter. The question then arose in Ireland as to whether the new clause retained the restrictions as to rank, or not, and the majority of the Cabinet determined that they were removed, and that the whole army and navy were thrown open to the Catholics. This determination was laid before the King, and for some reason or other he took no notice of it, conduct which the ministers (although the Bill undoubtedly exceeded what the King had already accepted) construed as giving the royal consent. It was then thought better to make a separate Bill instead of merely adding a clause to the Mutiny Act ; Lord Howick took the Bill to the King, and understood that he had his consent. But meanwhile Lord Sidmouth had had interviews with the King, and attempted to rouse his fears, and for the same purpose had sent in his resignation. Even more than this, Lord Malmesbury and the Duke of Portland thought they saw an opening for dislodging the ministry, and between them concocted a letter, exaggerating the difficulties of the situation, and containing an offer on the part of the Duke of Portland to form a ministry according to the King's wishes. Thus, apparently alarmed as to what he was doing, and feeling his hands strengthened by the Duke's offer, the King sent for the ministers, and told them he did not agree to anything beyond the completion of the Act of 1793. As soon as this determination of the King was known, the conduct of all Pitt's friends was fixed, and although they were at that moment thinking of joining the ministry, they now expressed their determination to oppose the Bill ; the whole party felt itself bound by Pitt's promise that the question should never be moved ; so strong was this feeling that even the ministry expressed themselves willing to drop their Bill. But in dropping it they were guilty of a most impolitic act. They drew up a minute of the Cabinet, reserving to themselves the right of avowing their sentiments if the petition from the Catholics,

which was at that time in preparation, was presented, and of submitting to the King from time to time such measures as they
deemed advisable for the good of the country.   Upon this the King
demanded from them a withdrawal of their minute, and a written
declaration that they would never offer him any advice upon the
The Grenville   subject of Catholic concession.   It was of course im-
ministry
resigns.   possible for any constitutional ministers to give such
March 18.   a pledge ; and it was upon this point—a point of real
constitutional importance—that the Cabinet were dismissed.   On the
19th of March the Duke of Portland received orders to form a
ministry in consultation with Lord Chatham.   The health of the
Duke was such that his Premiership could be little more than
nominal.   Indeed, from the first he suffered Lords Hawkesbury and
Eldon in fact to supersede him, and when Mr. Perceval became
Chancellor of the Exchequer he virtually assumed the lead of the
new administration.   Canning became Foreign Secretary, Lord
Hawkesbury Home Secretary, and Castlereagh Secretary for War
and the Colonies.

We have here, then, the final triumph of the policy of George III.
Constitutional   It was again his personal wish which overthrew the
importance of   ministry, it was again the underhand intrigues of those
the question.   professing to be his friends which strengthened his hands
in doing so, and we again find such things mentioned as that the
nephews of the Duke of Portland had had his distinct orders to vote
against the ministers' Bill should it be produced.   The same exercise
of prerogative that secured the ministry of Pitt and supported the
feeble ministry of Addington now again introduced into the ministry
men entirely after the King's own heart—pledged to oppose the great
Liberal measures of the day, and, say what they would, really answerable for the unconstitutional pledge the King had demanded from
his late ministry.   The conduct of the incoming ministry was not
allowed to pass without comment.   Attempts were made in both
Houses to establish two points of constitutional law now absolutely
received—first, that it is contrary to the first duties of the confidential
servants of the Crown to restrain themselves by any pledge, expressed
or implied, from offering to the King any advice which the course of
circumstances may render necessary for the welfare and security of
the Empire ; and, secondly, that it was impossible for the King to act
without advice.   In upholding this last point, Sir Samuel Romilly
asserted that there could be no exercise of prerogative in which the
King could act without some advice.   No constitutional doctrine is

more important than this, for without it the King, who theoretically can do no wrong, would be answerable for his own acts. On a motion by Mr. Brand supporting these doctrines, the Opposition thought themselves secure of a majority. But so great was the royal influence, so strong the Protestant feeling of the country, that they found themselves in a minority of more than thirty. A dissolution of Parliament followed on the 27th of April. And as the King, in the speech with which Parliament was closed, appealed as it were to the constituencies for the vindication of his conduct, the personal loyalty of the people, combined with their attachment to the old cry of Church and State, placed the ministry in possession of a majority which secured its permanence.

During the last days of the Grenville ministry it had been compelled to pursue the warlike policy of its predecessors, and had exhibited an incapacity which might have been expected from so mixed a body acting upon compulsion, and in contradiction to its preconceived ideas of policy. The renewed war which at once followed upon the cessation of the negotiations undertaken by Fox was on this occasion directed towards a new enemy. We have seen the contempt with which Bonaparte habitually regarded Prussia: his conduct seems to have been wilfully directed to drive that country into war, and it is interesting to observe that it was this unjustifiable conduct which gave the first obvious proof of the changed character of his policy, and roused that animosity, not of the Court, but of the people assaulted, which finally caused his ruin. All his late acts had tended to the detriment of Prussia. By the Confederation of the Rhine the constitution of Germany, in which Prussia might at all events have claimed some voice, was entirely changed; French fortifications had been raised on the German side of the Rhine at Mayence, and the fortress of Wesel had been re-established; the very bribe with which the apparent friendship of Prussia had been secured had been tampered with. Hanover, which in the winter had been given in full possession to Prussia, was in June without scruple offered to England; as a sort of counterpoise to the Rhenish Confederation, the King of Prussia had been invited by Napoleon to form a Confederation of the North; but he soon found how illusory the offer was, for he was everywhere practically thwarted by the diplomacy of the French. The Court, the army, and the official class smarted under the disgrace of the Treaty of Schönbrunn; and when Napoleon showed the temper in which he intended to interfere in Germany,—by the apprehension (in a neutral town which chanced to

Continuation of the war. 1806.

be occupied by French troops) of the bookseller Palm, and his cold-blooded murder on the charge merely of selling a book exciting the national feeling of Germany,—the popular anger grew so high, that the King of Prussia was obliged to act with some energy, especially when the young Queen put herself prominently forward as the leader of the national war party. A declaration of war with France was the consequence

Prussia declares war with France. Oct. 1, 1806.

But it was too late to be of any use. The French army, considerably more numerous than any troops Prussia could bring against it, was already in Franconia, a few marches from the frontier. There was no time to put to good account the strong national feeling which had been excited. Prussia could rely upon its army alone, and though strong in the military reminiscences of the Great Frederick and admirably appointed, the Prussian troops had not seen much war; the generals were old men wedded to obsolete traditions, while the King, in his anxiety to please Napoleon, had even gone so far as to discharge many of his troops in the previous year. The consequence of an encounter between such an army and the veterans of Napoleon might have been foreseen. The catastrophe was hastened by the bad arrangements of the generals. The King and his Court and crowds of enthusiastic nobility were with the army, but the chief command was in the hands of the Duke of Brunswick, an old man past seventy. Anxious to incorporate the troops of Hesse-Cassel, he repeated the error of the Austrians of the previous year, and advancing far beyond the Elbe, which forms the only good line of defence of which Prussia can boast, he took up a position between Eisenach and Weimar, covered by the Thuringian Forest, behind which the French could make any dispositions for the assault they pleased. The mistake was much too obvious to escape the eyes of Napoleon. His army passed rapidly through the defiles which lead to the upper waters of the Saal, and proceeding down the course of that river, interposed themselves between Brunswick and the Elbe. Perceiving too late his false position, the Duke attempted to withdraw towards Magdeburg. With the larger portion of his army he found himself stopped near Auerstadt as he approached Naumbourg on the Saal, by the division of Davoust, while the Prince of Hohenlohe, with a smaller division of the army, who was to have followed him, was fallen upon and overwhelmed at Jena by Napoleon himself with the greater part of his army. Beaten back from Auerstadt, Brunswick retired towards Weimar, only to meet the fugitives of Hohenlohe's army and their victorious pursuers. His

Mismanagement of Prussia.

Battle of Jena. Oct. 14, 1806.

troops were involved in the disaster, the whole Prussian army was broken and destroyed, and that one day's defeat drew with it the destruction of the monarchy. Such fugitive detachments as still kept together were one by one destroyed, and Napoleon entered Berlin in triumph (Oct. 27).

The temporary annihilation of Austria at Austerlitz, and the complete overthrow of Prussia at Jena, had made Napoleon master of nearly the whole of Europe. Nothing is more remarkable than the rapid expansion of his ambition ; each new success seemed to supply him with a new starting-point for further schemes. His mind, in spite of its practical character, had a strong tendency towards romance ; as in his youth he had been fired with the idea of a great Eastern monarchy, so now, as circumstances had been favourable to him, the idea of repeating the rôle of Charlemagne, and the re-establishment of the Empire of the West, seems to have been prominent in his mind. Already, in his dealings with the Pope, in the Confederation of the Rhine, and in the creation of vassal kingdoms, he had shown his wish to imitate the conduct of that great ruler. The idea was confirmed by the conquest of Prussia, and strengthened by a petition from one of his armies that he would take the title of Emperor of the West. Russia was the only opponent left upon the Continent. If Russia could be either conquered or won over, not only would he have been in truth the Western Emperor, but he would have the means, as he believed, of wreaking his vengeance upon his detested rival England, which still refused to yield to his ascendancy. Already in fact, he believed that this vengeance was in his grasp. On the 21st of November he issued the extraordinary measure known as the Berlin Decree. Even during the negotiations with Fox he had insisted upon Prussia closing against English traffic the mouths of the Elbe and Weser. The measure had not been a success, 400 Prussian vessels had been seized in reprisal, and the mouths of the North German rivers declared in a state of blockade. That blockade had been real. But the Emperor now, as he said by a just use of the law of retaliation (while he was unable with safety to place a single ship upon the ocean), declared that the whole of the British Isles were in a state of blockade, forbad on the part of all his dependent countries any commerce or correspondence with them, declared every subject of England found in a country occupied by French troops a prisoner of war, and all English merchandise, even all private property of Englishmen, confiscated. Thus was established what is known as the Continental system. It laboured

The Berlin Decree. Nov 21, 1806.

under three disadvantages. In the first place, it was absolutely
impracticable, Europe could not be supplied without England, as
Napoleon himself found in the course of the year when he authorized
the clothing of his own army with English cloth; secondly, it enabled
England by retaliatory measures to destroy every mercantile marine
in Europe except its own; thirdly, it was so distressing and vexatious,
and interfered so wantonly both with private property and the supply
of necessaries for the people, that, more than anything else that Napoleon did, it excited popular indignation against him, and tended to
his downfall. And yet it was not without a certain plausible excuse,
which rested on the difference then existing between the laws of war
as carried on by land and upon the sea. By land the property of an
enemy was not considered lawful prize unless it belonged to the
hostile government itself; by sea the property of peaceable merchants
was liable to seizure and confiscation. By land no one was considered a prisoner of war unless taken with arms in his hand; by sea
the crews of merchantmen were imprisoned as well as those of armed
vessels. The second point which formed Napoleon's excuse was the
extension given by England to the right of blockade. These two
points afforded the pretext under which the Decree was promulgated,
and was declared to be a fundamental law of the French Empire, till
England should recognize the laws of war to be the same by sea and
by land, and should consent to restrict the right of blockade to
fortified towns actually invested by a sufficient force. In issuing his
Decree, then, Napoleon put on a specious appearance of magnanimity, and took upon himself the part which he was fond
of assuming, that of champion of the rights of nations against the
tyranny of the English.

The necessity under which England as a belligerent lay of employing to the full the power which usage gave it of necessity
inflicted considerable inconvenience upon neutral powers. The
retaliatory measures which the Government thought it wise to
take still further injured the neutrals, and threatened almost to
annihilate the American trade. A series of orders in

Orders in
Council.
Council was issued, extending from January to November 1807. By the first of these orders vessels were forbidden to
trade between any ports in the possession of France, or of her allies
if under her control. By the second, issued in November, after the
extension of the Continental system to the Mediterranean, general
reprisals were granted against the goods, ships, and inhabitants of
Tuscany, Naples, Dalmatia, and the Ionian Islands. By the third,

all ports from which the flag of England was excluded were declared
in blockade, all trade in their produce unlawful, and their ships a
prize, while all vessels carrying certificates of origin (a measure which
Napoleon had insisted upon to prevent evasion of his system) were
declared liable to capture. By the fourth, another plan of evasion
was forbidden; the sale of ships by a belligerent to a neutral was
declared illegal, because the French had managed to preserve much
of their commerce by fictitious sales, enabling them to continue their
business under neutral flags. The Americans were the chief sufferers
by these orders, and the irritation already felt by them *Their effect*
was so increased that it ultimately ripened into .war. *on America.*
Their two special grievances were the constant search of their vessels
for deserters, and the refusal of the British authorities to recognize
their customhouse arrangements. By the English law as then existing an English subject could not get rid of his nationality. But
America was full of English and Irish emigrants and deserters from
English ships, and the Americans had the constant mortification of
seeing even their war-ships stopped and searched, and the asylum
of their flag violated by the apprehension, under the rough justice of
English naval officers, of many of their best seamen. By the neutral
laws direct trading between the colony of a belligerent and its
mother country was forbidden, but neutrals might trade for their
own supply with the colonies. More than this, if they imported
from the colonies more than they wanted they might re-export it
even to the mother country; the proof of a *bona fide* interrupted
voyage was the payment of the customhouse dues in the ports of
the neutral. But these dues were in America paid not in money but
in bonds, which were cancelled when the goods were re-exported.
The payment of goods was therefore fictitious, and English officials
refused to recognize them. The irritation produced by these two
causes was but slightly allayed by negotiations in 1809, and, as will
be subsequently mentioned, the people, especially the Southerners,
forced the States into war in 1812.

To enable Napoleon to carry out his idea either of a Western
Empire or of the complete annihilation of English trade it was
necessary that war with Russia should continue. As a means for
injuring that power he had already held out hopes of restoration of
liberty to Poland, and in December he was received as a national
saviour at Warsaw; but some remnant of the Prussian army had
formed a junction with the forces of the Czar, and Benigsen, in command of the combined armies, refused to give the French a resting

time in their new quarters. Napoleon had again himself to take the

Battle of
Eylau.
Feb. 7, 1807. field. The allies fell back northwards to Eylau, not far from Kónigsberg, and there, on the 7th of February, was fought a great battle, which, for almost the first time, the French could not claim as a victory. Their exhaustion was great. Three times within seven months fresh conscriptions had been ordered in France. The firmness of the Russians at Eylau gave rise to well-grounded hopes that the chance of checking Napoleon had arrived, but money and reinforcements of troops were sorely wanted.

But at this critical moment the Grenville ministry exhibited to the

Incapacity of
the Grenville
ministry. full its incapacity for carrying on war. The Emperor of Russia was told that he need expect no great assistance from England, and money was doled out to him with ridiculous parsimony. There was indeed in England a total mis-apprehension of the necessities of a great war. Since the time of Marlborough and Queen Anne the idea of war on a large scale, except upon the sea, seemed to have wholly disappeared from the minds of the public men of the country. Even the great successes of Chatham had depended principally upon his good fortune in securing the alliance of Frederick the Great, and now all the resources of England were frittered away in a ridiculous series of small expeditions. When a concentration of troops and a frank and open-handed assistance to its allies might have saved Europe, the English Government taught them by its conduct, that while urging them to fight it would practically desert them at the moment when its assistance was wanted, and spend its men and money on such isolated expeditions as the attack on Buenos Ayres, Alexandria, or upon the Dardanelles. These were the three military projects of the Grenville ministry.

In 1806 the English had recaptured from the Dutch the Cape of

Expedition to
Buenos Ayres.
May 1807. Good Hope. Sir Home Popham, who commanded the fleet, without orders from Government, determined upon a similar assault upon the Spanish colonies in America, and proceeded to capture Buenos Ayres. He thence wrote home a triumphant letter calling upon the English merchants to come to the magnificent new market he had opened. His triumph was of short duration. The colonists rallied under command of a French colonel, the city was recaptured, and the troops compelled to surrender as prisoners of war. In February 1807, 3000 men were sent out under Sir Samuel Auchmuty to assist Popham. Too late to save Buenos Ayres, he attacked and captured Monte Video. Before his success was known fresh reinforcements were sent out under General Whitelocke, with orders to assume the chief command, and with Popham's forces recapture Buenos Ayres. The attempt was a disgraceful failure; the troops were ordered to enter the city with unloaded muskets, and to rendezvous in the central square. The effect of so strange an attempt at street fighting may be easily conjectured. From the side-streets, housetops, and barricades thrown up across the roads, a destructive fire was kept up. Though Auchmuty met with some success, by nightfall 2500 of the English were either killed or prisoners, and Whitelocke was glad to accept the freedom of the prisoners both of the present engagement and of the past year, and to withdraw his troops, surrendering Monte Video and all he had conquered. In the judgment of the court martial which tried Whitelocke he was held totally unfit to serve his Majesty in any military capacity whatever, and the popular voice changed his name to General Whitefeather.

During the continuance of the great European war the friendship of Turkey had been a constant object with the great powers. The ambassadors from Russia, France, and England had used all their powers of persuasion and menace to secure the adhesion of the Sultan. Before the end of the year 1806 the threats of Russia had had the effect of driving the Sultan to the friendship of France, and the Porte had declared war with Russia just after the battle of Jena. Wanting his troops for the defence of his own country, and being at that time in close friendship with England, Alexander requested the English Government to take charge of his interests at the Turkish capital, and despatch a fleet to oblige Selim to give up his friendship with France. The plan, being one which could be carried out by the navy, suited the policy of the Grenville Government, and orders were sent to Lord Collingwood, then cruising off Cadiz, to send a squadron to the Dardanelles. He was not allowed to choose his own commander, but received orders from home to appoint Sir John Duckworth. Nothing could be worse managed than the expedition. Collingwood had given strict charge to Duckworth not to be drawn into negotiations. But when the passage of the Dardanelles, at that time almost unfortified, was forced, Duckworth, forgetful of Collingwood's advice, suffered himself to be entangled in negotiations. Sebastiani, the French ambassador, aroused the temper of the Turks, and instructed them in the best manner of fortifying their

Turkey declares war against Russia.

Expedition to the Dardanelles Feb. 1807.

coasts. The English fleet was in danger of being shut up in the Straits. It became necessary to withdraw; but that step was no longer easy. On the 1st of March the fleet sailed back through the Dardanelles. Batteries had been erected at every point, and though the fleet succeeded in running the gauntlet through the terrible fire, with the loss of only some 300 men, it found itself entirely prevented from any return. The object of the expedition had completely failed, and the only resource left was to keep the Turkish fleet blockaded.

In connection with this expedition a body of troops had been **Expedition to** despatched under General Fraser to capture Alexandria. **Alexandria.** **March to** It was hoped that on the receipt of the news of Duck- **August.** worth's expected success, it would have been able to advance to the reconquest of Egypt. Want of food necessitated an attack upon Rosetta. It was undertaken in the same foolish spirit as Whitelocke's attack upon Buenos Ayres. Entangled in the streets, the English soldiery were shot down in great numbers, and with the loss of a third of his troops the general in command withdrew to Alexandria. A subsequent effort was made to besiege Rosetta in form, but the forces of the Pasha of Egypt proved too strong for the besiegers; with heavy loss they withdrew to Alexandria, and in August 1807 were compelled to evacuate the country.

The only gleam of success which attended the military operations of **Expedition** the Grenville ministry was gained in the south of Italy. **to Sicily.** It will be remembered that immediately after the battle of **July, 1806.** Austerlitz the kingdom of Naples had been appropriated by France. Sicily, however, was not conquered, and in that island there was an English army commanded by Sir John Stewart. Urged to do something for the assistance of the Neapolitan Court, he landed in Calabria in July, and there fought and won the battle of Maida, in which the French general Reynier was completely beaten. The forces at Stewart's command were insufficient for the reconquest of the country, which fell again into French hands on the retirement of the English, after a lengthened opposition on the part of the peasantry.

The attempt made at the Peace of Westphalia to establish the **Complete dis-** balance of power in Europe, and to secure the rights of **solution of the** small states, had proved unsuccessful. It had been **coalition.** rudely shocked by the career of Frederick II., and almost annihilated by the partition of Poland. A spirit of jealousy and a desire for selfish aggrandizement had taken possession of the great reigning houses, and had proved a fatal obstacle to the formation of loyal coalitions for a general purpose. It is to this that may be traced the failure of united effort in the last war, and the terrible reverses which both Austria and Prussia had undergone; England had in the same spirit just been frittering away its strength in attempts to secure the mastery of the sea, and the opening of new markets for her trade; thus left without the assistance they had a right to demand, the Russians were completely defeated at the battle of Friedland (June 14). It was now the turn for Russia to seek its own ends, and to secure them by deserting its allies. Disgusted with the lukewarm assistance afforded by England, attached to the principles of the Armed Neutrality, and eager to carry on its schemes of aggression against Turkey, the Czar allowed himself to be dazzled by the flattering offers of Napoleon. The Emperor had found his difficulties increase with his empire; he had discovered that the Russians were more difficult to conquer than the Austrians or Prussians, and he was now willing to purchase the friendship of the Czar and his assistance against England by an arrangement by which Alexander should be Emperor of the East, while he kept for himself the envied position of Emperor of the West.

The meeting between the Emperors took place, as upon neutral ground, on a raft in the middle of the Niemer at Tilsitt. "I hate the English as you do," Alexander is reported to have said. "Then," replied Napoleon, "peace is made;" and the two Emperors set to work to arrange Europe according to their own fancies, upon the common basis of dislike to England, and under the showy pretext of checking her overweening pride upon the sea. As Russia was fighting not for herself but for her allies, a treaty of peace and amity was all that was wanted between her and France, and of course the lately conquered King of Prussia had to *Treaty of Tilsitt. July 7, 1807.* pay the price of the treaty, the terms being chiefly in favour of France. Prussia was deprived of all its provinces between the Rhine and the Elbe, and of its Polish possessions. The former were incorporated with Hesse, Brunswick, and a part of Hanover, to form a kingdom of Westphalia, which was given to Jerome Bonaparte; the latter were formed into the Grand Duchy of Warsaw, and given to the King of Saxony, one province only excepted, which was given to Russia, nominally to cover the expenses of the war. All the alterations which Napoleon had effected in Europe were accepted; the Duchies of Oldenburg and Mecklenburg were restored to their possessors, on the condition that the French should hold their ports till the conclusion of a general peace; Silesia and the German provinces on the right bank of the Elbe were restored to Prussia, but a military road was allowed to Saxony through Silesia, to afford the Saxon Prince access to his new dominions. Prussia was, however, to acknowledge the Berlin Decree, to reduce its troops to 42,000 men, to pay France £6,000,000 of money, in addition to the charges of the war, amounting to about £20,000,000, and to leave Berlin and its chief fortresses in the hands of the French till the debt was paid ; as the yearly revenue of Prussia was not much more than £3,000,000, this promised to be for some time.

But the real point of the treaty was its secret articles, which Secret articles of the treaty. were dimly suspected at the time, and the existence of which has subsequently been fully proved. By these articles, if England had not consented by the 1st of November to conclude peace — recognizing that the flags of all Powers ought to enjoy an equal and perfect independence on the seas, and restoring all conquests won from France or its allies since 1805—Russia was to make common cause with France against her, and oblige the Courts of Lisbon, Stockholm and Copenhagen to join in the alliance. In exchange for this, which was to wreak Napoleon's vengeance upon England, it was stipulated that if the Porte did not accept the mediation of France, France would make common cause with Russia against the Porte, and would agree to take from the Turks all the provinces of the Ottoman Empire in Europe, with the exception of the town of Constantinople and Roumelia. Napoleon had thus thrown over, for his own advantage, the Poles, on whose hopes of liberty he had traded, and the Turks, whom he had induced to declare war with Russia; Spain and Portugal were left open to his ambition ; Sweden was placed at the disposal of Russia, which was likewise rid of all difficulty from Poland.

The conduct of Alexander has an appearance of extreme treachery. Conduct of Alexander. Only a few days before he had written to the English King that "there was no salvation to himself or to Europe but by interminable resistance to Bonaparte;" moreover, he did not refuse to accept a considerable portion of the territories of his ally the King of Prussia. His apologists assert that his readiness to accept Napoleon's terms was assumed to afford him an opportunity for strengthening himself for future opposition to French aggrandizement. More probably he was led away, partly by his peculiar enthusiastic temperament, which made him wish to have a large share both in the establishment of peace and in the rearrangement of Europe, and partly by an undercurrent of ambition which laid him open to offers securing him the acquisition of Poland, and the command both of the Baltic and the Black Seas.

Already, before the signing of the Peace of Tilsitt, information had been brought to Canning, our Foreign Minister, that the fleets of Portugal and Denmark were to be taken by the French and used for an assault upon England. The secret articles of the treaty vindicate the truth of this information, and justify in some degree the immediate action which the English Government took upon it. For although there seems to be proof that the Danes themselves were anxious to maintain their friendship with England, it was more than probable that they would be unable to resist the combined pressure of Russia and France. Refusing the mediation offered by Russia, unless England was put on a fair footing with France by a frank disclosure of the nature of the late treaty, the English Government despatched a squadron to require the immediate surrender of the Danish fleet. It was no doubt a harsh measure, rendered still harsher by the courageous conduct of the Danes. Although Copenhagen was unprepared for an attack, the demand was refused, and it was found necessary to bombard the city. The effect of this step was, on the one hand, a surrender of the whole Danish fleet, which was brought to England, and on the other, to make Denmark, whatever its previous intention may have been, a close ally of France. In a second direction the consequences of the treaty became immediately obvious. Russia demanded of Sweden her adhesion to the Continental System. Christian IV., the king of that country, was chivalrous and impetuous to the verge of madness. He refused all solicitations to forsake his alliance with England, and became entangled in a war with France and Russia at once. When scarcely strong enough to defend his own country, he began an assault upon the Danish province of Norway, and consequently lost all his territory in Pomerania and Finland, which amounted to nearly a third of his kingdom. Sir John Moore, with an army of 10,000 men, were sent to his assistance, but found him so wild and unreasonable that he thought it better to sail home without even landing his troops. Frightened at the eccentricities of their sovereign, the Swedes removed him from the throne, setting up his uncle in his place.

In the North, then, the Treaty of Tilsitt had produced the effect which Napoleon had desired. Advantage had been taken of the

Consequences of the Peace of Tilsitt

Capture of the Danish fleet. Sept 8

War between Russia and Sweden. Oct 31.

bombardment of Copenhagen, which was held to be a fresh proof
Continental
System acknow-
ledged every-
where except
in Portugal. of the lawless ambition of England, to oblige Austria, Russia, and Prussia all to declare war with England. Denmark had joined the French alliance, Sweden had been compelled to forego the friendship of England. But there still existed one part of Europe where the Berlin Decree was unacknowledged, and the blockade of the British Isles was thus incomplete; this country was Portugal.

Napoleon had long had his eyes fixed upon the Peninsula; by the
Condition of
the Peninsula. Treaty of Tilsitt it had in fact been delivered into his hands as Finland into the hands of Alexander. The condition of the Peninsula was very favourable to his schemes. Charles IV., a weak old man, was on the throne, governed by his wife and by her favourite minister Godoy, the Prince of the Peace. In strong opposition to his father and to the Queen was Ferdinand, the Prince of Asturias. Both parties intrigued for the support of Napoleon, but Godoy had been able to offer the more tempting bait. Napoleon had induced the Prince of Asturias to enter into communication with regard to a marriage with a lady of the Bonaparte family. The secret correspondence had been brought to the knowledge of the King, and made use of by him and his minister to affix a charge of treason upon the Prince, and to imprison him for having conspired to drive his father from the throne. By the people the story of the conspiracy was regarded as a calumny of the minister to destroy the Prince, and fearful of the storm he had excited, Godoy now attempted to mediate a reconciliation between the King and his son. The Prince in his imprisonment was induced to write penitential letters, and a solemn pardon was given. But though the attempt to remove the Prince had thus failed, Godoy's own connection with Napoleon, who had probably been at the bottom of the late affair, was almost immediately shown by the publication, on the 29th of October, of the Treaty of Fontainebleau. This treaty disclosed the bait with which Godoy had been enabled to secure the alliance of Bonaparte. He suggested that France and Spain should join in appropriating Portugal if only he were allowed a principality out of the spoil. The house of Braganza was to be dispossessed; the northern province of Portugal was to be given to the King of Etruria,[1] whose own province, Tuscany, might thus be appended to the Italian kingdom; Godoy was to be rewarded with the principality of Alentejo and Algarves.

[1] The representative of the Bourbon Dukes of Parma and Placentia. His father had received Tuscany, with the title of King of Etruria, in exchange for his Duchies, by the Treaty of Lunéville.

Some excuse was of course wanted for this wanton attack upon Portugal. It was found in the way in which the Court of Lisbon obeyed the demand addressed to it after the Peace of Tilsitt, to close the ports of Portugal against England, to detain all Englishmen resident in Portugal, and to confiscate all English property. Meanwhile all Portuguese merchant ships in the ports of France were to be detained. The Prince Regent of Portugal was not strong enough to resist the demand. He obeyed the first order, without however forfeiting the friendship of England, which confessed the coercion laid upon him. To the other two demands he also at length conceded, but not till he had given plentiful warning to the English to withdraw and to sell their property. The delay was, however, sufficient to afford Napoleon the pretext he wanted. *Napoleon's pretext for war with Portugal.*

While negotiations were still proceeding with Portugal, the real intention of the Emperor—to appropriate both that country and Spain—became obvious. For this purpose nearly 30,000 French troops were to enter Spain, and 40,000 more were assembled at Bayonne. While Junot, with "the first army of the Gironde," poured through Salamanca (in October 1807), and proceeded to the conquest of Portugal, the domestic quarrels of the Spanish Court continuing, the 40,000 men assembled at Bayonne moved in two armies into Spain, and while apparently preparing to follow Junot, really occupied the line of mountains north of Madrid, and cut off that capital from the northern provinces, which were thus practically conquered without a blow. In March 1808 riots both in Madrid and Aranjuez, ending in the abdication of Charles and the accession of Ferdinand, gave the French, now under the command of Murat, an excuse for crossing the mountains by the Pass of Somo Sierra and occupying Madrid. By a series of shameless intrigues Napoleon attracted both Ferdinand and his father to Bayonne. Ferdinand was there induced to restore the crown to his father (May 5), who abdicated a second time, placing the crown in the hands of Napoleon. Napoleon immediately established his brother Joseph upon the vacant throne (June 15). *Junot's army enters Spain. Oct. 18. Ferdinand VII. succeeds his father Charles IV. March 19, 1808. Murat occupies Madrid. March 23. Napoleon places Joseph on the throne.*

But the Spaniards, especially the Castilians, were a people of high temper; in spite of a century's degradation, certain remembrances of a former greatness hung about them. They saw with scorn and disgust the treacherous conduct of their own rulers, who were handing them over, bound *Insurrection in Spain.*

hand and foot, to a foreign prince, whose very virtues rendered him doubly detestable to them; for the rule of the French meant splendid and centralized organization, restraint, self-denial, and wise government, very much opposed to Spanish feeling. While their rulers were basely truckling to the invader the people rose; the flame of insurrection spread far and wide; great riots in Toledo and Madrid were followed by similar exhibitions of national anger throughout the country, and Napoleon's armies, though they found no regular opposition, though intrigue and treachery had apparently removed all obstacles, found themselves in the midst of a hostile population, and masters only of the ground on which they stood. To meet this new difficulty the fertile mind of the Emperor had at once a plan ready. Madrid was to be a centre from which should radiate in all directions expeditionary armies to suppress the insurrections,

Operations of Napoleon's three armies from Madrid. Madrid itself resting for support on France. To hold the communications between Madrid and France therefore became a prime object. This work was intrusted to Bessières, while Duhesme operated in Catalonia, and expeditions were sent out from Madrid against Valencia under Moncey, and against Andalusia under Dupont. Bessières, though his general Lefèbvre failed before the desperate energy of the Saragossans, thoroughly defeated the Gallician troops under Blake and Cuesta at the Rio Seco. Duhesme effected nothing, and was obliged to raise the siege of Gerona. Moncey, though he reached the town of Valencia with success, was unable to take it, and had to retreat. Dupont pushed at first as far as Cordova, but losing heart, and badly supplied from Madrid, also attempted to retreat, was pursued by the Spaniards, and compelled to lay down his arms with 18,000 men,

Joseph evacuates Madrid. Aug 1, 1808. after the battle of Baylen, before he could recross the Sierra Morena. Unsuccessful, therefore, on all sides, and though victorious yet hard pressed upon the North, the French were obliged to retire, and King Joseph, evacuating Madrid, withdrew behind the Ebro.

Meanwhile Junot's army had proceeded direct to Portugal with

The Portuguese royal family emigrate to Brazil. Nov. 29, 1807. orders to occupy it by the 30th of November 1807. As Junot approached the capital, the Prince Regent, acting under the advice of Lord Strangford, the English ambassador, determined to leave his European dominions and to transfer the apparatus and seat of government to Brazil. On the 29th of November as many as 15,000 persons were carried by the English fleet down the Tagus. The last ship had

hardly sailed when Junot arrived. He had wished to stop and
reorganize his troops in Salamanca, but pressed by the Emperor,
he hurried forward in spite of the difficulties of the
way, and marched upon Lisbon with only a few
thousand weary and travel-worn soldiers. He however met with no opposition there, and after the manner of
Napoleon's lieutenants, at once set about Gallicizing the country.
The Portuguese army was chiefly sent away to France. The police
in the hands of the French was well administered, and though
the people of Lisbon obeyed unwillingly, order was successfully
maintained. The position of Spain and Portugal was thus closely
analogous ; in both cases the people had been deserted by their
natural rulers, in both cases the consequences were the same. The
insurrections in Spain were followed by similar movements in Portugal. The people took the government into their own hands, and
a popular Junta was established at Oporto under the influence of the
Bishop.

Junot's army occupies Lisbon. Nov. 30.

The insurrection in Spain had been observed with enthusiastic
admiration by the people of England. It seemed at
last as if that popular insurrection against the tyranny
of Napoleon, which had long been expected, had arrived.
Nevertheless, the total absence of central authority produced its
inevitable effects upon a country so ill ruled and so ignorant of self-
government as Spain. Ambitious men everywhere laid hold of the
local authority, and irresponsible juntas arose. The provincial feeling, always unreasonably strong in the Peninsula, found full vent.
Junta disputed with junta, and the whole country was involved in
the wildest anarchy. None the less the feeling of the English people
was a true one. Napoleon had reached the point when he came into
collision with that very power which formed the basis of his own
success—the power of the people. Already his behaviour in Germany had excited among the lower classes enthusiastic feelings of
hatred to their conquerors and of desire for national liberty; and the
outbreak of the Spanish insurrection added fresh vigour and raised
fresh hopes in the lovers of liberty throughout the whole
of Europe. To the English Government the arrival of
two Asturian envoys in the month of June seemed to
offer an opportunity which had long been wanted of giving a national
and unselfish character to our opposition to the great conqueror. In
the course of time it afforded also a battle-ground on which at length
the military power of the country found room to move in larger and

Enthusiasm in England for the Spanish insurrection.

Asturian envoys arrive in England. June 1808.

more combined action, than in the feeble expeditions of the earlier part of the war. But as yet this was not foreseen. For some years the great war in the Peninsula was starved, while money was lavished upon useless and isolated efforts in other parts of the Continent; it was only slowly and by degrees that the genius, the steadfastness, the success, of Wellington taught England the necessity of large and well-continued efforts in one direction. The Asturian envoys were received with enthusiasm not only by the Opposition but by the Government. But the opportunity offered was not wisely made use of. Spain was inundated with agents of no political ability, who were deceived by the boasting assertions of the Spaniards. Money and arms were sent over in lavish quantities to be left unopened on the quays, appropriated by the rival juntas for their own personal or local advantage, or to fall into the hands of the enemy, and the Spaniards, who did little or nothing for themselves, were taught to demand the assistance of England as a right.

The position of Portugal seemed to offer a more favourable ground for action, and thither it was determined to send an English armament. But the Government could not yet conceive of war upon a large scale, and in entire ignorance of the real condition of Spain believed that a mere handful of English troops, aided by the boasted enthusiasm of the Spanish nation, would be able to withstand the enormous armies Napoleon was ready to pour into the Peninsula. The army at first sent was little better than an expeditionary force. A body of troops ready at Cork for war in South America were despatched under Sir Arthur Wellesley, at that time Secretary for Ireland; but by some ridiculous mismanagement two senior officers, Sir Harry Burrard, and Sir Hugh Dalrymple, Governor of Gibraltar, were put over his head, and Sir John Moore, who was despatched with a second body of troops to reinforce him, though he had served as commander-in-chief both in Sicily and Sweden, also found himself in a subordinate position. The expedition touched first at Corunna, but was persuaded by the members of the local junta to proceed to Portugal, where they declared the numerous Spanish army was already collected, and whither they promised speedily to send reinforcements. Upon reaching Oporto, however, the commander found that there were no Spanish troops in the north of Portugal, neither were there any Portuguese troops; but upon the river Mondego there appeared to be a disorganized body of about 5000 men, representing 40,000 for

An English force sent to Portugal.

whom the Bishop of Oporto had received accoutrements. With them there were some 10,000 peasants without arms. Wellesley had now a choice left. He might land north of Lisbon and act against Junot, or proceed to Cadiz, and joining Spencer, who had a small command there, act against the French in Spain. He preferred the first alternative, and determined to land at the mouth of the Mondego, near Figueras. He sent to Wellesley lands at Figueras. Aug. 1, 1808. Cadiz for Spencer's troops, but fortunately that general, on hearing of the victory of Baylen, had already determined to sail for the Tagus. The two corps when joined amounted to about 12,000 men. The landing of the English at the Mondego confined the operations to that tongue of land which lies between the sea and the Tagus in its south-westerly course, and which is terminated by the city of Lisbon.

Wellesley determined to strike rapidly, and bring affairs in Portugal to a crisis at once. Therefore, although deserted by the Portuguese troops, he advanced directly southward towards Lisbon. Junot's troops were somewhat scattered, and the temper of the people prevented him from energetic action. He proceeded, however, to concentrate his troops, and while this movement was going forward the English army came into contact with one of his divisions under Laborde, occupying a strong position at the end of a valley leading from Obidos to Rorica. Here, after a sharp contest, the French general found himself out- Combat of Rorica. Aug. 17. flanked by the hills which line the valley, and withdrew, allowing Wellesley to proceed. Meanwhile Junot had been continuing his concentration, and had collected 14,000 men at Torres Vedras, to bar the road to Lisbon. Sir Harry Burrard, Wellesley's superior officer, had now arrived at the coast, and Wellesley begged him to allow Sir John Moore's division, on its arrival from England, to land on the Mondego river, and cross the tongue of land to the Tagus, thus cutting off the natural line of retreat into Spain, which would be up the valley of that river. He then proceeded to advance against Junot. But Burrard, a commonplace general, disregarding his advice, determined to bring Sir John Moore up as a reinforcement, and forbad Wellesley to undertake any offensive movement till that general's arrival.

Wellesley was therefore obliged to return to his army, which was in position at Vimiero. A little hill covered the village to the front. On either side of it ran a chain of heights, from which on the east a branch ran off southwards. There was a direct road between

Vimiero and Torres Vedras, and a second road from Torres Vedras
to a place called Lourinham ran along the top of the branch ridge
crossing the main ridge. On the hill before the village and upon
the ridge to the west Wellesley took up his position, expecting

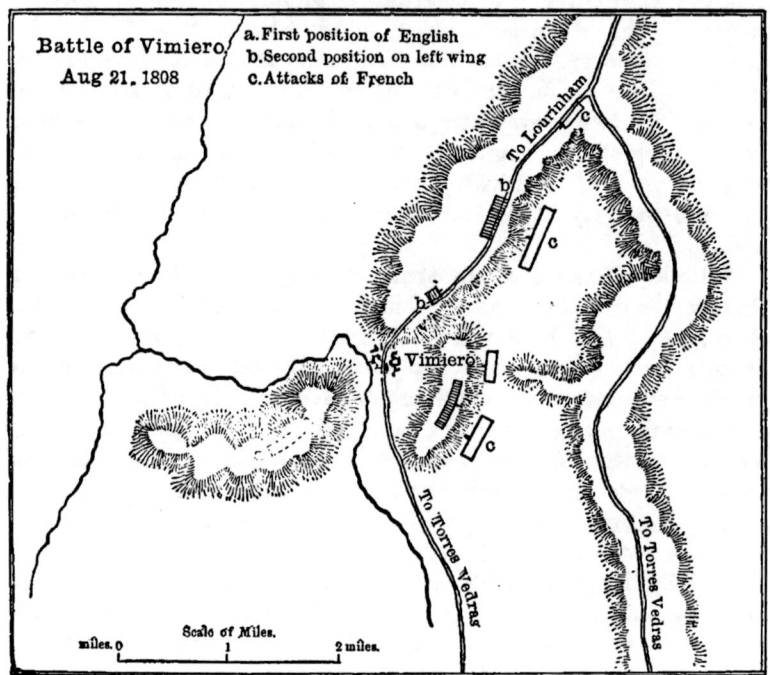

Battle of Vimiero
Aug 21. 1808

a. First position of English
b. Second position on left wing
c. Attacks of French

to be attacked on his right. But early on the 21st the French

came into view on the Lourinham road, and as they
pressed forward evidently threatened the left, and not
the right, of the English position. A considerable
body of troops was therefore moved from the right to the left
ridge, a movement unobserved by the French, for the valley
between the armies was thickly wooded. For the same reason
a ravine which rendered the left wing nearly unassailable was unobserved by the French. Junot directed two main attacks, upon
the central hill and upon the left ridge. The attack upon the
centre was defeated, for it was open on the flank to the fire of an
English brigade moving to the left, which halted half-way up the

hill when the strength of the central attack was seen; the left attack was ruined by the ravine. Meanwhile troops had been sent to turn the English left by the Lourinham road and to advance along the left ridge, which the French believed almost unoccupied; but, as has been mentioned, it was now covered with troops, and Ferguson's brigade beat the assailants back, and pursued them along the ridge till he had wholly separated them from the rest of the French army. They must have capitulated had not an unexpected order arrived to halt. Sir Harry Burrard, who had been on the field all day, had just assumed the command, and the change of leaders became at once perceptible. When the battle was over, thirteen guns, and many prisoners, including a general, were in the hands of the English, and the French had lost between 2000 and 3000 men.

The road to Torres Vedras from Lourinham, on which the beaten French army had collected, was two miles longer than the direct road from Vimiero. Wellesley designed to push forward with his victorious army, part of which had not been engaged, to forestall the French at Torres Vedras, and cut them off from Lisbon, a measure which, had Sir John Moore been landed from Mondego, must have completed their ruin. Again the prudence of Sir Harry Burrard thwarted Wellesley's plan. He was compelled to allow his army to rest in their old position. Sir Harry Burrard having thus spoilt a great victory, was almost immediately superseded by the arrival of Sir Hugh Dalrymple. Their combined wisdom allowed an advance upon Lisbon, but insisted on bringing Sir John Moore to join the army. While this was being settled, an envoy arrived from the French offering to treat, and finally the convention known as the Convention of Cintra was *Convention of Cintra. Aug 30* entered into, in many points against Wellesley's advice. It stipulated for the evacuation of Portugal, but for the transport of the whole French army, with their guns and horses, to France. It was at first suggested that the Russian fleet, at that time in Lisbon, should be regarded as in a neutral port; but as some English regiments had got possession of the mouth of the river, and had hoisted the English flag, this claim was overruled, and Siniavin, the Russian admiral, with his fleet, passed into the hands of the English.

It was not to be supposed that Napoleon would calmly watch the defeat of his troops even in an obscure corner of Europe, still less when their defeat seemed to thwart the completeness of his system, and was connected with events *Napoleon's position in Europe.* which had driven his brother from his throne. Though he knew that conquered **Prussia** beneath the surface was glowing with inextinguishable hatred, and though Austria, in spite of the war against England in which she was nominally engaged, was strengthening her army and re-establishing her finances in a way which seemed to threaten fresh efforts at freedom on her part, he determined to turn the full strength of his Empire upon the devoted Peninsula. He felt that so long as his friendship with Russia existed, so long as the Peace of Tilsitt held firm, his position was tolerably secure. He therefore renewed his alliance with Russia at a meeting with the Czar at Erfurth (Oct. 12), and suddenly ordered the widely scattered divisions of the grand army to concentrate on Paris preparatory to marching into Spain.

Unconscious of the coming danger and of the vast strength of its enemy, the central Junta at Madrid went on with its ill-arranged preparations to secure the freedom of Spain, and with its idle boasts as to the strength of the national armies. The English Government had not yet lost faith in Spanish assertions, nor learnt the absolute worthlessness of Spanish generals and armies ; the fables of the Junta gained credence, and while all the other generals who had gone to Portugal were recalled, some 25,000 men were intrusted to Sir John Moore, with orders to advance into Spain and assist the Spanish troops, which were now occupying the valley of the Ebro and closing the French frontier. Even had the Spanish troops been worth anything, there was an absurd disproportion between the forces prepared and the scene of action for which they were intended. Nor did this weakness fail to strike military men. The Duke of York, though by no means a first-rate general, called the attention of Government to the wide dissipation of the Spanish troops, and the great distance of Portugal from the scene of action, and gave it as his opinion that to employ less than 60,000 men was merely to waste them. . The Government refused to listen to his advice, Lord Castlereagh, the War Minister, was unmoved, and Moore was sent forward to certain failure. With a raw commissariat, and ill supplied with money, although it was at that very time being lavished upon the Spaniards, he embarked upon his dangerous march through a country where the roads were so bad that his artillery to reach Salamanca had to proceed all up the valley of the Tagus almost to Madrid and come back to meet him at Salamanca, where he was to be joined by reinforcements from England under Sir David Baird. Moore's concentration at Salamanca was wholly based on the supposition

Preparations in Spain.

Sir John Moore's march to Salamanca. Oct.

that the Spanish armies were strong enough at all events to retard, if not wholly to resist, the invasion of the French. Yet the grand army was rapidly approaching, and before long the forces collected upon the frontier rendered resistance hopeless. In September arrangements were made for the incorporation of the troops coming from Germany with those already in Spain, and eight great corps d'armée, commanded by six French marshals and Generals Junot and St. Cyr, besides the Imperial Guard, were collected to bear down all opposition.

While Moore was painfully completing his concentration at Salamanca, Napoleon himself arrived at Vittoria, and almost immediately the Spanish troops, which the English general was to support, were scattered to the winds. Napoleon arrives at Vittoria. Nov. 8, 1808.

From his central position the Emperor was able to concentrate his chief force now on his right, now on his left. In a rapid succession of victories Lefèbvre and Soult destroyed the armies upon the left and centre of the Spanish line, and on the 11th of November Blake was entirely ruined at Espinosa. Immediately the whole strength of the Destruction of the Spanish armies. Napoleon at Madrid. Dec. 4, 1808. French army was turned against the right, and on the 23rd of the same month Lannes crushed Palafox and Castaños at Tudela. All the boasted armies of Spain were thus swept away as it were in a moment, and Napoleon advanced upon Madrid, forced the passage of the Somo-Sierra, and after some slight opposition took possession of the capital on the 4th of December. The news of the defeats of Espinosa and Tudela reached Moore at Salamanca before his artillery had joined him. He resolved to await its arrival, and then to retreat.

Meanwhile, although Napoleon at the head of nearly 400,000 men was pressing onward rapidly to Madrid, in a few days to drive the members of the supreme Junta fugitives to Badajos, the old system of misrepresentation was kept up. Mr. Frere, the English plenipotentiary, had been persuaded to share in the illusions of the Junta, and he wrote peremptory letters, urging Moore to advance, and to rally the Spanish armies around him behind the Tagus. But news had at length reached Moore that those Spanish armies did not exist ; the national excitement he had been taught to expect was nowhere visible, and he presently heard that the capital itself was in the hands of Napoleon. For 25,000 or 30,000 English soldiers to oppose the grand army with Napoleon at its head was simply ridiculous ;

their retreat was a matter of necessity. But Moore determined before retreating to relieve if possible the pressure upon
the south of Spain, by pushing forward against Soult
and threatening the French communications with France.   In
acting thus he judged that Napoleon was far more likely to direct
his efforts against the English force than to spend his time in
subduing the southern provinces, which would easily fall into his
hands afterwards.   He therefore advanced towards the Carrion
river, where Soult had collected his army.   The measure succeeded.
Napoleon heard of the advance on the 21st ; dismissing all thought
of the Spaniards, he checked the further advance of his troops, and
turned all his attention to crushing the English.   On receipt of the
news that Napoleon had left Madrid, Moore, who had been hoping
to strike a blow before the arrival of Napoleon, at once began his
retreat.   He was closely followed by Soult, while Napoleon,
forcing the passes of the Guadarama, which were deep in snow,
came up from the south upon his flank.   The retreat was attended
with great difficulty.   Moore's troops were young, the subordination
was not perfect, and the enemy pressed him close; and at length, on
the 1st of January, Napoleon and Soult formed a junction at
Astorga, and their combined army amounted to 70,000 men.   In
ten days Napoleon had moved in the depth of winter 50,000 men
across 200 miles of hostile country.   But Moore's rapidity had
spoilt the effect of even this stupendous march ; he had already
passed Astorga.

There news reached the Emperor of the approaching declaration
of war from Austria, and he found it necessary to resign the command to Soult.   Some of his troops he took with
him ; but Soult himself, and Ney, who supported him,
still commanded upwards of 60,000 men, by whom the pursuit was
recommenced.   Amid many scenes of disorder the English army
pursued its career towards Vigo, where it was expected that the
fleet would be ready to receive it.   But information was brought
that the harbour was not fit for the embarkation of troops.   The line
of retreat was therefore changed to Corunna.   At Lugo, so close was
the pursuit that Moore thought it necessary to prepare for battle,
and the troops, though they had suffered much and become disorderly in retreat, at once showed that their spirit was unbroken.
To the number of 16,000 they formed willingly and regularly in
array of battle.   But as the French did not attack, and as the
supplies would not permit of more than one great battle, the army

Sir John Moore's retreat.

Napoleon leaves Spain.

being now concentrated and encouraged, Moore marched off at night, and resumed his course towards the sea. Although the movement was executed in the midst of a heavy storm, and though so much disorganization followed that the loss between Lugo and Betangos was more than in all the former part of the retreat, from thence to Corunna, the army being collected, marched in good order. As they approached the port, to their horror they discovered that the fleet had not arrived. Contrary winds were still detaining it at Vigo, " and the last consuming exertion made by the army was rendered fruitless." Battle was after all necessary. Large magazines of arms and ammunition left unappropriated and undistributed by the Spanish authorities, though their armies were in desperate want, were found and destroyed. The horses, many of them already broken down, were put to death. Soult's army, almost as exhausted by pursuit as Moore's by retreat, did not assemble till the 12th, but it was not till the 14th that the English transports arrived. The cavalry, who had lost their horses, the sick, and fifty pieces of artillery, were put on board, and preparations made for covering the embarkation of the troops. The ridge on which Soult's army was drawn up overlooked and commanded the position of the English, and some generals were desirous even then of entering into negotiations to secure the safe withdrawal of the army. Moore would not hear of it.

It was determined that upon the evening of the 16th the embarkation should take place, but about the middle of the day the French army began the attack. Even in the last hour of retreat the English showed their strength ; the assaults of the French were repulsed on all sides, and when night closed they were everywhere falling back in confusion. Moore had fallen in the battle, and the command devolved on Hope. Had he known that Soult's ammunition was nearly exhausted he would have continued the strife, and the disaster of the French would have been complete. As it was, he held it wiser to embark the English army during the night, an operation which was performed successfully and without confusion. The loss of the English was estimated at 800, that of the French at between 2000 and 3000. But though, no doubt, the battle of Corunna was an English victory, it was advantageous only in allowing the army to be withdrawn, and left the north-west provinces of Spain and the north of Portugal open to the French. Sir John Moore, whose character as a soldier had already been acknowledged, decoyed by false

Moore reaches Corunna. Jan. 10.

Battle of Corunna. Jan 16

hopes and misled by false information, had yet nobly succeeded in withdrawing for a time the pressure of the French from the south of Spain, and in the midst of overwhelming difficulties had saved the British army and closed his career with a brilliant victory.

The Convention of Cintra and the retreat of Sir John Moore,

Discouragement of the English ministry. the greatness of which was not understood, discouraged the English ministry with regard to its policy in the Peninsula. The cause of the Spaniards was however so popular that it was not deemed advisable wholly to desert them. For three months after the convention Portugal had been left a prey to its own anarchy, but in December Sir John Cradock was sent out to command the English troops. The armaments which had been sent to Cadiz having failed to effect anything there, collected at Lisbon. The Portuguese were at length wise enough to demand an

Beresford made commander of the Portuguese army. English general for their army, and Beresford was sent out to take the command, and thus something like order was re-established. But Napoleon had commanded the conquest of Portugal, the troops of Victor threatened it in the valley of the Tagus, while Soult had entered it from the north and mastered Oporto. Refusing to act with insufficient troops, and waiting for reinforcements, Sir John Cradock had wisely taken the position to defend Lisbon from the advance of Victor, and was stationed at Lumiar and Sacavem just above Lisbon. It was

Wellesley arrives. April 22, 1809. in this position that Wellesley found the English army when he came to take the command on the 22nd of April. With his arrival begins what is properly called the Peninsula War, a war which, by constantly sapping the strength of Napoleon, by exhibiting the possibility of his defeat, and by showing him and his rule, in opposition not to a government, but to a people, was to do more than anything else to complete his final overthrow.

But the English ministry, even while continuing the war, by no means regarded it in this light. Their hopes were not unnaturally turned rather to political coalitions in Europe and to expeditions which appeared more directly to attack the heart of the French empire. Moreover, political feeling in England was strongly excited. Though

Division of opinion in England. there was a general desire for the continuation of the war, there was no unanimity as to the means of carrying it on, or as to the people by whom it should be carried on. Every disaster was exaggerated for political purposes, every obstacle thrown in the way of ministerial action. Our system of party government is not well suited either to great European combinations (because the open hostility exhibited to the ministry of necessity gives an appearance of uncertainty to our engagements) or to the carrying on of war where secresy is necessary, and where reliance upon those to whom the war is intrusted, is required. In domestic affairs its effect is different, and at this time the Opposition was doing good service in bringing abuses to light and rendering salutary reforms necessary. Early in the spring they found grounds for assaulting the ministry in the conduct of the Duke of York, the commander-in-chief, who was accused by a certain militia colonel, Wardle by name, of being influenced by his mistress, Mrs. Clark, in his appointments, while her favour was said to be procured by money. The scandal excited was great, and the immoral details Scandal of of the story were in everybody's mouth. The inquiry the Duke made it evident that Mrs. Clark's influence had been of York. used, but it was not so clear that the Duke had ever himself acted otherwise than conscientiously. The majorities in his favour, however, were so small, that he felt it necessary to resign his office, and Sir David Dundas was appointed in his place. Before long his accuser was himself sued by a tradesman for the price of goods with which he had furnished a house for Mrs. Clark. This gave such an air of malice to the charge, and displayed Colonel Wardle's desire for purity in so strange a light, that it greatly lessened the feeling against the Duke, who was before long restored to his office.

This quarrel, in addition to the case of Lord Melville, excited attention as to the general purity of the administration. Considerable sums of money, amounting to nearly £20,000,000, were unaccounted for. Nor did a committee of inquiry, though it sent in its report, throw much light on the matter. But in March the Chancellor of the Exchequer brought in a Bill to prevent the sale and brokerage of office. Among other matters, attention was drawn to patronage in India, and Lord Castlereagh confessed to having pur- Charges against chased a seat in Parliament for a friend by a gift of an Lord Castle- Indian writership. Lord Castlereagh's frank confession May. induced the House to resolve that no criminating resolution was necessary. Again in May a fresh charge was brought involving Lord Castlereagh and Mr. Perceval also. They were charged with procuring the election of a certain Mr. Quintin Dick, and of afterwards influencing his vote. They were acquitted by a large majority. None the less, Romilly remarks in his Memoirs, "the decision of this night, coupled with some that had lately taken place, will do more towards disposing the nation in favour of a parliamentary reform than all the speeches that have been or will be made in popular assemblies." This question of parliamentary reform was now again beginning to occupy the public mind. Though still commanding majorities, the Cabinet was not at one with itself, and before the year was over the ministry had to be reorganized.

But meanwhile the war was proceeding in its course. The threatening news from Austria which checked Napoleon in his pursuit of Moore proved true. The cruelty and injustice of the attack upon Spain, and the spectacle of a people in revolt, had strongly excited the feelings of Germany. Earnest men of all ranks had enrolled themselves in the secret society known as the Tugendbund, which was shortly to show its strength. The same feeling of hostility to France had shown itself in irresistible force in Austria, smarting under its repeated disgraces. There the Court and Government put itself at the head of the movement, and the Archduke Charles, who was regarded as a military genius, issued a proclamation declaring that the liberty of Europe rested with the Austrian arms. There was no regular coalition formed, but Austria felt that it could rely upon the friendship of England (although still nominally at war with it), of Prussia, where the popular feeling ran high, and probably even of Russia. Armies numbering more than 200,000 men were set on foot, and on the 9th of April Austria declared war against Bavaria, an ally of France. The generals left in charge of Napoleon's army in Germany somewhat mistook his orders, and the Archduke succeeded in forming a partial concentration of his troops and occupying Ratisbon. The arrival of the Emperor on the field soon changed the face of affairs. A series of battles was fought; the left wing of Charles's army was separated from the right, and his forward advance entirely frustrated by defeats at Abendsberg (April 20), Eckmuhl (April 21), and Ratisbon (April 22). Napoleon again advanced to Vienna. But there he found the Archduke Charles still fronting him upon the northern side of the Danube, and the great bridge which crosses the river at Vienna broken down. Near that city the course of the Danube is divided by an island called Lobau, about three miles in length. Napoleon constructed bridges at the island, and brought his army across them into the level called the Marchefeldt on the northern side. There was fought the great battle of Aspern. Victory declared for neither party, and Napoleon found himself in an awkward situation,

Opposition to Napoleon in Germany. 1809.

Battle of Aspern. May 22, 1809.

for the river had risen, and aided by the efforts of the Austrians, had swept away the bridge, and he was thus cut off from reinforcements. He contrived to get back to Lobau, and there awaited his opportunity.

His position was indeed precarious. The secret societies had shown themselves, and a partisan insurrection had broken out under Colonel Schill and the Duke of Brunswick in Saxony and West-phalia. It was premature, and without much difficulty suppressed. The Tyrolese too, headed by Andrew Hofer, an inn- Revolt of the Tyrolese. keeper of the valley of Passeyr, had burst into revolt; 25,000 Bavarians which marched to suppress them had been beaten back. Again and again in the mountain passes they encountered and defeated both the French and Bavarian troops. The revolt was unsuppressed, when Napoleon determined to break from his difficult position. In July, while pretending to build a massive bridge across the river, he brought his army rapidly across it on a temporary structure. The Archduke, who had expected to attack the French while crossing, had now to fight another pitched battle, and two vast armies, numbering together be- Battle of Wagram. July 6, 1809. tween 300,000 and 400,000 men, encountered each other upon the tableland of Wagram. The French gained a hard-won victory. The Archduke was pursued to Zmaim, in Moravia, and there an armistice was made which Peace of Vienna. Oct. 14, 1809. ripened subsequently into the Peace of Vienna, signed on the 14th of October, by which fresh territory was torn from Austria for the advantage of Bavaria, France, and Russia; the kingdom of Spain was recognized; the insurgents of the Tyrol deserted, and a further pledge for the maintenance of the Continental System given. The close of the year was marked by a still further act of wickedness on the part of Napoleon, and a stronger proof of how completely he had deserted the principles of the Revolution. On the 6th of December he divorced his wife Josephine, and entered into negotiations, which were completed the following year, for his marriage with Maria Louisa, an Austrian princess.

The armistice of Zmaim was entered into on the 12th of July. On the 27th of that month, the very day on which the news of the armistice reached England, a great expedition left for the mouth of the Scheldt, for the English ministry had not deceived the hopes of the Austrians, and were determined to undertake what The Walcheren expedition. July 1809. they hoped would prove a diversion in their favour. For this purpose all the strength of England was to be employed. 40,000 soldiers were to be carried across in 400 trans ports under the charge of no less than 245 armed vessels. Yet, great as was the effort, the commonest precautions were neglected. Although it was well known that the climate of the islands at the mouth of the Scheldt was pestiferous, the medical officers were not consulted, none of the proper medicines were sent, and the force was accompanied, in spite of the protest of the surgeon-general, by only one hospital ship. Moreover, the pomp and publicity with which the expedition, which was intended to be secret, was prepared deprived it of much of its value ; and lastly, Court and ministerial favour secured the command for Lord Chatham, Master-General of the Ordnance, a man wholly unfitted for an important command. At length, after much delay caused by the want of harmony between the two branches of the service, the fleet set sail. ,It was the opinion of the best officers of the army that Antwerp might have been at once secured by a *coup de main*, yet it was determined to proceed more regularly and with deliberation; and Flushing (which, as the dykes had been cut, was regarded as impregnable) was taken in two days after the arrangements for the attack had been completed. It was not till the 21st of August that Lord Chatham began to think of moving towards Antwerp. But, as by that time the enemy's squadron had been withdrawn up the river to the city, and the intermediate fortresses had been so strengthened as to render the advance difficult, absolutely nothing further was even attempted. The army was kept lying in the plague-stricken swamps of Walcheren. Fever began to make fearful ravages. On the 29th Chatham wrote home that he could do no more—that already 3000 of the troops were sick. By September 11,000 men were stricken, and the great bulk of the army was ordered home. Lord Chatham, taking with him as many of the sick as he could, accompanied it. 15,000 men were left till the end of the year. Though the fever still spread with fearful rapidity, the only remedy supplied was a quantity of Thames water, which was constantly sent out. The roofs of the huts had fallen in, the men were removed to the churches, and the churches proved damp and worse than the roofless huts. At last 100 bricklayers were sent from England to repair the huts ; the bricklayers were speedily themselves in hospital. The death rate was now 200 or 300 a week ; and so terrible was the effect of the fever, that before the next June, of the 40,000 troops sent out 35,000 had been in hospital. Nor did this great folly produce the smallest effect on the general war. Even had the expedition not been so delayed that the Austrian armistice was already signed when it sailed, it could have done no good. Napoleon

Flushing taken. Aug. 15.

himself wrote of it, "Before six weeks, of the 15,000 troops which are in the Isle of Walcheren not 1500 will be left, the rest will be in hospital. The expedition has been undertaken under false expectations and planned in ignorance."

While wasting their strength in this idle display, the ministry were being taught, had they been willing to learn, where English forces might have been wisely employed. In Portugal, Wellesley, on taking the command, had marched against Soult in the north, *Wellesley* had brought his army across the Douro in face of the *victorious in* French, who were occupying Oporto, had recaptured *Portugal.* that city, and driven Soult to a desperate retreat. By extraordinary vigour and good fortune, Soult, though there were traitors in his camp, contrived to extricate his army, but Portugal was free. And Wellesley, victorious in the north, and deceived by the constant false information of the Spaniards as to the weakness of his enemies, determined to turn his arms against the other French army which was threatening Portugal in the valley of the Tagus. He was there to act with the Spanish army under Cuesta, an old man of crabbed temper and of great self-conceit. Victor's army fell back before the advancing English from Talavera behind the Alberche river.

By this march Madrid was threatened, and Joseph collected for its defence the troops of Victor, Sebastiani, and his own guard, amounting to about 50,000 men. As Wellesley had with him less than 20,000 English troops, and as he could place no reliance *Wellesley* upon the Spaniards of Cuesta though they were nearly *marches towards* 40,000 in number, it was a bold resolve to march against *Madrid* Victor. But Wellesley was ignorant of the extreme danger of his movement. Constantly misinformed by the Spaniards, he believed Soult's army in Castile and the plain of the Douro to consist of about 15,000 men; in reality it was more than 50,000 strong. With these it was possible, collecting them at Salamanca, to cross the mountains separating the plains of the Douro and the Tagus, to pass between Wellesley's troops and Portugal, and thus placing him between two armies, each virtually superior to his own, entirely ruin him. Ignorant as yet of the character of the Spaniards, Wellesley could not believe that he should be kept uninformed, nor could he believe that the Spanish troops supplied to occupy the passes of the mountains, and restrain, or at least check, Soult's movements, would give ground without striking a blow; nor, before entering on his enterprise, could he have conceived that his army would have been systematically kept without food. It is nevertheless true that the greatest difficulty was found in procuring rations, which often consisted merely of a few handfuls of grain, while the Spanish troops were very fairly fed. Victor and the King had taken up a position beyond the Alberche stream, a little river flowing from the north into the Tagus above Talavera. Beyond that stream, Wellesley, when he found how he was treated, positively refused to move Beginning to appreciate the character of the Spanish troops, he urged Cuesta not to venture on a forward movement without him; but the obstinate old man persisting in passing the Alberche, was roughly handled by Victor, and only saved from the consequences of his rashness by English assistance.

Soult had informed Joseph of his great plan. All the King had to do was to remain quiet, and check the advance of the English till Wellesley was caught in the trap. But there was a second Spanish army apparently threatening Madrid from the south. It might well be that before Soult's arrival the capital would be lost, although, if Soult's plan answered, it would be immediately regained. The King could not bring himself to bear even the temporary loss of his capital, especially as the hospitals and supplies for his army were there. He therefore rashly listened to the advice of Victor, which was contrary

Battle of
Talavera.
July 28, 1809. to that of Jourdan, his proper military adviser, and determined to attack the English. The position of Talavera is about two miles in length, crossing the plain from the river Tagus to a small range of hills which bounds the valley; beyond this range is a second valley of about half a mile in extent, and then come the mountains. The key of the position is the highest of the secondary hills, and this Wellesley occupied. The Spaniards he placed behind entrenchments in Talavera. Victor made a second error in making two preliminary attacks upon the key hill. Though these attacks failed, he still believed he could carry the position, and Joseph yielded to his desire for a general engagement. This was fought on the 28th of July. The advance of the French light dragoons so frightened the Spaniards that many regiments at once turned and fled, carrying the news down the valley that the English army was destroyed. Such as remained in their strong position proved sufficient to hold it, and were not seriously molested. The whole brunt of the battle fell upon the English in the centre and left wing. At one moment the centre was broken through, and disaster might have followed had not Wellesley at once seen what was wanted, and sent the 48th regiment down from the hill, though the fighting there was severe, and re-established the battle in the centre. An extraordinary and reckless charge of the 23rd light dragoons across an apparently impassable ravine, though carried out with the loss of almost half their number, had the effect of paralyzing a whole division of the French army, which was attempting to turn the English left by the valley between the hills and the mountains. When the evening closed the French had been defeated at all points, and the English remained masters of their position.

But by that time Soult had come almost unopposed through the mountains from Salamanca to Placentia and the direct road to Portugal was closed. All hopes of rendering the victory useful were therefore gone, and Wellesley was compelled to cross to the south of the Tagus, and take refuge among the mountains. After considerable loss and much suffering from the abominable usage he endured from the hands of the Spaniards, he came to a fixed determination that he would never again act in concert with them, that henceforward his first duty lay in saving Portugal, from which, if events favoured him, he might ultimately advance with an English and Portuguese army, and do for the Spaniards what they were totally unable to do for themselves.

The victory of Talavera was a great one, and the English ministry recognized it as such by raising Wellesley to the Peerage *Effect of* as Viscount Wellington. Nevertheless it was open to *the victory* the cavils of the Opposition, for it could be truly urged *in England.* that it had not produced any permanent advantage, and had been followed by a somewhat disastrous retreat. In Parliament some Opposition speakers even went so far as to urge that the name of the commander should be omitted from the vote of thanks to be given to the army. But it was in fact the weak war administration in England which rendered it useless. Our resources had been wasted in the pompous and ridiculous Walcheren expedition, and in a second expedition, almost as useless, which was despatched to Italy, where it was unable to effect anything, and had to withdraw to Sicily.

When Wellington withdrew from Talavera, after waiting some time on the Guadiana, he took up his position in the more northern part of Portugal, near Almeida, preparing for the defence of the country. During his inactivity there the advance of *French victories.* the French was nearly unchecked. They marched into *Nov. 1809.* Aragon and Catalonia, and defeated an army of 50,000 Spaniards at Ocana (Nov. 20), thus throwing open the province of La Mancha, and obtaining an opportunity for further advance into Andalusia.

This province was also overrun, with the exception of Cadiz, which was saved by General Albuquerque. The invasion thus formed itself into three defined divisions; an army for the invasion of Portugal, an army for the completion of the conquest of Andalusia, and an army in Catalonia, while the King and his Imperial Guards formed an army in the centre. Having thus borne down all opposition in Spain, Napoleon's intention was to overrun Portugal in the following year. His army for the purpose was placed under the command of Massena, while Soult was intrusted with the operations next in importance, and directed against Cadiz.

The assault which Wellington had been long preparing to resist was now to come. The ministers in England—in part despairing of his success, in part unable to comprehend the greatness of his schemes—distinctly told him that he must rely upon himself. But, with extraordinary steadfastness and courage, he undertook the task. Ever since the October of the preceding year he had foreseen what would happen; he had known that in all probability his troops would be outnumbered, and that he should be unable to make. head against the vast armies which Napoleon might set at motion against him. He had therefore designed a great defensive scheme, so that if the worst came to the worst he might still have some place to which to retire and avoid the necessity of evacuating Lisbon. He had therefore turned the promontory between the Tagus and the sea into a vast fortification. During the time of his delay on the

Guadiana, and while wintering near Almeida, thousands of Portuguese workmen were turning the hills
into impregnable fortresses. This great work, known as
the lines of Torres Vedras, was threefold. The outer line,
twenty-nine miles in length, extended from Alhandra on the Tagus to the mouth of the little river Zizandra close to Torres Vedras. The second, twenty-four miles in length, and which was intended originally to be the strongest of the two, was from six to ten miles in rear of the first, reaching from the Tagus at Quintella to the mouth of the St. Lorenza. In addition to this, a small fortification was erected to cover an embarkation in case the other two lines were forced. It enclosed an entrenched camp and Fort St. Julian, and was two marches in rear of the first line. Time had allowed Wellington so to strengthen the first line that it subsequently proved sufficient for all purposes. The General's great cares during the winter had been,—first, to instruct the Portuguese authorities to insist upon the inhabitants destroying all villages, mills, and crops

Wellington fortifies the Lisbon promontory. 1810.

in the course of the invading force when it should appear; secondly, to get the half-trained militia of the country over which he held command employed in such a manner as to oblige the French to act in a mass and prevent detailed fighting; and thirdly, so to arrange his troops that while spread abroad, for greater ease in procuring provisions, they should yet be within easy distance for concentration. He thus waited, fully prepared to carry out his great scheme when Massena should think fit to strike the first blow. So determined was he to adopt a waiting policy, that he even allowed the great fortress of Ciudad Rodrigo, the key of that part of Spain, to be taken before his eyes. Meanwhile he had to listen calmly to the assertions of the Opposition in Parliament, that no British soldier would leave the Peninsula but as a prisoner, and to see the City of London addressing the throne to inquire into his conduct, and protesting against conferring honours and distinctions on a general who had exhibited nothing but useless valour.

Ciudad Rodrigo fell on the 11th of July. It was not till September that the great attack began. Then Massena, with an army of 65,000 men, set forward towards Lisbon by the valley of *Massena advances against him. Sept. 1810.* the Mondego, having been informed by friendly Portuguese that the road was easy, and that there was no important position between him and Coimbra, where he believed he could forestall Wellington. An accident lost the English commander the advantage that any opposition from the fortress of Almeida might have given him. The explosion of a magazine rendered the capitulation of the fortress necessary almost immediately. In spite of Massena's attempts to deceive him as to the road he intended to pursue, in spite of the distance at which some of the English troops were stationed, Wellington contrived to collect his army and to place it between Massena and Coimbra. Down the valley of the Mondego the march was continued. The orders for the destruction of the property were carried out as far as possible, and crowds of wretched fugitive peasants accompanied the army. A panic began to spread in Portugal. The intriguing regency did not carry out the orders for destruction with sufficient activity. There was yet enough food left between Mondego and the lines to supply the French during the ensuing winter. To raise the temper of the country, and to excite the people to the voluntary destruction of their property, Wellington was compelled (in entire opposition to his original plans) to fight a great battle with *Battle of Busaco Sept. 29, 1810.* the advancing French. He selected the ridge of Busaco,

which almost closes the valley of the Mondego, just north of
Coimbra, as his battlefield.   The English and Portuguese there
stood at bay, and the French were completely defeated.   The moral
effect was all that could be desired—the Portuguese troops thence-
forward became fitting comrades for the English, and the waning
trust of the people was restored ; but as a military operation it effected
nothing.   Massena found a pass through the hills upon his right,
which enabled him though beaten to continue his advance, and Wellington, not attempting to attack him, fell back, giving orders to the
Portuguese militia to close upon the French rear.   Thus harassed in his
progress, Massena arrived before the famous lines (of the existence
of which he had only heard five days before), only to find them
thoroughly occupied by the English troops.   Against the works he
could do nothing ; his operations were in fact reduced to a blockade.
Massena's object, therefore, was to feed his army till reinforcements
arrived, Wellington's, by closing up the Portuguese militia behind
the French army, rapidly to reduce it to starvation.   The
expected reinforcements did not come, and on the 14th of
November Massena, who had lost upwards of 30,000
men since he had entered Portugal, was obliged to draw off his army
and begin a retrograde movement ; he moved leisurely, hoping to strike
another blow before he finally withdrew, but when reinforcements
arrived for the English he retreated with some haste to Almeida
and Ciudad Rodrigo.   The operations were closed by the combat of
Sabugal (April 3, 1811), where Massena was again worsted, and after
which he finally withdrew from Portugal.

*Massena
retreats.
Nov.*

While Massena was attacking Portugal, Soult had been vigorously
prosecuting the siege of Cadiz, and had there made dispositions which
would probably have ended in its capture, when he was ordered to
assist Massena, for the Emperor was more anxious to put an end to the
regular warfare in Portugal than to complete his conquests in Spain.
Portugal is assailable either by the northern line from Salamanca,
which Massena had followed, and which was covered by the fortress
of Ciudad Rodrigo, or by a line south of the Tagus through Estremadura and Alemtejo, which is covered by Badajos and Elvas.   In this
latter direction Soult had marched ; the fruit of his operations were
the victory of Gebora (Feb. 19), where the Spaniards were completely
defeated, and the capture of Badajos.   The two great frontier fortresses
between Spain and Portugal were thus in the hands of France.   But
the departure of Soult from Cadiz encouraged Graham, who commanded the English in that fortress, to attempt to drive Victor, who

was left in command, from his lines. A combined force of about 12,000 men sailed from Cadiz southward, intending to march upon the back of the French lines. Victor, marching out to defend them, was defeated at Barosa (March 5) by the vigour and generalship of Graham, La Peña, the Spanish commander, as usual, adding nothing to the victory, and failing when the victory was won to put it to any use. The battle was however so severe a threat that Soult, not wishing to lose all the fruit of his former arrangements, withdrew from his attack on Portugal. Yet, as both Badajos and Ciudad Rodrigo were in the hands of the French, in the following campaign there were two scenes of operation of which those fortresses were the centres.

The ministry in England had at last begun to feel some confidence in their general, but they would have been content with the success-ful defence of Portugal. Not so Wellington ; his mind Wellington's was full of great projects for the relief of Spain. The great plans. two points on which the French pressure was strongest were Catalonia and Cadiz ; and Wellington, believing that Massena, although his troops had been again raised to 50,000 men, would not be in a fit state for immediate action, had it now in his mind either to invest Almeida and Ciudad Rodrigo, betake himself with much of his army to Badajos, unite with the English and Portuguese troops there, and assault Soult in Andalusia ; or to engage in a still more magnificent plan,—to march his army right across Spain, taking Madrid on the way, which would cut off the resources of Soult's army and oblige it to withdraw, and then upon the eastern coast to enter into communica-tions with the English troops at that time in Sicily, and, working from a new base of operations, to attack the French in Catalonia. In either case the capture of Badajos was necessary, as its possession by the French was a constant threat to the Spaniards in Cadiz and to the southern provinces of Portugal. Wellington therefore, leaving the blockade of Almeida in the hands of Spencer, went to Elvas to arrange with Marshal Beresford, who commanded the troops in that direction, for the siege of Badajos. Before his arrangements were completed he was hastily summoned again to the north, where Massena had unex-pectedly shown signs of activity, and was moving to relieve Almeida Wellington was in time to check him at the hard-fought battle of Fuentes Onoro (May 5), which was followed by the evacuation of the fortress. He then returned to superintend the more important operation of the siege of Badajos. But before he arrived Battle of the operations had been interrupted. Soult had ad- Albuera. vanced to succour his late prize, and Beresford had May 16, 1811.

thought it necessary to fight a battle with him at Albuera. This battle, one of the bloodiest ever fought, took place on the 16th of May. The English and their allies had about 30,000 infantry and

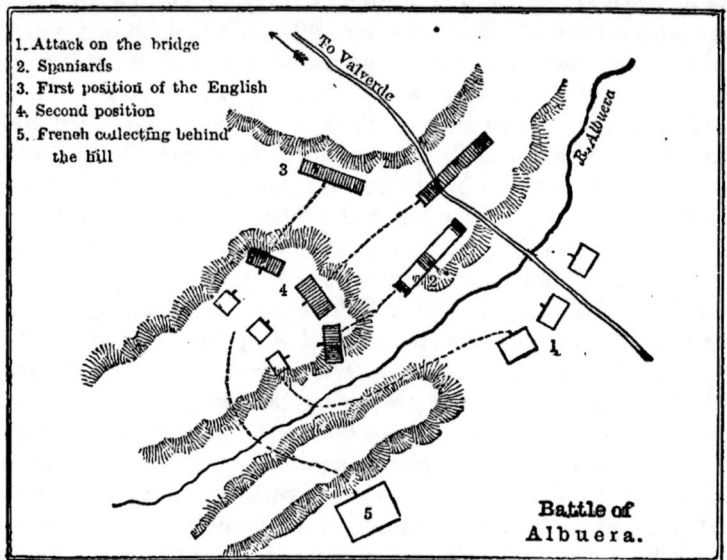

1. Attack on the bridge
2. Spaniards
3. First position of the English
4. Second position
5. French collecting behind the hill

Battle of Albuera.

2000 cavalry, but of these only 7000 were English, and the Spaniards were not to be trusted. Soult had with him only 19,000 good infantry and 4000 cavalry, but Beresford's faulty arrangements almost neutralized the superiority in forces. The English position was a ridge, in front of which ran the Albuera river. In the centre were the village and bridge of Albuera, through which ran the road to Valverde over the ridge. This road being Beresford's only line of retreat, he regarded a hill in the centre which defended it as the key of his position, and there put his best troops, intrusting the right to the Spaniards under Blake. He also neglected to place any troops across the river, and the enemy's movements were entirely hidden by the wooded heights on that side. For a direct attack Beresford's dispositions were correct, but upon his right a tableland stretched so far back as to command the Valverde road and to look along the back of the English position. Soult saw that by mastering this height he would cut off the English from retreat, oblige them to form a wholly new front, and in all probability destroy them. He therefore secretly, under cover of the hills, massed his troops upon his own left, and while a sufficiently important assault was made upon the bridge to attract Beresford's attention, tae bulk of the French army rapidly proceeded to place itself at right angles to the English position upon the tableland. The main point of the battle was in the struggle for the possession of this vantage-ground. In vain Beresford entreated Blake to change his front and cover the right. The Spanish general insisted that the real attack was upon the village. Beresford himself took the command of the Spanish troops, the change of front was effected, but even then they could scarcely be induced to move. At length the English second division moved from the centre and mounted the hill. But, brought too recklessly into action, they suffered much. Scarcely a third of the regiments remained standing, and Beresford was already thinking of retreat when Colonel Hardinge induced Cole with the fourth division, and Abercrombie with the third brigade of the second division, neither of whom had been much engaged, to advance to the rescue. At the head of 6000 men Hardinge advanced to cover the hill. The crowded formation of the French, who were in column, impeded their movements, and the advance of the English was so irresistible, that at length, unable to open out, they gave ground, and in the words of Napier, "slowly and with a horrid carnage were pushed by the incessant vigour of the attack to the furthest edge of the hill," and at length "the mighty mass, breaking off like a loosened cliff, went headlong down the steep; the rain flowed in streams discoloured with blood, and 1800 unwounded men, the remnant of 6000 unconquerable British soldiers, stood triumphant on the fatal hill." In four hours nearly 7000 of the allies and 8000 French were struck down. The victory was however won, and after occupying a threatening position during the 17th, on the 18th Soult marched away. The advantages of this bloody battle were little or none.

Yet though the battles of Fuentes Onoro and Albuera produced little result, although the French continued their successes in Catalonia, and Spain seemed entirely at their disposal, their position was by no means wholly prosperous. The broken armies of the Spanish had formed themselves into guerilla bands, their useless generals were superseded by daring partisan commanders, and troops wholly untrustworthy in pitched battles proved masters of the art of wild irregular warfare. It was only in large masses that the French were safe; yet, as Napoleon always acted on the principle that war should support war, and allowed only £80,000 for the maintenance of his armies in Spain, which at that time amounted to more than 300,000 men, the dispersion of the forces was an absolute necessity in order that food might be procured. No courier could be despatched except under escort; letters to Paris were guarded at first by 1400 dragoons, subsequently by 3000. Moreover, Joseph and the Emperor were not at one. The Spanish King did not wish to rule only as the agent of his brother in a conquered country, and at length the vexatious tyranny of Napoleon pressed so heavily upon him, that he went to Paris and resigned his crown. He was induced to take it back again, but the mere fact of his visit, coupled with Wellington's success and the late victories, which were complete if not decisive, raised the spirits of the patriots and increased the energy and number of the guerillas. Moreover, affairs in Europe were beginning to take a turn which compelled Napoleon to act with less vigour in the Peninsula. His marriage with the Austrian archduchess was a deadly insult to the Czar, for a princess of whose house he had previously been negotiating; the Continental System was becoming almost unbearable, coupled as it was with the French occupation of the northern ports of Germany; and the addition of territory to the Duchy of Warsaw seemed to threaten a restoration of the Polish kingdom, and to be a violation of the Treaty of Tilsitt. The estrangement of the Czar was becoming so evident that Napoleon's mind began to turn more and more towards an expedition against Russia. The number of troops in Spain was lessened, and first-rate soldiers withdrawn to give place to new conscripts.

But, in spite of this relaxation, this year forms in the opinion of the great historian of the war its most critical period. For Welling-

Position of Wellington. ton was miserably supplied from home, and sickness was rife among his troops, so that he could not bring more than 8000 men into the field, while the Portuguese Government, quarrelling with him, frequently refused supplies, and so starved their own troops, that instead of 40,000 soldiers who had been available on Massena's advance, only 19,000 badly-fed men were now with the army, and against this weakened force a new combination of the French had been arranged. The battle of Albuera had been followed by a renewal of the siege of Badajos. Want of proper material rendered the progress of the siege slow, and Marmont, who had succeeded Massena in command of the army of Portugal, was ordered to co-operate with Soult coming from the south to relieve it. Their junction was effected and the siege was raised. To all appearance therefore the battle of Albuera had been a French victory, and two armies instead of one appeared to threaten Portugal by the southern line. Wellington had brought his troops down and offered the combined generals battle upon the Caya. But, ignorant of the weakness of the English, and imposed upon by the confident front which Wellington with astonishing boldness showed them, the battle, which might easily have been decisive of the fate of the Peninsula, was refused by the French generals, and Soult moved southward, while Marmont returned to occupy the valley of the Tagus.

The French refuse the battle at Caya. June 1811.

This critical year of 1811 was a bitter disappointment to Wellington. He had hoped that his period of inactivity was over; that the defensive might have been changed to an offensive warfare. The blunders of his subordinates, the wretched jealousies of the Portuguese regency, and the poor support he received from home, had rendered his efforts futile. He still found himself when the year closed obliged to be contented with preserving his defensive attitude in Portugal. It was even worse than this. The French had succeeded in completing the conquest of the east of Spain, and the army of Suchet had advanced as far as Valencia ; while in the north Asturias and Galicia had again fallen into their hands. Some gleam of success had indeed been visible in the south, where Hill had checked Drouet in Estremadura, and where Soult had been beaten off in his attack upon the little fortress of Tarifa. But the reorganization of the French army (especially of the great army of the centre), and the threatened reappearance of Napoleon upon the scene, rendered the close of the year one of gloom and despair.

Yet events were occurring in Europe which allowed Wellington still to hope. Already before the end of the year 1810, the appropriation by Napoleon of the estates of the Duke of Oldenburg, a relative of Alexander, had induced the Czar to declare his freedom from the Continental System. It had become evident to him that, sooner or later, war would be forced upon him, and he had entered into open preparations. Under one pretext or another Napoleon had also been strengthening his troops upon the eastern frontier of his dominions, and though the forms of friendship were still kept up, it was plain that before long the two empires would be plunged into hostilities. During the whole of 1811 remonstrances and recriminations had passed between the courts. Alexander had at first intended to re-establish the kingdom of Poland, where the influence of Napoleon was still great, and to begin offensive movements. The success of Wellington at Torres Vedras is said to have suggested to him and to his counsellors

Threatened war between France and Russia.

the more prudent method of attracting the French into the heart of Russia, and of allowing the weather and the natural difficulties of the country to have their full force as his allies. He knew that, in spite of the marriage of the Austrian archduchess with Napoleon, he could rely upon the friendship of the Court of Vienna should any opportunity arise of successful opposition to France. Prussia likewise, since the battle of Jena, had undergone a complete though silent revolution ; feudalism had been almost destroyed, the peasants given a share in the property of the land, and the bourgeois at least endowed with some degree of self-government; the people and the government were absolutely at one. While ostensibly restricted to the treaty number of 42,000, the army had been practically increased to 150,000 men ; and, by an extraordinary effort of patience and good administration, the broken nation had been re-established. There, too, it was certain that any successful effort to check Napoleon would be hailed with delight. But Napoleon, observing that Russia did not take the initiative, and seeing that both Austria and Prussia were to all appearance still at his service, forgetting the lesson which he should have learnt from Spain, that the enmity of the people is more to be feared than the enmity of the government, seemed irresistibly led to the war which was to complete his ruin. In August 1811 there took place another of those scenes which had so frequently preluded war. At a public meeting of ministers in the Tuileries the Russian ambassador had to undergo a violent attack from the Emperor. From that moment all Europe knew that the war with Russia was determined on. It was upon the certainty of the approach of this event and the nature of the French warfare in Spain that Wellington rested his hopes.

Marmont's army had been moved for the sake of procuring food into the valley of the Tagus, which was thus called upon to support two armies, that of the centre and that of Portugal. Wellington did not believe that it could do this for long, but while the armies were there barring the valley of the Tagus offensive movements of any importance were impossible, as Soult and Drouet occupied the south, and the northern army in Asturias, capable of being reinforced by Marmont, prevented action in the valley of the Douro. But meanwhile Ciudad Rodrigo was not itself within immediate reach of the covering army; a sudden attack and capture of this fortress would almost certainly bring Marmont northward to save the neighbouring country and to relieve the valley of the Tagus. Even a weak army covered by the fortress

Wellington's plan for the campaign of 1812.

would probably be able to make good its position, while Wellington himself marching southward might also capture Badajos, and thence defeat Soult and Drouet in Andalusia. With infinite pains to avoid discovery he ripened his plan; preparations were secretly made at Almeida and at Elvas for the two sieges, and the first rapid blow was successfully struck, and Ciudad Rodrigo captured (Jan. 19). It had the effect expected; Marmont collected his troops at Salamanca, the scattered detachments of the French were everywhere drawn in, Hill's southern army was moved towards the north, and Wellington was sufficiently strong to fight a battle if necessary. Marmont for the present resigned the fortress and again distributed his troops. Wellington then proceeded to strike his second blow. Leaving one division behind him, with some Spanish troops and Portuguese militia, he moved southward, and at length succeeded in storming Badajos also, though with fearful loss (April 6). He acted with unusual skill, and the charge against him of having foolishly wasted life in the siege proves upon examination to be utterly groundless; for it was the extreme rapidity with which the fortress was captured which prevented Soult from coming to its relief. But again the fruits of his success were snatched from him; he was unable to follow out his plan of driving Soult from Estremadura, for he was badly seconded by the troops he had left in the north; Marmont, though somewhat slowly, had begun to carry out Napoleon's orders to regain Ciudad Rodrigo and to invade Portugal, and Wellington had to make all haste back to re-establish his affairs there. His rapid appearance from the south on Marmont's flank compelled that general to retreat, but the opportunity of a southern war was over, and the English army was again spread along the whole line of Portugal, but with this important advantage that the two key fortresses of Spain were now in its hands.

Capture of Rodrigo and Badajos.

It was as yet only the spring, Wellington had to choose in which direction he would arrange the ensuing campaign. He determined to make his attack on the northern line; a victory over Marmont would throw open the road to Madrid, and Soult would either have to retire from the south or be cut off from his communications. A portion of his army might indeed be sent to assist Marmont; but the harvest in the valley of the Douro is considerably later than in the south, and it was impossible that a large additional number of troops should be subsisted for at least a fortnight to come. Thus for a while he could act against

Wellington's attack on the northern army.

Marmont alone. Further to secure his position, he strengthened the army under Hill in the south, planned and executed an extraordinary capture of the French lines of communication at Ãlmaraz, thus rendering the intercourse between the two armies lengthy, and at the same time re-established the bridge of Alcantara, close to the Portuguese frontier, by which his own communications with Hill were rendered ten days nearer. It was thus against an army of about equal numbers with his own, but isolated for the present at all events from reinforcements, that Wellington advanced. Salamanca and its forts were captured, and Marmont fell back before him.

But his advance was not all triumphant, Marmont succeeded in turn in obtaining the ascendant. By a series of clever movements he compelled Wellington to retire, and moving towards the

Battle of Salamanca. July 22, 1812. right flank of the English, seemed to threaten the communications between Salamanca and Ciudad Rodrigo, while he kept himself in communication with the central

army under the king. Wellington saw that retreat was necessary, and he intended to return to Portugal. But Marmont was not contented with this success. He was eager to fight before his junction with the king, and brought on a battle beyond the Tormes, just south of Salamanca. The English occupied a sort of basin in a loop of the river; about the centre was a hill called the.

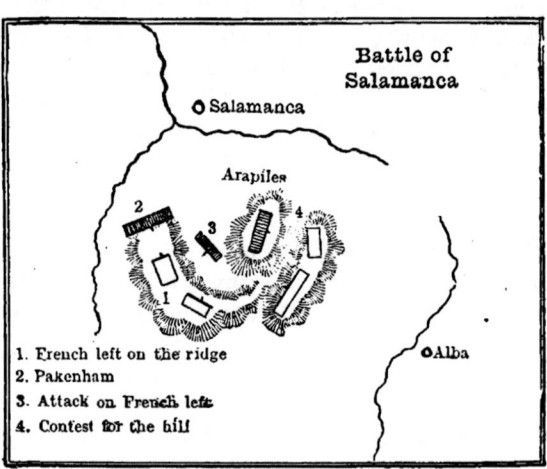

Battle of
Salamanca

O Salamanca

Arapiles

1. French left on the ridge
2. Pakenham
3. Attack on French left
4. Contest for the hill

O Alba

Arapiles; round the southern edge was a ridge which led to the point where the road by which the English must retreat ran. Marmont, hoping to envelop the English, sent forward his left along the ridge.

Wellington saw the advantage thus offered. Holding the Arapiles with his left, he fell on the flank of the advancing column, while Pakenham faced it upon the ridge. The French left was thus entirely destroyed, their attacks upon the central hill were unsuccessful, their confusion was increased by the loss of their commander, who was wounded early in the day, and it was only because a Spanish garrison which should have cut off their retreat across the Tormes at Alba had been withdrawn without Wellington's knowledge that their army escaped destruction. As it was, Clausel, who had succeeded Marmont, was able to bring off the greater part of his troops in safety.

The arrival of reinforcements under Sir Home Popham on the north of Spain had drawn a certain portion of the French troops in that direction, and against a weakened and defeated army Wellington proceeded in his triumphant advance toward Madrid. Joseph again left the city and retreated *Wellington enters Madrid. Aug. 12, 1812.* to Valencia, and with all the signs of wild rejoicing the conqueror was received in the capital of Spain. The effect of the late battle was exactly such as had been anticipated—King Joseph, acting as commander-in-chief, ordered Soult to evacuate Andalusia and the south. It was in vain that that general pointed out the possibility of holding his position there, and intreated the king to come with the other armies to his rescue: the orders were peremptory, and much against his will Soult withdrew and effected a junction with Joseph and Suchet in Valencia. The south and centre of Spain thus seemed clear of enemies, but the hold of the French was as yet shaken only, not broken; for in fact though Wellington's march had forced his enemies in two directions (Clausel, with the remainder of Marmont's army, having retired north, while the king withdrew south-east), such were their numbers that each division became the centre of an army as powerful as his own. Indeed, the very effect of his victory in drawing Soult from Andalusia had concentrated a vast power in Joseph's hands. Wellington was, however, aided by two circumstances. An expedition had been sent to Sicily under Sir William Bentinck; a portion of it under Maitland was landed at Alicante, and kept Suchet and the Catalonian army in play, while Sir Home Popham did the like for the army of the north.

Of the two armies against which Wellington had to contend by far the largest was the army of Soult and the king, on the south-east. On the other hand, Clausel's forces were *His great plans thwarted.*

beaten and retreating, so that it appeared to the general better to leave
a detachment under Hill to cover Madrid, while he himself repaired
with the bulk of his army to strike a final blow at Clausel by the
capture of Burgos, intending to return at once and with his whole combined forces fight a great battle with Soult and the king before the
capital. Again events occurred, upon which he could scarcely have
calculated, which thwarted his purpose. The Spanish army, which had
been intrusted with the duty of guarding his communications with
Salamanca and of completing the capture of the fortresses of the Douro,
and some English forces which had been left to assist it, were so badly
handled that the retreating army was in fact left unmolested, while
extreme want of money and political difficulties hampered Wellington's
own march. Clausel, too, proved a general of great ability; his retreat
up the valley of the Arlanzon towards Burgos was a masterpiece;
while, to crown all, the resistance offered by Burgos and the deficiency of proper artillery proved greater obstacles than had been
expected. The delay thus caused allowed the French to recover;
the crisis was met with energy, fresh troops were poured across the
frontier; Souham, who took the chief command, found himself at
the head of a force almost double that of Wellington; and as Soult
began to draw towards Madrid from Valencia, thus threatening the
safety of Hill, there was no course left but to summon that
general northward, and to make a combined retreat towards Salamanca and Portugal. It was not the most
glorious passage of our arms. Want of pay and some other causes
had somewhat slackened the discipline of the troops, and though
no disaster occurred, and though the French were more than once
checked, there were scenes of wild disorder and insubordination
which called forth stern reprimands from the general.

He retreats
to Portugal.

This was the last of Wellington's retreats. Events in Europe
lessened the power of his enemies; while fighting for
his very existence on the main continent of Europe,
Napoleon could not but regard the war in Spain as a very secondary
concern, and a great many old and valuable soldiers were withdrawn.
The jealousy which existed between Joseph and the generals, and
the dislike of the great generals to take upon themselves the Spanish
war, threw it into inferior hands for some little while, and there is
little more to chronicle than a succession of hard-won victories.
Moreover, Wellington's position was in other ways much strengthened; he had received from the Brazils full power of action in
Portugal, at Burgos he had been made commander-in-chief of th·

Improvement in
his position.

Spanish army, while the changes in the ministry at home, though they had deprived him of his brother's assistance, had yet been on the whole favourable to him; his greatness and success had become the chief support of the ministry. He had, moreover, by his personal authority established discipline in the Portuguese army, had used his power and influence to supply the commissariat and other trains, and even the Spanish troops which had been placed at his disposal had been brought into something like order. The whole active force of the French had been reduced to 197,000 men, while Wellington had contrived to prepare 200,000 allied troops for the campaign, although it was chiefly upon the 70,000 Anglo-Portuguese that he relied. The English fleets covered the coast, and every port thus became a little centre of action. A vigorous insurrection had arisen all along the northern provinces; and it was this more than anything else which decided Wellington's course of action. While leaving troops to occupy the attention of the French in the valley of the Tagus, he intended to march northwards, thus avoiding the obstacles offered by the passage of the Douro and Carrion, connect himself with the northern insurgents, and directly threaten the communications with France, either fighting for or turning every position in which the king might try to intercept him.

His movements, which had to be effected with considerable secrecy, were well carried out; the various divisions of his army met at Toro on the Douro. As he had expected, the French had to fall back before him; he compelled them to evacuate Burgos and attempt to defend the Ebro. Their position there was turned, and they had again to fall back into the basin of Vittoria. This is the plain of the river Zadora, which forms in its course almost a right angle at the south-west corner of the plain, which it thus surrounds on two sides. Across the plain and   <small>Battle of Vittoria. June 21, 1813.</small> through Vittoria runs the high road to France, the only one in the neighbourhood sufficiently large to allow of the retreat of the French army, encumbered with all its stores and baggage, and the accumulated wealth of some years of occupation of Spain. While Wellington forced the passage of the river in front south of the great bend, and drove the enemy back to the town of Vittoria, Graham beyond the town closed this road. The beaten enemy had to retreat as best he could towards Salvatierra, leaving behind all the artillery, stores, baggage, and equipments.

The offensive armies of France had now to assume the defensive and to guard their own frontier. Before advancing to attack them

in the mountains, Wellington undertook the blockade of Pampeluna
and the siege of St. Sebastian. It was impossible for the French

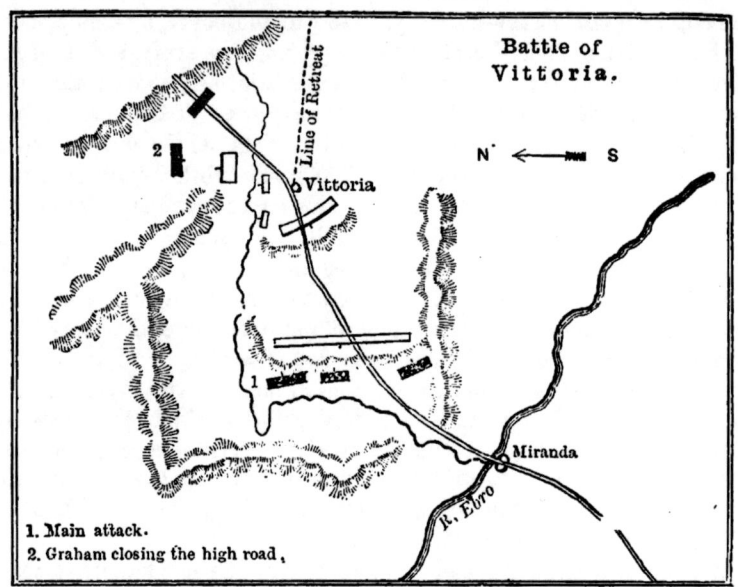

any longer to regard diplomatic or dynastic niceties. Joseph was
superseded, and the defence of France intrusted to Soult, with whom
the king had hopelessly quarrelled. He proved himself
Battles of worthy of the charge. A series of terrible battles was
the Pyrenees. fought in the Pyrenees, but one by one his positions
1813.
were forced. With fearful bloodshed, St. Sebastian was taken, the
Bidasoa was crossed (Oct. 7), the battle of the Nivelle fought and
won (Nov. 10), and at length, in February, the lower Adour was passed,
Bayonne invested, and Soult obliged to withdraw towards the east.

But by this time events on the other side of France had changed
the appearance of the war. Napoleon's threatened invasion of
Russia had taken place; the defensive plan adopted by the Russians
proved successful. The Emperor had himself hastened back to Paris
after the conflagration of Moscow, while his ruined and broken army
struggled home through the terrible suffering of the Russian winter.
As Alexander had foreseen, the reverse of the French had been followed by the defection at first of Prussia and shortly afterwards
of Austria. The powers of Europe were thus again formed in a

coalition. With such troops as he could collect, Napoleon had hurried, in the summer of 1813, to the very furthest confines of Germany, and fought the great battles of Lutzen and Bautzen. But the flower of his troops had been lost in Russia, his armies were no longer what they had been. His enemies in vast numbers began to gather round him. Though victorious at the gigantic battle of Dresden (Aug. 24, 1813), he was unable to make a final stand against the vast armaments of the coalition. Several of his lieutenants were defeated, and at length (Oct. 19), the battle of Leipzig, after three days of fighting, ended in his complete defeat. It is said that on the two sides the killed and wounded amounted to 110,000 men. The victorious allies swept onwards, and just at the close of the year 1813 entered France. The spring of the following year was occupied by the brilliant campaign in which Napoleon exerted all his genius in vain to check the huge masses of the invaders. While Wellington was making good his position in the south of France, in spite of the ability which he displayed, Napoleon was being constantly driven backward upon the east. The effect could not but be felt by the southern army, and Soult deserves great credit for the skill with which he still held at bay the victorious English. He was however defeated at Orthes (Feb. 27), lost Bordeaux (March 8), and was finally driven eastward towards Toulouse, intending to act in union with Suchet, whose army in Catalonia was as yet unbeaten. On the heights upon the east of Toulouse, for Wellington had brought his army across the Garonne, was fought, with somewhat doubtful result, the great battle of Toulouse. The victory has been claimed by both parties; the aim of the English general was however won, the Garonne was passed, the French position taken, Toulouse evacuated and occupied by the victors. The triumph such as it was had cost the victors 7000 or 8000 men, a loss of life which might have been spared, for Napoleon had already abdicated, and the battle was entirely useless. This was the last action of the Peninsula War, in which, after years of steadfast resistance, the English had at length triumphantly swept the French from the Peninsula, and done their full share in the great events which temporarily closed the career of Napoleon.

Battle of Toulouse. April 10, 1814

The negotiations which had terminated in the abdication of Napoleon had, as far as England was concerned, been carried on by the same ministry which had had the duty of conducting the war. The Tory party which

Long tenure of power of the Tory party.

the French Revolution and the policy of Pitt had called into
existence, robbed of the better and more liberal elements which
the presence of Pitt himself and his friends had introduced into
it, had succeeded in spite of its defects and of various opportunities
for a change in continuing its hold upon the Government. There
was at first one important member of it who kept up something

Policy of
Canning.

of the views of Pitt. This was Canning, the Foreign
Minister. But the presence of so incongruous an element tended rather to the weakness than to the strength of the administration ; nor is it certain that in the present crisis of Europe his
views were such as to render him the most efficient minister. Castlereagh, a man of narrower views and of much inferior talent, acted as
War Minister. Between him and Canning a strong antagonism
arose. Canning's errors were those of a liberal and noble mind. He
was anxious to see the Spaniards carry out their insurrection as much
as possible by their own means, and the wish led him to believe the
false tales of their patriotism and resources with which the braggart
spirit of the Spaniards supplied him. This credulity was strengthened
by the reports of Mr. Frere, whom he had sent to the Peninsula as
ambassador, and he was thus induced to misapply the wealth of
England, and to misuse the opportunities which his ·position as
Foreign Minister gave him, so as seriously to weaken the hands of
Wellington. His desire for the political regeneration of Spain blinded
him somewhat to the military necessities of the time, which required
that our general should be invested with almost absolute authority,
and the arrangement of political matters postponed till after the
favourable conclusion of the war. But though he thus not un-

Canning's
quarrel with
Castlereagh.

frequently threw obstacles in Wellington's way, Canning
by no means approved of the inefficient administration
of Castlereagh, and the constant starvation of the
military side of the Peninsula War. So far had the quarrel with
the War Minister extended that Canning had contrived, not perhaps
so openly and straightforwardly as could be wished, to extort from the
Prime Minister a promise that Lord Castlereagh should be removed
from his responsible situation, failing which he declared that he
would himself withdraw. His support was so necessary to the
Prime Minister that he had persuaded him to remain in office. But
Canning had throughout privately expressed the strongest disapprobation of the Walcheren expedition, and when its failure became
known, and when inquiries upon the subject brought to light the
fact that, while sitting in the same Cabinet with Castlereagh, he had

been in fact intriguing for his dismissal, the quarrel came to a point. Sharp words were exchanged between the ministers, and the consequence was a duel (Sept. 22), in which Canning was slightly wounded. It was of course impossible for the antagonists to serve longer in the same ministry. They both resigned, and their example was followed by the Duke of Portland, whose failing health had from the first rendered him unfit for his position, and whose weakness was exhibited in allowing so grave a quarrel to spring up within the limits of his Cabinet. It became necessary to reconstitute the ministry, and after a fruitless negotiation with Lords Grey and Grenville—with so little reality in it that Grey did not think it worth his while to come to London on the subject—Perceval, who had long been the most important person in the Cabinet, assumed the nominal direction, and Lord Wellesley, who had lately been serving as ambassador in Spain, where he had superseded Mr. Frere, was induced to accept the ministry of foreign affairs. Lord Castlereagh was succeeded by Lord Liverpool at the War Office, with Lord Palmerston as under secretary. The reconstruction of the ministry made no difference in its general tendencies. The introduction of Lord Wellesley was indeed a slight improvement; he entered the ministry chiefly for the purpose of supporting his brother's views in the Peninsula. This to the best of his abilities he did, but he was constantly thwarted by the mediocre men with whom he was joined, and with whom he was never able to work comfortably. By far the ablest and best writer in the Cabinet, his despatches were constantly criticised and altered. His colleagues could not understand the greatness of the openings afforded in the Peninsula, and after two years of office he withdrew (Feb. 19, 1812). The opportunity occurred in a great ministerial crisis caused by the renewed insanity of the King, which it was believed must have produced a change of ministry. The Regent, however, retained Mr. Perceval in office, and upon his death Lord Liverpool was called to succeed him, and continued in office till 1827, so that in fact from the fall of the Grenville ministry to that date, though with some change in the *personnel*, there was a continuance of the Tory rule.

Reconstruction of the ministry. Oct. 1809.

Continuation of the same ministry till 1827.

In November 1810 the King, who had never thoroughly got over the failure of the Walcheren expedition, and the disgrace of Lord Chatham and the Duke of York, was still further shaken by the death of the Princess Amelia, and before long it appeared that he had become hopelessly insane. After

Illness of the King Nov. 1810.

several prorogations it was resolved (December 20) that it was the duty of Parliament to supply the existing defect in the organization of Government. A precedent for the action of the ministry was drawn from Pitt's conduct under similar circumstances in 1788. It was determined to reproduce, though in a somewhat modified form, the restrictions then laid upon the power of the Regent.

The Regency Bill. Feb. 1811. But the Prince of Wales was by no means disposed to submit to these restrictions, and induced his brothers to join in a protest against them. Nor did the Opposition fail to see the probable advantage which would accrue to them from a more unlimited regency; they regarded it as certain that Grenville and Grey would be called to office, and they had no wish to curtail the power of the Crown when wielded by men ready to rectify the mismanagement under which they thought the country was suffering. But their hopes were destined to be speedily extinguished. In spite of his protest the Bill restricting the Regent was passed (Feb. 5), and the Prince took the oaths before the Privy Council. He had already made up his mind that it would be better to continue the present ministry, for a personal quarrel had arisen between him and his Whig friends. He had requested Grenville and Grey to draw up a reply to addresses from the two Houses which had been presented to him in January. They had found considerable difficulty in complying with his request, for Grenville had been a member of Pitt's ministry when he restricted the regency in 1788, while Grey then as now was a member of the Opposition ; but by careful suppression of the difficulties, a reply was drawn out and submitted to the Prince. Such a compromise was not what he had expected ; he summoned his friend Sheridan to assist him in criticising the reply. The paper was returned with pungent and witty marginal remarks, and a wholly different form of reply suggested. The Whig Lords took umbrage at the levity and rudeness of the Prince, and did not refrain from expressing their anger, a line of conduct which, as might have been expected, in the case of a man of such selfish and merely personal politics as the Prince, was warmly resented. Moreover, the flattery of the Queen, and the adhesion to him of his brothers, who wished for the

The Perceval ministry continued. continuation of the Perceval ministry, together with the falsely hopeful reports of the physicians, which led him to think that his regency would be a short one, induced him to accept the situation ; and immediately after having taken the oaths he declared his intention to retain Mr. Perceval. Although at first expressing his dislike to his ministers, before long entirely won over by their courtly language, he began to speak of his old friends as " the wicked politicians." The regency was at first fixed for one year only. . At the end of that time, that is, in February 1812, after a few more overtures to the Whig Lords to form a coalition with his present ministry, which he must have known was impossible, the Prince allowed the ministry to continue as before, Castlereagh being readmitted to office, and Lord Sidmouth becoming President of the Council. The joy of Mr. Perceval at the happy issue of   Assassination of the affair was proportionate to the fear he had felt at the   Mr. Perceval. thought of losing office ; but it was destined to be short-   May 1812. lived, for on the 11th of May, as he entered the House of Commons, he was assassinated by a lunatic of the name of Bellingham.

Again there was much negotiation, and an attempt to introduce Lord Wellesley and Mr. Canning to the ministry. Of   Lord Liverpool course they could not serve with Castlereagh ; they   made Premier. were then asked to form a ministry with Grenville and Grey, but these Lords objected to the Peninsula War, to which Wellesley was pledged. Grenville and Grey then attempted a ministry of their own, but quarrelled with Lord Moira on the appointments to the Household ; and as an American war was threatening, and the ministry had already given up their Orders in Council (one of the chief causes of their unpopularity), the Regent, rather than remain longer without a ministry, intrusted Lord Liverpool with the premier-ship, with Castlereagh as his Foreign Secretary, and the old ministry remained in office.

Before the day of triumph of this ministry arrived, while Napoleon was still at the height of his power, and the success of Wellington as yet uncertain, England had drifted into war with   War with America. It is difficult to believe that this useless war   America. might not have been avoided had the ministers been   May 1812. men of ability. It arose from the obstinate manner in which the Government clung to the execution of their retaliatory measures against France, regardless of the practical injury they were inflicting upon all neutrals. The causes of irritation have already been mentioned. America, adopting the policy of England, had proceeded to retaliate ; an embargo was laid upon trade both with England and France, and commercial relations with Europe practically broken off. An attempted arrangement between the two countries in 1809 had pro-duced but little result. But though foreign trade had diminished, the demand for home manufactures in America had largely increased ; the populations of the Northern and Eastern States were therefore satisfied with the existing state of things and decidedly averse to war, with its certain expenditure and probable injury to their manufactures. In the South the case was different. Without manufactures to supply the loss sustained by the restricted export of their tobacco and sugar, not in immediate contact with English territory, as were the Northern States, and led by an aristocratic and slave-owning race, the Whites of the South were inclined to war. The Presidents were Virginians, the Southerners had a superiority in Congress, and in May of 1812 it became plain that war must result unless the Orders in Council were repealed. But England was in confusion owing to the assassination of Perceval, and it was not till the middle of June, when war had been already declared, that Brougham's motion for the withdrawal of the Orders was carried. The concession, awkwardly made in the face of the American threats, came too late. The Americans had already made up their minds, and planned an invasion of Canada.

It was a war without great events. The attempts of the Americans upon Canada failed. Here and there a slight

Character of the war.

success attended the English arms, and the deep anger of our enemies was moved by the irksome blockade of their coast, and the employment of the savage Indian tribes as our allies. But if fairly successful on land, the English were to their great astonishment thoroughly worsted upon the sea. Ship after ship was taken by the American frigates. Nor was it till our commanders consented to recognise the fact that the classification of the two navies was wholly different, and that an American frigate was in tonnage and weight of metal a match for an English fifty-gun ship, that these disasters were brought to an end. It was an additional blow to the pride of England that the sailors by whom her ships were defeated were largely drawn from her own people. From the wretchedness prevalent in England, from high taxes, commercial difficulties, and the severe laws of impressment, men fled for refuge to America; and it is said that as many as 16,000 Englishmen were serving on board the American fleet.

The war was really so causeless and so prejudicial to the success of the allies in Europe, that the Emperor of Russia

Attempted negotiations.

attempted, in 1813, to bring it to a close by mediation, and although his offer was declined, a negotiation was entered into at Ghent which ultimately proved successful. But before the negotiators advanced far in their labours the war threatened to assume a more serious character. On the cessation of hostilities in the south of France, a considerable number of the English troops were embarked at Bordeaux direct for America, without even being allowed to return home, and increased energy began to show itself in all directions. A large fleet under Rear-Admiral Cockburn, and a body of troops under General Ross, were despatched to the Chesapeake, and a combined attack by land and water was made upon Washington, the Federal capital. The success of the expedition, which was complete, was stained by the destruction of   Capture of all public property, offices, and buildings in the city.   Washington. An outcry was raised, not only in America but in Europe, at what was regarded as an act of vandalism. It is said that the English Government had ordered it as a retaliation for the barbarities of the Americans on the Canadian frontier, and as it is confessed that private property was scrupulously spared, it may well be a question whether in fact such a destruction of national property is not a better manner of exhibiting the severity of war than the destruction of private property which so constantly attends it.

The capture of Washington was followed by other expeditions of a like nature with less satisfactory results. Large and systematic operations against a continent are at all times difficult, and certainly they were beyond the capacity of the English ministry as then constituted. They relapsed into all the old errors of the American War, and the military operations were reduced to mere piratical excursions. An effort was indeed made upon the only side where a base of operations existed, but on so small a scale and so badly directed as to be entirely useless. A combined attack by land and water was arranged against Plattsburg upon Lake Champlain. The dilatoriness of the commander, Sir George Prevost, allowed the flotilla to begin the fight unaided; it was completely beaten, and its destruction putting an end to all hope of success, the army withdrew. An attack on Baltimore met with no better fate, but the greater part of the province of Maine was taken and occupied. The arrival of the Peninsula troops, no longer well commanded, had produced but little effect; the negotiations at Ghent were gradually drawing to a conclusion. The Convention was signed on the 24th of December. It was, as might be expected from the temper of the two nations, little more than a compromise. The real points at issue were scarcely touched, the boundaries were left for future negotiation. Such as it was it came too late to save England from one more disaster. An expedition similar in character to those already mentioned had been directed against New Orleans. The place was vigorously defended by General Jackson. Natural difficulties and mismanagement met the English at every turn. The earth was too sandy to allow of redoubts ; while the Americans used cotton bales, which answered admirably as defences, the English found nothing better than barrels of sugar and molasses. When the storming parties reached the enemy's lines they found that their fascines and scaling-ladders had been neglected ; the assault became impracticable. As the approach of the town had been completely exposed to the fire of the enemy, very heavy loss had been sustained, three English generals, and among them Sir Edmund Pakenham, had been killed, and Lambert, who had succeeded to the command, thought it better to withdraw the army.

The American War was thus still at its height when the ministry
Abdication of   had been called upon to arrange the fate of the late Con-
Napoleon.   queror of Europe. When the allies, in their advance
towards France, had assembled at Frankfort, not yet certain of success, and conscious that their work would be easy could they separate Napoleon's interests from those of the nation, they had offered to negotiate at a general Congress upon the fixed condition that France should abandon Italy, Holland, Germany and Spain, and confine itself to its natural boundaries. Napoleon, suspecting not without reason their intentions in accepting the Congress, had refused the conditions. His refusal had been followed by a very able proclamation of the allies, separating the interests of the ruler from that of the people, and promising that France should retain its just weight in the balance of nations. Conscious of the effect of this declaration, which exactly suited the feelings of the majority of Frenchmen, Napoleon hastened to accept the conditions. But he was told it was too late. Traitors had already informed the allied sovereigns that they were strong enough to avoid compromise. The great campaign which followed had shown how much could yet be done by the Emperor's genius. Again negotiations were opened at Châtillon ; Napoleon expressed the utmost readiness to accept the terms of Frankfort. But the ultimatum of the allies had now risen, the Rhine boundary was no longer to be conceded. Napoleon could not make up his mind to allow France to issue from the war less than when he had first taken possession of the Government. The Treaty of Châtillon was broken off and war was again resumed ; and as though to express the completeness of their determination, the allied sovereigns entered into a treaty at Chaumont (March 1), by which

they bound themselves together for twenty years, promised each to supply 150,000 men, to which England was to add a subsidy of £5,000,000. The knowledge of this treaty made Napoleon feel that some desperate stroke alone could save him. He passed with his forces into the rear of the allies; he was nearer, as he himself said, to Vienna than they were to Paris. The movement put them in great perplexity. To leave so formidable a person upon their communications seemed too dangerous a step. Again treason served them in good stead. Their friends in Paris, at the head of whom was Talleyrand, urged them at once to move upon the capital. Joseph. Bonaparte, who had been left in charge there, with Marmont and Mortier, fought a last battle before the very walls. Joseph lost heart, and ordered the marshals to capitulate, the army was withdrawn behind the city, and Paris was in the hands of the allies. This was fatal to all Napoleon's hopes. He came to Fontainebleau, there found himself gradually deserted, heard how his marshals one after the other had joined the victorious allies, and on the 4th of April signed his abdication, consenting to withdraw to the Isle of Elba, which was to be constituted into a principality for his convenience. He was to be allowed 400 soldiers, his wife and child were to be placed in possession of Placentia and Parma, and he was to retain the title of Emperor. In the settlement of the affairs of France and Europe he was to have no voice. The last stroke of ill-fortune seemed to have come upon him when his Austrian wife, over-persuaded by her relations, deserted him, and set off with his young son to Vienna. During his ten months' residence in the Isle of Elba the settlement of Europe was being carried on by the diplomatists of all the powers assembled at Vienna.

Thus the Tory ministry seemed at last to have reaped the fruit of their lengthened efforts, and to have justified their long retention of office. But we shall look in vain for any merit in their policy but one, and that is steadfastness. The accidental discovery, General sketch for it was little more, of a general of surpassing genius of the Tory had enabled them to hide under his greatness their own policy. mediocrity; his skill had covered their constantly-repeated blunders, and fortune had supplied them with an enemy whose enthusiastic self-confidence, arbitrary temper, and insatiable ambition, had neutralized his transcendent genius, had forced upon them allies whom their own skill could not have secured, and had even alienated the people whose natural representative he was. With these advantages they had been able to obtain that success which a fixed line of

policy even when itself erroneous not unfrequently secures. They
had raised England to a position of the highest importance, the success of Europe against Napoleon was indisputably due to her. Yet
it cannot be said that they were urged by patriotic motives. Throughout their conduct had been dictated by the interests of their class.
They had recognized in Napoleon the great subverter of old institutions, the arch-enemy of the aristocratic order. It was in this
capacity chiefly that they had pursued him with such firm and
undeviating hostility. Of the events which took place during their
ministry, of the successful skill and bravery of soldiers and sailors, of
the establishment of national independence whether in England or
on the Continent, all Englishmen may be proud. Those who, reading history by the light of subsequent events, still hold that a
strong aristocratic element is a necessary ingredient of constitutional
liberty will admire their motives. But to those who feel that
growth and advance is the essential principle of the life of a nation,
and that those only are good governors who are capable of understanding and of carrying out the necessities of advancing civilization,
their sole claim to respect (and that is after all no small one) will be
that they knew their own minds, and in spite of all difficulties
realized their object.

The same motive of class aggrandizement which detracts from the
Home virtue of the foreign policy of this ministry underlay
government. the whole administration of home affairs. There was
an incapacity to look at public affairs from any but a class or aristocratic point of view. The natural consequence was a constantly
increasing mass of discontent among the lower orders, only kept in
restraint by an overmastering fear felt by all those higher in rank of
the possible revolutionary tendencies of any attempt at change.
Much of the discontent was of course the inevitable consequence of
the circumstances in which England was placed, and for which the
Government was only answerable in so far as it created those
circumstances. At the same time it is impossible not to blame the
complacent manner in which the misery was ignored and the
occasional success of individual merchants and contractors regarded
as evidences of national prosperity. At the beginning of the year
1810, Perceval, who in the interest of the Government had been
preventing as far as possible all inquiry into the Walcheren failure,
was bold enough at the opening of the session to take credit to himself for that expedition, and to declare that the national prosperity
was great, and that public works had been carried out as suc-

cessfully as in the times of profound peace. Such assertions could not have been made without some slight foundation. While the Continental System and the Orders in Council had together almost closed the European trade, certain other irregular doors had been opened; the removal of the Portuguese court to the Brazils had given hopes of an enlarged South American trade, and the two islands of Heligoland and Anholt had been fortified and turned into smuggling centres with some success. Certain public works, as the Waterloo and Vauxhall bridges, had been opened. But before the year was over the condition of the country surely proved that the prosperity boasted of was a mere phantom. The American trade proved ruinous to those who had rushed into it; the British goods on the Baltic had been seized and confiscated; the public works had been carried on by a lavish issue of paper money, which was now rapidly depreciating. A bad harvest came to increase the difficulties of the time. Early in the spring wheat was already at 102s. a quarter: though £7,000,000 worth was imported, it rose in August to 116s. But then, under the influence of a good harvest, it suddenly dropped to 94s.—thus the agricultural interest was also involved in ruin.

Under all these influences there was a collapse of credit. There were 273 stoppages of payment instead of Depression the ordinary average of 100, and before the year of trade. was out no less than 2314 commissions of bankruptcy were issued. This misery and depression lasted till the end of the war. Indeed, in the following years, 1811 and 1812, it was constantly increasing. The depression of commerce was so great and the collapse of credit so general that an advance of £6,000,000 to the merchants on due security was authorized by Parliament. The withdrawal of Russia from the Continental System, and its apparent inclination to throw off Napoleon's influence, slightly revived business. But this improvement was neutralized by the fearful winter and spring, which destroyed much of the harvest, and again raised the price of wheat. The apparent opposition between the interests of the manufacturing and agricultural classes was very curiously marked. A plentiful harvest in 1813, and the opening of many continental ports, did much to revive both trade and manufactures; but it was accompanied by a fall in the price of corn from 171s. to 75s. The consequence was widespread distress among the agriculturists, which involved the country banks, so that in the two following years 240 of them stopped payment. So great a crash could not fail to affect the manufacturing interest also ; apparently for the instant the very restoration of peace brought widespread ruin.

But whether for the moment it was the agriculturists or the merchants who suffered most, the lower classes were quite sure to suffer. Not only did the Continental System injure the great branches of English industry, the foreign corn ports were also closed. The increase of population since the large introduction of machinery in the last century had gone beyond the resources of home production. The high price of wheat has been already mentioned. Meat also went up from 4d. or 5d. to 10d. a pound. Considering the enormous rate of the price of corn, it was impossible to give wages sufficient to keep the operatives alive. Before the end of the year 1811, wages had sunk to 7s. 6d. a week. The manufacturing operatives were therefore in a state of absolute misery. Petitions signed by 40,000 or 50,000 men urged upon Parliament that they were starving ; but there was another class which fared still worse. Machinery had by no means superseded hand-work. In thousands of hamlets and cottages handlooms still existed. The work was neither so good nor so rapid as work done by machinery ; even at the best of times used chiefly as an auxiliary to agriculture, this hand labour could now scarcely find employment at all. Not unnaturally, without work and without food, these hand-workers were very ready to believe that it was the machinery which caused their ruin, and so in fact it was ; the change, though on the whole beneficial, had brought much individual misery. The people were not wise enough to see this. They rose in riot in many parts of England, chiefly about Nottingham, calling themselves Luddites (from the name of a certain idiot lad who some thirty years before had broken stocking-frames), gathered round them many of the disbanded soldiery with whom the country was thronged, and with a very perfect secret organization, carried out their object of machine-breaking. The unexpected thronging of the village at nightfall, a crowd of men with blackened faces, armed sentinels holding every approach, silence on all sides, the village inhabitants cowering behind their closed doors, an hour or two's work of smashing and burning, and the disappearance of the crowd as rapidly as it had arrived—such were the incidents of the night riots.

Perhaps, however, the agricultural labourer was still worse off. While farmers were selling their corn at 112s., or even at 170s., the

Misery of the lower classes.

The Luddite riots.

quarter—while it paid to take in bits of open down land, get three
crops off it without manuring, and then pass on to the   Misery of the
next piece,—the wretched labourers were told that prices agricultural
were so high that but little could be given them for their labourer.
wages.   The misery was therefore exceedingly great among them;
and even worse than this, the Poor Law stepped in and destroyed
their characters.   For the wages were so low that they could not live
on them, and they were forced to come upon the parish; and the old
Poor Law, in the hands of the farmer guardians, enabled those very
employers who kept the wages low to levy a rate upon their parishes
to support those people whom they were starving, and to give outdoor relief in aid of wages.   In other words, the employer had the
right to compel the country to give him the money to pay his
labourers enough to keep them alive.   Selfish views, too, were mixed
with false political economy.   Many labourers made cheap labour;
many hands, it was thought, made a strong country.   So this strange
grant in aid of wages came to be apportioned according to the number of the family of the recipient; and when the whole state of the
nation pointed to the necessity of a curtailed population, a premium
was given for its increase.

The termination of a war so new in its character, and so universal
as that which for the last eleven years had been wasting Difficulties
Europe, brought with it great difficulties.   On the one attending the
hand arose the question of the position to be taken up of Europe.
by the allies with regard to France; on the other, the reconstitution
of Europe, completely dislocated by the policy of Napoleon.   Both
questions were rendered difficult of solution by the various interests
and mutual jealousies of the powers of the victorious coalition.   But,
—while those European powers who had suffered most severely from
the French arms, and especially Prussia, on which the vengeance of
Napoleon had fallen most heavily, were desirous to treat France as a
conquered nation, so to curtail its dimensions as to render it harmless for the future, and to lay such burdens upon it as might in some
degree recompense them for their losses,—England, which had
never felt the sword of the conqueror, and Russia, ruled by a Czar
much influenced by notions of chivalry and magnanimity, had
already determined upon an opposite course.   Following the opinion
of the founder of their party, the Tory Government which had
succeeded Pitt declared its intention of acting towards France as
towards a friendly power, and of allowing it to retain the same
frontiers as in 1790.   There was not much magnanimity in such

conduct; the Tory party, the champions of legitimacy, could scarcely
avoid restoring the Bourbons ; their view of the balance of Europe
rendered a powerful France almost a necessity ; they could look for
no continental acquisitions for England, and took care to secure the
advantages they required for their maritime and commercial superiority in other directions. But, while restoring the Bourbons, the
English Government found itself compelled by the temper of the
time, the course of circumstances, and the liberal views of the
Emperor of Russia, to restore them only upon conditions. A constitutional government was granted to France, ratified by a charter
securing the chief personal and political rights of the people, such as
the maintenance of the public sales during the Revolution, freedom
of religion, and freedom of the press.

A France thus reconstituted, and holding friendly relations with
the other powers of Europe, would naturally claim its share in the
arrangements of the forthcoming Congress. It would probably have
been wiser had the French Government postponed all definite settlements as to its future limits till that Congress met ; the jealousies
which existed between the allies and their conflicting claims would
have afforded opportunity for securing favourable terms, for by the
Convention, by which France had surrendered the territories held by
her armies in Europe, her troops had been allowed to withdraw
unmolested, and a powerful army could have been rapidly reconstituted. But the allies, guided by Metternich, the Austrian minister,
and determined to keep as far as possible the management of the
Congress in their own hands, insisted on the immediate conclusion

Treaty of
Paris.
May 1814.

of the treaty with France. Eager to gain popularity
by the establishment of peace, the French Government
yielded, and in May the Treaty of Paris was concluded.
It was upon the whole more favourable than France, as a conquered
nation, could have expected. The frontier of 1790 was even slightly
increased : towards the north and towards the Rhine it was advanced
so as to include several important fortresses, especially the strong
place of Landau, and towards the Alps about half of Savoy was also
included. The demands of Prussia for a contribution towards the
expenses of the war were rejected by the influence of Austria and
England, and the treasures of art collected by Napoleon's armies
were allowed to remain in Paris. The one great loss sustained was
the Isle of France. It was upon the sea and among the colonies
that England looked for its reward ; it retained Malta, to secure its
influence in the Mediterranean, the Cape of Good Hope, which it had

won from the Dutch, and now, to complete its naval stations on the road to India, it insisted on the surrender of the Isle of France. The bases for the forthcoming Treaty of Vienna were also roughly laid by this peace. The published articles declared the independence of the States of Germany, the augmentation of Holland under the rule of the Prince of Orange, the independence of Switzerland and of the Italian States outside the limits of the Austrian possessions. Secret articles explained what these loose expressions meant. Belgium was to form the promised increase of Holland, and thus form with it a kingdom absolutely in the interest of England ; the left bank of the Rhine was to supply compensations for the German princes (which meant that it was to be given to Bavaria in exchange for the Tyrol) ; the Po, the Ticino, and Lago Maggiore were to form the boundaries of Austrian Italy, which thus included the territory of Venice ; and Sardinia was to receive Genoa in exchange for the portion of Savoy ceded to France.

The difficulties which were sure to attend the forthcoming Congress were already felt, and it was thought that the solution Visit of the would be rendered easier by the establishment of per- monarchs to England. sonal relations between the powers of the coalition. Aug. 1814. The great monarchs of Eastern Europe were therefore invited to visit the Prince Regent in England. The Emperor of Austria declined to come, but the Czar and the King of Prussia accepted the invitation, and were received with great pomp and enthusiasm. Several weeks were passed in universal gaiety, but the political object of the visit was not attained. The Czar seemed more than ever to occupy the first place among crowned heads ; and the dread of Russian influence, and the determination to oppose its claims in the Congress, were thus only rendered stronger.

The meetings at Vienna, at first appointed for August, had been postponed to September, and thither, after their visit Congress at to England, the monarchs themselves, and the ministers Vienna. who represented the various countries of the Congress, Sept. 1814. betook themselves. The interests of England were intrusted to Lord Castlereagh, a man of considerable firmness, but of mediocre ability, without accurate knowledge or broad views of the politics of Europe, and deficient in the conciliatory deportment so necessary for a successful diplomatist. The negotiators approached their difficult work in a spirit which promised no very good results. Almost of necessity the character of the Congress, and of the treaty it produced, belonged rather to the past than to the future. It was rendered

necessary by the changes created by the French Revolution, and was
in the hands of a coalition called into existence to oppose the Revolution, and consisting chiefly of monarchs whose views were both
absolutist and dynastic. The Czar alone had certain liberal tendencies, but they were so mixed with personal ambition as to excite
mistrust instead of co-operation among the assembled negotiators.
The Congress therefore assumed the form of an old European congress. It was occupied with the personal and peculiar interest of each
sovereign, the increase of territory and influence of each nation, instead
of attempting a settlement of Europe in accordance with any enlarged
or general theory suitable to the great change and growth of ideas
which had been at once the cause and effect of the Revolution.

As far as England was concerned, its interests had already been
The interests chiefly secured by the Treaty of Paris. The new king-
of the various dom of the Netherlands, it was thought, would be strong
countries at enough to hold the mouths of the great rivers of that
the Congress.
country, and thus prevent any revival of the Continental System ;
the road to India was rendered safe by the possession of the Cape
of Good Hope and the Mauritius, while Malta guarded English
influence in the Mediterranean. The maintenance of the old European balance was therefore the chief object which Castlereagh had
now in view, endangered chiefly by the overwhelming power óf
Russia, threatening alike the countries of Europe and our own
Asiatic dominions. The haste with which the Treaty of Paris had
been concluded tied the hands of France, which was represented by
Talleyrand ; and the very moderate ambition of Louis XVIII. limited
the claims of that country to the completion of the downfall of the
Napoleonic system by the removal of Murat from the kingdom of
Naples, and the establishment of the Spanish Princess, the Queen of
Etruria, in the Duchy of Parma, which had been promised to Maria
Louisa, Napoleon's wife. Louis was also anxious to save if possible
the kingdom of Saxony from annihilation. The really important
questions at issue regarded the settlement of the East of Europe and
the fate of Poland and Saxony, which appeared indissolubly connected, so closely were the Courts of Russia and Prussia united. The
Emperor of Russia was a man of enthusiastic temperament and
liberal theories, and at the same time of great ambition. He found
satisfaction for both sides of his character in a plan for the reconstitution of the kingdom of Poland, with a liberal constitution, either
under his own rule as king or under some prince of his house
acknowledging his supremacy. To complete this project he required

the possession of the whole of Poland, a reward which the over-weening value he set on his own services to the coalition induced him to regard as by no means more than his due. Both Prussia and Austria would have been called upon to restore certain portions of Poland which had fallen to their lot in the different partition treaties, but he supposed that his own resignation of certain portions would counterbalance these sacrifices, while Austria would be well rewarded by the possession of Lombardy and Venice, and Prussia by the whole of Saxony. The adhesion of the Saxon king to Napoleon was thought to justify the sovereigns of the coalition in confiscating his country, which, with the approbation of Russia, was claimed in its entirety by the Prussian Government. It is plain that the claims of Russia and Prussia could not but be in the last degree objection-able to Austria. Absolutist in its tendencies, it cared nothing for the freedom of Poland, while the possession of territory conterminous with the hereditary states of Austria would render Russia a most dangerous rival. At the same time, Prussia, the constant object of Austrian jealousy, if Saxony passed into its hands, would at once lose that broken and dislocated shape which had hitherto been its weakness, and would acquire a position in Germany which Austria could scarcely hope to equal. The policy of Austria was therefore clearly marked.

The position of England was not so obvious. It is possible to say now, guided by the light of subsequent events, and led by the spirit of freedom and nationality which has made such vast strides of late years, that the Government of England, the home of free institutions and avowedly the champion of national liberty, should have come forward even then in that capacity, should have rejoiced at the reconstitution of Poland, and have sought the unification of Germany by supporting the power of Prussia, and should have objected to the establishment of Austria in Italy, a country where her rule was certain to be disliked by the population. But the English Government at the time was a Tory Government, bent rather upon restraining than increasing popular tendencies, and under the dominion of three overmastering influences —the desire to secure England from any possibility of a renewal of the Continental System, an extreme jealousy of the pretensions and power of the Russian Emperor, and the wish to establish for some years at all events the peace of Europe. Its policy was therefore inconsistent and shortsighted, though good for the immediate object; fear of the advance of Russia made the English ministry blind to its duties towards Poland; the satisfaction and friendship of France

The policy of England at the Congress

were more important than the rights of Genoa; the immediate
balance of the powers of Germany was more important than the
national aspirations either of Italy or of Germany.

It so happened that the views of France were at this instant
The policy similar to those of England. Before the formal opening
of France. of the Congress an attempt had been made by the four
great powers to get the management of it entirely into their own hands.
France would thus have been excluded from the settlement of Europe;
but Talleyrand was not a man to bear quietly such an exclusion; he
appeared as the champion of the smaller states, and succeeded in
thwarting the efforts of the great powers. This, with other less important causes, had embroiled him with the Emperor of Russia, whose
objects he was thus bent on thwarting. The King of Saxony was a
friend and relative of Louis XVIII.; to save him and his country
from destruction was a part of the French programme. It therefore
suited Talleyrand to adopt the views of Castlereagh.

Thus Austria, France, and England, in conjunction with the smaller
Division of German powers, who looked with great dislike to the
the Congress. annihilation of one of the chief among them, were thrown
upon one side, in opposition to Russia and Prussia. The arrogant and
high-handed manner in which those two powers proceeded to take
temporary possession of the countries which they claimed still further
excited the anger of their opponents. So severe did the dispute grow,
so indissoluble did the knot appear, that war between the powers themselves seemed threatening. The Treaty of Ghent and the conclusion
of the English war with America allowed Castlereagh to act with
more vigour, and in January a secret treaty was entered into
between France, Austria, and England, by which each country
agreed to supply troops to compel, if necessary, the adoption of their
combined policy. Although this treaty was kept a secret, the firm
attitude and the combination of the three powers were so evident
Compromise that, as neither party really wished for war, a com-
agreed to. promise was discovered. About half of Saxony, with
a third of its population, was taken from the King and given to
Prussia, while the Czar, withdrawing from his extreme demand with
regard to Poland, allowed the Duchy of Posen to remain in the
hands of the Prussians, and a considerable portion of Gallicia,
together with the district of Tarnopol, to be retained by Austria,
while Krakow was to become a free and neutral republic. Poland
was thus in part reconstituted, but entirely in the hands of Russia.
These great questions being settled, the arrangements upon the

minor points proceeded with some rapidity; the left bank of the Rhine was given to Bavaria and Prussia; Genoa passed to Sardinia; the two ·houses of Hesse were re-established; Luxemburg was given to the Low Countries; Mayence became a Federal fortress; the Tyrol was restored to Austria; Switzerland was reorganized chiefly in accordance with the arrangements France had made there; the conduct of Murat, who began to show a tendency towards Napoleonism, facilitated the restoration of the Bourbons in Naples; Parma was given to Maria Louisa for her life; and the Congress completed its work by two great declarations of principle, one securing the freedom of the navigation of rivers, the other expressing, what was very dear to Englishmen at the time, a universal disapprobation of the slave trade.

Before the conclusion of these questions Castlereagh had been compelled by the meeting of Parliament to return to England, and the Duke of Wellington had taken his place at Vienna. His work there was not completed when the news arrived that Napoleon had broken loose from Elba, and the Duke was wanted to take command of the allied army in Belgium. The renewal of the common danger produced a temporary harmony among the negotiators at Vienna. The chief questions were rapidly settled, and a joint proclamation, issued by the eight powers which had signed the Peace of Paris, declared Napoleon the public enemy of Europe. The Congress continued its sittings, but military preparations for the time absorbed all attention. *Escape of Napoleon from Elba.*

It was agreed to act in accordance with the Treaty of Chaumont, each of the four great powers supplying its quota of troops, or in the case of England an equivalent in money. While the Prussians and the English with their allies were to advance into France and the Netherlands, the other powers were to pass the Rhine and join in a great advance upon Paris. It was hoped that by the end of April 500,000 men would be ready for the great movement. The French Court had taken refuge in the Netherlands, and as the people of that country were already half inclined to join the French, it seemed certain that that country would be the chief seat of operations; the war there was intrusted to the Anglo-allies under Wellington, and the Prussians under Prince Blücher. The hope of speedy action was quickly seen to be vain. Since the peace many countries had disbanded their troops, many of the best English regiments had been sent to America, and in spite of its long experience, the English Government *Military preparations against Napoleon.*

showed its usual weakness in the war administration. Wellington was convinced of the necessity of postponing the opening of the
campaign till June or July.

This delay gave Napoleon an opportunity of striking the first
blow, and although he could immediately dispose of not more
than 125,000 men, and although the English and Prussian armies
amounted to 220,000, the arrangement of the allied troops gave
him much hope of a successful campaign.   Bent upon covering
Napoleon enters Brussels, uncertain where the blow which he felt
Belgium. sure would soon be struck would fall and in order to
facilitate the subsistence of his troops, Wellington had spread his
army over a long line of frontier, from the neighbourhood of
Charleroi to Antwerp and Ostend. In like manner the Prussian
corps were spread eastward from Charleroi to Liège.   Trusting
to the wide dissemination of the allied troops to render concentration difficult, Napoleon thought to push between the English
and Prussian armies, and to crush them one after the other.
With all his old skill, he rapidly collected his army on the
Sambre, issued on the 14th June a stirring general order, and on the
15th attacked the Prussians at Charleroi, passed the Sambre, and
drove them back along the Namur road to a position near
Sombreffe, which Blücher had already appointed as a point of concentration should he be attacked from Charleroi. At the same time
the left of the French army under Ney was sent directly northward
along the road to Brussels, to clear it of English and prevent the
junction of the allies.

Up to this point Napoleon's plans seemed thoroughly successful.
He had already rendered any immediate junction of the armies
difficult, if not impossible ; with one part of his army he had
already reached the chosen ground of the Prussians, and found it
occupied by one only out of their four corps; with his left he had
advanced to the position of Quatre Bras against the English, where
as yet no considerable portion of the allies had arrived. But a strange
slowness marks his course in this campaign. Instead of bringing
up all his troops for an attack in both directions, in the early
morning of the 16th, he allowed his main body to pass the night on
the Sambre, while there was an interval of twelve miles between
Battle of Ney's position and that of his rear.   Consequently all
Ligny. the morning was passed in bringing up these troops,
and it was past noon before either at Quatre Bras or Ligny any
formidable attacks were made on the enemy. During that time two
more Prussian corps had arrived at Ligny, and Wellington's troops

were hastening to support the small force at Quatre Bras. Napoleon therefore, instead of being able to destroy a single Prussian corps, found himself involved in a bloody and hard-contested battle.   He was indeed victorious, but the victory was not of that crushing and decisive character which his precarious position rendered necessary for him.   At Quatre Bras, instead of a brief skirmish Battle of which would have enabled him to give assistance to Napo- Quatre Bras. leon at Ligny, Ney found it necessary to fight a battle, and that not a successful one.   The Allies, who in the morning were scarcely 8000 strong, made good their position till reinforcements arrived. When evening closed their preponderance was such that Ney was compelled to withdraw his troops to Frasnes.   So hard had he been pressed that he had found it necessary to summon to his aid the corps of D'Erlon, which almost at the same time received orders from Napoleon to fall on the Prussian right flank, and thus complete the victory of Ligny.   Confused by these contradictory orders, D'Erlon's corps of 20,000 men passed the day, without striking a blow, between the two battlefields, in either of which his presence might have had a decisive effect.   As it was, Napoleon overrated the success against the Prussians, and fell into a fatal error with regard to the line of their retreat.   Convinced that they would fall back towards Namur and Liège, he detached Marshal Grouchy with 30,000 men to follow them in that direction, while he himself brought his Retreat of main body to join Ney, with the intention of following Blucher's and destroying the English, who were compelled by army. Blucher's defeat to fall back towards Brussels.   But the Prussian generals, Blücher and Gneisenau, the chief of his staff, were not so easily shaken off.   Determined still to afford assistance to their allies, they withdrew northwards towards Wavre, while Grouchy and his troops were in vain seeking them towards the east.   From ‚ Wavre, which was reached late in the evening of the 17th, Blücher was enabled to assure Wellington of his approach, and to promise the assistance not of two divisions only, for which the English general had asked, but of his whole army.   Relying on this promise, Wellington determined to fight.

To give time for the arrival of the Prussians it was necessary · that his battle should be a defensive one.   The position, Position of which he had long before studied and selected, was Waterloo. admirably adapted for the purpose.   Nearly two miles south of Waterloo is the village of St. Jean, where the highroads from Charleroi and Nivelle towards Brussels join.   Just south of this the undulating country forms a somewhat continuous ridge, lying east

and west, crossed at right angles by the Charleroi road. Along
the south of the ridge lies a rich and cultivated valley, which
in about a mile swells again into a corresponding range of elevated
ground. Three or four farmhouses lie on the foot or on the southern
slope of the northern line of hills, so that the position resembles, as
Wellington said, a wall of a bastion with advancing angles. The

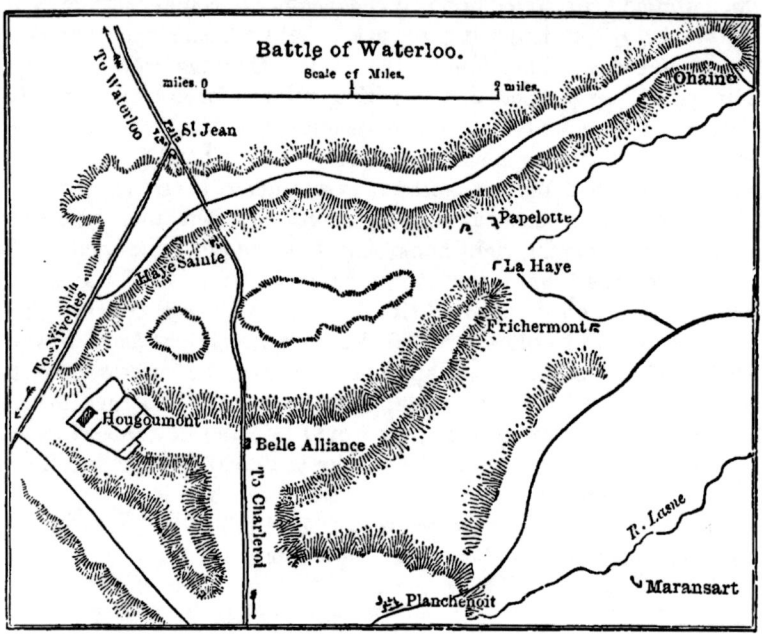

Battle of Waterloo.

English troops were placed along the ridge, and occupied the farmhouses. The centre was placed between the two highroads, having
in front the farm of La Haye Sainte standing on the western side
of the Charleroi road. The right was covered by the château of
Hougomont, with stone buildings and enclosures, while the left
stretched to the farms of Papelotte and La Haye. Wavre is about
seven miles from St. Jean, directly to the east, and expecting the
arrival of Blücher, Wellington allowed his left to be the weakest
part of his line. His care for his right was indeed exaggerated; he
thought it possible that an attempt might be made to reach Brussels
by outflanking him in that direction, and before all things desirous
of preserving the capital, he detached a body of 17,000 men to
Hal (eight miles to the west of his position), and thus seriously and
uselessly weakened his line of battle. The French position corresponded to the English Its centre also lay on the Charleroi road

and the range of heights parallel to those occupied by the English, on which is the farmhouse of La Belle Alliance. Its right extended to Frischermont, opposite to La Haye, having somewhat in its rear the village of Planchenoit; the left reached beyond Hougomont. In number the armies were not unequally matched. Wellington commanded about 68,000 men, Napoleon 70,000, but the English army consisted of troops of various nations, some of whom were thoroughly untrustworthy, and was inferior in cavalry by at least 3000 men, and in artillery by upwards of 100 guns.

By eight o'clock on the morning of the 18th the English were under arms, but Napoleon, ignorant of the movements of the Prussians, and anxious probably to excite the Battle of Waterloo. temper of his own troops, and display his power to those of the allies who were already wavering in their allegiance, delayed his attack till nearly mid-day, and employed the morning in a great review of his troops. The weather also on the 17th had been very stormy, the ground was saturated and heavy; and though this difficulty would likewise have affected his opponents, firm ground was no doubt more important for the attack than for the defence. It is probable that those wasted hours saved the English army, for the same condition of the ground told with terrible force upon the advance of the Prussians, who had to make their way through swampy defiles, where the artillery could scarcely be moved. Their advance was very slow, and nothing but the firm determination of their leaders to keep their word to Wellington would have enabled them to overcome the obstacles in their way. The battle began about half-past eleven by an assault upon Hougomont, which Napoleon intended to carry, and thus mask his real great attack upon the centre and left of the English. The firm resistance of the garrison, consisting of a portion of the English Guards and the troops of Nassau and Hanover, frustrated this first move. The capture of the château, which should have been a mere preliminary step in the great plan, became an object in itself; fresh troops were constantly brought against it, it was as constantly reinforced from the English line, and throughout the whole day its defence neutralized a considerable portion of the French infantry. It was not till five o'clock that Napoleon brought a couple of howitzers to bear upon it. Though the buildings were speedily in flames, the defence was continued, and it remained throughout the day uncaptured. During the first attack upon Hougomont skirmishing and firing had been going on along the whole line preparatory to the great movement against the left. That movement was rather hastened than post-

poned by a discovery which was made about one o'clock. About
that time troops were seen moving near a wood to the north-east of
the English position between Wavre and Ohain. At first Napoleon
took them for the troops of Grouchy, to whom he had sent information of the true direction of the Prussian retreat. They proved however to be the foremost troops of Bülow's Prussian corps. But the
Emperor, still believing that Grouchy would at all events prevent
the arrival of the main body of the Prussians, determined if possible
to complete the destruction of the English before taking notice of
the approaching troops. At half-past one, under a furious cannonade,
the first corps, D'Erlon's, marched against the English left between
Papelotte and La Haye Sainte. Although their peculiar formation, in
great closely-packed masses, exposed them fearfully to the fire of the
English artillery, they pressed forward up the English slope, threw
the first line, consisting of allies, into confusion, and were not repulsed
till Picton brought up the main body of the English left, who
charged them with the bayonet and drove them backward. As they
were already shaken, the English heavy cavalry, the Household
Brigade, and what is known as the Union Brigade, consisting of the
Scotch Greys, the Enniskillen Dragoons, and Royals, charged with
fearful effect. Carried away by their energy, they rode right up the
French slope to the battery of La Belle Alliance; scattered and
exhausted by their charge, they were fallen upon and very roughly
handled by the French Lancers, and only saved from destruction by
the advance of the English light cavalry. However, the first great
attack of the French had been triumphantly repulsed, though with
terrible loss. Both Picton and Ponsonby, who commanded the
cavalry, were killed. It was not long before a second attack was
made. Apparently about four o'clock, Ney was ordered to assault
the centre and right centre of the English to the west of the Charleroi
road. The attack was made chiefly with cavalry. Much of the
infantry were indeed employed round Hougomont and in the attack
of La Haye Sainte, which never ceased. For two hours the cavalry
charges continued; they were opposed by the allied troops thrown
into square, the squares being placed checkerwise behind the crest
of the ridge. It is uncertain whether any squares were broken; it is
certain at all events that though the line on the whole held firm,
reinforcements had to be brought from the right, and that there was
a moment between five and six o'clock when the centre was in the
greatest danger. After an heroic defence La Haye Sainte had been
abandoned for want of ammunition. The French held therefore a
position close to the English ridge, and the infantry of Donzelot's

division were gradually making their way to the line which the
cavalry charge had shattered. But to complete the lodgment effected
in the line on the ridge more infantry were absolutely necessary, and
these were not forthcoming. When Ney sent to demand them of the
Emperor, his messenger was met with the reply, "Does he want me
to make them?" In fact, since about half-past four o'clock the
advance of the Prussians had made itself clearly felt. The Comte de
Lobau had been sent to check them, and with him some battalions of
the Imperial Guard. But the numbers of the Prussians constantly
increased; it was in vain that they were more than once driven out of
Planchenois by the Guard, at six o'clock they had established themselves there, threatening even the rear of the French and the
Charleroi road, their line of retreat; and by seven o'clock Ziethen's
corps, which had pushed directly westward, had joined the left of the
English army, so that the French troops in Papelotte occupied an
advanced angle, surrounded both in front and flank by the enemy.
It was thus that reinforcements could not be sent to Ney, and the
second great effort of the French was rendered useless. But
Napoleon did not yet give up all for lost. He knew that the
English must be much exhausted, and determined to try one great
effort more with that portion of the Imperial Guard which had still
been kept in reserve. It was a general assault along the whole line,
but the most important part of it was the advance of the Guard upon
the English centre. To oppose them the English brigade of Guards
under Maitland had been brought forward. As the French columns
topped the ridge the Guards sprang to their feet, and at a distance
of fifty paces poured in a fire which shook the advancing masses, and
charged them with the bayonet. The columns of the Guard rolled
backward to the valley. At the same time a second column had met
with the same fate; the 52nd regiment under Colborne had advanced
so as to form an angle with the main line; as the French column
passed them they poured in a destructive fire, and charged directly
upon their flank. The course of that charge was unchecked, the 52nd
regiment continued to follow the flying French right across the valley.
Almost at the same time, the French in the angle at Papelotte had
also been driven back by the Prussians; and the English light
cavalry under Vandelour and Vivian had likewise charged, over-
throwing the troops opposed to them; thus in three parts of the field
the French were in flight. A general order to advance was given, and
after a short but broken resistance, the whole mass of the French
army fled in complete rout. About nine o'clock Wellington and
Blücher met at the farmhouse of La Belle Alliance, lately the

French headquarters. The pursuit was intrusted to the Prussians, less exhausted than their English allies, and was followed up by Gneisenau along the Charleroi road as far as Frasnes. The loss in this great battle was very heavy on all sides; that of England is put at 13,000, that of Prussia at 7000, and of France between 23,000 and 30,000. It was however decisive.

The advance of the allies into France was unchecked, and on the 7th of July Paris was again occupied. The entrance of the allies upon the country of France at once exhibited the different feelings by which they were actuated; while Blücher and the Prussians thought of nothing but vengeance, Wellington, true to the constant policy of England, insisted upon regarding France as a friendly country to which he was restoring its legitimate sovereign. He succeeded in restraining his violent colleague, who wished to put Napoleon to death, to lay a large contribution on Paris, and to blow up the bridge of Jena over the Seine, the name of which he considered an insult to Prussia. Wellington had no instructions how to act with regard to Napoleon, he therefore allowed him to follow his own course. The Emperor, embarking in an English frigate, the Bellerophon, attempted in his usual theatrical manner to claim the hospitality of the Prince Regent, but the dread of his name and ambition, and the proved danger of allowing him to remain in Europe, prevented the English Government from entertaining any such ideas, and Napoleon was sent to end his days as a prisoner in St. Helena.

The allies in Paris.

Napoleon banished to St. Helena.

The influence of England, naturally increased by the great part it had played in the war in Belgium, was sufficient to give the direction to the negotiations which followed the second restoration of the Bourbons. The Government succeeded in procuring that the Treaty of Vienna completed on June 9th and the first Treaty of Paris (May 1814) should be upon the whole maintained, but it could not refuse to allow some punishment to fall on France for the events of "the hundred days." The country was rigorously confined to its limits in 1790, losing all the additions which the first Treaty of Paris had given it; it was compelled to bear much of the expenses of the war; while its immediate good conduct was secured by an army of occupation, which was for five years to hold the northern fortresses under the command of the Duke of Wellington. The war contribution was to consist of 700,000,000 francs, a sum which was to be paid in five years, during which time the northern fortresses were held as guarantee. This treaty was signed on the 20th of November.

Second Treaty of Paris. Nov. 20, 1815.

England had one more piece of work to do before laying down her arms. The attention of the Congress of Vienna had been called to the condition of the Mediterranean, where commerce was interrupted, and the liberty of Christians imperilled by the piratical fleets of the slave-holding states of the Barbary coasts. A general co-operation against the pirates had been proposed, but no definite resolution was arrived at. To England, unquestioned mistress of the sea, and herself, by her new position in the Ionian Isles, a Mediterranean power, fell the duty of suppressing the evil. Early in 1816, therefore, Lord Exmouth, in command of the Mediterranean squadron, was instructed to visit the Mahomedan states ; he was to insist upon the release of Ionian slaves, and to negotiate a peace with the Mahomedans in the interests of Sardinia and Naples. From Algiers alone could opposition be expected. But the Government there made no objections to the admiral's demands ; the Ionian slaves were released freely, those of Naples and Sardinia upon the payment of a ransom. At Tunis, the next port visited, an accident changed the aspect of affairs. Lord Exmouth, took advantage of a mistake of his interpreter to declare that it was not the wish only but the fixed determination of the Prince Regent that slavery should cease altogether. Tripoli and Tunis submitted, and set free their slaves ; but Algiers, a stronger power, demanded time to refer the matter to Constantinople, promising to deal directly with the English Government. Meanwhile in Parliament the principle of ransoming the slaves had been strongly censured, and a general feeling that force should be used had arisen. A barbarous attack by Algerine soldiers upon the crews of some coral-ships at Bona allowed the Government to take advantage of this feeling, by despatching Lord Exmouth to complete his work. On the 27th of August, having been joined at Gibraltar by a small Dutch squadron, Lord Exmouth approached Algiers. After waiting two hours for a reply to his terms he placed his ships alongside the batteries in positions carefully marked out beforehand. The work of destruction was complete, the forts were reduced to ruins, the fleet that lay within the mole was burnt. For nine hours the battle raged, then when the ammunition was nearly expended the ships withdrew from their somewhat dangerous position. Their work had been effective : on the following morning the English terms were accepted, and on the 31st, 1200 slaves were embarked in the fleet, making in all more than 3000 whom Lord Exmouth had delivered.

The completion of the settlement of Europe had been carried out during the recess of Parliament. From July 1815 to February 1. 1816, the Government had been able to act entirely unchecked. On that day Parliament reopened, and Castlereagh resumed his seat in

Opposition in the Parliament. Feb. 1, 1816.

all the triumph of his completed negotiations. But with the conclusion of the war came the hour of trial for the Tory ministry. The mediocrity of their talent. the reactionary character of their political views, had been forgotten or even regarded as favourable points in their administration, while they stood forth firmly and energetically to express and give effect to the great wish of the nation, the destruction of the Napoleonic rule. With the return of peace the great questions of home politics were again becoming of importance, and the tendencies of the party fostered by their successful warfare were to call into existence an opposition not only in Parliament but among the nation at large. Already voices were raised against the late negotiations ; though, no doubt, the real magnanimity shown towards France, the advantages gained for England on the sea, and the security for some years of peace which the elaborate system of balance was thought to give, were fully in accordance with the wishes of the majority of the nation. There were men who, undazzled by the glories of the late war, saw that the policy of England had in fact favoured absolutism, —that, for the sake of the balance of power, countries had been handed over quite irrespective of the wishes of the people to sovereigns for whom they felt no natural affection,—that a dynasty disliked by a large section of the people had been forced upon France, and was upheld by English bayonets, and that in spite of the efforts of England the influence of Russia had been increased. It appeared to them that the intercourse with foreign powers had rendered our negotiators absolutists. Their conduct with regard to the Holy Alliance showed

The Holy Alliance. Sept. 1815.

that this was not in fact the case. The Holy Alliance, or Convention of September, by which the enthusiastic and sentimental Emperor of Russia joined with his brother sovereigns of Prussia and Austria to declare that henceforward their policy should be ruled on Christian principles alone, had been rejected by the English Government, which saw danger in this brotherly and religious bond between absolute monarchs, and declared through the Duke of Wellington that the English Parliament would require " something more precise." In fact, though in no way wishing to disturb the English Constitution, the Tory Government had been led into a course of policy which was not in accordance with English

traditions. The conclusion of a war the burden of which had been
upon the whole patiently borne, should have brought with it the
real blessings of peace ; but these were not found in the declaration
of the Government that it intended to keep up the war taxes, and to
keep on foot an army of 150,000, an intention which, when taken in
conjunction with the close alliances entered into with foreign powers,
seemed to mean that England was henceforward to attempt to take
its place as one of the great military powers of the Continent.

It was upon the two points of taxation and economy that the
Government first met with opposition. Mr. Vansittart, Extravagance
Chancellor of the Exchequer, declared his intention of of the
continuing half the income and property tax, which Government.
from the first had been avowedly a war tax. The Opposition to this
measure was headed in the Commons by Brougham. By a skilful
use of parliamentary tactics, he succeeded in gaining time, which he
employed in procuring a flood of petitions exhibiting the feeling of
the country so strongly that the Government was beaten. Apparently
in dudgeon at his defeat, the Chancellor of the Exchequer said that
as he had lost the income tax he should also throw over the malt tax,
a step which Castlereagh explained by saying that Government was
going to contract a loan, and £2,000,000 or £3,000,000 more or less
would make no difference. The recklessness of this assertion points
to one of the evils which the late war had produced ;—an unbounded
and lavish supply of money, and the habit of spending almost without question if success could be obtained, had destroyed all idea of
economy in the minds of the ministers. The angry feeling excited in
the people by this carelessness of the public money was not diminished by the extravagances of the Court, and the constant demands
for money to supply the deficiencies of the Civil List. Although
£800,000 was the sum granted in exchange for the hereditary
revenues, the average of late years had been considerably above a
million ; in 1815 it had reached nearly a million and a half. On
this point the ministers were themselves obliged to take the initiative,
and a Bill was passed for the better regulation of the Civil List.
But while the demand for economy, for the reduction of the war
expenditure, and the return of England to its usual independent
position with regard to the Continent, afforded themes for the Opposition in Parliament, an agitation of far more importance had sprung
into existence outside its walls.

At the opening of the session the Prince Regent's speech had con-
gratulated the country upon the prosperity of agriculture, and of all

branches of trade and manufacture. But it was, in fact, a time of
unexampled distress. The principle of protection which
had found favour with the mercantile world in the
seventeenth and eighteenth centuries had been extended to agriculture. In 1670, a period of great plenty having reduced the price of
corn, it was thought necessary to impose heavy dues on its importation. Up to 53s. 4d. a duty of 16s. a quarter was imposed, between
that and 80s., a duty of 8s. a quarter. The price at which importation, free or at a nominal duty, was allowed had been more than once
changed. In 1804 it had been set at 66s. During the latter years of
the war there had been constantly deficient harvests. In 1812 and
1813 the quarter of wheat had risen to 171s. The average price
during six years, from 1808 to 1813, had been 108s. During several
of those years the Continental System had virtually excluded foreign
competition. The effect of the high prices was most disastrous upon
agriculture ; while the suffering of the labourer had, as has been
explained, been very great, the class of farmer had changed, the
careful small cultivator had given place to ostentatious spendthrifts.
To secure great returns land wholly unfitted for the purpose had
been brought under the plough, crop after crop of corn had been
grown to the exhaustion of the soil, and many advantageous and
necessary forms of agriculture had been thrown aside for the cultivation of corn. The year 1813 was one of extraordinary plenty, the
surplus crop was enough to continue that plenty during the two
following years ; the effect was a very rapid fall in prices. Such a
fall naturally entailed the restoration of a better system of husbandry,
and the ruin of many of those who had embarked on the false course.
Peace added still further to this distress. Violent efforts were made
in Parliament by the landed interest, which was very strong, to
bolster up the evil system. It was proposed in 1813 that importation should be subject to a prohibitory duty till the price of wheat
reached 105s. the quarter. This demand was reduced to 84s. in
1814. Circumstances prevented its being carried then, but in 1815,
when the foreign markets were again opened, the terror of approaching cheapness enabled farmers and landlords to combine and hurry
through the House a Corn Law, fixing the price at which corn might
be imported at 80s. In spite of this, however, the distress continued. In fact, the false inflation of late years was giving way, and
agriculture entering upon a more natural course. The agricultural
interests still complained, and still asserted the necessity of relief,
but as, in order to win their support, the Government had already

Agricultural depression.

given up the malt tax, there was really scarcely anything left to give them, and their complaints remained unanswered ; and as the distress, although it was caused chiefly by the fault of the agriculturalists, and was but a fair counterpoise to the enormous profits they had lately been making, was a terrible reality, the poorer classes continued to suffer.

The depression was not confined to the agricultural interest. The removal of the restrictions caused by the Continental Commercial System excited lively hopes among the trading com- depression. munity. During the war our exports had chiefly depended upon an organized contraband trade. Even so, in 1811, shipments had been made to the Continent to the value of £11,000,000. It was supposed that, without restrictions, the sum might be doubled. Everybody wished for a share in the golden harvest, and much money was transferred from legitimate and lucrative trade to the purchase of colonial produce for exportation. But what is called effective demand for any commodity depends not on the desire of the purchaser, but upon his power of purchase. The exhausting wars of late years so limited that power of purchase that the exports of England either lay in the ports unsold or were got rid of at less than the cost price. Nor did our restrictive commercial policy allow a ready interchange of commodities, which might have tended to render the disaster less. Peace with America had produced somewhat the same effects. Thus, both in agriculture and in commerce, widespread suffering and distress existed.

The difficulties were increased at the time by a considerable reduction in the circulating medium. The fall in agricultural profits had ruined many banks in agricultural districts, and induced others to restrict their issue of paper money. A severe winter, a Riots and deficient harvest, and the rise of the price of wheat political before the close of the year (1815) again to 103s., meetings. came to complete the general misery. The effect was a widespread series of riots ; rick-burning and machine-breaking were constant, especially in the east of England. At Littleport, in the isle of Ely, the town was for two days in the hands of the mob (May 22), and the tumult was only suppressed after the military had been called out. In the coal and iron districts, though the people on the whole behaved well, great meetings of unemployed operatives took place ; while in Nottingham and the neighbourhood the Luddite disturbances broke out with fresh vehemence. The discontent and unhappiness of the people before long assumed the shape of a political movement.

The change must be attributed to the writings of Cobbett more than to any other single cause. For some years he had published a Liberal periodical called " The Weekly Political Register," in which, with remarkable clearness of style and simple power of argument, he had constantly attacked the Government. In 1816, he changed the price of his paper from a shilling to twopence, and it at once became the oracle of the working classes. His view was, that all the evils of the time might be cured by reform of Parliament. He indeed went far beyond what the nation was then fit for, demanding universal suffrage and annual Parliaments. But his work was the beginning of the great agitation which continued till the passing of the Reform Bill of 1832.

Against this new sort of opposition without the walls of Parliament the Government set to work with violent measures of repression. The Hampden Clubs, which had sprung up in all directions for purposes of parliamentary reform, no doubt had fallen in many cases into the hands of dangerous demagogues. In London they appear to have become connected with a body of men known as Spencean philanthropists, after Spence, who, at the beginning of the century, had made himself notorious by his socialistic plans. To this society belonged Thistlewood, the two Watsons, and a man of the name of

Meeting in
Spa Fields.
Dec. 2, 1816.

Preston. Castle, a spy of the police, crept in among them, and probably urged them to more reckless action than they would otherwise have taken. According to his account, a great plot was on foot for taking the Tower, seizing the Government, and establishing a Committee of Public Safety. A meeting in Spa Fields in connection with this plot was held upon the 2nd of December. It was to be addressed by Mr. Hunt, a vain and empty demagogue, but before he arrived the Spenceans had begun to act upon their own authority. Young Watson had led a number of men to Snow Hill to ransack a gunsmith's shop, and had there shot a gentleman who had remonstrated with him. The crowd then marched to the Royal Exchange, where they were met by the Lord Mayor, who courageously withstanding them, with only seven assistants, easily dispersed them. Preston appears also singlehanded to have climbed the wall of the Tower, and have summoned the guard to surrender. Beyond this nothing formidable was done.

While hunger and misery, the depression of trade, and the influence of a few able demagogues, were driving the poorer classes to acts of violence, and a dangerous union was being established between social and political discontent, the middle classes were

gradually arriving at the same conclusion as their inferiors with
regard to the necessity of a thorough change in the Petition from
constitution of Parliament. In December, only a few the Corporation
weeks after the uproar in Spa Fields, the Corporation of of London.
London, of late the firm supporters of the policy of Government,
addressed a petition to the Prince Regent, which throws a striking
light upon the feelings which the conduct of Government since the
war had excited. After a rapid summary " of the distress and misery,
no longer limited to one portion of the Empire, and under the irresistible pressure of which the commercial, agricultural, and manufacturing interests are equally sinking," the address goes on to say :
" Our grievances are the natural effect of rash and ruinous wars,
unjustly commenced and pertinaciously persisted in, where no
rational object was to be attained ; of immense subsidies to foreign
powers to defend their own territories or to commit aggressions on
those of our neighbours ; of a delusive paper currency ; of an unconstitutional and unprecedented military force in time of peace ; of the
unexampled and increasing magnitude of the Civil List ; of the
enormous sums paid for unmerited pensions and sinecures ; and of a
long course of the most lavish and improvident expenditure of the
public money throughout every branch of the Government, all arising
from the corrupt and inadequate state of the representation of the
people in Parliament, whereby all constitutional control over the
servants of the Crown has been lost, and Parliaments have become
subservient to the will of Ministers."

It began to be evident that, as the great common interest of the
war disappeared, and the popularity and influence Incapacity of
derived from its successful termination wore itself out, the Tory
the Tory party, with its repressive and reactionary doc- party.
trines, would find itself wholly unable to handle with success the
domestic questions which inevitably arose. For some years longer
it successfully held its position. Circumstances enabled it again to
separate the middle and lower classes, and full time was allowed it
to exhibit its repressive principles of home government.

The success of the Government was due to the excesses of the mob,
and to the exaggerated fear which it was found possible to excite
among the propertied classes. The Regent had scarcely opened
Parliament, with an assurance that he was well convinced of the
loyalty of the great body of his Majesty's subjects, but Attack on the
was determined to omit no precautions for preserving Regent.
public peace, when, as he was returning from the House, June 28, 1817.

he was ill-received by the people, and a missile thrown from the crowd even broke one of the windows of his carriage. This outrage encouraged the Government to take vigorous measures. It was not difficult to represent the whole project of reform as being indissolubly mixed with the extreme doctrines of Cobbett and the Spenceans. A secret committee of both Houses was appointed to inquire into the public disaffection; that of the Lords reported the existence of a great network of societies and clubs, which, under pretence of parliamentary reform, were attempting to infect the minds of all classes with a spirit of disaffection, and contempt of law, religion, and morality, while no endeavours were omitted to prepare the people to take up arms on the first signal of the accomplishment of their design. The Commons committee declared (Feb. 19) that the Hampden Clubs aimed at nothing short of revolution. Armed with these reports, which were no doubt extraordinarily exaggerated, Government introduced and carried Bills for preventing attempts to seduce soldiers and sailors from their allegiance, to give to the Prince Regent all the safeguards of an actual sovereign, to prevent seditious meetings, and lastly (March 3), for the suspension of the Habeas Corpus Act till the 1st of the ensuing July.

Repressive measures of the Government March.

The effect of these Acts was at once to give a certain reality to the dangers on the false apprehension of which they had been based. Public meetings being impossible, secret meetings, with all the dangers which invariably attend them, sprang into existence. The worse affected and more dangerous leaders of the people began to acquire influence, and desperate designs, fomented and betrayed by spies in the employment of Government, began to be entertained. It is impossible to suspect benevolent gentlemen such as Lord Sidmouth of wilfully entrapping ignorant artisans to their own destruction; but it is certain that use was constantly made of spies who found it to their own advantage to concoct and betray treasonable and atrocious conspiracies. The most notorious of these spies was a man of the name of Oliver, who, giving himself out as a delegate of London reforming societies, succeeded in giving a new impulse to the plots in various parts of the manufacturing districts of Yorkshire, Lancashire and Derbyshire. The violent suppression by the military and constables of a peaceable meeting, known as the meeting of blanketeers, at Manchester on the 29th of March, made the people more ready to listen to his suggestions. The meeting was a peaceful one, and acquired its

Secret political meetings.

name from the blankets or coats which many of those assembled had strapped upon their backs. A few of them set out upon a foolish march, intending to petition the Prince Regent in person ; but their intentions appear to have been quite peaceful, and though many were apprehended, they were all discharged before trial. It seems probable that what is known as the Derby insurrection was one of the consequences of Oliver's representations. A man of the name of Brandreth, known as " the Captain," went from house to house near Pentridge, spreading such assertions as that England, Ireland, and France were all to rise that night at ten o'clock, and that the " northern clouds," or men from the north, would come down and sweep all before them. A few men collected in arms at his summons. They do not seem ever to have numbered much more than an hundred, and were without difficulty dispersed, and many of them taken prisoners by the military at a short distance from Nottingham. Such disturbances as these were held to justify a second suspension of the Habeas Corpus.

The Derby insurrection June 10

But it was not only against seditious actions that Lord Sidmouth determined to proceed, but against seditious writings also. On the 27th of March he wrote a circular to the Lords Lieutenant of counties, in which he declared that in the opinion of the law officer the justices of the peace might issue a warrant to apprehend any person charged before them on oath with the publication of blasphemous or seditious libels, and compel him to give bail to answer to the charge. Considering the jealousy with which any political interference with the liberty of the press was regarded, and that by Fox's Libel Bill even the judges were held unfit to decide on the character of a libel, which was to be left to the decision of the jury, it is difficult to conceive a more high-handed interference with what was generally regarded as a constitutional privilege. Considerable use was made of the instructions, yet on the whole with so little success that the Government procured but a single conviction. The most important of these trials was that of Mr. Hone, which must have showed the Government, if nothing else could, how odious and useless their attempts to stifle the free expression of opinion was. Hone was a quiet and inoffensive publisher, a great collector and reader of old books. He had published certain political parodies, of which the subject can be pretty well understood from the titles they bore, " The Sinecurist's Creed," " The Litany, or General Supplication." It was against their alleged blasphemous character that proceedings were

Suppression of seditious writings.

Mr. Hone's trial. Dec. 18, 1817.

taken. Each parody was the subject of a separate trial, and the whole proceedings occupied three days. On the first day Mr. Justice Abbott, on the second and third Lord Chief-Justice Ellenborough occupied the bench. Hone defended himself, basing his argument on the essential difference between parodies intended to throw scorn upon the work parodied and those in which well-known writings were travestied for the purpose of ridiculing some other subject, and supporting himself by innumerable instances of political parodies couched in biblical forms coming from the pens of well-known and respected writers. His erudition enabled him to continue for many hours on each day producing instances of this kind. With astonishing firmness he refuséd to be browbeaten by Lord Ellenborough, and upon the third day even attacked his judge for the partisan spirit in which he had charged the jury the preceding evening. In all three trials, after a brief consideration, the jury acquitted him. The persistency with which the charges against Hone were pressed after his first acquittal entirely discredited the grounds of public morality on which the Government was professedly acting, and had all the appearance of a vindictive desire for revenge on the part of men smarting under deserved political satire.

The system pursued by the Tories, though for the time it was successful in keeping up a general dread of popular violence, and thus temporarily hushed the agitation for reform, was gradually alienating from Government all classes but the one immediately connected with it, and forcing the nation at large to look upon Government itself as its natural enemy, and to fix its hopes more and more upon some constitutional change. Indeed, though its large majority in the House enabled the Government to reject all liberal measures, and to pass those which it itself produced, a powerful Opposition began to show itself within the walls of the House, which the conduct of the Administration did not tend to conciliate. The extension of the

The Alien Act. May 5, 1818.

Alien Act, which reserved to the Government the power of removing aliens who were objects of suspicion, and which had already been twice renewed since the peace, for a further period of two years, was regarded as an attack upon the English right of asylum in favour of the Continental despotisms. It was warmly opposed, and a flaw found in it which secured its rejection. By the Act of Union, shareholders in the Bank of Scotland became naturalized subjects. An alien, by taking shares in the Bank, could therefore evade that Act. A clause was introduced to check this means of evading the Act; but as naturalized subjects had certain exemptions with regard to the payment of duties, the Lower House held that the introduction of the clause was an infringement of their privilege, as being in fact the introduction of a money clause. It had therefore to be dropped and a new Bill introduced. Even an attempt on the part of Government to gain popularity turned to its discredit. A show was made of destroying numerous sinecures; but as this destruction was coupled with a Pension List of an amount almost equal to that of the sinecures destroyed, the trick excited more anger than gratitude among the public. But the great contest of the time was on the subject of the indemnity demanded by the ministry to cover acts done during the suspension of the Habeas Corpus Act. A sealed bag of papers was laid upon the table of the House, which the Government demanded should be referred to a committee of secresy. The committee was to be appointed by ballot, but lists were circulated among the ministerial majority of the members for whom they should vote; in fact, therefore, the committee was nominated by the Government itself. The report declared· that the suspension was necessary, and that the Government had used the powers given them well. But the demand for an indemnity, while the grounds for that indemnity were kept studiously secret and examined only by the Government nominees, for the avowed purpose of keeping from the public the names of the witnesses who had given secret information, increased still further the bad impression which the employment of men like Oliver had already created.

The Indemnity Bill. March 13.

Under other circumstances loyalty for the Crown might have served to lessen the growing division between the Government and the people; the state of the royal family, and the character of most of its members, was now such as to weaken all such feeling. For the old King and Queen there was doubtless respect and pitying affection; but it was known that both the afflicted monarch himself and his faithful wife and guardian might at any moment die. As it was, they lived retired from the public view. The Prince Regent, the ostensible sovereign of the country, was understood to be little more than a selfish voluptuary. His reception on the opening of Parliament of 1817 shows how much he had lost the affections of the people. His unhappy domestic relations, shortly to become the ground of a keen party struggle, not only afforded a perpetual subject of scandal, but seemed to forbid the possibility of a direct male heir to the throne. The people's hopes were centred on the Princess Charlotte, the

Condition of the royal family.

Regent's only daughter, but lately married to Prince Leopold of Saxe-Coburg, and the blow was felt to be heavy when she died in 1817, immediately after giving birth to a child which did not live. It seemed for the instant highly probable that the large and strong family of the old King would come to an end in the first generation. Before the close of the following year this probability was lessened. No less than four members of the royal family were then married— Princess Elizabeth, the Duke of Clarence, the Duke of Cambridge, and the Duke of Kent, who married respectively the Landgrave of Hesse Homburg, the Princess Adelaide of Saxe-Meiningen, the Princess Augusta of Hesse, and Princess Victoria of Saxe-Coburg Saalfield, the widow of the Prince of Leiningen and sister of Prince Leopold. Had the family been at all popular such events, under the circumstances, would certainly have afforded joy to the nation. As it was, they only afforded an opportunity for the expression of a deeply fixed belief in the extravagance and wastefulness of the royal family. Of all the marriages that of the Duke of Kent with a sister of Prince Leopold was alone well received. The demand for an increase of income on behalf of the other princes was strongly resisted in Parliament ; the sum proposed for the Duke of Clarence was reduced by nearly half, and a grant of £6000 for the Duke of Cumberland, who had been married three years previously, was absolutely rejected by a majority of six members, a result which was received with loud cheers.

The insecurity felt by Government, in spite of its large majority,

The ministers' insecurity with the present Parliament.

in the present Parliament betrayed it into conduct which still further increased its unpopularity. The Parliament was now in its sixth session, and therefore approaching its time of dissolution. But several circumstances might call it again into existence. A clause in the Regency Act provided that Parliament should be summoned on the death of the Queen. The ministry had lately got the clause repealed ; but the death either of the King or Regent, if happening before the day appointed for the assembling of the new Parliament, would have caused the reassembling of the old. Both King and Queen might die at any moment ; nor was the Regent's health good. The dissolution was therefore hurried on in a manner which caused much anger. On the 10th of June Parliament was prorogued and dissolved at the same time, a form of proceeding unprecedented since the days of Charles II. The temper of the country was not improved by this step, and the elections were attended with the bitterest party strife. In Westminster Sir George

Murray, who stood on the Tory interest to replace if possible Lord Cochrane, who had withdrawn to take command of the navies of Chili, was so ill-used that his life was thought to be in danger. Several Radical candidates offered themselves, among others Hunt the orator; but the more respectable inhabitants contrived to save themselves from the disgrace of such representatives by bringing in Romilly, without any expense of his own, at the head of the poll. The other member was Sir Francis Burdett. In the same way the City of London elected four Liberals, rejecting three old ministerial representatives. This clearly showed the rising temper of the middle classes. But as the representation was then arranged no great change was possible, and the ministers found themselves still in possession of a large majority (July).

Before the assembling of the new Parliament (Jan. 14, 1819) one piece of foreign history deserves notice. A congress was held at Aix-la-Chapelle (Oct. 2, 1818), at which the final evacuation of France by the allies, although only three of the five years stipulated were accomplished, was agreed upon. This wise and just act seems to have been chiefly due to the Duke of Wellington, in opposition to some of the extreme Tories of the Cabinet. *Evacuation of France by the allies. Nav. 30, 1818.*

In spite of their parliamentary majority, the ministry did not feel very secure upon their seats, and it was perhaps more with a view of re-establishing their credit with the country than from increased wisdom that the Cabinet so far changed its views with regard to the currency question as to accept the truth of the doctrines which Francis Horner had some years (1811) before laid down, and introduced a measure in accordance with the plans of Ricardo, the political economist, for the resumption of cash payments. The Bank had already issued a considerable quantity of gold. Since 1817 as much as £6,000,000 had been put into circulation, but as the paper money still continued, as a matter of course this partial action produced no good effect; the gold had found its way out of the country, chiefly to France. It was now ordered that this voluntary payment in gold should cease. An examination of the affairs of the Bank proved that it was in excellent condition, and a series of resolutions were passed and subsequently embodied in Bills by Mr. Peel. By these, from the 1st of February 1820, the Bank was obliged to exchange its notes for gold ingots, in not less quantity than sixty ounces, at the rate of 81s. the ounce; in October of the same year the rate was to be reduced to 79s. 6d. the *Resumption of cash payments. May 1819.*

ounce ; on the 1st of May 1822 the rate was reduced to the regular mint price of £3, 17s. 10½d. ; and in May 1823 all notes were to be paid on demand in legal coin. As a fact, on the 1st of May 1821 the Bank resumed complete payment in cash.

Several divisions in Parliament clearly showed the growing weakness of Government. The Foreign Enlistment Bill, to prevent English subjects from serving in a foreign service or fitting out ships of war for foreign countries, was carried by a majority of thirteen only, the ground of opposition being that the Bill was in fact directed to the injury of the revolted colonies of Spain in America, in whose ranks many Englishmen were serving. Like the Alien Act of the preceding session, the Bill was considered as a proof of that legitimist and absolute tendency of which the Government was accused. Again, in the great question of Catholic emancipation, which was brought forward by Grattan in the best speech he ever made in the House, the Government were victorious by a majority of two only in a very full House ; while it was actually defeated by a majority of five on the question of the reform of Scotch burghs, which it had got rid of in the last session. The system in those burghs had been in existence ever since the fifteenth century, and so acted as to perpetuate the administration in the hands of one party, often of one family only, as the retiring members of the corporation had the right of electing their own successors. For years the burghs had been bent upon ridding themselves of this exclusive government; as in the case of other reforms, their efforts had passed out of sight during the tumult of the French wars, again to be called into existence on the resumption of peace. In 1817 certain irregularities of form in the burgh of Montrose had caused the elections to be set aside by the law courts. The Crown had been compelled to give a new charter, in which a certain popular element was admitted. Other burghs at once began to clamour for similar changes. To their petitions, however, the Government turned a deaf ear. When the elections in Aberdeen were quashed by the law courts, as those at Montrose had been, the old constitution had been re-established, and Lord Archibald Hamilton now took up the cause of the burghs. He demanded a copy of the new warrant, and was defeated by five only. Pressing his success, he demanded that the petitions of the burghs should be referred to a select committee. A large majority of the burghs themselves were loudly calling for reform. The population

Marginal notes:
Foreign
Enlistment
Bill.

Catholic
emancipation
rejected.
May 3.

Reform of
Scotch
burghs.
May 6.

of those who desired it amounted to 420,000, as opposed to 60,000, the population of those who had not petitioned. The proof of the wish of the people most interested was too strong for the House; in spite of the Government opposition, Lord Archibald's motion was carried in a House of nearly 300 by a majority of five. As the ground of opposition had been avowedly that a change in the burghs was but the beginning of parliamentary reform, this victory shows how the opposition to that measure was gradually breaking down.

In spite of these signs of weakness, the ministers were upon the whole well satisfied with the session. They believed in the success of their repressive measures in the year 1817, and thought that the state of the country was both quieter and more prosperous than it had been. Complaints of the depression of agriculture, Chronic and poverty and suffering among the agricultural poor, sufferings of were indeed chronic; they depended upon causes over the poor. which the immediate action of Government had little control. Exaggerated rents were seeking their natural level; over-cultivation, especially of corn, was giving place to more rational agriculture, and the enormous prosperity enjoyed by the agriculturists during the war was shrinking to modest and hard-won profits; the change could not but be attended with some depression and many painful contrasts. At the same time the action of the Poor Law as then administered, the injudicious fostering of the population which had gone on during the war, and the law of settlement which prevented free competition of labour, of necessity caused misery among the labourers. It was when the manufacturing and mercantile interests were also touched, when, under the action of restrictive corn laws, prices rose, while work was not to be had, that the social dangers of the country became from time to time great.

The prosperity of the year 1818 had been rather apparent than real; there had been much over-trading; a more healthy spirit appears to have arisen in the beginning of 1819, but the effects of the preceding folly were now to be felt. In the first half of the year the number of bankruptcies were almost double the average, the price of corn was still as high as 75s., work was scarce, and wages fell, and before the year was over the ministry found upon their hand difficulties even greater than those they had experienced in the gloomy year of 1817. For again the political question Political was ready to start to life, again leaders of a higher meetings. class were ready to take advantage of the sufferings of the people, and men of more extreme views among themselves were eager to lead them into desperate and revolutionary designs. There had been great meetings near Leeds, Glasgow, and at Ashton-under-Lyne, in June. On the 28th of that month, Sir Charles Wolseley and the Rev. Joseph Harrison had made violent speeches at a great assembly at Stockport, and Sir Charles had been elected the "legislatorial representative" for Birmingham. At the same time the reformers were found to be engaged in drilling. No arms were seen, and it is asserted by one of their leaders that the only object of their drilling was to secure order and regularity and the better appearance at a forthcoming great meeting at Manchester. On the other hand, it was held by those who dreaded popular movements that the drilling had been long and secretly continued, and was a part of a great plan for an exhibition of physical force. The object of the Manchester meeting, which was to be held on the 9th of August, was to choose a representative as Birmingham had already done. The meeting was declared illegal; a requisition was therefore sent to the proper officials, begging them to call it legally. On their refusal, it was determined to hold it, legal or not, on the 16th, in St. Peter's Field. Thither, on the day appointed, large bodies of men, well dressed and without arms, but in something like military array, marched from all

The Manchester Massacre. Aug. 16, 1819. the neighbouring towns, and collected round a hustings, from which Hunt was to address them. Their number perhaps amounted to about 80,000, all pressed together in a space of not more than three acres. The magistrates had formed no very definite notion of what to do. They had assembled a considerable military force, of which a troop of Manchester yeomen about forty strong and six troops of the 15th Hussars formed a part. A warrant was out against Hunt, and with extreme imprudence it was determined to execute it while he was on the hustings, as had been done in the case of Harrison on a previous occasion. Just as Hunt was beginning to speak, a strange pressure made itself visible to the crowd. The magistrates had come to a house overlooking the field; they had intrusted their warrant to the chief constable; he had declared he could not execute it without military aid, and the yeomen had pressed into the crowded space. As was natural, they had been separated and brought to a complete standstill. Upon this the magistrates seem to have lost their presence of mind, to have believed that the yeomanry were in danger, and to have ordered the 15th Hussars to extricate them. The consequence was a fearful charge, which swept everything before it, and, as one of the officers says, "by the time they had reached the other side of the field the fugitives were literally piled up to a considerable elevation above the level of the ground." The effect of the panic on so closely-packed a multitude, among whom the soldiers were using the sword, sometimes the flat and sometimes the edge, was fearful; about thirty wounded persons were carried to the infirmary, and forty more found their own way there in the course of the day. The actual wounds given by the soldiers do not appear to have been very many. Hunt and some of his followers were apprehended; the charge of high treason against them was subsequently dropped, and they were obliged to find bail to stand their trial for misdemeanour.

The Manchester Massacre, as it was called, was the result of accident and the bad management of the magistrates, Culpability of but the Government seemed to make the act entirely the Government. their own when they lavished approbation on the conduct of the authorities, and when they induced the Prince Regent himself to write an approving letter. As usual in England, the employment of the military except in the very last necessity excited the anger of very many even of the wealthier classes. Among those who had suffered from it its effect was simply to exasperate; for the time the temper of the people seems to have been really dangerous. The point, on the other hand, which struck the ministerialists was the weakness of the existing laws for the suppression of sedition, and in accordance with their view it was thought necessary to hold an autumnal session, which met on the 23rd of November, and which passed by large majorities a series of enactments known as "The Six The Six Acts. Acts." These were respectively entitled, "An Act to prevent delay in the administration of justice in cases of misdemeanour;" "An Act to prevent the training of persons in the use of arms and the practice of military evolutions;" "An Act for the prevention and punishment of blasphemous and seditious libels;" "An Act to authorize justices of the peace, in certain disturbed counties, to seize and detain arms;" "An Act to subject certain publications to the duties of stamps upon newspapers, and to make other regulations for restraining the abuses arising from the publication of blasphemous and seditious libels;" and "An Act for preventing the assembling of seditious assemblies." Having passed these repressive measures, the Parliament was again prorogued (Dec. 29) till February 1820. In the interval, on the 29th of January, the old King died, in his eighty-second year.

GEORGE IV.

1820—1830.

Born 1762=Caroline of Brunswick, 1795.

Charlotte=Leopold of Saxe-Coburg
Born 1796.
Died 1817.

CONTEMPORARY PRINCES.

France.	Austria.	Spain.	Prussia
Louis XVIII., 1814.	Francis II., 1792.	Ferdinand VII.,1813.	Frederick William
Charles X., 1824.			III., 1797.

Russia.	Denmark.	Sweden.
Alexander I., 1801.	Frederick VI., 1808.	Charles XIV., 1818.
Nicholas, 1825.		

POPES.—Pius VII , 1800.   Leo XII., 1823.   Pius VIII , 1829.

Lord Chancellors.	First Lords of the Treasury.
April 1807. Eldon	Jan 1812. Liverpool.
April 1827. Lyndhurst.	April 1827 Canning.
	Aug. 1827. Goderich.
	Jan. 1828. Wellington.

Chancellors of the Exchequer	Secretaries (Foreign and Home).
Jan. 1812 Vansittart.	June 1812 { Castlereagh. Sidmouth.
Jan 1823. Robinson.	Jan. 1822 { Castlereagh. Peel.
April 1827. Canning.	Sept. 1822 { Canning. Peel
Aug. 1827. Herries.	April 1827 { Dudley. Sturges-Bourne.
Jan. 1828. Goulburn.	Aug. 1827 { Dudley. Lansdowne.
	Jan. 1828 { Dudley. Peel.
	May 1828 { Aberdeen. Peel.

IT was no longer as Regent but as King that George, the new monarch, met the Parliament on its reassembling. He had so long acted virtually as sovereign that scarcely any visible effect was produced by the change. Yet during the first days there was considerable probability that the change of reign would be marked by a change of ministry ; for

Precarious position of the ministry.

there were two questions on which the ministers felt it their duty to oppose the new King—the one an increase of his private revenue, the other the divorce of his unfortunate wife. On the latter point, unfortunately for themselves, they were induced to make a compromise, believing that they were acting safely. Extremely anxious to avoid a public scandal, they refused at first to move in the matter of the divorce as long as the Queen remained quietly abroad, but promised to gratify the King's wishes should she make her appearance in England. On these terms they remained in office.

But, at the very time that their position as ministers was in danger, their lives were threatened by a conspiracy which in its atrocity and feebleness gives a fair measure of the power and intentions of the worst part of those engaged in the agitations of the day. As in the case of the Derby insurrection, it is impossible to acquit the authorities of the guilt of having employed spies who, though probably without Government authority, did in fact aggravate the crime of the conspirators. Information was given as early as November by a man named Edwards of a plot against the lives of the ministers, and from that time till the day of the explosion of the Cato Street conspiracy he continued to play the double part of conspirator and police agent. The form the plot ultimately assumed was the murder of all the ministers in a body at a Cabinet dinner, which Edwards informed the conspirators was to be held at Lord Harrowby's on the 23rd of February. The assassination was to be followed up by an attempt to fire the barracks, and to rouse the people to an assault upon the Bank and the Tower. As the ministry were well informed of the plot, the dinner was of course postponed. The guests arriving at the house of the Archbishop of Canterbury, who was giving a dinner-party that day, and who lived next door to Lord Harrowby, prevented the conspirators from discovering the postponement of the ministerial meeting; and they were arming themselves in a stable in Cato Street, near Edgeware Road, when the police came upon them. The capture was badly managed; the first officer who entered the room was stabbed, and in the confusion Thistlewood (already mentioned as the confederate of the Watsons), who was the soul of the present conspiracy, with fourteen others, contrived to escape; the rest, nine in number, were apprehended when the soldiers, who should have accompanied the police, arrived. Early the next morning, however, Thistlewood was captured. He and four others were executed, and five more transported for life. The terror excited

*Cato Street conspiracy.
Feb 23, 1820.*

[2 N]

throughout England was strangely exaggerated; the design appears to have been confined entirely to a few desperate men, and to have been scouted by all the more earnest Radicals to whom it had been suggested. About the same time the other prisoners, Hunt and his friends from Manchester (April), Wolseley and Harrison from Stockport (July), were tried, and sentenced to various periods of imprisonment. One advantage at least came from the trials; the true character of Hunt was discovered, his friends and companions learnt the worthlessness and egregious vanity of the man, and his influence was entirely destroyed.

The Parliament had assembled, according to law, upon the demise of the King, and after going through the necessary business, was dissolved. In April the new Parliament met. But any interest which

Importance of the Queen's trial. might otherwise have attended its labours disappeared before the absorbing interest of the year, the trial of the Queen. Though in itself wholly unconnected with politics, no event produced a stronger influence on the course of political growth. The loyalty of the country, and respect for authority and for the established powers, received a rude shock. It could not be otherwise when the people saw a ministry, many of whose severest and most unpopular measures had been based on the specious ground of the desire to maintain morality, forcing into public notice scandalous details, which the papers spread to every corner of the country for the satisfaction of prurient curiosity; when they saw the sovereign having recourse to all the foul and mean resources of the private inquiry office, which fill right-minded men with disgust even in the cases of private individuals, and the Government lending the whole weight of its authority to the vindictive prosecution of an unfortunate and ill-used woman. The effect was a complete severance between the Government and the more liberal-minded of the middle classes, whom fear of popular extravagances had hitherto united with it, and from the close of this trial may be dated the serious determination of the people at large to insist upon some great measure of reform.

Whatever may have been her folly or her guilt, no one can question the misfortune of the Queen. Giddy by nature and badly educated, she had been forced (1795) against her will upon a man whose immoral and selfish character wholly unfitted him for the difficult position of a husband of a frivolous and unwise wife. His distaste had been exhibited at their very first meeting, and he could only force himself to assume a gracious demeanour by having recourse to wine or spirits. From the very first he seems to

Position of the Queen.

have designed to part from her; she was early sent into a sort of banishment at Blackheath, a watch was set upon her conduct, an investigation before the Lords was set on foot, and though declared innocent of any grave offence, disgusted at such treatment, she unwisely withdrew abroad in 1814. She was followed in her retirement, by the advice of Sir John Leach, by emissaries to collect evidence against her, unknown to herself. It would have been wise had she remained abroad, but the treatment she had received rendered her desperate; she had been excluded from foreign courts, and when her husband came to the throne her name was omitted from the Liturgy. It seems to have been this last insult which roused her to action. In June she came to England, and was received with enthusiasm by the people, who regarded her as a persecuted woman. She thus placed the ministers in the awkward position of being obliged to fulfil the compromise under which they had retained office and to proceed to extremities against her. On the 6th of June the King sent a message to the Lords, ordering them to institute an inquiry into the Queen's conduct, and proofs were laid on the table. On the following day, Mr. Brougham, who undertook the management of her case as her Attorney-General, read a letter to the Commons demanding a public inquiry. Some efforts were made to effect a compromise, but as the King refused to demand her reception abroad or to insert her name in the Liturgy, all negotiations failed. The secret committee of the Lords therefore proceeded to make its report, declaring that a solemn inquiry was necessary; and Lord Liverpool shocked public feeling by introducing, for the purpose of producing such an inquiry, a Bill of pains *Trial of the Queen. Aug. 17.* and penalties to deprive her Majesty of her position as Queen, and to dissolve the King's marriage. The trial in fact came on with the second reading of the Bill, when the charges against the Queen were stated before the Lords; and for nearly a month the House was occupied in hearing witness. By this time the feeling in England was strongly excited. The ministers were insulted whenever they appeared abroad, and every opportunity was taken by the crowd of showing their sympathy with the Queen. The question had become in fact a political one, and the Queen lent herself only too readily to a somewhat ostentatious display of her sufferings. In October the defence commenced, and at length, on the 6th of November, the second reading of the Bill was passed by a majority of twenty-eight. Two days afterwards, on the third reading, there was a majority of only nine. As this was in the House of Lords, where the ministers were strongest, they saw it was useless to persevere, and Lord Liverpool declared that the Bill was abandoned. A burst of joy was heard throughout the country, for three nights London was illuminated, even Prince Leopold joining in the rejoicings. Declining all offers from the Government, the Queen placed her cause in the hands of the Commons. An annuity of £50,000 was given her the following session. But she was determined upon some more public announcement of her innocence; she still tried, though in vain, to secure the introduction of her name in the Liturgy, and was foolish enough on the occasion of the coronation in July of the following year to attempt to force her way into the Abbey. She had already begun to lose the sympathy of the people when, in August, she died.

However right it may have been to raise the question of the Queen's guilt, there was a general feeling that the ministers had at all events mismanaged the question, and after exciting strongly the temper of the people, had dropped their Bill without excuse or apology. Advantage was taken of the popular anger, excited by what was thought an act of oppression, to give currency to all sorts of charges against the ministry, and to impute to them unconstitutional principles, and connivance or even approbation of scandalous conspiracies against the Queen's character, of which they were certainly guiltless. But, before all, the late events had given a popular rallying-point for all sections of the Opposition, and had demonstrated how deep was the alienation between the ministry and the body of the people. It is from this time that we find serious and sometimes successful efforts made to begin the work of reform, which it was believed would render such an alienation impossible. Although, as was to be expected in a House elected under the old system, any wide measure, such as that produced by Lambton (subsequently Lord Durham, April 1821), recommending equal electoral districts, was sure to be defeated by a large majority, Lord John Russell succeeded in procuring the disfranchisement of Grampound, a notoriously corrupt borough in Cornwall (May 30). He and his friends were wise enough to accept this small beginning, even though his Bill was changed in the Upper House, where the vacant seat was transferred, not to one of the great unrepresented cities, as would have been just, but to the county of York. In the same way the great question of Catholic disabilities was brought forward with renewed strength. Those who were in favour of their removal were successful in the Lower House, and the Bill was only lost after passing through most of its stages in the Lords.

Consequent alienation between the ministry and people.

So shaken indeed was the predominance of the extreme Tory party, that in the year 1821 they found it necessary to strengthen themselves by a coalition with the Conservative section of the Opposition, hoping by this means to give a more broad and liberal appearance to the administration. Lord Grenville Peel joins
the ministry. himself declined office, but several of his followers were admitted to the ministry, while a still further improvement was made by the retirement of Lord Sidmouth, who had played so prominent a part in all the late repressive measures, and the substitution in his place of Mr. Peel, as yet Tory in his views, but capable, as was subsequently proved, of constant advance, and of an intellect so clear and sensible as to be able to learn, as his predecessor never could, the growing requirements of the time. At the same time Lord Wellesley was sent as Lord-Lieutenant to Ireland, with Mr. Plunkett as his Attorney-General, both of them supporters of the Catholic claims; and although Wellesley's statesmanlike character and moderation excited the anger of extreme men on both sides, the mere fact of such a man being placed at the head of the Irish Government was a clear mark of the relaxation of the principles of the Tory system. These new appointments were but the beginning, to be followed in a few months by other changes far more important, which were to effect an entire alteration in the position which England occupied in Europe, and in the principles which governed her financial policy. These changes were the admission, in 1822 and 1823, of Mr. Canning and Mr. Huskisson to the ministry. Throughout the trial of Queen Caroline, Canning had held himself studiously aloof. He had been early one of the Queen's advisers, had declared from the first his intention to avoid any participation in her trial, and had in fact remained abroad during its continuance. On his return in December, thinking it impossible for a minister to be entirely absent from his duties, but determined to take no part in the discussions on the trial which were inevitable, he insisted on resigning his place at the Board of Trade. He was therefore at first excluded from the new ministerial arrangements. The India Company indeed had decided upon sending him as Governor-General to India. His preparations for taking the post were being made, and he Death of
Castlereagh.
Canning
Secretary
of State.
Sept 11, 1822. was at Liverpool on a farewell visit to his constituents, when a piece of news was heard which caused a profound movement both at home and abroad,—Lord Castlereagh, now become Lord Londonderry, had committed suicide.

The man who was regarded as the real soul of the Tory party, as the type of the arbitrary and absolutist temper which distinguished it, had passed away. Honourable and amiable in his private life, he had contrived to render himself so unpopular that the news of his death was received with unseemly rejoicings, and his coffin was followed to the Abbey with shouts of gladness from his enemies. Europe was in a critical condition. Lord Londonderry had been in the act of going to an European Congress held at Verona. Canning appeared to be the only man fitted to supply his place. When asked to join the ministry as Secretary of State for foreign affairs, after some consideration, he threw up the great post for which he was at the moment destined, and accepted the office.

To understand the importance of this change it is necessary to say a few words on what had passed in Europe since the Peace. The hopes of the liberal party in Europe had received a heavy blow at the Congress of Vienna. England had so constantly put herself forward as the champion of freedom, and her influence had been so preponderating in the late events of tne war, that she was expected to have taken up strong ground in the settlement of Europe, and to have demanded and secured some sort of popular rights in the countries to which her assistance had been given. The nation had shown itself so full of resources, and had been so exceptional in the success of its opposition to Napoleon, that a general belief had arisen that there was something peculiarly excellent in the character of its constitution. So strong was this feeling, that many of the sovereigns of Europe promised constitutions to their people. It was forgotten that the freedom for which England had been fighting meant deliverance from external conquest, and had no connection with the internal freedom of national constitutions, that, on the contrary, the war against France had been originally undertaken, if not ostensibly yet really, to oppose the revolutionary temper of France. It was a severe disappointment when the English minister was seen joining with Talleyrand in upholding legitimacy, and for the sake of that principle, and to preserve in its old lines the balance of European power, himself demanding the destruction of the liberty of Belgium and of Genoa, and calmly acquiescing in the absorption of much of Saxony, the final division of Poland, and the destruction of Norway. Even the one constitutional effort which was made, the establishment of a limited monarchy in France, was rendered nugatory by the fact, that the privileges were given as a grant and charter from the crown, and the

Retrospect of the affairs of Europe.

Position of England abroad.

first principle of the English Constitution—that power is from the people—ignored.

But though in the general triumph of the moment his foreign policy was accepted and even approved, it will be remembered that even Castlereagh felt himself compelled to respect public opinion at home and to hold aloof from the Holy Alliance, which seemed to assert the unity of interests of the crowned heads and their sole right, as of divine origin, to be the governors of the world. It was the extension of the principles of the Holy Alliance which had produced the present critical state of Europe, *Effect of Castlereagh's policy.* with which his moderate abilities, his natural tendency towards repressive government, aggravated by domestic affairs, and the entanglements in which his policy at the Vienna Treaty had involved him, rendered Castlereagh unable to cope. It was no use to ignore the fact that the French Revolution had given a great impulse to the ideas of constitutional freedom. Even the conquests of Napoleon, followed as they always were by democratic changes, had fostered these ideas in the very countries which had suffered most from them; and when it appeared that all hopes and promises of freedom were entirely illusory, insurrections of the deceived people burst out in several parts of Europe, and where the strength of the government rendered such outbreaks impossible, secret societies, more dangerous and extravagant because they were secret, sprang everywhere into existence.

The first outbreak was in Spain, where Ferdinand had entirely refused the constitution to which he was pledged, and had shown his character by directing his vengeance chiefly against those very men who had been most prominent *Insurrection in Spain. 1820.* in saving his kingdom from the French. During the occupation of Spain by the French, when the central authority of the mother country was virtually destroyed, the South American colonies had, one after the other, thrown off their allegiance, and were still engaged in making good their independence. It was an army collected at Cadiz for the purpose of reducing the victorious colonies which set the example of insurrection. It mutinied in the beginning of the year 1820, and was so successful that the King was compelled, on the 7th of March, to accept the constitution of 1812, which had been drawn up under the influence of Napoleonic and American ideas. In August the constitutional spirit passed to Portugal. Since the departure of the royal family from Lisbon in 1808, the King had not returned to his European dominions.

Brazil became the seat of government, the restrictions formerly put
upon its trade were removed, it was elevated nominally to the rank of a kingdom, and Portugal seemed
to occupy the position of a colony of its former dependency. The
discontent which had thus been fostered displayed itself in August,
when national Juntas were established both in Oporto and Lisbon;
subsequently, on the 1st of October, the provincial assembly coalesced
with that of the capital, and the regency was compelled to resign its
functions. When at length in the following spring the King set out
for his continental dominions, it was a question whether he would
arrive in time to save them. Almost at the same time similar events
took place in Naples. Ferdinand IV. could not entirely disregard
popular wishes and rule despotically, as his nephew in
Spain had done, for the longer and more complete hold
which Murat, Napoleon's nominee, had obtained upon the throne had
given time for ideas of constitutional government to become prevalent,
and the army was full of Napoleonic soldiers. But in spite of the comparative liberality of his government, Ferdinand's army was full of
discontented soldiers, and the secret and revolutionary societies of
the Carbonari undermined society. At the same time, in the island
of Sicily a constitution had been established under the influence of
Lord William Bentinck, and had been swept away on the restoration.
In July the garrison at Nola mutinied, and before a week was over
the King was obliged to accept the Spanish constitution, which had
become the formula of the Liberal party, although there was actually
no copy of that document existing, and its contents seemed. to be
hardly known. Sicily soon followed Naples; but recollections of its
old independence prevented it at first from joining the revolutionary
government of the mainland, and its complete acquiescence in the
movement had to be secured by force of arms.

It was in presence of these disturbances that the true principles of
the Holy Alliance began to show themselves. The three
Eastern powers seemed to consider themselves authorized to introduce into Europe a new form of international
law. Regarding themselves as the only legitimate and divinely
appointed powers, and holding themselves pledged to mutual support
against their enemies, and having declared their intention to act as
a brotherhood in international questions, they appear to have believed that the enemies against whom their mutual assistance was
required were all those who resisted established authority, and that
any disturbances thus arising ought to be regulated by European

Insurrection in Portugal.

Insurrection in Naples.

Arbitrary action of the Holy Alliance.

congresses. In other words, they arrogated to themselves, for the sake of suppressing what they considered revolutionary movements, the right of federative action in the cause of legitimacy and absolutism. Already, at Vienna and Aix-la-Chapelle, they had acted more or less on this principle, and now they summoned a similar Congress at Troppau (1820). It was impossible for an English minister to accede to this new doctrine, however much he may have had at heart the cause which the allied sovereigns were supporting, and Lord Castlereagh, as early as April, declared that the alliance to which England was a party existed for particular cases only, and was not to be generalized as the Eastern sovereigns appeared to wish to generalize it. It shows how the position of England had sunk under Castlereagh's management, that the monarchs determined to act without England, and it shows the weakness of Castlereagh's mode of action that he allowed, under these circumstances, an English minister to be present at the meeting, not to take part in the discussions, but merely to report their progress to his Government. The Holy Alliance proceeded to act upon its own principles. In November the English minister learnt that the three powers intended to join and to act in common for the restoration of Ferdinand of Naples, whom they had invited to meet them at Laibach, whither the Congress was adjourned. Early in December 1820 a circular to that effect was issued in the name of the three sovereigns, which, in spite of what Castlereagh had said, proceeded to declare that, as what they were now doing was in accordance with the late treaties, they felt no doubt of the adhesion of France and England. On the 19th of that month, without knowledge of this circular, Castlereagh wrote an explicit declaration that England would not join in any united action. Had he openly declared this intention and withdrawn the English ambassador he would not have acted otherwise than as became an English minister. But on the 19th of January 1821 a letter of Castlereagh's, purporting to be an answer to the circular of December 8th, which had been published by some indiscretion in the public prints, while reasserting the position he had taken up in his previous declaration, went on to confess that the Government had looked with the strongest disapproval on the insurrection in Naples. This weak document, coming as it did just before the meeting of Parliament, after the popular temper had been roused by the knowledge of the arrogant circular of December, and taken in connection with the facts that diplomatic relations

England refuses to join.

Popular anger at Castlereagh's weak policy. 1821.

had not been renewed with the constitutional Government of Naples, and that an English fleet was cruising off the coast, seemed to show that the minister's heart was really with the sovereigns, and that his letter was only written to suit party purposes in England. At the opening of Parliament (Jan. 23, 1821) the Government had to withstand the most bitter assaults from the Opposition, headed by Lords Grey and Holland in the Lords, by Mackintosh, Brougham, and Tierney in the Lower House, and although a public vote of censure, considering the constitution of the House, was out of the question, it was plain that the feeling of all parties was strong against the action of the Holy Alliance. The attacks on the minister were still continuing when the uselessness of English interference was demonstrated by the entrance of an Austrian army into Italy, by which the revolution was summarily suppressed.

It was not only in the West of Europe that difficulties arose. The *Insurrection in Greece. March 1821.* Christian populations under the power of the Ottoman Porte rose in insurrection. They naturally looked, as they have always looked, to the Czar for protection. Their method of proceeding was closely analogous to that of the revolutionists in the rest of Europe; and in Greece, as in Italy, secret societies were organized against the existing powers. It has always been a part of Russian policy to secure as much influence in Turkey as possible. On the other hand, it was impossible for the English, at that time in constant diplomatic rivalry with Russia, to wish to see that power in possession of Constantinople or the Black Sea. In the affairs of Greece therefore a complete inversion of the principles which had been predominant at the Congress of Troppau was visible. The interests of Russia demanded that she should assist a revolutionary movement backed up by secret societies and directed against a legitimate sovereign, while England felt itself compelled to allege the doctrines of legitimacy and to call to its aid old alliances in order to shelter Turkey. The difficulty was so great that it was determined that this question also should be referred to a Congress, which was held first at Vienna, and subsequently moved to Verona.

But meanwhile fresh complications had arisen in the West. A *Complications between France and Spain. 1821.* terrible visitation of the yellow fever had come upon Spain. Under pretext of excluding the infection from their own country, the French had massed troops along the borders; but it soon became evident that something beyond sanitary precautions had inspired this movement. When the illness disappeared there was still an army of 100,000 men lying within reach of the Pyrenees. In fact, the Legitimists of France had seen with extreme dislike the revolution in Spain; it was political infection they were chiefly anxious to avoid, and the more advanced members of that party, which had a large majority in the French Houses, were thinking of the invasion of Spain, and the re-establishment by force of arms of the absolutist rule of Ferdinand. Lord Londonderry was preparing to attend the Congress at Verona when his health and reason gave way and he committed suicide. In his place the Duke of Wellington attended the Congress, and was somewhat surprised to find that, instead of the Greek question, the real point at issue was the demand of France for a joint action on the part of the Legitimist Courts of Europe to suppress the revolution in Spain.

Congress at Verona. Sept 1822.

It was to the management of this difficult affair that Canning was called. It cannot be said that he introduced a new system into our diplomacy. He had been a party to some of the declarations of his predecessor, and had accepted the responsibility of them. In fact, as has been seen in his public despatches, Castlereagh had already declared the impossibility of English co-operation in any general scheme of repressive action on the Continent, and his dislike to the government of Europe by congresses. It is the way in which Canning acted up to and rendered practical those declarations which makes it possible to say that his accession to office was an era in English politics. His instructions to Wellington were clear and precise. If a declaration of any such determination—that is, of joint action—should be made at Verona, come what might the Duke was to refuse the King's consent to become a party to it, even though the dissolution of the alliance should be the consequence of his refusal. Canning's object was to secure European peace and to allow nations freedom of choice as to their own government—to re-establish, in fact, in England and throughout Europe a policy based upon national grounds, as distinguished from that system of united and general policy by means of European congresses under which Europe since the peace had been labouring.

Object of Canning's policy.

In the first of his objects Canning was partially successful. The distinct refusal of Wellington to join in united action, and his subsequent withdrawal from the Congress, prevented a general European attack upon Spain. He could not entirely prevent the war, but he succeeded in reducing it to the dimensions of a national war. He used his best endeavours to

Partial success of Canning's diplomacy in Spain.

persuade France not to attack Spain. He declared that the free institutions of the Spanish people could not, as the French King had asserted, be only held legitimately from the spontaneous gift of the sovereign ; the Spanish nation could not be expected to subscribe to that principle, nor could any British statesman uphold or defend it ; it was in fact a principle that struck at the root of the British Constitution. In his eagerness to avert hostilities he even entreated the Spaniards to make changes in their constitution. His efforts on both sides were vain. The French invaded Spain ; on the 2nd of May 1823 they entered Madrid ; on the 1st of October Cadiz was surrendered, and Ferdinand and his absolute government were re-established. But in the matter of English interests Canning declared himself plainly. Portugal might be involved, and an effort might be made by Spain, with the assistance of France, to reconquer her colonies. Should Portugal join with Spain voluntarily, England would take no notice ; but if that country were invaded, England would of necessity come to the assistance of her old ally. With regard to the colonies he took a similar ground. They were virtually independent; during the contest, true to his principle of neutrality, he had abetted Government in preventing Englishmen from joining the insurgents ; but the trade with the colonies being now open, the interests of England were so involved with their independence that he would not allow any foreign nation to join in reconquering them ; if Spain was itself unable to subdue them, no foreign country, he declared, should subdue them for her. He followed up this policy by declaring that he would send English consuls to protect British trade, and their appointment was in fact the recognition of the independence of the colonies.

The new minister's conduct at the negotiations at Verona was subjected to warm discussion at the beginning of the year 1823. The firm attitude of neutrality which he had taken up did not satisfy the aspirations of those who looked upon his accession to office as the triumph of the Whig party. But his vindication was so complete that, upon the division, the opinion of the House appeared to be quite unanimous. The Opposition was only twenty in a House of 372, and of those twenty some were professed ministerialists, who had been shut out from voting by the crowd of their own adherents.

But it was not only in our foreign policy that a change of spirit
Change in commercial policy effected by Huskisson. now became obvious. In the winter of 1823, a few months after the accession of Canning to office, further changes took place in the ministry. Mr. Vansittart

resigned the place of Chancellor of the Exchequer, for which he was very unfit, and went into the Upper House as Lord Bexley. Mr. Robinson (afterwards Lord Goderich) succeeded him, and, much more important, Mr. Huskisson was in January made President of the Board of Trade, and with him a complete alteration came over our commercial policy, and the reign of restriction began to give way and yield place to free trade. The questions at issue had not yet become party tests, as they subsequently were, and Huskisson, as member of a Tory ministry, was able by his comprehension of the true principles of trade to set on foot a new system without separating from his colleagues.

The expenses of the war had been enormous, perhaps inevitably so, and the taxes were proportionately heavy. During the last year of the war in taxes and loans upwards of £170,000,000 had been raised. The National Debt amounted to nearly £800,000,000, and to meet the necessities of the moment this had been raised by very expensive methods, so that the nominal sum on which interest was paid was considerably higher than the actual money which had passed into Government hands. Mr. Vansittart, who had had the management of the finances, had no real knowledge of financial principles, and had acted on the simple plan of increasing taxes when more money was necessary, and supplying the deficit by loans contracted in an extravagant fashion, or taken from the sinking fund. He did not see that doubling a tax by no means doubled the returns from it, as it inevitably compelled some people, and those the most numerous and poorest, to surrender the taxed article; and in common with many people at the time, he believed in the magical effect of the sinking fund, although the sum yearly paid to it was derived from loans contracted at considerably higher interest than the fund itself bore. The sinking fund indeed had, in the hands of the present Government, almost lost its original object, and was openly declared both by Vansittart and Castlereagh to be chiefly useful for supplying the ministry with an easy means of getting money to meet emergencies, instead of a sacred deposit to be used only for the extinction of debt. The ease with which all money demands of Government were granted during the war had also engendered a spirit of extravagance, and economy had been one of the earliest cries of the Opposition on the resumption of peace. At first the support of the large standing army which still remained on foot, and other expenses which were regarded as necessary, had apparently prevented any

[margin note] Financial condition of England.

relaxation of taxes, but by degrees the universal discontent excited by their pressure had compelled Government to grant some relief, and a certain number of taxes had been taken off or reduced.

But all this time the real resources of England, the development of which would have largely increased the revenue, and at the same time have admitted of large decrease of taxation, had been restricted by unwise commercial legislation, having its origin in distant times and in a different state of society. The interests of the landowners and agriculturists were so closely connected with the predominance of the Tory party, and they had played so large a part in the conduct of England of late years, that the agriculturists had succeeded in making good the advantages of their class to the detriment of all others. They claimed nothing less than the exclusive right of supplying the whole nation with food, and by their clamour and influence in the House of Commons had succeeded in procuring corn laws which went far to secure them that monopoly. But meanwhile, within the last fifty years, the manufacturing interest, principally through the introduction of machinery, had relatively enormously increased. In the twenty years between 1811 and 1831, while the agricultural population increased but 2½ per cent., the manufacturing population had increased 31½ per cent. The time was rapidly approaching when the growing and increasing manufacturing and commercial element would of necessity claim its due position in opposition to the landed aristocracy. But at present the manufacturers themselves, ignorant of the true principles of political economy, were constantly seeking the benefit of their own class as distinguished from that of the general public, and restrictive, or, as they were called, protective, laws were extended over nearly every branch of industry.

The resources of the country restricted by protective laws.

Robinson, an exceedingly well-meaning man, had succeeded Vansittart as Chancellor of the Exchequer. But his plans and resources extended but little beyond those of his predecessor. He accepted and kept in operation some of his most unwise financial measures, and, without any change of general view, continued, what was no doubt a good thing in its way, to remit occasionally various small taxes. But he had beside him Huskisson as President of the Board of Trade, who acted in a very different spirit. Like his friend Canning, who gave him his full support, he was a self-made man, and belonging to none of the prominent ruling classes, was able to look at matters in a broader and more national light. And though, like his friend, he was constantly

Changes effected by Robinson and Huskisson.

spoken of as an adventurer, and in consequence had to undergo much opposition, he was able by the reasonableness of his views, and by the success which attended their execution, to launch England upon a new course of commercial policy, as Canning had been able to do with regard to foreign affairs. As yet free trade as a whole was not to be thought of, but Huskisson took every advantage of the demands of various classes of industrialists to introduce small reforms. In his first year of office, though he indicated the tendency of his policy, he was not able to affect much except with regard to the navigation laws. The three great industries of England were wool, silk, and cotton. Of these cotton alone had been left unrestricted, and there alone had a very remarkable increase been seen. In the wool trade considerable depression having been felt, numerous petitions from manufacturers were presented begging for the free importation of foreign wool, but at the same time asking that the export of British wool should be forbidden; in other words, claiming to buy the raw material of their manufacture at a price artificially lowered. Government replied that the import tax was a valuable source of revenue, but that it should be willingly foregone if free export was allowed also. As the manufacturers declined this, the movement for the present dropped. In the same way an attempt was made to free the Spitalfields silk manufacture from restrictions, such as the settlement of their wages by the magistrates. It was plain that as long as wages were not allowed to change with the varying requirements of the trade, the manufacturers were under disadvantages as compared with their rivals elsewhere. But 11,000 of the journeymen petitioned against this change, and although the Bill passed the Lower House by small majorities, it was so altered by amendments in the Upper House that Huskisson thought fit to drop it.

In dealing with the Navigation Act he was more successful. This law, passed in Cromwell's time, and completed in the 12th of Charles II., allowed the produce of Asia, Africa, and America to be brought to England in English ships only, and European goods only in English ships or in ships of the country producing the goods. The close of the American War had given the first blow to this system. American shipping, now become the shipping of a foreign country, was subject to the restrictions of the Act. The Americans retaliated, and the ships of both countries had to perform one half of the voyage empty; the consumers therefore paid double freight. This absurdity continued till the Treaty of Ghent in 1814, when the Governments agreed to drop their restric-

Change of the Navigation Act. June 1823.

tions. The course which had been successful with América was subsequently adopted by the mercantile states of Europe. Portugal, the Netherlands, and Prussia, all raised the dues on British vessels, and Huskisson, on the 6th of June 1823, took the opportunity of introducing the Bill known by the name of the Reciprocity of Duties Bill, by which the ships of British and foreign powers were put upon an equal footing, the right being retained to keep up restrictive duties upon the ships of nations who rejected the reciprocal equality of trade thus offered. The outcry against this change was very great, especially among the shipowners, whose business was trammelled by the heavy duty on Baltic timber. Huskisson expressed a hope that this duty might shortly be remitted, and meanwhile offered to return to shipbuilders all the duties paid on their materials. The offer was declined, and the grumbling continued, nevertheless the increase of British ships was enormous; in the last nineteen years of the restrictive duties the tonnage had increased ten per cent.; in twenty-one years after their abolition it increased forty-five per cent.

The first failure of his plans did not dishearten Huskisson, and the prosperity of the year 1824 enabled him to carry Bills for the relief both of the wool and silk trades. The silk trade had been principally established in England by the per-secuted Protestants in 1685, and to support it laws had been passed excluding from England foreign silks, which had previously been admitted free. Early in the eighteenth century the spinning of silk in the Italian method had been introduced by two brothers of the name of Lombe; to protect them heavy duties were laid upon foreign-spun silk. The material for the manufacture of silk goods was thus raised in price, and the manufacture had languished for many years, especially after the introduction of cotton. The production of spun silk in India, whence it was very plentifully supplied, had lately improved this state of things; it was believed that at this time 400,000 people were employed in the manufacture of silk goods. But there was a distinct preference for silks of French manufacture, and the smuggling of such goods into England was a serious damage both to the trade and to the revenue. The silk manufacturers, especially those about London, had immediately, upon Huskisson's accession to office, petitioned for the removal of duties on spun silk, but at the same time, with true class feeling, were eager to exclude foreign manufactured silks. In the same way the silk spinners were eager for the removal of duties upon raw silk, but bitterly opposed to the introduction of spun silk, while the journey-

Improvement in the silk trade.

March 1824.

men believed that ruin stared them in the face if foreign manufactured silks were introduced. Between these varying interests Huskisson had to steer his course. The duty on raw silk was immediately reduced to threepence from five and sevenpence halfpenny the pound. The clamour was too great to allow of a similar reduction in the duties on spun silk, which were lowered about half, from fourteen and eightpence to seven and sixpence ; and similarly, though Mr. Huskisson wished for an immediate change, the admission of foreign manufactured silks was postponed for two years, when they were to be admitted at an *ad valorem* duty of thirty per cent. The outcry against the change was great; the workmen thanked the House for the temporary postponement of the day of their destruction; the manufacturers expressed a hope that they should get out of the trade before the fatal day arrived. But the event thoroughly proved the wisdom of Huskisson's plans, and the truth of his prophecy that competition only was wanted to enable English manufacturers to rival the French; ten years after the passing of the Bill England exported to France £60,000 worth of manufactured silk.

The duties on wool, which came next into consideration, were of newer creation. In 1803 it had been subjected to a tax of a halfpenny a pound, raised by Mr. Vansittart in 1819 to sixpence. The same variety of interests was here at work as in the silk trade. The agriculturists and wool-growers wished for the retention of duties to secure a monopoly of the supply of wool, the manufacturers, to whom foreign wool for certain purposes is an absolute necessity, wished for free importation, but for the retention of an export duty to keep the price of English wool low. With perfect justice Mr. Huskisson determined to relieve both classes. Foreign wool was admitted, according to its excellence, at a penny or a halfpenny a pound ; English wool might be exported at a similar rate. Again the effect justified his view. The fear of a large exportation of English wool proved so completely groundless that by 1826 only 100,000 pounds weight had been exported, while 40,000,000 pounds of foreign wool had been introduced. The low price of wool of which the growers had complained had been caused by the increase of the article in England and the general slackness of the trade ; the large introduction of foreign wool had enabled the British producers to sell all their stock at remunerative prices to be worked up with it.

Improvement in the wool trade.

As befitted the dawning liberality of the English legislation, the question of the slave trade now again came prominently forward. It

was indeed the late changes in commercial legislation which again
brought it into notice. ·Since the opening of the Indian
trade in April 1814 a complete alteration had taken place
in the character of our commerce with that country.

Originally restricted to Indian produce paid for in bullion, it had lately
become much extended ; India received from England woollen goods to
the value of a million and a half, and strangely enough even cotton
goods, originally an Indian production, to the value of upwards of a
million. But as the duties on East India sugar were higher than those
charged on West India sugar, India was practically unable to pay for
the goods thus imported with its sugar. It was urged in Parliament,
that as the power of India to receive English goods was limited only
by what it could give in exchange, one great source of purchasing
power was thus denied it, and that an equality of duties should be
established. Of course the West India interests were violent in
opposition, but while objecting to the change at present, Huskisson
allowed that the production of slave labour was more costly than
that of free labour, and that slavery was not only a crime but a
commercial mistake. This confession called the abolitionists again
into activity. They had already succeeded in getting the trade
condemned by most civilized nations, and the slave who touched
English ground was free ; but the institution continued in all its
severity in our own colonies. Sir Fowell Buxton, who now became
the prominent supporter of abolition, brought in a resolution (May
15, 1823) declaring that slavery should be gradually abolished
throughout the British colonies. Gradual abolition presents great
difficulties. It is not logical, as slavery is either right or wrong ; it
is difficult to carry out, because slaves still left unenfranchized, while
others are freed, are naturally discontented. Canning therefore
distinctly objected to the motion ; he declared that no half measures
were possible, and that as for immediate abolition the Constitution
of England was against it. At the same time he proposed resolutions declaring the expediency of improving the condition .of the
slaves preparatory to freedom. This was followed up
in a circular issued on the 24th of May 1823, ordering
the cessation of the use of the whip in the field and of

the flogging of women. The circular excited great anger among
the planters, the House of Assembly in Jamaica began to talk of
independence and of addressing the King to remove Lord Bathurst,
the Colonial Secretary. In Barbadoes the mean whites, that is,
those who possessed no slaves and who were the outcasts of society,

rose in riot, and razed to the ground the chapel of a missionary who had spoken of them as an ignorant and depraved class.   In Demerara the purport of the circular and the way in which it was spoken of by the planters came to the ears of the negroes, and caused a rising (Aug. 18), which was only kept from becoming a dangerous insurrection by the influence of an Independent missionary of the name of Smith.   In two days the riot was quelled, with considerable bloodshed and nearly fifty executions of negroes.   But the importance of the affair lies chiefly in the conduct of the whites and the Government of the island towards Mr. Smith.   There had already been some efforts made to injure the influence of the dissenting missionaries, who had been most active in instructing the negroes, and although a clergyman of the Episcopalian Church who   *Persecution of* was in Demerara gave full testimony of Mr. Smith's   *Mr. Smith.* excellence, he was apprehended, kept in a disgraceful prison for two months, and then died of his hardships (Feb. 6, 1824).   Before he died he had been sentenced to death, as having been aware of the intended rising.   The sentence of the court-martial was quashed in England, but before the news arrived he was dead.   The treatment of Smith in his imprisonment, and of his widow, who was not even allowed to be present at his funeral, was marked by great cruelty, and his death was followed by a meeting of slave-owners, who petitioned that all missionaries should be expelled from the colony, and prohibited from coming there for the future.   In fact, they declared that any attempt to improve the moral or intellectual condition of the slaves was undesirable and a crime against the planters. The shock given by this violent action to the public feeling in England virtually secured the predominance of abolitionist views.

The years 1823 and 1824 were thus marked by a distinct advance in liberality on the part of the English Government.   But the beneficent action of Huskisson's legislation was postponed during the following year by a period of unexampled distress.   During the past year there had been much hope of increased prosperity.   The opening of new markets in South America had excited the hope of   *Misery caused* speedy profits, and introduced a spirit of rash speculation   *by wild* *speculation.* which has more than once disastrously affected British   *1825.* commerce.   The consequence was the very rapid formation of a vast number of joint-stock companies, with their attendant symptoms of unprincipled stockjobbing and dishonesty on the part of financial agents and promoters of companies.   It is impossible not to be reminded of the similar excitement in the tim of t e South Sea

Bubble,—again acts of fabulous folly were performed ; it is said that in their eagerness to get a sale for British goods both warming-pans and skates were exported in considerable numbers to the Tropics ; while a company of Scotch milk-maids was formed and transferred to Buenos Ayres, where, after conquering the preliminary difficulty of milking wild cattle, it was found that the inhabitants would not eat butter, and preferred the oil of their own country. Though many schemes to be carried on in foreign parts did not even take the trouble to secure charters, 286 private Bills were passed in the session of 1825. The speculation was assisted by a great apparent profusion of money, and by the careless action of both the Bank of England and the private provincial banks. In spite of signs that gold and silver were leaving the country, the Bank of England continued to increase its issue of notes, and the provincial banks followed its example ; there was far too much paper money in the country ; between June 1824 and October 1825 ten millions of coin and bullion were exported. At the same time the Bank of England lowered its rate of interest. Money was thus exceedingly easily obtained, and prices rose suddenly and very rapidly. The readiness of all the banks to discount bills even at long dates enabled speculators to buy up and hold back goods, thus still further raising the prices. There was naturally soon an end of this fictitious state of things. As the goods which had been bought up were brought into the market their prices necessarily fell ; foreign speculations could not produce very rapid returns ; the insecure bills, or those which had been discounted at very long dates, could not be realized, consequently the banks found it difficult to meet the demands upon them ; the Bank of England then took alarm, raised the rate at which it discounted bills, and contracted the issue of bank notes. In all ways therefore money began to get exceedingly scarce ; firms and companies began to break, credit was shaken, a run on the banks was the consequence. At length even the London houses were affected, and on the 5th of December the great banking-house of Pole & Company, on which as many as forty-four country banks depended, broke. In six weeks between sixty to seventy banks had stopped payment, of which six or seven were London houses.

The misery attendant on these disasters was so great that the
Success of Government thought it necessary to interfere. The
the healing
measures of the bank and the mint set hard to work to supply notes
Government. and coin ; 150,000 sovereigns a day were turned out,
but even thus, the story is told that the credit of the Bank was only

saved by the accidental discovery of a forgotten chest with 700,000 one-pound notes. By the end of the year the worst of the panic was over, but during 1826 bankruptcies continued with fearful rapidity. In the opinion of the Government some part of the late misfortune was to be attributed to bad legislation, and might be altered, but the greater part arose from a spirit of over-speculation, over which no legislative enactments could have any power. The healing measures proposed were the prohibition of the issue of one and two pound notes ; for it began to be generally acknowledged that unrestricted paper currency could not exist with coin, that in times of prosperity the paper would be preferred, gold and silver would seek other markets, and in times of necessity would be unprocurable. Many of the banks had paid for the privilege of issuing notes, but the Government risked the infringement on their rights, acknowledging it, and confessing that an Act of indemnity would be necessary. Secondly, they induced the Bank directors to give up one of their privileges, by which private banking-houses were restricted to six partners. Beyond a radius of sixty-five miles from London, the number of partners was henceforward unlimited, and much greater security was thus obtained. At the same time, for the instant relief of commerce, the ministers, unwilling to issue Exchequer bills, because they thought that commerce had better on the whole be left to right itself, succeeded in persuading the Bank to advance £3,000,000 to merchants upon the security of their goods. The effect of these measures was a restoration of credit and the gradual subsidence of the alarm.

But the misfortunes of the preceding years had of necessity been attended by extreme suffering among the poorer classes, and although they had on the whole borne their privations remarkably well, it was impossible, considering the excited temper of the times, Riots and to avoid riots. These were as usual directed principally machine breaking against machinery, which was still ignorantly regarded April 1826 by the artisans as the chief cause of their misery. The riots were very widely spread, every power-loom in Blackburn was smashed, the operatives in Manchester held stormy meetings, and in Carlisle, Staffordshire, and Norfolk uproars took place. To the miseries caused by depression of trade were added those of an unfavourable season ; the summer of 1826 was marked by a very severe drought. On all grounds, therefore, the ministers thought it their duty to introduce some measures which should Temporary tend to the lowering of the price of corn ; it was change in the corn laws. ordered that corn in bond in the warehouses, wait- May 26, 1826

ing till prices should rise to the level which allowed importation,
should be released at once and sent into the market, and that
Government should be authorized to import, within a space of two
months, 500,000 quarters more. Bills to this effect were passed
through the House, having been earnestly pressed forward because
the Parliament was on the point of dissolution, and had the ministers
been obliged to open the ports without leave, their conduct would
have been unconstitutional and would have required an Act of
indemnity. But, after all, their efforts were unavailing ; prices rose,
so that on the 1st of September the legal price was reached ; but as
it was only when the average price was above a certain point that
corn was admitted, and a month must elapse before that average
could be taken, it was thought desirable to forestall the time and
open them at once. The new Parliament assembled in November,
and remained a short time in session for the purpose of giving the
required indemnity.

The attention of Parliament was called to one other important
Canning's   topic, which may be regarded as the finishing stroke to
vigorous policy   Canning's foreign policy. It will be remembered that
in Portugal.
Dec. 1826.   he had always declared that any attack on Portugal
would be regarded as a sufficient cause for the entrance of England
into the war. The French troops still occupied Spain, and in the civil
war which was continued in that country the royalists had been joined
by several regiments of the Portuguese army. In spite of urgent
demands and repeated promises that these deserting troops should be
disbanded, they were allowed, if not encouraged, by the Spanish
royalists to make inroads into constitutional Portugal. The Princess
Regent applied to England for assistance ; Canning at once acted
vigorously according to his principles. At first the information
given was not accurate, but on Friday the 8th of December precise
information arrived, and Canning could triumphantly assert in the
House—"On Saturday his Majesty's confidential servants came to
a decision, on Sunday that decision received the sanction of his
Majesty, on Monday it was submitted to both Houses of Parliament,
and this day (Tuesday) on which I have the honour of addressing
you the troops are on their march for embarkation." It was plain
to all men that the honour of England was safe in such hands,
and proof was afforded to all Europe that England had distinctly
broken from her old connections, and that her sympathies were
on the side of political freedom and national independence.

It is not to be supposed that the changes worked by Canning and by Huskisson, and the decided preponderance of the more liberal-minded members of the Cabinet, were regarded with Division in the ministry favour by all their colleagues. Personally distasteful · to many of them because of their want of aristocratic connection, the innovating character of their policy, and their views, which were closely assimilated on most points to those of the Whigs, separated them entirely from the representatives of the old Tory party. They seem to have had but one point in common — their opposition to parliamentary reform. Lord Liverpool's Government had from the first been one of compromise. One of the greatest questions of the day, which had already caused the fall of more than one ministry, had been allowed to fall from the list of Cabinet questions, and it had been agreed that Catholic emancipation should stand entirely upon its own merits. But this was a point on which men felt very keenly, and there had thus arisen a complete division in the ministry ; on the one side were ranked the followers of Canning, including such men as Huskisson, Wellesley, Robinson, Sturges-Bourne, and Lord Palmerston; and on the other the high Tory or Protestant party, at the head of which was Liverpool himself, Lord Eldon, and the Duke of Wellington, and, although he was regarded as less bigoted, Peel. How great the split between the parties was is made plain not only by the strong if decorous language to be found in Lord Eldon's correspondence, but by the more outspoken expressions of Palmerston in his private letters. In the election of 1826, though himself a member of the ministry, Palmerston had been opposed at Cambridge by Goulbourn (also one of the administration), and all the influence of the Tory section had been used against him. In a letter describing the effects of that election, he says, "As to the commonplace balance between Opposition and Government, the election will have little effect upon it. The Government are as strong as any government can wish to be, as far as regards those who sit facing them ; but in truth the real Opposition of the present day sit behind the Treasury bench. It is by the stupid old Tory party, who bawl out the memory and praises of Pitt, while they are opposing all the measures and principles which he held most important, it is by these that the progress of the Government in every improvement which they are attempting is thwarted and opposed. On the Catholic question, on the principles of commerce, on the corn laws, on the settlement of the currency, on the laws regulating the trade in money, on colonial slavery, on the game laws, which are intimately connected with the moral habits of the people; on all these questions, and everything like them, the Government find support from the Whigs and resistance from their self-denominated friends." While again, speaking of the foolish obstruction to the Catholic claims, he writes of his colleagues in most unmeasured terms : " I can forgive old women like the Chancellor, spoonies like Liverpool, ignoramuses like Westmoreland, old stumped-up Tories like Bathurst, but how such a man as Peel, liberal, enlightened, and fresh-minded, should find himself running in such a pack is hardly intelligible." It is plain that a Government thinking so differently on the most important topics of the day must have been near its dissolution. It was held together in fact only by the

Illness of Lord Liverpool Feb 1827.

tact and personal influence of Lord Liverpool ; and when, on the 17th February, the Premier was found struck with an apoplectic fit it was certain that a ministerial crisis must arise.

The difficulty in the formation of a new permanent Government

Difficulties attending the formation of a new ministry

was likely to be increased by the two great questions which were expected to occupy the session. One of these was a change in the corn laws, and an attempt to bring them more into harmony with the new commercial views of Huskisson and his friends ; the other the Catholic emancipation, on which already the existing Cabinet was so much divided. The constant repetition of temporary measures required by the existing state of the law,

Necessity of a change in the corn laws.

the fluctuation of prices, and the consequent suffering of the poor, proved to those who were not pledged to the interests of the landowning and agricultural party that some alteration in the arrangements with regard to corn was necessary. With much care Canning and Huskisson, although both were too ill to allow of personal communication, had arranged a joint measure, by which foreign corn might be imported free of duty, to be warehoused and admitted to the market for home consumption, regardless of the price of corn, on the payment of duties varying in accordance with a certain scale ; when wheat was at seventy shillings the duty was to be one shilling, and to increase two shillings with every decrease of one shilling in price. The Bill was passed on the 12th of April, during the interval it was thought decent to allow for the possible restoration of Lord Liverpool's health. It did not come on in the Upper House till after the new Government was formed, but it was there thrown out in favour of an amendment produced by the Duke of Wellington, declaring that foreign corn should not be taken out of bond till corn had reached sixty-six shillings. The object of the Bill, which was to supply foreign corn whenever the sale of it was remunerative, was thus entirely frustrated and the Bill abandoned.

It was during the same period, while the Government was in abeyance, that the Roman Catholic question was brought on. The settlement of this question in one way or other had become almost a necessity. It has been seen how Pitt was compelled, by fear of the old King's health, to give up a cause which he undoubtedly regarded as just, and how the obstinacy of George III. upon the same point had ruined Lord Grenville's ministry. During Mr. Perceval's ministry, which was formed on the avowed principle of withstanding the claims of the Catholics, the dangers attendant upon the war afforded sufficient excuse for alleging that the time was inconvenient to move so critical a question ; but during the whole of that period they had, by means of an organization and the establishment of a central Catholic committee, kept their claims before the world, waiting till a favourable time should come. Lord Liverpool had found it impossible, as already stated, to form a ministry unanimous on the point, and year after year, as Bills in favour of the Catholics were introduced in the House, Castlereagh and Canning had been seen supporting them in opposition to most of their colleagues.

In Ireland, meanwhile, the question had naturally become the watchword of parties, and, like every other political question in that country, had assumed a national form and was leading to a division of races. Both the Protestant Orange Lodges and the Catholic Associations of White Boys had again sprung into existence, and so great was the disorder that in 1822 the Habeas Corpus Act had been suspended. At the same time, in agreement with the uncertain and half-hearted policy of Lord Liverpool's Government, Lord Wellesley, a favourer of the Catholic claims, was made Lord-Lieutenant, and Plunkett (in whose hands the chief management of Catholic parliamentary affairs was) Attorney-General, but yoked to Mr Goulbourn, who was a strong anti-Catholic, as Chief Secretary. The hopes of the Irish, not unreasonably raised by these appointments, were disappointed. Received upon his arrival with every sign of admiration and attachment, before long Wellesley was publicly assaulted and pelted in the theatres. He had attempted, in the midst of the wild excitement of the passionate Irishmen of both parties, to follow a cool and impartial policy. His chief object was to suppress secret

Marginal notes: Increasing importance of the Catholic question.

Disturbances in Ireland.

Failure of Wellesley's administration. 1822.

societies and to compel all parties to submit quietly to the law. By the use of very stringent measures, hy the suspension of the Habeas Corpus Act, and by the Insurrection Act, which allowed him to establish where necessary something nearly equivalent to martial law, he had succeeded in weakening the secret societies and in lessening the amount of crime; he thus earned for himself the hearty dislike of the extreme Catholics. At the same time the restraint which he put upon the Orange societies and Protestant demonstrations roused the extreme Protestants to fury, so that riots took place in Dublin which could only be checked by the military. He thus laid himself open to the charges brought against him by the ultra-Protestants of England, who urged, with a show of truth, that he had proved himself inefficient, and that it was plain that lenity and conciliatory measures would not produce the expected effect. And now, seeing that their hopes in their Lord-Lieutenant were

Formation of the Catholic Association. 1823. not realized, and wishing to gain favour with classes to whom secret societies were abhorrent, the Catholic party of Ireland, under the leadership of O'Connell, set on foot the great organization known as the Catholic Association, which, while it held aloof from secret societies, and kept itself as fai as possible within the limits of the law, was inspired as completely with fanaticism as any of its predecessors had been. Its avowed object was the preparation of petitions to Parliament; but it held regular sessions, had its committee of grievances, ordered a census of the population, and exacted a tax known as the Catholic rent. The effect of this Association was for a time to alienate the Catholics of England, and to make the question a more distinctly national one, and by 1825 the Association had become so formidable that, by a large majority, a Bill was passed rendering it illegal and attempting to dissolve it. The Bill declared that political associations were incapable of adjournment for more than fourteen days, incapable of having corresponding societies, of levying contributions, or of requiring oaths. The dissolution of the Association was only nominal, a new Association was immediately formed, and the Catholic body were advised to proceed by all political and legal means.

The Catholics had in fact gained a very important step in compel-

Rejection of the Catholic Relief Bill. 1825. ling Parliament to recognize the existence of the Association. It was no longer possible to postpone the consideration of their claims, and in March 1825, Sir Francis Burdett brought in what was called a Relief Bill, of which O'Connell, entirely falsely, claimed to be the chief author. Besides the Bill for the relief of disabilities there were two subsidiary Bills, the one raising the Catholic franchise to £10 instead of £2, which was thought to be a sop to the Protestants, the other to supply a State provision for the Catholic clergy, by which it was thought the other party might be pleased. Freed from the dread of the Association, the English partisans of the Catholic claims used all their influence and eloquence in favour of the Bill, and it passed the Commons by a considerable majority. Its fate in the House of Lords was different. It there encountered an opposition verging upon the unconstitutional; the Duke of York, the heir to the crown, adopting all his father's old scruples, declared, in distinct allusion to his probable succession to the throne, that under no circumstances and in no position would he assent to such a Bill. He succeeded in obtaining its rejection by a majority of forty-eight. The Duke's action was highly popular; it seems pretty certain that the feeling of the majority of Englishmen was against the Catholics. The plea that the Coronation Oath stood in the way of the royal assent to such a Bill no longer found defenders except with the extremest Tories, but the feeling of race which had been excited, the fear, not wholly ungrounded, that a measure so anxiously desired by the priests must hide some considerable advantage to the Roman Church, and the occasional rash declaration of some furious partisan that obedience to the Papal See was superior to any earthly obedience, made the majority of those who were not guided by reason and principle desire to retain the disabilities which still existed.

The effect of their defeat in the House of Lords was not to dishearten the Catholics, on the contrary, they took courage at their success in the Commons, and were only eager if possible to complete their triumph before the accession of the bigoted Duke of York should throw a fresh obstacle in their way. A Catholic petition was therefore prepared, which Sir Francis Burdett presented during the illness of Lord Liverpool, proposing at the same time a resolution that the affairs of Ireland required immediate and earnest attention. But an election had taken place since the last Bill had been introduced, and the anti-Catholic feeling had apparently gained ground in the new Parliament; in spite of all the support which Canning could give it, the resolution was rejected. It was the last defeat the champions of emancipation were destined to meet. *[margin: Rejection of Burdett's resolution. March 5, 1827.]*

While Canning was thus defeated on the two questions he had most at heart,—the improvement of the corn laws and the Catholic emancipation,—he found himself called upon to undertake the duties of Prime Minister. *[margin: Canning Prime Minister. April 10, 1827]*

There was indeed no one in the existing ministry who could well compete with him, and the popular voice at once nominated him as Lord Liverpool's successor. Yet from the first it was clear that his appointment implied a complete change of ministry. It was not to be expected that his opponents in the Cabinet, whether on aristocratic and personal or on political grounds, would consent to serve under him. The King, who had lately been drawing more towards the anti-Catholic party, himself hesitated, but when a cabal of Tory Lords threatened him with the loss of their support should he appoint Canning, his mind was at once made up to resent the affront, and Canning was sent for. His appointment was followed by the resignation of all the most important members of the ministry ; Wellington, R. Melville, Eldon, Bathurst, Westmoreland, Bexley, and Peel, chiefly on account of the obligations under which he felt as member for the Protestant University of Oxford, with several less important ministers, withdrew. As Canning was willing to consent that the Catholic question should still remain open, this great defection seems to show how clearly defined his general liberal tendencies had become. From among his own friends,

Canning's new ministry. 1827.
and such of the Tories as would still serve with him, by the 27th of April a new Government was formed. The Duke of Clarence, since the death of the Duke of York (Jan. 5, 1827) heir-presumptive, was made Lord High Admiral, Copley, made Lord Lyndhurst, became Chancellor, Lord Dudley, a very able though eccentric man, went to the Foreign Office, Mr. Robinson became Lord Goderich, and led the party in the Upper House as Secretary for the Colonies, Sturges-Bourne went to the Home Office, Mr. Huskisson remaining at the Board of Trade. These first appointments were however provisional; so also was Canning's own acceptance of the place of Chancellor of the Exchequer. The new Prime Minister, after the secession of his colleagues, was received with such marked approbation by the Whigs, that it was not difficult to see that his coalition with them would be only a matter of time; and as they would require their fair share in the administration, it was necessary to keep some of the high places in hand, or only provisionally filled. As far as the support of parties in the House went, the union between the Canningites and the Whigs was accomplished; Brougham, Burdett, and Tierney sat on the Government side of the house; but, although Lord Lansdowne had already a seat in the Cabinet, Canning did not live long enough to complete the fusion of parties in the ministry. After the Easter holidays,

during which the ministry were got together, little business of public importance was transacted, and the session was spent in a series of vehement attacks and personalities directed against Canning by his old friends. The only fact of importance was the failure of the Corn Bill in the Upper House, which has been already mentioned. In July, to the relief of all parties—for the bitter feelings lately excited had rendered the session an unusually disagreeable one—Parliament was prorogued. On the 8th of the next month Can- *Death of* ning died of an illness caught at the funeral of the Duke *Canning.* of York, and rendered worse by the effects of the con- *Aug. 8, 1827.* stant attacks to which he had been subjected acting upon his sensitive nature. Thus was prematurely terminated a change in the position of parties which, by uniting the moderate Tories and the Whigs, and placing the united forces under the command of so able a leader as Canning, seemed full of promise for the constitutional advance of England.

The death of Canning was felt to be a national loss. In spite of every effort to render his funeral private, vast crowds *Character and* attended, and Whigs and Tories joined in doing him *policy of* honour. It was only the exclusive clique which, like *Canning.* Chatham, he had broken through which retained its enmity and regarded him to the end as a renegade adventurer. His title to greatness can scarcely be questioned. Adorned with the richest gifts of body and mind, a noble and attractive presence, overflowing wit, and a majestic eloquence, he showed himself an essentially practical statesman. On most subjects his views were large and liberal; by his assistance his friend Huskisson was enabled to launch England upon a fresh course of commercial prosperity, and by so doing to alleviate the miseries under which the people were groaning. As a foreign minister he enabled the country to assume a great place among nations. Two principles formed the bases of his policy—peace, and the greatness of his native country, which he regarded as indissolubly connected with its national individuality. He thus broke from the trammels of the Holy Alliance, and set on foot the policy of non-intervention, which, though its misuse has much destroyed its credit, is, when the dignity of the country is properly supported, the true policy to be pursued by a people at once desirous to secure peace and to allow to other nations the opportunity of working out their own development, and of securing that national freedom of action which it claims for itself. There were undoubtedly inconsistencies in his political views. Like his successor, Peel, he belonged to a transition

time, and had a mind capable of growth. Several remnants of his
early political creed hung about him to the last. He was always a
firm opponent to parliamentary reform; while supporting continually the claims of the Catholics, he would listen to no arguments
in favour of the relaxation of the Test and Corporation Acts ; and he
always upheld the repressive measures of Lord Sidmouth. It is to
be remembered that his youth had been passed in the midst of the
French Revolution, against which all the weapons of his wit had been
directed, and that he was the favourite disciple of Pitt at the time
when that minister's energies were chiefly directed to the suppression of revolutionary and Jacobinical tendencies ; while, in his prime,
temperate reform had become so connected with the exaggerated views
of the radical reformers, that it is not to be wondered at that a statesman trained as Canning had been should object to measures which
might open a door to the admission of so violent a flood of change.

Though its chief was gone, it was determined to continue the
ministry which Canning had formed on the same principle of compromise on the subject of Catholic reform. The King could not
make up his mind to take any decided step one way or the other,
Goderich's and fixed upon Lord Goderich, a colourless man, as best
ministry. fitted to carry on the system. The changes necessary
were few, but some of them important for the future. Lord Goderich's own place was taken by Huskisson ; Lord Lansdowne accepted,
at the King's personal request, the Home Office ; the Chancellorship
of the Exchequer, which Canning had held, was, with some want of
wisdom, considering the connection of the Canningites and Whigs,
given to Mr. Herries, a Tory, an appointment which at once shook
the administration. Another important nomination was that of the
Duke of Wellington, who, immediately upon Canning's death, was
without difficulty persuaded to resume the command of the army,
showing how far personal enmity had been the cause of his previous
resignation. The accession of these two Tories was at the time
regarded as a sure augury for the early break up of the Cabinet.
" Before six months are over," said Lord Anglesey, who had been
the agent in securing Wellington's adhesion, " he will trip up all
your heels." These forebodings were speedily fulfilled. A quarrel
broke out about the appointment of a chairman to a Finance Committee which was to be formed at the opening of the session. The
position naturally belonged to Mr. Herries, but Tierney and Huskisson appear to have secured the appointment of Lord Althorp without
Mr. Herries' knowledge (Nov. 29). Both Huskisson and Herries

sent in their resignation; it seemed impossible to keep them both, and Lord Goderich, unable to take a firm course in the matter, sent in his own resignation, which, after he. had once weakly withdrawn it, was finally accepted (Jan. 8, 1828). After seven months of useless life the abortive ministry expired.

There was great difficulty in finding a successor for Goderich. Lord Harrowby declined the position. Huskisson, who was thought of, was supposed unable to lead the Commons, and the King, weary of compromise, determined to have recourse to the Tories, and, at the advice of Lord Lyndhurst, applied to the Duke of Wellington, whose supposed firmness of character in- Wellington made Prime Minister. Jan. 1828. spired him with confidence. But even yet George attempted to postpone the final settlement of the Catholic question; the conditions he laid on Wellington were only to avoid a union with Lord Grey and to establish a lasting Government. The Duke therefore, in spite of his late conduct, asked and received the adhesion of Dudley, Palmerston, Huskisson, and some others. The Whigs of the late Government naturally retired, and in their place the Tories of Lord Liverpool's Government resumed office. In fact the attempt was made to reconstitute the Liverpool Cabinet. Mr. Huskisson declared to his constituents at Liverpool that the presence of so many Canningites was a guarantee that that minister's policy would be continued, but it was generally understood that the accession of Wellington to the premiership was in fact a Tory triumph, and such it speedily proved. In a very few months an opportunity, arising from a slight difference of opinion, enabled the Duke to insist upon the resignation of Mr. Huskisson; with him the rest of Canning's party left the ministry, and the Government was constituted entirely on a Tory basis (May).

The continuation of Canning's policy in some way or other was indeed almost a necessity, but the way in which his Difficulty of the Turkish question. plans were completed by Wellington would hardly have satisfied Canning. He had died, leaving unfinished in the hands of his successors one of the most difficult diplomatic questions which he had undertaken. For six years a war, marked by extreme barbarity, had been carried on between the Turks and their Greek subjects. It will be remembered that on this point the Czar, who regarded himself as the natural protector of the Greeks, and who nourished the traditional desire of conquest on the side of Turkey, had found himself at variance with his own principles. His mind was divided between a wish to seize the opportunity offered of extending his influence over Turkey, and his love of legitimacy, which, as chief of the Holy Alliance, he constantly upheld, and which seemed to forbid him to take the part· of insurgents against their legitimate sovereign. Lengthened conferences between the representatives of the sovereigns of Europe had been held at St. Petersburg, where France and Austria, bitterly opposed to the English policy, both with regard to the constitutionalists of Spain, and the acknowledgment of the independence of the South American colonies, had shown themselves eager upon the side of legitimacy, and where Austria especially had expressed a constant wish that the Greeks should be treated merely as insurgents. Supported therefore by the advice of Austria, and trusting to the well-known feeling in favour of the Mahomedan rule in Turkey which existed among the Tories in England, the Porte had refused to listen to any offers of mediation. Nor did it seem possible that the English ministry, anxious at once to prevent Russia from attacking Turkey and yet to save the Greeks, could intervene with any hope of honourable success. At last, in 1824, an opening occurred, and the hope was raised in Canning's mind that these two apparently contrary objects might be obtained. The provisional government in Greece in its despair made a formal appeal to the English, and showed itself quite as fearful of the warlike views of Russia as Turkey itself, in the belief that the outbreak of a war with Turkey would ensure its own immediate destruction. The English minister now thought it possible to bring the conferences, from which he had hitherto held quite aloof, under his own hand in London. The course of events tended to assist his plan. In 1825 the conferences at St. Petersburg broke up without action, the other powers having refused to join Russia in mediation. It was the conduct of Metternich, who dreaded before all things any tampering with the principles of legitimate sovereignty, and constantly abetted the obstinacy of the Porte, which had rendered the mediation futile. Thus thwarted in his plans, and feeling that his failure was due to Metternich, the Czar found a point of union with Canning in their dislike to the Austrian minister. England was represented at Constantinople by Sir Stratford Canning, and by his skilful management the ambassadors of the two courts there began to draw together; and at last, in November 1825, Canning had a triumphant proof of the success of his policy and of the importance of England, when all the ministers of the great powers in London confessed that they saw no way out of their difficulty but by English intervention. This favourable

Canning's diplomacy on the subject.

state of things was for the moment crossed by the death of Alexander (Dec. 1, 1825). The view which his successor Nicholas would take became in the last degree important; Canning, with great wisdom, chose Wellington—opposed indeed to his policy, but personally acceptable to the Russian Czar—as his special ambassador to take the royal congratulations upon the new Emperor's accession, and to continue the negotiations if possible. The appointment met with universal approbation ; even Metternich believed that in the hands of Wellington the question must be settled in accordance with his views. It was with much surprise and anger that the Turks and Austrians heard that, on the 4th of April, an arrangement had been arrived at between the Courts of England and Russia. Taking advantage of the very moderate claims of the Greeks, who demanded no more than to be placed on the same footing as the Danubian Principalities, remaining as self-governing but dependent vassals of the Turkish Government, the English minister had succeeded in procuring the signature of a protocol embodying a plan for peaceful intervention.

Protocol between England and Russia April 1826.

The cause of Greek independence had already excited enthusiasm in England, many volunteers had joined the armies, and money had been subscribed for them. In this enthusiasm Canning in his heart fully joined ; from early youth one of his favourite dreams had been the independence of that race to which as an ardent lover of the classics he felt he owed so much. But, true to his principles, and determined to maintain the strict neutrality of England, he had done his best to check any active assistance to the insurgents. According to his view it was necessary that England should intervene with clean hands, and as the friend of both parties. He was also in constant dread of the watchfulness of his Tory enemies, fearing lest any sign of too great favour to Russia should enable them entirely to thwart his plans. Nevertheless the knowledge of the approaching intervention gave a great impetus to the feeling in favour of Greece in England, and men and money were poured in considerable quantities into the peninsula. Lord Cochrane, the most dashing and adventurous of English sailors, had joined the insurgents with an American frigate, General Churchill took command of their armies, yet their destruction seemed imminent. The Egyptians, under Ibrahim Pasha, had come to the assistance of their enemies; their fleet, which was little better than a body of pirates, was swept from the sea; Missalonghi was for the third time

Enthusiasm for Greek independence in England

taken, and in spite of General Churchill's efforts, Athens and the Acro-
polis had fallen. If the protocol was to be of any use the time for acting
upon it had arrived.   The allies received a great accession of strength
when, after a visit of Canning to Paris in the spring of 1826, the
French Government and the King himself entered heartily into their
plans.   It was plain that for the second time Canning had struck
a severe blow at the principles of the Holy Alliance. In April
1827 the three powers proceeded to act with renewed strength.
They demanded an immediate armistice, pointed out that the war did

Turkey refuses not seem to be approaching its conclusion, that it caused
the armistice interference with the traffic of the world, and that in
demanded by the interests of Europe it must cease.   Almost of course
the allies.
April 1827. the Turks, still trusting to Austria, and still unable to
believe in the changed posture of England, rejected this demand.
Therefore, in accordance with the expressed wish of the French, which
no doubt agreed with Canning's own wishes, the protocol was changed

The Treaty into a treaty known as the Treaty of London, signed
of London on the 6th of July by Lord Dudley, Count Lieven, and
consequently
signed. the Prince of Polignac.   In strict accordance with the
terms of the protocol, it set forth the necessity of European action,
it stated the terms which must be given to Greece, and which went
no further than establishing its self-government under Turkish
supremacy and saddled with a tribute to the Porte, and declared
that none of the parties to the treaty sought territorial increase or
commercial advantages.   Fear of Russian aggrandizement was thus
withdrawn, the intervention was at first to be purely friendly ; but
secret articles went on to say that, if the intervention were rejected,
more stringent means must be used to oblige its acceptance both by
one party and by the other, and that it would be necessary to show
countenance to Greece, by acknowledging her as a belligerent power,
and establishing consuls at her ports.   It was not expressly stated
what the further means of coercion were to be.   A month was given
to the Porte for consideration of the terms offered.   If no answer,
or an unfavourable answer came, the secret articles were to be put
into execution.   If the armistice was refused by the Turks, the
allied squadrons then in the Mediterranean were to unite, to enter
into friendly relations with the Greeks, and to intercept all ships
freighted with men and arms destined to act against the Greeks,
whether from Turkey or from Egypt.   At the same time they were
carefully to avoid hostilities.   It is doubtful whether Canning could
have succeeded in carrying out this his last measure of peace policy

and non-intervention without having recourse to war. When the affair had reached this point he died, and the completion of his work fell into weaker and less competent hands.

In August, a joint note having been again sent, and all satisfactory answer having been entirely refused by Reis Effendi, the Turkish minister, consuls were appointed according to the treaty, and the fleets ordered to compel the armistice. The execution of this delicate duty was intrusted to Admiral Codrington on the part of the English, to the French Admiral de Rigny, and to Count Heyden, who commanded the Russian fleet. Twenty-eight Turkish and Egyptian ships of war lay in Navarino Bay awaiting fresh reinforcements from Egypt. Had the union taken place, the combined fleets of Turkey and Egypt would have entirely destroyed the Greek Government then in the Ionian Islands, and have swept away what remained of the Greek fleet. The allies appeared before Navarino, explained to Ibrahim Pasha, who was in command, the negotiations which were proceeding, and declared that the Turkish fleet should not sail. Ibrahim, nothing daunted, while asserting that he would take orders from his own sovereign only, pledged himself, on the 25th of September, that the fleet should remain quiet for twenty days to enable him to receive an answer from Constantinople. In spite of this promise, Codrington, who had withdrawn, heard on the 1st of October that the fleet had left harbour. He at once went to meet it, and turned back the first squadron he encountered. On the 13th the combined fleets were in front of Navarino. Then Ibrahim in anger let loose his troops on the wretched people, and before the eyes of the allies terrible scenes of barbarity were enacted. Codrington, though with difficulty, kept himself in restraint, but on the 20th his fleet sailed into the harbour, to say that they would convoy the Turkish ships to Turkey, the Egyptian ships to Egypt. They found the Turks and Egyptians drawn up in the form of a horseshoe and ready for battle. Strict orders were given not to fire unless the enemy proceeded to hostilities, and Codrington, bringing his ship close to that of the Turkish admiral, opened communications with him. Meanwhile, a boat from the Dartmouth was fired upon, and a cannon shot was fired against the French flag-ship. In spite of this Codrington went on parleying till his pilot was shot by his side and a broadside fired upon his ship. The battle then began in earnest, and in four hours the hostile fleet was entirely destroyed.

The news of the victory was received with delight in France and

Attempt of the allies to compel the armistice.

Battle of Navarino. Oct 20, 1827.

Russia, and at first with triumph in England, where at the instant
Sir Edward Codrington met with the full approval of
the Government. None the less did it present to the
weak and tottering Cabinet of Lord Goderich difficulties

Goderich's inaction renders the victory nugatory.

of the gravest kind. The peaceful policy of their late chief had
ended in a fierce and destructive battle ; they hardly knew whether
to accept the whole responsibility of it or not. At all events they
did not follow up the blow or act with any vigour under the circumstances. The effect of this delay was to strengthen in Constantinople
the belief that the union between the three powers was not hearty,
and to encourage the Turks in their obstinacy. The foreign merchants in Constantinople were apprehended, the Porte determined on
war, demanding that the allies should refrain entirely from interfering on the Greek question, pay the fleet, and indemnify the Sultan
for his losses. In spite of the efforts of the ambassadors, before they
had left Constantinople, which they did upon the 8th of December,
nothing could be gained beyond an offer of a general amnesty to the
Greeks. Had the allied fleets proceeded at once to Constantinople,
which was the wish both of Sir Stratford Canning and of Codrington,
it is probable that they might have put an end to the war with
Greece, and have succeeded in carrying out at least one part of the
London Treaty, by saving Turkey from the invasion of Russia, which
now became inevitable. As it was, England had in fact only handed
the country up, weakened by the loss of its fleet, to the hands
of that power. The weakness of the Goderich Government prevented such efficient action, and the accession of Wellington to office rendered it still more impossible. True to his Tory traditions, while pretending

Wellington retains his alliance with Turkey 1828

to continue the policy of Canning, he fell back upon the words of
the London Treaty, which were no doubt intended to be pacific.
The speech at the opening of Parliament, on the 29th of January
1828, mentioned the battle of Navarino in somewhat disparaging
terms as "the untoward event," which it was hoped would not
be followed by further hostilities, and the Duke himself declared
that the preservation of the Ottoman Porte as an independent and
powerful state was necessary to the wellbeing of this country. In
fact, he suffered the matter again to fall back into negotiations.
England kept out of war, and Russia was allowed to overrun
Turkey, to take Adrianople (Aug. 20, 1828), and from thence to
dictate terms which left the Porte for ten years at least defence-
less in their hands. Among the terms demanded by Russia was

necessarily the independence of Greece. The limits were arranged by the three powers in London. Neither Turkey nor Greece were allowed a voice in the matter; the frontiers were fixed, and a monarchical form of government established ; the crown for a while went begging; it was declined by the Saxon Prince John, and by Prince Leopold (May 1830), subsequently King of the Belgians, nor was it till the year 1832 that Otho of Bavaria, a lad of eighteen, was found to undertake a post which offered almost insuperable difficulties and but very little honour.

The Duke of Wellington had been no doubt first called to the Premiership for the purpose of continuing as far as possible the system of the Tories. His conduct as head of the Government was so peculiar that it would scarcely have been tolerated in a less influential man. He regarded his office as he would have regarded a military command,—a trust not lightly to be laid down. He fought till his opponents became irresistible and then suddenly retreated, without thinking it necessary to resign office on account of his defeat. This view of his duty had the same practical results as the most determined place-hunting, and reduced his Government to that most dangerous form of weakness which consists in driving opposition to irresistible extremes, and then suddenly yielding to pressure. This peculiar tendency to give up his opinion and yet retain office was visible at the very outset. He had taken the Premiership, although a few months before he had declared himself wholly unfit for it ; he had formed a mixed Government, though his views and those of the King were in favour of a united one. His next concession was upon the repeal of the Test and Corporation Acts. In the first session of 1828, Lord John Russell moved for a Committee upon those Acts. Canning had always withstood their repeal ; the Duke and Mr. Peel were known to share the late minister's opinion. But when a majority of forty-four in a full House decided in favour of Lord John Russell's Committee, the leaders of the Government accepted their decision, and declared themselves satisfied with the substitution of a declaration that the incoming office-holder would do nothing to injure the Church, instead of the old sacramental test. After a lengthened and bitter opposition, led by Lord Eldon in the Upper House, the Bill was carried. The old Chancellor's view of the conduct of Government was very unfavourable. "They began in the Commons," he said, "by opposition, and then ran away like a parcel of cowards."

Character of Wellington's Government.

Repeal of the Test and Corporation Acts. May 1828.

The second important Bill of the session was the Corn Bill, to be
The Corn Bill substituted for that which Wellington had himself suc-
passed   ceeded in throwing out in the preceding session.   Here
again he yielded to circumstances.   Entirely leaving his previous
standing-ground, the Premier now supported the Bill on exactly the
same principle of duties on a graduated scale as that he had previously thwarted.   The fixed point in the scale was a few shillings
higher, but in principle the Bill was identical.

No doubt the necessity for such concessions was very irksome to
The resignation the Duke, and, as before mentioned, an opportunity
of Huskisson   soon occurred for ridding himself of the more liberal
and his friends.
May 1828.   members of his Cabinet, whose pressure he had been
unable to resist.   On a trivial question as to the disposition of the
seats of two disfranchised boroughs Huskisson had thought it his
duty to vote against his colleagues.   It had been before settled that
the question should not be a Cabinet one; but Huskisson, while
still under excitement, thought it right to send the Duke a letter
offering to retire should the Premier wish it.   The Duke seized his
opportunity, treated the letter as an absolute resignation, would
listen to no explanation, and obliged Huskisson to resign.   With
him went Palmerston, Dudley, Lamb, and Grant; their places were
filled with Tories, and the Government seemed at length thoroughly
homogeneous.

Yet the establishment of this Tory Cabinet was followed almost
The Catholic   immediately by a far greater concession than any of the
Emancipation   preceding ones, in the passage of the Catholic Emanci-
question.   pation Bill.   The Government had been constituted as
far as possible on a Protestant basis.   It was known that the King
was strong in his anti-Catholic propensities.   Although a small
majority in the Commons had, on the 8th of May, declared in favour
of bringing the question to a settlement, and although both the Chancellor and the Prime Minister had confessed, while opposing the
motion successfully in the Lords, that they saw no way at present out
of the great difficulty, thereby apparently implying a wish for a
settlement, the declarations both of Wellington and of Peel gave
little hope of any relaxation of the disabilities.   But meanwhile
events were occurring which rendered some settlement obviously
necessary.   There was indeed a general and growing feeling that
a question which in the last thirty-five years had ruined more
than one Cabinet, which was in fact uppermost in all men's minds
at the time of every new ministerial arrangement, and which had

kept Ireland permanently uneasy, could no longer be left uncertain. Events were now occurring in Ireland which would have rendered the further postponement of the settlement little short of madness.

The agitation in that country, which had almost subsided during the administration of Canning, a well-known supporter of the Catholic claims, and which had only slightly revived during Goderich's administration, broke out again in full force when the hostile ministry of Wellington came into office.   The law for the suppression of the Association would expire in the coming July, and meanwhile, keeping within the limits of the law, for all practical purposes the organization remained alive. The last general election had opened the eyes of the leaders of the Association to a new and irresistible source of power ; it had proved that the power of the priests was in some cases stronger than that of the landlords.   In their eagerness to secure their parliamentary influence, the landlords had followed the disastrous plan of breaking up their estates into small forty shilling freeholds, taking advantage of the low franchise which existed in Ireland.   Several instances had occurred in which the tenantry had broken loose from their landlords, and at Waterford, among other places, they had proved themselves too strong even for the great Beresford interest.   What had then been done in a few instances it was the intention of the Association to carry out in a large scale, and great efforts were made to secure the votes of those who were known as the Irish "forties" in the coming general election.   The anger of the proprietors thus assaulted in their strongholds was very great, and class animosity reached a terrible pitch.   The power of the Association was soon brought to the test. With the rest of the Canningites, Grant, President of the Board of Trade, had resigned ; his place had been given to Mr. Vesey Fitz-gerald, member for Clare, whose re-election thus became necessary. Aware that, even if they succeeded in excluding the Government candidate, the election of a Protestant representative would be of no great value to them, the Association determined to strike a great blow, and to bring forward O'Connell himself to dispute Mr. Fitzgerald's seat.   His triumph was complete ; after a few days' polling Mr. Fitzgerald withdrew.   But more wonderful and more terrible than his mere success was the admirable discipline and order with which it was obtained.   Lord Palmerston thus narrates the event :—" The event was dramatic and somewhat sublime.   The Prime Minister of England tells the Catholics in his speech in the House of Lords that if they will only be perfectly

Renewed agitation in Ireland.

Election of O'Connell for Clare. June 1828.

quiet for a few years, cease to urge their claims, and let people forget the question entirely, then after a few years perhaps something may be done for them. They reply to this advice, within a few weeks after it is given, by raising the population of a whole province like one man, keeping them within the strictest obedience to the law, and by strictly legal and constitutional means hurling from his seat in the representation one of the Cabinet ministers of the King. There were 30,000 Irish peasants in and about Ennis in sultry July, and not a drunken man among them, or only one, and he an Englishman and a Protestant, O'Connell's own coachman, whom O'Connell had committed upon his own deposition for a breach of the peace. No Irishman ever stirs a mile from his house without a stick, but not a stick was to be seen at the election. One hundred and forty priests were brought from other places to harangue the people from morning to night, and to go round to the several parishes to exhort and bring up voters. . . . All passed off quietly. The population of the adjoining counties was on the move, and large bodies had actually advanced in echelon, as it were, closing in upon Ennis, the people of one village going on to the next, and those of that next advancing to a nearer station, and so on." The sheriff and his assessor declared that the election was legal, the only obstacle to O'Connell's appearance in the House being the oaths he would have to take on his admittance. It was determined to follow up the success. O'Connell declared that Catholic representatives must be elected for all the counties of Ireland. The funds of the Association, which assumed its old form in July on the expiration of the suppression law, were partially devoted to the support of those on whom the vengeance of the landlords fell; and not content with declaring the necessity of the election of Catholic members, the Association drew up certain pledges to be required of all future Catholic candidates. These consisted in a promise to be the determined opponents of the ministry of Wellington and Peel till it granted Catholic emancipation, to support religious and civil liberty, to procure a repeal of the Subletting Act (which was an attempt to restrain the minute subdivision of property), and to support a reform of Parliament.

The power the Association had already exhibited, and its determination to have those representatives whom it should elect thus closely bound to pursue the line of conduct it dictated, much increased the Influence of the dread with which it was regarded. Symptoms were Association. already visible of the influence it might exert; only ten days after the establishment of the pledges (Aug. 2), Mr. Dawson, Peel's brother-in-law, and himself in the Administration, after a lively picture of the enormous power of the Association, concluded with the unexpected assertion, that as this power could not be crushed it ought to be conciliated. Coming from such a source the assertion was received as a certain proof that the cause of the Catholics was winning its way. Consequently the efforts of the Association were pressed forward with redoubled zeal. Parochial clubs were established, and great aggregate meetings held in various parts of Ireland. Mr. Shiel, one of its most ardent supporters, thus describes the condition of Ireland under its influence:—"Does not a tremendous organization extend over the whole island? Have not all the natural bonds by which men are tied together been broken and burst asunder? Are not all the relations of society which exist elsewhere gone? Has not property lost its influence? Has not rank been stripped of the respect which should belong to it? Has not an internal government grown up, which, gradually superseding the legitimate authorities, has armed itself with a complete domination? Is it nothing that the whole body of the clergy are alienated from the State, and that the Catholic gentry and peasantry and priesthood are all combined in one vast confederacy?" His description was true; the Association was omnipotent, and in nothing did it show its power so much as in the complete restraint it held over the excitable people. Faction and faction fights disappeared; crime of a graver sort almost vanished; and though the people were drilled and brought into something resembling military organization, although they were eager to know against whom they were to fight, the influence of the Association restrained them from all demonstrations likely to provoke hostilities, and on one occasion a few words from O'Connell at once broke up and dispersed a body of 50,000 men. This was the more admirable as the temper of the Protestants had naturally been roused, and Brunswick clubs had sprung up, to take the place of the Orange organization, which do not seem to have been as self-restrained as the Catholics. During the whole of this time the Duke was painfully making up his mind to his retreat. The peculiarity of his action was that he became absolutely silent; so complete was his silence, that Mr. Shiel thus describes the situation: —"The minister folds his arms as if he were a mere indifferent observer, and the terrific contest between Protestant and Catholic only afforded him a spectacle for the amusement of his official leisure; he sits as if two gladiators were crossing their swords for his gratification: the Cabinet seems to be little better than a box in a theatre from which his Majesty's ministers may survey the business of blood." Indeed, so strangely reticent was the Duke, that he ceased to correspond at all with his Lord Lieutenant, the Marquis of Anglesey. Unin-structed from home, Lord Anglesey, who was a Liberal, and inclined to the emancipation, naturally followed the dictates of his own opinions, and rendered the conduct of the Government almost treacherous from the indirect support he gave to the Liberals, while his chief in London was supporting the opposite party. The in-evitable consequence was that he shortly committed an indiscretion which necessitated his recall. His place was taken by the Duke of Northumberland, a strong Tory.

Resignation of Lord Anglesey. Jan. 1829

Peel, the most influential member of the ministry next to the Premier, had already, since the Clare election, arrived at the conclu-sion that the solution of the question could no longer be postponed, and that only one form of solution was pos-sible. The election of Catholics, while still unable to sit in Parliament, would deprive Ireland of its repre-sentation. So important an event as O'Connell's election could not possibly pass unnoticed and the question be left unmoved. With the present House a high-handed repression of the Association was impossible; were it attempted by a new House a civil war was inevitable: there remained but a third course—to give way. Early in August 1828, Peel had stated this opinion forcibly to the Duke, and told him that he considered that an attempt to settle the Catholic question was a lesser evil than to continue to leave it open; at the same time he wished himself to resign, and to leave the bringing in of the measure to other hands. Although aware of the penalty he should be called upon to pay for this change of opinion, the attacks to which he should be subject, and the loss of friends, he was at length persuaded by Wellington, who felt it impossible to carry on the Government without him, to retain his place. Peel's representations had had their effect upon the Duke's mind, and he was by degrees becoming convinced that further obstruction was impossible. Dur-ing the autumn he learned to see that his choice lay between the reconquest of Ireland, the repeal of the Union, or the emancipation of the Catholics. He could not hesitate which of the three to choose. But though his own mind and that of his colleague were made up, great difficulties lay in the way of the execution of their plans, the chief of which was the temper of the King, who had now begun to

Peel and Wellington see the urgency of the Catholic question.

declare that he, like his father, was troubled with conscientious scruples. At length, in January, the King consented that the question should be brought before the Cabinet. The two ministers found little or no opposition, and it was determined to take in hand the final settlement of the question. Accordingly, in the royal speech at the opening of Parliament (Feb. 5), it was stated that measures must first of all be taken to establish authority by the destruction of the Association, and that then the whole condition of Ireland should be taken into consideration, with a view to altering the laws so as to remove civil disabilities from his Majesty's Catholic subjects. The speech came as an unexpected blow to the high Tories, but immediate discussion was postponed at the request of the ministry till the actual Bill could be introduced in its completed form. Meanwhile the preliminary measure for the destruction of the Association was brought in. Its necessity was however forestalled by the clever tactics of the Irish, who dissolved their Association before the Bill obtained the force of law. Having declared his change of opinion, Peel, who throughout acted as honourably as circumstances would allow, thought it incumbent on him to resign his seat for Oxford, which he no doubt owed chiefly to his supposed anti-Catholic views. The events of the election proved that he was right, the seat was contested by Sir Robert Inglis, who was elected by a considerable majority. Peel found a seat at Westbury.

The coast seemed now clear for the great measure, but the King made a final stand. The very day before the Bill was to be introduced (March 4), he sent unexpectedly for Wellington, Lyndhurst, and Peel, declared he had been misunderstood, withdrew his sanction, and asked what they now intended to do about Ireland. In fact he had been incessantly worked on by the Tory Lords who had access to him ; and, weak and miserable, apparently thought that the fear of offending him might even yet postpone the measure. Peel at once declared that nothing remained for him but·to resign. The Duke and the Chancellor expressed the same intention, and they left the presence of the King, who bade them a most friendly farewell, in the belief that the ministry was at an end. Late at night Wellington received a letter, in which the King said that he was convinced of the impossibility of forming another ministry, and begged them to remain. Knowing his weak character, it was only on receiving express leave to declare that the measure was brought in with his consent that they agreed to remain, and it was with the assertion that he was acting in full accordance

with the King's wishes that Peel began his speech. The proposed Bill
Introduction of was of a sweeping but simple character. It substituted
the Bill, a new form of oath for the old oaths of supremacy,
March 5, 1829. allegiance, and abjuration ; thus, if a Catholic bound
himself to support the State and not injure the Church, he could
sit in either House of Parliament, had a perfect equality with his
Protestant neighbours, and was eligible for all offices, civil, military,
or municipal, with the exception of the office of Regent, of Lord
Chancellor, of Viceroy of Ireland, or royal commissioner of the
General Assembly of Scotland. From offices connected with the
Church, or participation in Church patronage, he was naturally excluded. The second point of the Bill was the position to be occupied
by the Roman Church. It was to be left as a dissenting community,
unendowed and unrestricted, but the use of episcopal titles, the
increase of monks, and the introduction of more Jesuits, were forbidden. This Bill for the remission of all restrictions was to be
coupled with another for the establishment of certain securities,
the chief of which consisted in the raising of the franchise to £10.
In a long and careful speech Peel explained his views, and vindicated his change of policy. The same course was pursued by
Wellington in the Upper House, where he alleged that the chief
grounds for his present conduct was his horror of civil war, which
he regarded as inevitable. " I am one of tnose who have probably passed a longer period of my life engaged in war than most
men, and principally, I may say, in civil war, and I must say this,
that if I could avoid by any sacrifice whatever even one month of
civil war in the country to which I am attached, I would sacrifice
my life in order to do it. There is nothing which disturbs property
and wellbeing so much, which so deteriorates character as civil
war, and that, my Lords, would have been the event to which we
must have looked, that the means to which we must have had
recourse." As was natural, there was a strong opposition, but in
both Houses Canningites, Whigs, and Ministerialists combined to
swell the majority ; on the first reading it numbered 188, on the
second 180. Not one amendment was carried in Committee, and the
Bill finally passed by a majority of 178 in a House of 452. In the
The Bill passed. House of Lords it was as favourably received, and on
April 1829. the 10th of April it was passed on the third reading by
213 to 209. There was yet one more struggle, in which the King
played a pitiful part. Lord Eldon relates two interviews he had
with him, in which George seemed inclined to deny that he had ever

authorized his ministers to bring in the Bill, and to represent him-self as forced to consent by repeated threats of resignation. Lord Eldon was honest enough to say, after he had seen written evidence of the fact, that the King's consent had been given, and that it could not now be withdrawn, and the interview closed in the midst of petulant and childish exclamations of anger on the part of the King. Lord Eldon probably hoped that in spite of what he had said there might be still some delay, but the royal assent was at once given, and the Bill became law on the 14th of April.

The Bill for the disfranchisement of the forty shilling freeholders passed at the same time as the Catholic Emancipation Bill, and received the royal assent with it. The conduct of O'Connell, who quietly allowed the passing of this Bill, caused much surprise. "The forties" had been his best supporters, he had pledged himself in the strongest language to support their claims, but he quietly allowed them to be disfranchised. It was strange how little commotion so sweeping a measure produced. A few of the more advanced reformers of England regarded it as an enormous price paid for a still greater advantage. But in fact the quarrel had been rapidly assuming the form of a division of races, and the English Catholics, without whom the measure could not have been carried, were far more anxious for the equality of their Church than for the enlargement of Irish liberty. To O'Connell the question assumed a different shape. Although he repeatedly declared that the passing of the Bill would quiet Ireland, he by no means intended that such should be the case. With him the question was far more Irish than Catholic, as was soon made evident by his conduct. He presented himself to take his seat in Parliament (May 15), and offered to take the new oath, but as he had been elected while the old law was in force, it was held that he was still under its requirements. With excellent temper and ability he argued his case, which was however given against him, and a new writ for Clare was issued. His return was unopposed (July 30), yet he allowed himself the utmost freedom of language, abused with all the powers of his invective the English Government, and gave it clearly to be under-stood that he meant to continue the struggle till it should end in the repeal of the Union. These preliminary operations took so much time that it was not till the next session that he could take his seat. From this time onwards it is impossible to regard him as the cham-pion of a good cause; he sank into the position of a demagogue, exciting the people for an impracticable object, which he must have

O'Connell agitates for the repeal of the Union.

known no English statesman or English Parliament could possibly grant.

The interest of this Catholic Bill had been so absorbing that little *Wellington's* else had been thought of, but when that obstacle was *foreign policy.* once cleared away, there was room to consider what was equally important, the foreign policy of the Government, in which there was much to excite the anger of the Liberal party, and to raise a belief that where Wellington could act without pressure his sympathies were in accordance with the system of Castlereagh rather than with that of Canning. While holding strictly to the principle of non-intervention, he appeared to use it so as to throw its advantages almost entirely upon the side of arbitrary power. It was the affairs of Portugal, of Greece, and of France which chiefly required his attention.

John VI. had at length come back from South America to attempt *Affairs of* to establish his power in Portugal in 1821. During his *Portugal.* absence Brazil declared itself independent, and put Don Pedro, John's son, upon the throne with the title of Emperor. On the death of John in 1826, Don Pedro was called to the throne of Portugal also. He had to choose between his South American and his European dominions. He preferred to remain in Brazil. He therefore gave a constitution to his Portuguese subjects, and then abdicated in favour of his young daughter Maria. For a while his sister acted as Regent, but in February 1828 Don Pedro thought it better to quiet his ambitious brother Miguel by appointing him Regent, and guardian of his niece, to whom he was to be ultimately married. Miguel always declared his intention, as was of course his duty, to uphold the constitution, which had been supported by English troops sent, it will be remembered, by orders of Canning, but had been opposed by a strong party of absolutists, and had not produced any marked improvement in the condition of the country. The priests, the nobility, and the soldiery were deeply infected with dislike to the constitution. In January 1828, just after Wellington had assumed the reins of power, Miguel had visited England for the purpose, it was understood, of studying the working of the constitution, and had voluntarily declared that if he violated the constitution in his own country he should be a perjured usurper. After some delay he accepted the constitutional oath, but with circumstances which made it doubtful even then whether he intended to keep it. So obvious were the signs of his intention to usurp the throne, that when Wellington determined to recall the English troops as though their duty was now completed, the English ambassador on his own authority retained them. Their retention was but temporary. On the 2nd of April they were recalled, although the Chamber of Deputies had been suddenly dissolved in the middle of March; for Wellington, clinging to the narrowest interpretation of the principle of non-intervention, held that the troops were sent to guard Portugal against foreign invasion, and not to be used in party quarrels. Their departure was almost immediately followed by open riots in favour of the absolutists. Restrained for a short time by the threat that all the ambassadors would leave his Court, on the 3rd of May Miguel began to throw away disguise. He summoned the three ancient estates of the realm instead of the new constitutional Parliament, and signed the decree as King {*Miguel usurps the throne. May 1828.*} Miguel I. This act of usurpation was followed by the withdrawal of all the ministers except those of Spain and Rome. A violent reaction set in, the uneducated masses, the aristocracy, and the clergy had it all their own way, and raised a general cry against the Freemasons, as they were pleased to call the Liberal party. While Miguel was planning his usurpation of the throne the act of abdication on the part of Don Pedro was finally completed, and the young Queen set sail for Europe. She was at first intended to visit her uncle the Emperor of Austria; but the news of what had happened in Portugal induced her guardians to bring her to England, where she was received with all the honour due to a queen both by {*Queen Maria acknowledged in England. Sept. 1828.*} the ministers Wellington and Aberdeen, and by King George himself. Meanwhile the government of the reactionists in Portugal had been marked by much violence and contempt of law. In the beginning of October, in the prisons of Lisbon alone, there were 2400 prisoners, of whom 1600 were confined for political crimes. The total number of prisoners throughout the kingdom amounted to upwards of 15,000, among whom were forty-two members of the Chamber of Peers and seven members of the Chamber of Deputies ; and so unrestrained was the wickedness of Miguel that he even attempted the life of his sister, the late Regent, because she refused to give up to him some of her jewels.

The withdrawal of the troops from Lisbon on the one hand, and the recall of the English minister and the acknowledgment of the young Queen on the other, appeared to be in accordance {*Wellington's adherence to the principle of neutrality.*} with the strictest rules of neutrality. At the same time it was obvious that that neutrality as yet had been

entirely in favour of Don Miguel. The principle had yet to be put
to harder trials; a number of Portuguese refugees of the constitutional
party were assembled in England, headed by the Marquis Palmella,
the Portuguese ambassador, and General Saldanha, late constitutional War Minister.   Besides their continental dominions, the
Portuguese possessed the islands of the Azores; and although the
islands had declared for Donna Maria, and therefore might be supposed to be under the protection of the English, Miguel had been
allowed to capture Madeira, and had attempted, though unsuccessfully, a similar attack upon Terceira.   In expectation of a repetition
of this effort, application was made to the Portuguese in England for
assistance.   A body of between 3000 and 4000 men, the relics of an
insurgent army which had attempted in vain to prevent Miguel's
usurpation, had been kept together at Plymouth, but the representations of the usurper had been listened to, and the Duke had ordered
that they should be distributed throughout England. Rather than submit to this, Palmella proposed to send them to Brazil; but Wellington,
mistrusting · their intentions when once they had left England,
declared his intention of placing them under the escort of the English fleet.   On receiving the application from Terceira, Palmella,
seeing an opportunity for employing his countrymen usefully, determined to send them thither, but unarmed, to avoid any breach of
the neutrality of England; and, in spite of the avowed intention of
Wellington to prevent this step by force, in the beginning of January
1829 the expedition actually sailed under Saldanha.   Some English
frigates were sent to prevent a landing, and fired upon the leading
vessel. Saldanha then retired to Brest.   Thus in the eyes of the
Liberals not only had the Duke been impartial, but he had fired
upon an expedition fitted out in favour of a sovereign acknowledged
by and at peace with England, and who intended to make good her
possession of an island of which she was at the moment actually
Queen. Such an interpretation of the duties of neutrality, especially
considering the bitter tyranny under which Portugal was groaning,
afforded good grounds for the anger of the English Liberal party.

In the affairs of Greece the same determination under no circumstances to draw the sword was obvious.   While the French sent an
army to the Morea and rescued the peninsula from the
Turks, and while Russia pursued her victorious course
towards Constantinople, the English clung tenaciously
to the peaceful side of the Treaty of London.   Their negotiations
were so far successful that Russia consented not to act as a belligerent

Non-interven-
tion in the
affairs of Greece.

in the Mediterranean, but the power of Turkey was none the less annihilated from the north. Meanwhile Wellington seemed chiefly bent in restraining the French from advancing beyond the Morea, and in curtailing as far as possible the limits which the powers intended ultimately to fix for the new kingdom of Greece.

In respect to France the effect of the sympathies of the English Government were perhaps rather fancied than real. The reactionary tendencies of Charles X.'s minister, M. de Villèle, and the contest in which he had engaged with the press had excited so much discontent, that the ministry had been compelled to resign in January 1827. There were in France three parties, the moderate royalists, of which Villèle was nominally representative, the ultra-royalists, and the liberals. On Villèle's retirement a colourless and inefficient ministry was called to office, and found itself opposed by a coalition between the liberals and the ultras. At the beginning of 1829 the most important and able of the ministers, De Peyronnet, retired. It was supposed that his resignation would break up the ministry, unless it was much strengthened by the admission of some new element; the arrival from London of Prince Polignac, a friend of Wellington and a strong royalist, was thought to mean that the English minister was using his influence to insist that the required strength should be derived from the introduction of a strong royalist element, and that an attempt should be made to rule France upon more strictly monarchical principles. The ministry however for the moment continued unchanged, but found itself in a complete minority in the Chamber of Deputies, and was defeated in an attempt to reform the departmental and municipal governments. Its plan ostensibly aimed at reducing the power of the prefects, who were government nominees, by the establishment of municipal councils, but in fact it secured the ascendancy of the more aristocratic part of the nation in the local government by rendering a high qualification necessary for the electors to these councils. So obviously inefficient had the ministry proved itself to carry on the business of the state, that immediately on the close of the session it was dismissed. But the King had no idea of replacing it by a more liberal Cabinet; his thoughts turned rather towards repression, and he summoned the ultra-royalists to his ministry.* While the new appointments were received with absolute distrust and dislike in France, they met with nothing but praise from the London journals; so clear did the connection between the Cabinets of the two countries appear, that

The Revolution in France.

Supposed influence of Wellington in Polignac's appointment.

the nickname of the Wellington Ministry was given to Polignac's administration.

It was a time of much depression both in trade and agriculture, and general discontent became prevalent. The mistrust with which the ministry was regarded was strengthened by the repeated and not always successful press prosecutions which were undertaken. It was even feared that, as the Chamber of Deputies was certainly hostile to the ministry, some attempt would be made to set aside the charter and to obtain a more favourable Chamber by unconstitutional means. But things had not yet reached that pass. The old Chamber was quietly opened on the 2nd of March with a speech in which the King, in the usual language of a constitutional ruler intending to have recourse to unconstitutional means of repression, after expatiating on the excellent condition of the country, went on to assert that if obstacles to the Government should arise, which he as yet did not foresee, he should find strength to overcome them in the loyalty of his people. The covert threat was not lost upon his audience ; the address moved in the Lower House expressed the prevailing mistrust. Concurrence between the sovereign and the interests of his people was, it declared, the necessary condition for the good working of the charter ; that sympathy was now broken, the administration had acted, and was continuing to act, as though the people were disaffected. The King was intreated to choose between his faithful Parliament and these evil counsellors. Charles did not refuse to receive the address, but stated in reply to it, that though grieved to hear that sympathy between himself and his people no longer existed, he had no intention of receding from his former view. The next day the Chamber was summarily prorogued, the first instance since the restoration of so strong a measure, and in May dissolved, a new Parliament being summoned for August. The elections went constantly against the Government, in spite of an attempt to rouse the love of glory in the people by an expedition to Algiers, and of a personal address by the King, who begged the electors to rally round him for the support of the royal prerogative. "It is your King who requires this of you, it is as a father he summons you, do your duty and I will do mine," were his closing words.

Their ill success in the elections reduced the ministers to a dilemma. They must either resign or again meet a hostile Parliament, or (a third alternative) proceed in some unconstitutional way. To all outward appearance they intended to pursue the second course, and the deputies actually set

[Marginal notes:]

Increasing opposition to the French ministry.

Unconstitutional conduct of the French ministry.

out on their journey towards Paris. Polignac and his friends had hoped to purchase leave to carry on the Government in their own way by introducing a popular budget, while the eyes of the people were dazzled by the military successes in Algiers. Finding this out of the question, at the last hour they determined upon an unconstitutional act. On the 21st of July, three ordinances were introduced to the Council, with an explanatory memorial. This memorial declared that the charter contained no promise of protection to the periodical press, and that the periodical press had been injurious, especially to the military affairs in Algiers, and that it must therefore be suppressed; while the highest duty of Government (its own preservation) authorized the setting aside of the charter, when all efforts to secure a favourable house had been exhausted in vain. The three ordinances suspended the liberty of the periodical press, dissolved the Chamber of Deputies, and altered, to suit the views of the Court, the structure of the chamber hereafter to be chosen.

The ordinances were kept a profound secret, and were given to the *Moniteur* to publish at midnight on the 25th of July. Outbreak of Their effect was an immediate outbreak, headed by the the Revolution opposition newspaper editors. A protest, signed by forty-four of them, was issued on the 26th, declaring that the Government had forfeited its right to obedience. There was a panic on the Exchange, and all things promised a revolution, the success of which could scarcely be doubtful, as the army was deeply infected with disaffection, and there were not more than 6000 trustworthy troops, under the command of Marmont, himself inclined to constitutional views. However, the ministry seem to have persuaded themselves that the effervescence was temporary, and on the 27th an attempt was made to suppress the protest of the press; the printing offices were closed, and while the police hammered at the doors unaided by the lookers-on, the papers were distributed by thousands from the upper windows. The case even came before one of the courts of law, as one of the printers was sued for breach of contract for refusing to print; the Tribunal of Commerce declared that the ordinance, being against the charter, could not be binding. So highly-strung a state of public feeling could not last long. Some deputies had assembled to discuss how they should act; the electors of Paris sent to them, and begged them to assume the command of the movement, asserting that the insurrection was already begun, the armourers' shops had been cleared, and that other signs of immediate revolution were visible. The deputies postponed their reply till the following morning; by that time the people had taken the law into their own hands. On all sides barricades were being rapidly thrown up; the Hôtel de Ville was seized, the tricolour flag hoisted, and the tocsin rang, while the troops were distributed in various parts of the town. Marmont, who knew the temper of the army, despatched a messenger to the King at St. Cloud to urge upon him the necessity of concession. The ministry was in permanent session in the Tuileries, and a state of siege having been declared, Marmont became head of the Government. With him the populace tried to treat. Himself inclined to peace, he could only answer that his orders were to use force. He however offered to send another messenger to St. Cloud ; the reply brought was to concentrate his forces, and to act with masses. The answer, which implied the suppression of the revolt at all hazards, was quite useless—the soldiers had rapidly deserted ; those who kept to their allegiance had not been supplied with food, and weary and dispirited, were gradually withdrawn. The uproar continued all night, and fresh barricades were hourly springing up. On the 29th the same scenes continued, the troops constantly fraternizing more and more with the mob, and in the afternoon Marmont found himself obliged to march with all the

Abdication of Charles X.

troops he could collect to St. Cloud to secure the safety of the King. It seems that up to that evening Charles and his courtiers still believed that they had only an émeute to encounter, but the next day, as no good news arrived, the King found himself gradually deserted, and at three in the morning of the last day of July himself drove off. When he heard that Louis Philippe, Duke of Orleans, had accepted the post of Lieutenant of the kingdom, he made a final effort to save his dynasty by abdicating in favour of his grandson, the Duke of Berri. The step was entirely fruitless ; he was recommended to withdraw quietly. He took the advice, repaired to Cherbourg, and arrived at Spithead on the 17th of August. After some residence at Lulworth, Charles accepted the hospitality of the English King, who had offered him the use of Holyrood House.

In the midst of this revolution, George IV., who had for some years been seriously ill, and who since the trial of his wife had

Death of George IV.

withdrawn himself much from public observation, died. His danger had been hidden from the people, probably at his own request. But on the 26th of June he died, a victim to a complication of diseases which had rendered his later years miserable.

Throughout the last session of the reign Wellington had occupied a position which could not long be maintained. There was no doubt that an earnest effort might immediately have driven his administration from office. He had broken with the old high Tories by the Catholic Emancipation and by his financial policy. He had quarrelled with the Canningites by insisting upon the resignation of Huskisson. He had indeed made some approaches towards the Whigs, and admitted both Scarlet and Lord Roslin to office, but his views rendered it impossible that any real union with them should be thought of. He thus stood absolutely alone, allowed to remain in office chiefly because men thought him the only minister fit to deal with the vacillating and unprincipled King, and because a speedy change on George's death was expected. Consequently the session was passed in somewhat meaningless discussions, and in attacks to which the arbitrary and self-confident character of Wellington laid him open. Though the settlement of Greece was finally completed, his foreign policy, as we have seen, which seemed to aim at little else than at keeping things exactly as they were, met with little approbation. Attacks against the press in which he engaged seemed at once somewhat to lower his dignity, and to give openings for the assaults of the Liberals. His financial measures, although he effected a saving of upwards of a million in the payment of the Civil Service, diminished but little the weight of taxation, while continued disturbances in Ireland, and widespread discontent and misery among the working-classes, especially in the silk trade, threw gloom over all the country.

Review of Wellington's administration.

His isolated position.

WILLIAM IV.

1830—1837.

Born 1765 = Adelaide of Saxe-Meiningen, 1818.

CONTEMPORARY PRINCES.

France.	*Austria.*	*Spain.*	*Portugal.*
Charles X., 1824.	Francis II., 1792.	Ferdinand VII.,1813.	Miguel, 1828.
Louis Philippe, 1830.	Ferdinand, 1835.	Isabella II , 1833.	Maria, 1834.

Prussia.	*Russia.*	*Denmark.*	*Sweden.*
Frederick-William III , 1797-1840	Nicholas, 1825.	Frederick VI., 1808-1839.	Charles XIV., 1818-1844.

POPES.—Pius VIII., 1829. Gregory XVI., 1831.

Lord Chancellors.	*First Lords of the Treasury.*
April 1827. Lyndhurst.	Jan. 1828. Wellington.
Nov. 1830. Brougham.	Nov. 1830. Grey.
Nov. 1834. Lyndhurst.	July 1834. Melbourne.
April 1835. In Commission.	Nov 1835. Wellington.
Feb. 1836. Cottenham.	Dec. 1834. Peel.
	April 1835. Melbourne.

Chancellors of the Excheque

Jan. 1828. Goulburn.
Nov. 1830. Althorp
Nov. 1834. Wellington.
Dec. 1834. Peel.
April 1835. Spring Rice.

Secretaries (Foreign and Home).

Nov. 1830	{ Palmerston. { Melbourne.
July 1834	{ Palmerston. { Duncannon.
Nov. 1834	{ Wellington. { Wellington.
Dec. 1834	{ Wellington. { Goulburn.
April 1835	{ Palmerston. { Russell.

IT was perhaps fortunate that George IV. was succeeded by a man of very different character, whose simplicity and geniality speedily made him as popular as his brother had been the reverse. The little care with which he preserved the outward forms of dignity shocked the older Tories ; the freedom with which he admitted men of both parties to his table and his Court seemed to promise a reign conducted on constitutional principles and without party bias on the part of the Crown. The popularity

Character of William IV.

of the King was at the time of great importance, because the excitement of the days of July in France spread rapidly over Europe, especially in Belgium and Poland, and met with great sympathy in England.   Had an unpopular monarch been upon the throne the Crown might easily have been involved in the quarrel with the people.

In Belgium the revolutionary spirit assumed the form of a national desire on the part of the French-speaking Belgians to sever themselves from the Dutch kingdom to which they had been attached by the Treaties of Vienna. There was good ground for their discontent.   The King of the Netherlands, a clever but injudicious man, had failed to fulfil his engagements, and had ruled entirely in the interests of the Dutch part of his kingdom.   The liberty of the press granted by the constitution had been superseded by a royal ordinance, intended to be temporary, but still remaining in force ; a judicial system by which the judges were the nominees of the Crown had superseded the enactments of the constitution, by which the judges were elective and irremoveable ; the King had twisted the clause recommending to his care the interests of education to mean that education should be entirely in the power of the Crown ; the French language had been proscribed in all public acts, and business had to be carried on in Dutch ; an undue proportion of the taxes was laid upon Belgium, and Protestants were chiefly employed both in public and educational offices, though absolute equality of religions had been guaranteed.   There is no need to explain the grievances of the Poles.   Destroyed as a nation, divided recklessly among their powerful neighbours, it was only too natural that they should at once accept any hope of freedom.

Effect of the July Revolution in Belgium and Poland.

In England the Revolution in France met with universal sympathy and admiration.   Among those classes which of late years had been in a constant state of discontent, it was accepted as an example to be at once followed.   But the orderly and self-restrained manner in which the change in France had been effected had a far different and more important effect than this. It seemed to show the possibility of great and thorough changes being carried out without the excesses which had hitherto accompanied revolutions, and had frightened the well-to-do middle classes from any co-operation with the more eager and innovating working-men. It seemed possible that the great question, which had been almost crushed by the French wars and by the lengthened tenure of office

Effect of the July Revolution in England.

by the Tories, might be revived and brought to a successful conclusion without opening the flood-gates of social anarchy. Parliamentary reform was at once taken up by the Whigs and by the great middle class of England, who determined to try whether they could not win it in some less objectionable form than it had assumed in the hands of radical demagogues.

In the midst of this renewed excitement both on the Continent

Position of Wellington's ministry.
and in England, the ministry of Wellington, cut off from its old friends and disowned by those whose policy it had been enforced to adopt, stood as representative of the bygone system. The minister, though he had already so frequently yielded to the pressure of circumstances, was regarded as the friend of Polignac, the fallen French minister. His foreign policy read by this light seemed to be directed entirely to uphold the principles which had actuated the Tory Government at the time of the Vienna Treaty. He was known to be at heart an enemy of all change, and his conduct was therefore watched at this crisis with extreme anxiety. It was felt at the time, and has since been confessed, that his ministry during the last session had existed only by the toleration of its enemies. With the death of the King the chief necessity for retaining the Duke in his position had disappeared, and the time seemed to have arrived for sweeping away the Government, which was merely obstructive and bent at the best in keeping things exactly as they were. The dissolution which necessarily followed the accession of the new King afforded the Duke's enemies the opportunity they required. In the midst of much excitement, for the reformers had already begun to cover the land with associations, the elections took place, with a result disastrous to Government. There was a loss of at least fifty Government seats. While the Liberals made extreme and successful efforts in places where the elections were open, the Tory proprietors of boroughs, in their hatred to Wellington, whom they regarded as their betrayer, brought in anti-ministerial nominees. The temper of the people was shown by the election of Brougham, voluntarily and without expense, to the representation of Yorkshire, by the loss of their seats by two brothers and a brother-in-law of Peel, undoubtedly the most important member of the Government after the Premier, and by the fact that of the eighty-two representatives of English counties not more than twenty were ministerial. Such a change no doubt offered much hope for the peaceful and parliamentary character of the constitutional advance which it seemed now impossible to avoid.

But there were still great dangers threatening the country. In Ireland O'Connell was spending all his energies in preaching the necessity of repeal, and heaping fierce and unmeaning words of hatred upon the ministry. *Danger from O'Connell's agitation for repeal,* He had re-established the Association under the name of "The Friends of Ireland," and when the Irish Government declared this illegal, it assumed a new form as the Society of Irish Volunteers. The lower classes were in a state of wild excitement, and their belief in their leader was not checked by the inconsistency with which he now extolled the Revolution in Belgium and in France, though hitherto, in his love of Catholicism, the Catholic and Jesuit-loving Bourbons had been the main subjects of his praise; nor did even the want of courage with which he refused to give satisfaction for the insults he had heaped on Lord Hardinge injure him with his followers. In October it was found necessary in Tipperary to take means for suppressing an outbreak by the use of the soldiery. In England events bearing a strong resemblance to the opening of a revolution began to be visible. The breaking of machines both in manufacturing and agricultural districts, and worse than that, in the South of England rick-burning, became con- *and from rick-burning.* stant. No efforts and no rewards could arrive at a true knowledge of the perpetrators of this crime. The farmers were kept in a constant state of nervous anxiety. A certain number of people were apprehended and hanged on the charge, but any man was still liable to find his ricks, in spite of all his care, suddenly and mysteriously bursting into flames. In London, too, the old demagogues began to make their appearance. Hunt and Cobbett were again haranguing crowds and filling their minds with hopes of social equality. Meanwhile the ministry took no step to declare its intention, and made no advances towards strengthening itself by union with any other party. It seemed indeed possible for a moment that the Duke would again yield, readmit the Canningites to his party, and produce some very moderate reform. If such a plan existed, it disappeared after the death of Huskisson. On the 15th of September a num- *Death of Huskisson.* ber of guests, among whom were the Minister, were asked to attend the opening of the first great railway in England, running between Manchester and Liverpool. The train, in which the guests were, stopped for water at Parkside. Several gentlemen left their seats, and a mutual friend brought Huskisson to the carriage where Wellington sat to attempt a reconciliation. The door was open as the old friends greeted each other warmly. Suddenly a train came up upon the other line, there was a cry of "Get to your seats;" flurried and unable, apparently, to pass the open door, Huskisson fell across the line, and was so severely injured that he died the same evening. The rest of Canning's followers, although their great leader had been an enemy to reform, at once made it plain that they had joined the Opposition.

It was thus, with unusual anxiety as to the conduct to be expected **Parliament** from the ministry, that the opening of Parliament on the **Nov. 2, 1830** 2nd of November was awaited. The worst enemies of the Duke could scarcely have hoped for a more ill-judged production than the King's speech. There was no sign that the very critical state of the country was even acknowledged. The change of dynasty in France was mentioned and accepted, the unpopular policy of the Government with regard to Miguel praised, the civil war in Belgium spoken of in terms of severe reprobation, and a determination expressed to uphold the present political system; the disturbed temper of the people in England and Ireland was mentioned with indignation, and the firm purpose of Government declared to repress it by every means in their power. Of recognition of the necessity of listening to what had now become the expressed wish of the nation there was not a word. If anything could be wanted to strengthen the impression caused by the speech, and to make it clear that the ministry was more conservative than ever, it was afforded by Wellington's words in the debate on the address in answer to Lord Grey's recommendation that some plan of reform should be undertaken. He declared his belief in the perfection of the legislative system. It possessed the full and entire confidence of the country; he was not therefore prepared to bring forward any measure of reform, and might declare at once that " as long as he held any station in the government of the country, he should always feel it his duty to resist such measures when proposed by others." It was a challenge to the reformers which was speedily answered. On the same night Brougham announced his intention of bringing forward a motion for reform on the 16th, and on that night the fate of the ministry must have been decided. In the interval before the critical day the excitement of the people was so great that the King's visit to the **Resignation of** City had to be postponed, because Wellington was afraid **the ministry.** to accompany him unless under a strong armed escort. But before that day arrived the ministry found an opportunity for resigning. Among the topics of the speech was the reform of the Civil List. On the 15th Sir Henry Parnell brought in a motion for a Select Committee; the ministry opposed it on the ground that no further economy was possible, and being beaten by a majority of twenty-nine, after taking one day to consider, announced on the 16th that their resignation had been accepted, and thus saved themselves from defeat on the more momentous question of reform. During the formation of the new ministry Brougham's motion was postponed, and it was almost immediately known that he had passed into the Upper House as Lord Chancellor, and that the first business of the new Government would be the production of a Reform Bill.

At such a crisis it was impossible that any statesman except Lord Grey should be intrusted with the formation of a Cabinet. Now nearly seventy years of age, he had been the prominent leader in every attempt at parliamentary reform for the last forty years. He found no difficulty in selecting his ministers. As far as talents and debating power went the Liberal party was very strong ; it was not yet discovered that the long absence of the party from office, and its consequent ignorance of the routine and traditions of official work had rendered most of its members rather weak administrators. The Chancellorship of the Exchequer was given to Lord Althorp, a most amiable and excellent man, a steady partisan of reform and retrenchment, but of an easy and not very vigorous character. Lord Lansdowne was President of the Council ; Lambton, now become Lord Durham, Grey's son-in-law, was Lord Privy Seal; the Secretaryships were supplied from the ranks of the Canningites ; Palmerston, Melbourne, and Goderich were respectively Foreign, Home, and Colonial Secretaries. Charles Grant was President of the Board of Control. Holland, Auckland, and Graham were also in the Cabinet. In office, but not of the Cabinet, were Lord John Russell as Paymaster-General, and Mr. Stanley, subsequently Lord Derby, as Secretary for Ireland.

The duty which this ministry undertook was by no means a light one ; for though it was plain that reform in some shape or other could no longer be delayed, its introduction was beset with difficulties, of which the greatest was by no means the opposition to be apprehended from the open opponents of the measure. Any advance towards a fair representation was certain to meet with the strongest opposition from men who regarded any change as revolutionary, and saw a diminution of their own interests in the slightest attacks upon the system of nominee boroughs. But such bigoted and selfish opposition might certainly sooner or later be overcome. A far greater danger was to be found

in the exaggerated hopes which had been fostered for many years
among the suffering artisans, who had been taught by their leaders
and demagogues to ascribe all their miseries to the want of fair representation. No measure which a ministry, aristocratic in its character as the present ministry was, could introduce, no measure which
could satisfy the intelligent middle classes, to whom social change was
almost as abhorrent as to the Tories, could fail to cause disappointment to the hopes of the lower classes ; and when they found how
little practical relief they would gain by the measure, there was only
too much danger lest the revolution of which the opponents of the
measure were so fond of talking might really come into existence.
Signs of popular discontent were, as has been already mentioned,
clearly to be seen.   Rick-burning still continued its course in the
South, and trades unions in their most aggravated form, and accompanied by murder, had made their appearance in the manufacturing
districts.   Extreme measures, such as the issuing of a special commission in the disturbed districts, were urged upon the Government ;
but Lord Grey replied that he considered the regular powers of the
Government, if properly used, were sufficient for all purposes.   In
fact, the ministry understood that the contest was not an ordinary
parliamentary one; it was scarcely to be expected that of its own free
will the House of Commons should accept a Bill which must exclude
many of its members from their seats ; it was as the spokesmen of a
great national wish that the ministers regarded themselves, and they
intended to rely upon the nation for their support.   Not only did
they therefore refrain from any exceptional measures for the suppression of disturbance, they also allowed to pass unquestioned the
legality of the numerous political unions which, following the example of the Union of Birmingham, of which Mr. Attwood was the
president, had sprung into existence all over England, and which
aimed at bringing into some sort of harmony the demands of the
wealthy and poorer classes.   The ministry had in fact determined
to use all expressions of the national temper, even when verging upon
breaches of the Constitution, to forward what they conceived to be
the great healing measure which the evils of the times demanded.
The struggle thus assumed a far more dignified form than that of an
ordinary political question.   In its first stage it was the people, as
usual with aristocratic leaders, who demanded and insisted upon
their will being heard by the Lower House.   When that House had
been reconstituted, and become favourable to the popular claims, it
was the people speaking by the voice of their constitutionally chosen

representatives, supported by an irresistible and probably unconstitu
tional action from without, which engaged in a life and death struggle
with the aristocracy, clinging tenaciously to their ancient privileges.

On the 3rd of February, when the Parliament reassembled, the
intention of the ministry to produce a measure of parliamentary
reform in both Houses was made known. The day for its introduction was fixed for the 1st of March. The interval was passed in
Parliament in the ordinary business of the session, and in the introduction of a budget which, betraying as it clearly did a tendency towards
the policy of Huskisson in favour of the manufacturing industries,
was received with an opposition which showed the temper of the
House, and which would probably under ordinary circumstances
have caused the fall of the ministry. But it was understood that it
was upon reform and upon no other question that the fate of the
Government depended. Without the walls of Parliament agitation
was vigorously at work. Petition after petition for and against the
approaching measure was prepared, and the whole country was upon
the tiptoe of expectation when on the appointed day Lord John
Russell made his statement as to the character of the Bill
Although it has since been found necessary more than
once to enlarge it, at the time the completeness of the
Bill surprised even the friends of Government, while it seemed to its
opponents little better than an ill-timed jest. As in all Bills for reform
of the representation, there were two points to be regarded : in the
first place, to secure that the representatives of the people should be
really representatives and not nominees; in the second place, to secure
by the arrangement of the franchise that they should as far as practicable represent all classes of the nation. On the first of these points
the Bill was complete, with very few exceptions rotten boroughs
were entirely swept away ; it is on the second point that subsequent
legislation has been found necessary. The Bill as originally presented destroyed at once sixty rotten boroughs, but with regard to
the franchise and the distribution of seats, as will be seen subsequently,
it showed considerable favour to the counties, that is to the landed
interest and to the middle classes, excluding entirely the artisan class,
which, when its members are prosperous and possess property, is one
of the most valuable elements in the constitution of the nation. As
Lord John Russell read the list of disfranchised boroughs, he was
greeted with shouts of laughter and ironical cries of " Hear " from
the members who represented them. The debate on the first reading
continued for seven nights ; the chief objection raised was that the

Reception of the Reform Bill March 1, 1831

balance of the Constitution would be changed and the power of the House of Lords diminished. It was, however, passed without divi- sion, the struggle being deferred to the second reading. Although its deficiencies were obvious enough to the advanced reformers, the importance of securing the one great step in advance which it pro- mised in the annihilation of rotten boroughs caused its general accept- ance, and " The Bill and nothing but the Bill " became the watchword of the Liberal party in England. There was considerable distur- bance, as was to be expected, throughout the country, and in antici- pation of a strong opposition many of the political unions came to the formal determination that, if necessary, they would refrain from paying taxes, and would even march to London ; they issued lists showing the numbers on which they could count, and it began to be plain that, if constitutional means failed, the Bill would be carried by unconstitutional pressure.

The second reading at length came on, and in the fullest House
The second reading of the Reform Bill. March 21 ever known, 608 members being present, the ministry secured a majority of one. Precedent would have de- manded their resignation, but regarding themselves as charged with a great national duty they kept their places, and all England illuminated at the news. The next process was to pass the Bill through Committee, and there the weakness of the Govern- ment at once disclosed itself. They were defeated by a majority of eight on a clause for reducing the whole number of members, and three days afterwards the House refused to go into a question of supply. The ministry, determined to bring matters to a crisis, re- garded this, not without some exaggeration, as a refusal of supplies, and declared that they could do nothing but resign; but the King, as yet true to them, refused their resignation, at the same time expressing a very strong wish not to dissolve the House. As the Parliament was now in its first session, this wish of the King was by no means unnatural, yet only by a dissolution could the ministers and the Reform Bill be saved. They themselves subsequently declared their belief that this was the real crisis of the question. The Opposition also felt the importance of the moment, and through their leader, Lord Wharncliffe, moved an address to the King, remon- strating against the intended dissolution. What the arguments of
Dissolution of the Parliament April 22. the ministry had been unable to effect was done at once by this ill-judged piece of violence, which the King con- sidered an attack upon his prerogative. He imme- diately declared his determination to dissolve the House. The

scene of excitement in the Lords has rarely been equalled when he suddenly made his appearance and demanded the presence of the Commons. An equally tumultuous scene had been going forward in the Lower House, the Speaker had himself been unable to obtain a hearing. At the summons of the Usher of the Black Rod, the Commons appeared at the bar of the Upper House, and were at once told by the King, in an unusually cheerful and firm tone, that he had come there for the purpose of proroguing them, with a view to immediate dissolution, in order to ascertain the sense of his people on the question of representation.

The dissolution thus taking place in the midst of the violent and strongly-organized agitation of the nation, virtually secured the passing of the Bill, although a long and dangerous period of contest had yet to be passed. That the mob should break out here and there in riots was inevitable; but it was the firm and determined attitude, not of the rioters, but of the great body of intelligent non-electors, which really influenced the elections. In all directions reformers were successful. Six county members only were opposed to the Bill, and when in July the second reading came on, the ministers found themselves in a majority of 136. Manifestly outnumbered, the opponents to the measure had recourse to an irritating form of warfare. Every single detail was fought over in Committee. There was a hope that, as the summer went on, the patience of members would be tired out, that the session must either be terminated or an accidental victory be snatched from the Government. So weary was the nation of the lengthened delay, that the political unions held a meeting to settle how much longer they would wait, but the question was too important to allow of any laxity on the part of its supporters, and on the 7th of September the report of the Committee was brought up. On the 21st, after another debate of three nights, the Bill passed the Commons by a majority of 109. Its fate now rested with the Peers, and they were not long in showing how they meant to deal with it. On the first reading it was thrown out by a majority of forty-one. The opponents of the measure fondly hoped that its fate and that of the administration were now sealed, but the Lords had not yet secured a victory. Indignant at the rejection of their Bill, the Commons at once passed a vote of confidence in the ministry, and all fear of their resignation was thus removed.

The Bill passes in the Commons Sept 23.

The Bill rejected in the Lords Oct 8.

But the indignation of the Commons was nothing to that of the
people at large, who saw the measure from which they
hoped so much snatched from them by the votes of a
few wealthy and important men, who in no sense represented them, and whose opposition bore in the popular eye all the
appearance of a selfish struggle for an exclusive and injurious
privilege. Again the disorderly mobs of London and other large
towns broke out into riots, but the number of rioters was usually few,
and many of them were known as belonging to the regular criminal
and ruffianly class. Of these riots the most important was that
which occurred in Bristol on the 29th of October. The occasion was
the public entry of Sir Charles Wetherell, a bitter opponent of reform,
into the city, of which he was recorder. It afforded another instance
of the mismanagement of the local magistracy. A mob, which seems
never to have reached a thousand in number, took possession of the
town for two days, broke into the mansion-house, and got drunk in
the cellars, and then, undisturbed, and after giving full notice of their
intention, set fire to Queen's Square, and burnt two sides of it to the
ground. The military had been in the town all day; at length they
proceeded to act, and re-established order with little difficulty, though
with some loss of life. · Their commander was Colonel Brereton. The
mayor and magistrates had weakly given him but a general authority
to act on his discretion, willing no doubt to shift the responsibility
to his shoulders. A man of kind heart, he had shrunk from acting
without more distinct authority; he had tried his best to calm the
crowd by friendly means, which only increased their confidence and
encouraged them with hopes of impunity. He was tried by court
martial, and, unable to face the prospect of a slur on his professional
character, committed suicide. But far more important than these
riots was the constantly increasing vigour shown by
the organized unions. Hitherto left untouched by
the Government, they now proceeded to measures which
clearly brought them under the action of the law. The London
Radicals held a great meeting on the 31st of October in Lincoln's
Inn Fields, presided over by Sir Francis Burdett, when a National
Union was established, intended to draw together the various unions
of the country, and to form a central directory of delegates. Before
the meeting separated, it was plain that some of its members were
ready to go much further than the unions had yet gone, and the
Metropolitan Union summoned a meeting for the 7th of November,
and issued a programme demanding the abolition of all hereditary

Marginal notes:

Consequent riots in the country.

Organized action of the political unions.

privileges and distinctions of rank. On this occasion the Govern
ment acted quickly and wisely. Lord Melbourne received a
deputation of the Union, and persuaded them to postpone their meeting, and shortly afterwards, on the 22nd of November, a proclamation was issued for the suppression of such political clubs.

This ·proclamation is believed to have been put forward at the
instigation of the King, who had been much frightened   Opposition of
by the riots at Bristol, and was constantly worked upon   the King.
by the ladies of the ;Court, who were strong anti-reformers. His
support could be no longer relied on by the ministry, and at this
time his help was more especially necessary, as it began to dawn upon
men's minds that nothing short of a large creation of Peers could
overwhelm the obstinate majority of the Upper House, and secure
the passage of the Bill. As the last Bill had been rejected, before the
fight in the Upper House could be recommenced the whole work
had to be gone through again in the House of Commons. It was not
long delayed there. Brought in by Lord John Russell   The Bill passes
on the 12th of December, it finally passed the Commons   on the second
                                                          reading in
by a majority of 116 on the 23rd of March. On the   the Lor⁴ₛ
14th of April the second reading of the Bill in the Lords   April 14, 1832.
took place, and it became apparent that a certain number of the
Peers had taken fright at the threatened increase to their numbers,
and had begun to recognize the danger of their obstructive policy;
the ministry succeeded in obtaining a majority of nine.

The 7th of May, after the Easter holidays, was the day fixed for the
Committee on the Bill. The holidays were well used   Preparations
by the reformers outside Parliament. Monster meet-   during the
ings were everywhere held, and the Political Union of   recess.
Birmingham, which held the first rank among the popular organiza-
tions, appointed a great meeting of all the unions of the counties of
Warwick, Worcester, and Stafford for the same day as the opening of
Parliament. The recess was not less eagerly employed by the anti-
reformers; his Tory friends, his courtiers, his wife, and his sisters,
worked upon the King's mind; he was persuaded to refuse the
creation of Peers, and to try once more what coercion could do in
suppressing the national ferment; the Duke of Wellington was
applied to, and orders to keep the troops in readiness were sent to
various parts of England, especially to Birmingham. Thus, when
the day arrived, while 150,000 men assembled at Newhall Hill in
Birmingham were swearing with bare heads and raised hands, "With
unbroken faith, through every peril and privation,·we here devote

ourselves and our children to our country's cause," Lord Lyndhurst,

The Bill rejected in the Lords. May 7.

who had been most active in organizing the present opposition, had contrived to secure a majority of thirty-five in the House of Lords for a motion postponing the disfranchising clauses of the Bill.

The antagonistic forces seemed to have come to a final issue, from

The ministry re-signs. The Duke of Wellington fails to form a ministry.

which there was no escape except by the creation of Peers, a measure as repugnant to the aristocratic feeling of Lord Grey as to the King. The Prime Minister, however, explaining the situation, demanded of the King the one necessary step. He was refused, and resigned. His resignation was accepted, and the Duke of Wellington was sent for to attempt to form a Conservative ministry. At the same time things had gone too far for complete repression, and the Duke was instructed to form a ministry which would introduce some extensive measure of reform. The news of the fall of the ministry was received in fierce anger by the whole people. The papers came out in mourning. The National Union decreed that whoever should advise a dissolution was a public enemy. Petitions praying that no supplies should be granted till the Bill was passed were signed in a few hours by many thousands of people, and sent to London, where they were joyfully received by the House of Commons. The great Birmingham Union made preparations to march to London 200,000 strong, and encamp on Hampstead Heath. Two insurmountable difficulties met the Duke of Wellington, and prevented the inevitable ruin which must have followed his success. It became clear to him that the military could not be trusted, that repression by force was out of the question, and he could find no Conservatives sufficiently courageous

The old ministry returns to office. May 15.

to join him in the ministry. The King was obliged again to have recourse to his former ministers. It was plain to the Lords that further opposition was useless, and would lead only to a public proof of the powerlessness of their resistance by the creation of new Peers. They therefore wisely

The Bill passes in the Lords. June 4.

attended to a circular letter from the King himself, begging them to withdraw their opposition. Wellington left the House, and was followed by about a hundred other Peers; the Bishops in a body withdrew their opposition, and the Bill was finally carried by a considerable majority.

The measure as passed was not and could not be final, but it

Description of the Reform Bill.

was a wide, comprehensive and judicious beginning. The chief evil of the representation had been the existence of nomination and rotten boroughs ; of these 56, having less than 2000 inhabitants, were disfranchised, and 111 seats left vacant. Thirty boroughs, with less than 4000 inhabitants, were each deprived of one member ; Weymouth and Melcombe Regis lost two. There were thus 143 seats to dispose of. Of these 65 went to the counties, an arrangement which showed the still unbroken power of the landed aristocracy, twenty-two large towns received the right of returning two members, and 21 the right of returning one. The remaining 13 were left for Ireland and Scotland. The second evil was the very irregular and restricted franchise. In some towns the freemen alone elected ; in others the suffrage was almost universal ; the whole number of electors on the roll was very small. A uniform £10 household franchise was now established in boroughs, but, as a concession to the rights of vested interests, freemen of corporate towns who resided within the borough, and who had been created before 1831, were allowed to retain their votes. In the counties copyholders and leaseholders were added to the constituencies, and by a clause introduced by the Marquis of Chandos, and carried in opposition to the Government, tenants at will paying a rent of £50 were also enfranchised. In this point again the landed interest showed its power, as such tenants were only too liable to be influenced by their landlords. At the same time, to decrease the disorders and expenses of elections, the duration of the poll was shortened. The period of fifteen days during which in county elections votes could be taken was restricted to two in England and to five in Ireland. Along with the English Bill, Reform Bills for Scotland and Ireland were also produced and passed. In Scotland the representation had been far more imperfect than in England ; it was now wholly remodelled. The county franchise was given to all owners of property, and long leaseholders of the value of £10 a year, and even to tenants for shorter periods paying a rent of £50 ; in the burghs the same £10 franchise was established as in England. The number of burgh representatives was changed from fifteen to twenty-three. The number of county members remained the same as before, but with some slight difference in distribution. To Ireland four additional boroughs were allowed, the counties there remained the same. But considerable discontent was caused by the adoption of the £10 freehold franchise in the counties, which very much restricted the number of the electors, from whom it will be remembered that till quite lately a 40s. qualification only was required.

Thus was completed, after a delay of nearly an hundred and fifty

years, the second act of the English Revolution. Incomplete and aristocratic in its character, the movement of 1688 yet established the superiority of Parliament as a whole, and its predominance over
the royal power. From that time onwards the Government
had been in the hands of the aristocracy, from whichever of the
political parties the members of the administration had been drawn.
The attempt of George III. to re-establish the power of the Crown
had been attended with some success as long as it was supported by
the good wishes of the people. Events had allied him with a party
bent on the repression of all popular movements and of all constitutional growth. Submissive during the war, the people on the return
of peace had been aroused to a sense of the injury under which
they suffered by their exclusion from all share in the Government.
Events in France had brought their discontent to a climax, and they
had now at length gained possession of that part of the Legislature
which had long pretended falsely to represent them.

Importance of the measure.

 But although the change effected by the Reform Bill at first sight
appears to have been political, it was in fact social. It
was the introduction of a wholly new class of society
into the duties of Government. The aristocratic classes,
which had hitherto had the monopoly of power, were forced to admit
to an equality with themselves the middle class, which the progress
of society, and the wonderful advance of material improvement during
the last half century, had raised to a position so important that its
claims could no longer be withstood. Its victory had been secured
by a twofold alliance. On the one hand it had taken advantage of
the real wants of the classes below it, and of the social ideas which
had been called into existence by the French Revolution ; it had
not scrupled to employ the modern arts of agitation, or to bring
what cannot be regarded in any other light than as an unconstitutional pressure to bear upon Parliament. On the other hand it had
worked constitutionally by an alliance with one of the governing
classes, namely, the Whigs. Long exclusion from office had as usual
made this party alive to the existence of abuses, the defensive and
obstructive attitude of the Tories had reawakened its desire for constitutional growth, and the philosophy and writings of the time,
especially those of Bentham and of the authors of the *Edinburgh
Review,* had taken considerable hold of its leading members. The
Whig Government therefore, with complete honesty, and in the
midst of considerable danger and difficulty, accepted the alliance
which the middle classes offered it, and honourably fulfilled its share

Introduction of the middle classes to power.

of the compact. Now that the great Bill was passed, it remained to be seen how far the Whigs were willing to forego their old aristocratic prejudices, and how far their strength would allow them to oppose the pressure of the extreme Radicals, whose alliance they had been forced to accept along with that of the middle class.

It was with the utmost anxiety that the character of the first reformed Parliament was watched. There was a general feeling of terror throughout England. Timid investors began to seek securities for their money in America or Denmark. There was a constant apprehension of a coming revolution which might resemble that in France; a feeling which was not appeased by occasional acts of violence throughout the country, and a fierce and dangerous assault by the London mob upon the Duke of Wellington himself. It is possible that in any other country such a revolution might have resulted; but the practical character of the English mind, which prevents it from being carried away by a passionate desire for ideal benefits, the wide diffusion and extremely strong love of property, the firm and dignified attitude of the nobility, the loyalty with which the really active part of the Tory party accepted the change and determined to make the best of it, secured tranquillity for the country during its passage through the dangerous crisis. It may also be reckoned as no small advantage to the cause of order, that the English Radicals found themselves thrown into the company of O'Connell and the Irish agitators; the clamour for repeal, the lawless violence which showed itself in the sister island, and the unscrupulous character of the demagogue who represented it, gave a strength and unity to the moderate Whig party which it would otherwise have wanted. At the same time the twofold connections and interests of the Government could not but, sooner or later, prove a cause of weakness. Their aristocratic tendencies, which remained unabated, prevented them from throwing themselves heartily into the wishes of their more popular supporters, and laid them open to the constant suspicion of an inclination towards Toryism. Their dependence on the popular party compelled them to take in hand many difficult questions for the solution of which the nation was clamouring. They had therefore to be constantly steering a middle course, and assuming an appearance of weakness which rapidly undermined their popularity, while the two tendencies which they represented, affecting the individual members of the Cabinet in different degrees, speedily led to a division among themselves. It is for these reasons that the work of the first reformed Parliament,

Anxiety as to the effect of the change.

great as it was, has an appearance of weakness as compared with the burst of popular reform which might have been expected after so great a change.

When Parliament assembled it appeared that the Whigs had on the whole a very large majority; but, besides an active and important body of Tories headed by Sir Robert Peel, there were a considerable number of Radicals, of whom Hume may be regarded as the leader, and the Irish members, for the most part the mere nominees and puppets of O'Connell, from whom opposition might be expected. There were changes both in the appearance and character of the House; the average age of the members was visibly increased, and it was evident that there would be more individual opinion, less distinctly party voting, and a greater necessity for convincing argument to ensure a majority. It was plain, too, that with much less of oratory there would be a far greater quantity of talking; and as the Government, in the King's speech, promised to introduce a number of very important Bills, it was found necessary greatly to lengthen the hours of business. At the same time, as there were no less than three hundred new members in the House, it was thought advisable to reappoint the old Speaker, Manners-Sutton, although he was a Tory in politics, a step which at once excited the displeasure of the more advanced Liberals.

Character of the reformed Parliament. Jan. 29, 1833.

The questions most generally occupying men's minds, and which it might be supposed would at once become prominent, were the disturbed and wretched condition of the poor, as evidenced by the late riots and constant rick-burning; the position of the Church; slavery; and the national relations to foreign countries, especially Belgium and the Peninsula; but, before all, the condition of Ireland, and the maintenance of the Protestant Church in that country.

Critical questions to be settled.

It was the Irish question which became at once the most important, and which ultimately caused the fall of the ministry. It was understood that some measures of coercion would be necessary to restore tranquillity in that country, but that they should go hand in hand with measures of reform and relief. As though to render the coming Coercion Bill more palatable, Lord Althorp, on the 12th of February, introduced a Bill for the regulation of the Irish Church. Since the Catholic Emancipation Act the state of Ireland had been becoming constantly worse. Instead of accepting the Act in a conciliatory spirit, O'Connell had used it as a stepping-stone for further demands, and had continued his course of

Condition of Ireland.

agitation. He had been prosecuted in 1831, had pleaded guilty to holding illegal assemblies, but by the carelessness of the Whig Government he had escaped without punishment. His present demand was repeal, but the outrages which filled Ireland were either agrarian or connected with the tithes ; and O'Connell skilfully managed, while by his agitation he continually kept up the discontent, to keep clear himself of any participation in the violence of his countrymen. Of course the repeal of the Union could not be for a moment thought of, but the Government could not deny that the position of the Irish Church and the collection of tithes for its support were real grievances.

In a country of which the population was somewhat over seven millions, there was established a dominant Protestant Position of the Church, the members of which numbered 853,000 only. Irish Church. It had a staff of no less than four archbishops and eighteen bishops, many of them with very large incomes, and a body of clergy supported principally by tithes, exacted not only from its own members, but from the six million and a half Catholics. To make matters worse, the tithe was paid by the tenants, and, as the land was infinitely subdivided, in minute sums which rendered its forcible exaction most irksome and ridiculous. In many instances a man's tithe was a farthing, and in some cases not more than seven parts of a farthing. So vexatious and unjust a tax was certain to cause exasperation. In 1831 the collection of tithes became almost impossible ; the collectors were murdered, the police who came to their rescue fired upon, cattle driven off that the tithe might not be paid, and the clergy were consequently reduced to such a miserable plight that some of them were actually brought to the verge of starvation. But in spite of the glaring anomaly of the existence of the Church at all, and of the ill-feeling and violence excited by the exaction of the tithes, neither Lord Grey nor Mr. Stanley, his Secretary for Ireland, could bring themselves to think of any wide measure of reform, so great was their dread of touching property or vested interests, or of in any way injuring the Church. In February 1832 committees were appointed to inquire into the system. They reported that the complete extinction of tithes by a commutation or charge upon the land was absolutely necessary. The Irish took this as an authorization of their proceedings ; the outrages increased, and a system of terrorism was established, which precluded the possibility of bringing the assassins and rioters to justice. In June the Government had adopted a plan which in fact made matters worse. They authorized the advance of £60,000 to the Irish clergy, who were unable to collect their tithes, and took upon themselves the duty of collecting former arrears, at the same time promising that the tithe commutation should be undertaken. A Bill to this effect was passed, rendering commutation necessary for a term of twenty-one years. Other Bills providing for the redemption of the tithe were unfortunately allowed to stand over to the next session. But Government had now made itself a tithe collector, and was so inefficient in that capacity that it had subsequently to allow that of £104,000 due £12,000 only had been levied, and that with some loss of life.

In the year 1833 a new arrangement was consequently attempted. The whole amount of arrears for the last three years amounted to about a million. This sum the Government proposed should be advanced by an issue of Exchequer bills, to be repaid gradually by a general land tax. As there seemed only too much probability that the land tax would be refused with as great determination as the tithes, most people regarded this sum as a mere gift to the Irish clergy. The Government was, however, able to pass the Bill. The final settlement of the tithe question was postponed for several years; meanwhile the violence which attended the attempts at collecting the tithes were the chief cause of the necessity of the Coercion Bill.

Irish Tithe Composition Bill passed. Aug. 23, 1833.

But the tithes, though the immediate cause of the disturbances, were only a part of the whole Church system; it was the Church itself which was the primary cause of the evil, and in the measure for the relief which was to accompany the Bill for the repression of disturbance, the ministers addressed themselves to lessen the more glaring defects of that institution; but at the same time they were as little disposed to injure the Church as the Tories themselves, and one of the chief objects of the proposed legislation was the improvement of the position of the clergy. It was thought that while the lessening of the hierarchy and the removal of some of the anomalies exhibited by the Church would be pleasing to the Irish, the Church would itself gain strength by the proposed changes. Besides the payment of tithes, a church cess, for the support of the buildings and expenses of the services, was paid indiscriminately by members of all religions, but managed by Protestant vestries. The annates, or firstfruits of livings, had been originally employed for these purposes, but in process of time had almost disappeared; such benefices as were still subject to them were to be now freed, a graduated tax was to be laid upon all livings,

Althorp's Irish Church Bill. Feb. 1833.

and with the produce the Church cess was to be extinguished. This was a direct boon to the Catholics. Another common complaint was the disproportion between the number of bishoprics and the Protestant population; it was now proposed to destroy ten of these bishoprics, or rather, as the ministry was careful to explain, not to destroy but to consolidate them with those which remained. The incomes of some of the larger bishoprics were also curtailed; the surplus money thus arising was to be paid into the hands of ecclesiastical commissioners. Thus far there was not much objectionable in the Bill, though the Tories and High Churchmen of England disliked the destruction of so many sees. But there was a further measure, which opened the door to grave opposition. It was proposed to change the terms on which church lands were let so as to improve the position of the tenant without injuring the clergy. The tenant would be willing to pay for this advantage, and the sum thus gained was calculated at between two and three millions. This money would, as the mover of the Bill expressed it, be available for the purposes of the State. This had all the appearance of an act of confiscation, the property of the Church was to be taken and applied to purposes not ecclesiastical. But the Irish Secretary had as strong a view as the Tories of the sanctity of Church property, and the danger of tampering in ever so small a way with the rights of property. It was therefore found necessary by the supporters of the Bill to invent a theory to secure unanimity in the Cabinet; it was argued that the sum derived from the change of tenure did not exist before, but would be created by the present act of the Legislature, that it was therefore not Church property at all, and might be applied to the purposes of the State. The Bill in this shape was introduced by Lord Althorp on the 12th of February. It at once appeared open to objections on two sides. While O'Connell and the Irish scoffed at the relief, which consisted only in removing the church cess, and the English Radicals declared that instead of twelve bishops one was amply sufficient for the needs of the Irish Protestants, the Tories, refusing to recognize the delicate line between Church property and money gained by the Legislature from Church property, raised the cry that it was but a first step in confiscation, and threatened not the security of Church property only, but that of all other property. It appeared necessary to choose between the views of one or the other of these sets of critics, and in spite of his own views, Lord Althorp consented to be governed by the Conservative element in the Cabinet and to withdraw what was called the appropriation clause. The removal of this clause, which contained the only important principle in the Bill, the right, namely, of Parliament to apply Church property to the wants of the State, rendered it so like a Tory measure, that with the assistance of that party it passed without difficulty in both Houses (July 30).

But three days after the introduction of the Irish Church Bill in the House of Commons, Lord Grey introduced into the House of Lords its complement, the Coercion Bill. Here again the absence of broad liberality in the ministry was apparent. It was conceived in the spirit of the most absolute government, and implied a distinct determination to make no attempt at pacification by liberal concessions. It was the work of Mr. Stanley, the Irish Secretary, a man of great ability and vigour, but without much sympathy for the Irish character, and, as his subsequent career proved, at heart a Tory. There was no difficulty in making out a case for the Bill. A narration of a few of the crimes which had of late filled Ireland with horror made it evident that something must be done. In the province of Leinster alone, in the three months July, August, and September, there had been 1279 crimes, in the following three months the number had risen to 1646. During the year the catalogue of Irish crimes contained 172 homicides, 465 robberies, 568 burglaries, 454 acts of houghing cattle, 2095 illegal notices, 425 illegal meetings, 796 malicious injuries to property, 753 attacks on houses, 280 arsons, and 3156 serious assaults: in all upwards of 9000 crimes connected with the disturbed state of the country. Well might Mr. Macaulay say that he "solemnly declared. he would rather live in the midst of many civil wars he had read of than in some parts of Ireland at this moment." It was not the number of crimes alone which rendered them terrible; they were carried on upon a system by which such terror had been excited that it was impossible to get juries to convict even after the clearest proof, or witnesses to give evidence as to what they knew. At the same time, the leaders of the people were teaching them, in public meetings and in assemblies of the so-called Association of Volunteers, to regard themselves as the victims of every form of oppression. To meet such a state of things it was proposed to place in the hands of the Lord Lieutenant, in accordance with the Proclamation Act of the 8th of George IV., 1828, power to suppress every meeting or association which he regarded as dangerous to the preservation of peace, under whatever name it might call itself, and further to declare any district to be in a disturbed state, which was then to be regarded as a proclaimed district; its inhabitants were

The Coercion Bill introduced Feb. 15, 1833, carried March 29 to be confined to their houses from an hour after sunset till sunrise, the right of meeting and petitioning was withdrawn from them without leave of the Lord Lieutenant, and they were placed under martial law. The Bill further gave power to enter houses in search of arms, forbade the distribution of seditious papers, and suspended the Habeas Corpus in the proclaimed districts. The Bill passed without difficulty in the House of Lords, where it was in harmony with the general feeling. In the Lower House it was introduced on the 27th of February by Lord Althorp, who, while corroborating the accounts of the outrages in Ireland, could not help showing his dissatisfaction at the extreme severity of the Bill. Not so Mr. Stanley, who, with the fiery vehemence which characterized him, turned upon O'Connell, and overwhelmed him with a flood of bitter invective, carrying the House completely with him, and securing the passage of the Bill, which was also most ably supported by Sir Robert Peel and his friends. Its effect was immediate and most satisfactory. Within a week of its passage the Marquis of Anglesey, who had returned to his office on Grey's accession to the ministry, had suppressed the Association of Irish Volunteers, the town and county of Kilkenny were then proclaimed, but so effective was the mere dread of the measure, that it was never found necessary to hold a single court-martial in the district, and within two months there was a decrease of two-thirds in the general list of crimes. A rapid rise in the funds showed that the moneyed public at least were pleased with the vigorous measure.

Mr. Stanley's share in the Bill, the severity of his views with regard to Ireland, and the personal bitterness between himself and O'Connell, rendered his further tenure of the office of Secretary undesirable. He was moved to the Colonial Office, from which Lord Goderich, now become Earl of Ripon, withdrew to accept the Privy Seal, while Lord Durham, who had hitherto held that office, retired from the ministry (March 12). Mr. Stanley was succeeded by Sir John Cam Hobhouse, who however only held the office for two months, and was in turn succeeded by Mr. Littleton (May). The withdrawal of Lord Durham, although attributed and partly due to ill-health, was probably caused principally by the growing divisions in the Cabinet. The Conservative tendencies of the Prime Minister and the severity of the Irish Act were not in accordance with Lord Durham's advanced liberalism. The shortness of Hobhouse's tenure of office may be traced to somewhat similar causes, or at least to the decrease of the popularity of Government. In company with several others he had at the late elections pledged himself to vote for the repeal of the house and window tax. In April the Chancellor of the Exchequer, Lord Althorp, brought in his budget. By careful economy, the abolition of sinecures, and the reduction of the public expenses, he was able to show a surplus of about a million and a half after replacing the deficit of the former year. This surplus he intended to employ in reducing some taxes which he regarded as particularly heavy, such as those on soap, on marine insurances, and some of the assessed taxes. But he impartially refused to listen either to the outcry of the towns for the abolition of the house and window tax, or to the clamours of the agriculturists against the malt tax; he regarded them both as necessary sources of revenue. The carelessness of Government subjected it to a temporary defeat on a subsequent motion for the reduction of the malt tax to one half. Though the defeat caused great irritation to the ministers it was speedily retrieved. A motion against the house and window tax was also brought in, and Lord Althorp, in opposing it, argued that the removal of either tax alone would be an unfair advantage to one or other of the rival interests, and that the removal of both was impossible; he introduced an amendment to the effect that the reduction of the malt tax and the repeal of the house tax would necessitate a general property and income tax, and a change in our financial system. As this amendment was carried, both the taxes were retained; but the ministers could not but feel that they owed their success to the support of their enemies, and the popular indignation was great. Hobhouse, unable to vote against Government, and thus to redeem his pledge, felt it incumbent on him to resign both his place and seat. On appealing again to his constituents at Westminster he was rejected for Colonel de Lacy Evans, a more advanced · Liberal. The same thing happened in the cases of Dr. Lushington and Mr. William Brown in the Tower Hamlets and Southwark. A great indignation meeting, attended with some violence, was held near Coldbath Fields, and several great towns passed resolutions to the effect, that the ministers, by violating the constitution of Ireland, refusing to inquire into the public distress, continuing the house and window tax, and by forcing the whole malt tax, already once repealed, upon the nation, had betrayed the confidence of the people.

Thus in all directions the power of the Government was decreasing; **Weakness of the ministry.** they were divided among themselves, and gradually losing the popularity of the country. Yet they were still able to carry out successfully some of the duties they had set themselves to perform; before the close of the session they had renewed the Bank charter, settled the affairs of the East India Company, and completed the emancipation of the slaves.

The last renewal of the Bank charter had been in 1800; since then events of the greatest importance with regard to currency and credit had taken place,—the resumption of cash payments at the close of the war, and the great commercial crisis of 1825 and 1826.   It was felt that the system of the Bank required close examination, and in May 1832 a very influential committee had been appointed to examine it preparatory to the renewal of the charter, which came to an end in August 1833.   Upon the information gained by this committee the ministerial propositions were based.   On the whole it appeared clear that a single bank of issue was better than several competing banks.   The Bank was therefore to retain its monopoly.   The principle of the Directors, that a third of the value of their obligations should be kept in hand in specie, was considered sound; but that the public might in future have control of the issue of notes, the Bank was required to publish a weekly account of its notes and deposits, and a quarterly average showing its general condition.   No other bank of more than six partners, within sixty-five miles of London, was to be allowed to issue paper, while notes of the Bank of England and its branches were made legal tender, except at the bank from which they were issued. It was hoped by this means that country banks, being able to meet their demands with bank notes, would be saved from the necessity of making large and rapid demands upon the Bank of England, and thus dangerously lessening the supply of gold.   The whole sum due from the Government to the Bank, and from which that institution derived its great credit, was fourteen millions.   This was regarded as too much; it was to be reduced to eleven millions, twenty-five per cent. being at once repaid to the Bank, while to balance its advantages the Bank was to receive £120,000 a year less than hitherto for the management of the National Debt.   On these terms the charter was to be renewed for twenty-one years, but with an option allowed to Government for breaking it off on a year's notice after eleven years. The two points which met with the greatest opposition were the terms which the Government had made with the Bank and the compulsory currency given to bank notes.   On the first of these points it seemed almost unanimously felt that the Bank had made too good a bargain; on the second it was hastily urged by many that it was a partial resumption of the inconvertible currency.   It was shown without much difficulty that this was not the case, as the Bank of

[margin note:] Renewal of the Bank charter. June.

England was bound ultimately to meet its liabilities in gold; but even Sir Robert Peel objected to the measure, avowing his fear that it would cause a depreciation of the paper. Experience has proved that this fear was groundless, and although the arrangements with the Bank had subsequently to be somewhat modified, the Bill passed, and was a distinct advantage.

But, if it had been thought well to continue the monopoly of the great banking corporation in England, the whole force of the commercial feeling of the time set directly against the perpetuation of the monopoly of the East India Company. The necessity for corporate trading had disappeared. The restrictions it laid upon free trade had become only so many obstacles in the way of extended commerce. Already, in 1813, this had been so clearly felt that the merchants of the great trading centres, Liverpool, Glasgow, Paisley, and Manchester, had succeeded in procuring the admission of traders to the territories of the Company, and to India generally, but the corporation still retained the trade with China. The accounts of the Company after this renewal of its charter rendered it plain that it could not compete with private merchants. It seemed clear that in China, as in India, the destruction of the monopoly would extend commerce. It was therefore determined to destroy the Company as a commercial body, allowing it to keep its territorial position. After April 1834 its commercial property was to be sold. It was, however, to retain the government of India, and to receive for forty years an annuity from the Indian revenue of £630,000, at the close of which period Parliament might redeem it by the payment of £12,000,000. It was further arranged that all restrictions in the way of the settlement of Europeans in the East should be removed, that natives and Europeans should have equal opportunities of employment and office, and should be under one law. The Bill was vehemently opposed by Lord Ellenborough, but was carried by large majorities, and proved to be the means of opening, in accordance with the principles of free trade, an enormous market for English commerce, so that in ten years the Chinese trade had doubled, and British exports to India and Ceylon had increased from two to six millions.

Settlement of the East India Company. July.

But the most important measure of the session was the Bill which was passed on the 30th of August for the emancipation of the slaves. The abolitionists had been successful in 1807 in putting an end to the traffic in slaves, but though raised in value and lessened in number, by means of smuggling

Emancipation of the slaves. Aug

and of the natural increase of the race the supply of human cattle had been kept up and slavery had continued. · The Resolutions of 1823 had aimed at the gradual extinction of slavery, at alleviating its worst horrors, and raising the slaves to a fitting condition to receive freedom ; but they had practically been inoperative : not only had they been continually thwarted by the Condition of planters, but the discovery that they had rights, and trade in the West India that those rights were acknowledged, caused a very Islands. natural uneasiness among the slaves, and had added greatly to the difficulties under which the planters laboured. Their position was constantly becoming worse. Injudicious protection had been afforded to sugar, their chief production. Enormous duties had been laid on it, with a preference always to the West Indian and slave-grown article. During the war the monopoly of production had fallen chiefly into their hands. They had been able to make enormous profits. As a consequence, just as in the case of corn in England, the cultivation of the sugar-cane had been carried on in the most reckless fashion. Plantations were temporarily occupied only to be exhausted or sold at a heavy loss, and fresh land taken in. In the midst of this false prosperity, a wasteful expenditure and a total want of economy, the natural consequences of easily-gotten wealth, had become prevalent ; the planters as a body had become deeply involved. The cessation of the war had admitted other competitors to the market. The commercial crisis in England had seriously affected the planters' credit, and just as the greatest efforts would have been necessary to restore them at all to their old state of prosperity, their supply of slaves was diminished, it became more difficult to work their exhausted land, and the Resolutions of 1823, and subsequent orders in Council, made the employment of slave labour, which economists had long known to be really an extravagant form of labour, more and more difficult. These evils were naturally attributed to the abolitionists in England and to the Government which had even partially listened to them. As long as the unreformed Parliament existed, the West Indian interest was very strong in the House, and the planters, who believed that with some help from England, and with the management of the slaves left in their own hands, they might yet retrieve their position, were not without hopes. The accession of the Grey ministry was a heavy blow to them, for a large section of the supporters of the Government were almost as anxious for the abolition of slavery as for the passage of the Reform Bill, and it was impossible that a ministry of which Lord Brougham was the Chancellor, who had owed his last election chiefly to the abolitionists' votes, should postpone the settlement of the question long.

The conduct of the planters forced on the crisis. A new series of orders in Council was issued in 1831 for the better and more merciful management of the slaves, for the limitation of the hours of labour, and for the establishment of official slave-overseers. All the colonies except the Crown colonies, where but little difficulty was met with, resented highly this interference with what they considered their rights and property. The language of their assemblies became disrespectful and almost rebellious. In Trinidad it was determined to stop the payment of taxes till the order was repealed, while on the other side the slaves in Jamaica burst into open rebellion, producing a loss estimated at £1,000,000. In April 1831, a great meeting in London declared that Government was liable for these losses, and claims were sent in to the Colonial Secretary for damages caused by the measures pursued by his Majesty's ministers. It was a sort of declaration of war, which was brought to a point when, on the 17th of April, Lord Harewood presented a petition from the West India interest begging for a full inquiry into the laws, usages, and condition of the West Indian colonies, and the possible future improvements, with due regard always to the rights of private property. This was in the very heat of the discussions on the Reform Bill. Bent upon his great measure, Lord Grey could not afford to risk anything at the moment. He therefore not only at once granted the committee, but allowed a sum of £100,000, which had been voted for the relief of the colonies, to be raised to £1,000,000 on account of a late destructive hurricane. On the 24th of May Sir Fowell Buxton, the leader of the abolitionists, brought the matter before the Lower House, while the Chancellor presented a gigantic petition, followed by many others, in favour of emancipation; for the great crisis was now over, Wellington's efforts to form a Government had proved futile, and the hope of the abolitionists were consequently high. But, somewhat strangely, Lord Althorp could not be induced in the Lower House to give up Canning's idea of gradual emancipation, and moved and carried amendments upon Buxton's motion in favour of the continuance of the policy of 1823. It must be remembered that the House of Commons was still unreformed, and that the great Bill was not yet carried.

With the change in the character of the House all prudential

Opposition of the planters to the orders in Council. 1831

reasons for opposition on the part of the ministry disappeared, and the pressure brought to bear upon them had become much stronger. They therefore now undertook the question, and the appointment of Mr. Stanley to the Colonial Office insured the success of the measure. The Emancipation Bill passed Aug. 30, 1833. It was not wholly satisfactory to the abolitionists. It still bore traces of the lingering wish for gradual emancipation. All children of slaves born after the passing of the Act, and all children of six years of age and under, were declared free, but the rest of the slaves were to serve a sort of apprenticeship ; three-fourths of their time was for a certain number of years to remain at the disposal of the masters, the other fourth was their own, to be paid for at a fixed rate of wages. The complete failure of the Resolutions of 1823 should have taught the Government the impossibility of this scheme. The period of apprenticeship was shortened from twelve to seven years, and subsequently, after a four years' trial, the plan was given up. The second part of the Government scheme was the remuneration of the planters by a loan of £15,000,000 ; but as Parliament regarded this as much too small a boon, it was subsequently changed for the enormous gift of £20,000,000. The vastness of the sum was held by many as totally disproportionate to the loss of the planters ; by others it was thought that, as slavery was in itself contrary to all right, the planters deserved no compensation for the loss of what they should never have possessed. On the whole, however, it was thought better that so great an act of justice should be generously completed, and the great sacrifice was willingly made. Wilberforce, the father of the movement, lived just long enough to bless God that the object of his life had been reached ; he heard the success of the second reading of the Bill, and died a few days afterwards, on the 29th of July.

Of the great questions of the day there still remained the all-important one, the condition of the labouring classes, but it was to another Prime Minister and to a modified Cabinet that the honour of the introduction of the new Poor Law was to belong. Weakness of the ministry shown in the Parliament. Feb. 4, 1834. In spite of their large majorities, no single measure of the Government had been passed without important modifications, no scheme had been introduced that did not bear upon it the marks of compromise, and afford a distinct proof of the inherent weakness of a Cabinet divided against itself. The speech from the throne in the opening of the year 1834 did not give any hope of a firmer and more united Government. The Duke of Wellington was not wrong in complaining that there was no

definite promise of a single Government Bill, that the foreign policy
of the Cabinet had not produced European peace, that in spite of
its majorities the Church policy of the Government had failed, and
that it had carefully avoided, even while vaunting the success which
had attended it, to state whether it intended the Coercion Bill to be
renewed in Ireland or not. Nor was it doubted that he was uttering
the opinions of some at least of the Cabinet itself when he warned
the Lords against the tendency visible in several of the late proceedings of the Government towards tampering with property and the
introduction of the beginnings of the policy of confiscation.

In the Lower House both the strength and weakness of the
Government were shortly to be displayed. O'Connell, who had
talked so long about the repeal of the Union, and had thus kept up
the agitation which was so lucrative to himself, was
compelled at length to make good his promises and to
introduce a substantive motion for repeal. A lengthened debate followed, but terminated in a most complete victory
for the Government; the division showing a majority of 485 in
favour of an amendment exactly contradicting O'Connell's motion.
The central position occupied by the Government enabled it, when it
occasionally joined heartily with one side or the other, still to command the House of Commons, but when questions arose of a more
doubtful sort its weakness became visible. Measures for the relief
of Ireland had been promised, and Mr. Ward, a private member,
determined to bring these promises to a test, by introducing a motion
(May 27) with regard to the difficult question of the Irish Church,
which the ministers would gladly have left quiet. Mr. Ward's resolution stated that the Protestant Episcopal Establishment of Ireland
much exceeded the spiritual wants of the Protestant
population, that it was the right of the State and of
Parliament to distribute Church property, and that the
temporal possessions of the Irish Church ought to be
reduced. This motion put the Government into the greatest perplexity; to uphold the direct negative was to resign its pretensions
to be the party of progress; to accept it was to shock some of its
most important members. The ministers determined to adopt a
middle course, and appoint a commission of inquiry. They hoped
thereby to induce Mr. Ward to withdraw his motion, because the
question was already in Government hands, but they seemed at
the same time to pledge themselves to act in accordance with
the recommendations of the commission. Armed with this com-

Rejection of repeal, a Government victory.

Ministerial difficulty on Mr Ward's motion on the Irish Church.

promise, Lord Althorp went to the House to meet Mr. Ward's motion. But the seconder, Mr. Grote, had advanced but a short way in the speech when the Chancellor of the Exchequer rose and said, that since the beginning of the debate information had been brought to him which induced him to beg for a postponement. His personal influence was so great that the House at once granted his request. The news he had received was the resignation of Mr. Stanley, the Colonial minister, and of Sir James Graham, First Lord of the Admiralty, who regarded any interference with Church property with great abhorrence. They were followed by the Duke of Richmond, Postmaster-General, and by Lord Ripon, Privy Seal. The more conservative members of the Cabinet had thus openly retired from it. It might have been expected that Lord Durham, who had previously left it upon opposite grounds, would have now returned to office, and the Government have assumed a more distinctly radical character. He was, however, personally obnoxious to such members of the party of Canning as still remained in office, and his influence was dreaded by Lord Grey, who, though he continued as yet to hold the Premiership in accordance with the generally expressed desire of the Liberal party, sympathized at heart more with the Tories than with the Radicals. He expressed his feelings in his answer to an address which Lord Ebrington got up intreating him to retain his place. "In pursuing," he said, "a course of salutary improvement I feel it indispensable that we shall be allowed to proceed with deliberation and caution; and, above all, that we should not be urged by a constant and active pressure from without to the adoption of any measures the necessity of which has not been fully proved, and which are not strictly regulated by a careful attention to the settled institutions of the country both in Church and State. On no other principle can this or any other administration be conducted with advantage or safety." No difficulty was found in filling the vacant places; Mr. Spring Rice, who had distinguished himself in the debate on the Union, became Secretary for the Colonies, and Lord Auckland succeeded Sir James Graham.

Under Lord Grey's leadership the Government was enabled to continue its course, because it was recognized at the time as the only possible Government; the Conservative feeling in England was far too strong to allow the success of a Radical Government with Durham at its head. On the other hand, on the great questions of the day it was impossible to go back. Sir Robert Peel clearly understood this position of affairs. He saw that a Tory

[side notes: Resignation of the most conservative ministers. Difficulties of Grey's position.]

Government would have no hope of permanence if it rested only on the support of the extreme members of the party. If the party was ever to be reconstituted it must loyally accept the changes which had been made, admit within its limits the more conservative-minded of the reformers, and take its stand on the great Conservative instincts of the nation—the love of the State Church, and the dread of any attack upon property. For the formation of a Liberal Conservative Government the time had not yet arrived, and the present Government of compromise was therefore allowed to continue. But the difficulties of the Premier, from the divergence of his opinions from those of his colleagues, soon became overwhelming. It was necessary to determine whether the Coercion Bill should be renewed or not. But it was possible to renew it in a softened form, and to omit the most objectionable parts—the suppression of the right of petition and the establishment of military courts. Such a course seemed advisable to Mr. Littleton, the Chief Secretary, and recommended itself also to the more liberal members of the Government, Lord Brougham and Lord Althorp. The mischievous activity of Lord Brougham led him to suggest to the Lord Lieutenant, Lord Wellesley, who had succeeded Anglesey, the advisability of officially informing the Government that he could do without these stringent clauses. Wellesley had already expressed himself privately to the contrary effect, but was overpersuaded, and followed the advice of Littleton and Brougham in his official despatches. These contradictory opinions from the chief of the Government were naturally very embarrassing to Lord Grey. To make matters worse, Littleton had attempted a personal reconciliation with O'Connell. Lord Althorp had known and approved of this step, but had warned Littleton against making any pledges. The Secretary unluckily allowed himself to be drawn into an admission that neither himself nor the Lord Lieutenant nor Lord Althorp approved of the renewal of the obnoxious clauses. To complete his blunder, he did not inform Lord Althorp what he had done, and trusted to a promise of secrecy on the part of O'Connell, the most untrustworthy of men. So strong was Lord Althorp's opinion on the subject, backed as he believed it to be by that of Wellesley and of Littleton, that after being outvoted in the Cabinet, he in fact tendered his resignation, but was overruled by Lord Grey.

On the 1st of 'July the Premier introduced the Bill in its full form, asserting, as from Wellesley's private letters to him he had a right to assert, that it was considered necessary by the Irish Government. On this, O'Connell, forgetful of his promise, disclosed in the Lower House his conversation with Littleton, which was in fact a direct contradiction of Lord Grey's asser- tion, at the same time implicating Lord Althorp in the deception played upon him. The Government seemed convicted Resignation of Grey's ministry. July 1834. not only of internal division, but of duplicity. Lord Grey reiterated his assertion in the Upper House with regard to the feelings of the Irish Government as expressed to him, while Lord Althorp admitted that he disliked the clause, and that Mr. Littleton was justified in telling O'Connell that the question was unsettled at the time of their conversation. The divergence of opinion in the Cabinet was thus fully brought out, and Lord Althorp was made to appear as guilty at once of having held out false hopes to O'Connell, and of having waived his own opinions for the sake of retaining office. Nothing could have been more alien to his nature than this charge, especially as, far from having really pledged himself to O'Connell, he had particularly warned Littleton against committing himself. But there seemed no way of escape without rendering still more glaring the weakness of the administration. On this ground, Littleton's offer to resign, which he felt in honour bound to. make, was rejected; but, when in their eagerness to embarrass Government the Opposition moved for the production of the private letters of the Cabinet, Lord Althorp, in dis- gust at his equivocal position and at the attempted introduction into Parliament of matters which he held to be wholly beyond its jurisdiction, determined to resign. Lord Grey, by no means wedded to office, and feeling that Althorp's personal influence was the main security of the Government, at once declared the administration at an end. The King had already shown, when giving an answer to an address from the Bishops, a strong feeling against any attack upon the property of the Church. This known division between the sovereign and his advisers, and the evident weakness of the Cabinet itself, rendered the resignation of the ministry less surprising than it otherwise would have been.

Seeing the impossibility of forming a distinctly Tory ministry, the King was persuaded by Lord Brougham to send for Lord Melbourne, whom he instructed to give effect as far as possible to his previously expressed wishes, and to Lord Melbourne's ministry. July 16. form a combined ministry, admitting to office some Tories and some of those who had left office on Conservative grounds. The attempt was fruitless. Peel did not yet see his desired opportunity, and foreseeing the gradual reaction which must arise from the unsatisfactory character

of the Whig administration, determined to await his time. The
King was therefore compelled to consent to the reconstruction under
Melbourne of the old ministry. There was very little change in the
construction of the Cabinet. Lord Melbourne's own place in the
Home Department was filled by Lord Duncannon (Ponsonby), Sir
John Cam Hobhouse obtained a seat in the Cabinet as First Com-
missioner of the Woods and Forests, and Lord Carlisle surrendered
the Privy Seal to Lord Mulgrave.

The change, such as it was, did not add to the strength of the
ministry. The introduction of the Coercion Bill on the 18th of
July, without the stringent clauses, seemed a confession that
some of the ministers at all events were acting contrary to conviction, or that they had weakly yielded to Irish clamour. The
Bill was however passed with a strong protest in the Lords. An
attempt on the 29th of July again to settle the tithe question
displayed still further the inefficiency of the ministry; they allowed
themselves to be beaten in the Lower House upon an amendment
of O'Connell, who, instead of the proposed land tax, suggested
the immediate payment of the tithes, diminished forty per cent.,
by the landlord. In spite of their defeat, which so completely
changed their Bill that out of 172 clauses 111 had to be removed,
Church policy   they proceeded with it, but suffered a heavy defeat
of Melbourne's   on the second reading in the Lords. Their Church
ministry.   policy was indeed throughout entirely ineffective. The
feeling that the Church was in danger had begun to take hold
not only of the Lords, who systematically resisted innovation, but of
the people in England. The efforts of the Dissenters, excited to
demand religious equality by the success of Irish agitation, were
fruitless. Their petitions were indeed of a character to cause some
fear. They begged for the separation of Church and State, for the
exclusion of Bishops from Parliament, for the admission of Dissenters
to all the privileges of the universities. On this last point a Bill
was introduced. Largely signed petitions were sent in against it
by the universities. All the leaders of the Conservative, or partially
Conservative party, combined to oppose it, and though it passed
the Lower House it was rejected in the Lords (Aug. 1). In the
same way the efforts of Government to relieve Dissenters from
the Church rates, and from the restrictions laid upon the right
of dissenting ministers to celebrate marriage, being all conceived
from a Church point of view, and assuming the form of concessions
rather than the granting of rights, were distasteful to the Dissenters

themselves, and came to nothing. The plan for the commutation of the English tithes met with the same fate. It was indeed a period of general ecclesiastical excitement; the introduction of the appropriation clause in the Irish Tithe Bill had closely touched the feelings of English Churchmen; the nature of the Church as distinct from an institution founded by and connected with the State began to be examined. A party in Oxford undertook to enlighten the nation upon the character of the Church in a series of tracts, which gained for the authors the title of Tractarians. In these they urged with great force all the tenets of what is now known as the High Church party—the doctrine of apostolic succession, the sole efficiency of the sacraments, the sacred nature of the priesthood, and the insufficiency of the Bible as apart from the explanations of Church tradition. Their principles rapidly spread. At the same time the Evangelical party lost several of its chief leaders and began to decline. And though three parties could still be traced, public opinion began to divide itself chiefly between the two great views of those who regarded the Church as an institution independent in itself, and beyond the reach of secular interference, and those Liberals who, attached as they might be to the Church as a political institution, regarded it as lying within the sphere of politics.

But if their liberal Church policy was doomed to failure, the ministry was able to do one great work by the reform of the Poor Law. The chief effects of the old Poor Law have been already mentioned. Its lax adminis- *Aug. 1834.* tration, the power of relief in the houses of the paupers, the system of allowances in aid of wages, and the distribution of relief in proportion to the number of children, had pauperized the agricultural poor, had withdrawn the chief restraints on early and imprudent marriages, had fostered immorality, and increased the amount of the poor rate till it seemed as though England would sink beneath the burden. It had become necessary to adopt some sounder principles, even although they had the appearance of harshness. Nor was the Government without experience by which to guide its action. Already in about a hundred parishes an improved administration had been tried, and in every instance it had succeeded; while, on the other hand, in certain parishes where the old system remained in vigour cultivation had been actually abandoned, and the neighbouring parishes having to support their poor, there was every risk of the plague spreading throughout England. The chief error in the old system was the complete confusion which existed between poverty and pauperism, between the industrious poor man and the self-pauperized idler.   It was this point on which a commission issued in 1832 chiefly insisted.   The Bill based on their report was in fact little more than a recurrence to the true principles enunciated in the first general Poor Law of the reign of Elizabeth.   To separate these two classes it was necessary that outdoor relief should be discontinued and the allowance system put an end to.   Those only who were really in want were to receive relief, but upon conditions which should render it certain that the want was real.   In the workhouse every able-bodied man must work; it was not fair that the industrious should be called upon to support an increasing race of paupers raised in the workhouse, husbands and wives must therefore be separated; for the sake of training and education, children must be kept from the possible contamination of the adult paupers; and as the maintenance of industry was one of the chief objects of the reform, free circulation of labour and the removal of most of the restrictions of the old law of settlement were indispensable.   The system no doubt had a very harsh appearance, but its principles could scarcely be questioned.   But these principles were in fact nothing new; all the evils to be rectified had arisen from the bad way in which such principles had been carried out.   The machinery then by which relief was to be administered was of almost more importance than the principles on which it was to be granted.   For economy, parishes were formed into unions, with one workhouse instead of several.   The method of collecting the rates was left unchanged, the distribution was still left to guardians and select vestries; but this local management was placed under a central board, consisting of three commissioners, with assistants, at first twenty-one, diminished subsequently to nine.   There was one other point which bore an appearance of extreme harshness, was much objected to at the time, and was subsequently changed; this was an attempt to check immorality by throwing the charge of the maintenance of illegitimate children upon the mother.   This appeared completely to shield the guilty father, and to punish only the weak and misguided mother, but in fact, as many wise people saw at the time, it roused a feeling of self-dependence and respect among women, and produced the very best effects; the decrease of illegitimate births was extraordinary.   The decrease in England was nearly 10,000, or thirteen per cent. in two years.   In one point only did it appear that party interests could interfere with the passage of the Bill.   It almost necessarily implied the subsequent repeal of the

Corn Laws. Freedom of labour, the abolition of the Act of Settlement, rendered such a change indispensable; but this the ministry,
very anxious to avoid the appearance of touching laws which were
very dear to the hearts of the agricultural interest, still refused to believe, and denied in the most absolute terms. Nevertheless, between
the second reading on the 9th of May and the third reading of the Bill
on the 1st of July, a very powerful opposition had been aroused. It
was spoken of as a Bill cruel against the poor. From a radical point
of view the centralization of the system was decried. The commissioners were spoken of as three-tailed Bashaws. It was however
carried by 157 to 50 votes. This was on the 2nd of July, when
Lord Grey was still in office. Under the new ministry the management of the Bill in the Upper House passed into the hands of Lord
Brougham; he supported it in one of his ablest speeches, and it was
carried on the second reading by a very considerable majority, and
became law on the 14th of August. Although some subsequent
amendments were necessary, it has on the whole proved highly
successful. The poor rate, which at the end of the American War,
when the population of England was about 8,000,000, amounted to
£2,132,487, which during the subsequent forty years of mismanagement had risen till in 1833, when the population was 14,000,000, it
had reached £8,606,501, was in the course of three years reduced by
upwards of £3,000,000.

But though its character was so free from taint of party, though its
action was on the whole so beneficial, the new Poor *Discontent*
Law was used, and used with effect, to excite the deep- *and misery*
felt discontent which was prevalent in the lower *of the poor.*
classes, and which continued to increase and to acquire form and
organization during the next four years, till it assumed the definite
form of Chartism, and produced the very dangerous outbreak in the
year 1839. It was scarcely possible but that such discontent should
exist; the hopes of the poor man, raised to an exaggerated height by the
excitement of the Reform Bill, had been cruelly disappointed. While
no doubt some good and useful measures of reform had been carried,
it was impossible to deny that the reform ministry had on the whole
proved itself unwilling and unable to handle the great social questions of the time, that disputes in Parliament had fallen back into
their old grooves, and had assumed the form of party contests rather
than of efforts for the improvement of the great mass of the people.
Hitherto trade had been fairly prosperous, but in 1835 symptoms
were evident that this prosperity was disappearing; and when want

was added to the justly-felt disappointment of the workmen, when
agitators were exciting them with dismal stories of the cruelty of the
Poor Law, of the tyranny of the manufacturing masters, and when
every good and popular measure seemed to be first stripped of half
its value by the ministry which introduced it, and then totally
rejected by an obstructive House of Lords, it is not to be wondered at
that the unrepresented masses believed that they had been used
merely as an instrument, and that if increased representation was so
good for their betters, it would prove the cure for them also, and
began to clamour for a wide extension of the franchise, and more
efficient security that the particular wants of their class should
receive attention.

Many signs of the growing discontent were visible. The most
formidable in the course of the year 1834 was the great
extension and changed character of the trades unions.
For some time trade societies had existed, and from time to time individual trades had combined to strike for advance of wages or other
trade purposes, but in this year a combination of many trades began
to make itself seen, which by mutual support should enable those on
strike to hold out against their masters, and though the system broke
down through the natural inefficiency of an uneducated body for
such a combination, the danger became great when it was extended to
the agricultural poor. To repress this symptom, so threatening to the
landowners and farmers, six labourers were indicted at Dorchester
under an obsolete statute against the administering of oaths. Amidst
much popular sympathy, they were sentenced to seven years' transportation. The whole body of unionists, in their indignation, summoned a general meeting in Copenhagen Fields on the 21st of April.
Besides a general intention to overawe the ministry, there seems to
have been among a knot of their leaders a distinct plan of somehow
or other securing the Government by violent means. It was intended
that the deputation of the trades should lay hands upon Lord Melbourne, who was then minister for home affairs, and proceed to further
acts of violence. Warned in time, Melbourne kept himself out of
sight, and sent his under secretary to receive the deputation, while
silently troops were held in readiness, the public offices defended
with artillery, and 5000 householders sworn in as special constables.
The under secretary declared that a petition accompanied by 60,000
men could not be received, and seeing the preparations made for
their reception, the crowd withdrew in quiet, and the day passed over
safely, but the incident shows both the power and temper of the

Increase of trades unions.

unionists. Even more formidable was the general feeling against the House of Lords which exhibited itself at the close of the next year. By that time the House had shown itself still more obstinate, and facts had been brought to light which rendered it particularly odious to the people.

In the autumn of 1834 the possession of office by the Whigs was regarded as secure, and while O'Connell returned to continue the agitation in Ireland, the ministers withdrew as usual to refresh themselves after the labours of the session. Among others, Lord Brougham travelled in Scotland, everywhere bringing both himself and the ministry into ridicule by his inconsistent and egotistical speeches. On the 15th of September the late Prime Minister attended a banquet held in his honour at Edinburgh, where he met Lord Durham, his son-in-law, Lord Brougham, and several of the other ministers. In returning thanks for the health of the ministry, the Chancellor appeared to rebuke the reformers for their impatience and for endangering all progress by their haste. These words by no means suited the views of Lord Durham, one of the chief authors of the Reform Bill, and a man of very popular tendencies. He replied that he entirely disagreed with his noble and learned friend, and frankly confessed that he was one of those persons who saw with regret every hour that passed over the existence of recognized and unreformed abuses. Brougham took this rebuke in the highest dudgeon, and in a very few days, at Salisbury, he replied severely upon Lord Durham, and uttered a sort of challenge to him to meet him in the House of Lords, and shortly after in the *Edinburgh Review* charged him with revealing the secrets of the Cabinet. Lord Durham's words at Edinburgh were eagerly accepted as proofs of a more frank acceptance of the principles of reform than they had hitherto met with from Government, and all minds were eagerly set upon the approaching duel in the House. But the King, who, as has been already mentioned, much disliked the Church policy of the Whigs, dreaded what must have given rise to a new assertion of the duty of rapid reform. He was eager to prevent the meeting in the House, and circumstances favoured him. Before the session Lord Spencer died, and Lord Althorp, his son, was thus removed to the Upper House. There was no reason why this should have broken up the ministry, but the King seized his opportunity, sent for Lord Melbourne, asserted that the ministry rested chiefly on the personal influence of Lord Althorp in the Commons, declared that, deprived

Dispute between Durham and Brougham.

Dismissal of the Melbourne ministry. Nov. 1834.

of it as it now was, the Government could not go on, and dismissed his ministers, instructing Melbourne at once to send for the Duke of Wellington.

Ever since the passing of the Reform Bill the conduct of Sir Robert

The Peel-Wellington ministry.

Peel had been extremely judicious. In his hands the Tory party had been entirely remodelled; there were indeed remnants of it unchanged, especially in the House of Lords, but gradually most of the party had separated themselves from this remnant, and had taken the name of Conservatives, declaring themselves as willing as the Whigs to foster reforms, although only in a Conservative manner. It was in vain that the old Tories had sought to keep the Duke of Wellington with them; he had wisdom enough to see that the hope of the party lay with Peel, and to keep up the closest connection with him. His first step therefore, when summoned by the King, was to send to Peel, who, believing that the time for a Conservative ministry had not yet arrived, had gone abroad, and was now in Rome. While waiting for his arrival, the Duke took upon himself the discharge of no less than five offices, conduct which, though in fact perfectly wise and reasonable, was foolishly complained of at the time as unconstitutional. Peel, although he was as yet by no means anxious for office, could not but obey the summons, and hurried home with extreme rapidity. He had hoped to obtain the support of Sir James Graham and Mr. Stanley, the late deserters from the Whig ministry, and it was a grave disappointment when they refused to act with him. Thus prevented from forming the moderate Conservative ministry he intended, Peel was reduced to fill his places with men of more pronounced opinions, which promised ill for any advance in reform. He himself became Chancellor of the Exchequer and First Lord of the Treasury. The Foreign, Home, War, and Colonial Offices were filled respectively by Wellington, Goulburn, Herries, and Aberdeen. Lord Lyndhurst became Lord Chancellor, Hardinge Irish Secretary, and Lord Wharncliffe Privy Seal.

With this ministry Peel had to meet a hostile House of Commons,

The Tamworth Manifesto. Jan. 1835.

for the approach of the Conservatives to power had combined Whigs and Radicals in opposition. The Prime Minister therefore thought it necessary to dissolve Parliament, and took the opportunity of declaring his policy in what is known as the Tamworth Manifesto. He declared his acceptance of the Reform Bill as a final settlement of the question, and promised to carry out its intentions as far as they consisted in a wise and careful improvement of old institutions. As to the other questions then at issue he would support the inquiry into the state of corporations which the late ministry had set on foot, and wished, as his predecessors had done, to relieve Dissenters from the Church rates and from all restrictions on their marriages; but upon the Irish Church, and upon admission of Dissenters to the universities, his mind was unchanged. He continued to object to the appropriation of Church revenues to secular purposes and to granting degrees to Dissenters. As to whether any reform was required in the organization of the English Church, his mind, he said, was not yet made up. The tone of this Manifesto was very different from that of the old Tory party, and shows that the Reform Bill had really done its work, that the country had entered upon a new era, when the lines between parties would be less coarsely drawn, when obstinate obstruction to all reform would be impossible, and the points at issue confined chiefly to the time, manner, and degree, in which reforms should be carried out. But it is impossible in a country where party government has once taken root that unprejudiced discussion of measures should become prevalent. The general principles of the men by whom the measures are suggested are, and must be, invariably taken into consideration, and the one party will not fail to feel mistrust of the other even though the plans suggested are as good, or better, than their own, and the contest between the rival parties for the Government of the country will not cease. Thus, in spite of Peel's moderation, the whole body of the Liberals were determined to oppose the new Government to the utmost, and not to trust the administration in the hands of one who had always represented the Tories, and who still received the support even of the extreme members New Parliament of that party. The elections, though they returned a Feb. 19, 1835. House, as is generally the case, more favourable to the existing Government than that which had been dissolved, still gave a considerable majority to the Liberals.

From the very first Peel held office upon suffrance; the only question was how to bring matters to a point, as the Overthrow of minister refused to accept as his dismissal anything but Peel's ministry. a direct vote of want of confidence. Meanwhile his April 8, 1835. temper and judgment daily increased the admiration which the public began to feel for him. He took up several of the late ministers' measures, and carried them through where they themselves had failed. A more complete liberty granted to the Dissenters with regard to their marriages won their approbation; and though he could not complete this measure, he was able on going out of office to leave it in the hands of Lord John Russell, by whom it was settled upon the principle that the State was only interested in the civil contract, while churches and sects were at liberty to add what religious ceremonies they liked. He introduced a measure for the voluntary commutation of tithes, which seemed to be successful, re-appointed all the committees of the preceding session for examining abuses, and continued with good effect the ecclesiastical commission for the organization of the arrangements of the Church. The common charge against him was that he was purloining the measures of his adversaries. However, although he had to stand constantly on the defensive, there appeared no sufficient grounds for a vote of want of confidence. At last, on the 30th of March, Lord John Russell brought the matter to a crisis by proposing as a sort of test question that the House should resolve itself into committee to consider the state of the Irish Church, with the intention of applying any surplus revenues which might be found to general education, without dis-tinction of religion. In other words, he reintroduced the old appro-priation clause. It is to be borne in mind that the Whigs themselves had abandoned that clause, that they had voted against it in the case of Mr. Ward's measure, and that they afterwards entirely rejected it. But for the time it served the party purpose. Although Peel declared, and declared rightly, that the feeling of England was against it, the votes of the Scotch and Irish members carried the day, and the ministry was beaten on the 3rd of April by a majority of thirty-three. On the 8th Sir Robert Peel announced his resig-nation.

The Whigs were thus again triumphant. The history of their weakness and their difficulties belong to a period of history which lies beyond the limits of this work. But one measure which they brought to a satisfactory conclusion requires mention as completing in one very important point the work of the Reform Bill. This was the reform of corporations. With this exception it would be impos-sible to describe the course of their measures without following them so far that they become a part rather of present politics than of past history. But this reform to which they at once pledged themselves was scarcely less important for the purification of local government than the Reform Bill itself had been with regard to the central Legislature.

On the extension of the franchise on the passing of the Reform Bill, attention had been drawn to the fact that in a great number of corporate towns many of the electors who had the right to join in choosing members for Parliament had no voice at all in the management of their own local affairs. It was clearly for the interest of the reform party to remove this abuse, and to secure still stronger support from the middle class of citizens among whom their strength already lay.   In 1833 a commission of ten members had been issued to inquire into the condition of the corporations of England and Wales.   Nominated during the first days of the popular triumph, and with a party object, it was natural that the commissioners should be drawn entirely from the ranks of the reformers.   Their report was therefore open to the charge of onesidedness, but it brought a state of things to light which thoroughly justified the Government in introducing a great measure of reform.   The constitution, originally popular, of the English boroughs had in lapse of time been completely altered. The rights of citizenship, originally belonging to all fully qualified freemen residing within the borough, had been gradually confined to a small class technically spoken of as the Freemen, many of whom were so decayed as not only to pay no rates, but in some cases to be themselves dependent on the poor rates.   The government of the town and administration of the corporate property, and, before the Reform Bill, the election of parliamentary representatives, had in some instances fallen into the hands of an exclusive council, who had the right of filling up the vacancies in its own numbers.   A variety of circumstances had contributed to these changes.   Birth, marriage, apprenticeship, or membership of some guild, originally tests of residence, had after a time acted so as to exclude large numbers of residents from the ranks of the freemen. Wealth introduced a division of classes, and unchecked encroachment on the part of the wealthy had gone still further to exclude many from their rights.   Political reasons had induced the Crown to seek the support of the boroughs in Parliament, and, especially in the time of the Tudors, new charters had been granted which placed the local government entirely in the hands of self-elected councils, much more easily handled for political purposes than widespread constituencies.   The same process had been continued by the Stuarts. James II. even went further, and his attempt to nominate corporations of boroughs was not the least of the causes of the Revolution. Though the project failed, the close corporation system was continued both by Whigs and Tories, who found their political advantage in it. This perversion of municipal arrangements for political purposes had

Condition of municipal corporations

been attended with many practical abuses. In the first place, the corporations, which had in their hands the government of large and important towns, by no means represented the property, intelligence, or population of those towns. Thus in Ipswich, of 2000 ratepayers only 287 belonged to the corporation. At Cambridge, out of 20,000 inhabitants, only 118 were freemen, while of the property, which was valued at £25,000, only £2100 was the property of freemen. In Norwich, £25,500 was the value of the rated property, £18,200 of this belonged to those who were not freemen. Again, these self-elected governors constantly misappropriated the corporate funds, which, as the gross income of the corporations was £366,000, was a matter of considerable importance; the corporate offices were filled by favour, the charities employed for the purchase of votes, and large sums spent upon feasting and other useless shows, while the townsmen at large were rated for all local purposes. The distribution of these rates again was in the hands of the same people who exacted them, and no account of how they were employed could be obtained. To cure this general state of corruption was the intention of the new measure.

The measure included 178 boroughs. It began by marking out their boundaries, where possible in accordance with the boundaries of the electoral borough. The object of the Bill was not to centralize, but on the contrary to improve local administration; it was not therefore proposed to withdraw business from the hands of the corporation, with the exception of the administration of charities and church funds, which were respectively placed in the hands of trustees named by the Lord Chancellor and of the ecclesiastical commissioners. It was the nature of the corporation itself which was to be improved. In accordance with the principle of the Whig party, the new governing bodies were to be elected by constituencies of considerable breadth, but confined to the middle classes. A three years' residence and payment of the poor and borough rates was to be the qualification of an elector. By them the new governing body, called the town council, was chosen, which together with the constituency formed the corporation. To committees of the town council were intrusted the administration of the various branches of local government. To the whole body collectively was given the management of the borough funds, the proper expenditure of which was to be guaranteed by a publication of the accounts, properly audited by auditors not themselves town councillors. The Government reserved in its own hand the right of appointing justices of the peace and paid magistrates when required.

The Municipal Reform Bill. Sept. 7, 1835.

Though the change was sweeping, and seemed somewhat to affect the rights of property, the abuses were so glaring that the Bill easily passed the Lower House. In the Lords several amendments were passed against the Government, especially one retaining their old privilege to existing freemen, but somewhat to the disappointment of the Tories, the Commons accepted the amendment, and the Bill was passed on the 7th of September.

So absorbing had been the interest of domestic questions that foreign affairs had been somewhat disregarded. Yet from time to time they had come before the public attention, and were in themselves of considerable im- *Foreign diplomacy of Palmerston.* portance. They had fallen chiefly into the hands of Lord Palmerston, a disciple of Canning's, and therefore by principle an upholder of peace and of the doctrine of non-intervention, but inspired also as his master had been with an admiration and love for the institutions of constitutional monarchy, which led him into a line of conduct which it is difficult to harmonize with his professed principles. The most striking characteristic of our foreign policy in his hands was the close apparent union with France in opposition to the three Eastern powers, which Palmerston still regarded as tainted with the old principle of the Holy Alliance, and of one of which, namely Russia, he was sensitively mistrustful on all points connected with the policy of the East of Europe. The sympathy between England and France was inevitable. In some sense the kings of the two countries were both citizen kings, the great change which had taken place in England was the counterpart of the Revolution of July. In both countries it was the middle class which had just obtained the predominance. In both countries there was the same character of government, and both expressed the same desire for peace. At the same time the questions which agitated Western Europe were all more or less connected with the establishment of that form of government which both countries admired.

The influence of the Revolution of July had, as has been mentioned, spread far and wide over Europe, but had made itself most prominently felt in Belgium, which had broken loose from its enforced connection with Holland, *Absorption of Poland. 1831.* and in Poland, which rose in insurrection to free itself from the rule of Russia. With Poland England had little to do. In the existing state of circumstances, though the sympathy of all classes was strongly with the Poles, armed interference was not to be thought of, and it was impossible to prevent the total subjugation of that gallant nation, after a very brave but ineffectual attempt to withstand the might of Russia. The fall of Warsaw sealed its fate; it was incorporated, contrary to all the stipulations of the Treaty of Vienna, with the Russian empire.

But Belgium was nearer home. Its creation into a strong kingdom Formation had been the pet scheme of English diplomatists; it was of Belgium. impossible to leave it to be overwhelmed by Holland, in conjunction with the Eastern powers, or to be absorbed by France. The difficult duty of the English minister was so to undo the work of his predecessors as if possible to prevent a war which would inevitably have arisen in either of the above cases, and so to preserve the independence of the Belgians that they might yet serve in some degree to fulfil the object of the negotiators of Vienna, as a check upon the power of France. To gain these ends he induced the five great powers to send representatives to a Congress in London. The first difficulty was to restrain the ambitious desires of France, where the propagandist and conquering spirit seemed for the moment to have been reawakened by the late revolution. The original plan of mediation was rejected by the King of the Netherlands, who, trusting to the assistance of Russia, invaded Belgium, and was only dislodged by the appearance of a French army. After a period of some anxiety, the firmness of Palmerston was successful in causing the withdrawal of the French troops, and the rejection of the crown by the King's son the Duc de Nemours. The immediate danger of war being thus averted, the London Conference drew up twenty-four articles (Nov. 15, 1831), on which, though they were not thoroughly acceptable to either party, it was determined to insist. They specified the limits of the new kingdom more favourably for Holland than had been the case in the preceding and rejected scheme, and settled the division of the public debt. Upon the understanding that these arrangements were final, Prince Leopold, the husband of the late Princess Charlotte, accepted the throne, not however, as Palmerston was careful to explain, as the English candidate, but as a man generally acceptable to the powers. He shortly rendered his position more secure by marrying a daughter of the French King. But the difficulties did not end with his acceptance of the throne ; the King of the Netherlands continued to refuse the proferred terms, till at length the two Western powers lost patience, and unable to procure the assistance of the other members of the Conference, took the matter into their own hands, laid an embargo on the Dutch ships, blockaded the mouth of the Scheldt, and laid siege to Antwerp with a French army. After a very gallant defence, Antwerp yielded, and though the final settlement between the countries was postponed till 1839, a provisional armistice was entered into which practically put an end to the difficulties.

As important as Belgium were the affairs of Portugal and Spain. Don Miguel had pursued his career of cruelty and folly. Acts of unjustifiable violence committed on the subjects Affairs of
Portugal. of France had compelled the French Government, in July 1831, to send a squadron to the Tagus to obtain satisfaction, a measure which threatened for an instant serious consequences, as the English Government still felt itself pledged to uphold Portugal, its old ally. Fortunately Miguel was too foolish to see his opportunity. Still worse behaviour towards some English subjects brought a British fleet to Portugal in the following spring also to demand satisfaction. It became certain that the two Western powers would act in union there as they had already done in Belgium. While continuing nominally a strict neutrality, all sorts of volunteer assistance was allowed to join Don Pedro, when in July 1832 he landed at Oporto, again to assert the claims of his young daughter. An Englishman commanded his fleet, a Frenchman his army, and his troops were largely composed of volunteers from both nations. On the other hand, the French Legitimists, with Marshal Bourmont at their head, crowded to assist Don Miguel. For a while Don Pedro's expedition met with poor success ; he could barely make good his position in Oporto, but in the middle of the next year, Admiral Sartorius having given place to Napier, the tide of victory changed, Miguel's fleet was destroyed off St. Vincent, and before the end of June Lisbon was in the hands of the Queen's adherents. For some while longer the strife was continued ; but the Whigs could boast that the question was practically settled, and constitutional government established, although the assertion they made that they had held a strict neutrality, and without helping either side had allowed them to fight the matter out, was scarcely consistent with truth.

The success of constitutional principles in Portugal was speedily followed by events which produced the same results in Affairs of
Spain. Spain. The law of succession in that country had been again and again changed ; the liberal constitution of 1812 had excluded females ; Ferdinand in 1830 had again admitted them to the succession, but, frightened by a dangerous illness, and under pressure from the priests, he subsequently withdrew this decree, thus leaving his brother Don Carlos, an extreme absolutist, heir to the throne. The return of health brought him under other influences. He had married a young Neapolitan Princess, Christina, by whom he had two daughters, and through her influence he was induced, in 1832, to re-establish the old law, settling the crown on his daughter Isabella. In September 1832 he died, and when Isabella was proclaimed Queen and Christina Regent, Carlos met with considerable sympathy, especially among the clergy, the peasantry and the old nobility, as they considered him tricked out of his inheritance by Christina's influence. But Christina had sense enough to throw herself heartily upon the side of the Liberal government, and rallied round her all the friends of constitutionalism in Spain and elsewhere. Thus there were in each of the neighbouring countries of the Peninsula a young Queen representing constitutional principles, opposed to an uncle with absolutist views claiming the throne. The Queen was successful in Spain ; the Cortes was summoned under a Liberal minister, and Don Carlos was driven from the country. The similarity of their positions made the cause of the two Princes one, and Carlos betook himself to Don Miguel, who was still after his expulsion from Lisbon lying at Santarem. Lord Palmerston saw in this position of affairs an opportunity for carrying out his great object, of supporting constitutionalism and aiming a blow against the absolute powers of the East. He arranged, early in the year 1834, a Quadruple Alliance, primarily between Spain and Portugal, for the purpose of expelling the claimants to both countries from the Peninsula, a movement which was to be supported in case of necessity by a French army and an English fleet.

Thus, as in the affairs of Belgium, France and England had been successful in thwarting the Eastern powers and estab-

The Quadruple Alliance. 1834.

lishing a constitutional power, so now again they had induced Spain and Portugal to add their weight to the constitutional cause. " I reckon this to be a great stroke," said Palmerston ; " in the first place it will settle Portugal, and go some way to settle Spain also, but what is of more permanent and essential importance, it establishes a quadruple alliance between the States of the West, which will serve as a powerful counterpoise to the Holy Alliance of the East." The treaty did in fact at once put an end to the opposition of Don Miguel. A Spanish army marched to attack him on the rear, and he surrendered, and promised to leave the Peninsula. In the affairs of Spain the treaty was not so effectual. Don Carlos escaped in an English ship, to return subsequently and carry on a civil war, which lasted till 1840. During that period the English, though still preserving external neutrality, allowed an English legion, under the command of Sir De Lacy Evans, to go to the assistance of the Queen, whose final triumph he materially assisted in gaining. The whole fruit of the Whig foreign policy, and of the friendship with France, which the similarity of feeling in the two countries had engendered, was to consolidate for the time the West of Europe upon constitutional principles, in well-defined opposition to the East. But this had not been done without the exertion of an amount of influence, and an indirect employment of physical force, which could scarcely be honestly veiled under the name of neutrality ; nor had the joint influence of the two countries been sufficient to check the growth of Russia in the East. Mahomet Ali, the Pasha of Egypt, had formed the idea of creating an Arabian monarchy from portions of the Turkish Empire. His adopted son and heir, Ibrahim Pasha, overran the whole of Syria, and, in 1832, seemed on the highroad to Constantinople. In its extremity the Porte applied to Russia for assistance, and although the French ambassador contrived a temporary arrangement with the Pasha which postponed for a time the interference of the Russians, the further advance of Ibrahim compelled a renewed demand for help, and finally, on July 8, 1833, most of the demands of Mahomet Ali were granted, and the Treaty of Unkiar Skelesi was signed with Russia, which opened the Bosphorus to the Russians, and closed the Dardanelles to the ships of war of other nations ; the protests of England and France remained entirely unheeded.

Unavailing against Russian advance.

Treaty of Unkiar Skelesi.

Palmerston's dislike to the advance of Russia in the East rested not only on his general antipathy to the prince, whom he regarded as the head of the absolutist party, but arose from the feeling that it was necessary to secure our road to India, which has been the chief spring of the policy of England in the Mediterranean, and indeed, that nothing should interfere with our Indian possessions, became yearly more important. Uninfluenced in its general course by the changes of parties, the Indian Empire had been steadily increasing for the last thirty years. Though Wellesley's view stated broadly, that England must be the one great power of India, was not accepted by several of his successors, without wish of their own they had been compelled to act much as he would have acted, constantly to increase the English dominions, and to complete the system of

Retrospect of affairs in India.

subsidiary treaties with those powers which were still allowed a separate existence.

Lord Cornwallis' second tenure of office, interrupted by his speedy

Cornwallis.
July—Oct.
1805.
death, was too brief to allow him to reverse his predecessor's policy, as seems to have been his intention.

Sir G. Barlow.
1805—1807.
Nor was the government of Sir George Barlow, one of the civil servants of the Company, who devoted himself chiefly to the financial business of his office, of sufficient length

Lord Minto.
1807—1813.
to produce much effect. But during the rule of Lord Minto, sent out to replace him by the Grenville administration in 1807, some events of importance took place. Of these the most important were the capture of the Dutch and French possessions in the East, the check which was given to the rising kingdom of the Sikhs in the Punjaub, and the strange incident of a mutiny of the English officers in Madras. In July 1810 the Island

Capture of
Batavia and
Mauritius.
of Bourbon was taken with little loss, and in the following November, General Abercrombie, with an expedition consisting of troops from Bengal and Madras, attacked the Isle of France; within three days of his reaching the island he succeeded in overcoming all opposition, the island was surrendered, and the last remnant of French power in the East disappeared. In February of the same year the possessions of Holland, then forming a part of the French Empire, were also attacked, and in 1811 a considerable army was landed in Java. Batavia at once surrendered, but it was not till after a severe battle with the Dutch General Jansens, and the loss of about a thousand men, that the island was subdued; it was intrusted to the government of Mr. Raffles, afterwards Sir Stamford, and was much improved under his hands, but at the Peace of Vienna it was restored with most other colonial conquests. It has been believed that its value and wealth were not thoroughly known or appreciated by the ministry at the time. It was the interest of the European war also which brought Lord Minto's government into contact with powers on the north-east of India. A French embassy to Persia,

Check of
the Sikhs.
really directed against the Russians, was thought to have reference to an intended attack upon India, which was known to have been at an earlier time a favourite project of Napoleon's. It became therefore necessary for the English Government to attempt to secure the friendship of the Affghans and the Sikhs. This latter race, originally organized in a sort of confederacy, had been gradually brought under the subjection of one

family, the representative of which was now Runjeet Singh. In their dread of the French, the English were for a while blind to his encroachments even on the east of the Sutlej, but as events in Europe showed that Napoleon's Eastern dreams were for the present over, a firmer tone was adopted, and in 1809 the appearance of English troops proved to Runjeet that his hopes of further conquest were futile, and he consented to enter into a treaty of perpetual friendship. The mutiny at Madras was somewhat similar to that which Clive had suppressed in the Bengal army. The withdrawal of an allowance known as the tent contract was the imme- ^{Mutiny at} diate cause of the disaffection, but there had been for ^{Madras.} some time discontent among the officers, unfortunately supported by some whose age and position gave them influence over their juniors. General Macdowell, having been refused a seat in the Council, had thrown up his command, and was returning to England in disgust. He entered into an unseemly quarrel with the Quartermaster-General, Colonel Munro, and published a general order declaring that had he remained in India he would have brought him to a court-martial. The Government, in great anger, suspended those officers who had assisted in publishing the general order, and finding them largely supported by their fellow-officers, proceeded to remove a considerable number from their command. This was followed by an open mutiny which broke out in Hyderabad, Seringapatam, and elsewhere. At Seringapatam the mutineers were suppressed by force of arms, else- where they came to their senses, and accepted the conditions imposed on them by Lord Minto, who had come to Madras to attempt to meet the difficulty. Lord Minto returned to England in 1813, after an honourable discharge of his duties, and was succeeded by the Earl of Moira, afterwards Marquis of Hastings.

It was during Lord Moira's administration that the work of Wellesley was completed and the position of England ^{Marquis} rendered absolutely paramount in India. His first ^{of Hastings} difficulties were with Nepaul, where the Goorkhas had ^{1813—1823} succeeded in establishing a power of some importance, and had not refrained from attacking English territory. The war ^{War with} was a severe one ; on more than one occasion the Eng- ^{Nepaul.} lish troops were defeated or foiled by the strong fortifications of their opponents. But after two campaigns, in 1815, Sir David Ochterlony succeeded in securing the hill-fortresses and compelling the Goorkha chief to come to terms. The Nepaulese surrendered to the English a portion of the Terrai, a territory lying to the south of their country, reinstated a considerable number of the small princes they had lately dispossessed, and received an English resident at Catmandoo, their capital. It was at the close of this war that Lord Moira received his marquisate. But events, to which Lord Hastings owes his chief celebrity, arose in a more important quarter. The centre of India was occupied by the great princes of the Mahratta nation, who, though subdued by Lord Wellesley, were uneasy under their altered circumstances, and were dreaming of the restoration of their national greatness. Their nominal head was the Peishwa resident at Poonah, and now placed under a subsidiary treaty with the English. These princes kept up communications among themselves. Agents from Poonah were at all their courts, and some of them certainly engaged

War with the Pindaries and Mahrattas. in intrigues both with the Nepaulese and Runjeet Singh, the late enemies of the English. Besides these covert and dangerous enemies, there existed a body of freebooters called the Pindaries. Recruited from all nations and all religions, their hordes found employment sometimes with the armies of the native princes at war with each other, sometimes in predatory excursions of their own. The reward for which they served was nearly always the right to rob. Their expeditions were of the most destructive character; all mounted and lightly armed, they crossed the country in marches of from forty to fifty miles a day, fell upon the devoted district, and carried off everything moveable in it, frequently burning what they could not carry away, and having recourse to the cruellest tortures to wring from the wretched inhabitants a knowledge of their hidden treasure. They had found their chief support among the Mahrattas, and had established themselves in the country between the Nerbudda and the Vindhya hills. Till 1815 they had refrained from attacking the English, but during the Nepaulese war they had crossed the river into the Deccan, and had ravaged the territory of our ally the Nizam; and the year after they had even passed the British frontiers and plundered more than three hundred villages. Lord Hastings determined to put an end to these robbers, supported as he believed that they were by the Mahratta confederation, before he dismissed the army collected for the war of Nepaul. He applied for leave to act on a great scale, and, having received it, brought into the field large armies from all the Presidencies, and prepared for war on such a scale as rendered it plain that he intended to make a final settlement of Central India. It was the complicity of the Mahrattas with the Pindaries which rendered his work difficult. The Peishwa had already shown his intentions. His favourite,

Trimbucjee, had procured the murder of the agent of the Guicowar, who, in union with the English, was negotiating for a new lease of the Peishwa's property in Gujerat. The murderer was screened, and signs were everywhere visible that the Peishwa was meditating treachery. Yielding to the pressure of the English resident, he surrendered Trimbucjee; but on the escape of his favourite he again gave him refuge, and eluded the English demands. At length, yielding to the strong measures taken by them, he apparently gave up the point, and in June 1817 entered into a new treaty considerably more stringent than the Treaty of Bassein, and designed to destroy the Peishwa's nominal superiority over the Mahratta confederation, which was the source of so much danger. The effect of the treaty was very temporary. The Peishwa continued his measures against the English, attacked and burnt the British residency, was defeated after a severe battle and fled, intending to make common cause with his compatriots. Meanwhile events of a somewhat similar character had been taking place at the courts of the other Mahratta chiefs. It was thought necessary not only to separate them from the Pindaries, but to oblige them to join in the suppression of those freebooters. In November Sindia was compelled to make a treaty to that effect, containing a most important clause, as it allowed the English to make separate treaties, which had hitherto been forbidden, with those chiefs, especially the Rajputs, who were dependent upon Sindia. The unity of his kingdom was thus broken up. A treaty of a similar character was concluded with Ameer Khan, the head of a large body of freebooters in close connection with Holkar, though at the time resident at Jeypoor. With the other two great chiefs, the Rajah of Nagpoor and Holkar, more violent measures were found necessary. Appa Sahib, the uncle of the late prince, had obtained the government of Nagpoor, and had pretended a close friendship with England. But the same national aspirations as had moved the Peishwa acted upon him too. As the Peishwa was the nominal viceroy of the Mahrattas, so was he their nominal commander-in-chief. He repeated the treachery at Poonah, and attacked the British residency; and as his army was strong, and consisted largely of Arabs, he was only defeated after a battle of eighteen hours' duration. By December, however, he was thoroughly conquered, and had given himself up to the English; Nagpoor had been evacuated, and the Arabs dismissed. Just about the same time the forces of Holkar had been also defeated at Mahidpoor, in the neighbourhood of Oojein. On the insanity of Holkar himself, his power had passed into the hands of his young wife, Toolsee-Bhye, as regent for the young prince; but she was mistrusted by the war party, seized, and put to death. The chiefs then plunged into war, but were thoroughly defeated by Hislop's forces, and the young Holkar was compelled to enter into a treaty, which, among other things, bound him to perpetual peace, and established the Company as the arbitrator in all his quarrels. As in the case of Sindia, the Rajput princes subject to his dominion were allowed to contract separate treaties with the English, and gladly seized the opportunity. Thus the great confederation was defeated in detail, and the Peishwa alone, a fugitive from his capital, was capable of making resistance. It was found nearly impossible to come up with him; though combats were occasionally fought, no general battle resulted. But a new plan was devised which before long completed his destruction. The strongholds of his country were one by one reduced; and among others, in February, Satara, the residence of the descendants of Sevaji, whose nominal minister the Peishwa was. The authority of this prince was re-established, and the Peishwa was deposed, and thus the national character of his resistance destroyed. Soon after, also (Feb. 19, 1818), he was forced to battle at Ashtee, near Bunderpoor, and there thoroughly beaten. His power of resistance was now at an end, his fortresses had fallen one by one; his motley army, consisting largely of Pindaries, was broken up, and in June, finding himself surrounded, he surrendered to Sir John Malcolm. He accepted an allowance of £80,000 a year, with leave to withdraw and reside at Benares, where he remained quietly during the rest of his life. He had refused even to the last to surrender Trimbucjee, who was, however, shortly afterwards captured, and kept a prisoner till his death. The destruction of the Mahratta power had gone hand in hand with that of the Pindaries. Wherever they had been met with they had been beaten. By the end of February all their leaders had surrendered, and such remnants of them as were left had been removed to Goruckpoor, where they settled quietly down. There was one exception; their great chief, Chetoo, was still at large, and when Appa Sahib of Nagpoor, continuing his treachery after the treaty, and still holding communication with the Peishwa, was dethroned, the two chiefs took refuge in the Mahadeo hills on the south of the Nerbudda, and there assembled a mixed army of Mahrattas, Arabs, and Pindaries, to the number of about 20,000. The destruction of these troops closed the war. The English forces were concentrated for a great attack; seeing the hopelessness of resistance, the leaders fled, and took refuge in the fort of Aseerghur, which belonged to Sindia, with whom no doubt Appa had still relations. The fortress could not long shelter him. Sindia, in fear, refused to receive him; he fled to Runjeet Singh, and was finally allowed to return and live peaceably in Judpore. Chetoo, deprived of most of his followers, also took flight; he attempted to retire into the Malwa, but during his retreat sought refuge in a thicket, and was there devoured by a tiger. As a punishment for having received the fugitives, Aseerghur was besieged and taken, and as clear proofs were found in it of Sindia's treachery, it was retained. This was the last act of the war. At its conclusion the whole dominions of the Peishwa, with the exception of a district given to the Rajah of Satara, and all Appa Sahib's dominions in Berar, passed directly into the , hands of the English. All the Rajput rajahs had placed themselves under British protection, and Sindia was the only prince with whom there had not been concluded a satisfactory subsidiary treaty. Lord Hastings had thus the merit of thoroughly completing the great plans of the Marquis of Wellesley.

When Hastings left his office, which he had held for nine years, he was succeeded by Lord Amherst, who reached Calcutta Lord Amherst. in August 1823, and held the Governor-generalship till 1823—1828. 1828. During that period the dominions of England received a still further accession, and the difficulty of putting a stop to a course of conquest once begun was shown. At the same time that Clive had laid the foundation of the English Empire, a man of the name of Alompra had established a great empire on the other side of the Ganges. He had succeeded in bringing into one the kingdoms of Siam, Pegu, Ava, and Aracan. By degrees the two empires of Burmah and of India had become conterminous. The Burmese had been rendered so confident by their successes that they had demanded of Lord Hastings the surrender of Chittagong, Dacca, and other places, as having been originally dependencies of Aracan; their demand had of course been absolutely disregarded, but they were now proceeding to conquer Cashar, a district in North-Eastern Bengal, the rajah of which applied for help to the English. A further act of encroach-ment on their part brought on a war; they seized, on the coast of Chittagong, a little island in the possession of a small British outpost. No satisfaction could be obtained, and in March 1824 war became inevitable, much against the will, and somewhat to the surprise, of Lord Amherst, who had intended to be peaceful. The The Burmese attack of the English was made upon Rangoon at the War. mouth of the Irawaddi. It was easily occupied, but the Burmese

were a warlike race, and being strengthened in their wish for resistance by successes on the Bengal frontier refused to come to
terms. Again and again the great pagoda of Rangoon, which had
become the English citadel, was assaulted. In December a final
unsuccessful attack was made under the command of Maha Bun-
doola, who had distinguished himself in the north. From May to
February the fighting about Rangoon had continued, the chief
difficulty met with being the skill of the enemy in the defence
of stockades. Then, at last, Sir Archibald Campbell found it
possible to advance up the Irawaddi towards Prome. In April he
reached that place and found it deserted. There the English remained during the rainy season. In November hostilities were
renewed, and the English gradually forced their way up to within
forty-five miles of Ava, the capital. There at length, in February
1826, a treaty was concluded by which the Burmese ceded Assam,
Aracan, and the country south of Martiban along the coast. They
also gave up their claims upon the English provinces, paid a large
sum of money, and established friendly relations between the courts,
to be kept up by an interchange of ambassadors.

The occupation of England in a foreign war had given rise to
hopes among the princes of India that an opportunity had come
for reasserting their freedom. But all such thoughts were dashed
to the ground by the capture and destruction of the
fortress of Bhurtpore, hitherto considered impregnable.

Capture of
Bhurtpore.

At the beginning of 1825 a disputed succession had occurred.
The expelled Prince was under British protection; it remained
to be seen how far it now availed him. Lord Amherst was at
first inclined to non-intervention, but the army was in the hands
of Lord Combermere, an old Peninsula officer, not likely to shrink
before difficulties. He at once undertook to reduce the stronghold.
Having demanded the dismissal of women and children, which was
refused, he proceeded to bombard the town. After two months of
siege, the assault was given, and in two hours the town was secured ;
the fortress was then razed to the ground, and the rightful prince
reinstated, and the great movement against the English which had
been dreaded by many thinking men in India thus at once checked.
The Indian Empire had now reached the limits which were not
increased for many years. The subsequent conquests of the Punjaub
and Sinde have set a natural and geographical boundary to it, which,
it may be hoped, will prevent the necessity of those wars of conquest, which were really wars of defence, to which it owes its present
gigantic dimensions.

INDEX

CONSTITUTIONAL MONARCHY

CPSIA information can be obtained
at www.ICGtesting.com
Printed in the USA
LVOW07s0135181217
560124LV00026B/2979/P